4th Annual International Conference on Wireless Communication and Sensor Network (WCSN 2017)

ITM Web of Conferences Volume 17 (2018)

Wuhan, China
15 - 17 December 2017

Editors:

Kei Eguchi
Tong Chen
Chen Wang
Ning Zhang
Hongzhi Wang

ISBN: 978-1-5108-5725-4

Printed from e-media with permission by:

Curran Associates, Inc.
57 Morehouse Lane
Red Hook, NY 12571

Some format issues inherent in the e-media version may also appear in this print version.

Printed by Curran Associates, Inc. (2018)

For additional information, please contact EDP Sciences – Web of Conferences at the address below.

EDP Sciences – Web of Conferences
17, Avenue du Hoggar
Parc d'Activité de Courtabœuf
BP 112
F-91944 Les Ulis Cedex A
France

Phone: +33 (0) 1 69 18 75 75
Fax: +33 (0) 1 69 28 84 91

contact-edps@webofconferences.org

Additional copies of this publication are available from:

Curran Associates, Inc.
57 Morehouse Lane
Red Hook, NY 12571 USA
Phone: 845-758-0400
Fax: 845-758-2633
Email: curran@proceedings.com
Web: www.proceedings.com

TABLE OF CONTENTS

Preface

WCSN 2017

4th Annual International Conference on Wireless Communication and Sensor Network (WCSN 2017) was held in Wuhan, China, from 15-17 December 2017. WCSN2017 is to offer scholars, professionals, academics and graduate students to present, share, and discuss their studies from various perspectives in the aspects of wireless communication and sensor network. These proceedings tend to collect the up-to-date, comprehensive and worldwide state-of-art knowledge on information technology and application. All accepted papers were subjected to strict peer-reviewing by expert referees. The papers have been selected for this proceedings based on originality, significance, and clarity for the purpose of the conference. The selected papers and additional late-breaking contributions to be presented will make an exciting technical program on conference. The conference program is extremely rich, featuring high impact presentation. We hope this conference will not only provide the participants a broad overview of the latest research results on information technology, but also provide the participants a significant platform to build academic connections.

The Technical Program Committee worked very hard to have all papers reviewed before the review deadline. The final technical program consists of 56 papers. There are three keynote speeches and three invited sessions. The keynote speakers are internationally recognized as a leading expert in the research field of information technology who has demonstrated outstanding proficiency and has achieved distinction in his profession. The proceedings were published as a volume in by EDP science.

We would like to express our sincere gratitude to all the members of Technical Program Committee and organizers for their enthusiasm, time, and expertise. Our deep thanks also go to many volunteers and staffs for the long hours and hard work they have generously given to WCSN 2017. Finally, we would like to thank all the authors, speakers, and participants of this conference for their contributions to WCSN 2017, and also looks forward to welcoming you to WCSN 2018.

Prof. Hyunsung Kim

Program Chair
Prof. Hyunsung Kim, Dept. of Cyber Security, Kyungil University, Full Professor, Korea.

Program Chair
Prof. Chen Wang, Associate Professor, School of Electronic Information and Communications, Huazhong University of Science & Technology, China.

Co-Chair
Prof. Hui Yang, Associate Professor, Beijing University of Posts andTelecommunications (BUPT), China

Editor
Tong Chen, Professor in Affective Computing,School of Electronic & Information Engineering Southwest University Chongqing,China
Chen Wang, School of Electronic Information and Communications, Huazhong University of Science & Technology, Associate Professor, China
Kei Eguchi, Department of Information Electronics, Fukuoka Institute of Technology, Professor, Japan
Ning Zhang, Beijing Union University, China, Professor, China
Hongzhi Wang, School of computer science and technology, Harbin Institute of Technology, Professor, China

Technical Program Committee
Jianlun Wang, China Agricultural University, Associate Professor, China
Lan Luo, University of electronic science and technology, Professor, China
Tie Qiu,Dalian University of Technology, Professor, China
Li Tan, Beijing Technology and Business University, Professor, China
Lixiang Li, School of Cyberspace Security, Beijing University of Posts and Telecommunications, Professor, China
Xianjin Fang, Anhui University of Science and Technology, Professor, China
Hui LI, Hainan University, Vice dean of College of Information Science and Technology, China.
Saman Shojae Chaeikar, Khaje Nasir Toosi University of Technology, Professor, Iran
LORENZ Pascal, University of Haute Alsace, Professor, France.
RAJDEEP CHOWDHURY, JIS COLLEGE OF ENGINEERING, Professor, India
Felix J. Garcia Clemente, University of Murcia,Associate Professor, Spain
Mardeni Roslee, Multimedia University, Senior Lecturer, Malaysia
Bai Li, Zhejiang University, PhD Candidate, China
Imran Memon, Zhejiang University, Research Assistant, Pakistani
Xianfang YUE, University of Science and Technology Beijing, Associate

Dr.Md Ileas Pramanik, City University of Hong Kong, Hong Kong, China
Assistant Professor, Bangladesh Sattar Ameri, Wayne State university, PhD., Iran
Dr. Youssef SAID, Tunisie Telecom, Professor, Tunisia
Jiannan Zhai, Institute for Sensing and Embedded Network Systems Engineering, Florida Atlantic University, Chief Engineer, Assistant Research Professor, China
Mahtab Jahanbani Fard, Wayne State University, Researcher scholar, Iran
Dr. R. Raja, Alagappa University, Assistant Professor, India
Svetlana Zhelyazkova Vasileva-Boyadzhieva, Varna University of Management, Lecturer, Associate professor, Bulgaria
Ray-Hwa Wong, Department of Mechanical Eng., Hwa-Hsia University of Technology, Associate professor, Taiwan, China
A.D.N.SARMA, Centre for Good Governance, Hyderabad, Sr. Technical Consultant, India
Bogdan Tiganoaia, Politehnica university of Bucharest, Assistant Professor, Romania
Dimitris Kanellopoulos, University of Patras, Research Fellow, Greece
Hyunsung Kim, Kyungil University, Professor, Korea
Mumtaz Karatas, National Defense University, Turkish Naval Academy, Assistant Professor, Turkish
Trong- Minh Hoang, Telecoms Faculty, Posts and Telecommunication Institute of Technology, Dr, Lecturer, Vietnam
Akhlaqur Rahman, Swinburne University of Technology, PhD Researcher, Bangladeshi
Bhadrachalam C, Amrita University, Associate Professor
Jasmine Seng K. P., Charles Sturt University, Adjunct Professor
Mohamed Mahmoud Gomaa, National Research Centre, Associate Professor, Egypt
Amir R. Ali, German University, Assistant Professor, Egypt

General Chair Prof. Hyunsung Kim

POSITIONS HELD

•Full Professor (2014 - present), Dept. of Cyber Security, Kyungil University, Kyungbuk, Korea. Teaching the computer engineering and security related subjects.

•Visiting Professor (2016, two years), Dept. of Mathematical Sciences, University of Malawi, Zomba, Malawi. Visiting Prof. Levis Eneya

•Associate Professor (2012 - 2013), Dept. of Cyber Security, Kyungil University, Kyungbuk, Korea.Teaching the computer engineering and security related subjects.

•Associate Professor (2002 - 2011), Dept. of Computer Engineering, Kyungil University, Kyungbuk, Korea.Teaching the computer engineering and security related subjects.

•Visiting Professor (2009, a year), School of Computer, Dublin City University, Dublin, Ireland. Visiting

•Editorial Board (2002 - present), Korea Institute of Information Security and Cryptology, Seoul., Korea. Gave advices for the domestic journal

•Senior Researcher (2000 - 2002), Ditto Technology, Daegu., Korea. Directing research on the hardware implementation of the basic architectures for the public-key cryptosystem

COURSES TAUGHT:

•Network Security (Each Fall 2004-present; 3 credits). Department of Computer Engineering, Kyungil University, Korea

•Data Structure (Each Spring 2004-present; 3 credits), Department of Computer Engineering, Kyungil University, Korea.

•Formal Languages and Automata (Each Spring 2002-present; 3 credits). Department of Computer Engineering, Kyungil University, Korea

•Information Security (Each Fall 2002-present; 3 credits). Department of Computer Engineering, Kyungil University, Korea

•Computers (Every Semester 1998-2001; 3credits), Department of Computer Engineering, Kyungpook, National University, Korea.

Co-Chair Prof. Hui Yang

Hui Yang received B.E and Ph. D degree in communication and information systems from Beijing University of Posts and Telecommunications (BUPT), Beijing, China, in 2009 and 2014. He is currently an associate professor of Institute of Information Photonics and Optical Communications at BUPT, working on many China national (including NSFC, 973, 863, etc.) and international projects regarding optical networking and communication technologies. His main research interests include network architecture, software defined optical network (SDON), dynamic optical network, flexible band width optical network, cross-stratum optimization (CSO) and network protocols and algorithms. He has authored or coauthored more than 60 peer-reviewed papers related to the previously mentioned research topics in prestigious international journals and conferences, and he is the first author of more than 30 of them. He presented several invited papers in international journals and conferences, including many prestigious ones such as Scientific Reports, IEEE Communications Magazine, Optics Express, IEEE JOCN, Optical Switching and Networking, INFOCOM, OFC, ECOC and GLOBECOM etc. He got the Best Paper Award in NCCA 2015. Also, he is an active reviewer for several international journals, and I have previously reviewed more than 30 manuscripts in the following journals.

Program Chair & Editor Associate Professor Chen Wang,

Associate Professor, School of Electronic Information and Communications, Huazhong University of Science & Technology, China

EDUCATION

Sept. 2008 – Jun. 2013: Ph.D Degree, Dept. of Automation, Wuhan University, Wuhan, ChinaDoctoral Dissertation: Energy Efficient Schemes and Algorithms for Underwater
Sept. 2004 – Jun. 2008: B.E. Degree, Dept. of Automation, Wuhan University, Wuhan, China

WORK EXPERIENCE

Jun. 2017 – present: Associate Professor, School of Electronic Information and Communications, Huazhong University of Science and Technology, Wuhan, China
Jun. 2013 –Jun. 2017: Pos-Doc, School of Electronic Information and Communications, Huazhong University of Science and Technology, Wuhan, China Supervised by Prof. Hongbo Jiang

RESEARCH INTERESTS

Internet of Things / Wireless Sensor Networks / Pervasive and Mobile Computing / Location Based Services / Privacy Preserving / Mobile Crowdsensing / Topology Identification and Geometric Algorithm / etc.

COMPETENCE

In-depth knowledge of communication protocols and algorithms in wireless network
Skilled at C/C++, Java, Matlab and OpenGL
Proficient in Android application development
Familiar with Graph Theory, Stochastic Process, Machine Learning, Data Mining, Optimization, etc.;
Talented in problem solving and analyzing, Ability to work in fast-paced, intense environment, and under pressure to meet deadlines, Excellent team player

Editor Prof. Tong Chen

Professor in Affective Computing,School of Electronic and Information Engineering Southwest University, Chongqing,400715, China

RESEARCH EXPERIENCES

Signal Processing & Image Processing: Algorithm development, mathematical modeling, image enhancement, data visualization.

Affective Computing: Stress detection using hyperspectral imaging technique, affective physiological signal acquisition, affective feature extraction and selection, emotion understanding and recognition. In charge of a lab since 2012 for remote sensing human emotions (there are hyperspectral imager, somatosensory cameras, HD cameras available for the research).

Biomedical Engineering: Developing algorithms for remote measuring physiological signals including HR, HRV, breathing rate, GSR, and tissue oxygen saturation.

EMPLOYMENT

11/2016-present Professor, Southwest University, China

11/2011----10/2016 Associate Professor, Southwest University, China

11/2006---11/2011 Lecturers, Southwest University, China

07/2002---11/2006 Assistant Professor, Southwest University, China

RESEARCH PROJECTS

01/2014-12/2016 Hyperspectral Imaging Human Blood Oxygenation and Emotion (Natural Science Foundation China, [CNY280,000]): Principle Investigator, developing robust and real-time algorithm for generating tissue oxygen saturation (StO2), investigating facial StO2 patterns under positive and negative affective states, and investigating the relationship between HR response and StO2 response to affective states.

01/2013-12/2015 Remote Sensing Human Emotions Using StO2 (China Ministry of Education [CNY300,000]): Principle Investigator, selecting optimized wavelength for generating StO2, investigating facial StO2 patterns under two kinds of emotions, and extracting features for discriminating the two emotions.

2008-2011 Remote Detection of Stress Using Imaging Technique (UK MOD): This is a 3-year project with £433.8K support. My work focused on developing algorithm to produce StO2, detecting stress using hyperspectral imaging technique.

2011-2014 Research on Emotion Interaction between Human and Computer Based on Physiological Signal (China MOE): This is a 3-year project with 1 Million CNY support. My work focused on investigating the techniques that can be used for remote sensing physiological signals, and developing algorithms for remote measuring HR, HRV, and RR.

Editor Prof. Kei Eguchi

Professor, Department of Information Electronics, Fukuoka Institute of Technology, Fukuoka, Japan

RESEARCH TOPICS:

Switching converters, Intelligent systems, Non-thermal food processing

EDUCATIONAL BACKGROUND:

1990.4-1994.3: Department of Electrical Engineering and Computer Science, Kumamoto University

1994.4-1999.3: Graduate School of Science and Technology, Kumamoto University

1999.3 : Received Ph.D.

EMPLOYMENT RECORD:

1999.4-2000.12: Lecturer
Department of Information and Computer Sciences, Kumamoto National College of Technology

2001.1-2003.3: Associate Professor
Department of Information and Computer Sciences, Kumamoto National College of Technology

2003.4-2006.3: Associate Professor
Department of Electronic Engineering, Kumamoto National College of Technology

2006.4-2012.3 : Associate Professor
Department of Technology Education, Shizuoka University

2012.4- Present : Professor
Department of Information Electronics, Fukuoka Institute of Technology

2015.9-2015.11: Visiting Scholar, California State University, Eastbay, USA

Editor Prof. Ning Zhang

Dr. Ning Zhang, male, Professor, Beijing Union University, China. Ning Zhang received the MS degree in Physics science from Hefei University of Technology in 1992, and the PhD degree in Optics science from the department of Optics Engineering, University of Tianjin in 2002. From 2002-2004, as a postdoctoral research fellow, he worked in Beijing University of Posts and Telecommunications. He is currently a professor in Beijing Union University. His research interests are in the areas of Communication Science, Computer Network Technology, Information Systems, Software Engineering, Education Management, etc. Dr. Ning Zhang, is invited reviewer for the following international journals: Chinese Journal of Electronics (China, SCI), Mathematical Problems in Engineering (USA.SCI), Optics Communications (USA. SCI),etc. Areas of Interest: Communication Science, Computer Network Technology.

Editor Prof. Hongzhi Wang

Harbin Institute of Technology

RESEARCH INTERESTS

Big Data Management and analysis, Data Quality, Web Database, Graph, Database, Information Integration,

WORK AND RESEARCH EXPERIENCES

Professor Harbin Institute of Technology Harbin, China, 2015.12-Now
Teach and research on database research, including big data management and analysis, data quality, and graph management

Associate Professor Harbin Institute of Technology , Harbin, China, 2010.9 –2015.12
Teach and research on database research, including XML database, data quality, sensor network and information integration
Visiting Scholar University of California Irvine, USA, 2012.9-2013.9 Research on Big Data Management

Lecturer Harbin Institute of Technology Harbin, China, 2008.7 –Present
Teach and research on database research, including XML database, data quality, sensor network and information integration

Star Track Program of Visiting Researcher, Microsoft Research Asia Beijing, China 2011.4 – 2011.10
Research on distributed graph management

Graduate Student Researcher, Harbin Institute of Technology Harbin, China, 2000.4 – 2008.7
Focused on database research, including XML database, compressed database and information integration

Visiting Research Associate University of New South Wales Sydney, Australia, 2004.5-2005.4
Researched on efficient query processing of XML

Keynote Prof. Ting Yang

School of Electrical Engineering and Automation, Tianjin University, Tianjin, China

Dr. Ting Yang is currently a Chair professor of Theory and Advanced Technology of Electrical Engineering, at the School of Electrical Engineering and Automation, Tianjin University, China. He was the cooperative research staff of Imperial College London (2008), University of Sydney, Australia (2011, 2015). Prof. Yang is the winner of the "New Century Excellent Talents in University Award" from Chinese Ministry of Education. He is the leader of tens of research grant projects, including the International S&T Cooperation Program of China, the National High-Tech Research and Development Program of China (863 Program), the National Natural Science Foundation of China, and so on. Prof. Yang is the chairman of two workshops of IEEE International Conference, and the editor in Chief of one of Special Issues of the international journal of DSN. He is the author/co-author of four books, more than one hundred publications in internationally refereed journals and conferences. Prof. Yang is a senior member of the Chinese Institute of Electronic, the fellow of Circuit and System committee, the fellow of Theory and Advanced Technology of Electrical Engineering, and the member of International Society for Industry and Applied Mathematics. His research fields include Smart Grid, advanced metering infrastructure, and information and communication technologies in electric power system.

Keynote Prof. Lei Zhang

Lei Zhang received his Ph.D degree in Circuits and Systems from the College of Communication Engineering, Chongqing University, Chongqing, China, in 2013. He was selected as a Hong Kong Scholar in China in 2013, and worked as a Post-Doctoral Fellow with The Hong Kong Polytechnic University, Hong Kong, from 2013 to 2015. He is currently a Professor/Distinguished Research Fellow with Chongqing University. He has authored more than 50 scientific papers in top journals, including the IEEE Transactions on Neural Networks and Learning Systems, the IEEE Transactions on Image Processing, the IEEE Transactions on Multimedia, the IEEE Transactions on Instrumentation and Measurement, the IEEE Transactions on Systems, Man, and Cybernetics: Systems, the IEEE Sensors Journal, Information Fusion, Sensors & Actuators B, and Analytica Chimica Acta. His current research interests include machine learning, pattern recognition, computer vision, electronic olfaction and intelligent systems.

Keynote Prof. Hui Zhang

Hui Zhang received the B.S. degree and PhD. degree respectively in 2005 and 2010, both from Beijing University of Posts and Telecommunications. In 2010, he became a faculty member in the School of Information Science in Nankai University, Tianjin, China. From 2013-2014, he was a postdoctoral research fellow respectively in University of Southampton and Korea Advanced Institute of Science and Technology. He is currently an associated professor in Nankai University. His research interests are in the areas of Wireless Networks, Visible Light Communication, Social Networks, Energy Internet, etc. Currently He is the reviewer for the following journals: IEEE Transactions on Wireless Communication, IEEE Transactions on Mobile Computing, IEEE Transactions on Vehicular Technology, EURASIP Journal on Wireless Communications and Networking, IEEE Globecom, IEEE VTC, Chinese Journal of Electronics.

Keynote Prof. Lei Zhang

Lei Zhang received his Ph.D degree in Circuits and Systems from the College of Communication Engineering, Chongqing University, Chongqing, China, in 2013. He was selected as a Hong Kong Scholar in China in 2013, and worked as a Post-Doctoral Fellow with The Hong Kong Polytechnic University, Hong Kong, from 2013 to 2015. He is currently a Professor/Distinguished Research Fellow with Chongqing University and also the founder of Learning Intelligence & Vision Essential (LiVE Group). He has authored more than 70 scientific papers in top journals, including the IEEE Trans. Neural Networks and Learning Systems, the IEEE Trans. Image Processing, the IEEE Trans. Multimedia, the IEEE Trans. Instrumentation and Measurement, the IEEE Trans. Systems, Man, and Cybernetics: Systems, etc. His current research interests include machine learning, pattern recognition, computer vision and intelligent systems. He has been a reviewer for more than 50 journals such as IEEE Transactions (T-IP, T-MM, T-CSVT, T-CYB, T-SMCA, T-IM, T-IE), and so on. He also serves as keynote speaker, area chair, session chair, and program committee for more than 20 international conferences. Dr. Zhang was a recipient of Outstanding Reviewer Award of Sensor Review Journal in 2016, Outstanding Doctoral Dissertation Award of Chongqing, China, in 2015, Hong Kong Scholar Award in 2014, Academy Award for Youth Innovation of Chongqing University in 2013 and the New Academic Researcher Award for Doctoral Candidates from the Ministry of Education, China, in 2012.

Keynote Prof . Xiong Li

EDUCATION BACKGROUND

PhD in Weapon System Engineering, Academy of Armored Force Engineering, 2003-2009
Masters of Command Information System, Academy of Armored Force, 1997-2000
Bachelor of Command Technology and Engineering, Academy of Armored Force Engineering, 1993-1997

TEACHING EXPERIENCE

Military Operations Research (Undergraduate Course), 2003-2013
Complex System Modeling (Graduate Course), 2007-2016
System Analysis and System Engineering (Graduate Course), 2011-2016
Intelligent Decision-making (Graduate Course), 2011-2016

SELECTED ACADEMIC AWARDS

PhD thesis entitled "*Study on Warfare System Modeling Based on Meta-agents Interaction Chain*" was nominated as one of the **30 Chinese PLA most excellent doctor theses** in 2010 and the **100 national most excellent doctor these**s in 2011, respectively.

Keynote Prof. Wei Chih Hsu

Department of Computer and Communication Engineering, National Kaoshiung First University of Science and Technology

EDUCATION

Ph.D, Graduate Institute of Electrical Engineering, National Taiwan University, Taiwan, 09/1978 to 04/1984

Visiting scholar, Purdue University, U.S. 02/1984 to 02/1985

WORK HISTORY

Professor, Department of Computer and Communication Engineering, National Kaoshiung First University of Science and Technology, 02/1986-Present

Associate Research, Chunghwa Telecom Co., Ltd.,04/1984—01/1986

AWARDS:

Excellent teachers (counseling students admitted to "IPMA International Professional Management Project ", 2011,2012,2013

Statement of Peer review

In submitting conference proceedings to *Web of Conferences*, the editors of the proceedings certify to the Publisher that

1. They adhere to its **Policy on Publishing Integrity** in order to safeguard good scientific practice in publishing.
2. All articles have been subjected to peer review administered by the proceedings editors.
3. Reviews have been conducted by expert referees, who have been requested to provide unbiased and constructive comments aimed, whenever possible, at improving the work.
4. Proceedings editors have taken all reasonable steps to ensure the quality of the materials they publish and their decision to accept or reject a paper for publication has been based only on the merits of the work and the relevance to the journal.

Title, date and place of the conference

2017 4th International Conference on Wireless Communication and Sensor Network (WCSN2017)
Wuhan, China, from 15-17 December, 2017

Proceedings editor(s):

Kei Eguchi
Department of Information Electronics, Fukuoka Institute of Technology, Professor, Japan.

Date and editor's signature

15/1/2018

A Study on the Node Centrality Based Multi-social Attributes Weighted in Mobile Social Networks

Yanhong Meng[1,*], *Xianxian* Liu[1], *Peirong* Zhao[1], and *Yunhui* Yi[1]

[1]State Key La Laboratory of Integrated Services Networks, Xidian University, Xi'an, China

Abstract. Mobile social networks (MSNs) exploit human mobility and consequent device-to-device contact to opportunistically realize data communication. Thus links in MSNs is dynamic changing over time and strongly influenced by people activities, mining influential nodes is one of the important questions for effective information transmission in MSNs. While traditional centrality definitions are based on the static binary network model and not suitable for time-varying topology structure in mobile social network. Furthermore previous centrality metrics often referred to social attributes about neighbor nodes and contact times, and did not take the contact duration time into consideration. Therefore, this paper proposes a centrality measurement method based on multi-social attributes weighted. We first use the temporal evolution graph model which more accurately depicts the dynamic nature of topology in MSNs. Quantifying human social relations and mobility model as weights for the links, and then we redefine degree of centrality and the measurement of shortest path. Finally, the superiority of the concepts we posed are evaluated in the real data set.

1 Introduction

The rapid development of Internet, the advent of the era of 4G mobile Internets, the fast growth of mobile terminals technology and the massive popularity of mobile terminals prompt the mobile social networks emerging at the historic moment. MSNs can take advantage of mobile features of wireless devices users and ubiquitous accessibility, and finally realize information transmit among interested mobile users without relying on mobile networks operators' communication infrastructures [1-3, 10].

In mobile social network, node is represented as people and group, meanwhile relation shows the relationship between nodes [4-5]. The problem is how to find the most influential node in the network. The number of important nodes is generally very small, but their impact can more quickly spread to most other nodes in the network. Many scholars use the central metric method to measure the importance of the nodes. The most typical one is proposed by Freeman [17]. While traditional centrality definitions are based on the static binary network model and not suitable for time-varying topology structure in MSNs. So

* Corresponding author: yhmeng@stu.xidian.edu.cn

some researchers extend centralities measures to weighted networks [6, 7] and dynamic networks[9-11, 16]. Opsahl et al. [7] generalizes Freeman's three centralities, not only focusing on tie weights, but also on the number of ties. Temporal network can be modelled in terms of time-varying graphs, which are time-ordered sequences of graphs over a set of nodes, centralities measurement must obey the time [9-11].

The sum of various human relations form social attributes, what's more, links in MSNs is dynamic changing over time and strongly influenced by people's activities. Paper [16] puts forward entropy degree centrality (EDC) and social-based global centrality that both based on social relations (neighbor nodes and contact times), when contact time equals 1, no matter how many neighbor numbers are, we get the same EDC. While common neighbor is zero, no matter how big the contact time is, the social-based global centrality always is same, thus ignore impact of the different contact times. According to the above discussions, in this paper, we add contact duration time and propose a centrality measurement method based on multi-social attributes weighted.

The rest of this paper is organized as follows: Sec.2 gives a brief overview of preliminary works. Measurement of centrality based multiple social attributes in MSNs are described in Sec.3. In Sec. 4, we present the experiment results of all proposed concepts. Finally, we offer conclusions in Sec. 5.

2 Preliminaries

2.1 Temporal evolution graph model

We use temporal evolution graph model [9-11, 16] to provide a concise and general formulation that takes into account time order, contact duration times and contact times to capture the dynamic topology of MSNs. The relations between entities are assumed to take place over a time span T. We use ω to denote the time duration of each snapshot (or time window size). $Q^T = T/\omega$, expressed numbers of time units. So dynamic networks will be represented as $G^T = (V^T, E^T, M^T)$, $G^T = \{G^T_{t_1}, G^T_{t_2}, \cdots, G^T_{tQ}\}$ during the duration time T. $V^T\!: V^T \subseteq V$, the set of all individuals in the network during T. $E^T : E^T \subseteq E$, the set of edges that represent contact events between individuals during T. M^T:a sequence of connectivity matrices which record contact events of between individuals during T.

We introduce the following illustrative example in Fig.1, the left graph is the total static graph in time T, the connections between two points indicate the contact times (black number) and the total contact duration time (blue number). The right graph depicts dynamic connect graphs in different time units. We assume $T = 8\,\text{mins}$, $\omega = 1\,\text{min}$ and $Q^T = 8$. Observing edge A-F, there are only four contact times in time units 2, 4, 6, and 8. While contact duration time is 2mins, so the half time must be invalid in four times connection. However, due to the window size is bigger this fact cannot be observed precisely. Then analysing edge B-C, we can see that it exists 3 times connect in 1, 4, and 6/7/8 time units, because B and C are always connected in 6, 7 and 8, we consider it as one time connect.

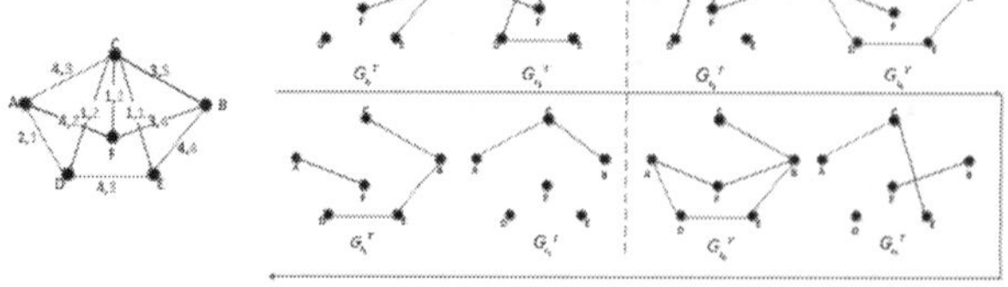

Fig. 1. A simple example about temporal evolution graph

2.2 Measurement of centrality in opsahl weighted network

2.2.1 Degree centrality

Freeman [17] asserted that the degree of a focal node is the number of adjacencies in a binary network. For one node, the greater the number of neighbors are, the stronger the connect ability to other nodes. So we give the definition $k_i = C_D(i) = \sum_j^N x_{ij}$, where i is the focal node, j represents all other nodes, N is the total number of nodes, and x is adjacency matrix, in which x_{ij} denotes 1if node i is connected to j, and 0 otherwise.

Degree has generally been extended to the sum of weights when analyzing weighted network, and labeled node strength, the definition is $s_i = C_D^{w}(i) = \sum_j^N w_{ij}$, where w is the weighted adjacency matrix, in which w_{ij} is greater than 0 if the node i is connected to node j, and the value represents the weight of the tie.

However, measurement of degree in binary network and weighted network focuses on either tie weights or the number of ties, and they are both incomplete measurement. In an attempt to combine both degree and strength, Opsahl et al.[7] import a tuning parameter, α, which determines the relative importance of the number of ties compared to ties weights. The formula is as follows:

$$C_D^{w\alpha}(i) = k_i \times \left(\frac{s_i}{k_i}\right)^{\alpha} = k_i^{1-\alpha} \times s_i^{\alpha} \tag{1}$$

Where α is a positive tuning parameter, if this parameter is between 0 and 1, then having a high degree is taken as favourable.

2.2.2 Closeness centrality and betweenness centrality

The closeness and betweenness centrality measures rely on the identification and length of the shortest paths among nodes in the network. In binary network, Freeman [17] defined the shortest path formulation as $d(i,j) = \min(x_{ih} + \cdots + x_{hj})$, from which we can observe the shortest path in binary network can only impacted by the number of relay nodes passed by.

In weighted network, there were several expressive methods, Dijkstra [12] proposed an algorithm that finds the path of least resistance, and was defined for networks where the weights represented costs of transmitting. Newman et al[13] and Brande et al.[14] defined Dijkstra algorithm as $d^{w}(i,j) = \min(1/w_{ih} + \cdots + 1/w_{hj})$, from which we can also find the shortest path in weighted network can only impacted by the weights between nodes.

In order to focus both on the number of relay nodes and the weights between nodes, Opsahl et al.[7] also import a tuning parameter, α, and redefine the shortest path as follows:

$$d^{w\alpha}(i,j) = \min\left(\frac{1}{(w_{ih})^{\alpha}} + \cdots + \frac{1}{(w_{hj})^{\alpha}}\right) \tag{2}$$

The impact of different tuning parameters will be analyzed, when $\alpha = 0$, the proposed measure produces the same outcome as the binary distance measure, whereas when $\alpha = 1$, the outcome is the same as the one obtained with Dijkstra's algorithm. A value for

$0 < \alpha < 1$ assigns the path with the greatest number of intermediary nodes has the longest distance.

3 Measurement of centrality based multiple social attributes in MSNs

In mobile social networks, the sum of various human relations form social attributes, so the human mobility bring fierce impact. Paper [8] suggested that the strength of a relationship is dependent on four components: the frequency of contact, the length or history of the relationship, contact duration, and the number of transactions. In this paper, we take contact times, contact duration time, the number of neighborhood node and common neighborhood node into consideration to quantify the weight between nodes.

3.1 Dissimilar weight and similar weight

Literature [13] lists weight measurement in the social network and non-social network, generally speaking, a social network, the connection weights are a fuction of duration, emotional intensity, intimacy and the exchange of service.

According to different meaning of weight, weights can be divided into two categories: dissimilar weight and similar weight. In general, the most we have studied is the dissimilar weight which corresponding to the distance and the larger the weight the further the distance between two nodes. However, the similarity weight stands the opposite. In fact, similar weight is prevalent in the social network, for example, in the cooperative process of scientists, the weight is higher on behalf of the cooperation between the two scientists is more frequently and more closely. So we can assume that the smaller the distance between them.

The differences between dissimilar weight and similar weight directly affect the definition of shortest path length of network. Given a path from node i to j and pass by node k, for dissimilar weight, and the distance between node i and node j is $d_{ij} = w_{ik} + w_{kj}$, while the distance is defined $d_{ij} = 1/w_{ik} + 1/w_{kj}$ for similar weight.

3.2 Determination of tie strength (or weight)

Due to similar weight is prevalent in the social network, in this paper, we take contact times, contact duration time, the number of neighborhood nodes and common neighborhood nodes into consideration to quantify the tie strength (or weight) between nodes. Tie strength between nodes is determined by multiple social attributes. Give a time period T, we assume that there are M factors, $factork, k = 1,\cdots,M$ and $g_i(factork)$ means the contribution to tie strength between node i and j for any factor. Then the contributions of M factors are as follows: $TieStrength^T(i,j) = \{g_1(factor1),\cdots,g_M(factorM)\}$.

Basagni et al. [15] shows the high correlation between contact times (regularity) and contact duration (familiarity) in four datasets, and they define four kinds of relationships between a pair of nodes: community, familiar strangers, strangers, and friends. For a pair of nodes, the greater the encounter frequency, the greater the chance to communicate.If two nodes stay a longer time, the like is more stable. On other hands, if two nodes have more other acquaintances in common, they may have a higher probability of two people being acquainted. So we propose the tie strength, as:

$$TieStrength^T(i,j) = F(i,j)^{\delta + sim(i,j)} + D(i,j)^{\delta + sim(i,j)} \quad (3)$$

Where $F(i, j)$ and $D(i, j)$ represents contact times and contact duration time between node i and node j during the time span T, respectively. δ is correction factor, whose value range is $0 < \delta << sim$, which makes the equ.(3) not equal 1, when their common nodes is 0, but contact times and duration time are not 0. Where $N(i)$ is the neighborhood number, $sim(i, j)$ stands for density of common nodes, and is denoted as follows:

$$sim(i,j) = \frac{|N(i) \cap N(j)|}{|N(i) \cup N(j)|} \tag{4}$$

3.3 Multi-social attributes degree centrality

According to the tie strength proposed in Sec.3.2, we get the node strength during a time span T as:

$$S^T_{iM-social} = \sum_{1}^{N} TieStrength^T(i,j) \tag{5}$$

Where N is the neighborhood of node i, but equ.(5) also does not consider neighborhood number, so from the discussion of Sec. 2.2.1, multi-social abttributes degree centrality is denoted as:

$$C^T_{DM-social}{}^{wet}(i) = k_i \times \left(\frac{S^T_{iM-social}}{k_i} \right)^{\alpha} = k_i^{1-\alpha} \times \left(S^T_{iM-social} \right)^{\alpha} \tag{6}$$

We also create a tuning parameter α as:

$$\alpha = \frac{\left(S^T_{1M-social} \times \cdots \times S^T_{iM-social} \times \cdots \times S^T_{NM-social} \right)^{\frac{1}{N}}}{\max\left\{ S^T_{1M-social}, \cdots, S^T_{iM-social}, \cdots, S^T_{NM-social} \right\}} \tag{7}$$

After analyzing the equ.(7), we know $0 < \alpha < 1$. Combing with equ.(1), under the same consederation, neighborhood number is much more, the degree centrality is bigger.

3.4 Multi-social attributes closeness centrality and betweenness centrality

From the discussion of Sec. 3.1, we see that the greater the weight, the smaller the distance between two nodes, and that is to say the tighter between two nodes the distance of two nodes in MSNs. In addition, when the information goes through more nodes, the more likely it is to be stolen or tampered. Thus less hops is hoped in MSNs.

Assuming a path from node i to node j will pass m nodes in a span time T, $n_1, n_2, \cdots, n_m$, $w_{ij} = TieStrength^T(i,j)$, then the distance from node i to node j defined as:

$$d^{wet}_{M-social}(i,j) = \min\left(\frac{1}{\left(w^T_{in_1}\right)^{\alpha}} + \frac{1}{\left(w^T_{n_1n_2}\right)^{\alpha}} + \cdots + \frac{1}{\left(w^T_{n_mj}\right)^{\alpha}} \right) \tag{8}$$

Where a tuning parameter denoted as:

$$\alpha = \frac{\left(w^T_{in_1} \times w^T_{n_1n_2} \times \cdots \times w^T_{n_mj} \right)^{\frac{1}{m+1}}}{\max\left\{ w^T_{in_1}, w^T_{n_1n_2}, \cdots, w^T_{n_mj} \right\}} \tag{9}$$

After analyzing the equ.(9), we know $0 < \alpha < 1$. Comparing with equ.(2), under the same consederation, a path of two nodes has less hops, the distance is samaller.

4 Experiment results and analysis

4.1 MIT reality data set

The Reality Mining project[18] was conducted from 2004–2005 at the MIT Media Laboratory. They used mobile phones pre-installed with several pieces of software to record the researchers' data. Subjects were observed using these measurements over the course of nine months and included students and faculty from two programs within a major research institution. The bluetooth scan interval was 5 min. We use the bluetooth traces over one month in 2004 October and define the contact as the link during which two devices are in mutual radio transmission range and can exchange data. If two scan time less than 30 min, we believe the two adjacent contact as one contact.

4.2 Experimental results of the tightness between nodes

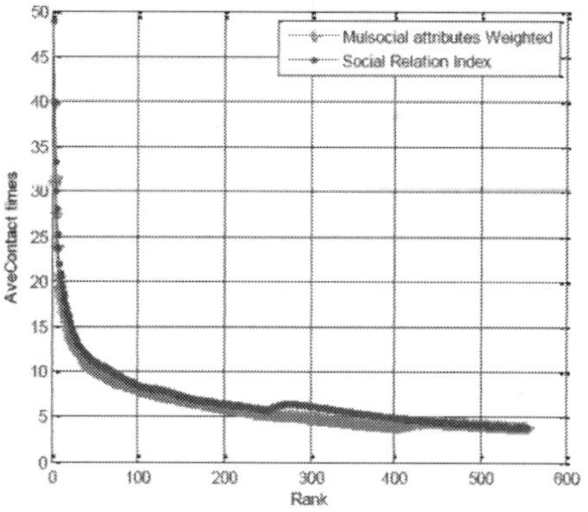

Fig. 2. Average contact times in tightness Ranking top N.

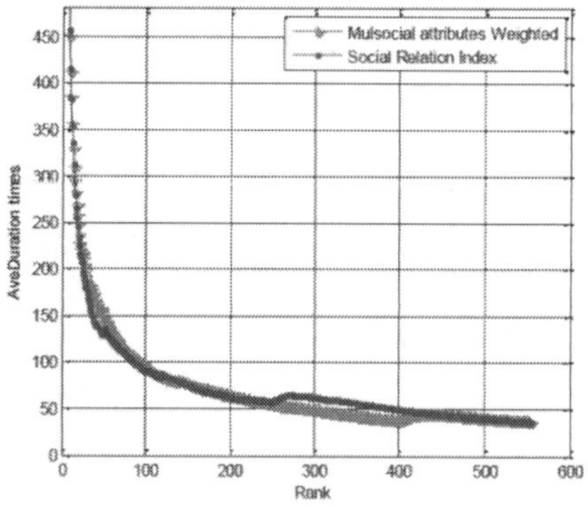

Fig. 3. Average duration time in tightness ranking top N.

In order to evaluate the centrality based on multi-social attributes, we first campare the tie strength proposed in this paper with social relation index defined in paper [16] about average contact times, average contact duration time, and average common node number in tightness ranking top N. Figure 2, 3 and 4 report the tie experiment results between strength and SRI by MIT traces, and horizontal axises are the tightness ranking top N in three figures, besides vetical axises represent average contact times, average contact duration time, and average common node number in three figures, respectively. Because contact duration is a new factor added in tie strength and its constraint to contact times, figure 2 shows that the average contact times in SRI is slightly high campared with tie strength. Coversely, figure 3 shows that the average duration times in tie strength is slightly high campared with SRI before rank 251. In Fig. 4, it shows most rank tie strength is higer, while only rank between 18 and 108, the average common node number in SRI is slightly high campared with tie strength. Becasue when common neighbor is 0, no matter how big the contact times and duration are, SRI equal 1, which lead to ingnoring the influences of differen contact times. This is why the curse about SRI in figure 2 rises abruptly after rank 251, and also goes up suddenly in figure 3. A sharp decline appears in figure 4 becasue of common nodes become 0. Above all, mesurement of tightness proposed in this paper can considers more comprehensive factors and get more smooth curse compared with SRI.

4.3 Experimental results of multi-social attributes degree centrality (MSADC)

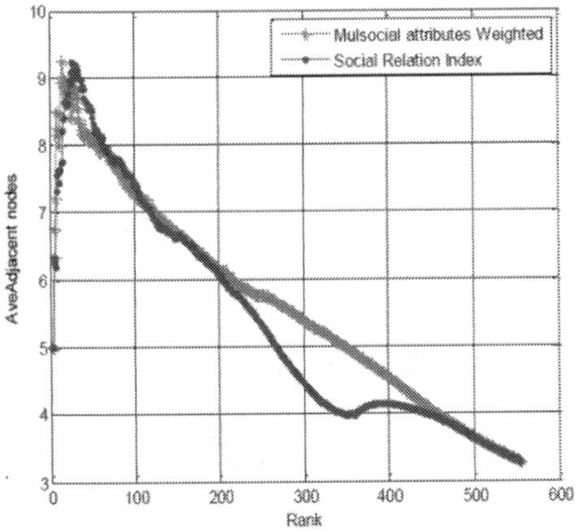

Fig. 4. Average adjacent nodes in tightness ranking top N.

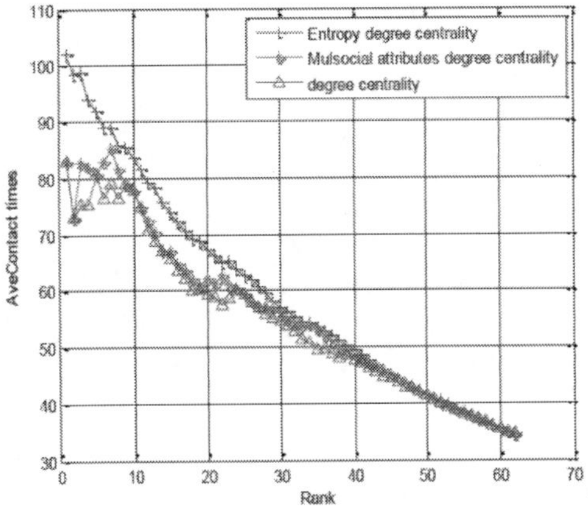

Fig. 5. Average contact times in MSADC ranking top N.

We compare MSADC with entropy degree centrality[16], degree centrality[17], and weighted degree centrality[14]. Figure 5 shows the the curves of average number of contacts of the top-N nodes which are ranked by MSADC, entropy degree centrality, and weighted degree centrality. Owning to duration time the new factor added in MSADC and its constraint to contact times, the curse about MSADC is lower than entropy degree centrality and higher than degree centrality. But the average number of contacts of the top-N nodes about MSADC is most higher than others in Fig. 6. For not thinking over the duration time in entropy degree centrality, figure 7 just reports the the curves of average duration time of the top-N nodes which are ranked by MSADC and weighted degree centrality. We can learn that MSADC precedes degree centrality in the aspect of duration time. In conclusion, although MSADC is not superior to entropy degree centrality in contact times, it has best performance in neighbor number, and precedes degree centrality in the new factors.

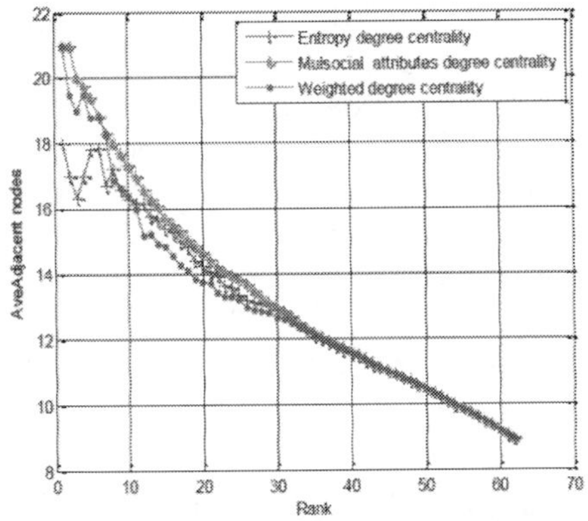

Fig. 6. Average adjacent nodes in MSADC ranking top N.

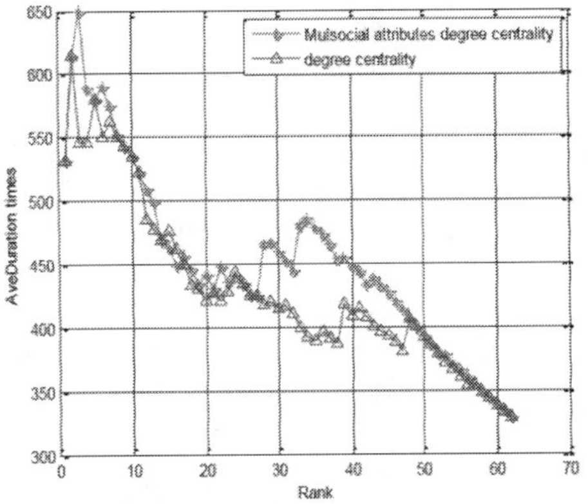

Fig. 7. Average duration time in MSADC ranking top N.

4.4 Experimental results of multi-social attributes degree centrality (MSADC)

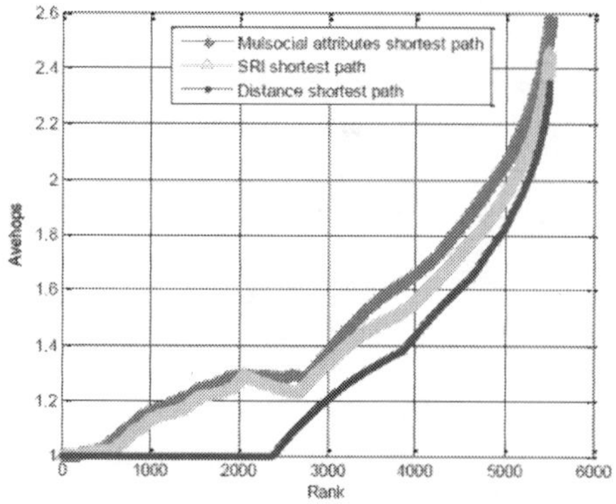

Fig. 8. Average hops in shortest distance ranking top N.

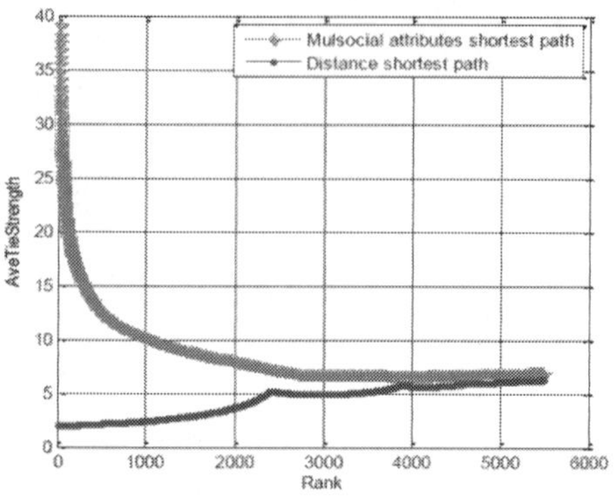

Fig. 9. Average weight in shortest distance ranking top N.

Closeness centrality and betweenness centrality rely on shortest paths among nodes to identify influential nodes in the network. In order to evaluate the effectiveness of the proposed centrality metrics in MSNs, we first evaluate the effectiveness of the proposed MSASP by MIT data set. We compare MSASP with SRI shortest path [16] and distance shortest path [17]. Figure 8 shows the the curves of average hops of the top-N nodes which are ranked shortest distance by MSASP, SRI shortest path, and distance shortest path. Because the distance between nodes is shorter, the path has less hops and higher weight. Figure 8 clearly shows that the average hops in MSASP are very close to SRI shortest path, and they are both higher than distance shortest path. Due to measure standards are different between tie strength and SRI, we cannot contrast their values. So there only exist MSASP and distance shortest path to compare the average weight between nodes ranking top N in figure 9.We obviously learn about MSASP is higher than distance shortest path. Above all, MSASP can better measure the shortest distance between nodes.

5 Conclusion

In mobile social networks, the sum of various human relations form social attributes, so the human mobility bring fierce impact. How to find the influential node in MSNs is the focus for many researchers. Therefore, this paper proposes a centrality measurement method based on multi-social attributes weighted for MSNs. Firstly, using the temporal evolution graph model, we quantify human social relations and mobility model as weight for the links and the experiment prove that mesurement of tightness proposed in this paper can consider more comprehensive factors and get more smooth curse compared with SRI. Then MSASP is come up with, and the experiment shows it can better measure the shortest distance between nodes. What's more, we redefine degree of centrality and its superiority is evaluated in the real data set.

As future work, we are planning to analyze the correlation between multi-social attributes degree centrality and multi-social attributes closeness and betweenness centralities. We will also discuss other data sets for the applicability.

References

1. D. M. Boyd and N. B. Ellison, *Comput.-Mediated Commun.*, **13**, 210, (2007).
2. X Hu, T H S Chu, et al. *IEEE Communi.* Surveys & Tutorials, **17**, 1557(2015).

3. X Wang, H Wang, et al. *IEEE Inter. Conf. on Sen.*, Communi., and NET. 1(2017).
4. W Stanley, F Katherine. New York: *Cambridge University Press.* 17(1994)
5. Q Xingqin, P Eddie, et al. *Information Sciences.* **194**, 240(2012).
6. Y Yustiawan, W Maharani, A Gozali. *Pro. Com.* **59**, 419(2015), .
7. T. Opsahl, F. Agneessens, J. Skvoretz, *Soc. Networks* **32**, 245 (2010).
8. E M Daly, M Haahr. *IEEE Trans. Mobile Computing* **8**, 606 (2009)
9. H Kim, R Anderson. *Phys. Rev. E*, **85**, 026107(2012).
10. V Nicosia, J Tang, C Mascolo, et al. Temp. Net. *Springer Berlin Heidelberg*, **15**(2013).
11. C Magnien, F Tarissan, 1200 (2015).
12. E W Dijkstra, *Numerische Mathematik*, **1**, 269 (1959).
13. M. E. J. NEWMAN, *Phys. Rev. E,* **64**, 016132. (2001)
14. A Barrat, M Barthélemy, et al. *Proce. National Academy. Sciences,* **101**, 37472004(2004).
15. S Basagni, M Conti, S Giordano, et al. *Wiley-IEEE Press*, 360-418(2013).
16. Gao Zhenxiang, Shi Yan, Chen Shanzhi, I*nte. Jou. Mod. Phys. C*, **26**, 1550107(2015).
17. L. C. Freeman, *Soc. Networks* 1, 215 (1979).
18. N. Eagle, A. S. Pentland and D. Lazer, *Proc. Nat. Acad. Sci.* **106**, 15274 (2009).

A Novel Analysis Method of Pre-adjusting System for Self-interference Cancellation in Analog Domain

Hui-Hui Li[1*], *Nan* Chen[1] ,*and Xiandeng* He[1]

[1]Skate Key Laboratory of Integrated Services Networks, XiDian University, Xi'an, Shaanxi, China

Abstract. Pre-adjusting system, which computes the attenuation coefficients of self-interference cancellation, is one of the most important parts in a practical self-interference cancellation system. In this paper, a new way is given to analyze the pre-adjusting system in analog domain, and a clear theoretical analysis is carried out. Meanwhile, a method for solving the optimal attenuation vector is introduced. The simulation results show that the Interference Cancellation Ratio(ICR) can reach up to 62.8 dB in an ideal environment and 50.4 dB in a real environment, which are much better than the ordinary demand of 40 dB in analog domain. Finally, an amplitude modulation signal is verified in our method, with shows good performance, too.

1 Introduction

With the rapid development of wireless communication technology, a large number of wireless electronic devices have been widely used in various fields[1]. The electromagnetic interference is being produced when people are enjoying the convenience of these equipments, especially in a limitted range of space, where a variety of radio transmission devices compete for a certain spectrum of resources[2]. These mutual interferences among the radio transmission equipments have seriously affected their functions. Interference cancellation is becoming important in both advanced wireless devices and future wireless networks[3]. In limitted space of communication platforms, the radios are often self-interference limited rather than external-interference or noise-limited. Meanwhile, in the fifth generation of wireless mobile communications, the co-time co-frequency full duplex(CCFD) technology will play an important role[1]. What's more, the self-interference cancellation problem is the core challenge of CCFD. So it's meaningful to do some research on self-interference cancellation.

Certainly, self-interference cancellation can be divided into three stages: antenna cancellation, analog domain cancellation, and digital domain cancellation[2][4]. In this paper, we major in the analog domain cancellation. Earlier studies on the self-interference cancellation algorithms in the analog domain mainly focus on the structure. The authors in [4]-[6] provided a self-interference estimation structure in the analog domain, and adjusted

* Corresponding author: 15891027098@163.com

its phase, amplitude and delay to cancel the self-interference. Besides, [7]-[11] gave some skills to got the attenuation coefficients. In this paper, the algorithm is optimized and verified in the actual system.

This paper studies the interference cancellation based on a Six-channels Interference Canceller as Fig 1, which is made by our laboratory. In Fig 1, every channel means a different frequency, widely from 30MHz to 512MHz randomly. Each channel is similar to others. And details of the single channel is given as Fig 2, which will be described below. Actually the canceller is divided into two parts from a functional point of view. One is pre-adjusting system and the other is cancellation system.The pre-adjusting system which estimate the attenuation coefficients, and depends on them, the cancellation system do the cancellation job. Naturally, the pre-adjusting system is the pivotal one. In this paper, a new analysis method based on mathematical equation is proved. Firstly, a structure of pre-adjusting system is given. Secondly, some theoretical analyses are done in detail. Thirdly, the method is verified by System View.

This paper is structured as follows. Section 2 presents the model of the pre-adjusting system. At the same time, a theoretical analysis is given in detail. Simulation results are given in Section 3. Conclusions are made in Section 4.

2 System model and analysis

In our Six-channels Interference Canceller, each channel is similar to others. Without loss of generality, as show in Fig 2, a general pre-adjusting system model of single channel is given.

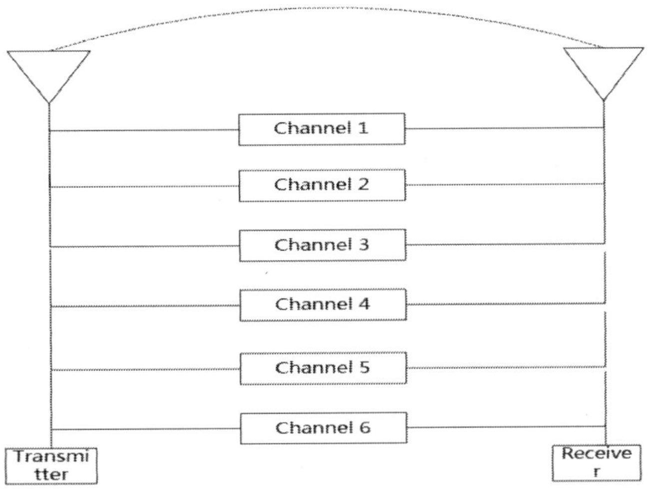

Fig. 1. Six-channels interference canceller

Obviously, the block of "Transmitter" transmits interference signal and the block of "Receive Signal" receives signals. There must be something to explain that the desired signal is not given in this structure. Because the canceller has three steps to finish a job: first, the pre-adjusting system finds the attenuation coefficients; second, the cancellation system do the cancellation job by using the attenuation coefficients from the first step; third, the desired signal can be transmitted.

In Fig 2, the block of "Reference Signal" get some portion of the signal from the block "Transmitter". Then we get $s_1(t)$and $s_2(t)$ after the block of "Hibert Transform". The value of the block "Control" and "Integrals" is to get attenuation coefficients. Finally, the block "Merger Offset" merges signals.

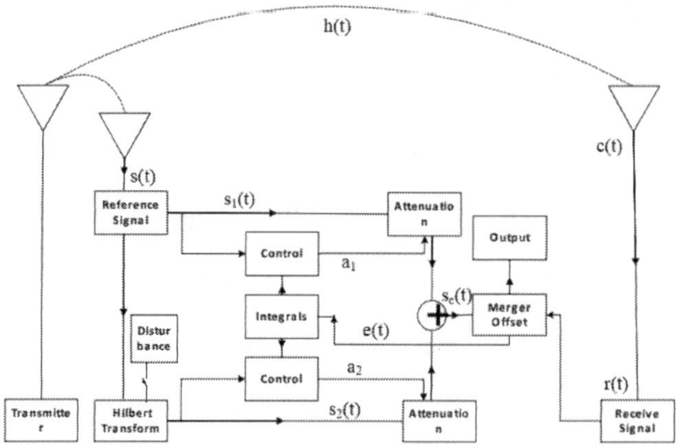

Fig . 2. Pre-adjusting system of single channel

2.1 Theoretical analysis

As show in Fig 2, $s(t)$ is the reference signal which is coupled from transmitting antenna. The channel characteristics of transmission path is $h(t)$.

$$h(t)=a\delta(t-\tau)e^{j\theta} \tag{1}$$

Where a, τ are the amplitude attenuation and time delay of the self-interference channel, respectively. And θ is the random phase shift of this channel. Then $s_1(t)$ and $s_2(t)$ are the same phase and orthogonal component of $s(t)$,respectively. The orthogonal component is achieved by Hibert filter. So the received signal can be written as

$$\begin{aligned} \mathrm{r}(t) &= c(t) + n(t) = \mathrm{Re}\{[s(t) + j\hat{s}(t)] * h(t)\} + n(t) \\ &= \mathrm{Re}\{\textstyle\int_{-\infty}^{+\infty} h(\tau-t)[s(\tau)+j\hat{s}(\tau)]d\tau\}+n(t) \\ &= \mathrm{Re}\{a[s(t-\tau)+j\hat{s}(t-\tau)]e^{j\theta}\}+n(t) \end{aligned} \tag{2}$$

where $c(t)$ is the real self-interference and $n(t)$ represents the additive white Gaussian noise. And r(t) is a receive signal which contains interference signal and noise. Meanwhile, $*$ represents the convolution operation. $\mathrm{Re}\{x\}$ denotes the real part of x, and $\hat{s}(t-\tau)$ is the Hibert transform of $s(t-\tau)$.

Given $\vec{a}=[a_1,a_2]^T$,where a_1 and a_2 are the attenuation coefficients of the same phase and orthogonal branch. So it is supposed that $\vec{s}(t)=[s_1(t),s_2(t)]^T$. Obviously, from Fig 1, the equivalent cancellation signal, by orthogonal vector synthesized , can be given as

$$s_c(t)=\vec{a}^T \bullet \vec{s}(t) \tag{3}$$

where $s_c(t)$ is the synthetic signal of the same phase and the orthogonal component. It's easy to see that the phase and amplitude of the synthetic signal can be adjusted by changing the elements of $\vec{a}$. From (3) and Fig 2, the residual self-interference signal after offsetting is written as

$$e(t) = r(t) - s_c(t) = r(t) - \vec{a}^T \bullet \vec{s}(t) \tag{4}$$

According to the irrelevance between $c(t)$ and $n(t)$, the analysis of the residual self-interference signal is equivalent to calculate the optimal attenuation coefficient vector $\vec{a}$. The aim is to minimize the power of the residual self-interference signal, just as

$$\min_{\vec{a}} E\{| e(t) |^2\} = \min_{\vec{a}} E\{(\mathrm{r}(t) - \vec{a} \bullet \vec{s}(t))^2\} \tag{5}$$

2.2 Optimal attenuation coefficients solution

From the previous section, the problem of self-interference cancellation can be changed to get the optimal solution of $\vec{a}$ when the power of residual signal is minimum. Considering the details of the error signal,

$$\begin{aligned} E\{| e(t) |^2\} &= E\{[r(t) - \vec{a}^T \bullet \vec{s}(t)][r(t) - \vec{a}^T \bullet \vec{s}(t)]\} \\ &= E\{r(t)^2 - 2r(t)\vec{a}^T \bullet \vec{s}(t) + \vec{a}^T \vec{s}(t) \bullet \vec{s}^T \vec{a}\} \end{aligned} \tag{6}$$

It can be assumed that the power of self-interference signal is P_c and the power of noise is σ_n^2. Then, from (2) and (6), a simplified form of (6) can be expressed as

$$\begin{aligned} E\{| e(t) |^2\} &= E\{c(t)^2 + n(t)^2 - 2[c(t) + n(t)]\vec{a}^T \bullet \vec{s}(t) + \vec{a}^T \vec{s}(t) \bullet \vec{s}^T(t)\vec{a}\} \\ &= P_c + \sigma_n^2 - 2E\{c(t)\vec{a}^T \vec{s}(t)\} + E\{\vec{a}^T \vec{s}(t) \bullet \vec{s}^T(t)\vec{a}\} \end{aligned} \tag{7}$$

Without loss of generality, suppose self-interference signal and reference signal are all stable. Then,

$$\vec{p} = E\{c(t)\vec{s}(t)\} \tag{8}$$

$$\vec{R} = E\{\vec{s}(t)\vec{s}^T(t)\} \tag{9}$$

where $\vec{p}$ is the correlation vector between reference signal and received signal, and $\vec{R}$ is the autocorrelation matrix of the reference signal. then (7) can be simplified as

$$E\{| e(t) |^2\} = P_c + \sigma_n^2 - 2\vec{a}^T \vec{p} + \vec{a}^T \vec{R}\vec{a} \tag{10}$$

From (5), the optimal solution can be get as by $\vec{a}$ when (10) gets the minimum. That is $\vec{a}$ should satisfy the requirement of (11).

$$\frac{\partial E\{|e(t)|^2\}}{\partial \vec{a}} = -2\vec{p} + 2\vec{R}\vec{a} = 0 \tag{11}$$

It can be seen that the error mean square function is a quadratic function of the attenuation coefficient vector $\vec{a}$. To solving the optimal value of the attenuation coefficient is to get the result of the Wiener Hoff's equation defined by (11).

However, the accurate estimation of the correlation vector $\vec{p}$ and the autocorrelation matrix $\vec{R}$ are difficult to get. However, the recursive method of the conventional Wiener Hoff's equation is restricted by the range of the eigenvalue of the relevant matrix , and it is impossible to get a fast and accurate answer[12]. In addition, if the relevant matrix from (11) is a singular matrix, the optimal solution can't be get usually. Therefore, we propose a method of iterative weighting to estimate the correlation vector $\vec{p}$ and the autocorrelation matrix $\vec{R}$, effectively. Furthermore, the least squares solution is obtained by using the generalized inverse matrix of autocorrelation matrix from (11). Then, the procedure can be expressed as (12), (13), (14) and (15).

$$\vec{p}_n = \mu\vec{p}_{n-1} + (1-\mu)\vec{p}' \tag{12}$$

$$\vec{R}_n = \mu\vec{R}_{n-1} + (1-\mu)\vec{R}' \tag{13}$$

$$\vec{p}' = \int_{t_0}^{t_1} r(t)\vec{s}(t)dt \tag{14}$$

$$\vec{R}' = \int_{t_0}^{t_1} \vec{s}(t)\vec{s}^T(t)dt \tag{15}$$

where μ is the weighting factor, t_0 and t_1 are the start time and end time , respectively. $\vec{p}_n$ is the nth iteration estimates of the correlation vector and $\vec{R}_n$ is the autocorrelation matrix. The initial values $\vec{p}_0$ and $\vec{R}_0$ can be set to zero.

On the basis of (11) to (15), the optimal value of the attenuation coefficient vector, corresponding to the nth iteration, is

$$\vec{a}_n = \vec{R}^+_n \vec{p}_n \tag{16}$$

where $\vec{R}_n^{+}$ is the Moore-Penrose inverse of the autocorrelation matrix $\vec{R}_n$. When $\vec{R}_n$ is not singular, $\vec{R}_n^{+} = \vec{R}_n^{-}$.

2.3 Interference cancellation ratio (ICR)

In addition to the convergence rate, another important performance indicator of pre-adjusting system is the ICR. According to section B, we can give a define of ICR as (17).

$$ICR = 10\lg\left(\frac{E\{|c(t)|^2\}}{E\{|e(t)|^2\} - E\{|n(t)|^2\}}\right) = 10\lg\left(\frac{P_c}{E\{|e(t)|^2\} - \sigma_n^2}\right) \quad (17)$$

Then, considering all the condition, the simplest form of ICR can be achieved as (18).

$$ICR = 20\lg\left(\frac{A_c}{A_e}\right) \quad (18)$$

where A_c is the amplitude of self-interference and A_e is the amplitude of the residual signal.

3 Simulation results

To verify the self-interference cancellation performance of the pre-adjusting system model as show in Fig 2, simulations are performed by the System View simulation software in this section. And some analysis also are done in an ideal environment and a real environment , respectively.

Without loss of generality, the reference signal is a sinusoidal signal . Its frequency is 300MHz. At the same time, the number of samples in this paper is set to300,000 in order to have better statistical properties.

As the reference signal may have other complex representations, we consider an amplitude modulation signal as reference signal, and other parameters remain the same.

3.1 Ideal environment

In this section, the disturbance is not given. Fig 3 shows the amplititude of the residual self-interference signal. Fig 4 and Fig 5 displays the frequency spectrum characteristics of the self-interference signal before and after cancellation. It is clear that the method of this paper has a significant effect on self-interference cancellation.

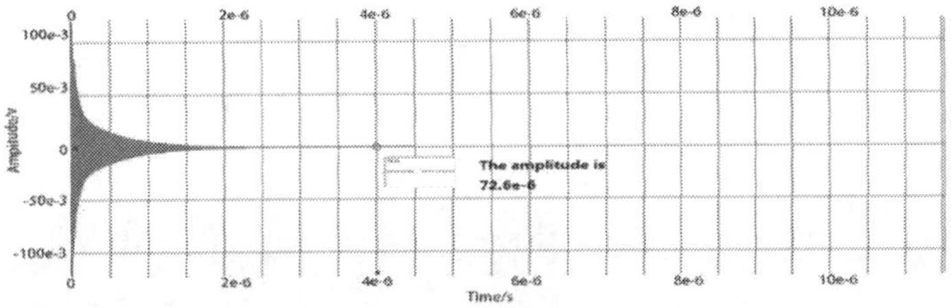

Fig. 3. Residual signal of self-interference in an ideal environment.

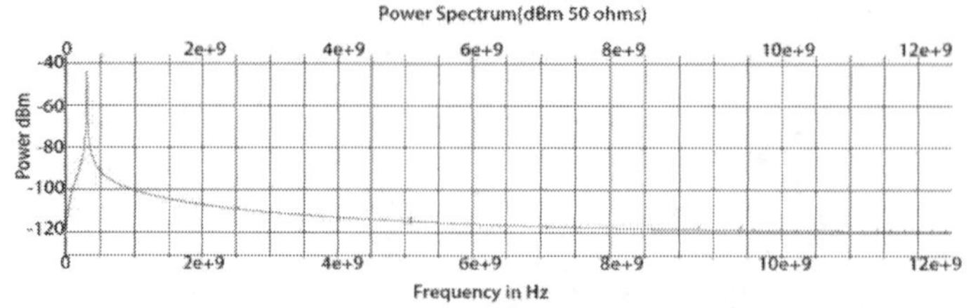

Fig. 4. The frequency spectrum of residual signal in an ideal environment.

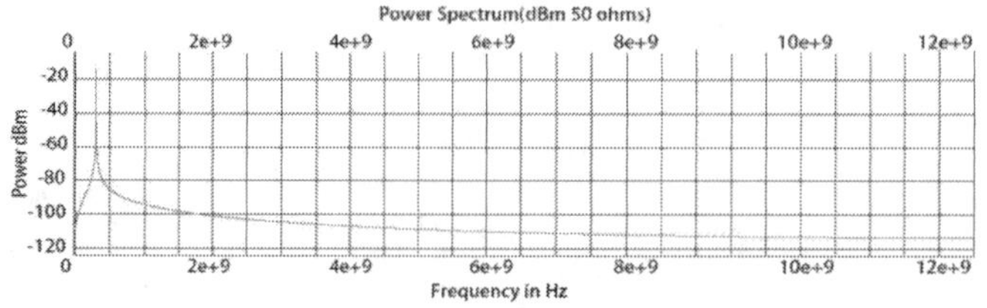

Fig. 5. The frequency spectrum of self-interference before cancellation

$$ICR = 20\lg\left(\frac{A_c}{A_e}\right) = 20\lg\left(\frac{0.1}{72.6\times10^{-6}}\right) = 62.8dB \tag{19}$$

As show in Fig 4, it is only 2 μs when the system converges to a steady state. Actually, the convergence process is to find the optimal attenuation vector. When the waveform tends to be stable, the optimal solution is found which is promised by 300,000 samples. Then, the ICR is 62.8 dB , which is shown in Fig and calculated by (19).

3.2 Real environment

As it is difficult for us to get an ideal Hilbert filter in reality, the inherent characteristic should be considered. In the simulation, we simulate the non-ideal part by give a disturbance in -60 dBm. Before interference cancellation, the mixed frequency spectrum of the self-interference and the disturbance is given by Fig 8.

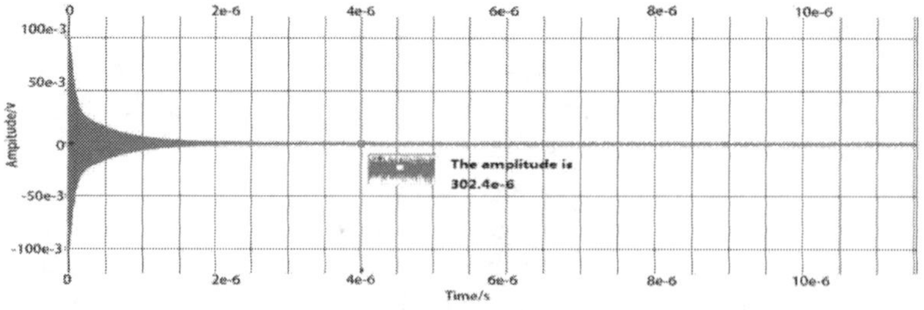

Fig. 6. Residual signal of self-interference in a real environment.

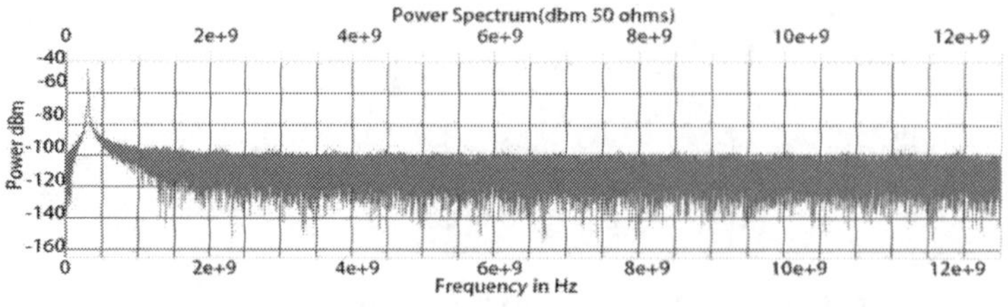

Fig. 7. The frequency spectrum of residual signal in a real environment.

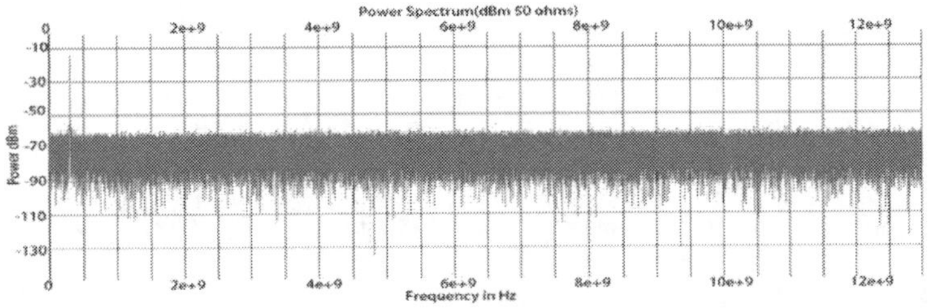

Fig. 8. The frequency spectrum in a real environment before interference cancellation.

Comparing the ordinates in Fig 7 and Fig 8, it can be seen that the amplitude has a disdinct decline after interference cancellation.

In Fig 6, it can be observed that the convergence time is about 2.5 μs which means we will get an optimal solution after 2.5 μs . The ICR is 50.4 dB which is shown in Fig 6 and calculated by (20), and the disturbance decrease 40 dBm, which is shown in Fig 7 and calculated by (21).

$$ICR = 20\lg\left(\frac{A_c}{A_e}\right) = 20\lg\left(\frac{0.1}{302.4\times10^{-6}}\right) = 50.4dB \tag{20}$$

$$-60dBm-(-100dBm)=40dB \tag{21}$$

Comparing Fig 4 with Fig 7, it can be seen that the main frequency components at 300MHz are close to each other, about -45 dBm. Note that when take the disturbance in, our method is influenced. It is the inherent characteristic of Hilbert filter that makes the self-interference cancellation performance be deteriorated. Obviously, this performance is 10.4 dB better than the ordinary demand of 40 dB in analog domain[13].

3.3 Amplitude modulated signal

In reality, there are lots of modulated signals. In this paper, the amplitude modulated signal is considered. Now, the reference signal can be expressed as (22),

$$s(t)=A\cos(2\pi ft)\cos(2\pi f_c t) \tag{22}$$

where A is the amplitude, f and f_c are the frequency of signal and carrier, respectively. The values of f , f_c are 300MHz and 3GHz respectively. It is possible to get (23) by simplifying (22).

$$s(t)=\frac{A}{2}\left\{\cos 2\pi(f_c+f)t+\cos 2\pi(f_c-f)t\right\} \tag{23}$$

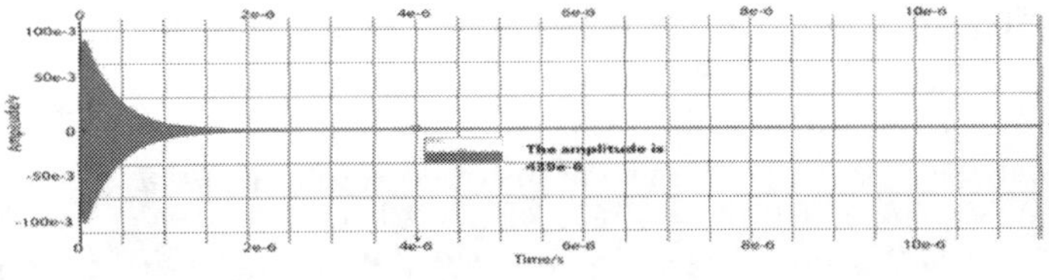

Fig. 9. Residual signal of self-interference.

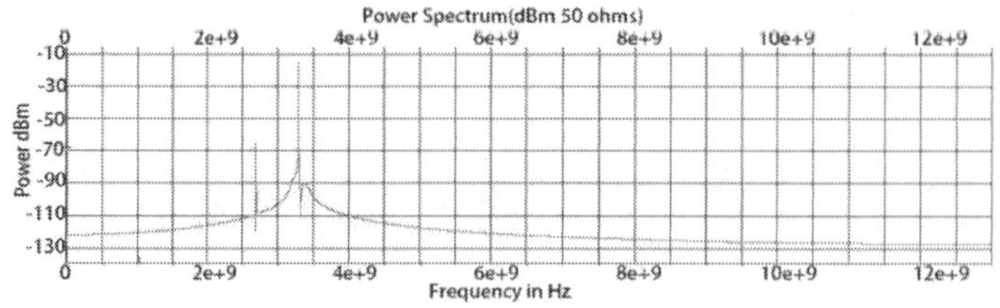

Fig. 10. The frequency spectrum before interference cancellation.

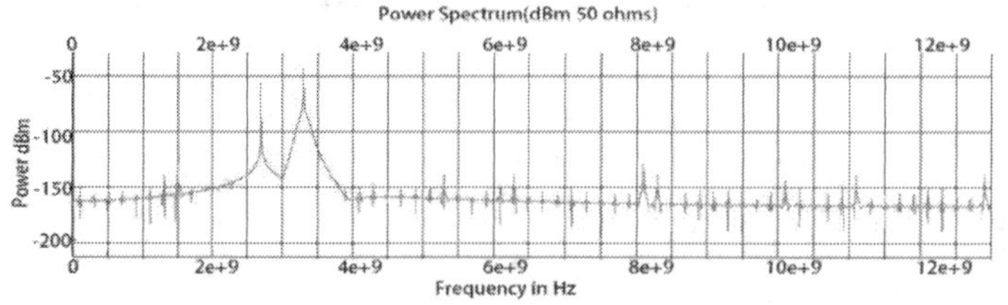

Fig. 11. The frequency spectrum after interference cancellation

$$ICR = 20\lg\left(\frac{A_c}{A_e}\right) = 20\lg\left(\frac{0.05}{439\times10^{-6}}\right) = 41.1dB \tag{24}$$

Depending on the symmetry, only the upper sideband need to be considered. The simulation of residual signal is expressed as Fig 9. Comparing Fig 10 with Fig 11, we can see that our method has a good performance in 3.3GHz. Meanwhile, there is a spectrum line in 2.7GHz, which is produced by the non-ideal characteristics of the band-pass filter. And the ICR is 41.1 dB from (24), which has an advantage of 1.1 dB than [13]. Obviously, it has a good job.

Conclusion

Based on the Six-channels Interference Canceller, this paper presents a new method of pre-adjusting system. Not only the clearly theoretical analysis is proposed, but also a way to solve the optimal attenuation vector is given. The results of simulation in System View tell us that this method has a 10.4 dB better performance than the ordinary demand. Meanwhile, it also has a good performance when the reference signal has a complex form. At the same time, a large number of samples are used in this paper to achieve a better performance, which increases the time loss. Therefore, the algorithm would be optimized in the future. Meanwhile, the environment of CCFD will be studied at a later time.

References

1. J. Lu, ZTE TECNOLOGY JOURNAL.23,2(2017)
2. J. Wang, H. Zhao, Y. Tang, *IEEE ICC*, pp. 5622-5627(2016)
3. H. Wang, J. Wang, H. Li, Jou&Mag, 23,858(2012)
4. J. Choi, M. Jain, K. Srinivasan, P. Levis, S. Katti , *MOBICOM*, 49,1(2010)
5. M. Jain, J. Choi, T. Kim, D. Bharadia, S. Seth, *ICMCN*. ACM pp. 301-312(2011)
6. S. Hong, J. Mehlman, S. Katti, *ASCCR*, 42,37(2012)
7. X. Liu, J. Liu, F. Zhao, W. Zhang, *IEEE ICCPS*, PP. 138-141(2015)
8. J. Liu, H. Quan, Z. Li, D. Liu, H. Zhao, J. E&I. T 39,654(2017)
9. I. Hwang, B. Song, N. Cong, SS. Soliman, IEEE Jou&Mag, 34,2838(2016)

10. Y. Xie, J. Liu, M. Li,S. Ouyang, G. Liao, Jou on Comm, 36,122(2015)
11. Y. Zhao, J. Lei, Ele Sci & Tec, 35,145(2016)
12. S. HAYKAN, *Adaptive Filter Theory*, pp. 440-465(2008)
13. Y. Tang, *Full Duplex Principles and Applications,* pp. 34-173(2016)

Joint Digital Self-interference Cancellation in Full-duplex Radios under IQ Imbalance and Transmitter Non-linearity

Meijing Zhou[1*], *Nan* Chen[1], *Changhua* Zhu[1], and *Yunhui* Yi[1]

[1]State Key Laboratory of Integrated Services Networks, Xidian University, Xi'an, Shaanxi, China

Abstract. RF imperfections can significantly degrade the performance of full-duplex wireless communication system by introducing non-idealities and random effects, which make it difficult to cancel the self-interference completely. In this paper, we first address the adverse benefits of both the transmitter non-linearity and the IQ imbalance. Then on the basis of these, a joint digital self-interference cancellation scheme is proposed, in which not only the effect of IQ imbalance and power amplifier non-linearity individually, but also the comprehensive function of them are taken into account. Furthermore, the simulation is implemented in the MATLAB platform using standard WiFi 802.11ac PHYs. The results show that the proposed canceller can eliminate more compared with other cancellation schemes, and the overall self-interference attenuation can attain 108dB, which makes the residual self-interference closer to the noise floor.

1 Introduction

Recently, full-duplex communication has become one of the research hotspots in the field of wireless communication [1-3], since it can increase the capacity of the communication system theoretically [4, 5]. However, the key problem in achieving a full-duplex wireless communication is the existence of strong self-interference (SI) signal.

At present, the commonly used method of SI cancellation is a combination of antenna separation, analog cancellation and digital cancellation [7-12]. However, the experimental data in [2, 3, 5] show that it's impossible to realize the complete SI elimination in practical full-duplex system by only classical linear SI cancellation. This is mainly affected by the RF impairments in the transceiver chains, such as: transmitter and receiver non-linearity, IQ imbalance, oscillator phase noise, quantization noise and receiver Gaussian noise, etc. The strength of each noise source at different received SI signal has been shown in [13]: The nonlinear distortion is the main limiting factor. It's pointed out that the mirror component caused by IQ imbalance in the direct-conversion transceiver chains is generally 25-40dB [6, 14, 15]. This means that the effect of IQ imbalance is not negligible, and must be taken into consideration.

In this paper, we first take both IQ imbalance and power amplifier (PA) non-linearity into account in the design of SI canceller for a 16QAM-based full-duplex radio. Based on

* Corresponding author: mjzhouxd@163.com

the discussion of the IQ imbalance and transmitter non-linearity in digital domain, we proposed a joint cancellation scheme, which can eliminate not only the image component and PA nonlinear distortion, but also the combination of the two items. Moreover, the unknown parameters are estimated according to the least-square (LS) criterion. Finally, the performances of the proposed scheme together with other three SI cancellers in digital domain are compared, and the results show that the residual SI in our scheme is minimal and closest to the noise floor.

The remainder of the paper is organized as follows. In section 2, the structure of the considered full-duplex radios is presented, alongside with analysis of RF impairments. Then we propose a joint digital SI cancellation scheme in section 3. In section 4, the entire system is simulated and the performances of different algorithms are evaluated. Finally, the conclusions are drawn in section 5.

2 System model and RF impairments

A full-duplex transceiver with SI cancellation is depicted in Fig. 1, where dual antennas are installed with distance of 20cm [5]. Physical isolation is used to maximize the attenuation of SI in antenna separation, and here the antenna cancellation is assumed to be 25dB. As to analog cancellation, it's just assumed that the amount of SI cancellation is 30 dB according to the typical cancellation scheme in [7] since the emphasis of this paper is placed on the cancellation of the effects introduced by RF impairments in digital domain.

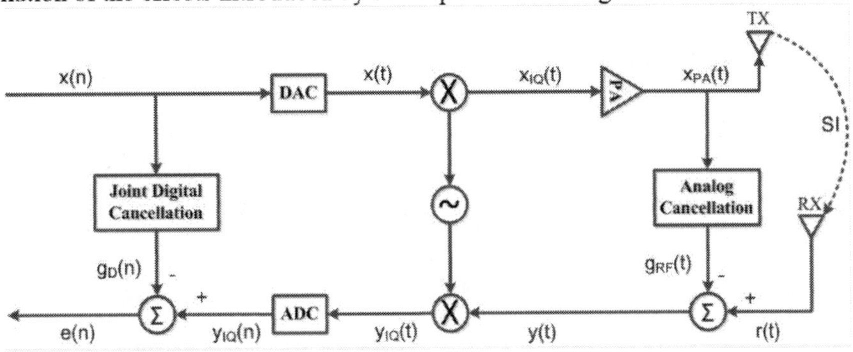

Fig. 1. A block of diagram for full-duplex transceiver with SI cancellation

In practical systems, it can't be negligible that each component of the transceiver is non-ideal, so we must take the impairments of these components into account. According to the previous discussion, we mainly consider the effect of IQ imbalance and PA nonlinear distortion. And in order to make the model simple and convenient, other RF impairments are ignored temporarily in this paper.

2.1 IQ imbalance

IQ imbalance is a prominent problem in most of the transceiver chains, which is mainly caused by the mismatch between I and Q branches of the quadrature modulator. The ideal quadrature modulator generally has a constant gain and a linear phase, thus the gain of I and Q branches is equal, and also the phase of the local oscillator signal is orthogonal [16]. However, in practical circuit, the quadrature modulator always has a certain amplitude and phase deviation, which leads to the imbalance of the gain in I and Q branches, and finally results in the mirror-frequency interference. The structure of quadrature modulator with IQ imbalance is presented in Fig. 2.

The signal $x(t)$ is up-converted into the signal at desired medium frequency by quadrature modulator, i.e. $x_I(t)$ and $x_Q(t)$, which represent the in-phase signal and quadrature-phase signal respectively. The symbol k and ϕ in Fig. 2 represent the imbalance of amplitude and phase in local oscillator. Then the signal $y(t)$ can be written as

$$\begin{aligned} y(t) &= x_I(t)\cdot\cos(2\pi ft) + x_Q(t)\cdot(1+k)\sin(2\pi ft+\phi) \\ &= g_1(t)\otimes x(t) + g_2(t)\otimes x^*(t) \end{aligned} \tag{1}$$

where $g_1(t)$ is the response for the direct signal component, and $g_2(t)$ is the response for the image component [15]. Here $\otimes$ indicates the convolution operation, and $(\cdot)^*$denotes the complex conjugate. The performance of quadrature modulator can be defined as image rejection ratio (IRR), and the expression of IRR is

$$IRR(dB) = 10\log 10\frac{1+(1+k)^2+2(1+k)\cos\phi}{1+(1+k)^2-2(1+k)\cos\phi} = 10\log 10\left(\left|G_1(f)\right|^2 \Big/ \left|G_2(f)\right|^2\right) \tag{2}$$

where $G_1(f)$ and $G_2(f)$ are the Fourier transformation of $g_1(t)$ and $g_2(t)$ respectively.

2.2 PA non-linearity

The non-linearity of PA in transmitter is the most widely researched source of distortion in the existing literature. We use Taylor series expansion to approximate the non-linear function, which is a standard way to model non-linear functions [7]. Generally, the output of the nonlinear PA block can be written as

$$y(t)=\sum_{m=1}^{M} a_m x^m \tag{3}$$

It can be shown that for practical wireless systems, only the odd orders of the polynomial contribute to the in-band distortion [9], and the third order item is the main influence factor, so the higher orders are ignored in this paper. Thus we can rewrite (3) as

$$y(t)=a_1x(t)+a_3x^3(t) \tag{4}$$

where a_1 and a_3 are the weights of linear item and third order item respectively.

2.3 SI cancellation model

Based on the above analysis, the following cancellation model of the whole system only considers the PA non-linearity and IQ imbalance. According to the research in literature [9], we make some simplification to the analysis procedure, and expand the final SI signal model with the cross combination items of IQ imbalance and PA non-linearity.

The baseband signal is represented by $x(n)$, and $x(t)$ is the corresponding RF signal after digital-to-analog converter (DAC). The signal $x(t)$ is then up-converted into the required frequency for transmission by quadrature modulator with the error k and ϕ. Then according to (1), we can obtain the up-converted signal $x_{IQ}(t)$

$$x_{IQ}(t)=g_{1,TX}(t)\otimes x(t)+g_{2,TX}(t)\otimes x^*(t) \tag{5}$$

where $g_{1,TX}(t)$ and $g_{2,TX}(t)$ are the response of each item in the transmitter chain.

It should be amplified by PA in transmitter to the specified power before transmitting. The output of PA can be acquired according to (4)

$$x_{PA}(t)=a_1x_{IQ}(t)+a_3x_{IQ}^3(t) \tag{6}$$

For simplicity, $x_{IQ3}(t)$ is used instead of $x_{IQ}^3(t)$ in (6), which refers to the third order non-linearity. As mentioned in section 2.2, the transmission path and analog canceller are regarded as a whole channel here, and $h_{RF}(t)$ is the response of the channel. So the signal before the quadrature modulator in RX radios can be written as

$$y(t)=h_{RF}(t)\otimes x_{PA}(t) \tag{7}$$

Similar to the transmitter chain, the signal is down-converted to the baseband frequency through quadrature modulator in the receiver chain, which also produces the mirror-frequency interference. The equation for $y_{IQ}(t)$ is as follows

$$y_{IQ}(t)=g_{1,RX}(t)\otimes y(t)+g_{2,RX}(t)\otimes y^{*}(t) \tag{8}$$

where $g_{1,RX}(t)$ and $g_{2,RX}(t)$ are the response of each item in the receiver chain. Finally, the signal is digitized by analog-to-digital converter (ADC), $y_{IQ}(n)$ is the expression of $y_{IQ}(t)$ in digital domain.

To obtain the final digital cancellation model, we substitute (5) to (6), then take the results into (7), (8) successively. The signal $y_{IQ}(n)$ can be written as

$$y_{IQ}(n) = h_1(n)\otimes x(n) + h_2(n)\otimes x^{*}(n) + h_{IQ3}(n)\otimes x_{IQ3}(n) + h_{IQ3,im}(n)\otimes x^{*}_{IQ3}(n) + w(n) \tag{9}$$

where $w(n)$ is the overall other noise in the transceiver, and $h_1(n)$, $h_2(n)$, $h_{IQ3}(n)$ as well as $h_{IQ3,im}(n)$ represent the channel response of $x(n)$, $x^{*}(n)$, $x_{IQ3}(n)$ and $x^{*}_{IQ3}(n)$ respectively, they can be expanded as

$$h_1(n) = a_1 g_{1,TX}(n)\otimes h_{RF}(n)\otimes g_{1,RX}(n) + a_1^{*} g_{2,TX}^{*}(n)\otimes h_{RF}^{*}(n)\otimes g_{2,RX}(n) \tag{10}$$

$$h_2(n) = a_1 g_{2,TX}(n)\otimes h_{RF}(n)\otimes g_{1,RX}(n) + a_1^{*} g_{1,TX}^{*}(n)\otimes h_{RF}^{*}(n)\otimes g_{2,RX}(n) \tag{11}$$

$$h_{IQ3}(n)=a_3 h_{RF}(n)\otimes g_{1,RX}(n) \tag{12}$$

$$h_{IQ3,im}(n)=a_3^{*} h_{RF}^{*}(n)\otimes g_{2,RX}(n) \tag{13}$$

From (9), it can be found that the total SI in the digital domain contains not only the linear components and the image components, but also the items $x_{IQ3}(n)$ and $x^{*}_{IQ3}(n)$, which are the cross combination items of IQ imbalance and PA nonlinear distortion. However, $x_{IQ3}(n)$ and $x^{*}_{IQ3}(n)$ are expressions about $x(n)$, $x^{*}(n)$, and can't be obtained directly from the transmitted signal, so it's necessary to expand the two items continuously.

Following the polynomial expansion formula $(a+b)^3 = a^3 + 3a^2b + 3ab^2 + b^3$, $x_{IQ3}(n)$ and $x^{*}_{IQ3}(n)$ can be written as

$$\begin{aligned} x_{IQ3}(n) &= \left[g_{1,TX}(n)\otimes x(n)+g_{2,TX}(n)\otimes x^{*}(n)\right]^3 \\ &= a_1(n)\otimes x^3(n)+3a_2(n)\otimes\left[x^2(n)x^{*}(n)\right]+3a_3(n)\otimes\left[x(n)(x^{*}(n))^2\right]+a_4(n)\otimes(x^{*}(n))^3 \end{aligned} \tag{14}$$

$$\begin{aligned} x^{*}_{IQ3}(n) &= \left[(g_{1,TX}(n)\otimes x(n)+g_{2,TX}(n)\otimes x^{*}(n))^3\right]^{*} \\ &= a_4^{*}(n)\otimes x^3(n)+3a_3^{*}(n)\otimes\left[x^2(n)x^{*}(n)\right]+3a_2^{*}(n)\otimes\left[x(n)(x^{*}(n))^2\right]+a_1^{*}(n)\otimes(x^{*}(n))^3 \end{aligned} \tag{15}$$

where $a_1(n) \sim a_4(n)$ and $a_1^*(n) \sim a_4^*(n)$ are the weights of individual signal components. The signal $y_{IQ}(n)$ can be simply rewritten by substituting (14), (15) to (9) as

$$\begin{aligned} y_{IQ}(n) &= h_1(n) \otimes x(n) + h_2(n) \otimes x^*(n) + h_3(n) \otimes x^3(n) + h_4(n) \otimes (x^*(n))^3 \\ &+ h_5(n) \otimes (x^2(n)x^*(n)) + h_6(n) \otimes (x(n)(x^*(n))^2) + w(n) \end{aligned} \tag{16}$$

where $h_1(n)$ and $h_2(n)$ are the same as which in (9), $h_3(n) \sim h_6(n)$ are the response for the corresponding signal components, we can expand them as follows

$$h_3(n) = h_{IQ3}(t) \otimes a_1(n) + h_{IQ3,im}(t) \otimes a_4^*(n) \tag{17}$$

$$h_4(n) = h_{IQ3}(t) \otimes a_4(n) + h_{IQ3,im}(t) \otimes a_1^*(n) \tag{18}$$

$$h_5(n) = 3h_{IQ3}(t) \otimes a_2(n) + 3h_{IQ3,im}(t) \otimes a_3^*(n) \tag{19}$$

$$h_6(n) = 3h_{IQ3}(t) \otimes a_3(n) + 3h_{IQ3,im}(t) \otimes a_2^*(n) \tag{20}$$

Now the individual signal components can be easily obtained by some elementary manipulations, what need to do is estimating the responses and reconstructing a cancellation signal, then subtracting it from the SI in digital domain at last.

3 Joint digital SI cancellation

As discussed in section 2, the residual SI in the digital domain considering both IQ imbalance and PA nonlinear distortion has been analyzed. Different from [9], the equation about SI is expressed as the sum of six distrinct parts rather than four components. Next, the corresponding unknown coefficients will be estimated and then the final SI cancellation will be carried out. In Fig. 3, the structure of digital SI cancellation is depicted.

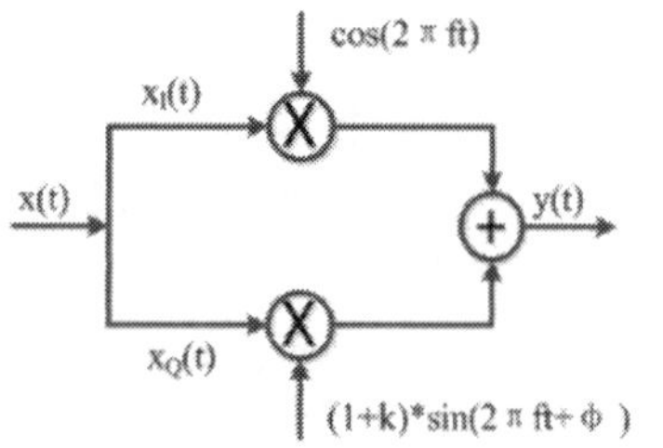

Fig. 2. The structure of quadrature modulator with IQ imbalance.

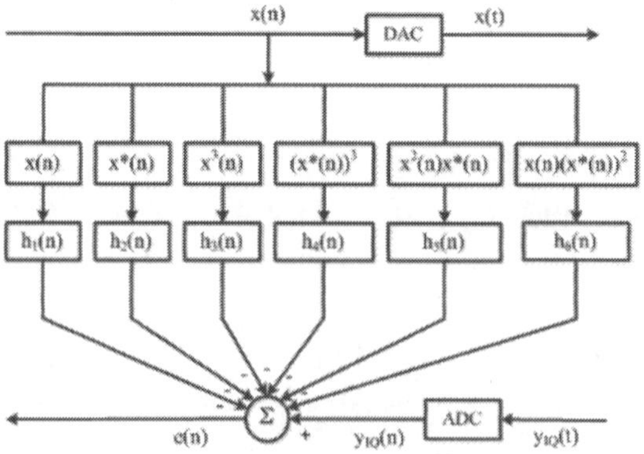

Fig. 3. A schematic diagram of the proposed joint digital SI cancellation.

From (16), $x(n)$ is the original signal in the baseband, $x^*(n)$ denotes the complex conjugate, $x^3(n)$ represents the third order non-linearity, and the others are the cross combination items of IQ imbalance and PA nonlinear distortion. Since the transmitted signal is known, the above six items are also available. It's assumed that the number of signal samples is N, then (16) can be rewritten with vector-matrix notation

$$\begin{aligned} y_{IQ} &= Xh_1 + X^*h_2 + X^3h_3 + (X^*)^3h_4 + (X^2X^*)h_5 + (X(X^*)^2)h_6 + W \\ &= [X\; X^*\; X^3\; (X^*)^3\; (X^2X^*)\; (X(X^*)^2)][h_1\; h_2 \;\mathrm{L}\; h_6]^T + W \\ &= X_{aug}h_{aug} + W \end{aligned} \tag{21}$$

where $y_{IQ} = [\; y_{IQ}(1) \quad y_{IQ}(2) \quad \cdots \quad y_{IQ}(N)\;]^T$, $[\cdot]^T$ indicates the transpose of vector and W is the corresponding vector form of $w(n)$.

Here, the values of signal at further/before times than n are used to estimate the value of signal at time n [7]. For example, X is the Toeplitz matrix of $x(n)$

$$X = \begin{bmatrix} x(k) & \cdots & x(1) & \cdots & x(-k+1) \\ x(k+1) & \cdots & x(2) & \cdots & x(-k+2) \\ \vdots & \ddots & \vdots & \ddots & \vdots \\ x(N+k-1) & \cdots & x(N) & \cdots & x(-k+N) \end{bmatrix} \tag{22}$$

where k is the numbers of pre- and post-cursor filter taps. Similarly, the other signal matrix in (21) can also be written in the form of Toeplitz matrix and will not be enumerated.

The goal is to find the optimal estimation of the vector h_{aug}, it can be calculated following the LS criterion

$$\hat{h}_{aug} = (X_{aug}^H X_{aug})^{-1} X_{aug} y_{IQ} \tag{23}$$

where $[\cdot]^H$ indicates the conjugate transpose of matrix. From the augmented channel estimation, the individual channel estimations can be directly obtained as follows

$$\hat{h}_1 = \left[\; \hat{h}_{aug}(0) \quad \hat{h}_{aug}(1) \quad \cdots \quad \hat{h}_{aug}(2k-1) \;\right]^T \tag{24}$$

$$\hat{h}_2 = \left[\; \hat{h}_{aug}(2k) \quad \hat{h}_{aug}(2k+1) \quad \cdots \quad \hat{h}_{aug}(4k-1) \;\right]^T \tag{25}$$

and

$$\hat{h}_6 = \left[\; \hat{h}_{aug}(10k) \quad \hat{h}_{aug}(10k+1) \quad \cdots \quad \hat{h}_{aug}(12k-1) \;\right]^T \tag{26}$$

The equations of $\hat{h}_3 \sim \hat{h}_5$ are omitted here.

As mentioned above, the cancellation signal $g_D(n)$ in Fig. 1 can be successfully constructed with good estimations of the responses of individual signal components. Thereby, we can eliminate it from the SI after RF cancellation to the level of noise floor as close as possible and render the residual SI negligible.

4 Simulation results and analysis

In this section, the validity of the above analysis results is verified with full waveform simulations of a complete full-duplex transceiver. A similar transceiver model, as shown in Fig. 1, will be implemented in MATLAB platform, and the IQ imbalance as well as the PA non-linearity will be both taken into consideration.

Firstly, the whole simulation is implemented in a dual-antenna case at WiFi 2.4GHz with an average transmit power of 20dBm and a bandwidth of 10MHz. The signal of interest and the noise floor is set to -85dBm and -100dBm separately. Besides, PA and quadrature modulator in transceiver chains are installed with typical parameters in practical systems. The adverse benefit of IQ imbalance is modeled by introducing some offsets both in amplitude (k) and phase (ϕ) to I and Q branches, and the IRR is set to 30dB. Moreover, the channel is first estimated through the transmitted training samples, and then together with the signal samples, is subtracted from the SI. The performance of the simulation is analyzed mainly based on the metric: the cancellation of residual SI in digital domain.

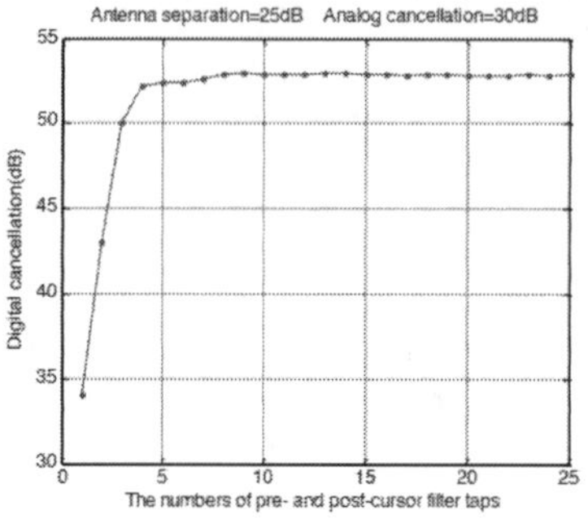

Fig. 4. The amount of digital cancellation obtained using the proposed canceller with different numbers of pre- and post-cursor filter taps

In the first simulation scenario, we investigate the relationship between the amount of digital cancellation and the value of k by changing the number of pre- and post-cursor filter taps. Fig. 4 shows that the digital cancellation is improved with the increase of k to some degree, but when k is higher than 10, there are no significant differences in the obtained digital cancellation. It suggests that the nearby signal having great correlation with the estimated signal, which then affects the accuracy of channel estimation, and the signals much further have little impact on it. Thus we should choose an appropriate number of filter taps for digital SI cancellation. In order to achieve the best performance, we fix the value of k to 10 in the following simulations.

Next, four different cancellation schemes are compared considering both IQ imbalance and PA nonlinear distortion: classical linear canceller; linear canceller with image components, the channel response function can be estimated as $\hat{\boldsymbol{h}}_{augl} = (\boldsymbol{X}_{augl}^H \boldsymbol{X}_{augl})^{-1} \boldsymbol{X}_{augl}^H \boldsymbol{y}_{IQ}$, and $\hat{\boldsymbol{h}}_3 \sim \hat{\boldsymbol{h}}_6 = \boldsymbol{0}$, where $\boldsymbol{X}_{augl} = \begin{bmatrix} \boldsymbol{X} & \boldsymbol{X}^* \end{bmatrix}$ and $\hat{\boldsymbol{h}}_{augl} = \begin{bmatrix} \hat{\boldsymbol{h}}_1 & \hat{\boldsymbol{h}}_2 \end{bmatrix}^T$; nonlinear canceller with third order non-linearity, the channel can be estimated as $\hat{\boldsymbol{h}}_{aug2} = (\boldsymbol{X}_{aug2}^H \boldsymbol{X}_{aug2})^{-1} \boldsymbol{X}_{aug2}^H \boldsymbol{y}_{IQ}$, and $\hat{\boldsymbol{h}}_2, \hat{\boldsymbol{h}}_4 \sim \hat{\boldsymbol{h}}_6 = \boldsymbol{0}$, where $\boldsymbol{X}_{aug2} = \begin{bmatrix} \boldsymbol{X} & \boldsymbol{X}^3 \end{bmatrix}$ and $\hat{\boldsymbol{h}}_{aug2} = \begin{bmatrix} \hat{\boldsymbol{h}}_1 & \hat{\boldsymbol{h}}_3 \end{bmatrix}^T$; the proposed canceller. The measured power spectral densities (PSD) are shown in Fig. 5 and Fig. 6 respectively.

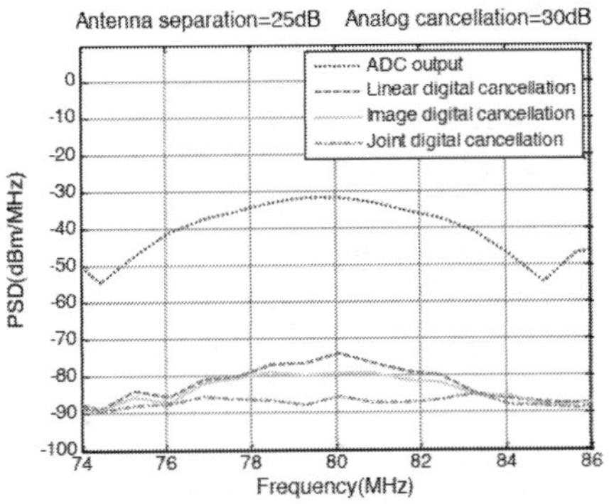

Fig. 5. The achieved power spectral densities with three different cancellers respectively, compared with ADC output.

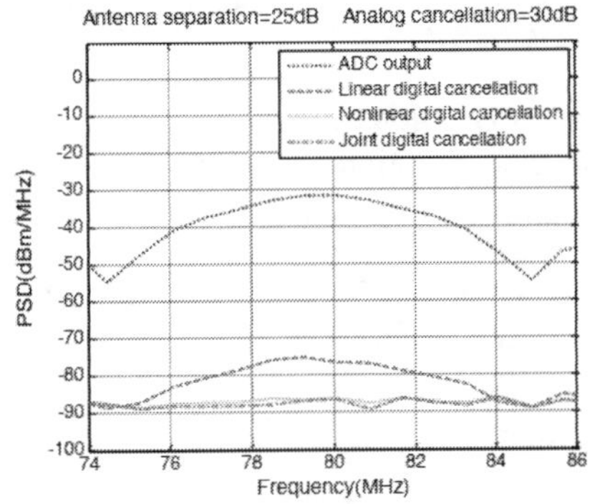

Fig. 6. The achieved power spectral densities with three different cancellers respectively, compared with ADC output.

The analysis results show that: the performance of the proposed canceller is superior to the other three cancellers. The linear digital canceller can attenuate the SI signal only by 45dB after RF cancellation, while the linear canceller with image components and the nonlinear canceller with third order non-linearity achieve 47dB and 52dB at the frequencies from 75MHz to 85MHz respectively. Intuitively, the proposed canceller obtained the best performance up to 53dB. To summarize, the simulation results prove the validity of the proposed model foregoing. Meanwhile, it illustrates clearly that only eliminating the linear components is not enough, the effects of RF impairments must be taken into consideration and attenuated in the digital domain. Although the joint digital cancellation scheme increases the complexity of the model and computation to some extent, it does improve the interference cancellation ratio in the digital domain. Combined with antenna separation and analog cancellation, the overall amount of cancellation can be the same level as 108dB.

In Fig. 7, the whole amounts of SI attenuation of above four schemes under different signal-to-noise ratios (SNR) are presented. The result of (a) shows that when SNR is increased, the PA non-linearity becomes the dominant noise component. The difference between (a) and (b) is that IRR=30dB in (a) and IRR=25dB in (b). It can be observed that the distances between the upper two lines and the lower two lines are both little bigger than these in (a) as SNR is increased. That is to say, with the increasing of the IQ imbalance, the advantage of the joint digital cancellation is more prominent.

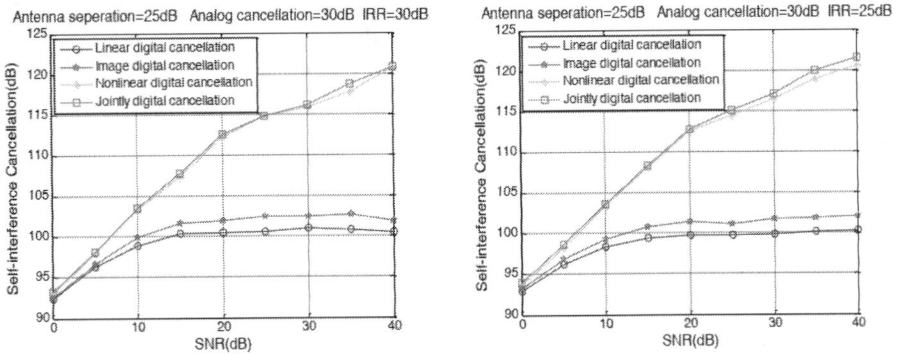

(a) (b)

Fig. 7. The amount of SI cancellation as a function of SNR under the circumstance of 25dB antenna suppression and 30dB analog cancellation, with (a) IRR =25dB and (b) IRR=30dB.

5 Conclusion

In this paper, a joint digital SI cancellation scheme for full-duplex radios is proposed, and the adverse benefits of IQ imbalance and PA non-linearity are analyzed in detail. The proposed canceller increases the amount of cancellable SI signal power up to 108dB by taking all the distortions caused by IQ imbalance and PA non-linearity into account rather than partially, which means that it's able to suppress the SI to the next significant noise component. Accordingly, we will consider the LNA non-linearity together in the cancellation model to make the residual SI signal equal or even lower than the noise floor in the future.

References

1. D.W. Bliss, P.A. Parker, A.R. Margetts, IEEE/SP **2** , 478(2007).
2. M. Duarte, A. Sabharwal, IEEE. ASILOMAR **3**, 1558 (2010).
3. JI. Choi, M. Jain, K. Srinivasan, P. Levis, S. Katti, ACM MOBICOM **49**, 1 (2010).
4. A. Sabharwal, P. Schniter, D. Guo, D.W. Bliss, S. Rangarajan, R. Wichman, IEEE. Journ. Sel. Areas Commun. **32**, 1637 (2014).
5. M. Duarte, C. Dick, A. Sabharwal, IEEE. Trans. Wirel. Commun. **11**, 4296 (2012).
6. Y. Sun, H. Zuo, L. Song, Journ. Electr. Sci. Tech. **45**, 873 (2016).
7. D. Bharadia, E. Mcmilin, S. Katti, ACM SIGCOMM. **43**, 375 (2013).
8. T. Chen, S. Liu, IEEE. GLOBECOM 1 (2015).
9. D. Korpi, L. Anttila, et al, IEEE. Journ. Sel. Areas Commun. **32**, 1674 (2014).
10. L. Samara, M. Mokhtar, O. Ozdemir, et al, IEEE. Commun. Lett. **21**, 314 (2017).
11. M. Sakai, H. Lin, K. Yamashita, Phys. Commun. **18**, 2 (2016).
12. A. Masmoudi, T. Le-Ngoc, IEEE. Trans. Vehi. Tech. **65**, 5122 (2017).
13. E. Ahmed, A.M. Eltawil, A. Sabharwal, IEEE. Asilom. Confer. Sig. Syst. Comput. **118**, 1199 (2013).
14. L. Anttila, D. Korpi, V. Syrjala, M. Valkama, IEEE. Asilom. Confer. Sig. Syst. Comput. **118**, 1193 (2013).
15. L. Anttila, M. Valkama, M. Renfors, IEEE. Trans. on Circ. & Syst. II Expr. Bri. **55**, 359 (2008).
16. S. Hu, M. Li, Acad. Semin. Commun. Depart. Chin. Univ. (2009).
17. J. Lu, Modern Radar **21**,100 (1999).

Multi-hop Fast Conflict Resolution Algorithm for Ad Hoc Networks

Shengwei Wang[1], *Jun* Liu[2,*], *Wei* Cai[2], *Minghao* Yin[2], *Lingyun* Zhou[2], and *Hui* Hao[3]

[1]Power Emergency Center, Sichuan Electric Power Corporation, Chengdu, China
[2]National Key Laboratory of Science and Technology on Communications, University of Electronic Science and Technology of China, Chengdu, China
[3]Information Technology Center, Tsinghua University, Peking, China

Abstract. Media access control is an important technology in ad hoc networks. Based on the multi-hop Pseudo Bayesian (PB) algorithm and the single-hop Fast Conflict Resolution algorithm (FCR), in this paper, we propose a Multi-hop Fast Conflict Resolution (MFCR) algorithm for ad hoc networks. We make the detailed introduction of the theoretical model, the pseudo Bayesian analysis and the algorithm deign. MFCR employs a competition probability forecasting method, which is similar to the back-off counter used in FCR, combined with the handshake process used in PB to solve the utilization and the fairness problems of the time slot allocation. Simulations show that the MFCR has evident improvement in the network performance.

1 Introduction

The media access control is an important technology in Ad-Hoc networks [1]. Because of the limitation of frequency, the wireless channel resource is relatively scarce. Meanwhile, the channel fading, the interference and the transmission collision will deteriorate the transmission capacity [2][3]. Hence, the channel resource allocation will play an important role. The channel of Ad-Hoc networks is a multi-hop broadcast shared channel, only the nodes are far away from each other can reuse the same frequency at the same time [4].

In Time Division Multiple Access (TDMA) Media Access Control (MAC) protocol [5][6][7], the wireless channel is divided into periodic frames in time dimension, and each frame consists of some time slots. The goal of channel resource allocation is making nodes rationally utilize limited slot resource according to the network situation.

The static TDMA protocol can't adjust the slot allocation scheme to the network situation, which will cause the waste of the channel resource. In contrast, the dynamic TDMA protocol can adjust the slot allocation flexibly to adapt to the network situation [8], so it can effectively use the slot resource.

The Five-Phase Reservation Protocol (FPRP) is a typical dynamic TDMA protocol based on competition [9]. The nodes in the network obtain their own delivery slot through competition mechanism, so the slot allocation of each time frame is different.

* Corresponding author: liu_jun@uestc.edu.cn

Due to the distributed characteristic, the FPRP protocol can be executed independently by each node. That is to say, the nodes more than two hops can simultaneously use the same slot. For each node, the slot reservation process can be regarded as a local reservation procedure, which only involves the slot reservation within two hops. Through the local reservation process, it makes the network have a good scalability.

In FPRP protocol, the single wireless channel is logically divided into the reservation channel and the information channel. To TDMA frame, it is the reservation frame and the information frame. Each reservation frame and information frame has the same number of time slots. In the reservation phase, the node reserves time slot by a five phase handshake mechanism. In this way, FPRP can realize a conflict-free slot allocation for packet delivery. The reservation frame is followed by a number of information frames, the nodes in the network can transmit data in the information slot until the next reservation frame.

2 System model

We use graph $G(V, E)$ to represent the network topology, where V is the node set and E is the link set in the network. If there is a link between node i and node j, we use an undirected edge $e_{i,j}$, $e_{i,j} \in E$, to represent the one-hop neighboring relationship. If there is no direct link between node i and node j, but they have a common neighbor k, we define node i and node j as two-hop neighbor. We use matrix $\mathbf{C}(G)=[c_{ij}]_{N\times N}$ and $\mathbf{D}(G)=[d_{ij}]_{N\times N}$ to represent the one-hop connection relationship and the two-hop connection relationship respectively 10. The c_{ij} and d_{ij} are defined as

$$c_{ij}=\begin{cases}1, & e_{ij}\in E, i\neq j\\ 0, & else\end{cases} \tag{1}$$

$$d_{ij}=\begin{cases}1, & e_{ik},e_{jk}\in E, e_{ij}\notin E, i\neq j\\ 0, & else\end{cases} \tag{2}$$

Owing to the nodes in a half-duplex wireless network cannot receive multiple packets simultaneous and cannot transmit and receive at the same time 11, the time slot of each node must be different from the one-hop neighbors and the two-hop neighbors to avoid transmission collision.

The main goal of the slot assignment algorithm is to maximize the channel utilization with the minimum number of time frames. Consider a time frame has M slots and each node's slot number is at least one. We use a $M\times N$ matrix $\mathbf{T}=[t_{mi}]_{M\times N}$ to represent the slot allocation scheme in network. If time slot m belongs to node i, we set $t_{mi}=1$, otherwise $t_{mi}=0$, and define the slot utilization of node i as

$$\rho_i=\frac{\sum_{m=1}^{M}t_{mi}}{M} \tag{3}$$

The slot utilization of the whole network can be expressed as

$$\rho=\frac{1}{N}\sum_{i=1}^{N}\rho_i=\frac{1}{MN}\sum_{m=1}^{M}\sum_{i=1}^{N}t_{mi} \tag{4}$$

As a result, the slot allocation can be summarized as the following mathematical model

$$\min M \text{ and } \max \rho \tag{5}$$

$$\begin{aligned} s.t.\,C1&: \sum\nolimits_{m=1}^{M} t_{mi} \geq 1 \ \ (i \in N) \\ C2&: c_{ij} + t_{mi} + t_{mj} \leq 2 \ \ (i,j \in N, i \neq j, m \in M) \\ C3&: c_{ik} t_{mi} + c_{jk} t_{mj} \leq 1 \ \ (i,j,k \in N, i \neq j \neq k, m \in M) \end{aligned} \tag{6}$$

where $C1$ denotes that each node takes at least one slot, $C2$ represents two one-hop neighbors can't be allocated with the same slots, $C3$ stands for that two-hop neighbors can't use the same slots.

3 Pseudo baysian algorthm

In this paper, we use the Pseudo Bayesian algorithm 12 to calculate the probability of nodes participating in the slot reservation. Through the five phase handshake reservation mechanism in FPRP, the node in the network can sense the current slot reservation status, such as success, idle, and conflict. Because the reservation process is a local process within two-hop, the node needs to maintain two parameters: one is the number of competition nodes within its two-hop; the other is the number of nodes want to reserve the slot, but can't compete for the current slot due to the slot being reserved by others. When a node is informed that the current slot is allocated to one of its neighbors, it stops the competition for the current slot, but can still participate in the competition for the next slot. The status of idle, conflict, and success will affect the number of competition neighbors within two-hop, so the nodes can participate in the remaining reservation process with a modified competition probability.

According to Pseudo Bayesian algorithm, the competition probability of each node is related to the number of competing nodes within two-hop. That is, the number of competitors in two-hop is inversely proportional to the competition probability. Consider two situations in the network, the one is in the dense area (such as the network center area), the other is in the sparse area (such as the edge of the network). Because there are more neighbors in the dense area, more reservation activities will take place, and there will be more conflicts. As it is hard to find the idle state in the reservation process, the possibility of decreasing the competition probability is high. On the other hand, because there are fewer neighbors in the sparse area, there will be fewer conflicts, and it is easier to sense the idle state in the reservation process. According to the Pseudo Bayesian algorithm, once a node finds an idle state in the current sot reservation process, the competition probability will be increased. So the possibility of increasing the competition probability in the sparse area is higher than that in the dense area. Thus, the difference of node density in two-hop will result in unfair slot allocation.

4 Multi-hop fast conflict resolution algorithm

In order to solve the problem in multi-hop pseudo Bayesian algorithm, we propose a Multi-hop Fast Collision Resolution (MFCR) based on single-hop Fast Collision Resolution (FCR) [13]. In FCR, when the node senses the idle slot, the value of back off counter decreases by one. When a node checks continuously idle slots, once the slot been idle again, the value of back off counter decreases by half. On the other hand, when a node senses the collision, it doubles the value of contention window (CW). Set a random number between 0 - CW as the value of back off counter. In this way, when collision emerges, the node defers its channel access to decrease the collision possibility.

MFCR applies the Fast Conflict Resolution in the multi-hop ad hoc networks. In MFCR, n_c is used to predict the number of neighbors within two-hop, the role of n_c is similar to the back off counter used in FCR. The larger n_c is, the smaller the competition probability of a slot achieves. Considering the fairness of slot allocation, we limit n_c between $n_{\min}$ and $n_{\max}$. Through the five-phase handshake process taken in FPRP protocol, each node can sense the reservation status of the current slot. At the beginning of reservation process, n_c is initially set to the minimal value $n_{\min}$. After the reservation process finished in a round, the node updates n_c according to the following algorithm.

Algorithm 1 Competition probability adjustment

Input: Reservation status
Output: Competition probability
Note: x denote the number of continuous idle and k is the threshold of continuous idle state, $0 < \beta < \alpha < 1$. h denote the number of hops to the successful reserving node, and $0 < a_3 < a_2 < a_1 < 1$. P denote the competition probability.
1. **switch** (reservation status)
2. **case** idle:
3. **if** $x < k$, then
4. $n_c = \max(\alpha n_c, n_{\min})$
5. **else**
6. $n_c = \max(\beta n_c, n_{\min})$
7. **case** conflict:
8. **if** the node is the reservation initiator
9. $n_c = n_c + random(0, \min(2n_c, n_{\max}) - n_c)$
10. **case** success:
11. **if** $h == 0$, $n_c = n_{\max}$
12. **if** $h == 1$, $n_c = \max(a_1 n_c, n_{\min})$
13. **if** $h == 2$, $n_c = \max(a_2 n_c, n_{\min})$
14. **if** $h \geq 3$, $n_c = \max(a_3 n_c, n_{\min})$.
15. **end of switch**
16. $P = 1 / n_c$

Then repeat the above steps

In Idle state, MFCR takes α and β as the amplitude factors to multiply by n_c, the reduction of β to n_c is greater than that of α to n_c. When the number of the continuous idle states detected is less than k, MFCR uses α to reduce n_c, and the competition probability of the node increase slowly. If the number of continuous idle state is equal to or bigger than k, which means that only a few competition nodes are within two-hop, and the collision probability is low.

When a node encounters a conflict, it will decrease the competition probability rapidly b sharply increase of n_c. In other words, in MFCR, while the reservation collision occurs within two-hop, the proposed conflict resolution algorithm can decrease the reservation collision rapidly.

After successfully reserving a time slot, the node updates n_c with the maximum value n_{max} to decrease the competition probability of the next time slot, which guarantees the fairness of slot allocation. If a node gets the information that a one-hop or two-hop neighbor reserves the current slot successfully, the node decreases n_c with factor a_1 and a_2 to increase the competition probability of the next slot, which speeds up the convergence of slot allocation algorithm. If a node receives a successful reservation message comes from three or more hops away, the node increase its competition probability with factor a_3 due to the spatial reuse of the time slot 14.

5 Performance evaluation

In this section, the performance of the proposed MFCR is evaluated. We set the network scene in a 1500m×1500m rectangle area, the communication range is 300 meters. The detailed simulation parameters are listed in Table 1.

Table 1. Simulation parameters.

Network range	1500 m × 1500 m
Communication range	300 m
Send buffer length	64 packets
Packet size	1024 bits
Packet transmission rate	1 Mbps
α	0.9
β	0.5
n_{min}	2
n_{maxn}	24
a_1	1/1.1
a_2	1/1.2
a_3	1/1.3

In addition to the above simulation parameters, we also define the following performance parameters.

Network throughput: The total number of packets sent successfully per second.

Packet delivery rate: The total number of packets received divides by the total packets that the network generates.

Average access delay: The sum of the packet delay of all the received packets divides by the total number of the received packets.

Success rate of competition: The number of nodes that successfully reserve the slot divides by the total number of nodes in the network during a frame time.

Fairness of slot allocation: The variance of slot number allocated to each node in a frame time.

Slot utilization: The total times of successful slot reservation divides by the slot number in a frame time.

5.1 Average successful competition rate and average time slot utilization rate

The packet generation rate is set to 20 packet/second/node and the other parameters are the same as table 1. The number of nodes in the network is gradually increased from 20 to 60. The network topology is randomly generated according to the node number. We simulate the success rate and the average slot utilization of FPRP and MFCR for 20 independent simulations.

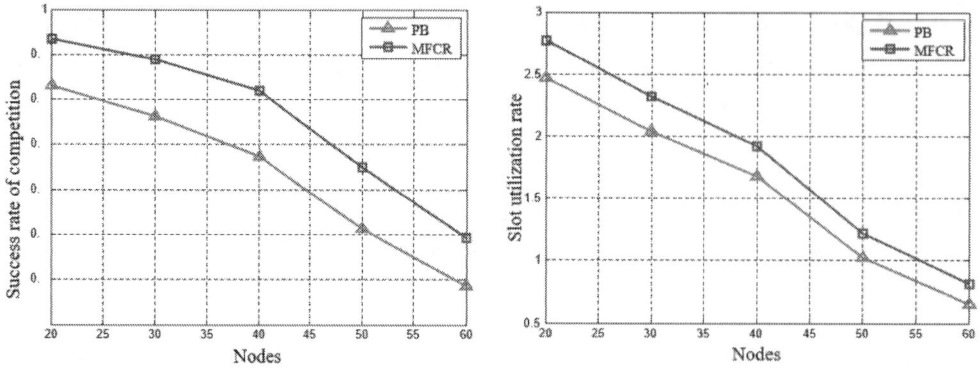

(a) Success rate of competition (b) Slot utilization rate

Fig. 1. Comparison of the success rate and the utilization rate.

As shown in Fig. 1(a), the average successful competition rate decreases with the increase of the nodes. The reason is that with the increase of nodes, more conflicts will emerge, thus causing the decline in the success rate of competition. MFCR has a higher success rate than PB, which is because MFCR significantly reduces the competition probability when it encounters conflicts, reducing the potential conflicts in the future.

As shown in Fig. 1(b), the slot utilization rate of MFCR is higher than PB. It reflects that MFCR has a better spatial reuse capability than PB. Moreover, with the increase of the node density, the competitors between two-hop increased, which leads more conflicts. So the slot utilization decreases with the increase of nodes.

5.2 Fairness of the slot allocation algorithm

The number of nodes is 25, packet generation rate is 20 packet/second/node, and the other parameters are the same as table 1. The network topology is randomly generated according to the node number. We simulate the fairness of slot allocation for MFCR and PB for 20 times.

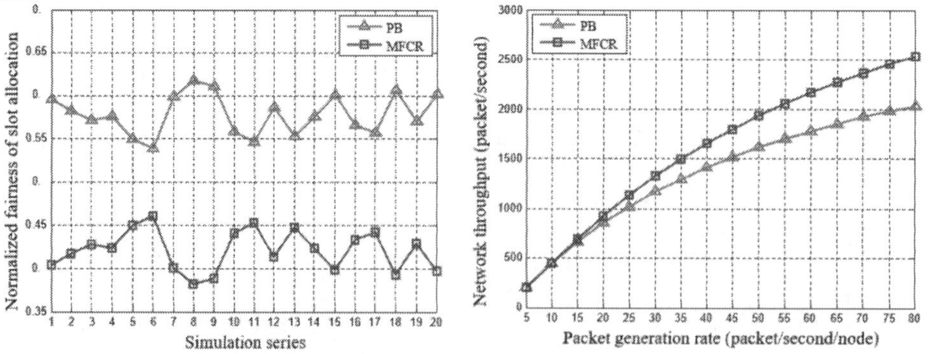

(a) Normalized fairness of slot allocation (b) Network throughput vs packet generation rate

Fig. 2 Comparison of the fairness and the network throughput.

As shown in Fig. 2(a), the variance of the slot number per frame of MFCR is less than PB. In MFCR, the node successfully reserving a slot will set the contention probability to the smallest value, and the possibility to participate in the next slot competition decreases fast. However, in PB algorithm, the node that successfully reserves a slot will participate in the next slot competition with the unchanged probability, while the competition probability of those nodes suffering continuous conflict is reduced, which will result in unfairness of slot allocation. Therefore, MFCR performs better than PB algorithm on the fairness of slot allocation.

5.3 Network communication performance

The number of nodes is 50. The network topology is randomly generated according to the node number. The network throughput, the average access delay and the packet delivery rate are achieved respectively under conditions of different packet generation rate.

Fig. 2(b) is the network throughput comparison, the difference between the MFCR and the PB algorithms isn't obvious when the packet generation rate is low due to the light load. With the increase of the packet generation rate, because of the higher slot utilization and the fairness of slot allocation, the throughput of MFCR is higher than PB. With the increase of the packet generation rate, the throughput of these two algorithms both tend to saturated due to the limited slot resources.

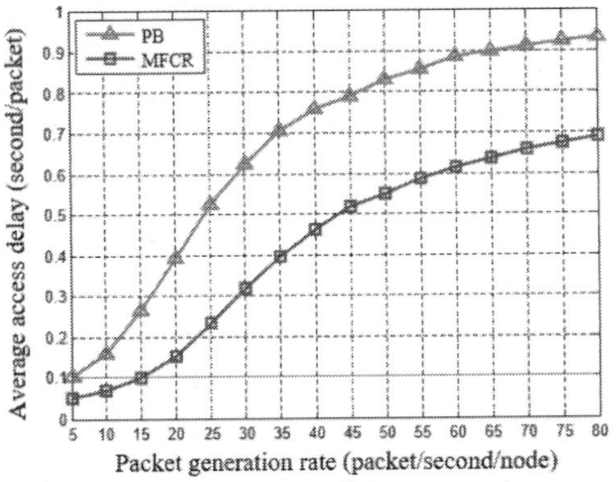

(a) Average access delay vs packet generation rate

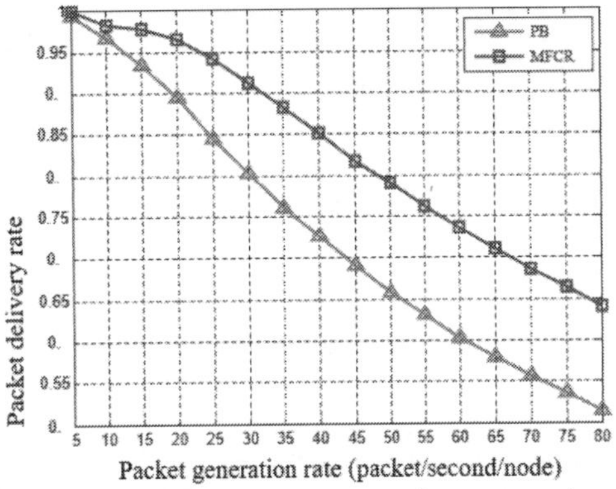

(b) Packet delivery rate vs packet generation rate

Fig. 3 Comparison of the average access delay and the packet delivery rate.

As shown in Fig. 3(a), with the increase of packet generation rate, the number of the packets that accumulated in the send buffer increase rapidly, so the average access delay in the network gradually increases. However, owing to the higher time slot utilization and the higher success reservation rate, the average access delay of MFCR performs better than PB.

Fig. 3(b) is the packet delivery rate comparison. When the packet transmission rate is lower than the packet arrival rate, the send buffer will overflow and the new arrival packets will be discarded. Hence, the packet delivery rate will decrease. Because of the higher spatial reuse capability, more packets are sent simultaneously at different node beyond two hops, the packet delivery rate of MFCR is higher than PB algorithm.

6 Conclusion

In this paper, we propose a multi-hop fast conflict resolution algorithm, namely MFCR for ad hoc networks. We make detailed introductions of the theoretical model, the pseudo Bayesian analysis and the algorithm design. MFCR employs a competitive probability forecasting method, which is similar to the back-off counter used in single-hop FCR, combined with the handshake process used in multi-hop pseudo Bayesian to solve the utilization and the fairness problems in distributed time slot allocation. We compared the network throughput, the packet delivery rate, the average access delay, etc. between MFCR and PB. Simulations show that MFCR has evident improvement in the network performance.

Acknowledgement: This work was supported in part by State Grid Corporation of China 2015 Scientific Research Project under grant no. 521999150031, and the National Natural Science Foundation of China under grant no. 61271168.

References

1. C. Chrysostomou, L. Lambrinos, C. Djouvas. The need for a system design methodology to address challenges in wireless access in vehicular ad hoc networks. International Congress on Ultra Modern Telecommunications and Control Systems, pp. 1226 - 1231, 2010.
2. M.R. Mili, L. Musavian, K.A. Hamdi, F. Marvasti. How to Increase Energy Efficiency in Cognitive Radio Networks. IEEE Transactions on Communications, Vol. 64, no. 5, pp. 1829 - 1843, 2016.
3. Y.P. Zhang, B. Li, M. Yang, Z.J. Yan. Capacity analysis of wireless ad hoc networks with improved channel reservation. 2015 IEEE Wireless Communications and Networking Conference (WCNC), pp. 1189 - 1194, 2015.
4. Y. Kim, F. Baccelli, G. Veciana . Spatial Reuse and Fairness of Ad Hoc Networks With Channel-Aware CSMA Protocols. IEEE Transactions on Information Theory, Vol. 60, no. 7, pp. 4139 - 4157, 2014.
5. X.X. Jiang, D.H.C. Du. PTMAC: A Prediction-Based TDMA MAC Protocol for Reducing Packet Collisions in VANET. IEEE Transactions on Vehicular Technology Vol. 65, no. 11, pp. 9209 - 9223, 2016.
6. M. Sami, N.K. Noordin, M. Khabazian. A TDMA-Based Cooperative MAC Protocol for Cognitive Networks With Opportunistic Energy Harvesting. IEEE Communications Letters, Vol. 20, no. 4, pp. 808 - 811, 2016.
7. M. Hadded, P. Muhlethaler, A. Laouiti, R. Zagrouba, L.A. Saidane. TDMA-Based MAC Protocols for Vehicular Ad Hoc Networks: A Survey, Qualitative Analysis, and Open Research Issues. IEEE Communications Surveys & Tutorials, Vol. 17, no. 4, pp. 2461 - 2492, 2015.
8. B. Shrestha, K.W. Choi, E. Hossain. A Dynamic Time Slot Allocation Scheme for Hybrid CSMA/TDMA MAC Protocol. IEEE Wireless Communications Letters, Vol. 2, no. 5, pp. 535 - 538, 2013.
9. C.X. Zhu, M.S. Corson. A Five-Phase Reservation Protocol (FPRP) for Mobile Ad Hoc Networks. Wireless networks, Vol. 7, no. 4, pp. 371-384, 2001.
10. D. Arivudainambi, D. Rekha. Broadcast Scheduling Problem in TDMA Ad Hoc Networks using Immune Genetic Algorithm. International Journal of Computers Communications & Control, Vol. 8, no. 1, pp. 18-29, 2012.
11. V. Aggarwal, N.K. Shankaranarayanan. Performance of a Random-Access Wireless Network With a Mix of Full- and Half-Duplex Stations. IEEE Communications Letters, Vol. 17, no. 11, pp. 2200 - 2203, 2013.
12. D.Y. Kim, H. Nam, H. Jin. Pseudo-Bayesian Broadcasting Algorithm for Opportunistic Splitting Scheduling Systems. IEEE Transactions on Vehicular Technology, Vo. PP, no. 99, pp. 1 - 6, 2016.
13. Y. Kwon, Y.G. Fang, H. Latchman. Design of MAC protocols with fast collision resolution for wireless local area networks. IEEE Transactions on Wireless Communications, Vol. 3, no. 3, pp. 793 - 807, 2004.
14. M.H. Chaudhary, B. Scheers. High spatial-reuse distributed slot assignment protocol for wireless ad hoc networks. 2012 Military Communications and Information Systems Conference (MCC), pp. 1 - 8, 2012.

Neural Network-Based Receiver in Band-Limited Communication System with MPPSK Modulation

Zixin Wang[1], *Fan* Meng[1,*], and *Lenan* Wu[1]

[1] School of Information Science and Engineering, Southeast University, Nanjing 210096, China

Abstract. As a type of the spectrally efficient modulation, the m-ary phase position shift keying (MPPSK) has been considered to meet the increasing spectrum requirement in the future wireless system. To limit the signal bandwidth and cancel the out-band interference the band-pass filters are used, which introduce the waveform distortion and inter-symbol interference (ISI). Therefore, a single hidden-layer neural network (NN)-based receiver is proposed to jointly equalize and demodulate the received signal. The impulse response of the system is static and the network parameters can be obtained after off-line training. The number of the hidden nodes is also determined through simulations. Simulation results show that the NN-based receiver works well in the communication system with different allocated bandwidths. By observing the modified confusion matrix, the false symbol decision is relevant to modulation index, waveform distortions and the ISI.

1 Introduction

To satisfy the fast-growing broadband wireless service, more high-speed transmission of information within the unit band is required. Since the frequency resources are valuable, a class of efficient modulation techniques named as "Ultra Narrow Band (UNB)" has been concerned [1-4]. Based on the extended binary phase shift keying (EBPSK) [5], an m-ary phase position shift keying (MPPSK) modulation is considered as a multi-level form of EBPSK.

In the wireless communication systems, the band-pass infinite impulse response (IIR) filters [6,7], which have less orders than the FIR filters to satisfy the same specifications, are adopted to suppress the sidelobe of the transmitted signal and eliminate the out-band interference at both the transmitter and receiver. Meanwhile, the waveform distortion, the inter-symbol interference (ISI) of adjacent symbols and the band-pass Gaussian noise can be caused by the IIR filters. Therefore, in that case the traditional demodulation methods based on matched filter (MF) [8] or impacting filter [9, 10] cannot work well. To solve these problems, the following two modules can be adopted: 1) an equalization to reduce the confirmed ISI; 2) a MF to match the distorted waveform. However, the communication system is usually assumed to be FIR rather than IIR for the traditional equalization methods

*Corresponding author: mengxiaomaomao@outlook.com

[11,12]. In addition, the received signal is filtered symbol by symbol instead of at a sampling interval, and the computational complexity increases with more orders (up to several dozen) of the equalization.

The neural network (NN) [13], which has been successfully applied in many scenarios such as control engineering [14], computer vision [15] and recently communication engineering [16,17]. With its remarkable capacity to infer the mapping implied by the training data, we propose a single hidden- layer NN-based receiver. The joint equalization and demodulation task can be finished by a single NN-based receiver. Since the impulse response of the system is static, the network parameters can be obtained through off-line training with large amount of data. The number of the hidden nodes is also determined through simulations. The simulation results show that the NN-based receiver can overcome the waveform distortions and ISI in a single network. Besides, by observing the modified confusion matrix, the false symbol decision can be mainly attributed to ISI, especially in the region of higher SNR. The waveform distortions also decrease the constellation point distance, which means the system requires higher SNR to obtain the same SER.

The rest of this paper is organized as follows. Section 2 introduces the system model of a band- limited wireless communication. In Section 3, we introduce the structure of a single hidden-layer feed-forward NN (FNN), hyper-parameter settings of the network and the input/output data. Then, in Section 4, the single-layer NN-based receiver is tested and the simulation results are analyzed. Conclusions and discussion are given in Section 5.

2 System model

The MPPSK modulation [18] is considered with the symbol guard interval factor being $r_g = 0$ and the phase shift being $\theta = \pi$, respectively. Finally, for symbol $m \in \{1,\cdots,M\}$, the modulated MPPSK signal is written as

$$g^m(t) = \begin{cases} \sin(2\pi f_c t) & 0 \le t < (m-1)KT_c \\ -\sin(2\pi f_c t) & (m-1)KT_c \le t < mKT_c \\ \sin(2\pi f_c t), & mKT \le t < NT_c \end{cases} \tag{1}$$

where $T_c = 1/f_c$ denotes the carrier period. K and N represent the number of carrier periods in each time slot and in each symbol, respectively. Apparently, we have $N = KM$ and $T = NT_c$, where T denotes the MPPSK symbol duration. The diagram of a wireless band-limited communication system used in our paper is shown in Fig. 1.

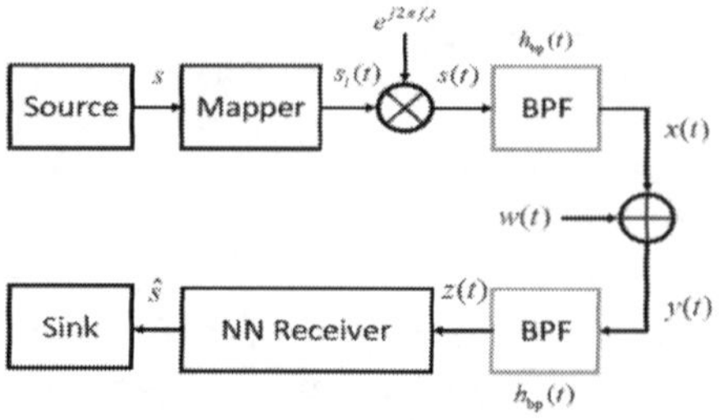

Fig. 1. The diagram of the band-limited communication system

The symbol sequence s is produced from the source, and mapped into a baseband signal $s_l(t)$, which can be represented as

$$s_l(t) = \sum g_n(t - nT), \tag{2}$$

where $g_n(t) \in G = \{g^1(t), \cdots, g^M(t)\}, n \in \mathbb{N}$.

Then $s_l(t)$ is up-converted into the band-pass signal $s(t) = s_l(t)e^{j2\pi f_c t}$ by the carrier frequency f_c, and it is shaped by a bandpass filter. Finally, the transmitted signal is denoted as

$$x(t) = s(t) * h_{bp}(t), \tag{3}$$

where the $*$ represents convolution operator and $h_{bp}(t)$ denotes the impulse response of the filter. The channel impulse response is assumed to be $\delta(t)$ and $w(t)$ is the additive white Gaussian noise (AWGN) with zero mean and variance σ_w^2. Then the received signal $y(t)$ can be described as $y(t) = x(t) + w(t)$.

At the transmitter, a same passband filter is used to reduce the out-band interference. Signal $z(t)$ after the passband filter is obtained as:

$$z(t) = y(t) * h_{bp}(t) = s''(t) + w'(t). \tag{4}$$

The notation $s''(t)$ represents that the signal $s(t)$ is filtered twice, and noise $w'(t)$ is filtered once.

The task is to equalize and demodulate the band-limited signal. Since the band-pass filter is used, the waveform distortion and ISI are introduced. A MF corresponding to the distorted symbol waveform can be designed by a NN-based method. The convoluted signal also can be equalized by a NN-based module. Moreover, the function of the two modules working as the MF and the equalizer separately can be realized by a single NN-based module. The NN-based receiver can jointly equalize and demodulate the signal and directly produce the estimated symbol sequence $\hat{s}$.

3 NN-based receiver

The core part of the NN-based receiver is a FNN. Generally, it is a composition of one input layer, L hidden layers and one output layer of computational units [19]. Particularly, the single-hidden layer $(L = 1)$ NN is considered in our paper, which is illustrated in Fig. 2.

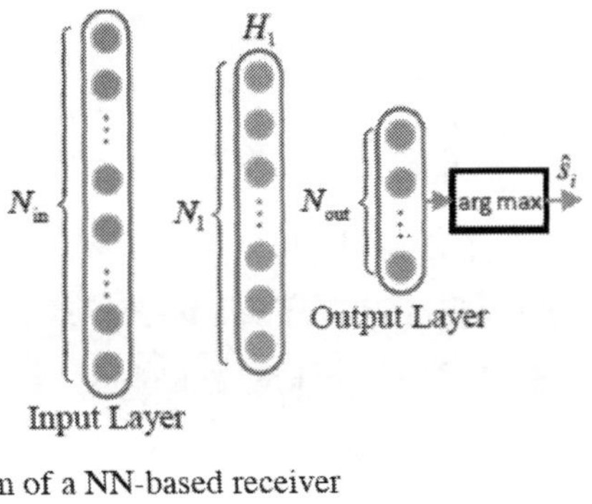

Fig. 2. The schematic diagram of a NN-based receiver

3.1 Feed-forward neural network

A mapping function $F_{\text{FNN}} : R_{\text{in}}^{N} \Rightarrow R_{\text{out}}^{N}$ of FNN is defined as:

$$F_{\text{FNN}}(\mathbf{x};\theta) = g_{\text{out}} \circ f_{\text{out}} \circ g_1 \circ f_1 \circ (\mathbf{x})^{\circ} \tag{5}$$

where $\mathbf{x}$ denotes the input vector, $f_1 \circ$ denotes a linear pre-activation function and $g_1 \circ$ denotes a nonlinear activation function of the hidden layer. The activation of the input layer is linear. The parameter θ is composed of weight matrix $\mathbf{W}_1 \in R^{N_1 \times N_{\text{in}}}$ and bias vector $\mathbf{b}_1 \in R^{N_1}$, and the $\mathbf{W}_{\text{out}}$, $\mathbf{b}_{\text{out}}$ of output layer are also included. The output of the hidden layer is vector $\mathbf{x}_1 = [x_{1,1}, \cdots, x_{1,N_1}]^T$, it is computed from the activations of the preceding layer, i.e. the input layer. Given the input vector $\mathbf{x}$, the pre-activation of the hidden layer is given as

T

$$f_1(\mathbf{x}) = \mathbf{W}_1\mathbf{x} + \mathbf{b}_1. \tag{6}$$

After the corresponding non-linear activating nodes, the output of the hidden layer can be written as

$$\mathbf{x}_1 = g_1(f_1(\mathbf{x})), \tag{7}$$

where the activation functions g1 used in FNN are all rectified linear unit (ReLU) [20], which is $g(x) = \max(0, x)$. It is shown that ReLU is much faster than widely used sigmoid in terms of calculation speed [21]. Besides, there is no nonlinearity in this task and extra nonlinear approximation capability is unnecessary.

3.2 Data and hyper-parameters

The input vector $\mathbf{x}$ for the corresponding symbol s_i to be inferred is composed of a piece of windowed sampled received signal $z(n)$. Considering the convoluted signal, the window size is set larger than one symbol interval. Meanwhile large window can introduce a large amount of uncorrelated data, which can make the training process hard to converge. Therefore, a window of medium size is proposed. The size of input vector is denoted by N_{in}, and it can be written as:

$$N_{\text{in}} = N \times N_s \times f_s / f_c, \tag{8}$$

where N_s represents the corresponding normalized window size (divided by symbol duration). More concretely, the sampled data of $N_s = 1.25$ successive symbols is used in our simulations. The parameters of MPPSK modulation is list as follows: $M = 64, K = 4$. The carrier frequency is $f_c = 70$ MHz and the sampling frequency is $f_s = 280$ MHz. Therefore the final N_{in} is 1280.

This is a classification problem to classify the convoluted signal with colored noise. By assigning a generalization of the logistic function, i.e. soft-max activation function [22] for categorical target variables $(M > 2)$, the number of target variables $N_{\text{out}} = M$ for classification. The output of softmax activation function g_{out} is $\mathbf{y} = [y_1, \cdots, y_M]^T$, and the element y_i is defined as:

$$y_i = \frac{e^{x_i}}{\sum_{j=1}^{M} e^{x_j}} \tag{9}$$

where x_j is j-th unit output of previous layer, i.e the last hidden layer. The estimation $\hat{s}_i$ can be obtained by selecting the maximal element in the output vector, which is shown in Fig. 2.

Since $N_{\text{in}} = 1280$, the input dimension is very high and serious over-fitting can be introduced in the training process. Therefore a callback is proposed in the training process. The validation loss is stored after each training epoch and finally the network parameter θ with the lowest loss is loaded in the NN-based receiver. The loss function is cross-entropy error minimizing, and it is optimized by Adam algorithm [23] with default settings. Besides, the detailed network and training settings are list in Tab. 1 and the parameter will be particularly mentioned if modified.

Table 1. Simulation parameters

Variables	Values
Number of Train Samples	9×10^4
Number of Validation Samples	1×10^4
Epoch Number for Network	20
Batch Size	128
Active Function	ReLU

There are several advantages on NN-based methods. Firstly, the whole system is time-invariant and the impulse response is known, which means plenty of training data can be easily obtained by simulations. Secondly, the accuracy of inference can be easily adjust by changing the network scale, which means the design of the NN-based receiver is flexible. Lastly, the NN can realize the functions of equalizer and demodulator in a single module, which simplifies the receiver design. Therefore, the receiver based on NN is used in the following simulation section.

4 Simulation results

After MPPSK modulation, the main lobe of the signal is up to 35 MHz, while the allocated bandwidth B = 10 MHz as shown in Fig. 3. This communication system is a wide band transmitting system.

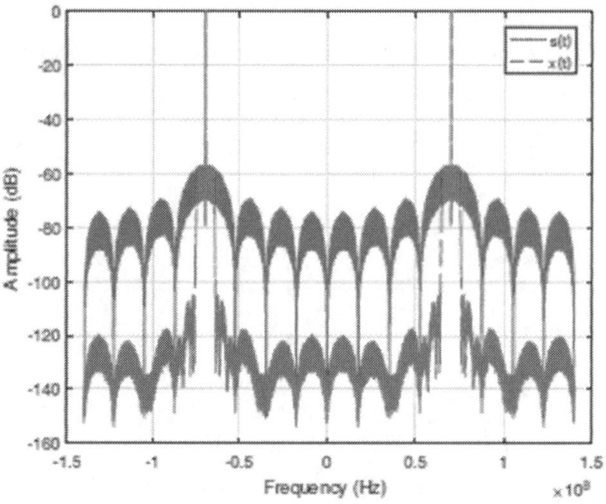

Fig. 3. PSD of the transmitted signals before and after the band-pass filter (B = 10 MHz)

For the bandpass filter (Chebyshev type II), the maximum passband ripple is $R_p = 3\text{dB}$, the minimum stopband attenuation is $R_s = 45\text{dB}$, and the frequency interval $\Delta f = 2\text{MHz}$. The normalized power spectrum densities (PSD) of the received signals after and before the bandpass filter are shown in Fig. 3. The sidelobe of $x(t)$ is sharply filtered to lower than 105dB compared to band MPPSK signal $s(t)$ is about -57dB. Under these parameters, the order of designed band-pass filter is 21.

4.1 Number of hidden nodes

We begin by comparing the performance of different numbers of hidden nodes N_h. The increasement of N_h can enhance the approximation ability of the network, while it requires greater computations and complexity of the receiver. The fast processing speed is more important under high transmitting symbol rate. Therefore we need to find a suitable size of network first, taking account of both performance and efficiency. The bandwidth is B = 10 MHz, and the training data, validation data and testing data are all the same to different networks.

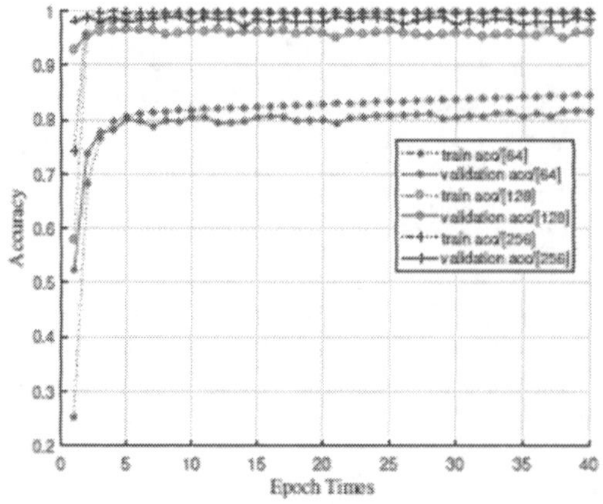

Fig. 4. Training and validation accuracy of different networks

The network of single-hidden layer is considered in this simulation, and $\{64\}$, $\{128\}$ and $\{256\}$ nodes, which are all integer multiples of M. In Fig. 4 the curves of accuracy and cross-entropy loss in training process are plotted. After about 5 epoch times, all validation loss and accuracy go stable with small jitters, while training accuracy remains rising and training loss keeps declining. This over-fitting issue can be solved by a callback, which selecting the best model parameters corresponding to the least validation loss in all training epochs.

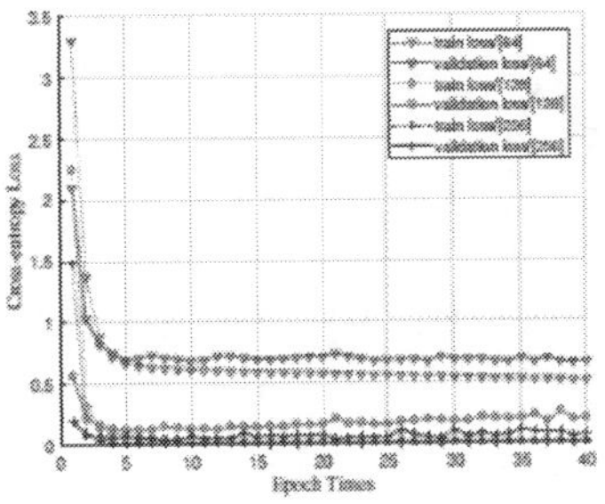

Fig. 5. SER/SNR curves of different numbers of hidden nodes (B = 10MHz)

As the nodes increases, the convergence values of validation accuracy increase, which are 0.85, 0.96 and 0.98 for N_h = 64, 128 and 256 in Fig. 4(a). Generally the trend of variation has an inverse relation with its corresponding loss, and therefore the values of loss decrease as the accuracy rise when comparing Fig. 4(a) and Fig. 4(b).

The SER/SNR curves of networks of different N_h are shown in Fig. 5. The SER performance of {64} nodes is poor, which can only achieve about 3.5×10^{-3} when SNR = 8dB. Meanwhile the network of $\{256\}$ nodes can obtain about 2.7×10^{-5}. In the region of SER=1.0×10^{-4}, the network of $\{256\}$ nodes can achieve about 1.4 dB gain over the $\{128\}$ nodes. In summary, the network of $\{256\}$ nodes works the best of all networks and we use it in the following simulations.

4.2 Bandwidth

In this subsection the bandwidth B is considered, while the other parameters remain as before. The bandwidths are set to be $B=\{6,10,20\}$MHz, and the corresponding training data is collected with SNR regions $\{[14,18],[6,8],[-2,0]\}$ dB. The simulation results are illustrated in Fig. 6. Generally it can be seen that as the bandwidth decreases, the SER performance of the NN-based receiver degrades with a higher value and a slower downward trend.

There is about 4.2 dB SNR gain to achieve the same SER = 1.0×10^{-3} when comparing curves of B = 10 MHz and B = 20 MHz. Moreover, the SNR gap goes larger as the SER decreases, and up to about 6.5 dB in the region of SER= 5.0×10^{-5}. As for the curve of allocated bandwidth is only B = 6 MHz, the SER is much poorer than the other two considering the more serious ISI.

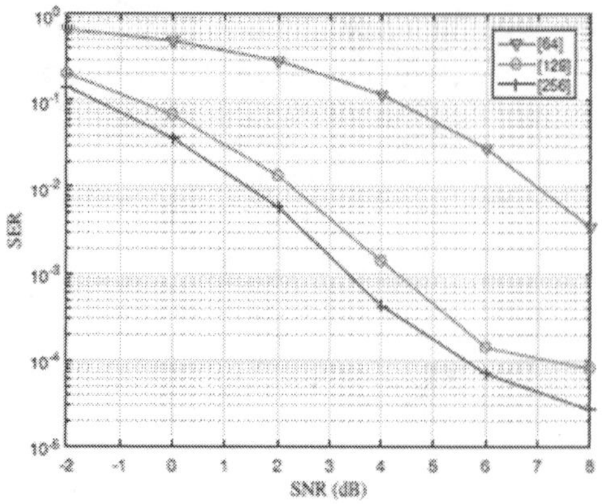

Fig. 6. SER/SNR curves of different numbers of hidden nodes(B=10 MHz)

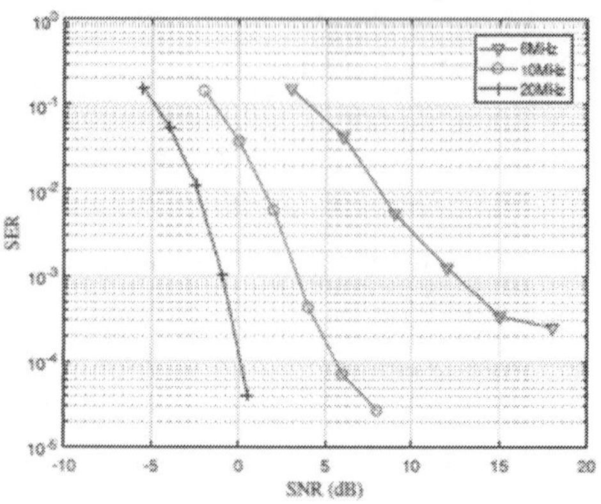

Fig. 7. SER/SNR curves under different bandwidth

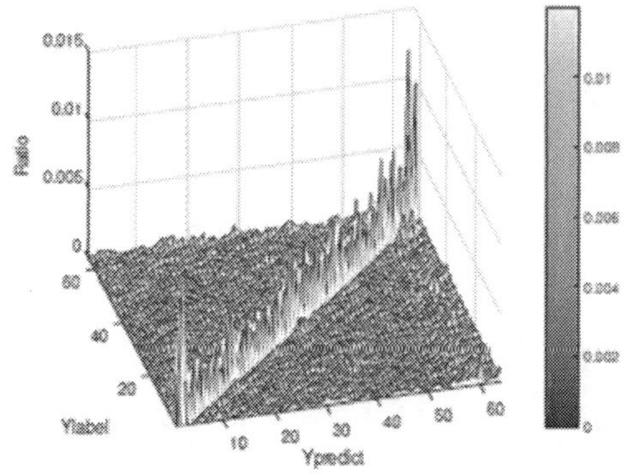

Fig. 8. A 3-D normalized conditional SER illustration when SNR=0 dB

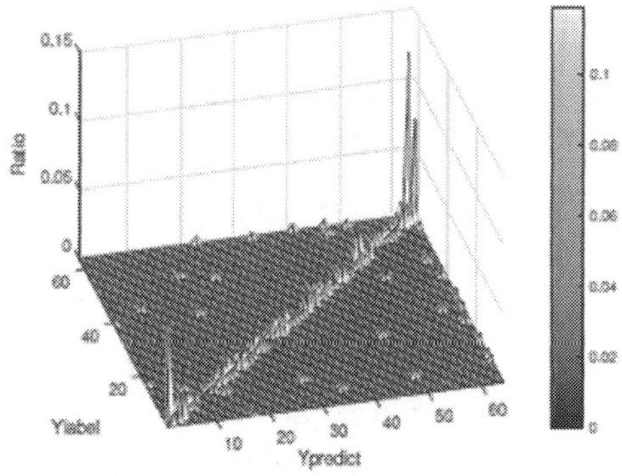

Fig. 9. A 3-D normalized conditional SER illustration when SNR = 4 dB

To further study the reasons for the symbol error, the modified confusion matrix is plotted in Fig. 7. The x-axis, y-axis, z-axis represents the estimated symbol labeled as Ypredict, the true symbol labels as Ylabel and the joint symbol error ratio R , respectively. The notation $R_{i,j}$ denotes the joint symbol error ratio for the pair of the estimated symbol $i \in \{1,\cdots,M\}$ and the true symbol $j \in \{1,\cdots,M\}$. We set $R_{i,j} = 0$ when $i = j$, to make the modified confusion matrix show only the error information, and the R can be normalized with $\sum_{i,j} R_{i,j} = 1$.

Firstly by observing Fig. 8 and Fig. 9, most errors occur at the neighborhood regions of $i, j = 1$ and $i, j = M$, whose locations of changing phase are at the fore-end and the back-end of the waveform. These errors are introduced by interference of the nearby symbols. Secondly, at the region of $|i - j| = 1$ the errors are easily introduced and the $R_{i,j}$ remains a constant when SNR is set. As the (1) shows that the MPPSK modulates the signal by locations of changing phase. The use of filters smooths the waveform of the signal, but it also aggravates the vagueness of the location information, which means the constellation point distance decreases. This type of mistakes can be reduced by increasing SNR. Lastly, all the other errors are caused by the noise and their probabilities remains a constant at a given SNR region.

5 Conclusions

The equalization and demodulation problem for MPPSK signals in a band-limited communication system with IIR filters at both the transmitter and receiver has been investigated. We propose a NN-based receiver and introduce its diagram and training process. The NN-based receiver works well under different bandwidth limitations with a single-hidden layer of 256 nodes. After inference result analysis, we find that the false symbol decision is relevant to modulation index m and can be attributed to ISI and waveform distortions. In the future work, more complex communication scenarios will be considered for the efficiently modulated signals.

Acknowledgments: This work was supported in part by the Fundamental Research Funds for the National Natural Science Foundation of China (Grant No. 61271204), and the SAST (Grant No. SAST2016071).

References

1. L. Wu, "UNB modulation in high speed space communications," Proc. of ICSIT, **6795**, 679 (2007)
2. M. Feng, L. Wu, "Special non-linear filter and extension to Shannon's channel capacity," Digital Signal Processing, **19**, 5, (2009)
3. M. Feng, L. Wu, P. Gao, "From special analogous crystal filters to digital impacting filters," Academic Press, Inc. (2012)
4. C. Lu, L. Wu, P. Chen, J. Wang, "M-ary phase position shift keying with orthogonal signalling," IET Communications, **9**, 12, (2015)
5. L. Wu, M. Feng, "On BER performance of EBPSK-MODEM in AWGN channel," Sensors, **10**, 4, (2010)
6. P. P. Vaidyanathan, P. Regalia, S. K. Mitra, "Design of doublycomplementary IIR digital filters, using a single complex allpass filter," *in Acoustics, Speech, and Signal Processing, IEEE Interna- tional Conference on ICASSP*, (1986)
7. A. V. Oppenheim, R. W. Schafer, "Discrete-time signal processing," **23**, 2, (1989)
8. C. Qi, L. Wu, "Pll demodulation technique for m -ray position phase shift keying," Journal of Electronics (China), **26**, 3, (2009)
9. L. Wu, H. Feng, "Extended binary phase shift keying modulation and demodulation method for frequency spectrum compression," (2009)
10. Z. Chen, L. Wu, P. Chen, "Efficient modulation and demodulation methods for multi-carrier communication," IET Communications, **10**, 5, (2016)
11. J. G. Proakis, M. Salehi, *Digital Communications*. (New York: McGraw-Hill, 1995)
12. C. A. Belfiore, J. Park, John H, "Decision feedback equalization," Proceedings of the IEEE, **67**, 8, (1979)
13. P. E. Keller, *Artificial Neural Networks: An Introduction* (2005)
14. H. Wei, H. Huang, S. S. Ge, "Adaptive neural network control of a robotic manipulator with time-varying output constraints," IEEE Transactions on Cybernetics, **47**, 10, (2017)
15. A. Krizhevsky, I. Sutskever, G. E. Hinton, "Imagenet classification with deep convolutional neural networks," in International Conference on Neural Information Processing Systems, (2012)
16. P. A. Haigh, Z. Ghassemlooy, I. Papakonstantinou, S. Rajbhandari, "Online artificial neural network equalization for a visible light communications system with an organic light emitting diode based transmitter," in Network and Optical Communications, (2013)

17. O. B. Belkacem, R. Zayani, M. L. Ammari, R. Bouallegue, D. Roviras, "Neural network equal- ization for frequency selective nonlinear mimo channels," in Computers and Communications, (2012)
18. P. Ying, L. Wu, "New scheme of MPPSK modem," Journal of Southeast University, (2012) Abramson2006Pattern
19. V. Koltchinskii, "Neural network learning: Theoretical foundations," Annales De L Institut Henri Poincare Probabilites Et Statistiques, **39**, 6, (2003)
20. X. Glorot, A. Bordes, Y. Bengio, "Deep sparse rectifier neural networks," in International Con- ference on Artificial Intelligence and Statistics, (2011)
21. Y. LeCun, Y. Bengio, G. Hinton, "Deep learning," Nature, **521**, 7553, (2015)
22. N. Abramson, D. Braverman, G. Sebestyen, *Pattern recognition and machine learning*. (Springer, 2006)
23. D. P. Kingma, J. Ba, "Adam: A method for stochastic optimization," Computer Science, (2014)

A Digital Image Denoising Algorithm Based on Gaussian Filtering and Bilateral Filtering

Weiying Piao[1,*], *Yibao* Yuan[2], and *Haijun* Lin[1]

[1]Harbin University of Science and Technology, School of Test and Control Techniques and communication engineering, 150080 Harbin, China
[2]Harbin Institute of Technology, School of Electronic engineering and Automation, 150001 Harbin, China

Abstract. Bilateral filtering has been applied in the area of digital image processing widely, but in the high gradient region of the image, bilateral filtering may generate staircase effect. Bilateral filtering can be regarded as one particular form of local mode filtering, according to above analysis, an mixed image de-noising algorithm is proposed based on Gaussian filter and bilateral filtering. First of all, it uses Gaussian filter to filtrate the noise image and get the reference image, then to take both the reference image and noise image as the input for range kernel function of bilateral filter. The reference image can provide the image's low frequency information, and noise image can provide image's high frequency information. Through the competitive experiment on both the method in this paper and traditional bilateral filtering, the experimental result showed that the mixed de-noising algorithm can effectively overcome staircase effect, and the filtrated image was more smooth, its textural features was also more close to the original image, and it can achieve higher PSNR value, but the amount of calculation of above two algorithms are basically the same.

1 Introduction

Image shall be such a very important information carrier, but during the process of image forming, transmitting and receiving, due to the existence of various interference factors, it may systematically introduce certain noise, and some detailed features may also be submerged in noise, this shall bring great difficulty on subsequent image processing procedure. To adopt proper method to eliminate the pollution noise in image shall be a very important preprocessing procedure.

The noise in image was usually eliminated by filtering method. The non-linear filtering technique can protect the edge of image while eliminating the noise, such as bilateral filtering [1]. Bilateral filtering shall be the non-linear filtering technique in spatial domain, same as the classical Gaussian filter, bilateral filtering do also utilize the spatial distance information (geometric distance) among the pixels in neighborhood for locally weighted average, the difference between these two methods is that, bilateral filtering do also utilize the grey similarity information of the pixels in neighborhood, this enables such algorithm

* Corresponding author: pwying@163.com

maintaining the edge of image quite well, and effectively smoothing Gaussian noise. Due to the simple, non-iterative and local characteristics of bilateral filtering, it then has been widely applied in image processing accordingly [2-5].

In practical application, it found that in the high gradient region of grey value, there's the "staircase effect" with bilateral filter, that the grey value in such region of original image is smoothly changed, after the bilateral filter treatment on its noise image, the grey value in such region can be changed like ladder. In addition, while the noise variance is quite big, the de-noising effect of bilateral filtering shall not be quite ideal.

In order to solve such problem and improve the de-noising effect of bilateral filter, there are many scholars proposed some improved algorithms. Choudhury et al proposed the trilateral filter[6], the trilateral filter can achieve quite smooth image but with quite large calculation amount. Yu Bo proposed the bilateral filtering algorithm with controllable kernel function[7]. Eisemann, Petschnigg et al proposed the joint bilateral filter[8.9], Laurent et al proposed guided bilateral filter[10], Ba T et al proposed semi-guided bilateral filter[11], but the joint bilateral filter, guided bilateral filter and semi-guided bilateral filter may only need the guiding image in high quality to achieve quite good de-noising effect, but it's very hard to estimate the guiding image in high quality from noise image[12].

According to the grey value of pixels in neighborhood bilateral filter can allocate the weight value accordingly. In the neighborhood, if the grey value of a certain pixel is more closer to the central point, its weight value shall be bigger then. While there's Gaussian noise in the image, the observed grey value of each pixel shall deviate from the original real grey value of such point, and fluctuate around the real grey value accordingly, the bigger noise variance, the more obvious deviation it may have accordingly. By taking the grey value of central point as reference datum, it may cause the fluctuation of reference datum accordingly. In the high gradiant region of image, such fluctuation shall be more obvious, bilateral filter may regard such kind of edge as the ladder-shaped edge incorrectly, so as to generate the "staircase effect".

From above analysis it can be seen that, the reason of bilateral filter generating the "staircase effect" shall be that it takes the grey value of central point as reference datum and does not fully utilize the characteristic of white Gaussian noise –"zero-mean". in order to solve such problem existed in bilateral filtering, in this paper such a mixed de-noising algorithm based on both the Gaussian filter and bilateral filtering is proposed. In such mixed de-noising algorithm, the input for range kernel function of bilateral filtering can be determined by reference image and noise image mutually. In this paper, it first introduces the principle of such mixed de-noising algorithm, then compares the de-noising effect of both the mixed de-noising algorithm and bilateral filtering through experiment.

2 Basic principle of mixed de-noising algorithm

In digital system, the additive white Gaussian noise is a common noise type. To assume that through a degradation process, it can get the observed signal I from the original "true" signal X, the degradation process means to add the white Gaussian noise V with zero mean into X, then the observed signal I can be expressed as below,

$$I = X + V \tag{1}$$

The purpose of filtering is to recover the original signal X from the observed signal I.

Bilateral filtering can be regarded as such a particular form of local mode filtering[13]. the local mode filtering can be came down to a minimization problem, as shown in equation (2),

$$\underset{X_p}{Min}\sum_{q\in S_p} h\left(\left\|p-q\right\|\right)\rho\left(X_p-I_q\right) \tag{2}$$

In equation (2), p, q represents the pixels, S_p represents the neighborhood of pixel p, I_p, I_q represent the grey value of the signal (image) at pixels p, q, X_p represents the grey value of pixel p that need to be solved, $\|p\text{-}q\|$ represent the Euclidean distance between point p and point q. $h(\cdot)$ represents the weight function of 2-dimensional linear phase filter, its expression can usually be Gaussian function. $\rho(\cdot)$ is error norm. In order to solve equation (2), it can differentiate the equation (2) to get equation (3),

$$\sum_{q\in S_p} h\left(\left\|p-q\right\|\right)\psi\left(X_p-I_q\right)=0 \tag{3}$$

In equation (3), $\psi(\cdot)$ is influencing function. To set $\delta\left(x\right)=\frac{\psi\left(x\right)}{x}$, and substitute it into equation (3), then get the equation (4),

$$\sum_{q\in S_p} h\left(\left\|p-q\right\|\right)\delta\left(X_p-I_q\right)\left(X_p-I_q\right)=0 \tag{4}$$

By simplifying equation (4), to get equation (5),

$$\begin{aligned} X_p &= \frac{1}{W_p}\sum_{q\in S_p} h\left(\left\|p-q\right\|\right)\delta\left(X_p-I_q\right)I_q \\ W_p &= \sum_{q\in S_p} h\left(\left\|p-q\right\|\right)\delta\left(X_p-I_q\right) \end{aligned} \tag{5}$$

Equation (5) is the filtering Equation of local mode filtering, W_p represents the normalization coefficient of filtering formula. If $h(\cdot)$ and $\delta(\cdot)$ are taken as Gaussian functions, the equation (5) can be expressed with equation (6),

$$\begin{aligned} X_p &= \frac{1}{W_p}\sum_{q\in S_p} G_{\sigma s}\left(\left\|p-q\right\|\right)G_{\sigma r}\left(X_p-I_q\right)I_q \\ W_p &= \sum_{q\in S_p} G_{\sigma s}\left(\left\|p-q\right\|\right)G_{\sigma r}\left(X_p-I_q\right) \end{aligned} \tag{6}$$

In equation (6), $G_{\sigma s}(\cdot)$ represents the Gaussian function with the standard deviatio as σ_s, it's so called as spatial kernel function, $G_{\sigma r}(\cdot)$ represents the Gaussian function with standard deviation as σ_r, it's so called as range kernel function, σ_s and σ_r can respectively determine the expansion degree of spatial kernel function and range kernel function. In order to solve equation (6), it then can rewrite equation (6) into equation (7),

$$\begin{aligned} X_p^{(t+1)} &= \frac{1}{W_p}\sum_{q\in S_p} G_{\sigma s}\left(\left\|p-q\right\|\right)G_{\sigma r}\left(X_p^{(t)}-I_q\right)I_q \\ W_p &= \sum_{q\in S_p} G_{\sigma s}\left(\left\|p-q\right\|\right)G_{\sigma r}\left(X_p^{(t)}-I_q\right) \end{aligned} \tag{7}$$

In equation (7), t=1,2,3,... in order to solve equation (7), it may need to estimate the initial value of $X_p^{(1)}$, one of the most simple methods is to let $X_p^{(1)}=I_p$, then to perform iterative computation only once. At this time, equation (7) can be converted into standard bilateral filtering equation, thus bilateral filtering shall be such a special solution for local mode filtering, it can also be regarded such a special form of local mode filtering. From the analysis in previous paragraph it can be seen that, bilateral filtering does not fully utilize the characteristic of white Gaussian noise in "zero mean", thus it can not be the optimal solution of local mode filtering at all.

The de-noising effect of local mode filtering does relate to the value of σ_r parameter closely. When σ_r has quite small value, the local mode filtering shall have better edge maintaining effect accordingly, but it can easily converge to local extreme point, and its de-nosing effect may also become bad; along with the raised σ_r value, the local mode filtering may gradually approach to global extreme point with enhanced de-noising effect, but the edge maintaining effect may become bad accordingly; while σ_r value tended to infinity, the local mode filter will then turn into Gaussian filter. From above analysis it can be seen that, to avoid filtering equation converging so quickly to local extreme point can effectively improve the de-noising effect of local mode filtering. Based on such analysis, in this paper a mixed de-noising algorithm based on both the Gaussian filter and bilateral filtering is proposed. First of all it uses Gaussian filter to filtrate noise image, then takes the image treated with Gaussian filter as reference image and input it into bilateral filter, then to take both of reference image and noise image as the input for range kernel function of bilateral filter. The reference image provides the low frequency information of image, and noise image provides the high frequency information of image. Due to the existence of reference image, the mixed de-noising algorithm can more effectively utilize the characteristics of white Gaussian noise- "zero mean", thus it then can better eliminate white Gaussian noise.

3 Selection of parameters of σ_s and σ_r

The performance of bilateral filter is mainly determined byσ_s and σ_r parameter, the bigger σ_s parameter, the higher degree of smoothness in the image, and there would be more textural features have been smoothed out. In comparison with them, σ_r parameter shall have more obvious influence on filtering effect, and σ_r can control the smoothness and edge maintaining ability of bilateral filter at the same time. The less σ_r parameter, the better edge maintaining effect the bilateral filtering may get, but its de-noising effect may become bad; the bigger σ_r parameter, the better de-noising effect bilateral filtering may have, but its edge maintaining effect may become poor accordingly.

C.Liu has studied the relation between σ_r parameter and noise variance σ_n^2 [14], when σ_s=3, σ_r=1.95σ_n, bilateral filtering may have quite good de-noising effect.

In this paper, the given value of σ_s, σ_r parameters in the algorithm are different from normal bilateral filtering. The effect of Gaussian filter is to mainly eliminate the noise and achieve the "zero mean" of white Gaussian noise. The bigger given value for standard deviation of Gaussian function shall be beneficial for eliminating noise, but the bigger σ_s parameter value, the more obscure edge the image may have, and it may also lower the PSNR accordingly. In order to reduce the obscure degree of the edge, the given value of σ_s parameter should be quite small, but too small value may be hard to effectively eliminate noise, through several experiments, it was found that when σ_s=1 the effect was quite good and it then got the better balance between de-noising and edge maintaining.

For the given value of σ_s parameter in Gaussian filter, thus it cannot effectively eliminate noise at all, it may need subsequent bilateral filter to further eliminate noise and protect image's edge. In mixed de-noising algorithm, the effect of reference image is to act as the "zero mean" of white Gaussian noise. For the white Gaussian noise in reference image is lower than that in noise image, thus the given value of σ_s parameter in bilateral filter can be smaller than that in general bilateral filter, thus it can be beneficial for achieving better edge maintaining effect and to offset the loss in high frequency caused by Gaussian filter to the certain extent.

Through several experimental validation, while σ_s=1 in Gaussian filter, and σ_s= 3 in bilateral filter, and both the σ_r parameter in bilateral filter and noise variance σ_n^2 meet the relation in equation (8), it can achieve very good de-noising effect on most images, and the image's PSNR value after filtration was also quite high.

$$\sigma_r = 0.02\sigma_n^2 + 0.8\sigma_n \tag{8}$$

In equation (8), the value range of σ_n parameter can be within 10-40.

4 Experiments

In this section, it compares the de-noising effects of mixed filtering algorithm and bilateral filtering on white Gaussian noise, and uses imnoise function in Matlab to add white Gaussian noise in the image. In this paper, it uses the peak signal-to-noise ratio (PSNR) value to evaluate image's quality, the definition of PSNR is shown in equation (9),

$$PSNR = 10\log\left\{\frac{L^2 \times M \times N}{\sum_{i=1}^{M}\sum_{j=1}^{N}\left[X(i,j) - I(i,j)\right]^2}\right\} \tag{9}$$

In equation (9) M, N represent the size of images, $I(i,j)$ is original image, $X(i,j)$ is the filtered image, L is the dynamic range of image grey value, the L value of 8-bit image is usually set as 255. In this paper, the grey level of grey image is 8bit with resolution as 512×512.

The template size of Gaussian filter is 3×3 and σ_s=1. The template size of bilateral filter in the mixed algorithm is 15×15, σ_s=3, σ_r parameter value is set as specified in equation(8). The template size of bilateral filter is 15×15, σ_s=3, σ_r=1.95σ_n.

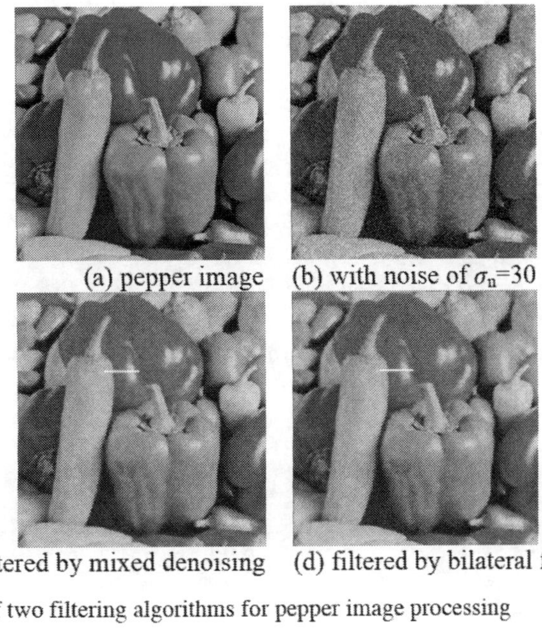

(a) pepper image (b) with noise of σ_n=30

(c)filtered by mixed denoising (d) filtered by bilateral filtering

Fig. 1. Comparison of two filtering algorithms for pepper image processing

Figure 1(a) is the original image of pepper image, (b) is the image with added white Gaussian image in σ_n=30, (c), (d) are the images treated with mixed de-noising algorithm and bilateral filter processing. From figure 1 it can be seen that, in comparison with bilateral filtering, the image treated by the mixed de-noising algorithm was more smooth, and the textural features of the image was more closed to original image, for the edge maintaining effect, the two algorithms basically maintained the equal level.

Figure 2 is the one-dimensional horizontal gray section of the original pepper image and the filted image (the white underlined part in figure 1).

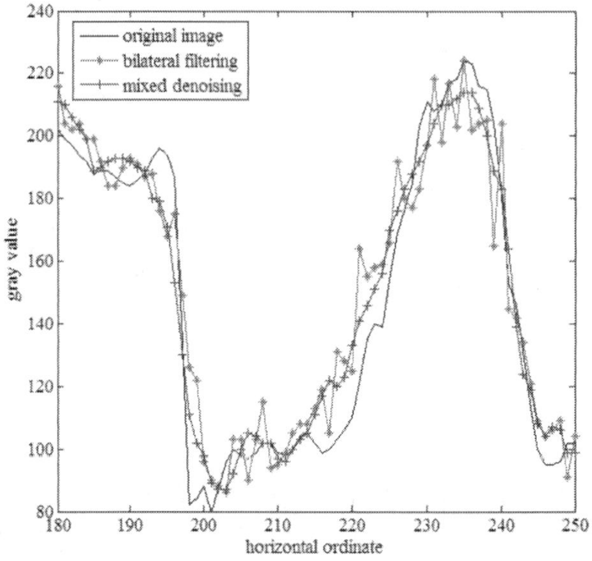

Fig. 2. One dimension horizontal gray level profile of pepper image

From figure 2 it can be seen that, in comparison with bilateral filtering, the image treated with the mixed de-noising algorithm was more smooth. In the section of 210-240 at the horizontal ordinate, the grey value of original image was changed smoothly, bilateral filtering did not have the good effect for processing such kind of edge, and there occurred the obvious "staircase effect", but the mixed de-noising algorithm did have quite good effect for processing such edge. In the section of 190-200 at the horizontal ordinate, there's the mutation in grey value of original image, the mixed de-noising algorithm did basically have the same processing effect on such edge as well as that of bilateral filtering.

Table 1 shows the comparison on the PSNR value of pepper image processed by mixed de-noising algorithm and bilateral filtering respectively under different noise variance conditions. It can be seen that, while the noise variance was quite small, in comparison with bilateral filtering, the mixed de-noising algorithm did not have the obvious advantage, but along with the enlarged noise variance, the PSNR value of the image processed by the mixed de-noising algorithm was obviously higher than that processed by bilateral filtering.

Table 1. Comparison of PSNR values of Lena images with different algorithms

σ_n	Noise image	Mixed denoising algorithm	Bilateral filtering
20	21.43	29.56	28.95
30	18.37	28.49	26.88
40	16.28	27.51	25.48

Figure 3(a) is the original image of Lena image, (b) is the image with added white Gaussian noise in σ_n=20, (c), (d) are the images processed by mixed de-noising algorithm and bilateral filtering respectively. Similar with figure 1, in comparison with bilateral filtering, the mixed de-noising algorithm did retain more textural features of the image while eliminating the noise, the image after filtration was more closer to the original image.

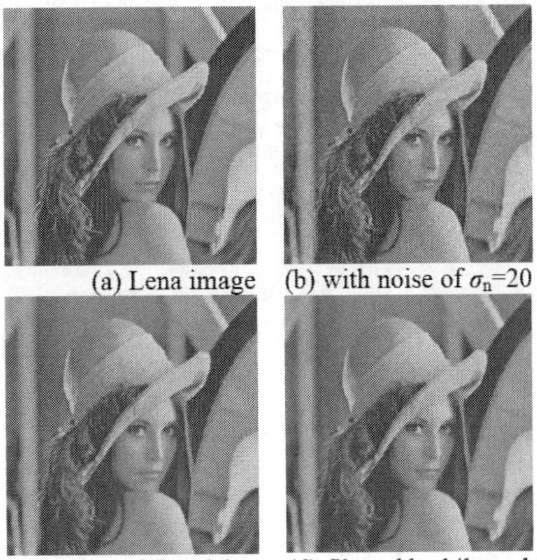

(a) Lena image (b) with noise of σ_n=20

(c) filtered by mixed denoising (d) filtered by bilateral filtering

Fig. 3. Comparison of two filtering algorithms for Lena image processing

Table 2 shows the comparison on the PSNR value of Lena image processed by mixed de-noising algorithm and bilateral filtering respectively under different noise variance conditions. From table 2 it can be seen that, the PSNR value of Lena image processed by mixed de-noising algorithm was obviously higher than that processed by bilateral filtering, its advantage was more obvious than that of pepper image. In addition, the comparative experiments were also carried out on many other images, the results showed that the mixed de-noising algorithm were always better than bilateral filtering.

Table 2. Comparison of PSNR values of Lena images with different algorithms

σ_n	Noise image	Mixed denoising algorithm	Bilateral filtering
20	21.52	31.14	28.82
30	18.35	29.26	26.84
40	16.16	27.87	25.51

Gaussian filter can be realized by frequency domain fast algorithm, in comparison with bilateral filtering, its calculation amount can be basically ignored, thus the calculation amount of mixed de-noising algorithm was basically the same as the traditional bilateral filtering. Experimental results showed that the two methods did spent the basically same time to process the same image. From experimental results it can be seen that, the de-noising effect of the mixed de-noising algorithm proposed in this paper on Gaussian noise was obviously better than that of bilateral filtering, But because Gaussian filter has been carried out, thus there may be some losses in the high frequency information of the image, it shall be a defect of mixed de-noising algorithm.

5 Summary

In this paper, a mixed de-noising algorithm based on both Gaussian filter and bilateral filtering is proposed. In comparison with routine bilateral filtering algorithm, the mixed de-noising algorithm did more effectively utilize the characteristics of white Gaussian noise with "zero mean", while eliminating the noise it can select quite smaller σ_r parameter, according to the experimental results, in comparison with bilateral filtering, the image treated with mixed de-noising algorithm was more smooth with more natural shading effect, its textural feature is more closer to original image, and such method can get even higher PSNR value. The mixed de-noising algorithm inherited the local and non-iterative characteristics of bilateral filtering, its calculation amount only had a little bit increase in comparison with bilateral filtering, and its de-noising effect was obviously better than that of bilateral filtering, thus such method can be expected to be widely used then.

References

1. C. Tomasi, R. Manduchi., *Proceedings of the IEEE International Conference on Computer Vision* (1998)
2. F. Durand, J. Dorsey., ACM Tran. on Grap., **21**, 257 (2002)
3. B. Zhang, J. P. Allebach., IEEE Tran. on Imag. Proc., **17**, 664 (2008)
4. C. Xiao, J. Gan, Visu. Comp., **28**, 713 (2012)
5. S. V. M. Sagheer, S. N. George, *International Conference on Recent Advances in Information Technology* (IEEE, 2016)
6. P. Choudhury, J. Tumblin., *Proceedings of the Eurographics Symposium on Rendering*. (2003)
7. B. Yu, L. Guo, X. L. Qian, T. Y. Zhan, J. of Jilin Uni., **42**,1553 (2012)
8. E. Eisemann, F. Durand., ACM Tran. on Grap., **23**, 673 (2004)
9. G. Petschnigg, M. Agrawala, H. Hoppe, R. Szeliski, M. Cohen, K. Toyama., ACM Tran. on Grap., **23**, 664 (2004)
10. L. Cara_a, J. P. Tarel, P. Charbonnier., IEEE Tran. on Image Proc., **24**, 1199 (2015)
11. T. Ba, M. Ai-Nasrawi, G. Deng, et al., Let Imag. Proc., **11**, 512 (2017)
12. F. Y. Hu, S. H. Si, Y. N. Zhang, J. Q. Sun, J. of imag. and grap., **18**,1237 (2013)
13. J. V. D. Weijer, R. V. D. Boomgaard, *Proceedings of the conference on IEEE Computer Vision and Pattern Recognition* (2001)
14. C. Liu, W. T. Freeman, R. Szeliski, S. Kang. *Proceedings of the Conference on IEEE Computer Vision andPattern Recognition* (2006)

A Low-voltage Programmable Frequency Divider with Wide Input Frequency Range

Yilong Liao[1*], and *Xiangning* Fan[1]

[1]Institute of RF-&OE-ICs, School of Information Science and Engineering, Southeast University, 210096 Nanjing, China

Abstract. A low-voltage programmable frequency divider with wide input frequency range is fabricated in standard 0.18μm TSMC RF CMOS technology and presented in this paper. Considering the frequency division ratio of dual-modulus prescaler is relatively smaller, a programmable divider with full custom design is used to increase the frequency division ratio and the maximum operating frequency. The frequency division ratio of the programmable frequency divider covers from 64 to 255. And the measured results show that the programmable divider works correctly when the input frequency varies from 0.5 GHz to 6.0 GHz, with 1V supply. Besides, the power consumption is 3.5 mA at the maximum frequency of 6.0 GHz.

1 Introduction

With the rapid development of wireless communication, various kinds of wireless communication mode are springing up constantly, making the integration of a variety of wireless communication in a mobile terminal a development tendency. The RF transceiver which supports multiple standards also therefore becomes a research hot spot. Many domestic and foreign scholars have made a thorough research about multi-mode multi-frequency broadband frequency synthesizers [1-3] which is indispensable in a multi-mode RF transceiver.

The programmable frequency divider as a critical module in multi-mode multi-frequency frequency synthesizers, is required to work under the broadband and high frequency [4-5]. Because of the simple structure, the programmable frequency divider made up by dual-modulus prescaler and programmable divider is extensively applied. The programmable counter is constituted by a *Programmable* counter (P-counter) and a *Swallow* counter (S-counter). Usually, the two counters are designed by semi-custom design approach, which can only work at a low frequency band. In order to obtain a higher working frequency, the counters presented in this paper are designed by full custom design approach. At the same time, the frequency division ratio of dual-modulus prescaler is designed to be small to lower the minimum frequency division ratio of the whole programmable frequency divider. So, the programmable frequency divider presented in this paper also has a large frequency division ratio range.

* Corresponding author: yilongliao@seu.edu.cn

2 Circuit design

2.1 Architecture of programmable frequency divider

The architecture of the programmable frequency divider is shown in Figure 1. The full programmable divider used in this design is based on the pulse-swallow topology and it contains a 8/9 (N/N+1) dual-modulus prescaler, a 5-bit P-counter and a 3-bit S-counter [6]. Signal DMPout is the output signal of the dual-modulus prescaler (DMP). Signal DIVout is the final output of the whole programmable frequency divider. The total division ratio (TD) is given by

$$TD = S(N+1) + (P-S)N = PN + S, \tag{1}$$

where P and S are the loaded initial values in the P-counter and S-counter, respectively. Equation (1) states that the programmable frequency divider presented in this design can cover the consecutive division ratio from 64 to 255.

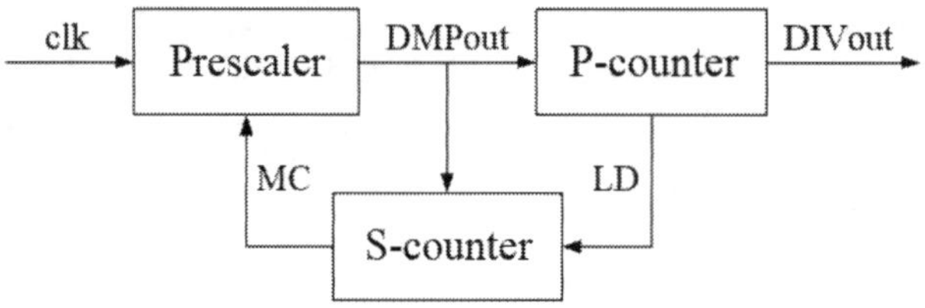

Fig. 1. Topology of programmable frequency divider.

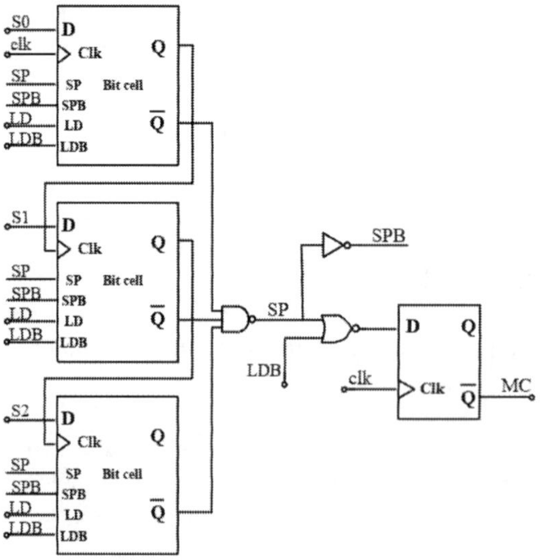

Fig. 2. Swallow counter.

2.2 Programmable divider

The 3-bit swallow S-counter used in the programmable divider is shown in Figure 2. It consists of three asynchronous loadable bit-cells, a DFF and logic gates to achieve programmability from 0 to 7. The asynchronous loadable bit-cell, as shown in Figure 3 is similar to the bit-cell reported in [7], except the five transistors M1 M5 M6 M9 M14 whose inputs are controlled by the logic signal SP or SPB. SPB is inversed to SP and when SP is switched to logic ‘1’, S-counter stops counting. When the S-counter finishes counting down-to-zero, SP switches to logic ‘1’ and MC switches to logic ‘0’, then the precaler changes to the divide-by-9 mode for the left (P-S) clock cycles [8]. The S-counter can work correctly whatever the loading value is.

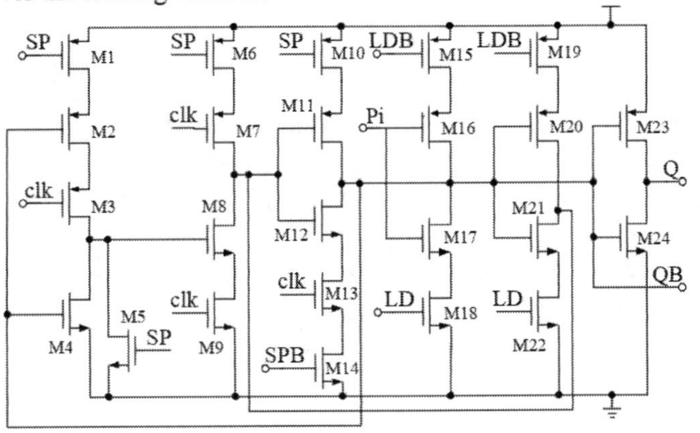

Fig. 3. Bit-cell used in S-counter.

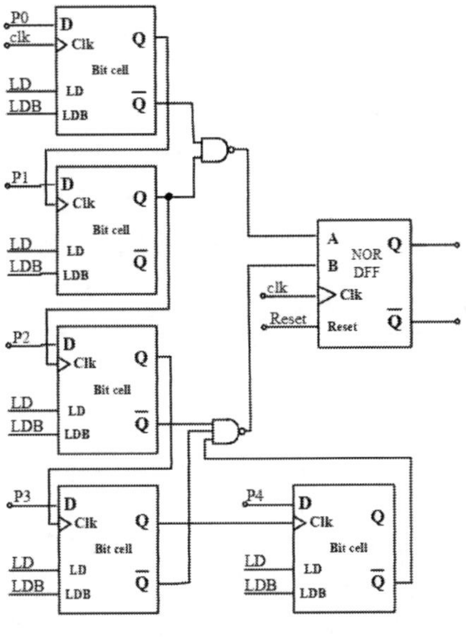

Fig. 4. Programmable counter.

The 5-bit programmable P-counter used in the fully programmable divider is shown in Figure 4 [8]. It consists of five asynchronous loadable bit-cells, a NOR-embedded DFF and logic gates to allow it to be programmable from 2 to 31. The bit-cell used in the P-counter is similar to the bit-cell reported in [7] with optimized transistor size for low power consumption. When the P-counter finishes counting down-to-two, LD switches to logic ‘1’ and keeps the state for a clock cycle. It makes sure that bit-cell have enough time to load new counting value [9]. The NOR-embedded DFF shown in Figure 5 can be reset by the signal Reset. When Reset switches to logic ‘1’, LD switches to logic ‘1’ and both P-counter and S-counter load the new counting values. Note that the P-counter can work correctly when the loading value is not less than 2. Beside, in this design, the loading value of P-counter is not less than 8.

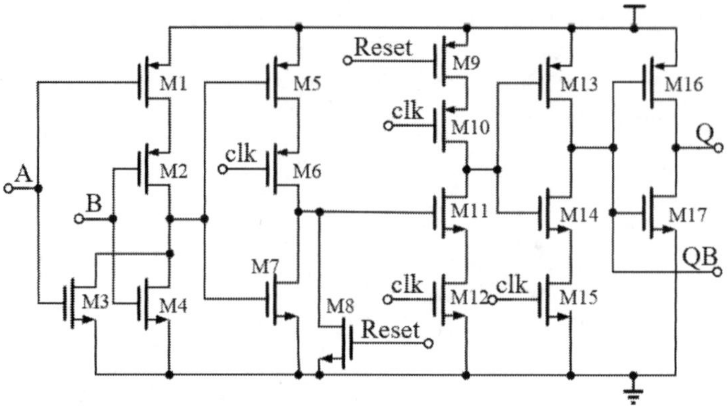

Fig. 5. NOR-embedded DFF with reset function.

2.3 Dual-Modulus prescaler

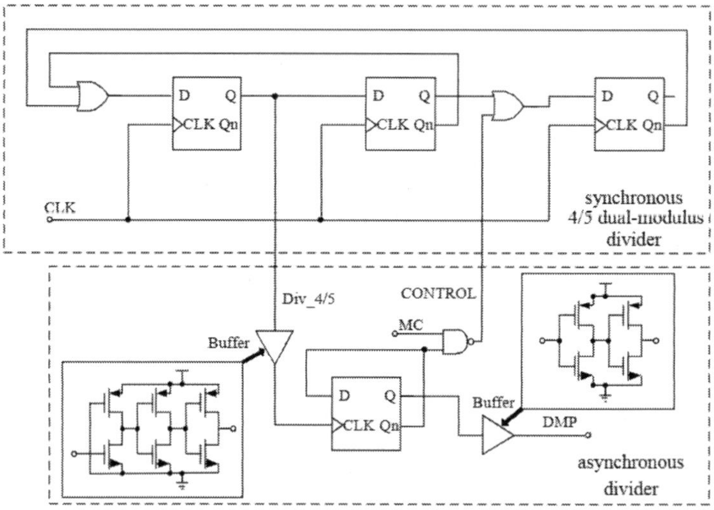

Fig. 6. Dual-modulus prescaler.

The prescaler as shown in Figure 6 employs a synchronous 4/5 dual-modulus divider and an asynchronous divider. The synchronous divider is constructed by three DFFs and two OR logic gates. When the mode control signal CONTROL switches to logic '1', only DFF1 and DFF2 are working in fact. So signal Q2b of DFF2 feedback to DFF1, consequently the synchronous divider divides the signal clk by 4. When the mode control signal CONTROL switches to logic '0', Q3bn+1=Q2bn and Q1n+1=Q2bn|Q3bn. So the synchronous divider divides the signal clk by 5.

In this design, source coupled logic (SCL) circuit as shown in Figure 7 is chosen as the DFF [10]. To increase the operating frequency and save the power consumption, the OR logic gate is integrated in the SCL circuit directly [10], as shown in Figure 8. Asynchronous divider is constructed by True-signal-phase-clock (TSPC) circuit [11] and it divides the signal from the synchronous divider by 2. When MC switches to logic '0', the division ratio of prescaler is $2\times4 = 8$. When MC switches to logic '1', in a whole dividing cycle, the prescaler divides clk by 8 for 0.5 cycle and divides clk by 10 for the other 0.5 cycle, so the division ratio of prescaler is $8\times0.5 + 10\times0.5 = 9$.

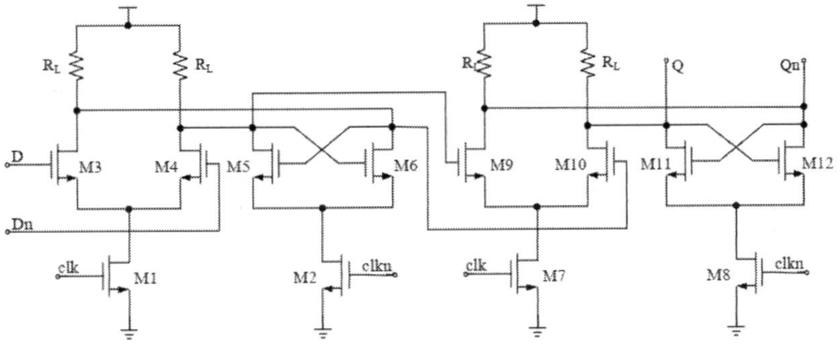

Fig. 7. SCL circuit.

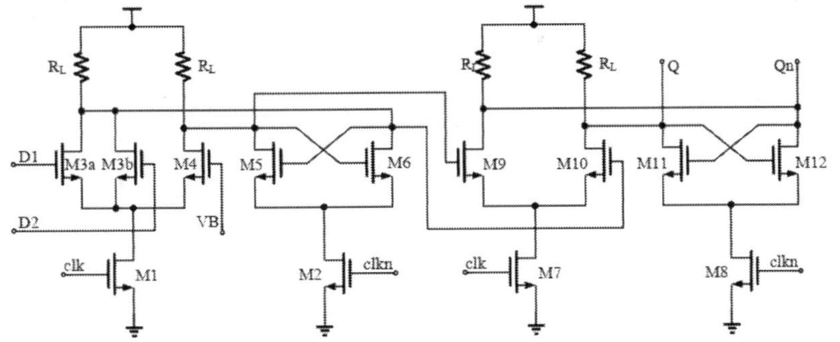

Fig. 8. SCL circuit integrated with OR logic gate.

3 Simulated results

The layout of the programmable frequency divider is shown in Figure 9. It consists of a S-counter, a P-counter and a dual-modulus prescaler. The area of the whole circuit is 0.258 mm×0.168 mm.

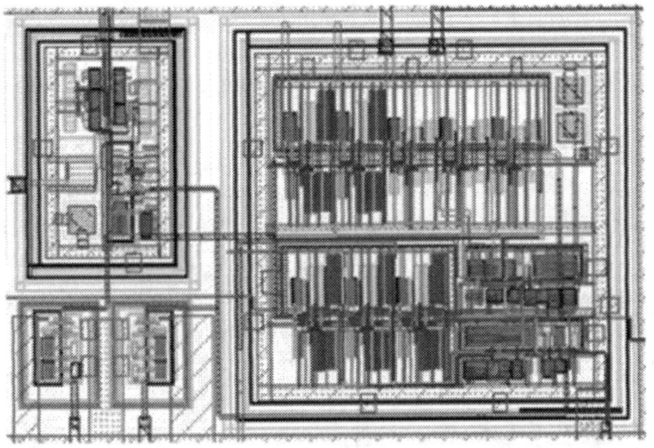

Fig. 9. Layout of the proposed divider.

The post simulation is performed in Cadence. When the frequency is 6.5 GHz, the inputs and outputs of the prescaler are shown in Figure 10. According to the markers placed in the waveforms in Figure 10, we know the division ratio is 8/9 by simple calculation. The prescaler can work correctly with 0.5-6.5 GHz input range and consumes 3.19 mA when the frequency is 6.5 GHz and supply voltage is 1V.

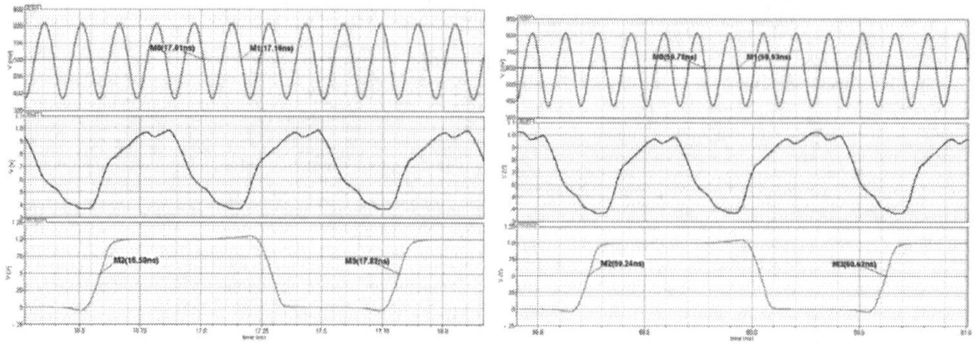

(a) Divide-by-8 (b) Divide-by-9

Fig. 10. Post simulated prescaler input and output waveforms.

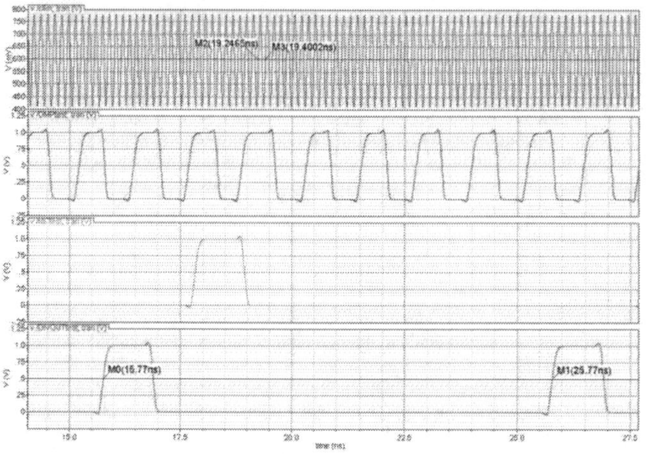

Fig. 11. Post simulated programmable frequency divider input and output waveforms.

The post simulation result of input and output of the whole programmable divider is presented in Figure 11. The counting value of P-counter is 8 and the counting value of S-counter is 1, so the division ratio of the whole programmable divider is 65, as calculated by Equation (1). In the Figure 11, the first waveform is the input signal clk, whose frequency is 6.5 GHz, the second waveform is the output signal DMPout, the third waveform is MC, and the fourth waveform is the output signal of the whole programmable divider DIVout. According to the markers placed in the waveform in Figure 11, the division ratio is 65, which is consistent with the value calculated by Equation (1). The highest frequency that P-counter and S-counter designed by the full custom approach can work at is around 900MHz. The programmable divider can work correctly with the input range of 0.5-6.5 GHz. And it draws 4.99 mA current from 1V supply voltage at the maximum frequency.

4 Measured results

The proposed programmable divider is fabricated using standard 0.18-μm CMOS technology with six metal layers. The whole circuit (including pads) occupies a chip area of 0.675mm × 0.378mm, and the die micrograph is shown in Figure 12.

The measured results of input and output of the whole programmable divider is illustrated in Figure 13. The counting value of P-counter is 16 and the counting value of S-counter is 4, so the division ratio of the whole programmable divider is 132, which is calculated by Equation (1). The frequency of input signal clk is 6 GHz. In Figure 13, the first waveform is the output signal of the whole programmable divider DIVout, whose frequency is 45.45 MHz ; then, the second waveform is the output signal MC ; finally, signal DMPout is shown in the third waveform. Figure 14 shows the output frequency spectrogram of the programmable divider. According to the data in the waveform in Figure 13, we can obtain that the division ratio is 132. The measured results states that, when the input frequency varies from 0.5 GHz to 6.0 GHz, the programmable divider can work effectively. With 1V voltage supply, the consumed current is 3.5 mA at the maximum input frequency.

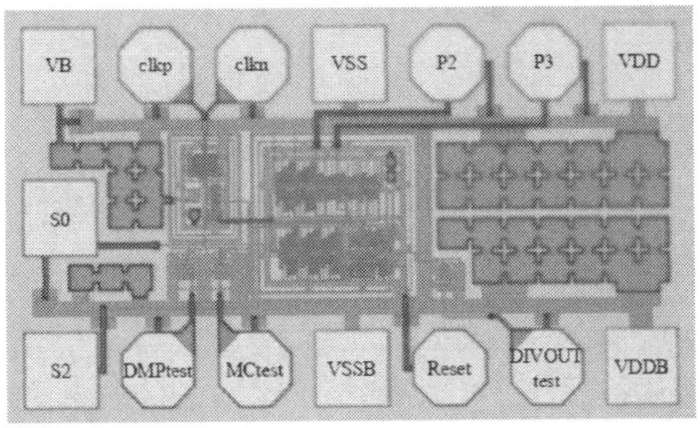

Fig. 12. Chip micrograph of the programmable frequency divider.

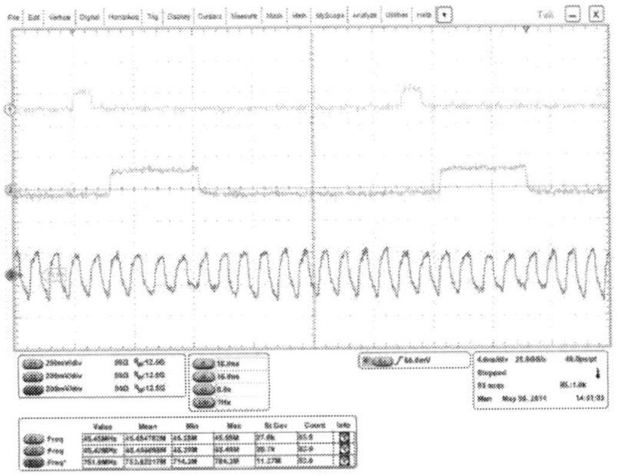

Fig. 13. Programmable frequency divider's input and output waveforms.

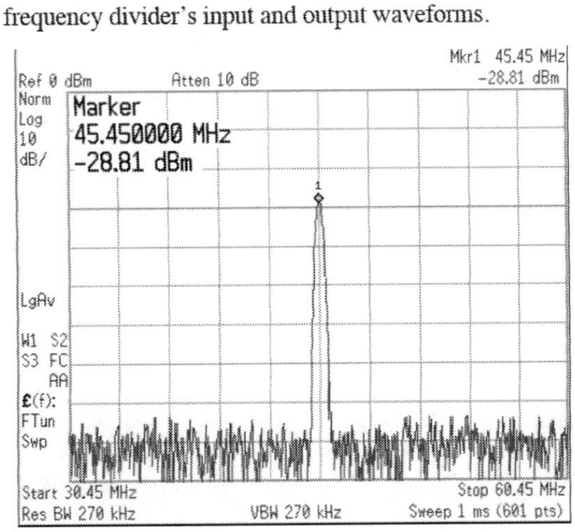

Fig. 14. Frequency spectrogram of the output of programmable divider.

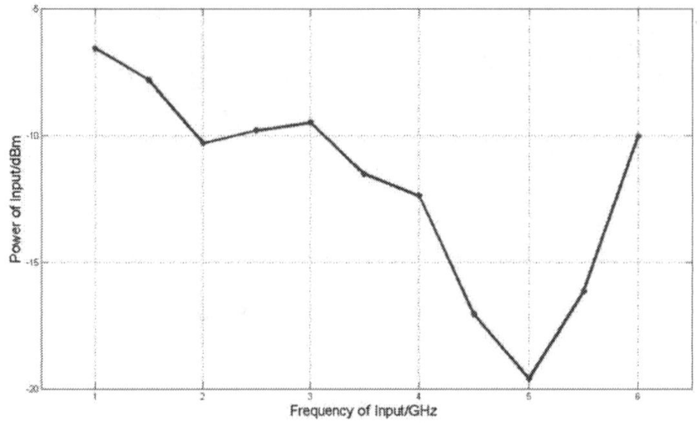

Fig. 15. Input sensitivity curve of the programmable divider.

Shown in Figure 15 is the input sensitivity curve of the programmable divider. As is seen in Figure 15, when the frequency of the input is 5 GHz, the required input power is minimum. Consequently, the programmable divider is most sensitive when the input frequency is around 5 GHz.

5 Conclusion

A 1V low-voltage programmable divider in standard 0.18μm TSMC RF CMOS technology is presented. The measured results show that the programmable divider operates correctly with the 0.5-6.5GHz input. At the maximum input frequency, a current of 3.5 mA is drawn from the 1V supply. The Input sensitivity curve of the programmable divider states that when the input frequency is around 5 GHz, the programmable divider is most sensitive and the required input power is minimum.

References

1. J. Zhou et al., IEEE T MICROW THEORY, **61**, 2, (2013)
2. D. Huang, W. Li, J. Zhou, N. Li and J. Chen, IEEE J SOLID-ST CIRC, **46**, 6, (2011).
3. R. Chen and H. Hashemi, 2013 IEEE Radio Frequency Integrated Circuits Symposium (RFIC), Seattle, WA, (2013).
4. E. Tatschl-Unterberger, S. Cyrusian and M. Ruegg, 2005 IEEE International Symposium on Circuits and Systems, **6**, (2005).
5. Y. H. Peng and L. H. Lu, IEEE T MICROW THEORY, **55**, 1, (2007).
6. Z. Gao, Y. Xu, P. Sun, E. Yao and Y. Hu, 2010 International Conference on Computer Application and System Modeling (ICCASM 2010), Taiyuan, (2010).
7. X. P. Yu, M. A. Do, L. Jia, J. G. Ma and K. S. Yeo, IEEE T VLSI SYST, **13**, 9, (2005).
8. V. K. Manthena, M. A. Do, C. C. Boon and K. S. Yeo, IEEE T VLSI SYST, **20**, 2, (2012).
9. M. Vamshi Krishna, J. Xie, M. A. Do, C. C. Boon, K. S. Yeo and A. V. Do, 2010 18th IEEE/IFIP International Conference on VLSI and System-on-Chip, Madrid, (2010).
10. B. Razavi, *RF Microelectronics*, Prentice Hall, 432-440, (2011).
11. M. V. Krishna, M. A. Do, K. S. Yeo, C. C. Boon and W. M. Lim, IEEE T CIRCUITS-I, **57**, 1, (2010).

A Quantum Cryptography Communication Network Based on Software Defined Network

Hongliang Zhang [1,*], *Dongxiao* Quan [1,*], *Changhua* Zhu[1,*], and *Zhigang* Li[1,*]

[1]Skate Key Laboratory of Integrated Services Networks, XiDian University, Xi'an, Shaanxi, China

Abstract. With the development of the Internet, information security has attracted great attention in today's society, and quantum cryptography communication network based on quantum key distribution (QKD) is a very important part of this field, since the quantum key distribution combined with one-time-pad encryption scheme can guarantee the unconditional security of the information. The secret key generated by quantum key distribution protocols is a very valuable resource, so making full use of key resources is particularly important. Software definition network (SDN) is a new type of network architecture, and it separates the control plane and the data plane of network devices through OpenFlow technology, thus it realizes the flexible control of the network resources. In this paper, a quantum cryptography communication network model based on SDN is proposed to realize the flexible control of quantum key resources in the whole cryptography communication network. Moreover, we propose a routing algorithm which takes into account both the hops and the end-to-end availible keys, so that the secret key generated by QKD can be used effectively. We also simulate this quantum cryptography communication network, and the result shows that based on SDN and the proposed routing algorithm the performance of this network is improved since the effective use of the quantum key resources.

1 Introduction

The one-time-pad encryption scheme can guarantee unconditional security of information transmission in the traditional communication network. But one-time-pad is unrealistic until QKD is raised. The unconditional security of QKD is guaranteed by the basic principles of quantum mechanics, that is, Heisenberg's uncertainty principle and quantum non-cloning theorem. The quantum cryptography communication network which is based on QKD and one-time-pad can achieve the secure transmission of information. The architecture of the quantum cryptography communication network generally includes three layers: application layer, key management layer, and quantum layer.

The quantum layer is used to implement the end-to-end QKD and upload the generated key to the key management layer. The key management layer is used to store the keys generated by the quantum layer and select the appropriate route. Application layer is used for the access of diverse transaction, including voice, video and other transaction. The

*Corresponding author: luffyliang@163.com

information is encrypted with the key stored by the key management layer for secure transmission. Compared with the classical network, the session key is transmitted by a sequence of links that protected by QKD protocols in quantum cryptography communication network. Apparently, the establishment of communication is limited by link keys[1]. So it is important to be able to control link keys throughout the network.

In the traditional network, most of proposed algorithms can usually realize the local optimal solution, because the topology of the whole network is unknown. Besides, if we continue to use the classical routing algorithms in quantum communication network, such as RIP algorithm. Since this alogrithm is based on hops, it means the routes that have the minimal number of hops will be chosen repeatedly as optimal routes, which implies the network will eventually fail to communicate, due to the keys in those links will be depleted in a short time. Meanwhile, the keys in the links that are rarely used will be severely wasted, since those links are never considered as the optimal routes.

SDN is an emerging and fast growing technology for interconnecting network devices and forwarding packets based on unified policies and security enforcements[2][3]. SDN offers deep programmability of the network at all layers and even extends the network state into applications for enabling better pathing decisions. The OpenFlow protocol plays a key role in enabling SDN architectures through its simple, flexible and adaptable programming interface[4] At present, the mainstream SDN architecture is mostly devised according to the three-tier model, that is, the application layer, the control layer, and the forwarding layer , which are illustrated in Fig. 1.

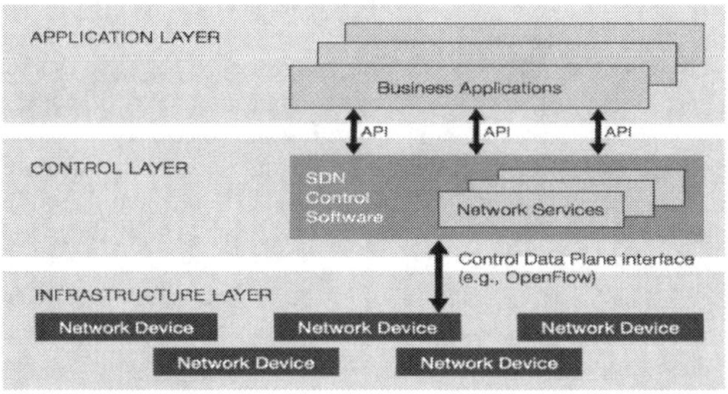

Fig. 1. Mainstream SDN architecture

In this paper, first, we propose a quantum cryptography communication network model based on the traditional SDN architecture, which makes full use of the characteristics of SDN and can realize the visualization of link keys in the whole network and select the global optimal route of point-to-point according to the key statistics result. Second, we propose an adaptive routing algorithm, which can automatically select the optimal route.

The rest of this paper is organized as follows. In section 2, we will describe in details the composition and operation principle of the quantum cryptography communication network we designed. In section 3, a simulation platform is set up and is used to count the amount of the available keys in the whole network links. Then in section 4, we propose a quantum communication network routing algorithm and make a simulation on it. In the last section, we make our main conclusion and discuss some remaining questions in this paper.

2 Design of network architecture model

We design the quantum cryptography communication network based on trusted repeaters[5]. The nodes in the network are divided into relay nodes and terminal node. The terminal node has three layers: the application layer, the network layer and the quantum layer. The main function of the application layer is to access voice, video, ftp and so on. The role of the network layer is to establish a network connection and provide services for the upper. Quantum layer implements end-to-end QKD. In the division of the protocol layer, the terminal node of both our network and the traditional network are consistent in function. The reply node is divided into quantum layer[6]and middle layer[4][7].

We will explain our network reply model architecture in details with end-to-end communications as shown in Fig.2.

The quantum layer we design refers to the QKD module[8], and it utilizes QKD protocols to generate keys. Considering all implementations of practical QKD systems are based on optical apparatus, so we suppose the quantum layer consists of single photon sources, modulators, detectors and other optical components[9]. It would be very ideal if the QKD module can communicate directly with the controller, but it is not yet possible[10]. So we design the middle layer. The middle layer has two parts: the key storage layer and the OpenFlowAgent (OFA) layer. The key storage layer is used to store the keys generated by the quantum layer, and report the number of keys to OFA in time. The OFA is an extended OpenFlow switch that acts as a proxy for QKD modules to communicate with the key management layer. We choose the SDN controller as the key management layer because it can monitor the whole network topology information in real time and control the network resources such as bandwidth in the traditional network, and effectively improve the utilization of network resources. Since key resources are relatively valuable in quantum cryptography communications, so we take advantage of of SDN controllers to effectively manage key resources. The key management layer has two roles, one is to act as a traditional SDN controller, and the other is to control the entire network key state. This means it will send two kinds of flowtables to the OpenFlowAgent, one of them is responsible for the direction of traditional network data, and the other is responsible for the direction of data encrypted by the quantum key. The reason we designed the two flow tables is the encrypted data can not be transmitted due to the key amount is insufficient, but the transmission of the conventional data can not be affected by this reason. When a data message passes through the SDN relay node, it will selectively match the flowtable[2].

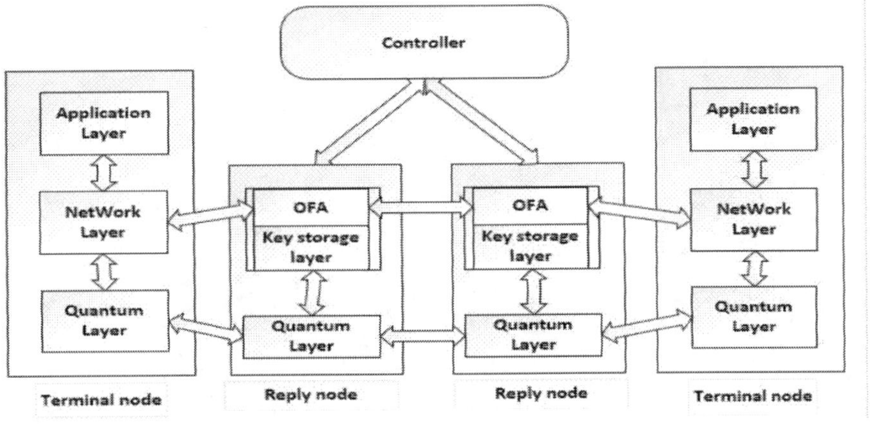

Fig. 2. Hierarchical model architecture

The communication process of each layer is shown in Fig.3 The OFA layer is in charge of encapsulating the key information, which is stored in the key store layer, into the PacketIn packet and uploading the packet to the key management layer[10]. At this point, the key management layer knows the keys state in the entire network. The key management layer selects the globally optimal route according to the key state of the whole network, then it sends the routing information to the OFA through the flow table. Finally, the application layer communicates with each other through the route[4].

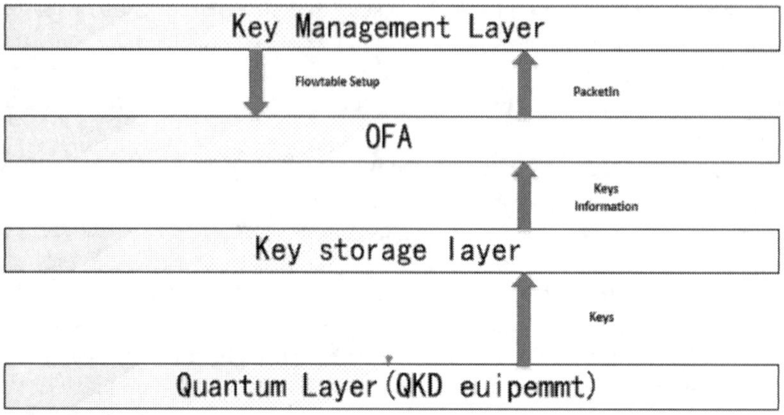

Fig. 3. Communication process

We make a network simulation according to the model and ideas mentioned in Sec.2 to verify the performance of the SDN controller manages the network key state.

We use Mininet to generate the network topology. Mininet is a powerful network simulator that is especially useful for experimenting with SDN applications[4]. To simply explain, one can pass it a file specifying the topology that one want to simulate and it establishes the environment using the Linux namespace software. The controller used in our simulation model is the mainstream SDN controller Floodlight since its stability and ease of use have been praised by SDN professionals. With these two softwares, we build our experimental simulation platform on the Linux system.

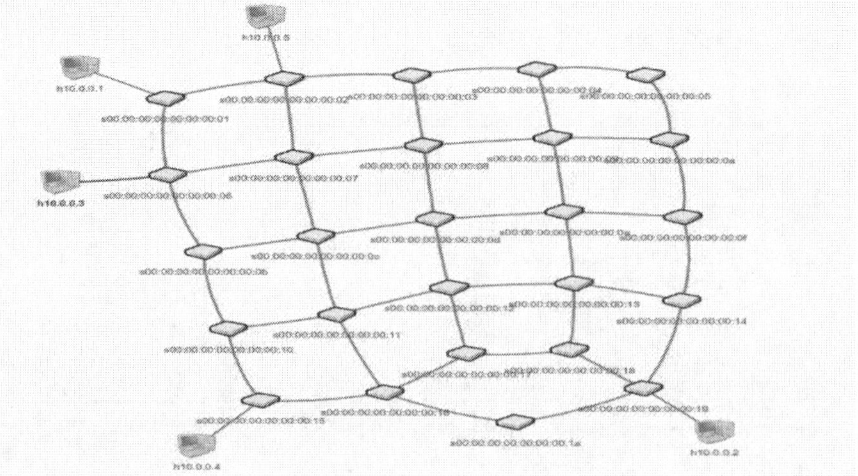

Fig. 4. Network topology

Now we assume that the quantum layer has already generated keys and upload the key to the key store layer. The key management layer needs to poll the nodes in a certain cycle to obtain the global network key state. The network topology generated by Mininet is shown in Fig.5. Here, Each switch node in the topology can be connected to a number of host nodes. We configure five hosts (h10.0.0.1 , h10.0.0.2 , h10.0.0.3 , h10.0.0.4 and h10.0.0.5) in this topology.

3 Quantum key management simulation

We will find the link through the following steps and learn the information of key in this link:

1. The link discovery module of the key management layer initiates a thread to monitor on the entire network topology, and the thread runs according to a certain time interval.
2. The key management layer uses the Link Discovery Protocol (LLDP) to learn the link state.
3. The link discovery module updates in time the key state of each link stored in the key management layer and timely displays in the console.

The following is a small part of the display as shown in Fig.5.

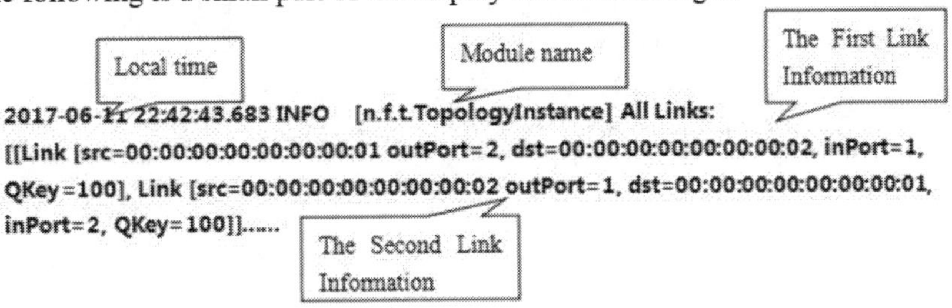

Fig. 5. All links

The information that each link stores contains the source address, the destination address, and the amount of remaining keys on the link. For example, given [src = 00: 00: 00: 00: 00: 00: 00 :01,outPort = 2, dst = 00: 00: 00: 00: 00: 00: 00: 02, inPort = 1, Qkey = 100], this means the switch named ID 1 is connected to port 1 of the switch named ID 2 through port 2 and there are still 100 kbits of keys on this link.

4 A routing algorithm for quantum cryptographic communication network

In the cryptography communication network, due to the existing conditions, the quantum key generation rate is relatively low, but a secure network requires massive keys. Thus, it is not feasible to consider only the number of links. So in addition to the link hops, we also use the number of available keys on the link as a routing condition[1][11].

4.1 Implementation steps of routing algorithm

Now that the key management layer has obtained the key's information of each link on the whole network, we can implement the routing based on the following steps:

1. First, the key management layer uses the Yen's algorithm (an extended version of the Dijkstra algorithm that solve the k shortest path problem) to select the k shortest path.
2. Then it traverse each path to learn the amount of keys on each path.
3. Now it compares the amount of keys of the bottleneck link on the path and removes the inappropriate paths that the amount of the available keys on their bottleneck link is lower than a certain threshold. The communication process of the service such as voice and video is considered to be bidirectional, and we can get the following equation:

$$V_A T = 2(V_K T + W) \tag{1}$$

Where V_A denotes the coding rate of the communication service, V_K is key rate, W denotes the demand for link keys Ideally. Taking into account the case of key loss, we set the link key threshold to $1.2W$. T is communication time. We can adjust the threshold according to the values of V_K and V_A.

$$W = \frac{V_A T - 2V_k T}{2} \tag{2}$$

4. In the remaining paths, it selects the path with the least number of hops as the optimal choice.

Because we use the one-time-pad encryption scheme, the amount of available keys on *ith* link is related to the total number of keys generated, we denote it by S_i, and the length of each packet, denoted as Pj, through this link. The amount of the available keys on the link, denoted as *Ri*, is calculated as follows:

$$R_i = S_i - \sum_{j=1}^{N} P_j \tag{3}$$

where N denotes the number of packets that pass through the link.

Assume the total number of links that this path traverses is L, The amount of the available keys in the bottleneck link, denoted by \$m\$, can be expressed as

$$m = min\{R_1, R_2, \ldots, R_L\} \tag{4}$$

4.2 Experimental simulation

Using the topology of figure 4 and our designed program, three alternative paths from h5 to h2 are generated.

In the quantum cryptography communication network, we refer to the coding rate of voice services and we can set V_A is 8kbit/s and V_K is 5kbit/s. Through the formula (2), we can get the 1.2W is 70kbit. So we modify the core code of floodlight to simulate the process of our algorithm.

Then let h5 continuously send UDP packets to h2, and we record the path was selected at different time as shown in Fig.6.

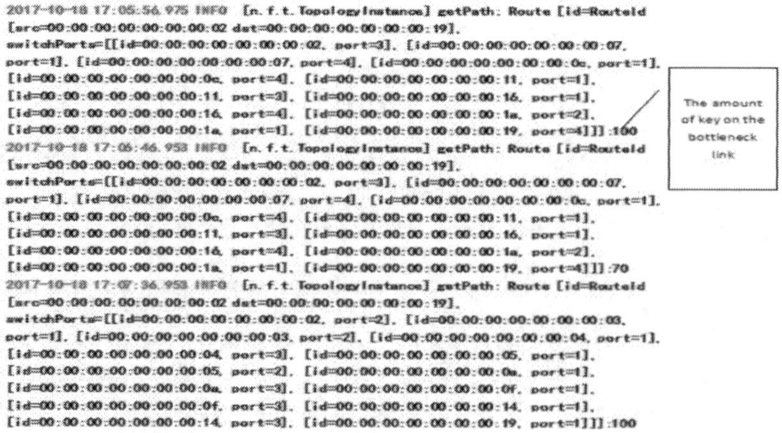

Fig. 6. Optimal path

The experimental results show the system automatically changes the route when the key value of bottleneck link of the first path is below the threshold. Experiments show that our algorithm is feasible.

5 Conclusion

The quantum key generated by QKD is a very valuable resource, and its management is of great significance.

This is the first time to integrate the idea of SDN into the quantum cryptography communication network, which is a quite reasonable innovation. In this paper, a quantum cryptography communication network model based on SDN is proposed to realize the flexible control of quantum key resources in the whole cryptography communication network and on this basis we propose a routing algorithm. Compared to other routing algorithms, the routing algorithm is more globally optimal.

SDN is one of the hot spots of the current network research. We will pay our attention on this domain constantly. We will study how to develop the flowtable, so that our quantum cryptography communication network model is more practical. And the number of switching nodes and host nodes in the actual network is much larger than the number of our simulation experiments, so we will expand our model for multi-controller mode. We believe that multiple controllers work together to manage the entire network and its control efficiency can increase significantly.

We will use further simulation experiments to demonstrate that quantum cryptography communication network that contains SDN thought has a great advantage in the management of keys and other network resources.

References

1. M. Li, "Stochastic routing in quantum cryptography communication network based on cognitive resources," in The Ninth International Conference on Wireless Communications and Signal Processing, 2016.network based on cognitive resources," in The Ninth International
2. M. M. K. Maurya A K, "A survey on software-defined network and openflow: From concept to implementation.," IEEE Communication
3. K. Govindarajan, "Interoperability issue between ipv4 and ipv6 in openflow enabled network," in 2014
4. V. R. Dasari1 and T. S. Humble2, "Openflow arbitrated programmable network channels for managing quantum metadata," The Journal of Defense Modeling and Simulation: Applications, Methodology, Technology, vol. 14, pp. 1 – 11, 2016.
5. M. M. K. Maurya A K, "Two-way quantum communication: Generalization of secure quantum information exchange to quantum network[j].,"Pramana, pp. 515 – 526, 2016.
6. R. S. TS Humble, "Software-defined quantum communication systems,"
7. Optical Engineering, vol. 53, 2014.
8. V. R. D. . R. J. S. . R. P. . B. P. W. . T. S. Humble, "Programmable multi-node quantum network design and simulation," Proceedings of the SPIE, vol. 9873, 2016.
9. T. S. Humble, "Quantum security for the physical layer," The Journal of Defense Modeling and Simulation: Applications, Methodology, Technology, vol. 51, 2013.
10. R. V. M. J. Touch, "Designing quantum repeater networks," IEEE Communications Magazine, vol. 51, pp. 64 – 71, 2013.
11. N. Y. Xiaoyuan Cao, "Dynamic openflow-controlled optical packet switching network," Journal of Lightwave Technology, vol. 33, pp. 1500 – 1507, 2015.

 https://doi.org/10.1051/itmconf/20181701008

12. T. L. W. M. K. N. RV Meter, T Satoh, "Path selection for quantum repeater networks," Networking Science, pp. 82 – 95, 2013.

A Joint Subcarrier Assignment and Power Allocation with Statistical Delay QoS Provisioning in Full-Duplex OFDMA Systems

Shuai Yan[1], *Xuefen* Chi[1,*], *Linlin* Zhao[1], and *Yuhong* Zhu[1]

[1]Dept. of Communication Engineering, Jilin University, Nanhu Street 5372, Changchun, China

Abstract. In this paper, we explore a joint subcarrier assignment and power allocation with statistical delay QoS guarantees for full-duplex OFDMA systems. Effective capacity theory which evaluates wireless channel capacity from a novel view of link layer provides a theory basis for modeling the system capacity under the conditions of delay QoS constrains. After modeling the aggregate effective capacity of the system, we formulate joint subcarrier assignment and power allocation problem as a mixed integer programming problem, whose target is to maximize the aggregate effective capacity. To solve this integer programming problem, we allocate initial power on each subcarrier and decompose it into two sub-problems, which are subcarrier allocation problem and power allocation problem respectively. Further, we propose an alternative algorithm to achieve joint subcarrier assignment and power allocation, which can meet the "subcarrier continuity" constraint of uplink resource allocation. Simulations have shown that the performance of our proposed scheme is favorite. Additionally, we investigate the effect of the residual self-interference, inter-node interference (INI) and statistical delay QoS exponent on the performance of systems.

1 Introduction

Due to the shortage of radio spectrum, traditional radio communication systems suffer from limited channel capacity. Fortunately, full-duplex communication technologies provide an effective way to improve the spectrum efficiency via enabling a full-duplex node to transmit and receive simultaneously in the same frequency band [1-3].

The cellular communication system with full-duplex enable physical layer calls for a re-design of resource allocation algorithms in higher layers. The resource allocation algorithms in full-duplex OFDMA systems have been studied to maximize the sum-rate by assigning subcarriers and allocating transmission power under a limited power budget. The authors in [4-6] have formulated the joint problem of subcarrier assignment and power allocation in full-duplex OFDMA networks, and developed an iterative solution that achieves local Pareto optimality. The authors in [7] have proposed a three step subcarrier and power allocation algorithm to maximize the system throughput for the OFDMA full-

[*] Corresponding author: chixf@jlu.edu.cn

duplex system. The authors in [8] focused on a full-duplex multi-user OFDMA cellular system, and they proposed a subcarrier allocation, power allocation and uplink and downlink user-pairing scheme to maximize the system sum-rate by integrating the dual method and the sequential parametric convex approximation method. For OFDMA systems, the uplink resource allocation is subject to subcarrier "continuity" constraints, which refers to the subcarriers or resource blocks (RBs) allocated to each user having to be continuous. However, the above-mentioned resource allocation algorithm for full-duplex OFDMA systems, no attempts have been devoted to propose resource allocation algorithm, which meet uplink resource allocation's "subcarrier continuity" constraint.

Furthermore, quality-of-service (QoS) guarantees play a critically important role in future communication networks. The next generation communication networks are required to provision high data rate and reliable service for delay sensitive applications. That is, more attention must be paid to evaluate the performance not only on the throughput, but also on the QoS guarantees.

Recently, the concept of statistic delay QoS in effective capacity theory has captured increasing attention of researchers. Different from the traditional Shannon capacity theory, effective capacity presents a novel perspective on the capacity of channel in terms of delay QoS metric in the link-layer [9-10], which can measure the throughput performance of the network under the statistic delay QoS constraint. However, for full-duplex OFDMA systems, how to maximize effective capacity while satisfying the given QoS requirement is an open problem.

In this paper, we consider a single-cell full-duplex OFDMA system, where the BS and nodes have power constraints and all nodes have QoS requirements. We aim to maximize the aggregate effective capacity by optimizing the uplink and downlink resource allocations while meeting the delay QoS requirements of transmission services in the presence of the full-duplex transmissions.

In order to obtain the aggregate effective capacity of the system, we define the subcarrier scheduling probability function to represent the subcarrier occupied by the node, and then get the probability of the service rate when the node occupies the subcarriers. Based on this, and combined with effective capacity theory, the effective capacity of a node under a subcarrier is modeled. Finally, we accumulate the effective capacity of all nodes to obtain the aggregate effective capacity of the system.

Relying on the derived system aggregate effective capacity, our joint subcarrier assignment and power allocation problem is formulated as a mixed integer programming problem with the target of maximizing the aggregate effective capacity. We target to support statistical delay QoS constraints. In view of the existing literature, the transmit power not only depends on the channel gain but also is influenced by statistical delay QoS. Therefore, we derive a QoS-driven power allocation strategy based on effective capacity theory. To solve this integer programming problem, we first allocate initial power on each subcarrier based on the given QoS-driven power allocation strategy, then the joint allocation problem can be decomposed into two sub-problems, which are subcarrier assignment problem and power allocation problem.

The subcarrier assignment is affected by the initial power, and also affects the final power allocation. Considering that subcarrier assignment and power allocation are intertwined, we solve these two sub-questions in two steps. First, for the uplink, we propose an iterative maximum expansion algorithm to solve the subcarrier allocation problem, which meets uplink resource allocation's "subcarrier continuity" constraints; for the downlink, we solve the subcarrier assignment problem based on a bipartite matching approach to make sure that a subcarrier is assigned only to one node. The uplink and downlink subcarrier assignment pattern is obtained, respectively. Second, according to the uplink and downlink subcarrier assignment pattern, we reallocate the power on each subcarrier based on the given QoS-driven power allocation strategy. In this way, an alternative algorithm to achieve joint subcarrier assignment and power allocation is formed.

The rest of this paper is organized as follows. The full-duplex OFDMA system model is described, and aggregate effective capacity maximization problem is formally formulated in Section 2. Our proposed subcarrier assignment and power allocation strategy are presented in Section 3. We evaluate our solution in comparison with other resource allocation schemes in Section 4. Finally, we conclude our paper in Section 5.

2 System model and problem formulation

In this paper, we consider a single-cell OFDMA system that consists of a full-duplex base station (BS), N half-duplex uplink nodes and M half-duplex downlink nodes. The system model is illustrated in Fig. 1. For the OFDMA system, the entire available bandwidth is equally divided into S subcarriers, each of them with a bandwidth of B. $\mathbf{S} = \{1, 2, . . . , S\}$ is the sets of subcarriers, $\mathbf{N} = \{1, 2, . . . , N\}$ and $\mathbf{M} = \{1, 2, . . . , M\}$ are the sets of uplink nodes and downlink nodes, respectively. Each subcarrier is assumed to be perfectly orthogonal to any of other subcarriers, so there is no interference between different subcarriers. Owing to the BS operates in full-duplex mode, the BS can transmit and receive signals on the same frequency at the same time, there exists inter-node interference (INI) from uplink nodes to downlink nodes. Meanwhile, the BS is assumed to be imperfect full-duplex that exists residual self-interference. We regard the residual self-interference and INI as increasing the noise power[3], the INI of all nodes is the same, and let σ_{BS} and σ_{INI} be the residual self-interference of the BS and inter-node interference (INI), respectively.

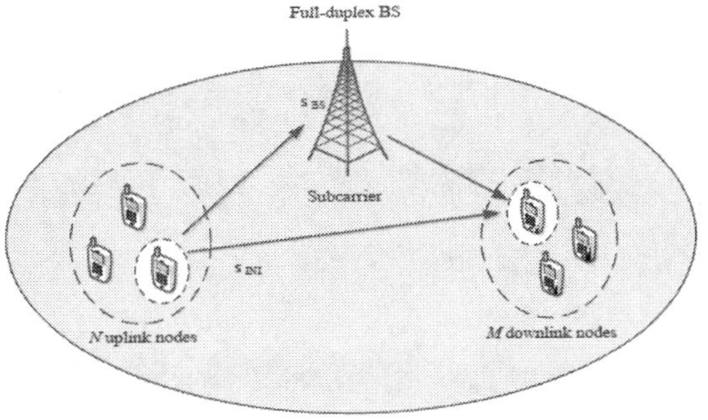

Fig. 1. A single-cell full-duplex OFDMA system

2.1 Channel model

In this scenario, we assume that the BS has the full knowledge of channel state information (CSI). We consider a block fading channel, and the channel fading gain includes the location-dependent path loss and the fast fading effect. The channel coefficient from node n to BS, and that from BS to node m, over subcarrier s are denoted by $h^u_{n,s}$ and $h^d_{m,s}$, respectively. Additionally, the transmit power from node n to BS, and that from BS to node m, over subcarrier s are denoted by $p^u_{n,s}$ and $p^d_{m,s}$, respectively. Then, the uplink and downlink transmit power vector are denoted by $\mathbf{P}^u := \{p^u_{n,s}\}_{n\in\mathbf{N},s\in\mathbf{S}}$ and $\mathbf{P}^d := \{p^d_{m,s}\}_{m\in\mathbf{M},s\in\mathbf{S}}$, respectively. Finally, we define $\mathbf{P} := (\mathbf{P}^u, \mathbf{P}^d)$ as the power allocation vector. Owing to the residual self-interference and INI, the signal to interference plus noise power ratio (SINR) for uplink and downlink are $g^u_{n,s} = \left|h^u_{n,s}\right|^2 / (\sigma_{\mathrm{BS}} N_0)$ and $g^d_{m,s} = \left|h^d_{m,s}\right|^2 / (\sigma_{\mathrm{INI}} N_0)$, respectively, where N_0 denotes the receiver noise. Then, we define $\mathbf{G} := \{g^u_{n,s}, g^d_{m,s}\}$ as the SINR vector. Thus, the rate of uplink transmission can be expressed as:

$$R^u_{n,s} = B \cdot \log_2(1 + P^u_{n,s} g^u_{n,s}) \tag{1}$$

The rate of downlink transmission can be expressed as:

$$R^d_{m,s} = B \cdot \log_2(1 + P^d_{m,s} g^d_{m,s}) \tag{2}$$

2.2 Statistical delay-QoS guarantee

Effective capacity theory, which is proposed by Wu and Negi in 2003 [11], is the dual problem of effective bandwidth. It characterizes the maximum constant arrival rate of a given service process under the statistical delay QoS constraint. Assume that $\{R[i], i = 1, 2, ...\}$ is an ergodic stochastic service process, $R[i]$ is the service rate of system in the i slot. Then, the effective capacity of the service process is defined as:

$$EC(\theta) = -\frac{1}{\theta}\log_2(\mathrm{E}\{e^{-\theta R[i]}\}) \tag{3}$$

where the θ is the QoS exponent [12]. It should be noted that a small θ corresponds to a loose delay constraint, while a large θ indicates a stringent delay constraint.

According to (3), the uplink effective capacity can be expressed as:

$$EC_{n,s}(\theta^u_n) = -\frac{1}{\theta^u_n}\log_2(e^{-\theta^u_n(R^u_{n,s}=0)}(1-\gamma_{n,s}) + e^{-\theta^u_n(R^u_{n,s}>0)}\gamma_{n,s}) \tag{4}$$

the downlink effective capacity can be expressed as:

$$EC_{m,s}(\theta^d_m) = -\frac{1}{\theta^d_m}\log_2(e^{-\theta^d_m(R^d_{m,s}=0)}(1-\gamma_{m,s}) + e^{-\theta^d_m(R^d_{m,s}>0)}\gamma_{m,s}) \tag{5}$$

where θ^u_n and θ^d_m is the QoS exponent of uplink traffic and downlink traffic, respectively. $\gamma_{n,s}$ and $\gamma_{m,s}$ are the probability that node n and node m are scheduled on subcarrier s, respectively, if the node n and node m are scheduling, $R^u_{n,s} > 0$, $R^d_{m,s} > 0$; otherwise, $R^u_{n,s} = 0$, $R^d_{m,s} = 0$.

Then, the aggregate effective capacity of uplink and downlink can be expressed as:

$$EC_{n,m,s}(\theta^u_n, \theta^d_m) = EC_{n,s}(\theta^u_n) + EC_{m,s}(\theta^d_m) \tag{6}$$

For the OFDMA system, each subcarrier can only be assigned to a single node. To better express the node and subcarrier pairing, we define the uplink and downlink subcarrier assignment indication vector as $\mathbf{X}^u := \{x^u_{n,s}\}_{n\in\mathbf{N}, s\in\mathbf{S}}$ and $\mathbf{X}^d := \{x^d_{m,s}\}_{m\in\mathbf{M}, s\in\mathbf{S}}$, respectively, in which $x^u_{n,s} = 1$ denotes that subcarrier s is assigned to uplink node n and $x^d_{m,s} = 1$ denotes that subcarrier s is assigned to downlink node m. Finally, we define $\mathbf{X} := (\mathbf{X}^u, \mathbf{X}^d)$ as the subcarrier assignment vector.

2.3 Problem formulation

In this paper, we let P_{BS} and P_T denote the total transmission power for the BS and for uplink node n, respectively. Thus, the joint subcarrier assignment and power allocation for aggregate effective capacity maximization is formulated as:

$$
\begin{aligned}
\text{P: maximize} \; & \sum_{n=1}^{N}\sum_{m=1}^{M}\sum_{s=1}^{S} x_{n,s}^{u} \cdot x_{m,s}^{d} \cdot EC_{n,m,s}(\theta_n^u, \theta_m^d) && \text{(a)} \\
\text{s.t.} \; & \sum_{s=1}^{S} p_{n,s}^{u} \le P_T, \;\; \forall n \in \mathbf{N} && \text{(b)} \\
& \sum_{m=1}^{M}\sum_{s=1}^{S} p_{m,s}^{d} \le P_{BS}, && \text{(c)} \\
& P_{n,s}^{u}, P_{m,s}^{d} \ge 0, \forall n \in \mathbf{N}, m \in \mathbf{M}, s \in \mathbf{S} && \text{(d)} \\
& \sum_{n=1}^{N} x_{n,s}^{u} \le 1, \sum_{m=1}^{M} x_{m,s}^{d} \le 1, \forall s \in \mathbf{S} && \text{(e)} \\
& x_{n,s}^{u} \in \{0,1\}, \forall n \in \mathbf{N}, s \in \mathbf{S} && \text{(f)} \\
& x_{m,s}^{d} \in \{0,1\}, \forall m \in \mathbf{M}, s \in \mathbf{S} && \text{(g)}
\end{aligned}
\qquad (7)
$$

where the objective of the optimization Problem (7) is the sum of the effective capacity of in the system. Constraint (b) guarantees the limit of the total transmission powers for the node n. Constraint (c) guarantees the limit of the total transmission powers for the BS. Constraint (e), (f) and (g) guarantees each subcarrier is exclusively assigned to one uplink and downlink node.

3 Subcarrier allocation and power allocation scheme

The original problem P is an integer optimization problem. The subcarrier assignment and power allocation are intertwined: the subcarrier assignment is affected by the initial power, and also affects the final power allocation. In order to make the problem tractable, we first allocate initial power on each subcarrier based on the given QoS-driven power allocation strategy, then the joint allocation problem can be decomposed into two sub-problems, which are subcarrier assignment problem and power allocation problem. After that, an alternative algorithm that mixing the subcarrier assignment algorithm and QoS-driven power allocation strategy is proposed. We first describe QoS-driven power allocation strategy, and then consider the uplink and downlink subcarrier assignment algorithm.

3.1 QoS-driven power allocation

Given a certain determined subcarrier assignment pattern $\mathbf{X}^*$, the original optimization problem P is transformed into a power allocation problem. We target to support statistical delay QoS constraints, in view of the existing literature, the transmit power will depend on not only the channel gain but also the statistical delay QoS[10]. Then, the transmit power of node n on subcarrier s to BS can be derived as:

$$p_{n,s}^{u}=\begin{cases}\left[\beta_n\cdot\left(\dfrac{\alpha(\theta_1)^{\alpha(\theta_2)+1}}{\alpha(\theta_2)^{\alpha(\theta_2)}\cdot g_{n,s}^{u}{}^{\alpha(\theta_1)+\alpha(\theta_2)}}\right)^{\frac{1}{\alpha(\theta_1)+\alpha(\theta_2)+1}}-\dfrac{1}{g_{n,s}^{u}}\right]^{+} & \text{if } x_{n,s}^{u}=1,\\ 0 & \text{if } x_{n,s}^{u}=0,\end{cases} \tag{8}$$

where $\alpha(\theta_1)=\theta_n^u/\ln 2$ is the constraint of statistical delay QoS for uplink, $\alpha(\theta_2)=\theta_m^d/\ln 2$ is the constraint of statistical delay QoS for downlink. The water level β_n is a variable, which dependent on users' statistical delay QoS requirements and satisfying $\sum_{s=1}^{S}p_{n,s}^{u}=P_T$. Similarly, the transmit power of BS on subcarrier s to node m can be derived as:

$$p_{m,s}^{d}=\begin{cases}\left[\beta\cdot\left(\dfrac{\alpha(\theta_2)^{\alpha(\theta_1)+1}}{\alpha(\theta_1)^{\alpha(\theta_1)}\cdot g_{n,s}^{d}{}^{\alpha(\theta_1)+\alpha(\theta_2)}}\right)^{\frac{1}{\alpha(\theta_1)+\alpha(\theta_2)+1}}-\dfrac{1}{g_{n,s}^{d}}\right]^{+} & \text{if } x_{m,s}^{d}=1,\\ 0 & \text{if } x_{m,s}^{d}=0,\end{cases} \tag{9}$$

where β can be numerically obtained by constraint $\sum_{m=1}^{M}\sum_{s=1}^{S}p_{m,s}^{d}=P_{BS}$.

3.2 Subcarrier assignment

Note that the constraints of P indicate the matching relationship between nodes and subcarriers, so we can transform P into a maximum weighted bipartite matching problem. We denoted the uplink and downlink weight matrix as $\mathbf{W}_{N\times S}$ and $\mathbf{W}_{M\times S}$, respectively. The elements of $\mathbf{W}_{N\times S}$ and WM ×S are $w_{n,s}=EC_{n,s}(\theta_n^u)$ and $w_{m,s}=EC_{m,s}(\theta_m^d)$, respectively.

3.2.1 Uplink subcarrier assignment

In this paper, we propose an iterative maximum expansion (IME) algorithm to solve the uplink subcarrier allocation problem, which meet uplink resource allocation's "subcarrier continuity" constraint. The basic idea of IME is that the maximum value is selected from all the weight values of each user on each subcarrier, and the subcarrier corresponding to the maximum weight value is assigned to the corresponding user, and then the subcarrier position is centered and to expand the resources for this user on both sides, until the extended weight of this user on the subcarrier is less than the other user and get the uplink maximum weighted matching F^u.

3.2.2 Downlink subcarrier assignment

The Hungarian algorithm is an algorithm for solving assignment problems, the basic idea is to transform the original efficiency matrix C into a new efficiency matrix $\overline{C}$, so that the new matrix $\overline{C}$ contains many zero elements, but the optimal solution does not change. In the new efficiency matrix $\overline{C}$, If you can find n (equal to the order of the matrix) zero elements which different rows and different columns, you can make their corresponding x_{ij} is equal to 1, the other x_{ij} is equal to 0, then the solution must be the program Optimal solution.

However, the Hungarian algorithm requires that the number of elements on both sides be equal, and in fact, the number of subcarriers is usually greater than the number of nodes. To this end, we re-use the Hungarian algorithm until all of the subcarriers are assigned to the nodes and get the downlink maximum weighted matching F^d.

The detailed algorithm can be summarized as the following procedures. In the first step, calculate $p^u_{n,s}$ and $p^d_{m,s}$ according to (8) and (9), respectively. Then, calculate $EC_{n,s}(\theta^u_n)$ and $EC_{m,s}(\theta^d_m)$ according to (4) and (5) based on the results of $p^u_{n,s}$ and $p^d_{m,s}$, respectively. In the second step, adopt the IME algorithm to get the uplink maximum weighted matching F^u with the weight matrix $\mathbf{W}_{N\times S}$; adopt the Hungarian algorithm to get the downlink maximum weighted matching F^d with the weight matrix $\mathbf{W}_{M\times S}$. Then, we can get the subcarrier assignment $\mathbf{X}^* := (\mathbf{X}^u, \mathbf{X}^d)$, where $\mathbf{X}^u = F^u$ and $\mathbf{X}^d = F^d$. Finally, allocate uplink power $\tilde{p}^u_{n,s}$ by (8) and downlink power $\tilde{p}^d_{m,s}$ by (9) according to $\mathbf{X}^*$, so, we can get the power allocation $\tilde{\mathbf{P}}$.

4 Simulation results

In this section, we conduct simulation experiments to evaluate the performance of the proposed resource allocation scheme for full-duplex OFDMA systems under the LTE specifications[5]. We assume that the number of uplink and downlink nodes is equal to N. The detailed simulation parameters are listed in Table 1. In addition to the path loss P_{loss} (dB), it is obtained from the modified Hata urban propagation model, which is calculated as:

$$P_{loss}(d) = 69.55 + 26.16\cdot \log f - 13.83\cdot \log h_{BS} - C_H(f) + (44.9 - 6.55\cdot \log h_{BS})\log d \quad (10)$$

where d (km) is the distance between BS and nodes, h_{BS} (m) is the height of the BS, f (MHz) is the center frequency. $C_H(f)$ is the antenna height correlation factor, which is defined as:

$$C_H(f) = 0.8 + (1.1\cdot \log f - 0.7)h - 1.56\cdot \log f \quad (11)$$

where h (m) is the height of the node. We assume that each node is placed at an equal distance d from the BS.

Table 1. Simulation parameters.

Parameter	Settings
Carrier center frequency	f = 2.1 GHz
Subcarrier bandwidth	B = 180 kHz
Noise power	N_0 = -119 dBm
Maximum BS power	P_{BS} = 43 dBm
Maximum Node power	P_T = 24 dBm
The height of the BS	h_{BS} = 30 m
The height of the node	h = 1.5 m

Fig. 2 illustrates the effect of the number N of nodes on the aggregate effective capacity when S = 30, d = 200m, $\sigma_{BS} = 1$dB and $\sigma_{INI} = 3$dB. For any n∈N and m∈M, we let $\theta^u_n = \theta^d_m = 10^{-5}$. Observed from Fig. 2, with more nodes, the aggregate effective capacity of each scheme increases towing to the multi-user diversity. Our resource allocation scheme can achieve a greater aggregate effective capacity than the iterative allocation scheme[6] does, and the advantages of our resource allocation scheme would be greater with the increase of the number of nodes.

Fig. 3 demonstrates the impact of statistical delay QoS requirements on the aggregate effective capacity when $S = 30$, $N = 30$ and $d = 200$ m. Observed from Fig. 3, the aggregate effective capacity reduces upon increasing the downlink required statistical delay QoS exponent, the full-duplex OFDMA system is sensitive to the statistical delay QoS requirements, and the effective capacity degrades rapidly for θ_m^d in the range 10^{-4} to 10^{-2}.

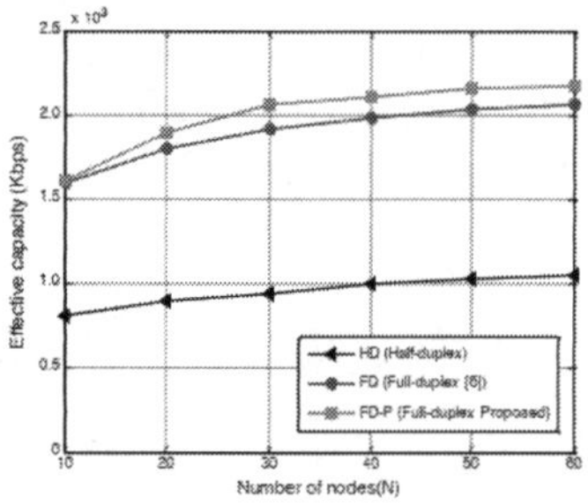

Fig. 2. Performance comparison according to N values

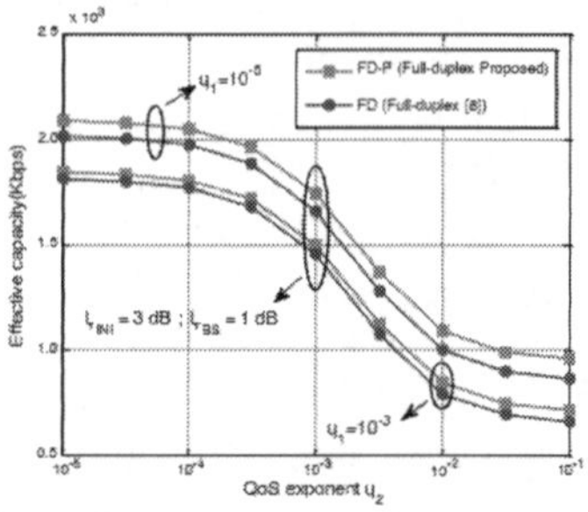

Fig. 3. Performance comparison of different uplink statistical delay QoS requirements

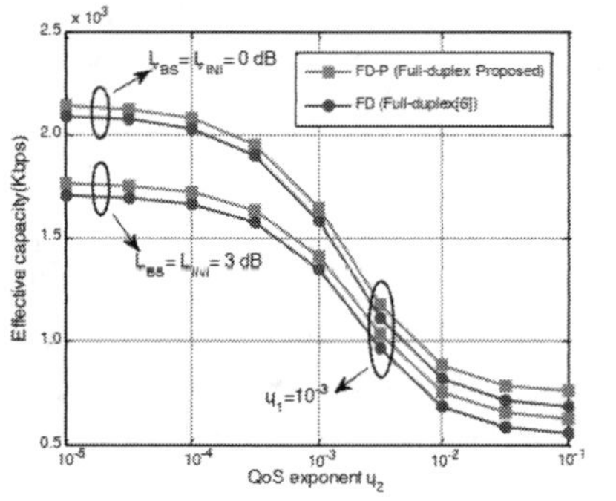

Fig. 4. Performance comparison according to downlink statistical delay QoS values With different interference

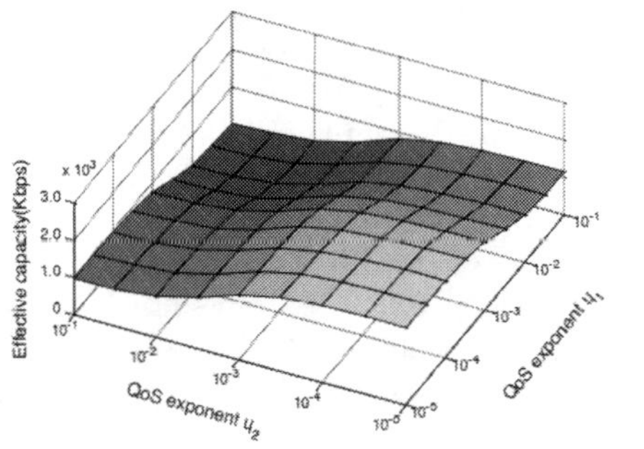

Fig. 5. The impact of heterogeneous statistical delay QoS requirements on the aggregate effective capacity

Fig. 4 demonstrates the impact of the statistical delay QoS requirements and interference on the aggregate effective capacity when the uplink required QoS exponent (θ_n^u) is 10^{-3}, $S = 30$, $N = 30$ and $d = 200$ m. Observed from Fig. 4, for any statistical delay QoS requirements, the aggregate effective capacity reduces upon increasing the residual self-interference or INI. When statistical delay QoS exponent is very small, residual self-interference or INI has a large effect on system aggregate effective capacity, this is because with the statistical delay QoS exponent gradually smaller, the statistical delay QoS requirements is very loose, system aggregate effective capacity is largely unconstrained by statistical delay.

Fig. 5 evaluates the aggregate effective capacity versus uplink required QoS exponent (θ_n^u) and downlink required QoS exponent (θ_m^d) corresponding to heterogeneous statistical QoS provisioning when $\sigma_{BS} = 1\text{dB}$ and $\sigma_{INI} = 3\text{dB}$. As shown in Fig. 5, the aggregate effective capacity decreases with the uplink required QoS exponent and the downlink required QoS exponent. In addition, when statistical delay QoS is very loose, the system can get the maximum aggregate effective capacity.

5 Conclusion

In this paper, we investigated the joint subcarrier assignment and power allocation problem with statistical delay QoS guarantees for users in full-duplex OFDMA systems. Our joint subcarrier assignment and power allocation problem was formulated as a mixed integer programming problem whose target is to maximize the aggregate effective capacity. In order to make this integer programming problem tractable, we allocate initial power on each subcarrier and decompose it into two sub-problems, which are subcarrier allocation problem and power allocation problem respectively. Based on IME algorithm, Hungarian algorithm and QoS-driven power allocation strategy, we proposed a new resource allocation scheme to solve this aggregate effective capacity maximization problem with polynomial computational complexity. The numerical simulations demonstrated that our proposed scheme was more effective to the system effective capacity than the iterative allocation scheme in [6], especially when the number of subcarriers and nodes was large. In addition, when statistical delay QoS was very loose, the system can get the maximum aggregate effective capacity, and compared with the very stringent requirements for statistical delay QoS, residual self-interference or INI has a greater impact on system aggregate effective capacity.

References

1. J.I. Choi, M. Jain, K. Srinivasan, P. Levis, S. Katti, MOBICOM, pp. 1-12, (2010)
2. M. Jain, J.I. Choi, T. Kim, MOBICOM, pp. 301-312, (2011)
3. D. Bharadia, E. Mcmilin, S. Katti, CCR, **43**, 4, pp. 375-386, (2013)
4. C. Nam, C. Joo, S. Bahk, ICTC IEEE, pp. 924-927, (2014)
5. C. Nam, C. Joo, S. Bahk, IEEE Transactions on Wireless Communications, **14**, 6, pp. 3018-3119, (2015)
6. C. Nam, C. Joo, S. Bahk, IEEE ICC, pp. 3885-3890, (2015)
7. A.C. Cirik, K. Rikkinen, R. Yue, T. Ratnarajah, EuCNC, pp. 11-15, (2015)
8. Y. Jiang, H. Chen, F.C.M. Lau, P. Wang, Y. Li, Transactions on Emerging Telecommunications Technologies, pp. 1-19, (2015)
9. W. Cheng, X. Zhang, H. Zhang, IEEE ICC, pp. 5286-5290, (2012)
10. W. Cheng, X. Zhang, H. Zhang, Computer Communications. IEEE, pp. 55-63, (2015)
11. D. Wu, R. Negi, IEEE Transactions on Wireless Communications, **2**, 4, pp. 630-643, (2003)
12. J. Tang, X. Zhang, IEEE Transactions on Wireless Communications, 6, 8, pp. 3058-3068, (2007)

Electromagnetic Pulse Generated by a Horizontal Electric Dipole over a Perfect Conductor Covered with a Dielectric Layer

Juan Zheng[1], *Tong* He[1], *Ping* Cao[1], *Zhuhong* Lin[1], and *Kai* Li[1]

[1]Zhejiang University, College of Information Science and Electronic Engineering, China

Abstract. In this paper, the electromagnetic pulse due to a delta-function current excitation has been derived on the planar surface of a perfect conductor coated by a dielectric layer. The approximate expression of wave component is obtained when both the transmitting source and the receiving antennas are located on the surface of the dielectric. When the thickness of the intermediate layer is subjected to the condition of $k_1 l \ll 0.6$, this physical model is applied to the microstrip circuit. Analysis and computations of the wave components are carried out on the microstrip circuit, including the surface trapped wave vector which had been ignored in former studies. It is shown that the trapped-surface-wave terms should have been taken into consideration as the main contribution in total transient field in the far-field radiations.

1 Introduction

The electromagnetic fields of vertical and horizontal electric dipoles on or near the boundary of two dielectrics have been well known in terms of closed-form expressions for many years [1][2].

In early 1990's, the simple analytical formulas were derived for the electromagnetic fields generated by horizontal and vertical electric dipoles in the presence of a three-layered region. The details of the research findings are well summarized in the classic two books [3][4]. It was demonstrated that the total field on or near the air-dielectric boundary is determined primarily by lateral wave, where the amplitude of the field along the boundary is $1/\rho^2$.

In the late 1990's, Wait (1998) and Mahmound (1999) wrote comments on the work by King and Sandler (1994) and considered that the surface wave, varying as $\rho^{-1/2}$ in the far-field region, should not be overlooked in the three-layered case [5][6].

After that, many researchers had revisited the old problem and some new progresses had been made [7-10]. Over the past two decades, the existence or nonexistence of the trapped-surface-wave term in the solution had been a controversial subject for the electromagnetic field radiated by a dipole source in the presence of three-layered region. The details of the study on the controversial subject were summarized in the book by Li [11]. However, it should be noted that the trapped-surface-wave terms were indeed underestimated in the classic book [4].

According to Wait, it is known that the total transient field should include the trapped surface wave as the primary wave in the far-field radiation when both the transmitting source and receiving antennas are located on the planar surface of dielectric. Therefore, the electromagnetic pulse of a vertical electric dipole in the presence of three-layered region was treated analytically in the former research by Cheng et al. [12].

Following the research line, the transient field generated by a horizontal electric dipole with delta-excitation in the presence of three-layered region has been investigated including the trapped-surface-wave term in the present study for the applications of microstrip circuit [13-17].

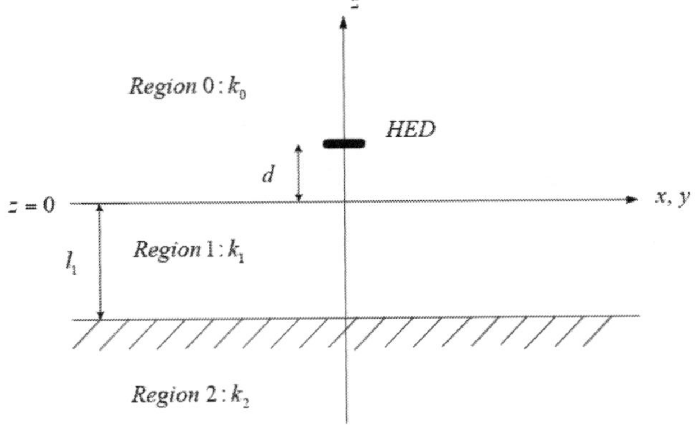

Fig.1. Horizontal electric dipole at height d in air near the surface of a perfect conductor coated with a dielectric layer.

2 Transient field of horizontal electric dipole with delta-function excitation

2.1 The simplified representations for the field components in frequency excitation

Captions should be typed in 9-point Times. They should be centred above the tables and flush left beneath the figures. The geometry under consideration is illustrated in Fig. 1, where the horizontal electric dipole in the $\hat{z}$ direction is located at *(0, 0, d)*. Region 0 $(z \geq 0)$ is the upper half-space filled with air characterized by the permeability μ_0 and the relative permittivity ε_0, region 1 is occupied by the dielectric layer characterized by the permeability μ_1, relative permittivity ε_1, and conductivity σ_1, and region 2 $(z \leq 0)$ is a perfect conductor. Then the wave numbers of the three layers are

$$\begin{aligned} k_0 &= \omega\sqrt{\mu_0\varepsilon_0} = \frac{\omega}{c}, \\ k_1 &= \omega\sqrt{\mu_0\varepsilon_0\varepsilon_1} = \frac{\omega\sqrt{\varepsilon_1}}{c}, \\ k_2 &\to \infty. \end{aligned} \tag{1}$$

The approximated formulas were derived for the electromagnetic field in frequency domain excited by a horizontal electric dipole in the presence of three-layered region [8]. The time dependence $e^{i\omega t}$ is applied throughout the analysis. The field components can be written in the simplified form.

$$
\begin{aligned}
E_{0z}(\rho,\varphi,z) = \frac{i\omega\mu_0 Idl}{4\pi k_0^2}\cos\varphi\cdot\Bigg\{ & -\frac{\rho}{r_1}\cdot\frac{z-d}{r_1}\cdot(\frac{k_0^2}{r_1}+\frac{3ik_0}{r_1^2}-\frac{3}{r_1^3})e^{ik_0 r_1} \\
& +\frac{\rho}{r_2}\cdot\frac{z+d}{r_2}\cdot(\frac{k_0^2}{r_2}+\frac{3ik_0}{r_2^2}-\frac{3}{r_2^3})e^{ik_0 r_2}+2\pi k_0^2 \\
& \cdot\sum_j \frac{\gamma_L^* \tan\gamma_L^* l\cdot e^{i\gamma_{0E}^*(z+d)}}{q'(\lambda_{jE}^*)}\cdot\lambda_{jE}^{*2}\cdot H_1^{(1)}(\lambda_{jE}^*\rho) \\
& +2ik_0^3 A\sqrt{\frac{1}{\pi k_0\rho}}\cdot e^{ik_0 r_2}\cdot\Bigg[\sqrt{\frac{\pi}{k_0\rho}}+\frac{\pi}{\sqrt{2}}\cdot e^{i\frac{\pi}{4}} \\
& \cdot A\cdot\exp\left[-i\frac{k_0\rho}{2}(\frac{z+d}{\rho}+iT)^2\right] \\
& \cdot erfc(\sqrt{-i\frac{k_0\rho}{2}(\frac{z+d}{\rho}-iA)^2})\Bigg]\Bigg\}
\end{aligned} \tag{2}
$$

In above formula, A and T are expressed by

$$
A = \frac{k_0}{k_1^2}\sqrt{k_1^2-k_0^2}\tan(\sqrt{k_1^2-k_0^2}\cdot l), \qquad T = \frac{\sqrt{k_1^2-k_0^2}}{k_0\tan(\sqrt{k_1^2-k_0^2}\cdot l)}. \tag{3}
$$

With $r_{1,2}=\sqrt{\rho^2+(z\mp d)^2}$, $q'(\lambda_{jE}^*)$ and $p'(\lambda_{jB}^*)$ are expressed as

$$
\begin{aligned}
q'(\lambda_{jE}^*) &= -\frac{k_1^2\lambda_{jE}^*}{\gamma_{0E}^*}+i\frac{k_0^2\lambda_{jE}^*}{\gamma_{1E}^*}(\tan\gamma_{1E}^* l+\gamma_{1E}^* l\sec^2\gamma_{1E}^* l), \\
p'(\lambda_{jB}^*) &= -\frac{\lambda_{jB}^*}{\gamma_{1B}^*}+i\lambda_{jB}^*(\frac{\tan\gamma_{1B}^* l}{\gamma_{0B}^*}+\frac{\gamma_{0B}^* l}{\gamma_{1B}^*}\sec^2\gamma_{1B}^* l).
\end{aligned} \tag{4}
$$

In above formulas, both γ_{mE}^* and γ_{mB}^* are written as

$$
\begin{aligned}
\gamma_{mE}^* &= \sqrt{k_m^2-(\lambda_{jE}^*)^2}; \quad m=0,1, \\
\gamma_{mB}^* &= \sqrt{k_m^2-(\lambda_{jB}^*)^2}; \quad m=0,1.
\end{aligned} \tag{5}
$$

Where m denotes the region numbers 0, 1 and j denotes the number of poles (0~n), λ_{jE}^* and λ_{jB}^* are the roots of the following two equations, respectively.

$$
\begin{aligned}
q(\lambda) &= k_1^2\gamma_0 - ik_0^2\gamma_1\tan\gamma_1 l = 0, \\
p(\lambda) &= \gamma_1 - i\gamma_0\tan\gamma_1 l = 0.
\end{aligned} \tag{6}
$$

In general, the thickness of the intermediate layer satisfied to the condition of $k_1 l \le 0.6$, we have

$$
\tan\sqrt{k_1^2-k_0^2}l \approx \frac{wl}{c}\sqrt{\varepsilon_1-1} \tag{7}
$$

Defining $Q_j^*=\frac{\lambda_j^*}{k_0}$, thus we write

$$
q'(\lambda_j^*) \approx -\frac{\omega^2 Q_j^*}{c^2}\left(\frac{\varepsilon_1}{\sqrt{1-Q_j^{*2}}}-i2\frac{\omega l}{c}\right) \tag{8}
$$

Both the formulas of the lateral wave and the surface wave can be reduced as follows

$$E_{0z}^{l}(\rho,\phi,z) = -\frac{\omega\mu_0}{2\pi}\cos\phi\cdot k_0^2 l\cdot e^{ik_0 r_2}\cdot\left(\frac{1}{k_0\rho}+k_0 l\sqrt{\frac{\pi}{k_0\rho}}\cdot e^{-ip^*}\cdot F(p^*)\right),$$
$$E_{0z}^{s}(\rho,\phi,z) \cong \frac{\mu_0 Idl}{2}\cos\phi\sqrt{\frac{2}{\pi\rho'}}\times\sum_j \frac{(\varepsilon_1-Q_{jE}^{*2})(Q_{jE}^{*})^{\frac{1}{2}}\sqrt{1-Q_{jE}^{*2}l}}{2c\sqrt{1-Q_{jE}^{*2}l}\cdot(\omega-b)}\cdot i(\omega)^{\frac{5}{2}}e^{i\frac{3\pi}{4}}e^{iQ_{jE}^{*}\omega\rho'}. \tag{9}$$

With above approximations, the electromagnetic field in frequency domain excited by a horizontal dipole can be rewritten in the following simplified forms

$$\begin{aligned}E_{0z}(\rho,\phi,z) = &-\frac{i\omega\mu_0 Idl}{4\pi k_0}\cos\phi\cdot\left[\left(\frac{\rho}{r_1}\right)\left(\frac{z-d}{r_1}\right)\left(\frac{k_0}{r_1}-\frac{3i}{r_1^2}+\frac{3i}{k_0 r_1^3}\right)e^{ik_0 r_1}\right.\\ &\left.-\left(\frac{\rho}{r_2}\right)\left(\frac{z+d}{r_2}\right)\left(\frac{k_0}{r_2}-\frac{3i}{r_2^2}-\frac{3i}{k_0 r_2^3}\right)e^{ik_0 r_2}\right]+\frac{\mu_0 Idl}{2}\cos\phi\sqrt{\frac{2}{\pi\rho'}}\\ &\times\sum_j \frac{(\varepsilon_1-Q_{jE}^{*2})(Q_{jE}^{*})^{\frac{1}{2}}\sqrt{1-Q_{jE}^{*2}l}}{2c\sqrt{1-Q_{jE}^{*2}l}\cdot(\omega-b)}i(\omega)^{\frac{5}{2}}e^{i\frac{3\pi}{4}}e^{iQ_{jE}^{*}\omega\rho'}\\ &+\frac{\omega\mu_0 Idl}{4\pi}\cos\phi\cdot k_0^2 l\cdot e^{ik_0 r_2}\\ &\cdot\left[\frac{1}{k_0\rho}+k_0 l\sqrt{\frac{\pi}{k_0\rho}}\cdot e^{-ip^*}\cdot F(p^*)\right]\end{aligned} \tag{10}$$

With $\rho' = \frac{\rho}{c}$, p^* can be written as

$$p^* = -\frac{\omega^3 l^2\rho'}{2c^2}\cdot\frac{(\varepsilon_1-1)^2}{\varepsilon_1^2} \tag{11}$$

The Fresnel function $F(p^*)$ is defined by

$$F(p^*) = \frac{1}{2}(1+i)-\int_0^{p^*}\frac{e^{it}}{\sqrt{2\pi t}}dt \tag{12}$$

2.2 Approximately formulas for transient field

Obviously, the analytical solution of the transient electromagnetic field can be obtained from the inverse Fourier transformation of the frequency-domain solution. The three time-dependent field components are described as follows

$$\begin{aligned}E_{0z}(\rho,0;t) &= \frac{1}{\pi}\mathrm{Re}\int_0^\infty E_{0z}(\rho,0;t)e^{-i\omega t}d\omega\\ &= \frac{\mu_0}{2\pi c}\cos\phi\sqrt{\frac{1}{2\pi\rho'}}\cdot\sum_j\frac{(\varepsilon_1-Q_{jE}^{*2})(Q_{jE}^{*})^{\frac{1}{2}}\sqrt{Q_j^{*2}-1l}}{\sqrt{1-Q_{jE}^{*2}l}}I_1\\ &-\frac{\mu_0}{2\pi}\cos\phi\left(\frac{l}{c^2\rho'^2}I_2+\frac{\varepsilon_1^2}{c(\varepsilon_1-1)^2}\sqrt{\frac{\pi}{\rho'}}I_3\right)\end{aligned} \tag{13}$$

Where

$$
\begin{aligned}
I_1 &= \frac{1}{\pi}\mathrm{Re}\int_0^\infty e^{i\frac{3\pi}{4}} \frac{i\omega^{\frac{5}{2}}}{\omega - b} e^{i\omega Q_j^*\rho'} e^{-i\omega t} d\omega, \\
I_2 &= \frac{1}{\pi}\mathrm{Re}\int_0^\infty (-i\omega)^2 e^{-i\omega(t-\rho')} d\omega, \\
I_3 &= \frac{1}{\pi}\mathrm{Re}\int_0^\infty \omega^{\frac{3}{2}} \varepsilon^{*2} e^{-ip^*} F\left(p^*\right) e^{-i\omega(t-\rho')} d\omega.
\end{aligned} \tag{14}
$$

It is noted that the integrals I_1 and I_3 corresponds to the trapped surface wave and the lateral wave. Under the condition of $k_0\rho \geq \frac{8}{(k_0 l)^2}$, we have

$$
e^{-ip^*} F\left(p^*\right) \approx \sqrt{\frac{k_0\rho}{\pi}} \frac{1}{k_0^2 \varepsilon^*}\left(\frac{ik_0}{\rho} + \frac{1}{\rho^2 \varepsilon^{*2}}\right) \tag{15}
$$

The above three integrals I_1, I_2, and I_3 can be approximated in the following forms

$$
\begin{aligned}
I_1 &= \sqrt{\frac{1}{\pi}}\left\{-b^{\frac{5}{2}}\left[C_2 \cos\left[b\left(t - Q_j^*\rho'\right)\right] + S_2 \sin\left[b\left(t - Q_j^*\rho'\right)\right]\right]\right. \\
&\quad \left. + \frac{b}{2}\left(t - Q_j^*\rho'\right)^{-\frac{3}{2}}\right\} U\left(t - Q_j^*\rho'\right), \\
I_2 &= \delta''\left(t - \rho'\right), \\
I_3 &= -\sqrt{\frac{1}{\pi\rho'}} \frac{(\varepsilon_1 - 1) l}{c\varepsilon_1} \delta''\left(t - \rho'\right) + \sqrt{\frac{1}{\pi\rho'}} \frac{c\varepsilon_1}{(\varepsilon_1 - 1)\rho' l} U\left(t - \rho'\right).
\end{aligned} \tag{16}
$$

The Fresnel cosine integral C_2 and sine integral S_2 are written as

$$
\begin{aligned}
C_2 &= \int_0^{b\left(t - Q_j^*\rho'\right)} \frac{\cos t}{\sqrt{t}} dt, \\
S_2 &= \int_0^{b\left(t - Q_j^*\rho'\right)} \frac{\sin t}{\sqrt{t}} dt.
\end{aligned} \tag{17}
$$

With $b = \frac{c\varepsilon_1}{2l\sqrt{Q_j^{*2} - 1}}$, the Heaviside unit step function $U(x)$ is defined by

$$
U(x) = \begin{cases} 0 & x < 0 \\ 1 & x \geq 0 \end{cases} \tag{18}
$$

With the substitutions of (16) into (13), the approximated formulas of the time-dependent field components can be derived readily. The component E_{0z} can be expressed in the following forms

$$
\begin{aligned}
E_{0z}\left(\rho, 0; t\right) &= -\frac{\mu_0}{2\pi c}\cos\phi \cdot \left(\frac{1}{\rho'}\delta'\left(t - \rho'\right) - \frac{1}{\rho'^2}\delta\left(t - \rho'\right) + \frac{1}{\rho'^3} U\left(t - \rho'\right)\right) \\
&\quad + \frac{\mu_0}{2\pi c}\cos\phi \sqrt{\frac{1}{2\pi\rho'}} \cdot \sum_j \frac{\left(\varepsilon_1 - Q_{jE}^{*2}\right)\left(Q_{jE}^*\right)^{\frac{1}{2}} l}{\sqrt{1 - Q_{jE}^{*2} l}} \cdot \frac{\varepsilon_1 - 1}{2\varepsilon_1} \sqrt{\frac{1}{\pi}} \\
&\quad \cdot \left\{-b^{\frac{5}{2}}\left[C_2 \cos\left[b\left(t - Q_j^*\rho'\right)\right] + S_2 \sin\left[b\left(t - Q_j^*\rho'\right)\right]\right]\right. \\
&\quad \left. - \frac{b}{2}\left(t - Q_j^*\rho'\right)^{-\frac{3}{2}} - \sqrt{\pi} \cdot b^{\frac{5}{2}} \cdot \cos\left[b\left(t - Q_j^*\rho'\right) + \frac{3\pi}{4}\right]\right\} \\
&\quad \cdot U\left(t - Q_j^*\rho'\right) + \frac{\mu_0}{4\pi}\cos\phi \frac{\varepsilon_1^2}{c\left(\varepsilon_1 - 1\right)^2}\left[\frac{1}{\rho'^2} \frac{c\varepsilon_1}{l\left(c\varepsilon_1 - 1\right)} U\left(t - \rho'\right)\right]
\end{aligned} \tag{19}
$$

With similar procedures, the rest five components can be obtained readily.

3 Computations and discussions

In practical applications, the radiation of a horizontal electric dipole in the three-layered region is useful in the microstrip circuit. However, it is difficult for microstrip circuits to meet the far-field approximation, since the Fresnel integral has the above approximation only when the propagation distance ρ is greater than the Sommerfeld distance. For example, assume the thickness of the intermediate medium layer of the microstrip circuit is l = 0.1cm, the operating frequency f ~ 0.8GHz. Hence,

$$k_0 = \frac{2\pi f}{c} = 1.6\pi \times \frac{10^9}{3\times 10^8}, \quad k_0 l = 0.01675. \tag{20}$$

The far zone condition is

$$\rho \geq \frac{8}{k_0^3 l^2} = 445.5m \tag{21}$$

The size of the circuit device usually cannot meet the above conditions. It can be seen that the size of the media material is particularly important, generally, if it satisfies to

$$k_0\rho << \frac{1}{k_0^2 l^2} \tag{22}$$

The electromagnetic field in the air and the dielectric layer includes only the direct wave and the ideal reflected wave. Therefore, the expressions for each component of the horizontal electric dipole can be approximated as follows:

$$\frac{k_1^2}{k_0^2} E_{1z'}(\rho,\varphi',0) = E_{0z'}(\rho,\varphi',0) \sim \frac{i\omega\mu_0}{2\pi k_0}(k_0 l)\cos\varphi' \cdot e^{ik_0\rho}\left(\frac{ik_0}{\rho} - \frac{1}{\rho^2}\right) \tag{23}$$

The above are the expressions of the electromagnetic field in the near zone which have a wider range of applications compared to that in far zone.

According to the previous results, the transient components of a horizontal electric dipole include the direct wave, the ideal reflected wave, the lateral wave and the surface wave. Among these terms, the lateral wave and the trapped surface wave of a vertical electric dipole converge with ρ^{-2} and $\rho^{-1/2}$, respectively, and will not be discussed here. In this part, some numerical results of the electromagnetic field excited by a horizontal electric dipole will be given, where the variations of the distance and the dielectric parameters are considered as the main influence, the excitation source is $\delta(t)$.

With ε_1 =2.85, the magnitudes of the component E_{2z} and $B_{2\varphi}$ due to a horizontal electric dipole on the surface of a dielectric-coated conductor are computed at ρ = 15, 20, 25, 30 km, respectively and shown in Fig. 2. and Fig. 3.

With ε_1 =2, 2.65, 2.85, and 3.65, the magnitudes of the trapped-surface-wave terms E_{2z}^S in (19) are computed at ρ = 300 km and the result are shown in Fig. 4. Obviously, it is seen that the trapped-surface-wave terms are contributed by the poles λ_j^*, which are determined by both the thickness of the dielectric layer and the dielectric parameters. In another word, the trapped-surface-wave terms can be computed readily when the poles λ_j^* are determined.

https://doi.org/10.1051/itmconf/20181701010

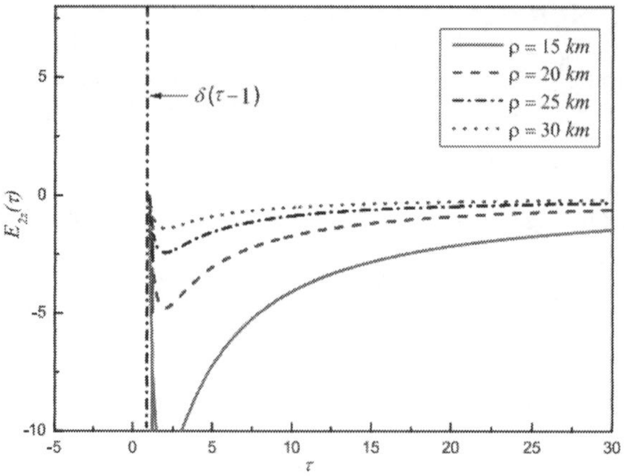

Fig.2. Magnitudes of E_{2z} due to a horizontal electric dipole with delta-function excitation. $\varepsilon_1 = 2.85$.

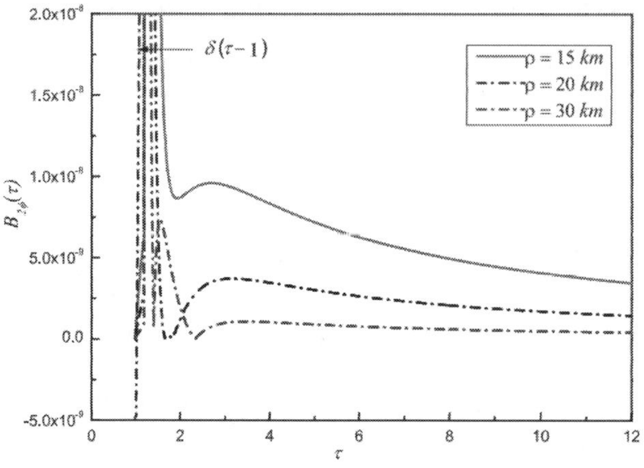

Fig.3. Magnitudes of $B_{2\varphi}$ due to a horizontal electric dipole with delta-function excitation. $\varepsilon_1 = 2.85$.

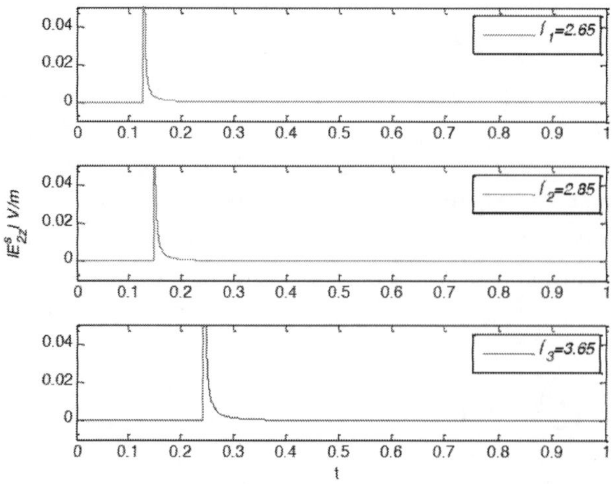

Fig.4. Magnitude of the trapped-surface-wave term $E^S_{2z}(\rho,t)$ due to a horizontal electric dipole with delta-function excitation $\rho = 300$km and $\varepsilon_1 = 2.65$, 2.85 and 3.65, respectively.

4 Conclusions

In this paper, the transient electromagnetic field excited by a horizontal electric dipole with delta-function on the surface of a dielectric-coated conductor has been studied analytically. At different distances the time-dependent vertical electric field is computed and discussed, respectively. It is shown that the trapped-surface-wave terms should not be neglected in the total transient field when both the horizontal electric dipole and the observation point are on or near the surface of the dielectric-coated earth. This physical model is applied to the microstrip circuit for far-field radiations.

References

1. A. Zenneck, Annalen Physik (Leipzig), **23**, 846-866 (1992)
2. A. Sommerfeld, *Annalen Physik* (Leipzig), **28**, 665-736 (1909)
3. J. R.Wait, Pergamon Press, New York (1970)
4. R. W. P. King, M. Owens, and T. T. Wu, Springer-Verlag, New York (1992)
5. J. R. Wait, Radio Science, **33**, 251-253 (1998)
6. S. F. Mahmoud, IEEE Transactions on Antennas and Propagation, **46**, 1745-1946 (1999)
7. R. W. P. King and S. S. Sheldon, Radio Science, **29**, pp. 97-113 (1994)
8. R. E. Collin, IEEE Transactions on Antennas and Propagation, **52**, 3133-3137 (2004)
9. R. E. Collin, IEEE Antennas Propagation Maginze, **46**, 64-79 (2004)
10. H.-Q. Zhang, W.-Y. Pan, K. Li, and K.-X. Shen, Progress in Electromagnetics Research, 163-186 (2005)
11. K. Li, ZJU Press, Springer (2009)
12. D. Cheng, T. T. Gu, P. Cao, T. He, and K. Li, International Journal of Antennas & Propagation, 1-7 (2015)
13. B. F. Dong, SWJTU (2016)
14. G. Q. Zheng and B. H. Sun, The National Natural Science Fund (2017)
15. H. W. Sun, Applied Mechanics and Materials, 462-463 (2014)
16. E. A. Hajlaoui, Circuit World, 56-62 (2017)
17. S. Majidifar and G. Karimi, Ace Elsevier Journal (2016)

Research on Outfitting Virtual Assembly based on Ergonomics

Zuhua Jiang[1*], *Junguo* Lu[2], *Yongjun* Ji[1], and *Hongyuan* Zhu[1]

[1]Department of Industrial Engineering and Management, Shanghai Jiao Tong University, 800 Dongchuan Road, Shanghai 200240, PR China
[2]Research Institute of shipbuilding technology, Shanghai Waigaoqiao Shipbuilding Co. Ltd., 3001 Zhouhai Road, Shanghai 200137, PR China

Abstract. To improve the present situation where the assembly work of ship outfitting depends on manual experiential operation, the thesis, taking outfitting assembly operation as the research object and optimal assembly path as the target, puts forward the simulation method and procedure of outfitting virtual assembly considering operational posture, operational load, reachability and visibility and other ergonomic factors, taking pipe assembly operation of ship section as the application example. The results show that the method can obtain better assembly operation path, avoid interference of workers' operation process and improve the efficiency of assembly operation.

1 Introduction

The outfitting work in shipbuilding is characterized by a large amount of work, wide work scope and intensive labor force, accounting for more than half of the total work of shipbuilding. In the process of outfitting, the assembly sequence of outfitting equipment is design according to the experience of designers, while the assembly trajectory depends on the experience of field operating persons, which results in that there are some problems, such as unreasonable operational posture of the field operating person, assembly interference and poor reachability and visibility, and that it costs too much time for the assembly of outfitting equipment to influence shipbuilding cycle in the process of practical assembly. Therefore, the research on the method and procedure of outfitting virtual assembly combined with ergonomics that can carry on the simulation analysis of manual assembly through the virtual environment and find the ergonomic problems that may appear in the process of outfitting assembly, can improve the feasibility of outfitting operations.

2 Related works

The core concept of outfitting virtual assembly on the basis of ergonomics is that by means of virtual simulation, the assembly sequence and assembly path of the fitting parts in the

* Corresponding author: Zhjiang@sjtu.edu.cn

hull section are optimized to get the assembly path which is best suited to the workers in the field. Chaffin expounded that the digital human model has been increasingly used in industrial design system and ergonomic methods can evaluate the reachability of assembly design to reduce production cost and improve the comfort level of operation[1,2]. T. DUKIC et al proposed to add human model to the virtual assembly process, considering that the multifaceted ergonomic factors and methods can improve the authenticity of virtual simulation[3].Dan Lämkull et al. added virtual human into virtual assembly simulation, and by comparing with the actual operation result, concluded that digital human model can improve the operational posture and tooling design of the work, and can get better assembly sequence by forming a benign feedback process[4].Shiguang Qiu et al.decomposed the virtual human movement into three kinds of movement, the original motion, fine motor and transient motion, realize the rapid generation of virtual people virtual human posture movement through hybrid control method of virtual human applied in the DMSP interactive assembly maintenance simulation system, which shows that the method can improve the generation efficiency of the virtual human movement[5].

For research on outfitting virtual assembly, most of the existing research focused on the single-site studies of assembly model building, design of assembly sequence, assembly path planning and the ergonomic evaluation methods without studying virtual assembly in different stages as a whole system. The optimization of assembly path is mainly focused on the optimization of the algorithm without optimizing the outfitting virtual assembly path in combination with ergonomic methods, which leads to poor practicability of optimized results. Focusing on above problems, this thesis, based on traditional outfitting virtual assembly methods and combined with ergonomic methods, puts forward the simulation method and procedure of outfitting virtual assembly considering operational posture, operational load, reachability and visibility and other ergonomic factors, constructs a systematic virtual assembly method and takes the pipe assembly operation of ship section as the application example.

3 Outfitting virtual assembly method based on ergonomic analysis

The virtual assembly processes based on ergonomics are shown in Figure 1. The virtual assembly process planning is a systematic work. Firstly, the design model is imported into the simulation system, and the initial assembly sequence is simulated and the assembly path is produced. The system can ensure the feasibility of outfitting assembly process by collision detection and constraint recognition. Combined with ergonomics, the outfitting assembly sequence and assembly process are optimized to ensure the reachability and visibility of assembly. Transfer the generated work files to the site, guide the field work, and feedback the work situation to the designers, so as to form the closed-loop feedback mechanism. The basic work processes are as follows.

(1) Designers firstly create a data model by CATIA, import the data model (including fittings equipment model, auxiliary tool model and model attribute information) model into the simulation software, DELMEL, and build the virtual assembly environment.

(2) the assembly designer shall, combined with the design experience, design the assembly sequence of the outfitting equipment according to the assembly process rules of the outfitting. According to the initial outfitting assembly sequence designed, control the assembly sequence of outfitting equipment and auxiliary tooling in virtual environment, set up the assembly sequence of outfitting parts, and generate the assembly path by the simulation system.

(3) In virtual assembly, simulation system can detect interference in virtual assembly through collision detection and constraint identification. If there is interference in the

virtual assembly process, assembly designers will modify and optimize the assembly sequence and assembly path.

(4) If there is no interference, the virtual assembly process of the outfitting will be carried out ergonomic analysis, and the assembly sequence and assembly path of the outfitting shall be optimized.

(5) Finally, output the optimized assembly sequence and assembly path, generate the assembly process animation, the results of the assembly process planning, analysis results of assembly process and other process documents, transfer process documents to the field through the enterprise's integrated platform and provide guidance to on-site operating persons.

(6) Operating workers conduct actual assembly according to virtual assembly process documents provided, and feedback the problems existing in the actual assembly process through the enterprise integration platform to outfitting assembly designer to help them improve.

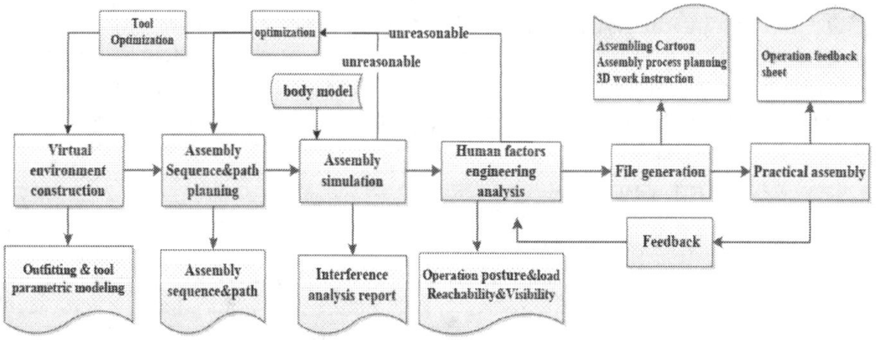

Fig. 1. Detailed process of outfitting virtual assembly based on ergonomic analysis

4 Application example

4.1 Construction of virtual environment

Taking the pipe virtual assembly of marine oil separator of a certain type as an example, build assembly scene, digital prototype 3D entity model, tool model and human model, and incorporate these models into the virtual environment. In order to build the model quickly, the model structure needs to be simplified, and some geometric information and constraint information should be removed. The virtual assembly maintenance environment created is shown in Figure 2.

Fig. 2. The pipe virtual assembly environment of marine oil separator of a certain type

 https://doi.org/10.1051/itmconf/20181701011

4.2 Virtual assembly path and simulation

According to the path information of a piping system, establish the corresponding assembly path data file, generate the traditional assembly path in the DELMIA, and add the virtual human model, as shown in Figure 3.

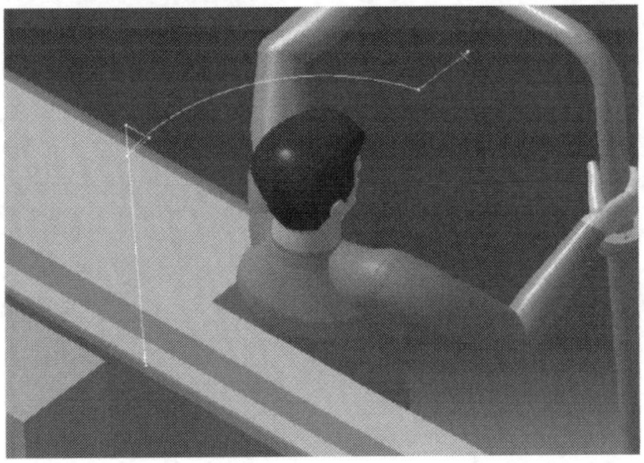

Fig. 3. Traditional assembly path

4.3 Ergonomic analysis and optimization

Because the size of the hull section is fixed and limited, the principle of global layout should be met in the installation of fittings and equipment. The general position of fittings and equipment has been determined, which limits the selection of people's installation posture. It is usually necessary to combine the activity space of the work, to analyze the traditional assembly path by ergonomic methods, and optimize the operational posture and operational load of the assembly to meet reachability and visibility.

4.3.1 Ergonomic analysis

Based on the traditional assembly path generated in DELMIA, according to the pipe assembly process, the simulation of virtual human operation can detect the situation of interference and invisibility in some sections of traditional assembly path generated previous, as shown in Figure 4.

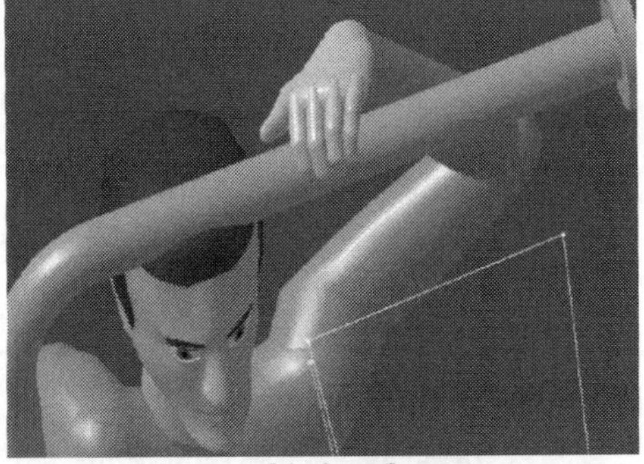

(a) Assembly interference

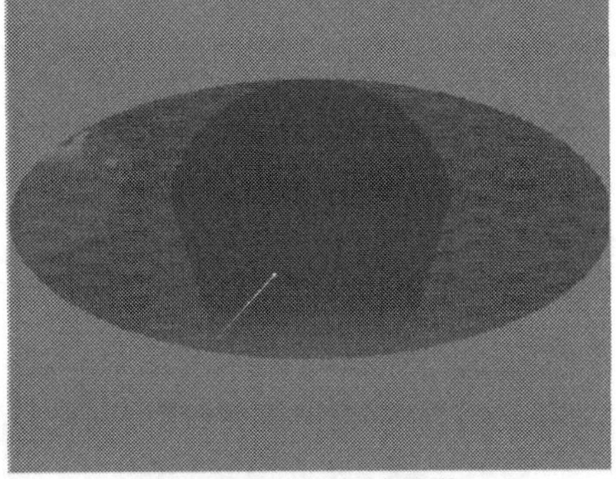

(b) Assembly invisibility

Fig. 4. Problems of traditional assembly path

4.3.2 Optimization of operational posture and load

Using DELMIA RULA analysis method, grade the position comfort evaluation of virtual people , and give the load and the analysis scores of the various parts, to facilitate the optimization of operational posture and load. First analyze the traditional assembly path. As shown in figure 5, it can be seen under the scheduled posture, the right hand load of traditional assembly workers is bigger, and the left and right operational posture scored five points and three points, and even some of those joints up to 9 points, which is not conducive to workers in assembly operation and needs to be improved on the man-machine factors as soon as possible.

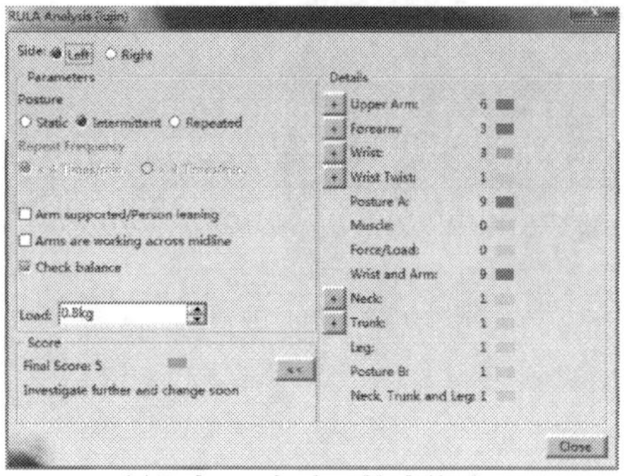

(a)Rula analysis of left limb

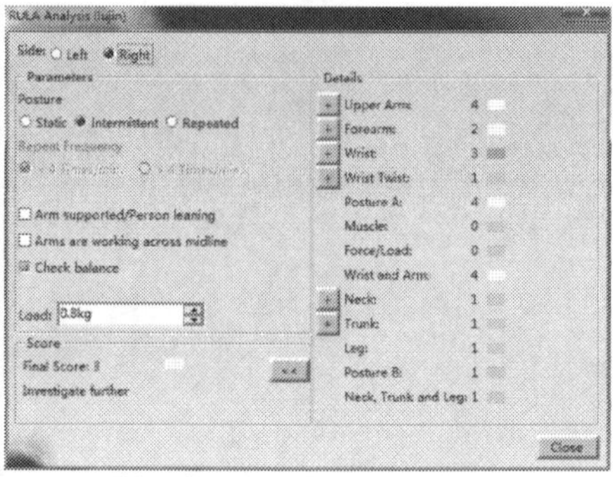

(b)Rula analysis of right limb

Fig. 5. Assembly posture of traditional assembly path and Rula analysis

(a)Optimized assembly path and assembly posture

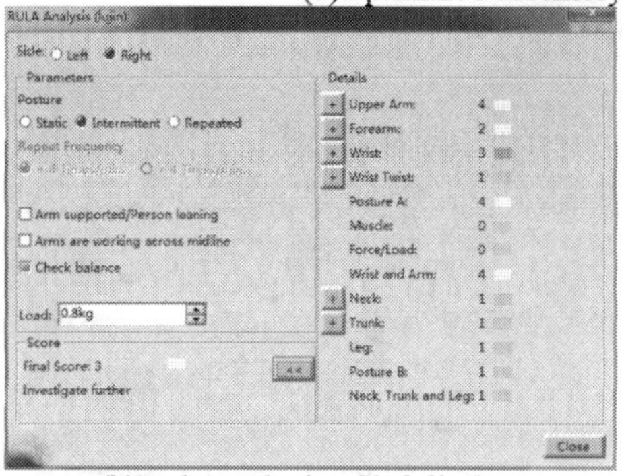

(b)Rula analysis of left limb

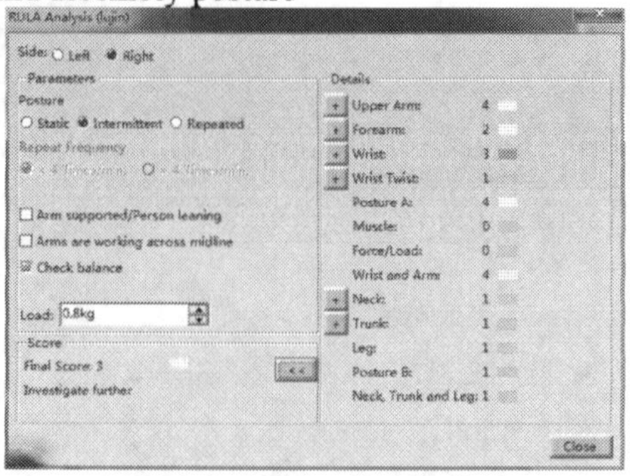

(c)Rula analysis of right limb

Fig. 6. Assembly posture and Rula analysis of new assembly path

Combined with ergonomic factors, replan the pipe assembly path by DELMIA so that the operating load on the left and right side is relatively balanced during the assembly operation, and the operating posture scored 5 points and 3 points, as shown in Figure 6. The suggestion is to further investigate. However, due to the influence of special space and part shape, the staff needs to adopt the uncomfortable posture to finish the work. But since the staff should hold the same position for a long time, this position is allowed.

4.3.3 Analysis and optimization of reachability and visibility

When workers carry out assembly operation at the installation site, the motion range of the hands and the vision at the posture are directly related to the feasibility of the assembly operation. Seen form Figure 7, the operating part is within the arm motion space and the operation reachability as well as visibility of pipe parts can be determined initially. But the location of the installation deviates from the center of the field of vision, that is, this is not the area with optimal field of vision, so it's necessary to adjust the orientation of the human model to find the best angle and position. The adjusted posture is shown in Figure 7. After the adjustment and the test, the operation reachability and the visibility are great.

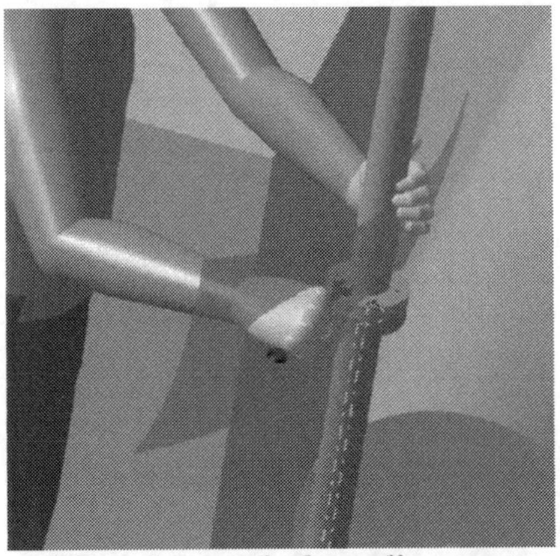

(a)Reach range before adjustment

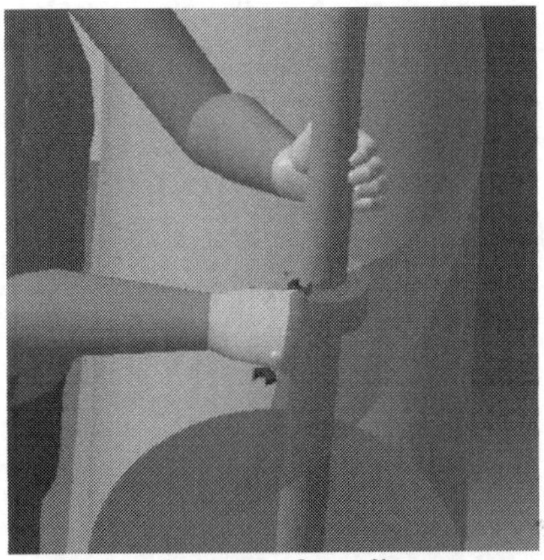

(b)Reach range after adjustment

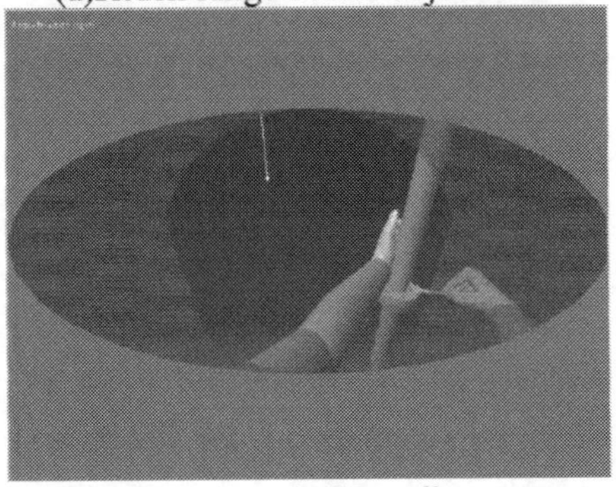

(c)Reach range before adjustment

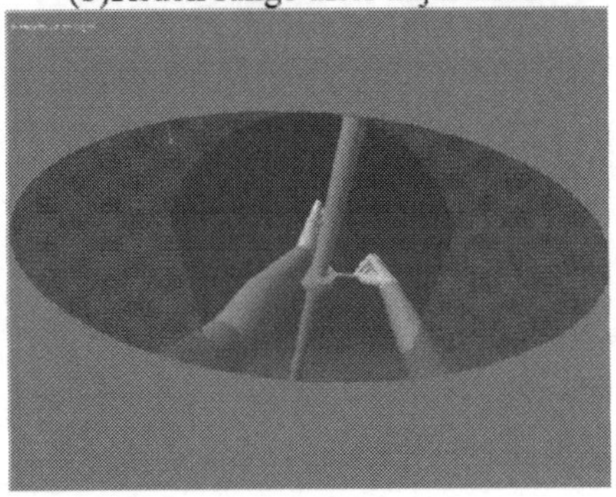

(d)Reach range after adjustment

Fig. 7. Reach range and visual range before adjustment

5 Generation of Operation Instruction Documents and On-site Assessment

Simulation and optimization can determine the assembly method that is to be used in practice. Transfer the virtual simulation documents of the final assembly scheme into the process documents that have the guiding effect on the process layout and operation of the actual assembly. Mainly include: making video data of virtual assembly process and matching with corresponding voice and subtitle, to form the guidance video of the pre-employment training; making an operation instruction book of document format printed in paper version, provided to the field operator.

On-site staff, based on the virtual simulation of the process document, carry out the construction and evaluation, feedback the results to the designer, forming a virtuous cycle of virtual assembly.

6 Conclusion

In this thesis, an outfitting virtual assembly method is put forward based on ergonomic analysis, and DELMEL software is used to optimize the pipe assembly path of the hull section. The study shows that in outfitting virtual simulation, the introduction of the man-machine engineering is able to optimize the workers' operational posture and operational load, test the assembly reachability and visibility and ensure the feasibility of outfitting assembly, so as to effectively guide the assembly of workers, ensure the quality of assembly and improve work efficiency.

This research was financially supported by Ministry of Industry and Information Technology of the People's Republic of China(The Ministry mounted Letter No.545[2016]).The authors gratefully acknowledge this support.

References

1. Chaffin D, On simulating human reach motions for ergonomics analyses, Human Factors and Ergonomics in Manufacturing, 12 (2002) 235–247
2. Chaffin D, Human motion simulation for vehicle and workplace design, Human Factors and Ergonomics in Manufacturing, 17 (2007) 475
3. T. Dukic, M. Rönnäng, M. Christmansson, Evaluation of ergonomics in a virtual manufacturing process, Journal of Engineering Design, 18 (2007), 125-137
4. Dan Lämkull, Lars Hanson, Roland örtengren, A comparative study of digital human modelling simulation results and their outcomes in reality: A case study within manual assembly of automobiles, International Journal of Industrial Ergonomics, 39 (2009) 428-441
5. Shiguang Qiu, Qichang He, Xiumin Fan & Dianliang Wu, Virtual human hybrid control in virtual assembly and maintenance simulation, International Journal of Production Research, 52 (2014), 867-887

ITM Web of Conferences **17**, 01012 (2018) https://doi.org/10.1051/itmconf/20181701012
WCSN 2017

A Method for Detecting Large-scale Network Anomaly Behavior

Huimin Hu[1,]·, *Wenping* Ma[1], and *Wei* Luo[1]

[1]State Key Laboratory of Integrated Services Networks, Xidian University, Xi'an, China

Abstract. A clustering model identification method based on the statistics has been proposed to improve the ability to detect scale anomaly behavior of the traditional anomaly detection technology. By analyzing the distribution of the distance between each clustering objects and clustering center to identify anomaly behavior. It ensures scale abnormal behavior identification while keeping the processing mechanism of the traditional anomaly detection technology for isolation, and breaking through the limitation of the traditional anomaly detection method assumes that abnormal data is the isolation. In order to improve the precision of clustering, we correct the Euclidean distance with the entropy value method to weight the attribute of the data, it optimizes the similarity evaluating electric of the nearest neighbor clustering algorithm, and simulated. Experimental results show that the statistical method and the improved clustering method is more efficient and self-adaptive.

1 Introduction

With the rapid development of the Internet and the information technology, the network application and information sharing are becoming more and more extensive. In the face of the increasingly complex network environment, the static defense which relies solely on the firewall is not enough to deal with all kinds of attacks, but the network intrusion detection technology with active monitoring system can effectively make up the shortage of the firewall, which can be divided into host-based system and network-based anomaly detection system according to the different monitoring objects. The host-based system anomaly detection detects the abnormal behavior of the network by monitoring and analyzing the host system log file, but it is poor interaction. At present, the anomaly detection technology based on network behavior is a research hotspot of the network-based anomaly detection. Judging whether the data flow in the network is abnormal by data mining technology, that is, the clustering is regard as normal behavior by clustering algorithm and the isolated is abnormal, and the detection performance is obviously superior to the host-based intrusion detection system. However, due to the rapid expansion of the network scale, various newly and large-scale attacking methods are endless, and it has obvious defects in flexibility, adaptability and so on. They cannot to deal with the changing network intrusion, so it is an important challenge of how to effectively detect the new large-scale attack.

· Corresponding author: 1304237049@qq.com

There have been many scholars have made improvements to this, the literature [1-3] are based on data mining network intrusion detection technology, by reducing data used in the network and the dimension of attributes to raise the accuracy of clustering to improve the efficiency of network intrusion detection through the clustering process, but the algorithm focuses on the clustering data itself, ignoring the clustering. In the literature [4-5], they detect the anomaly behavior of the online network by constantly updating the behavior pattern library, but the method of distinguishing between normal and abnormal behavior is not given in essence. In literature [6], the anomaly behavior is similar to that of isolated points, ignoring the case of scale anomaly behavior would be clustered. The improvements above to the network anomaly detection are essentially based on the fact that the abnormal behavior is very small compared with the normal behavior, and the two are very far apart, that is, assuming that the abnormal behavior of the data is the isolated point. But the actual network anomaly behavior is often a large number of occurrences by camouflage, and close to the normal data cluster. Using the improved method above to detect the anomaly behavior effect is not ideal, and the anomaly behavior clusters are regarded as normal data and cause attacks successful invasion.

In the information theory, information entropy is used to measure the degree of chaos of information, and the concepts used in literature [7] solve multi-decision problems. This article uses it to measure the degree of discretization of individual attributes. In the clustering algorithm, the larger the degree of discretization is, the smaller the information entropy is, the greater the amount of information it provided, and the larger the weight. Otherwise, contrary to the above; based on the entropy method, the nearest neighbor clustering algorithm is improved, and the entropy method is used to evaluate the attributes of the objects. The weights of each attribute are calculated to measure the importance of the attributes. Euclidean distance is modified to make the clustering results more objective. The clustering algorithm completes the clustering of data, but the clustering does not indicate which clusters are normal behavior and which are clustering of abnormal behavior.

In order to solve the problem that the improved algorithm is not effective for large-scale abnormal behavior detection, this paper proposes a clustering model identification pattern method, which combines the statistical model with the traditional cluster-based anomaly detection technology. The distribution of the euclidean distance is analyzed to distinguish the normal and abnormal data clusters, and preserving the large-scale abnormal behavior recognition while keeping the processing mechanism the traditional anomaly detection of isolated points as abnormal data. Analyzing how to apply it to abnormal behavior and the improvement of the clustering method .In the end, it was verified by experiments.

2 Algorithm analysis

For the nearest neighbor clustering algorithm, the number of clusters does not need to be given in advance which can be dynamically generated in the process of clustering, with great flexibility and adaptability. The accuracy of clustering algorithm directly affects the effect of network anomaly detection. Considering the contribution of each attribute of data object generated by network behavior to clustering, an attribute weighting method based on entropy method is proposed. The attribute weights are determined objectively according to the characteristics of each object's attribute itself to improve the accuracy of clustering. Based on the statistical class cluster **pattern recognition** method to identify the cluster model and to detect scale anomaly behavior.

The traditional nearest neighbor clustering algorithm is only suitable for dealing with numerical attributes. For the nominal attribute, the frequency of each state of the cluster attribute is taken as the corresponding attribute value. To analyze the algorithm, we assume that there is a data set which have m objects, each data object is characterized by n

attribute values, which constitute the data matrix X, each row corresponds to an object, which is the j dimension of the i data object, $i = 1,2,3,...,m$, $j = 1,2,3,...,n$. The distance between the two objects is the matrix $D(i,j)$, the larger the $d(i,j)$, the smaller similarity between the two objects. So if $d(i,j) = 0 \&\& d(i,j) = d(j,i)$,the matrix is symmetrical. As follows,

$$X = \begin{pmatrix} x_{11} & x_{12} & \cdots & x_{1n} \\ x_{21} & x_{22} & \cdots & x_{2n} \\ \vdots & \vdots & x_{ij} & \vdots \\ x_{m1} & x_{m2} & \cdots & x_{mn} \end{pmatrix} \tag{1}$$

$$D(i,j) = \begin{pmatrix} 0 & & & \\ d(2,1) & 0 & & \\ \vdots & \vdots & \ddots & \\ d(m,1) & d(m,2) & \cdots & 0 \end{pmatrix} \tag{2}$$

In order to improve the stability and accuracy of clustering and reduce the error caused by the existence of extreme values, the maximum and minimum values of each column in the data matrix X are set to the average of the remaining $m-2$ values.that is,

$$x_{ak\,max} = x_{bk\,min} = \sum_{j(j \neq a,b)}^{m} x_{jk} \Big/ (m-2) \tag{3}$$

Which $x_{ak\,max}$ and $x_{bk\,min}$ are the maximum and minimum values of the columns $a,b \in [1,m]$.

2.1 Improved nearest neighbor clustering algorithm by entropy method

2.1.1 Calculate the weight of each attribute by entropy method

The entropy method determines the weight of each attribute according to the degree of difference between the attribute values of the characterization object, which is determined by the data object itself avoiding the influence caused by the human factors, making the objectivity more accurate and the clustering result more accurate. The calculation steps are as follows.

1. Normalized the attribute value

The similarity between the calculation object and the center of each cluster is the key of the clustering algorithm. The difference of the attribute units of the object will directly affect the clustering result. The attribute of the larger initial range is relatively large. The clustering object attributes must be normalized before compiling the similarity between objects. In order to maintain the correlation between the original data, we use the minimum-maximum normalization method to linearly transform it. For the j dimension attribute, we use the following formula to calculate it,

$$x_{ij}' = n\_min_j + \frac{(x_{ij} - x_{jmin})}{x_{jmax} - x_{jmin}}(n\_max_j - n\_min_j) \tag{4}$$

The attribute values x_{ij} are mapped to $[n\_max_j, n\_min_j]$, and the attribute values are normalized.

2. *Calculate the proportion* x_{ij}' *of the* j *attribute value of object* i

$$p_{ij} = x_{ij}' \Big/ \sum_{i=1}^{m} x_{ij}' \tag{5}$$

3. *Calculate the* j *dimensional attributes of the entropy*

$$e_j = -\sum_{i=1}^{m} p_{ij} \ln p_{ij} \Big/ \ln n \tag{6}$$

4. *Calculate the weight of each dimension*

$$w_j = (1 - e_j) \Big/ \sum_{j=1}^{n} (1 - e_j) \tag{7}$$

That, $\sum_{j=1}^{n} w_j = 1, 0 \le w_j \le 1$.

2.1.2 Similarity measure

In the nearest neighbor clustering algorithm, we need to calculate the similarity between objects. In this paper, Euclidean distance is used as the basis of similarity measure [8], Euclidean distance formula is

$$d(i,j) = \sqrt{\sum_{k=1}^{m} \left(x_{ik}' - x_{jk}'\right)^2} \tag{8}$$

Where the k attribute values of the data objects i and j are the sum of all the attribute distances between the data objects i and j. The formula (1-6) ignores the differences in the proportion of each attribute in the clustering algorithm, which leads to the difficulty of clustering. In this paper, we use the entropy method to calculate the weight of each attribute of the object, the weighted Euclidean distance is used as the basis for the similarity measure, and the euclidean distance formula after the weight correction is

$$d_w(i,j) = \sqrt{\sum_{k=1}^{m} w_k \left(x_{ik}' - x_{jk}'\right)^2} \tag{9}$$

Which w_k is the weight of the attribute calculated by (1-5). The value of the weights reflects the role of the attributes of the objects while clustering, so that the measurement of the distance between objects is more accurate and the nearest neighbor.

2.2 Cluster-based pattern recognition based on statistical methods

The traditional network anomaly behavior detection assumes that the abnormal behavior is a small amount and is very different from the normal behavior data. It can find the isolated point by cluster analysis to detect the occurrence of the anomaly, but does not recognize the clustering model. The number in real network of the normal and abnormal behavior cannot be predicted. In the real network environment, if the attacker send a large number of intrusion data with high similarity to normal data, the detection is low efficiency, or even failure.

To break the limitation of the traditional network anomaly detection, we detect the abnormal behavior by detecting the pattern of the cluster of the number of balanced between the abnormal and the normal behavior in the real network environment and preventing the large-scale abnormal data object invasion. Compared with the traditional, we add the clustering pattern recognition mechanism of the statistical, and the isolated point is the same as the traditional anomaly detection, which is regarded as abnormal data. In this paper, we assume the normal behavior is independent and random, and the large-scale anomaly data generated by the intruder does not meet the assumption of independent randomness [9]. In probability theory, the central limit theorem (CLT) establishes that, in most situations, when independent random variables are added, their properly normalized sum tends toward a normal distribution even if the original variables themselves are not normally distributed. In the clustering algorithm, the Euclidean distance is the sum of the distances between the various attributes of the object. In the case of large sample, theoretically approximating the normal distribution, we confirm the conclusion by Matlab simulation experiment.

We randomly generate the matrix with $1000*12$ (1000 objects of 12 attributes), and select an object as a central point, then calculate the distance d of the remaining objects to the center and the distance d_w using the entropy method. Figure 1 is the distribution of the characteristics d and d_w. This result verifies that both are similar to the normal distribution.

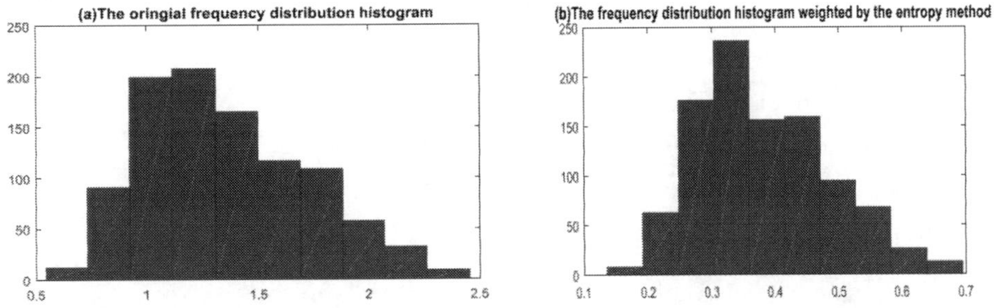

Fig. 1. The frequency distribution histogram of d and d_w

Based on the above characteristics, the clusters of network behavior are detected by statistical distribution, the normal behavior cluster and abnormal behavior cluster can be detected efficiently.

$$f(x,\mu_{dX},\sigma_{dX}) = \frac{1}{\sqrt{2\pi\sigma_{dX}^2}} exp\left(\frac{-(x-\mu_{dX})^2}{2\sigma_{dX}^2}\right) \tag{10}$$

Algorithm description: record the intermediate data generated by the nearest neighbor clustering algorithm: the mean μ_{dX} and variance σ_{dX}^2 of $d_w(i,j)$, and analyze whether the Euclidean distance $d_w(i,j)$ of each cluster obeys the normal distribution of (1-8), if they obey ,the data produced for normal behavior, else the data generated by abnormal behavior. Since the statistical method does not need to know the prior knowledge about the abnormal behavior object, it can detect new intrusion and improve the detection rate and adaptability of intrusion detection.

3 Experiments and results analysis

To verify the effectiveness of the improved algorithm and the detection effect of the abnormal data object, this paper uses Matlab programming to simulate and compare the experiment from the following two aspects:(1) the clustering effect of the improved algorithm, the higherthe detection rate of the algorithm, the better the clustering; (2) cluster pattern recognition effect, and simulating all kinds of cluster distribution to judge whether the various types of cluster model is correct intuitively.

3.1 Data

The experiment using the "corrected.gz" data set in the KDD CUP99 [10] , select three classes of neptune, smurf, mailbomb, each class has 2000 anomaly data objects.

Table 1 List of attributes and weights

num	attribute	Attribute description	weight
1	duration	Connection duration (seconds)	0.0872
2	Protocol_type	Protocol Type	0.0602
3	service	The type of network service of the target host	0.0405
4	flag	Connect to normal or wrong state	0.0914
5	Wrong_fragment	The number of pieces of error	0.1023
6	Num_failed_logins	The number of failed attempts to log in	0.1077
7	Num_file_creation	The number of times to create file	0.0906
8	count	The number of connections with the same destination host is connected to the current connection Over the past two seconds	0.0724
9	srv_count	The number of connections with the same service as the current connection Over the past two seconds	0.0917
10	serror_rate	The same as the current connection host and the percentage of SYN error connections Over the past two seconds	0.0781
11	srv_serror_rate	The same as the current connection host and the percentage of SYN error connections Over the past two seconds	0.0872
12	diff_srv_rate	The same percentage of the current connection to the target host but the different connections Over the past two seconds	0.0907

For the normal data, randomly extract 2000 packets by wireshark. There are 8,000 objects as experimental data set. Each data object in the data set is characterized by several attributes. Because the properties of the object are too complicated to concisely depict the behavior of the network. It is not ideal to use all the attribute clustering directly. ①The increase of dimension will leads to the difficulty of processing the data of clustering algorithm. ②Some properties are very small and even affect the clustering effect. Therefore, the choice of attributes directly affect the effect of clustering, so we must select a set that can distinguish normal and abnormal behavior efficiently. In this paper, we use feature selection method to select the attributes of clustering [11]. Table 1 lists the 12 feature attributes selected for each object and their corresponding weights.

3.2 Results analysis

Next, compare the detection results of the nearest neighbor clustering improved by entropy method with the original method by matlab programming. And verification the result through the statistical clustering model.

3.2.1 The detection rate of the nearest neighbour clustering improved by entropy method

The clustering analysis of the same experimental data set is respectively carried out by using the traditional nearest neighbor clustering algorithm and the improved nearest neighbor clustering algorithm. The clustering algorithm is estimated by comparing the detection rate of the two experimental methods. And the detection rate is defined as

$$\text{Detection rate}=\frac{\text{The correct number of objects}}{\text{The total number of objects}}*100\% \tag{11}$$

Table 2. Comparison of two algorithms

Num	Data Type	Traditional algorithm detection rate	Improved algorithm detection rate	Increment
1	neptune	83.94%	88.32%	4.38%
2	smurf	82.35%	86.76%	4.41%
3	mailbomb	76.31%	78.95%	2.64%
4	normal	89.90%	93.94%	4.04%

From the table above we can know that the data is clustered into four clusters through the clustering algorithm, which coincides with the experimental data set. Compared with the traditional nearest neighbor clustering algorithm, the improved clustering algorithm is better. The accuracy of the nearest neighbor clustering algorithm is improved by 3.87% and treat the isolated points as abnormal data according to the traditional clustering algorithm.

3.2.2 Cluster model detection based on statistics

Figure 2 is the sum of the attribute similarity that the improved frequency distribution of the distance $d_w(i,j)$ between the clusters and the centers. The clusters can be detected to be normal and abnormal efficiently by statistical analysis.

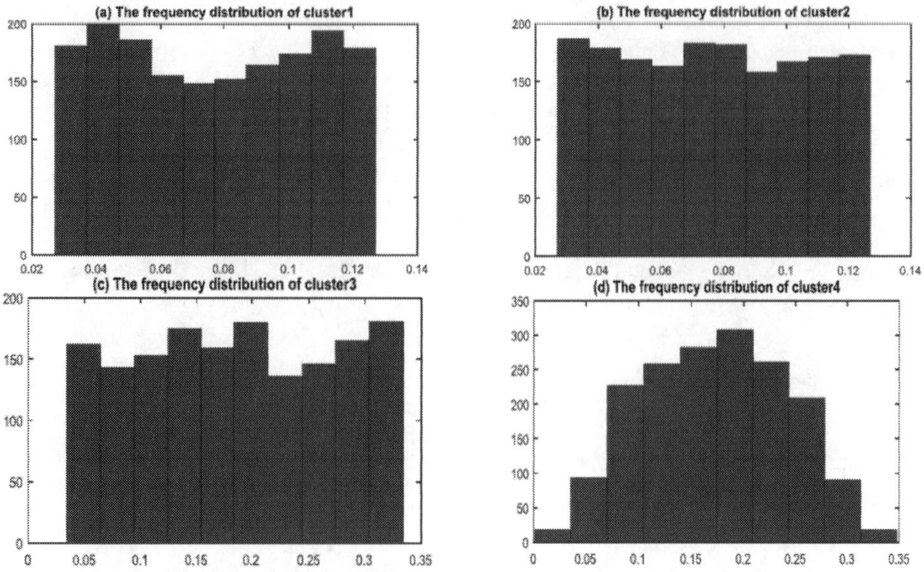

Fig. 2. The frequency distribution histogram of $d_w(i,j)$

It can be seen from the experimental simulation that cluster4 approximates the normal distribution and is normal. The other three categories are not the abnormal. It is consistent with the dataset that cluster1, cluster2, cluster3 for the neptune, smurf, mailbomb data clusters, cluster4 for the normal data cluster. There are two obvious advantages of class clustering pattern recognition based on statistics, ①the complexity of the algorithm is low, ②the normal and abnormal behaviors are identified from the nature and the detection ability of network anomaly detection in large-scale abnormal behavior is improved. It is proved that the statistical detection method is reliable and efficient for cluster detection.

4 Summary

The author studies how to improve the accuracy of clustering and the detection efficiency of large-scale abnormal behavior based on the traditional method of network anomaly detection and proposed that the weights of clustering data object attributes are set by entropy method and clustering pattern recognition method based on statistical analysis. Using the entropy method to calculate the attribute weights and modify the similarity measure formula of the nearest neighbor clustering algorithm which improved the objectivity of the attribute value and the accuracy greatly. For the clustering algorithm, the cluster-based pattern recognition mechanism based on the statistical method is added. The normal and abnormal behavior of the network is efficiently identified by analyzing the statistical distribution characteristics of the parameters. The isolation point is still think as abnormal data based on the traditional intrusion detection method to improve the reliability and applicability of intrusion detection and to overcome the low efficiency for large-scale network abnormal behavior detection, and achieved the expected aims.

Acknowledgement: This work was funded by National Key R&D Program of China under grant No. 2017YFB0802400, National Natural Science Foundation of China under grant No. 61373171 and 111 Project under grant No. B08038.

References

1. Guo Chun. Research on Key Technologies of Network Intrusion Detection Based on Data Mining [D]. Beijing University of Port and Telecommunications for the Degree of Doctor of Engineering.(2014).
2. Cui Wen Ke, Design and Implementation of Intrusion Detection System Based on Clustering Algorithm [D]. A Master Thesis Submitted to University of Electronic Science and Technology of China.(2016).
3. Sun Jian-hua ,Jin Hai,Chen Hao,Han Zong-fen , MA-IDS: A Distributed Intrusion Detection System Based on Data Mining[J]. WuHan University Journal Of Natural Sciences-english,(2005,10(1):111-111).
4. Juliette Dromard;Gilles Roudière;Philippe Owezarski .Online and Scalable Unsupervised Network Anomaly Detection Method[J]. IEEE Transactions on Network and Service Management,(2017,14(1):34-47).
5. Martin Grillab;Tomáš Pevnýab;Martin Rehakab, Reducing false positives of network anomaly detection by local adaptive multivariate smoothing[J]. Journal of Computer and System Sciences,(2017,83(1):43-57).
6. He Z, Xu X, Deng S. Discovering Cluster-Based Local Outliers [J]. Pattern Recognition Letters, (2003, 24(9):1641-1650).
7. Kordecki, H;Karmowski, M;Knapik-Kordecka, M;Karmowski, A;Gworys, B.Method of Component Importance Evaluation in Complex Data Structure Analysis[J].Advances in clinical and experimental medicine,(2011,20(2):205-209).
8. Nguyen T T, Chang K, Hui S C. Supervised Term Weighting Centroid-Based Classifiers for Text Categorization [J]. Knowledge and Information Systems, (2013,35(1): 61-85).
9. Liu Shuai.Research on Analysis and Detection of Multi-layer Abnormal Behavior for Network Data Stream[D].A Dissertation Engineering University for the Degree of Doctor of Engineering.(2015).
10. Hettich S, Bay S D. Kdd cup 1999 data. UCI KDD Archive [DB/OL], 1999. http://kdd.ics.uci. edu//databases/kddcup99/kddcup99. html].
11. Amiri F, Rezaei Yousefi M M, Lucas C, et al. Mutual Information-Based Feature Selection for Intrusion Detection Systems [J]. Journal of Network and Applications, (2011, 34(4):1184-1199).

Research and Mass Deployment of Non-cognitive Authentication Strategy Based on Campus Wireless Network

Dapeng Huangfu[1], *Xiaoping* Tian[1], *Xingjian* Wang[1], and *Ping* Chen[1,*]

[1]Center Information & Network Technology, Beijing Normal University, Beijing, 100875, China

Abstract. With the rapid development of Internet +, the dependence on wireless networks and wireless terminals are increasing. Campus wireless network has become the main network of teachers and students in campus on the internet. As there are uneven clients and a wide variety of intelligent terminals now. Simplified authentication and network security become the most urgent problem for wireless network. This paper used the Portal + Mac authentication method to realize the non-cognitive authentication of teachers and students on basis of the analysis of the advantages and disadvantages of mainstream authentication of campus wireless network, such as 802.1X authentication, Portal authentication, Mac authentication and DHCP authentication. Teachers and students only need portal certification at the first time, then surf the internet with non-perceived authentication at the second time and later. This method increases network security, and is better to meet the needs of teachers and students.

1 Campus wireless network authentication mode analysis

With the rapid development of Internet+ and the popularity of intelligent terminals, the dependence on wireless networks and wireless terminals are increasing. Teachers and students hope to easily access the network anywhere in the campus. In recent years, with the rapid development of 5G wireless network technology, the construction of wireless network in colleges and universities have been completed, and the basic construction of campus wireless network have been completed. How to provide convenient and safe authentication method to users is one of the important research topics in wireless network construction [1].

At present, in the campus wireless network environment, the mainstream authentication method are 802.1x certification, Portal certification, DHCP access certification and Mac address certification.

1.1 802.1x certification

The IEEE 802.X protocol has a more complete authentication function, by controlling the port limit of the Ethernet access device to the non-certified user[2,3]. In the cable network,

* Corresponding author: chenping@bnu.edu.cn

the 802.1X protocol divides the switch port into a physical port and a logical port. The logical port is closed without authentication, and only EAPOL data packets can be passed. After the successful authentication, the logical port opens and allows the normal data package to pass. Cable network users mainly use windows operating system. It needs to configure the client or install terminal software, bring greater challenges for ordinary users.

In the wireless network, the wireless handheld terminal are mostly integrated with the 802.1x client. Users only need to fill in the account and the password which could be realized. After the first successful certification, the authentication terminal would automatically log on. This process realized the non-perceived authentication based on 802.1x. But the terminal compatibility was poor. The operating systems such as windows XP and windows 7 still needed to install software or configure clients. At present, all colleges and universities are using a SSID-Mobile signal, mainly providing service for mobile terminals. At the same time, global alliance signal Eduroam is also based on the 802.1X protocol.

1.2 Portal authentication

Portal authentication [3,4] is one of the most popular authentication methods, and its compatibility is better. After the user access the wireless network to obtain the address, the gateway would be able to redirect the non-certified user to the Portal authentication page, and then access the network resources after the success. Portal could achieve network access and release, but there was a difference between the way and the mechanism.

At present, there were three main types of Portal authentication. (1) Two times authentication. The first authentication through AC Portal could achieve the access and users could access the campus resources. The second authentication could be realized by the Portal authentication billing system, and the user could access the outside network resources. The tedious process of 2-time authentication process reduced the efficiency of the network and the user experience. (2) One time authentication. After AC Portal and certification billing system Portal docking, users could connect to AC. The billing system would give a response to the AC authentication request, while AC Portal carried the account and password to the certification billing system to send a request. Simultaneously the certification billing system issued the strategy to the server, in order to realize the user's accurate release. AC Portal achieved the user access, and one time authentication could achieve access and release. This authentication could simplify the user authentication process. But each manufacturer's AC needed to meet with the billing system to achieve the docking debugging, so the backstage maintenance was very difficult. (3) The independent Portal server. An independent Portal server was set up in the wireless core switch and the campus exit. It was used to realize the access of wireless network, and the release by the Portal sever of the linkage authentication billing system at the same time. This authentication solved the difficulties of docking between different manufacturer controllers, and it was more convenient to maintain. But the wireless network needed to adjust the topology and increase the Portal server.

The Portal authentication had several problems: (1) Users need to have the active authentication each time and it could not achieve no perception; (2) This authentication could not get the user Mac address. The user's identification was not accurate, so the user with the same IP address would be treated as the same user in a short time.

1.3 Mac address authentication

The Mac address authentication was based on the EAP authentication protocol framework, which was matched by the Mac address of the terminal equipment to the user[4]. Network managers needed to maintain a Mac address list to record all terminal Mac addresses that accessed to the network. When the user accessed the network, the Mac address of its terminal would match the address in the Mac address table firstly. Only the successful matching terminals were allowed to access the network. This authentication had several advantages. It was convenient, fast, more practical, adapt to small-scale wireless network environment or a few special users under the large-scale wireless network. But it also had few shortcomings. This authentication needed administrator to bind the terminal Mac address and user information and record to the authentication server. It would undoubtedly be a disaster for a large-scale network environment and the maintenance work would be more than imagination. In addition, this method had the risk of forging the Mac address. The user's network flow would be stolen easily, and the network security had some risks.

1.4 Non-perception authentication with the combination of Portal and Mac

The non-perceived authentication with the combination of Portal and Mac addresses overcame their shortcomings and retained their respective advantages [4,5]. The first certification was realized through Portal authentication, and completed the binding work of accounts and terminal Mac address. After the authentication, users could login on the network when the terminal Mac and the Mac address table matched successfully. Users did not participate in this process, while AC completed the automatic certification initiatively. At present, there are differences in the network mode of various colleges and universities. The realization form of Portal and Mac was different, but the principle was the same. So this method was relatively perfect and feasible.

Through the study of the above four authentication methods, the terminal adaptability of the 802.1X certification was not suitable for the popularization of the masses. The complexity of the Mac address authentication operation was not suitable for independent deployment. Portal certification required certification every time and was so inconvenient. Only Portal and Mac were integrated address authentication methods, which had the implementation and convenience, were suitable for large-scale application and deployment.

2 Methods of no sense of authentication

The original authentication methods of the wireless network of Beijing Normal University is the 802.1X certification, BNU-Mobile (the mobile phone and the flat terminal), Portal certification: BNU (Teaching area), BNU-Student (Dormitory area). In order to facilitate users to use the free resources on campus and IPv6, the Portal had only been enabled the access function. But there was safety problems.

2.1 Non-sensory authentication topology

As the wireless network became the main Internet way and the country's attention was drew to the network security, it was imperative to enable Portal access certification [6-10]. In order to implement the deployment of Portal access, and to improve the experience of the Internet, the combination of Portal and Mac were used in the whole school. The whole authentication way was made up of the following parts, as shown in figure 1:

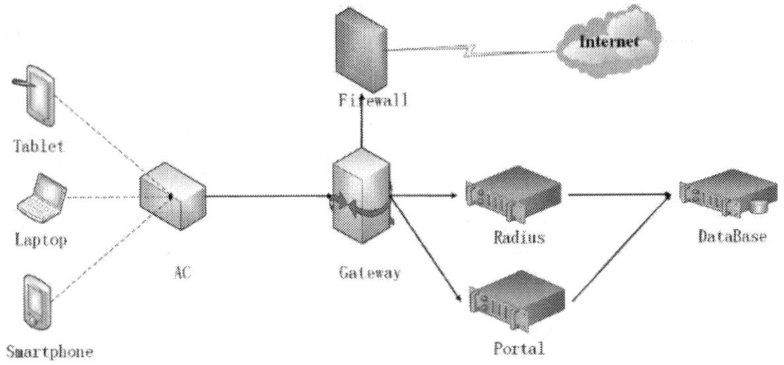

Fig. 1. Mac and Portal no-cognitive authentication logic diagram.

1) The user terminal were usually a notebook, intelligent mobile phone, tablet and so on with the installation of the browser terminal. These terminals contained wireless network card. The browser was used to trigger Portal authentication, and the network card provided the only user Mac address.

2) As a wireless user access gateway, AC equipment carried several functions. The first was the security access function, which was responsible for access to the user's legitimacy detection. The second was pushing Portal certification page for the user terminal. The third was the linkage line function. AC would kick the user while the wireless terminal was off the wireless network or the long-term no traffic. At the same time, the billing system linkage kicked off the user after received the offline information. If the billing system had long-term non-flow and then kicked off the terminal, AC would kick off the user after receiving the information.

3) Portal server was the user authentication entrance. The user terminal first accessed to the wireless network, the AC re-directional web interface to the corresponding billing Portal server. It would push the web authentication page to the user terminal based on the HTTP protocol and submit the information containing the user account/password to the billing database.

4) RADIUS server could achieve certification, authorization and accounting services, which was usually considered as the AAA server. It had four functions as the scalability of the RADIUS. The first function was responsible for receiving information of Portal server and AC device, such as user name/password, Mac address, online time and flow, etc. It realized the user authentication after comparing these information with the billing database. The second was sending the control strategy of users to AC device, and authorizing the user terminal online (offline) certification request. The third was accounted based on the user's online time or flow. The last was binding the user Mac address and user account (first automatic binding), and storing the user terminal information into the billing database.

5) Billing database was responsible for user terminal information, corresponding relationship of account and Mac address, and authentication billing data storage.

2.2 Non-perceived authentication process

The non-perception of the combination of Portal and Mac was in application in Beijing Normal University. The first certification achieved access and accuracy through the Portal certification. At the same time, that certification achieved the binding of the user account and the Mac address, and storing into the billing system. The authentication realized the user's access and accuracy certification by comparing the Mac address in the terminal and billing system Mac table. The whole process was initiated by AC, cooperated with the completion by Radius and the billing system database. The user had no sense of authentication, so it was called non-perceived authentication.

The specific authentication process was shown in figure 2.

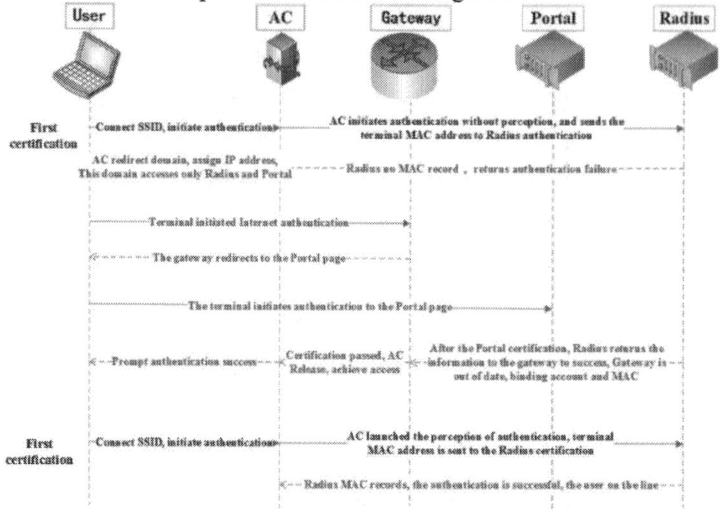

Fig. 2. Non-perceived authentication process.

(1) When the user connected to the SSID firstly, the user terminal initiated an authentication request to AC. AC got the Mac address of the user terminal and initiated the Mac authentication request to the RADIUS server. At this time, the Mac address of the user terminal was not recorded in the billing database connected by the RADIUS server, so it would reject the authentication, and the Mac address authentication failed. AC would re-assigned the user to the Guest VLAN for the next certification.

(2) AC took the initiative to push portal certification page after Guest VLAN opened Portal certification. In other case, the terminal send HTTP requests to AC when a user visited a web site, and AC would redirect the user's HTTP request to the Portal authentication page. The user could complete the Portal authentication on the portal page, while the Radius server was bound to the user's account and the Mac address.

(3) After the successful Portal certification, the user could access the network normally. The first certification is the regular Portal authentication.

(4) When the user connected to the SSID, the AC sent the Mac authentication request to the RADIUS server firstly. As billing database corresponding to the RADIUS server had the user's account, Mac address and other information records, the authentication would be successful and the user would be on line without the Portal certification. The following-up authentication was completed by the terminal, AC, and RADIUS server automatically, which did not need users' participation. So it was no sense to the user.

From the authentication process, the non-perceived authentication was not free of certification, which was to reduce the user's participation in the authentication process, and reduce the complexity of the operation. The non-perceived authentication was completed with no sense of perception, both guaranteeing the online security management, and improving the user's Internet experience. This authentication was suitable for teachers and students' wireless network service in campus.

3 Large-scale deployment of non-perceived authentication

Portal and Mac authentication combinations were relatively mature for non-sensory authentication tests and small-scale cases [4]. But in the process of mass deployment, it would meet the problem of software and hardware bottlenecks and the adaptability of users. The work that needed to be prepared in advance included:

(1) Billing strategy adjustment

(2) Portal and Radius server: Portal service used Apache software to realize the function. As the Apache service's bottleneck, it did not respond to the problem when the number exceeded 10000. Therefore, it was necessary to calculate the number of Portal and share the pressure on multiple Apache servers before a large-scale deployment. The wireless online users of Beijing Normal University would exceed 30,000 in the rush hour. However, the Portal page request was not more than 20000. We had set up 2 Apache servers, the dormitory area and the teaching area of the wireless Portal certification respectively. Then, the Portal certification page requested no more than 10000, and the controller had no pressure in general.

(3) Wireless controller: Previously, the controller system needed to be upgraded to the latest stable version, which was used to solve the controller version and enhanced the performance of the controller. At the same time, the configuration of the user without traffic offline and the linkage line was build, preventing the terminals of users to take up the charge and send a number. It was recommended that the HTTPS protocol be closed, because the protocol could lead to an Apache pressure, while the controller's CPU would be consumed by the agreement.

(4) Billing database optimization: The campus wireless network of Beijing Normal University configured a VLAN address pool in the teaching district and the dormitory area. At the same time, the user terminals could achieve cross-controller roaming. Therefore, the IP address obtained by the user terminals would not change. The billing system would generate online logs only when the user was active or long-time no traffic was forced to get off the line. So, the users produced only a few online logs every day. When the Portal authentication and the Mac authentication were not cross-controllers, the billing system would produce a web log when the teachers or students cross the controller. In this case, the billing system would produce a large number of web logs a day. So many web logs would generate great pressure to the billing database.

4. Conclusion

The coexistence of wired and wireless network is the trend of campus network construction in the future. The combination of MAC and Portal technology is the security of MAC address authentication and the security of Portal authentication. This integrated authentication for the flow or length of billing colleges and universities, that is to protect the legitimacy of users, but also to avoid the use of non-perception of authentication methods resulting in unknown traffic or economic losses.

But this authentication method also has some disadvantages, although it can bring convenience to users, but if there is no limit to the number of user terminals, it will inevitably lead to the number of terminals flooding. According to each user will generally hold computer, tablet and mobile phone 3 terminal equipment to consider, in accordance with the user terminal number of Beijing Normal University Teachers and students were 3 and 5, the subsequent terminal access to campus network Radius with terminal access to campus network order kicked off the front of the terminal.

References

1. Xie Sheng jun, Yin Feng, Zhou Xu chuan. Cable and wireless integrated flat campus network design. Journal on Communication, **9**, 80-81(2013).

2. Long Jun jun, Yuan Aimin. ANRD-DPM Algorithm Based on MAC Certification and AS Level Related Decomposition. Bulletin of Science and Technology. **9**, 131-134(2016).
3. Steven K. Brawn, R. Mark Koan, Kelly Caye. Staying secure in an insecure world: 802.1x secure wireless computer connectivity for students, faculty, and staff to the campus network. Proceedings of the 32nd annual ACM SIGUCCS conference on User services. **4**, 273-277(2004)
4. Feng Lei, Lin Chunjian, Zhao Jun. Research on the technology of certification without perception based on MAC with Portal. Journal of Central China Normal University (Nat. Sci.), **5**, 4-8 (2017).
5. Wang Dao jia, Ma Yan, Huang Xiao hong. Research of DHCP based campus network admission control and senseless authentication method. Hua Zhong Univ. of Sci. & Tech.(Natural Science Edition). **10**, 181-185(2016).
6. Amna Saad, Mohd Izzat Mohamat Roseli, Muhammad Saufi Zullkeply. A smart e-voting system using RFID authentication method for a campus electoral. Proceedings of the 8th International Conference on Ubiquitous Information Management and Communication Publisher: ACM.**14**, (2014).
7. Li, X., Yuan, H., Xiaofeng, C., Xinyi, H., Ticket-based handoff authentication for wireless mesh networks journal of Computer Networks.**73**, 185-194 (2014).
8. S. T. Ali, V. Sivaraman, and D. Ostry. Secret key generation rate vs. reconciliation cost using wireless channel characteristics in body area networks. 2010 IEEEIFIP International Conference on Embedded and Ubiquitous Computing. 644–650(2010).
9. Li, C., Nguyen, U.T. Fast Authentication for Mobility Support in Wireless Mesh Networks. Intconfof WCNC. 1185–1190(2011).
10. Yi, P., Wu, Y., Zou, F. and Liu, N. A Survey on Security in Wireless Mesh Networks. IETE Technical Review.**27**, 6–14(2010).

A IF Signal Precessing System Design Based on Software Radio Platform

Jing Zhao[1,*], *Hao* Nie[1], and *Jing* Yu[1]

[1]Aviation Maintenance NCO Academy of Air Force Engineering University Xinyang Henan, 464000, P. R. China

Abstract. Software radio is a definition of a design thought about how to implement flexible functions by using fixed hardware platform. Any platform based on this is characterized to be universal, standardized, modular, open and highly flexible. Due to some realistic reasons, a software radio platform is hard to be realized. So, most signal processing is operated after mixing. According to software radio requirements, a "FPGA+ADC+DAC" structure is designed. Compared with former processors, this module has broad application prospects with the small size, low power, configurable and programmable feathers. It has multifunction, such as generating IF signals, performing digital down conversion and realizing the synchronous demodulation and the other functions. This module also provides the extended host interface to communicate with upper computers. According to the practical test, take MSK signal for example, if the bit rate is 1Mb/s, bit error rate is lower than 10^{-6}.

1 Introduction

The main design philosophy of software radio [1,2,3] is to make A/D and D/A converter close to the antenna, if possible, and realize hardware functions with method of editing software, such as frequency selection, modulation and demodulation, data format conversion, encoding and decoding, communication protocols and so on. Considering the processing speed of DSP or FPGA and data storage capacity, normally, A/D and D/A converter only can be placed before intermediate frequency (IF) module. Currently, IF sampling software radio structure is widely employed into digital transceiver.

The classic IF transceiver structure is shown on fig. 1. It includes T/R switch, low noise amplifier, mixer, wide-band IF amplifier, power amplifier, wideband filter and digital signal processing.

For the digital signal processing, it might be implemented by ASIC, DSP and FPGA. To a software radio system, ASIC is no longer suitable in system design because it is detrimental to module interchangeability and increases the system complexity and power consumption. Early SDR platform generally uses DSP as the core processor, but the DSP line mode reduces the system parallelism. Afterward, the structure of FPGA+DSP is used to improve the real-time and parallel processing capabilities instead of DSP. However,

* Corresponding author: sherilljames@163.com

differences between FPGA and DSP work mode will make it a long time to transfer the data between them. With the increase of data processing capacity in communication systems, data transmission between FPGA and DSP will have more influence over the processing speed of the whole system. Therefore, FPGA used as the system processor is a development trend of SDR structure.

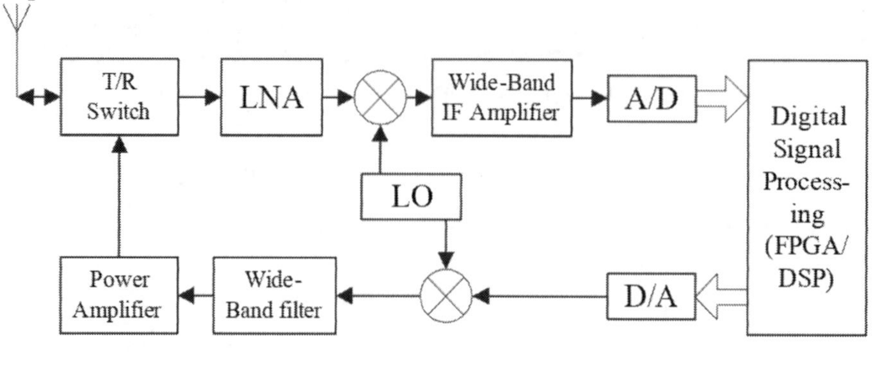

Fig.1. IF Transceiver software radio structure

In this paper, the hardware structure of ADC+FPGA+DAC is applied, and a common host interface is designed to extend the functionality. Its block diagram is shown on fig. 2.

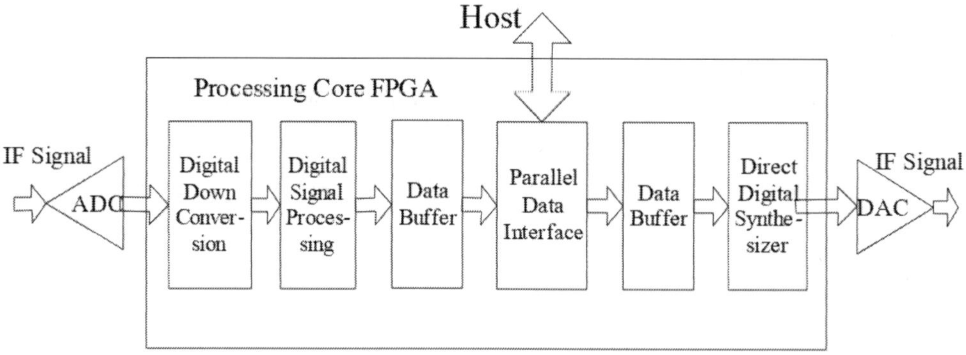

Fig.2. System structure

In this way, the signal processing could be adopted for many communication systems, such as ASK, MSK, PSK, MSK and DQPSK etc.

2 System realization

In the system, the Xilinx FPGA XC2V3000, ADI's ADC AD9430 with maximum sampling frequency 210MHz, and ADI's DAC AD9753 with maximum sampling frequency 300MHz are applied. Taking MSK IF signal for example, analyze its realization process.

MSK is minimum frequency shift keying. It is a binary frequency shift keying signal with minimum bandwidth. So, it is widely used in digital communication systems. To demodulate MSK IF signal, the system might have digital direct synthesis (DDS), down digital down conversion (DDC), synchronous (coherent) demodulation etc.

Fig. 3 shows the FPGA internal signal processing flow chart. According to DDS theory, FPGA controls DAC to generate the MSK IF signal and deliver it to the ADC front-end of this module through analog channel. According to the bandpass sampling theorem, FPGA controls ADC to sample the MSK signal and transmits the results to the host through the communication interface after digital down conversion, demodulation, frame alignment, parity check, and so on. Firstly, the sampled data is transmitted into the DDC unit through the registers; secondly, the baseband signal is extracted above to mixer and low-pass filter to complete the MSK demodulation; thirdly, FPGA performs the frame alignment and parity check; finally, the processing results is buffered into RAM so as to transmit to host.

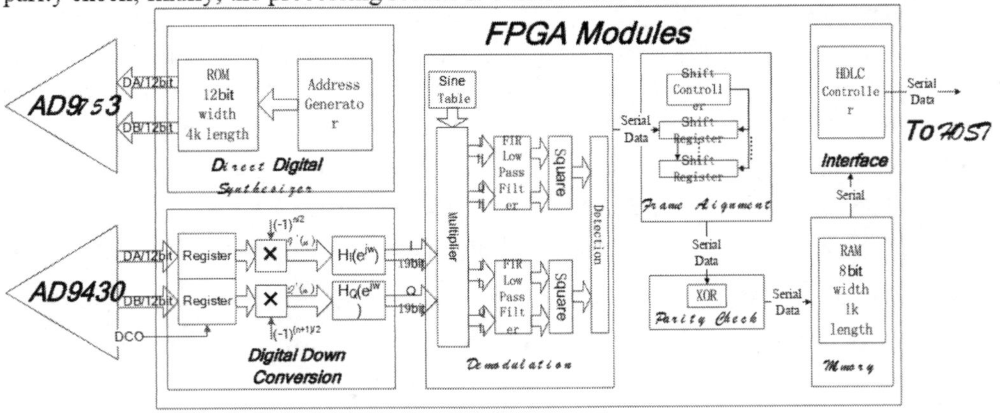

Fig. 3. FPGA internal signal processing flow chart

2.1 DAC control

The AD9753 is a 12-bit dual digital input digital-to-analog converter. Since the internal Phase-Locked Loop (PLL) circuitry is able to double frequency of input clock, the two input digital data is converted to analog signal at twice the speed of the input clock and sent out. Therefore, FPGA can control the DAC using half the sampling frequency.

Two 12-bit wide, 4096 deep read-only memory (ROM) is generated inside the FPGA, which stores 4096 sampled single cycle sinusoidal wave data. According to DDS theory, we can get the frequency control word K. Two memories take 0 and K as the initial address respectively and 2 K as the increment address. FPGA inputs the clock signal at half of the sampling frequency to DAC in the differential form through the clock chip MC100LVEL16. At this rate the data read from two memories is sent to the P1B and P2B port of DAC. The DAC output analog signal becomes a single frequency signal through low-pass filter and amplifier circuit.

We can get signals of different frequencies according to different control word K and do the coding combination of the two signals on the basis of sending codeword required, thus, the transmission of MSK signal is realized.

2.2 ADC sampling control

AD9430 is a 12-bit dual digital output analog-to-digital converter. Since the internal clock management circuitry is able to divide frequency of input clock by two, the output data at half the speed of the input clock is latched and then transmitted to the processor. Therefore, FPGA can do the data processing using half the sampling frequency.

MSK IF signal becomes a differential signal after the transformer, and then is input to the ADC. Meanwhile, FPGA generates the sampling clock and input it to the ADC in differential form through the clock chip MC100LVEL16. ADC sends the sampling data to FPGA through digital ports DA and DB and divides sampling frequency by two simultaneously, which is provided to FPGA in differential form as data synchronous clock DCO. The data of ADC is assigned to the internal registers for digital down-conversion by FPGA on falling edge of DCO.

2.3 Digital down conversion (DDC)

As the data sampled by AD9430 is two parallel output, the parity extraction of the FPGA input is not necessary. The input data from port DA and DB is regarded as I Road and Q Road signal directly. By taking the opposite sign of another I signal point and another Q signal point respectively, the processing of signal multiplied by $(-1)^n$ is realized.

By eight parallel multiplier and an 3-level adder with 8-input, 1-output, we can obtain the eight-band FIR filter. Two sets of filter coefficients are designed with the phase delay difference of $2\pi/T'$. Then, I signal after the filter is delayed $T'/2$ sampling period more than Q signal, thus, the time alignment of I Road and Q Road is realized.

In the process of implementation, we change the sampling frequency as $f_S = 4f_L/3$. From the preceding analysis, f_H becomes $2\Delta f$ and f_L becomes direct current (DC) signal after DDC processing. Then, only the mixing of $2\Delta f$ is necessary to be processed inside the FPGA, saving the FPGA internal resources of multipliers and logic units.

2.4 MSK demodulation

Since the low frequency signal has been converted into DC signal in the process of ADC sampling and DDC, the demodulation is divided into two parts, as shown in Fig. 4.

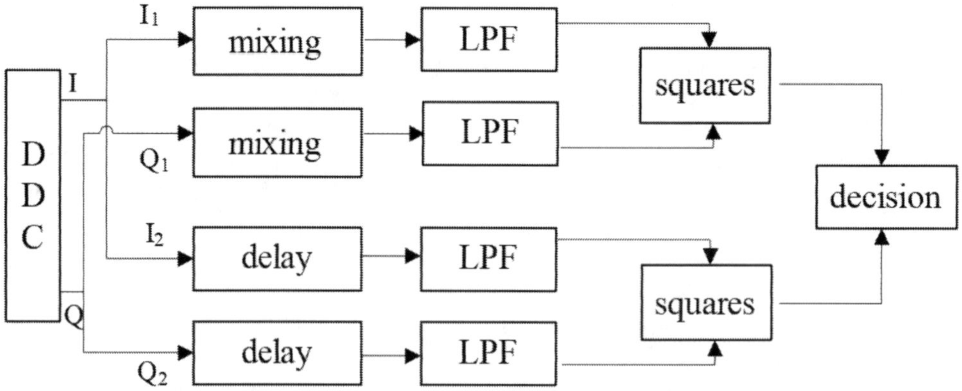

Fig. 4. MSK demodulation block diagram

A memory is generated inside the FPGA, which stores a sampled single cycle sinusoidal wave data. Then, by reading data from the memory at the processing-frequency, the look-up table method is realized and local oscillator (LO) signal at frequency of $2\Delta f$ is generated. After I1, Q1 and the LO signal above are mixed in the Mixer, frequency components are DC, $2\Delta f$ and $4\Delta f$ respectively. To ensure that four signals are sent into the LPF simultaneously, the I2 and Q2 signals go through the Delay Line Device with the same processing time as the Mixer.

After that, we generate a FIR low-pass filter by using the same method as polyphase filter and change the specific coefficient in order to make the cut-off frequency be 500 KHz. After the LPF, the high frequency components are filtered and only the DC component is retained. Take the sum of squares of the DC components of I1and Q1, I2 and Q2 respectively to get the amplitude information of MSK signal components with two frequencies. Then, the MSK symbol is achieved by joint judging the amplitude values.

2.5 Frame alignment

After the video symbol is obtained, the data symbol alignment and frame alignment is processed. For frame alignment, the matching method uses shift-register. We assume the symbol length of frame header is N, and then M shift-register with N-bit is constructed inside the FPGA. When the input symbol is detected, start the current register and prepare the next register at the same time, and then start the M shift-registers successively and circularly. Judge the register before each shift, if the symbol of any register is exactly the same as specified frame header before, the frame alignment is successful; otherwise, keep shifting until it is successful. The process of frame alignment is given in Fig. 5.

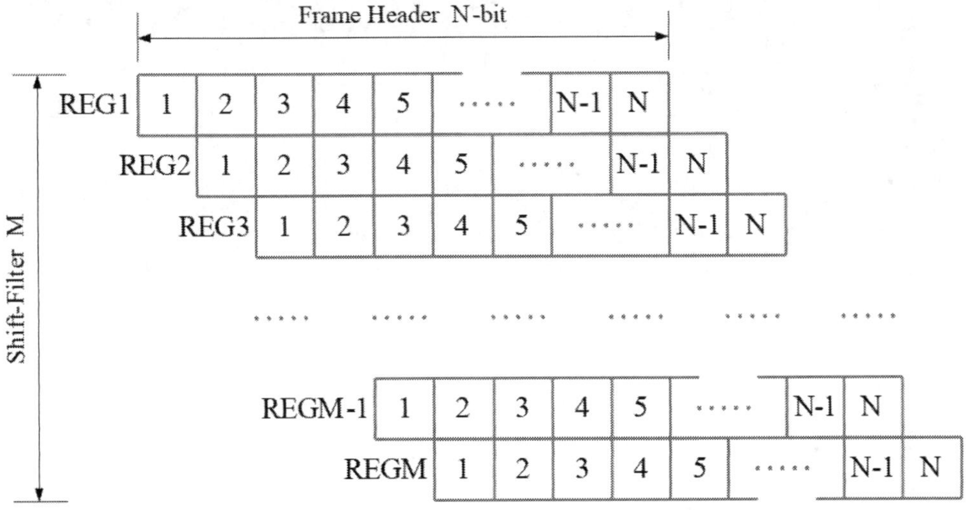

Fig. 5. Process of frame alignment

2.6 Data processing and transmission

After the success of frame alignment, the MSK data is collected according to timing relationship of the data frame. Then we decode each group of collected data, including removing the prefix, suffix and parity bit, and so on. Do the bitwise operation XOR to the data decoded and, compare the results with the parity bit. If both are the same, the data is judged to be valid and is stored in the FPGA internal memory in the form of bytes. If not, discard this frame of data and send an error report to the host.

To communicate with the host, we generate a SPI communication module inside the FPGA and do the optical coupling isolation and voltage conversion by convert devices on the communication interface. The host sends the encoded data and corresponding request through SPI interface. The SPI communication module receives the encoded data and sends the MSK data to be stored and error report to the host according to the command.

3 System test

During the test, we set the parameters as follows: IF 120MHz, bandwidth 10MHz, signal rate 1Mbps, frame rate 100fps, and take the MSK signal output of the module as the IF signal input of the module, the communication rate 2Mbps. The test time is 30 hours and the number of frame tested is 107.

 https://doi.org/10.1051/itmconf/20181701014

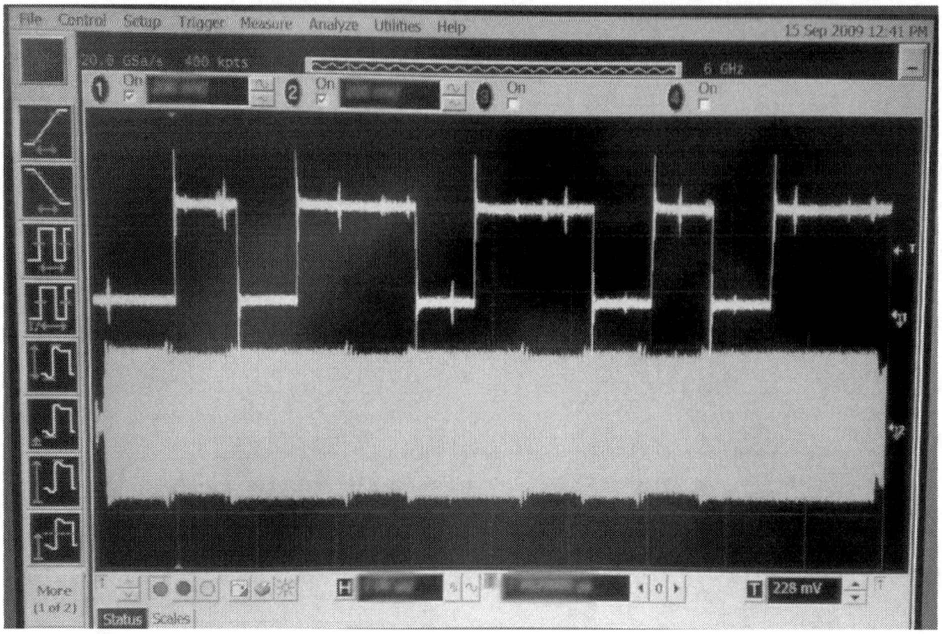

Fig. 6. comparing results

The comparison of the output MSK symbol and input MSK signal results is shown in Fig. 6.

After the actual test, the delay of output symbol is 1.05μs. When the signal-to-noise (SNR) of the input IF signal is greater than 10dB, the bit error rate (BER) of MSK demodulation is better then 10-6 and the bit error rate (BER) of communication is better then 10-6, meeting the general requirement of wireless communications.

4 Conclusion

According to the idea of SDR, the MSK communication module of ADC+FPGA+DAC is designed in this article, including the bandpass sampling and the generation of the IF MSK signal. The data processing such as DDC, polyphase filtering and MSK demodulation is realized inside the FPGA. As the system is based on the SDR architecture of broadband IF sampling and all of the signal controlling and data processing is realized in one FPGA, it can meet the requirement of various communication systems by modifying the hardware program. Since digital down conversion is applied in the course of signal sampling, the processing of IF signal at higher carrier frequency can also be achieved. The system has good versatility and reconstruction, with a broad application prospects.

References

1. Alsliety, M., Aloi, D.N. Signal processing choices and challenges for SDR in Telematics [J]. International Symposium on Signal Processing and Its Applications, Feb. 2007, pp1-4.
2. Hatai, I., Chakrabarti, I. FPGA implementation of a digital FM modem for SDR architecture [J]. International Conference on Computer and Devices for Communication, Dec. 2009, pp1-4.
3. Zhao DeAn, Lian XianGuo and Yang Ping. Multi-rate Signal Processing for Software Defined Radio (SDR) and Realize on FPGA [J]. International Forum on Computer

Science-Technology and Applications, Dec. 2009, pp251-254.
4. Pan Yun, Ge Ning and Dong Zaiwang. Mixed-Signal Modeling and Analysis for a Digital RF Direct Sampling Mixer [J]. IEEE International Conference on Circuits and Systems for Communications, May 2008, pp623-627.
5. Jie-Cherng Liu. Bandpass sampling of multiple single sideband RF signals [J]. International Symposium on Communications, Control and Signal Processing, March 2008, pp863-866.
6. Yamamoto, T., Kasahara, M. and Matsuura, T. A 63-mA 112/94-dB DR IF bandpass Modulator with direct feed-forward and double sampling [J]. Custom Integrated Circuits Conference, Dept. 2007, pp61-64.
7. Mitola, J. The software radio architecture [J]. IEEE communication magazine 1995 Volume 33, Issue 5,pp26- 38.
8. Zhang Rui, Li Jiandong. A New Type of Practical Software Radio Architecture [J]. ACTA EL ECTRONICA SINICA, Nov.1999,pp39-41.
9. Zhang Jianli, Yang Jiawei, Huang Pengyu. Study And Realization Of A Software Radio IF Modulation demodulation Platform Based On Dual DSPs [J]. Space Electronic technology, S1,2006,pp158-162.
10. Wei Zheng, Zhou Chunhui Zhao Ming. Software Radio Platform Design Based on High-Performance DSP [J]. Microcomputer Information, 02.2007, pp198-200.

Digitized Modeling and Machining Simulation of Equal Base Bevel Gear

Bin Wang[1], *Yunpeng* He[1,·], *Peiyao* Feng[1], *Xun* Sun[1], *Aijun* Xu[1], *Jubo* Li[1], *Tianxing* Li[1], *Xinjie* Jia[1], and *Bo* Zhang[1]

[1]School of Mechatronics Engineering, Henan University of Science and Technology, Luoyang 471003, China

Abstract. In order to achieve the NC machining to the equal base circle bevel gear with a standard cutter, to plan the machining path efficiently and to predict machining interference, based on the equal base circle bevel gear theory, the machining coordinate system for the bevel gear was established, according to gear tooth surface equations of the bevel gears, the tooth surface discretization function was derived, and through the calculation and get the discrete points, the gear surface was modeled in the software UG, and then the planning of the machining path, automatic programming and simulation processing were done. At last, simulation processing, analysis and comparison to the gear surface were carried on with the software VERICUT, improved that the gear surface modeling and NC machining methods were correct and feasible.

1. Brief introduction of the equal base circle bevel gear

According to the traditional theory of the equal base circle bevel gear, using the finger-shaped milling cutter to machine the bevel gear, through controlling the finger-shaped milling cutter and wheel billet to achieve specific relative motion, to make sure that the base circle radius of the bevel gear at different cone distances is same, the tooth profile will not change suddenly, in which way to machine the entire tooth surface accurately with only one milling cutter. However, since the finger-shaped milling cutter is special tools, the profile accuracy of its shaft cross-sectional shape depends on the accuracy of the sample plate and the technical level of the worker, which means the high production cost and low precision of the cutter, what's more, the cutter must be changed many times due to the wear and tear of the cutters during the machining to large size gear, Because the difficult of making sure the accuracy is consistent to multiple cutters, so, it's more difficult to manufacture the cutter and the manufacturing costs is high, and the gear machining accuracy is low. Therefore, using a common ball end milling cutter to achieve the finishing of the gear surface, which is an effective way to improve the machining accuracy and reduce the manufacturing cost [1,2].

The software UG combines the process of geometric modeling, cutter Location, graphic display and post processing together during the components machining, the problems

· Corresponding author: heyunpeng06@163.com

accrued in programming source, graphic display, cutting simulation and interactive modification of complex components can be effectively solved, which is an effective measure to avoid collision due to the interfere between the machine tool, cutter, and fixture during CNC machining. Therefore, in order to plan the machining path during the NC programming to the bevel gear and automatically programming in UG software, the digital processing based on the equal base circle bevel gear theory is necessary, and accurate modeling in UG software, this is the key points to the NC machining to the equal base circle bevel gear with UG software[3,4].

For this reason, based on the equal base circle bevel gear theory, through the establishment of the machining coordinate system, gear surface analysis and discretization, the gear surface modeling was finished in UG software, and further simulation processing to the gear surface was done, in order to verify the correctness of the tooth surface modeling, the CNC machining code generated by UG software was imported into VERICUT software, and simulation processing was done, and the simulation process and the theoretical tooth surface flanks virtual contrast detection was carried on to verified the correctness and feasibility to the tooth surface modeling and NC machining method[5].

1.1 Characteristics of the equal base circle bevel gear

By the way of numerical control, the special tooth trace is processed by controlling the finger-shaped milling cutter and wheel billet to achieve specific relative motion, and the bevel gear, whose base circle radius of equivalent gear at different cone distances is same, namely, equal base circle curve bevel gear. The features of these gears are as follows:

$$r_{vb} = \frac{zm_t \cos\alpha_n}{2\cos\delta\cos^2\beta} = \frac{zm_{te}\cos\alpha_n}{2\cos\delta\cos^2\beta_e} \equiv const \tag{1}$$

According to the Eq. (1), the relationship between the helix angle β of the tooth trace and cone distance R is:

$$\beta = arc\cos\sqrt{\frac{R\cos^2\beta_e}{\mathrm{R_e}}} \tag{2}$$

where: z --the number of teeth for the bevel gear;

δ --the indexing angle of bevel gear(°);

α_n --the normal pressure angle of tooth profile(°);

R, Re--cone distance at an arbitrary point and of the big-end respectively(mm);

m_t, m_{te}--the transverse modules at the cone distances R and Re(mm);

β, β_e--the helix angles of tooth trace corresponding to R and Re(°).

2. The modeling of equal base circle bevel gears tooth surface

2.1 The establishment of machining coordinate system

Figure 1 shows the relationship between the relative position of the cutter and the blank in the gear cutting coordinate system during the cutting of the equal base circle bevel gears as the ball end milling cutter. While the ball end milling cutter move from the big end to the small end in a certain speed, wheel blanks rotate according in a variable speed regularly, the center of the ball end cutter move along line isometric of the actual tooth line, that's how the tooth surface of the equal base circle bevel gears was enveloped.

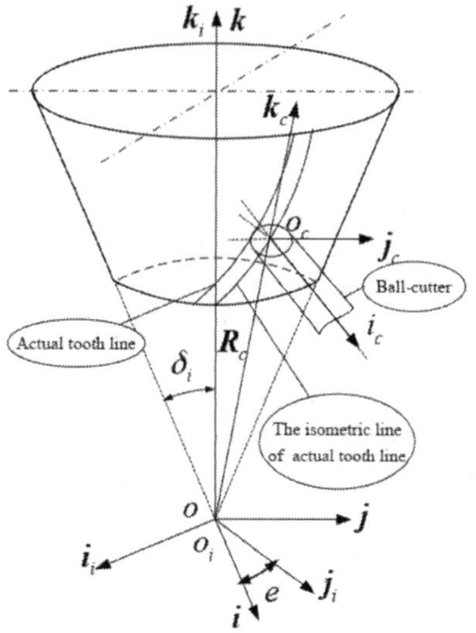

Fig. 1. Gear cutting coordinate system of the equal base circle bevel gears.

$\sigma_i(O_i - i_i j_i k_i)$ is the coordinate system fixed to the wheel blanks, the origin O_i is at the top of the cone, and the big end of the theoretical tooth line is in the $j_i o_i k_i$. $\sigma_c(O_i - i_i j_i k_i)$ is the coordinate system fixed to the cutter .It is used to describe the cutter surface formed by the rotation of the cutter shaft about axis i_c. During the cutting process, the tool axis is always perpendicular to the conical busbar, the cutting coordinate system moves along the conical busbar, and O_c is located on the conical busbar. $\sigma(O - ijk)$ is the space fixed coordinate system, used to realize the transformation between σ_i and σ_c, the origin o coincides with the origin o_i of the coordinate system of the wheel blanks. During the process of cutting, the tool axis is always in the iok plane of the fixed coordinate system, axis j_c and axis j remain parallel.

The vector relation between the origin σ and the origin σ_c is:

$$\overline{OO_c} = \overline{R_c} = R_c(\sin\delta_i \vec{i} + \cos\delta_i \vec{k}) \tag{3}$$

By sub-cone tooth crown line gear on the rolling relationship between the wheel axis j_i coordinate system and the axis i of the fixed axis angle:

$$e = \theta_c / \sin\delta_i \tag{4}$$

In the formulas (3) and (4): R_c is the vector between the tool center and the cone tip; δ_i is processed gear root cone angle (i = 1,2 corresponding to the small round, big round); θ_c is the polar angle of the tool center at the taper R_i.

The transformation matrix between each coordinate system is:

$$\sigma_c \rightarrow \sigma : \left[M_{0C}\right] = \begin{bmatrix} \cos\delta_i & 0 & \sin\delta_i \\ 0 & 1 & 0 \\ -\sin\delta_i & 0 & \cos\delta_i \end{bmatrix} , \sigma \rightarrow \sigma_i : \left[M_{i0}\right] = \begin{bmatrix} \sin e & -\cos e & 0 \\ \cos e & \sin e & 0 \\ 0 & 0 & 1 \end{bmatrix} \quad (5)$$

2.2 Discretization of tooth flank surface

The equal base circle bevel gears tooth surface equation was obtained originally based on finger-shaped milling cutter theory. In the cutter coordinate system, the contact point between the tool surface and the gear tooth surface satisfies the meshing equation, and the tooth surface equation of the equivalent equal base circle bevel gear is obtained by solving the meshing equation [6, 7]:

$$\overline{r^{(i)}} = [M_{iO}][M_{OC}]\overline{r^{(c)}} + [M_{iO}]\overline{R_c} \quad (6)$$

According to the tooth surface equation, substitute the parameters, simplified processing, get the gear tooth surface concave point formula:

$$\begin{cases} X = \sin e(X_i^{(c)}\cos\delta + Z_i^{(c)}\sin\delta) - Y_i^{(c)}\cos e + R_c\sin e\sin\delta \\ Y = \cos e(X_i^{(c)}\cos\delta + Z_i^{(c)}\sin\delta) + Y_i^{(c)}\sin e + R_c\cos e\sin\delta \\ Z = -X_i^{(c)}\sin\delta + Z_i^{(c)}\cos\delta + R_c\cos\delta \end{cases} \quad (7)$$

Where: $R_c = \sqrt{R^2 + (r_0 - s)^2 + 2R(r_0 - s)^2 \sin\beta}$

$X_i^{(c)}$ corresponds to $X_{cd}^{(c)}$, $X_{bc}^{(c)}$, $X_{ab}^{(c)}$ in CD, BC and AB;

$Y_i^{(c)}$ corresponds to $Y_{cd}^{(c)}$, $Y_{bc}^{(c)}$, $Y_{ab}^{(c)}$ in CD, BC and AB ;

$Z_i^{(c)}$ corresponds to $Z_{cd}^{(c)}$, $Z_{bc}^{(c)}$, $Z_{ab}^{(c)}$ in CD, BC and AB .

$$\text{CD:} \begin{cases} X_{cd}^{(c)} = rk\bullet\cos(Tk + sk / rk) - rv \\ Y_{cd}^{(c)} = -rk\bullet\sin(Tk + sk / rk)\bullet\cos\gamma \\ Z_{cd}^{(c)} = rk\bullet\sin(Tk + sk / rk)\bullet\sin\gamma \end{cases}$$

$$\text{BC:} \begin{cases} X_{bc}^{(c)} = rk\bullet\cos(Tk) - rv \\ Y_{bc}^{(c)} = -rk\bullet\sin(Tk)\bullet\cos\gamma \\ Z_{bc}^{(c)} = rk\bullet\sin(Tk)\bullet\sin\gamma \end{cases}$$

$$\text{AB:} \begin{cases} X_{ab}^{(c)} = rf + Rb\bullet\left[1 - \cos(\theta k)\right] - rv \\ Y_{ab}^{(c)} = -Rb\bullet\sin(\theta k)\bullet\cos\gamma \\ Z_{ab}^{(c)} = Rb\bullet\sin(\theta k)\bullet\sin\gamma \end{cases}$$

sk-- the tooth profile modification at the radius of sk ;

Rv--radius of the equivalent gear indexing circle(mm);

Tk--The angle between the straight line $O_a K$ and the axis of the cutter(°), O_a is the equivalent spur gear center ;

rf—— $r_v - h_f$;

Rb-- the radius of the cutter arc(mm);

θk --The center angle between the K point and A point on the arc of the cutter(°);
γ --Tool axis truncation around its axis clockwise rotation angle(°).

2.3 The establishment of the gear three-dimensional model

On the base of conical gear tooth surface equation, a series of different values of the cone distance parameter R, according to the above formula of discrete points can get the discrete point coordinates of the tooth surface. Table 1 shows the geometric parameters of the example gear. The calculated instantaneous discrete point coordinates are connected, constituting the tooth surface contact wire. According to this series of contact lines, you can constitute a space curved surface gear. Extracting these discrete points, importing UG can constitute a lamellar tooth surface to complete three-dimensional model of the gear. As shown in figure 2 is the lamellar tooth after finishing.

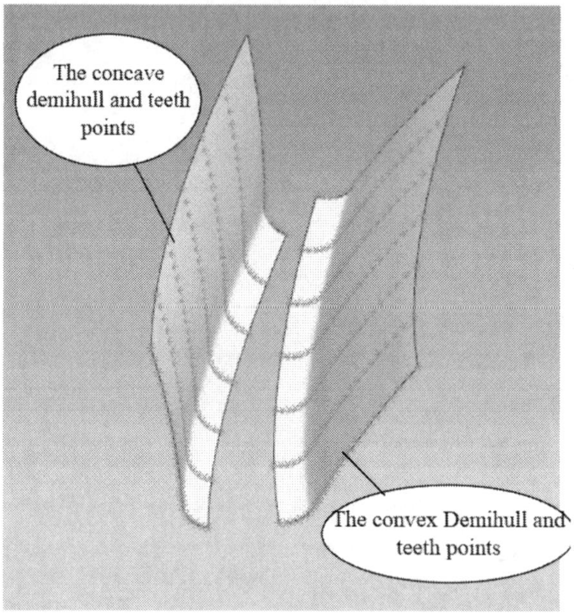

Fig. 2. The lamellar tooth.

Table 1. Basic parameters of gear pair.

parameters of gear pair	Numerical value
Number of pinion Z_1	22
Number of Bull wheel Z_2	27
Big end transverse module M_{te}	12
Breadth of tooth B	40
Big-end helix Angle β	6°
Shaft Angle γ Normal pressure Angle α_n	90° 20°

As shown in figure 3, generating design gear precise three-dimensional model through the lamellar tooth.

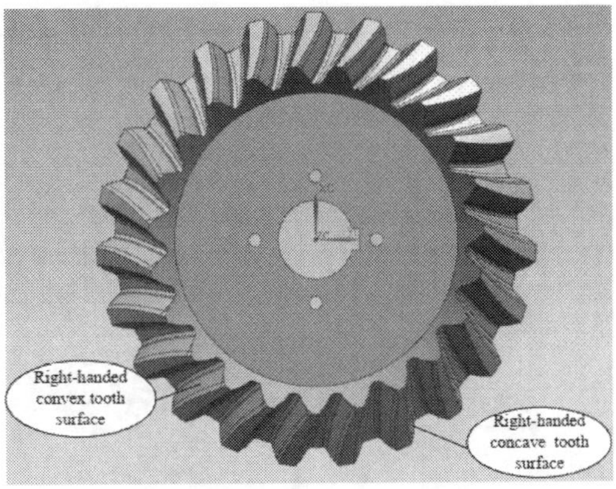

Fig. 3. The design of the three - dimensional model of the equal base circle bevel gears.

3. Simulation processing

In order to improve the processing efficiency of the equal base circle bevel gear, the ball milling cutter is only used in the fine finishing, the forming milling which is more efficient is still used in the process of rough machining and semi-finishing. The three-dimensional model of the gear which is semi-finished was built as the gear blank which was then imported to the software UG.

The coordinate system for fine finishing was set in the gear blank. The ball milling cutter was chosen and built as the finishing tools, the parameters of the cutter was set and the diameter of the cutter is 6mm. Select [Cavity milling] as the processing methods for the finishing machining, select [Fixed shaft contour milling] in the subtypes. Select the convex surface of the gear as the cutting area. Set the driving method as [streamline driver], use the streamline driving method to make sure the cutter move in the radial direction along the cutting routes during the machining processing, in which way the finishing process to the gear surface can be done, select reciprocating cutting as the cutting mode for the finishing machining, set the step distance as the residual height, then generate the tool path for the finishing machining to gear convex surface, set the remaining machining parameters, then do the simulation processing (figure 4), verify the correctness of the gear processing method initially. Generated NC codes suit for the cutting machine through the post-processing, and put the NC codes above into the software VERICUT, in which further simulation and validation can be done. The simulation results were shown in figure 5[8].

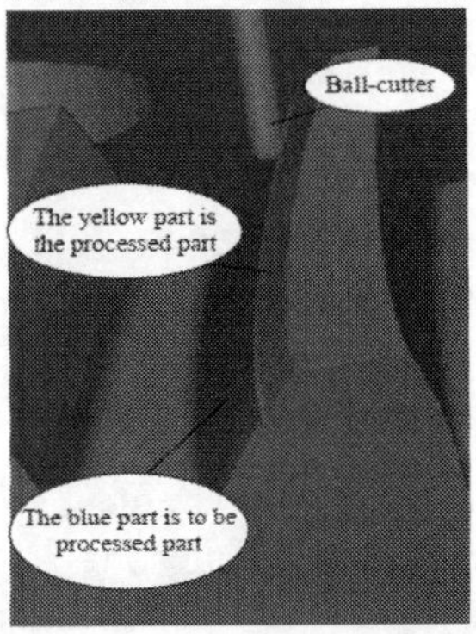

Fig. 4. UG software simulation processing view.

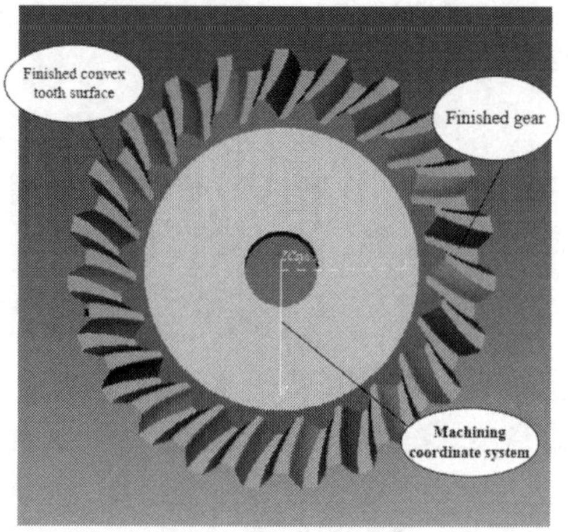

Fig. 5. VERICUT software simulation of the processed gear.

The simulated tooth surface and the theoretical tooth surface were compared and analyzed, Figure 6 shows the result. In the figure, the red area is overcut, the blue area is undercut, and the error less than 0.01 mm is displayed in green. As can be seen from figure 6, there is a slight overcut of the concave end of the gear tooth and a small amount of undercut at the large end. A small amount of overcut is machined on the large end of the convex end, and the rest is overlapped with the theoretical tooth surface. Figure 6 shows a slight error between the machining flank and the theoretical flank, which can be improved by controlling the tool pitch and tool diameter. The analysis and comparison results show that the method of tooth surface modeling of the equal base circle bevel gear and its processing method are correct and feasible[9].

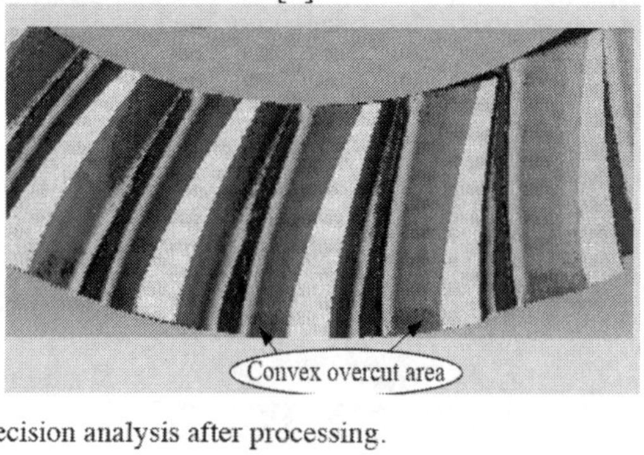

Fig. 6. Tooth surface precision analysis after processing.

4. Conclusion

According to the theory of the equal base circle bevel gear, the tooth surface of the equal base circle bevel gear is completed in UG software through discretization of the surface of the equal base circle bevel gear, and is simulated in UG. Finally, VERICUT software is used for further simulation of CNC machining and verification, the results show that:

1).Based on the tooth surface equation, the calculation, extraction, introduction and 3D modeling of the equivalent base tooth surface are correct.

2).Based on the ball-end milling cutter, the NC machining of the equal base circle bevel gears in the UG software is automatically programmed, the NC code and the simulation machining are generated correctly and practically.

Acknowledgement: The research reported here is partially supported by the National Natural Science Foundation of China (Grant No.51405135,51575161,U1504522), Henan Universities Key Scientific Research Project of China (Grant No.15 A460003,17A460002,16A460033),The Doctoral Scientific Research Foundation of Henan University of Science and Technology.

Reference

1. Gong Y P. Study on Transmission Theory, Strength Analysis and Running-in Simulation of Equal Base Circle Bevel Gear [D]. Shenyang: Northeastern University 1996.
2. Cai Chunyuan, Cheng Naishi. Principle of Equal Base Circle Bevel Gear [J]. Chinese Journal of Construction Machinery, 1992, 28 (3): 61-64.
3. Zhang W H, Gong Y P, Wang D. Analysis of Tooth Geometry and Modification of Equal Base Circle Bevel Gear [J]. Journal of Northeastern University (Nature Science) 2000, 21(4): 390-393.
4. Wang B, Deng X Z, Dang Y G. Processing Principle and Tooth Surface Determination of Equal Base Circle Bevel Gear Using Disc Cutter, Journal of Aerospace Power, 2014, 29(3): 663-671.
5. Wang B, Deng X Z, Jia X J. Calculation of Tool State and Trajectory Processing Equal Base Circle Bevel Gear Using Disc Cutter [J]. China Mechanical Engineering, 2013, 24(19): 2664-2670.
6. Wang Fulin, Yi Chuanyun, Wang Tao. et a1. A generating method for digital gear tooth surfaces[J]. Int Adv Manuf Technol (2006) 28: 474-485.
7. Wang Bin, Fan Mingxing, Sun Xun. Cutter position calculation of machining equal base circle bevel gears with a pot-shaped milling cutter[J]. International Journal of Advance Manufacturing Technology, 2016: 87, 2625-2637.
8. Kong Deying, Chong Kai, Wang Xiao. NC machining simulation and optimization based on UG / CAM and VERICUT [J]. Machine Tool & Hydraulics,2011,39 (23): 147-149+153.
9. Wang Bin, Deng Xiaozhong, Chen Jun. Simulation for the NC machining to the equal base circle bevel gear with figer-shaped cutter based on VERICUT software [J]. Manufacturing technology and machine tools, 2013, (09): 124-128.

An Adaptive Contention Window Scheme for 802.11ah WLANs

Renzheng Gao[1], *Xiaoying* Lei[1·], *and Qiang* Hu[1]

[1]College of Information Enginnering Yangzhou University, Yangzhou 225127, China

Abstract. In order to cope with the rapid development of the Internet of things, IEEE working group has proposed a new wireless network technology, 802.11ah. IEEE 802.11ah operates at sub 1GHz band, and can provide long transmission range, wide coverage, while supporting more than 6,000 of station to be connected. In order to alleviate the high collision probability, 802.11ah MAC protocol involves in the RAW (restricted access window) mechanism combined with grouping mechanism. However, in 802.11ah WLAN (wireless local area network), most of the stations operate at sleep mode, and it is expected that at the start of a BI, the network suffers much higher collision probability than at the latter period of the BI. In order to improve these drawbacks, we propose an adaptive contention window scheme based on which an optimum contention window size is adapted at the start of the BI, and then gradually halved when the transmission completes successfully. Through conducting simulations, we prove that our proposed protocol can enhance the performance of 802.11ah WLAN.

1 Introduction

The Internet of things (IoT) is an important part of the new generation of information technology, and it is also an important stage of development in the "information" era. IoT describes a vision where everyday objects can be equipped with identifying, sensing, networking and processing capabilities that allow them to communicate with one another over the Internet [1]. Nowadays, IoT has been used in the major developed countries in the world, but the global system of networking industry is still in the process of establishing and perfecting. In order to provide ubiquitous connectivity, the IoT (Internet of Things) requires wireless network technologies which can provide high performances even in a dense network environment.

The IEEE 802.11ah working group has proposed a WLAN (wireless local area network) technology that can work on unlicensed frequency bands below 1GHz. Due to the advantages of low frequency propagation, 802.11ah WLAN (wireless local area network) technology can achieve a wide range of network transmission function, and accommodates multiple stations [2]. The 802.11ah MAC (media access control) proposes an RAW (restrict access window) mechanism working under the support of a grouping scheme. This protocol can provide long transmission range, wide coverage, and support more than 6,000 of

· Corresponding author: xylei@yzu.edu.cn

stations to be connected, and applies packet technology, it assumes that each group of stations has the same number, and takes BI (beacon interval) as the cycle to carry out data transmission. Here is the process: during a beacon interval (BI), AP initiates several restricted access windows (RAWs), and an RAW is sliced into equal time slots which can be allocated to single station or a group of stations. Stations contend to access channel according to the allocated RAW [3].

However, the 802.11ah MAC layer is still based on the 802.11DCF (distributed coordination function) protocol. And it is proved that the legacy DCF (distributed coordination function) protocol raises severe channel contention and hidden terminal problems in large size networks. On the other hand, most of the stations in 802.11ah operate under PSM (power saving mode), according to which the stations wake up periodically to transmit packets, and then enter into sleep mode. It can be expected that, there are more contending stations at the start of BI than in the later period, therefore, these collisions will cause the waste of channel resources and the consumption of energy.

In order to improve 802.11ah, we propose an adaptive contention window scheme, based on which the initial value of the current contention window is set according to the number of competing stations, and with the successful transmission, the value of contention window is reduced, or else the contention window size sustains to be the current value in case of collision occurs. More details will be present in Section 3.

The rest of the article is organized as follows: Section 2 provides an overview of the IEEE 802.11ah, IEEE 802.11DCF and the related works of this paper while Section 3 presents the details of the proposed scheme. Section 4 conducts the discrete simulations to evaluate the performance of proposed scheme, and finally, section 5 draws conclusion remarks.

2 Preliminaries

2.1 IEEE 802.11DCF

Figure 1 illustrates the IEEE 802.11 DCF scheme [9]. In the basic DCF, we choose two stations as sender and receiver, first, the sender should sense the channel for a period of DIFS (DCF inter frame space) before its transmission. If the channel remains idle for DIFS (DCF inter frame space), the station can access the channel to transmission. Otherwise, the station starts a backoff process by randomly selecting a number from [0, w] as the value of the BC (backoff counter), where w is the value of the current contention window of this station. The 802.11standard has defined the maximum and minimum values of contention windows (CWmin, CWmax). The initial value of w is CWmin, it doubles in case the station encounters a collision, otherwise, if a transmission is successful, the value will be set back to CWmin. On the other hand, when the value of w reaches to CWmax, the station has to sustain it even if it encounters another collision. However, when the number of collisions of the station is too high to reach the upper limit, we will discard the packet that the station needs to transmit, and it must reselect the new BC to compete channel with others. While staying in backoff procedure, the station continues to sense the channel, and as soon as an idle channel is sensed, the station reduces its BC for one time slot. When the BC of the station reaches to 0, the station can access to the channel and start its transmission immediately. When the sender transmits data successful, a SIFS (short inter frame space) later, the receiver returns a reply packet and the sender catch it. At this point, the entire data transmission between the stations is completed.

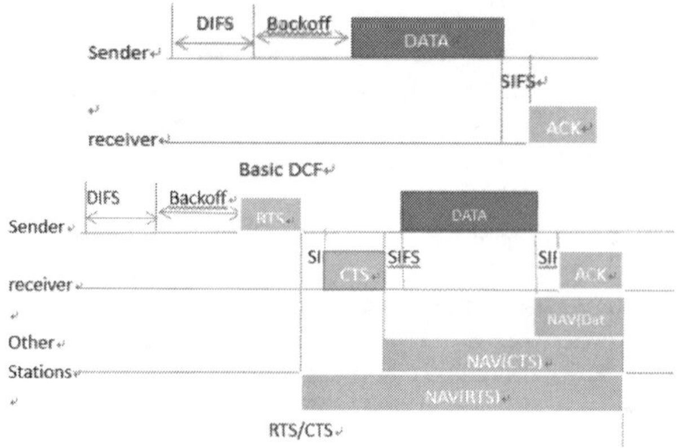

Fig. 1. IEEE 802.11 DCF.

In addition to the basic access, an optional four way hand-shaking technique, known as request-to-send / clear-to-send (RTS/CTS) mechanism has been standardized. Before transmitting a packet, a station operating in RTS/CTS mode "reserves" the channel by sending a special Request-To-Send short frame. The destination station acknowledges the receipt of an RTS frame by sending back a Clear-To-Send frame, after which normal packet transmission and ACK response occurs. Since collision may occur only on the RTS frame, and it is detected by the lack of CTS response, the RTS/CTS mechanism allows to increase the system performance by reducing the duration of a collision when long messages are transmitted. As an important side effect, the RTS/CTS scheme designed in the 802.11 protocol is suited to combat the so-called problem of hidden terminals, which occurs when pairs of stations result to be unable to hear each other.

In Figure 1, a sender that wants to transmit a packet, waits until the channel is sensed idle for a DIFS, follows the backoff rules explained above, and then, instead of the packet, preliminarily transmits a special short frame called request to send (RTS). When the receiver detects an RTS frame, it responds, after a SIFS, with a clear to send (CTS) frame. The transmitting station is allowed to transmit its packet only if the CTS frame is correctly received. The frames RTS and CTS carry the information of the length of the packet to be transmitted. This information can be read by any listening station, which is then able to update a network allocation vector (NAV) containing the information of the period of time in which the channel will remain busy. Therefore, when a station is hidden from either the transmitting or the receiving station, by detecting just one frame among the RTS and CTS frames, it can suitably delay further transmission, and thus avoid collision.

2.2 IEEE 802.11 AH

The 802.11ah TGah (Task Group) has started establishing the IEEE 802.11ah amendment since November 2010, which is completed in March 2016[4]. Comparing with the existing IEEE 802.11 WLAN (wireless local area network) technology, 802.11ah revision involves many unique features in the PHY (physical) protocol and MAC (media access control) protocol.

IEEE 802.11ah physical layer reuse a series of 802.11ac technology [5] and make it improved so that it can work in the S1G unlicensed band. As shown in Figure 2, the 802.11ah of the channel definition is different in various countries: e.g., the United States, South Korea, 902-928 MHz; 917.5-923.5 MHz; 863-868 MHz; Chinese, Europe, Japan, 755-787 MHz; 916.5-927.5 MHz [6]. Singapore uses two independent available frequency bands, 866-869 MHz and 920-925 MHz. The PHY layer adopts OFDM (orthogonal frequency division multiplexing) and works at 1 GHz frequency, which is 10 times lower than the main frequency version. The proposed channel bandwidth includes 1 MHz, 2 MHz, 4 MHz, 8 MHz and 16 MHz, of which 1 MHz and 2 MHz channel bandwidth are widely adopted in many countries [7].

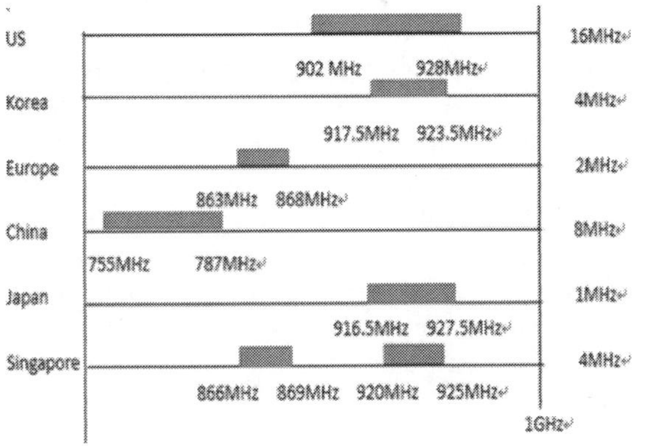

Fig. 2. IEEE 802.11ah Global channel allocation.

Because the IEEE802.11 MAC protocol uses 802.11 DCF (distributed coordination function), it can cause large packet collision probability and trigger hidden stations problems in large size networks. The IEEE 802.11ah MAC proposes to an RAW (restrict access window) scheme. The core idea is that a BI (beacon interval) is divided into equal time slots, named, RAW, and each of the time slots can be assigned to a station or a group of stations [8]. AP stores RAW relevant information into the beacon frame, including the starting time, length, the number of time slot and the AID of stations that can be allowed to transmit in each time slot. The information to the initiated RAWs is broadcasted through short Beacon frames by the AP. A station can access channel during the allocated RAW, following the process defined by DCF protocol.

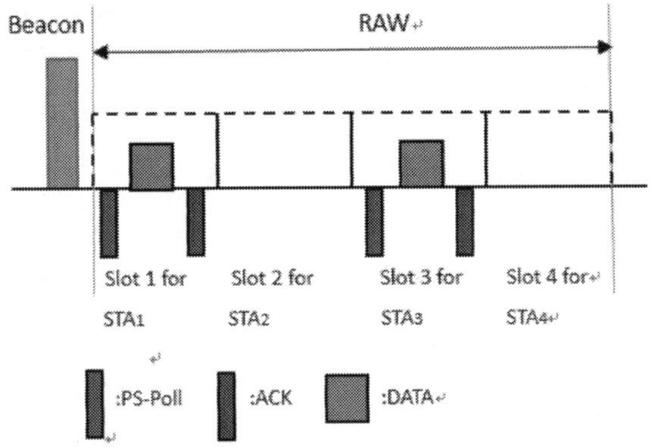

Fig. 3. RAW based channel access.

Figure 3 depicts a RAW-based media access approach. In a BI, AP allocates the time slots to 4 stations, STA1, STA2, STA3 and STA4, STA1 and STA3 are in active mode, while STA2 and STA4 are in doze mode. STA1 and STA3 by sending PS-Poll frames tell the AP that the station is in active mode. The AP receives the station information and to assign time slots to stations, at the same time, the station starts listening beacon frame, which carry the relevant information about RAW, including the beginning time of RAW, time length of RAW, the number of Slot in the RAW and which RAW will be allocated to the transmission, etc. When the STA1 and STA3 receive this information, they will know that the AP is allocated to their access time, Slot1 for STA1 and Slot2 for STA3. Then, the stations access the channel within the time slot assigned to each other and carry out data transmission. This mechanism reduces the number of devices trying to access channel at a given time period, and thus alleviates the channel contention.

However, the above mechanism does not guarantee effective channel utilization. No matter what the state of the device is, the AP will allocate the time slot for them, in case the station is in sleeping mode, the allocated time slot will be wasted. In order to improve the efficiency of channel utilization, many scholars have studied the protocol in depth, and proposed a series of effective improvements, such as the introduction of RA (resource allocation) frames in 802.11ah improving the problem of the allocated time slot of the dormant stations, and 802.11ah uses the TWT (target wake-up time) mechanism, which allows AP to manage the wake-up time of the stations below BSS, the stations can be in different time periods to wake up, thereby reducing competition conflict, improve the efficiency of the system, but also greatly reduce the power consumption of the stations. On this basis, we will also do more research on this problem in the future.

2.3 Related works

However, the random backoff method can encounter collisions, stations can choose a same BC value because they have no idea of the BC selected by others. Previous works have presented different approaches for solving this problem [10-14]. [10] proposed station can reserve a BC value through the data packet being transferred and store the reserved BC into the packet header, other stations can monitor this packet and know the value of BC according to the broadcast characteristics based on wireless networks; [11] is suggested that when a station accesses the channel successfully, it can reuse its BC by increasing the value of M. Here, M is the number of stations that belong to the same BSS (basic service set), this station can continue to occupy channel and transmit data packet, without choosing a new BC to compete channel; [12], according to this scheme, when a station wants to transmit a packet, it stores the next backoff counter to be used in the MAC header of current packet.

The other stations which overhear this packet avoid choosing the same backoff counter. This reservation-based scheme successfully reduces the collision probability in certain level while increasing whole network throughput; In [13] a virtual backoff algorithm is proposed. When multiple stations select an identical BC, the channel accesses of these stations are rearranged according to their sequence numbers, in other words, the stations that choose the same BC are made out of the sequence numbers in the virtual space, and these serial numbers are used to access the channel, it can effectively relieve collisions in this way; [14]design a collision-free backoff method to improve the backoff function, that enable the stations to reserve their own BCs using previously delivered control packets, after these stations complete their data transmissions they release the reserved BCs to stations having not reserved a BC.

These approaches still suffer some drawbacks: when a station chooses the value of BC randomly in [10], the randomly selected BC may be with a large value, thus brings in long access delay and waste of resources; in [11], the number of stations contending for channel can be much less than M, when the M value is far greater than the number of stations, the scheme is meaningless; in[12], when there a hidden station in the network, other stations may cause collisions because they cannot monitor its reservation BC; [13] requires for hardware modification, the realization of which is complicated, which is not operable in the process of experiment; in [14], we assume that each station sends a packet and can be monitored by other stations, that may fail if all the stations work in CAM (continual active mode), because the control packet transmission will not occur, thus, the BC reservation process cannot be activated. If in this case, we will do more research on it in our future work.

3 Adaptive contention window scheme

In this section, we design an adaptive contention window method to improve the performance of IEEE 802.11ah. Our proposal is based on the following observations: In 802.11PSM (power saving mode), stations periodically wake up according to BI (beacon interval), it is expected that at the start of a BI, there are much more active stations, which can bring in a high collision probability. And with the passing of BI, the number of active stations decreases, thus the channel competition eliminates. Furthermore, RAW scheme is supported by a grouping mechanism, therefore, it's reasonable to obtain the number of stations per group.

In proposed scheme, instead of utilizing a minimum contention window at the beginning of the backoff process and doubles it each time a collision occurs, we propose to begin with an optimum contention window, CWopt. And if the stations transmission completes successfully, the value of the CW decreases to half, or else with collision occurs, the value of the CW sustains. The value of CWopt is provided in [9] as follows:

$$CW_{opt} \approx N\sqrt{(2Tc)} \quad (1)$$

Here, N is the number of stations in the network, Tc is the average time to detect the collision of each station, which can be obtained according to (2):

$$Tc = H + E[P] + DIFS + \delta \quad (2)$$

where H is the packet header, the value of which equals to

$$H = PHYhdr + MAChdr \quad (3)$$

PHYhdr is the header of physical layer and MAChdr is the header of MAC (media access control) layer. E[P] is the average length of the longest packet payload involved in a collision, and δ is the propagation delay time.

Since 802.11ah is based on a grouping mechanism, we assume there are Nt stations in the network, and they are divided into G groups then the number of stations in each group is Nt/G=n, according to (1), The optimum CW applied by stations at the beginning of backoff process is Nt/G *√ (2Tc), and for each of successful transmission, this value reduces to 1/2, otherwise it sustains. In this way, at the start of a BI, the stations contend channel with a large window size, which can effectively reduce the collision probability. And as more and more stations complete their transmissions and enter into sleep mode, a smaller value is applied as contention window, which can reduce the channel access delay and improve network transmission performance.

4 Performance evaluation

4.1 Simulation environment

OPNET is an excellent network simulation and modeling tool. It supports object-oriented modeling and provides a graphical editing interface that is more convenient for users to use. The powerful capabilities and comprehensiveness provided by OPNET can almost simulate any network device and support various network technologies. In addition to the ability to simulate fixed communication models, OPNET's wireless modeler can also be used to build models of packet radio networks and satellite communication networks. At the same time, OPNET has outstanding performance in the design of the new network and the analysis of the existing network. It provides the same environment as the real network for the research of communication protocols and algorithms, and the perfect result analyzer provides an effective and intuitive tool for network performance analysis.

In this paper, we mainly use its WLAN (wireless local area networks) environment model, and based on this model, the network environment is modified as the experimental model we need. First, we are modifying the protocol to 802.11ah, including the width of transmission channel and the data transmission rate, on the other hand, we modify the backoff algorithm for our proposed scheme.

Figure 4 depicts the transmission process model of WLAN including 10 working modules. INIT: Initialization of the process model, BSS_INIT: Schedule a self interrupt to wait for mac interface, IDLE: The purpose of this state is to wait until the packet has arrived from the higher or lower layer, FRM_END: The purpose of this state is to determine the next unforced state after completing transmission, WAIT_FOR_RESPONSE: The purpose of this state is to wait for the response after transmission. The only frames which require acknowledgements are RTS and DATA frame, DEFER: This state defer until the medium is available for transmission, BKOFF_NEEDED: In this state we determine whether a back-off is necessary for the frame we are trying to transmit, BACKOFF: Processing Random Backoff, TRANSMIT: In this state we complete data transmission, SCAN: Record the state name if running in debug mode. The proposed scheme is to modify the backoff algorithm in the BACKOFF working module.

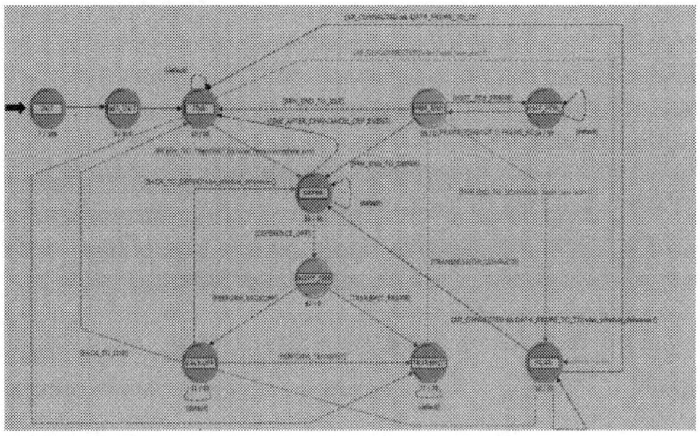

Fig. 4. WLAN process model.

4.2 Results

In this section, we evaluate the performance of the proposed scheme using the OPNET simulator. The network is composed of a AP and several stations, and the number of stations is varied to evaluate the performance of the scheme comparing with the legacy protocol. We select the number of stations as 60,80,100,120 and 140, and then create network work environment for them, simulate these projects. We compare these projects with the results of the simulation. All stations send or receive packets periodically. More details of the parameters are shown in the Table. 1.

Table 1. Simulation parameters

Physical Characteristics	OFDM(802.11a)
Data Rates(bps)	2.6Mbps
Channel setting	Channel 1
Transmit power(W)	0.05

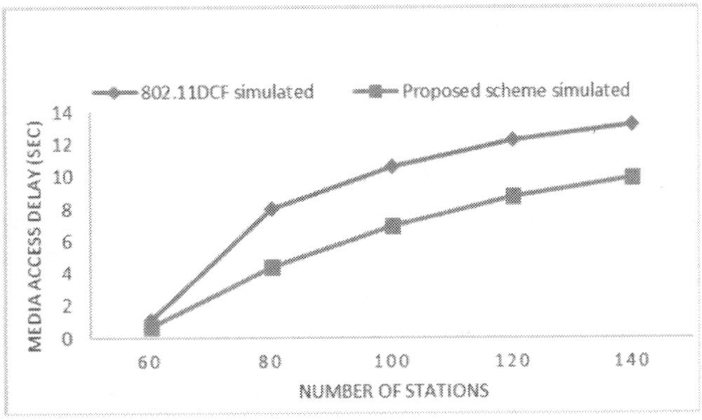

Fig. 5. Media access delay (sec).

Figure 5 describes the obtained media access delay as varying the number of stations under the legacy scheme as well as the proposed scheme. We can find that when the number of stations increases, the media access delay increases gradually, but the proposed scheme significantly reduces the media access delay. It is because by applying an adaptive contention window size, proposed protocol can reduce the time consumed in backoff process, thus decrease channel access time.

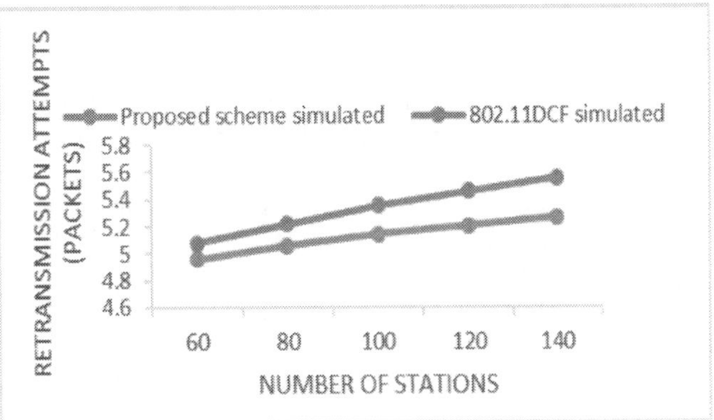

Fig. 6. Retransmission attempts (packets).

Figure 6 depicts the transformation of the retransmission attempts as varying the number of stations of the whole network. We can find that with the number of stations increasing, the network retransmission attempts grow up in both scheme, but in a lower level in proposed scheme. It is because by adapting the contention window size, our protocol can reduce the collision probability, thus bring in high performance.

5 Conclusion

Based on the fact that there are more contending stations at the start of a BI then in later period, we have proposed an adaptive contention window scheme to improve the performance of 802.11ah. Instead of utilizing a minimum contention window at the start of a BI and doubles it when collision occurs, we utilize an optimum contention window at the start. And sustains its value in case of collision, or else reduces it to be half of its previous value for success transmission. By conducting simulations, we confirmed that the proposed scheme can effectively reduce the media access delay and the network retransmission attempts, improving the overall performance of the network.

References

1. Xiaoying Lei,Seung Hyong Rhee. "Performance Improvement of Sub 1 GHz WLANs for Future IoT Environments",(2017).
2. BiKaichun, Xia Wan Li, Li Weina. "Foreign networking perspective. Electronics Industry Press",(2014).
3. Bel A. Adame T. Bellalta B. Barcelo J. Gonzalez J., and Oliver M "CAS-based channel access protocol for IEEE 802.11ah WLANs", European Wireless 2014, 20th European Wireless Conference, (2014).
4. J.-O Seo, C. Nam, S.-G. Yoon, and S. Bah"Group-based contention in IEEE 802.11ah networks, "IEEE, (2014);
5. Ji B., Song K., H u Y., and Chen H., "Cooperative Transmission Mechanisms in Next Generation WiFi: IEEE 802.11ac," International Journal of Distributed Sensor Networks, vol. **2014**, (2014).
6. Aust S., Prasad R.V., and Niemegeers I.G., "IEEE 802.11ah: Advantages in standards and further challenges for sub 1 GHz Wi-Fi," In Proceedings of IEEE International Conference on Communications (ICC), IEEE, June (2012).
7. Khorov E., Lyakhov A., Krotov A. and Guschin A., "A survey on IEEE 802.11ah: An enabling networking technology for smart cities," Computer Communications, vol. **11**, pp.53-69,(2015).
8. Hazmi A., Rinne J., and Valkama M., "Feasibility study of IEEE 802.11 ah radio technology for IoT and M2M use cases," In Globecom Workshops (GC Wkshps), IEEE, (2012).
9. Bianchi G., "Performance analysis of the IEEE 802.11 distributed coordination function," IEEE Journal on Selected Areas in Communications, vol.**18**, no.3, pp. **535-547**, (2000)
10. J. Choi, J. Yoo, S. Choi, and C. Kim, "EBA: An enhancement of the IEEE 802.11 DCF via distributed reservation," IEEE Trans. Mobile Comput., vol. **4**, pp. 378–390, (2005).
11. Y. He, J. Sun, X. Ma, AV. Vasilakos, R. Yuan, W. Gong, "Semi-random backoff: towards resource reservation for channel access in wireless LANs," IEEE/ACM Trans. Netw. (TON), vol.21, no.**1**, pp.204-217,(2013).
12. Choi, J., Yoo, J., Choi, S., & Kim, C. EBA: An enhancement of the IEEE 802.11 DCF via distributed reservation. IEEE Transactions on Mobile Computing, 4, **378–390**, (2005).
13. P.V. Krishna, S. Misra, M.S. Obaidat, V. Saritha, "Virtual backoff algorithm: An enhancement to 802.11 medium-access control to improve the performance of wireless networks," IEEE Trans. On Vehicular Tech., vol.59, no. **3**, pp.1068-1075,(2010).
14. Xiaoying Lei Yangzhou, ChinaSeung Hyong Rhee"Design of a Collision-free Backoff Method to Improve the IEEE 802.11 DCF ",(2016).

Key Technologies in Massive MIMO

Qiang Hu[1,·], *Meixiang* Zhang[1], and *Renzheng* Gao[1]

[1]College of Information Enginnering Yangzhou University, Yangzhou 225127, China

Abstract. The explosive growth of wireless data traffic in the future fifth generation mobile communication system (5G) has led researchers to develop new disruptive technologies. As an extension of traditional MIMO technology, massive MIMO can greatly improve the throughput rate and energy efficiency, and can effectively improve the link reliability and data transmission rate, which is an important research direction of 5G wireless communication. Massive MIMO technology is nearly three years to get a new technology of rapid development and it through a lot of increasing the number of antenna communication, using very duplex communication mode, make the system spectrum efficiency to an unprecedented height.

1 Introduction

In recent years, the growth of mobile data traffic has been increasing rapidly and is expected to reach 200 to 1,000 times by 2020. At the same time, with the increasing energy consumption of the communication system, reducing the energy consumption of the system has gradually become one of the important goals of mobile communication development. The fourth generation mobile communication system (4G) is hard to meet people on the spectrum efficiency and power efficiency of higher demand, the future of the fifth generation mobile communication system (5G) need to be in network architecture, network protocols and new breakthrough in wireless transmission technology, etc, in order to achieve higher spectral efficiency and green dual goals of wireless communication [1][2].

Multiple-input multiple-output (MIMO), also known as the multiple antenna technology, through the communication link of sending and receiving set up multiple antennas at both ends and make full use of space resources, can provide diversity gain in order to enhance the system reliability, provide multiplexing gain in order to increase the frequency spectrum of the system efficiency, provide array gain in order to improve the power efficiency of the system, and in the past 20 years has been one of the mainstream technology in the field of wireless communications. Currently, MIMO technology has been adopted by The 3rd Generation Partnership Project (3GPP), 3GPP's LTE/LTE-Advanced and The Institute of Electrical and Electronics Engineers's WiMAX and other 4G standards [3]. However, the existing 4G system base stations have fewer antennas (generally no more than 8), and MIMO performance gains are severely limited.

In response to the lack of traditional MIMO technology, Marzetta of bell laboratories in the US proposed the concept of massive MIMO in 2010 [4]. In a massive MIMO system,

· Corresponding author: huqiang1210hq@163.com

the base station is configured with tens to hundreds of antennas, which is an order of magnitude larger than that of the traditional MIMO system. The base station makes full use of the space freedom of the system and serves a number of users at the same time. Study found that when a village on the number of base station antenna becomes infinite, different user channel will tend to be orthogonal, additive white gaussian noise and small scale fading, all negative effects can be neglected, only limited to single user throughput is the same in the other community pilot sequences of interference users, system throughput than traditional MIMO system more than one order of magnitude [5][6]. The evolution of traditional MIMO to massive MIMO is a process from quantitative to qualitative change. Due to the large number of base station antenna MIMO and air separation users than traditional MIMO is orders of magnitude increases, both in the wireless communication on the basic principles and specific methods had different both in common, it provides researchers with contains many high research value of "gold mining and metallurgy" [7]. In recent years, the basic theory of massive MIMO, channel measurement and modeling, channel information acquisition, wireless transmission, experiment and testing have yielded fruitful results.

The structure of this paper is as follows: the second section analyzes the MIMO technology standardization process in detail, and the third section analyzes the technical advantages of massive MIMO and the main application scenarios compared with the traditional MIMO technology. The fourth and fifth sections are introduced from the point of view of channel measurement and channel modeling, and the channel estimation techniques for massive MIMO systems are analyzed in detail. Then precoding technology and signal detection technology are introduced. The eighth section illustrates the technical challenges faced by massive MIMO technology today. At the end of this paper, the summary of this paper is made.

2 Traditional MIMO technology

MIMO technology was first established in 1908 by Marconi, it by the sender and the receiver are equipped with multiple antennas to improve the capacity of communication system, system data transmission rate and transmission reliability. MIMO technology is one of the key technologies of the third generation mobile communication system (3G) and 4G communication systems.

2.1 Single user MIMO technology

The earliest point to point MIMO communication transmission technology, that is, single user MIMO (SU-MIMO), SU-MIMO using multiple antennas at both the transmitter and receiver to carry out wireless communication. In the actual system, if the multiple lines between the transmitter or the receiver are not related to each other, the distance between the adjacent antennas must be greater than the carrier wavelength. For handheld mobile terminals, physical size is limited, placing multiple antennas and uncorrelated antennas is very difficult, which limits the actual gain of SU-MIMO system. The basic model of SU-MIMO is shown in Figure 1.

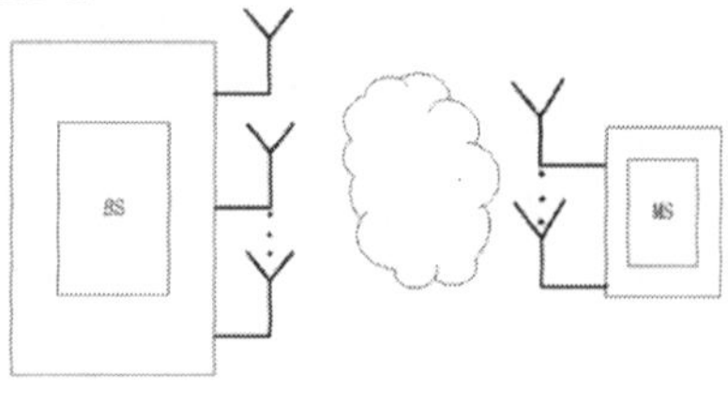

Fig. 1. The basic model of SU-MIMO.

2.2 Multiple user MIMO technology

The actual wireless communication system tends to be a base station (BS) communication with multiple mobile terminals (MS), so a multiple user MIMO (MU-MIMO) appears [8]. In more community MU-MIMO case, inside the village interference can be through the night, frequency division and reduce or eliminate the code classification and simple technology, but the interference between zones must adopt some more complex technology to reduce or eliminate, such as using Maximum Likelihood Multi User Detection(MLMUD) in the uplink or in the downlink using Dirty Paper Coding (DPC) technology. Inter cell interference leads to bottlenecks in MU-MIMO and cooperative MU-MIMO that limit spectrum and power efficiency enhancement. The basic model of MU-MIMO is shown in Figure 2.

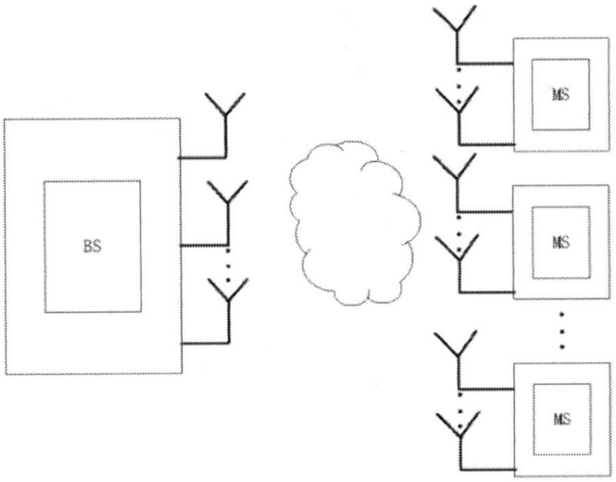

Fig. 2. The basic model of MU-MIMO

2.3 Standardization of MIMO Technology

The MIMO technology standardization process in LTE/LTE-A is shown in Table 1.

Table 1. MIMO technology standardization process.

Standard	MIMO Technology	Characteristic
Rel-8	Transmit diversity Space-division multiplexing Beamforming MU-MIMO	Supports up to 4 layers of transmission only support single-layer transmission up to two rank1Ue
Rel-9	Dual stream beamforming	SU / MU flexible switch up to 4 data streams(Up to 2 layers per UE)using non-codebook transmission support opportunity channel reciprocity feedback
Rel-10	High-order MIMO	Supports up to 8 layers of transmission High Precision Feedback Based on Two Level Multi - granularity Codebook
	Uplink MIMO	Supports up to 4 layers of transmission
Rel-11 Rel-12 Rel-13	CoMP CoMP/3DMIMO 3D MIMO	Multi-cell support for collaborative MIMO Multi-cell collaborative MIMO / 3D Expand to three-dimensional (3D) antenna array

3 Massive MIMO technology

In 2010, the Bell laboratory scientist Marzetta proposed the concept of massive MIMO in the multi-cell and Time Division Duplexing (TDD) scenarios, thus discovering some different features of the single cell and the limited number of antennas [4]. Massive MIMO technology refers to the large number of antennas deployed by the base station, usually one hundred or hundreds of antennas [9], which is increased by several orders of magnitude over the existing communication system. More than one user is served at the same time frequency resource, and the mobile terminal generally uses a single antenna reception [10]. The basic model of massive MIMO is shown in Figure 3.

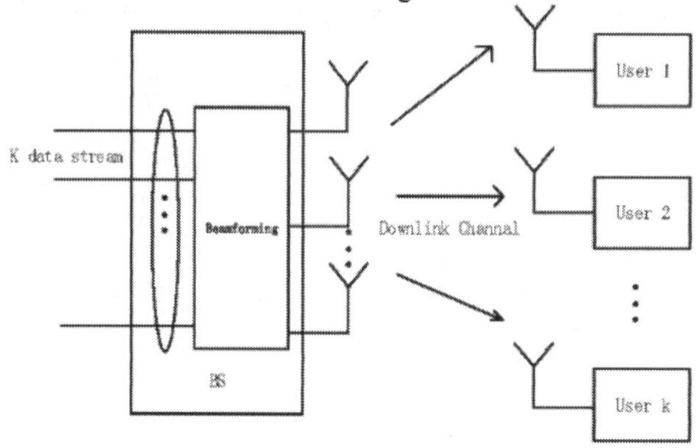

Fig. 3. The basic model of massive MIMO.

3.1 Technical advantages of massive MIMO

The main advantages of massive MIMO technology are as follows:
1) The power of the antenna is very low: Under ideal conditions, the transmitting power of each antenna is inversely proportional to the number of antennas, and under certain conditions of transmitting signal-to-noise ratio (SNR), the total emission power is also inversely proportional to the number of antennas. Therefore, the emission power required for each antenna is inversely proportional to the square of the number of antennas. This can effectively reduce the power consumed in massive MIMO applications.
2) Channel "hardening": The number antennas tends to infinity, the channel matrix of random matrix theory may be used for analysis of channel matrix singular value would be known gradually distribution, and channel vector will tend to be orthogonal, the simplest signal processing method is optimal.
3) The effects of thermal noise and small scale decline are eliminated: Using linear signal processing method, the thermal noise and small scale fading effect the performance of the system increases with the decrease in the number of antennas, and the effect of thermal noise and small scale fading are negligible in comparison with interference between zones.
4) Spatial resolution enhancement: In massive MIMO systems, with the increase of base station antennas, beamforming can transmit the transmitted signals to one point of the space, that is, the base station can accurately distinguish each user, thus improving the spatial resolution [11].

3.2 Massive MIMO comparison with traditional MIMO performance

In 3GPP, MIMO technology is generally evolving along SU-MIMO, MU-MIMO to network MIMO development. Compared with the traditional MIMO technology, the performance of massive MIMO technology is reflected in many aspects. Table 2 gives the performance comparison between traditional MIMO and massive MIMO.

Table 2. Traditional MIMO and massive MIMO performance comparison

Technical content	Traditional MIMO	Massive MIMO
The number of antennas	≤8	≤100
Channel angle value	uncertain	As the matrix field grows to form a deterministic function
Channel matrix	Low demand	High demand
Channel capacity	Low	High
Diversity gain	Low	High
Technical content	Traditional MIMO	Massive MIMO
Link stability	Low	High
To resist noise	Low	High
Array resolution	Low	High
Antenna correlation	Low	High
Coupling	Low	High
SER	High	Low
Pilot pollution	no	yes

3.3 Massive MIMO application scenarios

The application scene of the massive multi-antenna MIMO technology in the fifth generation mobile communication system is shown in Figure 4. The two cell of macro cell and micro cell coexist in the application scenario of 5G massive antenna array. The network is mainly divided into two types: isomorphism and heterogeneous network, and scenes are divided into indoor scenes and outdoor scenes. According to the test related literature, about seventy percent of the mobile communication system on the land is from indoor. Therefore, massive MIMO channels can be divided into micro cell base stations, indoor or outdoor users, macro cell base stations for indoor or outdoor users. At the same time, the micro cell can be used as the relay base station to transmit information, and the channel can be divided into the macro cell base station and the micro cell base station. The number of antennas in the base station can be increased infinitely, and the number of mobile users in the cell can also be increased [12].

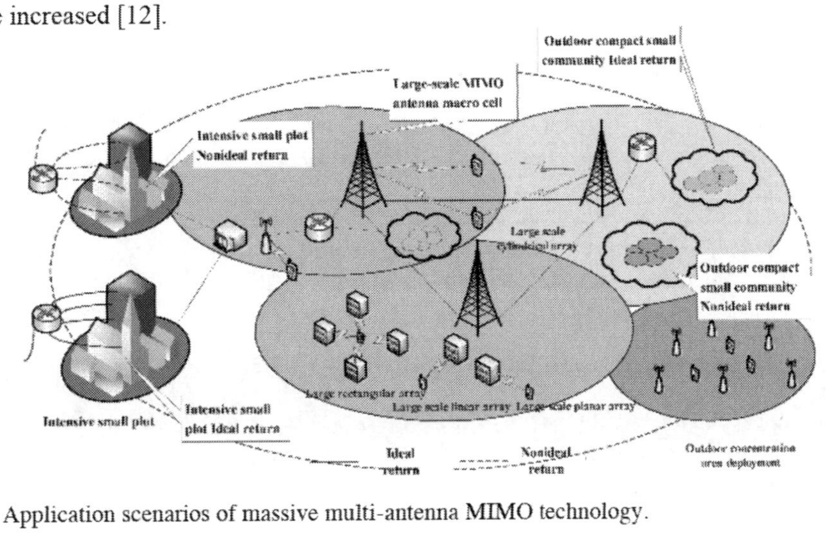

Fig. 4. Application scenarios of massive multi-antenna MIMO technology.

4 Measurement and modeling of massive MIMO channels

When the wireless transmission conditions are ideal, the channel vectors of the transmitter and receiver are gradually orthogonal due to the increase of the large number of MIMO system antennas. The following main research and analysis of massive MIMO channel measurement and modeling.

4.1 Measurement of massive MIMO channel

Through the channel measurement in the actual wireless communication environment, the theoretical channel model of the massive MIMO system can be effectively verified. The performance of the whole communication system is improved by measuring the actual channel. And the perfect result analyzer provides an effective and intuitive tool for network performance analysis.

1) The distributed MIMO channel is measured under 2.6GHZ microcellular conditions : In order to study the crosscorrelation characteristics of large-scale fading of distributed MIMO consisting of four base stations and a mobile station between different base station links, the channel in 2.6GHZ microcell environment has been measured in the previous literature [6]. In these four base stations, three base stations have deployed four groups of highly polarized antenna units. Another base station has deployed only one antenna unit. The mobile station has deployed a cylindrical uniform array consisting of 64 groups of dual polarized antenna units. By using the above measurement method, we can get the large scale channel fading at different locations by analyzing the large-scale fading and cross-correlation characteristics between different base station links [13].

2) Measurement method of unit 128 linear array: The literature[7]considers26 line-of-sight communication users, 10 non-line-of-sight communication users, the system working in 2.6HZ, and the base station equipped with 128 unit linear arrays. In addition, the antenna array length and the antenna spacing are set to 7.3m and half wavelengths respectively. In this paper, the massive MIMO channel is studied in the above scenario, and the Rciean K factor, the received power value of the array, the antenna correlation and the eigenvalue distribution are analyzed. The results show that due to the presence of some invisible scattering and the variation of the scattering power value, the propagation channel of large antenna arrays can not be regarded as a generalized stationary process. However, near-field effect and non-stationarity on array help to eliminate the correlation among users, thus providing a good, stable and low interference channel condition.

4.2 Massive MIMO channel modeling

Because of the rapid development of 5G technology, massive MIMO channel modeling has shown some new features. For example, spherical waves need to be replaced by a plane wave at the base station terminal large array antenna deployment, and the channel energy is concentrated in a limited space [14]. The channel is no longer independent and distributed. With the ever-increasing array of base station antennas, only different antenna units can see different scatterers and characterize the decline with non-static characteristics.

5 Channel status information acquisition technology

Bell laboratory, put forward the massive transmission scheme of MIMO system TDD mode, namely in the number of users equipped with single antenna is far less than the number of base station antenna assumptions, by receiving pilot signal to the target base station, according to the uplink channel estimation value of the CSI, reciprocity, TDD using TDD system has link with uplink CSI conjugate transpose down link of CSI. To transmission of uplink signal detection and descending precoding, the number of users in the village gains momentum, the pilot channel estimation cost will increase, especially in the high-speed mobile communications, pilot overhead will occupy most of the time and frequency resource. Therefore, it is of great practical value to study the massive MIMO CSI technology when TDD transmission mode pilot frequency is limited. Compared to Frequency Division Duplexing (FDD) mode, TDD mode can provide more ideal methods for obtaining CSI [15].

6 Massive MIMO precoding technology

Studies have shown that massive MIMO precoding technology plays a critical role in the bottleneck of breaking down the system's downward capacity. Nowadays, in massive MIMO downlink transmission, the purpose of using a large number of transmitter signal processing technology is to transform the complexity of massive MIMO system from the terminal side to the base station side. At present, there are mainly linear and nonlinear precoding algorithms, which are composed of zero forcing precoding (ZF), matched filtering precoding (MF) and block diagonalization (BD). The nonlinearity includes DPC, auxiliary grid method, vector perturbation (VP) and so on.

6.1 Linear Precoding

The linear and non-linear precoding technique has made extensive research [16], makes the massive MIMO precoding technology can reduce the system performance is affected by the pilot pollution, the following typical linear precoding algorithm will be introduced.

1) ZF precoding: In the literature [10], ZF precoding adopts the channel parameters replaced by pseudo inverse matrix [17]. In the literature [11], when meet the ratio of base station antenna number M and the terminal number K is constant, by increasing M and K at the same time, the matrix can be trace $\{(G^H G)^{-1}\}$converges to $1/(\propto -1)$ in which A^Hrepresent the Hermite matrix A conjugate transpose.

2) MF precoding: The inverse calculation of KxK dimension matrix in ZF precoding will increase the complexity of the algorithm. In the massive MIMO, $(G^H G)/M$ gradually approach the identity matrix, and by simplifying the matrix to solve the inverse operation, the performance of the ZF precoding tends to MF precoding performance. With the expansion of the antenna array, the MF precoding matrix will be infinitely close to ZF.

3) MMSE Precoding: In the multi-cell massive MIMO system, the assignment problem of the training sequence should be considered when the pre coding scheme is designed. The minimum mean squareerror estimation precoding (MMSE) scheme proposed in the literature [12] can reduce the pollution of pilots. Compared with the single cell scenario, the MMSE precoding matrix A_l^{opt} is obtained from the optimal solution of the objective function. In this paper, the target function is set up mainly by the mean square interference between the signal both received by the user in the same community and the user in the cross cell.

6.2 Nonlinear Precoding

Nonlinear precoding is by VP, DPC and auxiliary network method, etc, in the cell in the M and K is not especially large, non-linear precoding can show some advantages. In literature [15], the expression of SNR approximation in the VP of complete CSI is mentioned.

7 Massive MIMO system signal detection algorithm

The station will be time-frequency resources among different users, to a large number of users to provide services in massive MIMO system in multi-cell multi-user terminal in the area of the transmitted signal is sent to the base station at the same time, the base station can by the spatial signature of the uplink signal received for testing.

7.1 Linear detection

When the base station is equipped with a large antenna array, if we can satisfy the condition of low SNR, the performance of the MRC receiver can achieve optimal linear receiver (OLR) performance. However, when the SNR is below OLR, the performance of OLR will be optimized compared with the typical MMSE receiver system when the interference is relatively large.

7.2 Nonlinear detection

1) Algorithm based on tree structure (TB): Sphere decoding (SD) is a typical nonlinear detection algorithm, SD is a maximal likelihood (ML) decoder [18]. SD algorithm shortcoming is only considering the specific radius point, in order to find any signaling point, to increase the radius, the existing of low complexity of TB in only some of the most valuable nodes are added can effectively reduce the complexity of the search.

2) Random Step (RS) method: The principle of this algorithm is: select an initial vector, evaluate its peripheral vector N_{Neigh} needs MSE as the condition, and select MSE as the minimum vector, repeat the above procedure N_{iter}.

8 The technical challenges of massive MIMO

Massive MIMO technology is one of the most promising technologies in mobile communication. However, from the perspective of system design and engineering implementation, there are still many key technical problems that need to be solved effectively.

8.1 Channel model

All wireless communication systems need to specify a corresponding system model to be used as a basis for performance evaluation and comparison. Considering that the array aperture of the massive MIMO is limited, the traditional linear array is no longer applicable and may need to be extended to the antenna array in three-dimensional space. There are few theoretical modeling and practical modeling of massive MIMO channels, and there is no widely accepted channel model.

8.2 Channel information accuracy and feedback overhead

Massive MIMO antennas require high precision CSI, and channel estimation accuracy, delay, and huge feedback overhead and processing will be the key factors to gain a better gain. The changing speed of the channel, the complexity of the coverage environment, the interference intensity of the cellular signal and the speed of the feedback information are also the key factors that affect the effect and successful deployment of massive MIMO.

8.3 Control broadcast channel design and algorithmic stability

Although there has been a great deal of research on massive MIMO, it has not enough practical experience in the joint design with control broadcast channel and the stability of each algorithm in the actual complex environment. Therefore, it is inevitable for a certain time scale deployment and running in period.

8.4 Resource scheduling

In order to improve the capacity of the system, in the massive MIMO transmission, it is necessary to pair the antenna with the user to form a virtual MIMO channel. This process consists of grouping between users and the selection of antennas at the base station. At the same time, the allocation of spectrum resources needs to be considered when the number of users is relatively large.

8.5 Active integrated antenna

Due to the need of beamforming, the antenna design needs to combine the active circuit with the antenna to form a highly integrated active antenna system. It challenges the structure, size, weight, heat dissipation, cascade and maintenance of the antenna system. Especially in the aspect of antenna sharing, massive MIMO cannot share antennas with 2G, 3G and existing systems. Under the increasingly tense antenna resources, there is a certain risk that the antenna form can be successfully commercialized.

9 Conclusion

Massive MIMO technology is considered to be a key technology in the future 5G. It has a significant effect on the channel capacity, energy efficiency and spectrum efficiency of wireless communication systems. This paper analyzes the standardization process of MIMO technology in detail, and the performance advantages of massive MIMO compared with traditional MIMO. On this basis, we analyzed and compared the application scenarios, channel measurement and channel modeling of massive MIMO, and analyzed the channel estimation technology, precoding technology and signal detection technology of massive MIMO system. In the future, due to the higher requirements of massive MIMO on hardware complexity, the presence of pilot pollution limits the improvement of system performance, and there are still many challenges to be completed.

References

1. CHIHLIN I,ROWELL C,HAN S F., "Toward green and soft: a 5G perspective", IEEE Communication Magazine, vol. **52**, pp. 66-73,(2014).
2. HUH HCAIRE GPAPADOPOULOS H C, "massive mimo spectral efficiency with a Not-sołLarge Number of Antennas", IEEE Transactions on Wireless Communications, vol. **11**, no. 9, pp. 3266-3239, (2011).
3. S.-Y. Lien and K.-C. Chen, "Massive access management for QoS guarantees in 3GPP machine-to-machine communications," IEEE Commun.Lett., vol. **15**, no. 3, pp. 311-313,(2011).
4. FOSCHINI G., "Layered space-time architecture for wireless communication in a fading environment when using multi-element antennas," Bell Labs Technical Journal, vol. **8**, pp. 41-59, (1996).

5. D. Gesbert, M. Kountouris, R. W. Heath, C.-B. Chae, and T. Salzer,"Shifting the MIMO paradigm: From single-user to multiuser communications," IEEE Signal Process. Mag., vol. **24**, no. 5, pp. 36-46, (2007).
6. MARZETTA T L., "Noncooperative cellular wireless with unlimited numbers of base station antennas", IEEE Transactions on Wireless Communications, vol. **9**, no. 11, pp. 3590-3600, (2010).
7. TULINO A MVERDU S, "Random matrix theory and wireless communications," Communications and Information Theory, vol. **1**, no. 1, pp. 1-182, (2004).
8. WEI H,WANG D M,ZHU H L,et al., "Mutual coupling calibration for multiuser massive MIMO systems," IEEE Journal on Selected Areas in Communications, vol. **15**, no. 1, pp. 1-1, (2015).
9. D. Gesbert et al., "Multi-cell MIMO cooperative networks: A new look at interference," IEEE J. Sel. Areas Commun., vol. **28**, no. 9, pp. 1380C1408,(Dec. 2010).
10. GAO XTUFVESSON FEDFORS O, "Massive MIMO channels- Measurements and models," Conference on SignalsSystems and Computers, pp. 280-284, (2013).
11. A. Paulraj, R. Nabar, and D. Gore, "Introduction to Space-Time Wireless Communications," Proc. of Cambridge Univ. Press, 2003, Cambridge, U.K,(2003).
12. WANG Dongming,ZHANG Yu,WEI Hao, "An overview of transmission theory and techniques of large-scale antenna systems for 5G wireless communications," Science China:Information Sciences, vol. **46**, no. 1,pp. 3-21, (2016).
13. VIEIRA J,MALKOWSKY S,NIEMAN K,et al., "A flexible 100-antenna testbed for massive MIMO," Proceedings of 2014 IEEE Globecom Workshop. Texas, USA:IEEE, pp. 287-293, (2014).
14. FADLALLAH Y,AISSA A,AMIS K,et al., "New iterative detector of MIMO transmission using sparse decomposition," IEEE Transactions on Vehicular Technology, vol. **68**, no. 8, pp. 3458-3464, (2014).
15. JOSE JASHIKHMIN AMARZE'ITA T Let a1, "Pilot contamination and precoding in multi-cell TDD systems", IEEE Transactions on Wireless Communications, vol. **10**, no. 8, pp. 2640-2651,(2011).
16. YU X,SHEN J C,ZHANG J,et al., "Alternating minimization algorithms for hybrid precoding in millimeter wave MIMO systems," JIEEE Journal of Selected Topics in Signal Processing, vol. **10**, no. 3, pp. 485-500, (2016).
17. LI HLEUNG V C M., "Low complexity zero-forcing beamforming for distributed massive MIMO systems in large public venues," Journal of Communications and Networks, vol. **15**, no. 4, pp. 370-382, (2013).
18. R. Wang and G. B. Giannakis, "Approaching MIMO channel capacity with soft detection based on hard sphere decoding," IEEE Trans. Commun.,vol. **54**, no. 4, pp. 587-590, (2006).

Reliability Assessment of the Wind-solar-battery Storage System Based on Optimized Configuration

Yuan Wang[1*], and *Haojie* Liu [2]

[1]Xi'an Aeronautical University, 710077 Xi'an, Shaanxi Province, China
[2]State power grid Baoji power supply company, 721004 Baoji, Shaanxi Province, China

Abstract. In order to analyze the impact of new energy power generation on the power grid system, the reliability evaluation of the wind-solar-battery storage system is carried out. Proposed to wind power, solar, thermal power, different sodium-sulfur battery storage combined optimal dispatch of scenery. The shortest variance of the net load and the maximum variance of the wind storage system are taken as the objective function. The short-term optimal scheduling model of the power grid is established based on the characteristics of the wind farm, the characteristics of the solar field and the electric field of the sodium flow battery. Multi-objective particle swarm optimization The algorithm solves the model and obtains the output power of wind, light, storage and fire under different new energy strategies. The reliability is evaluated by Monte-Carlo method. Taking the IEEE-30 node as an example, it is proved that the proposed model is reasonable and the new energy can improve the clean energy consumption ability and minimize the impact on the power grid under the optimal scheduling strategy.

1 Introduction

In recent years, wind and solar energy with their wide distribution, abundant resources, clean and renewable energy, have been widely used and developed. However, the counter-peak load regulation of wind power indirectly widen peak-valley difference of load, leading to thermal power depth peak shaving or shutdown[1-2]. The substantial, frequent fluctuations of solar power will have serious impact on the active balance of system, influencing active power economic dispatching, increasing the risk of frequency quality cross-border[3]. Therefore, the study of how to maximize the acceptance of wind power and solar power generation, while minimizing its impact on the system is of great importance.

Aiming at this problem, researches focus on energy storage system and hybrid systems consisting wind power plant and photovoltaic power plant, by controlling the charging and discharging of the energy storage system, the fluctuation of wind power and solar power generation is reduced. Literature [4] established a multi-objective energy storage

* Corresponding author: 578101618@qq.com

optimization configuration model based on the minimum cost, the best power matching and the smoothest output power. Literature [5] proposed micro-grid storage margin calculation method based on scene generation and reduction technology, battery charge and discharge optimization technology chord method. Grid system is complex and diverse, not just consider the energy storage system. Only when the energy storage system is operated in a complex power grid can we better reflect the impact of energy storage optimization on the power grid. Therefore, this paper simulates complex power grids based on recent loads, wind power and solar power generation forecast, and the energy storage impact is evaluated by reliability.

Based on daily load forecast, wind power and solar power generation output forecast, combined with Na/S battery storage system and TOU, a wind-solar-battery hybrid system which can declare next day output plan was proposed. The wind-solar-battery hybrid system maximum profit and minimum net load were set as objectives, considering the Na/S battery storage internal characteristics. A 96-period all-day optimal dispatch model was established. Multi-objective Particle Swarm Optimization (PSO) is used to solve the model. The output power of wind, light, storage and fire under different new energy strategies is obtained. And the reliability of the model is evaluated by Monte-Carlo method. the correctness and feasibility of model and algorithm were verified by an example.

2 Wind-solar-battery hybrid system dispatching process

2.1 Wind-solar-battery hybrid system operation mode

The wind-solar-battery hybrid system operation mode mainly including the following steps:
Step1: Power grid dispatching center, wind power plant and solar power plant will forecast the next day load output curve, as well as wind and solar power curve.
Step2: Wind-solar-battery hybrid system jointly considers TOU, reducing abandoned wind, abandoned light, punishment assessment and other factors, the improved ratio method is adopted to declare next day output plan to the dispatching center.
Step3: The dispatching center will arrange the output of regular power unit according to the declaration of wind-solar-battery hybrid system.

2.1 Batteries, wind power and solar power generation dispatching strategy

The real time predicted power of wind power and solar power is compared with declaration planning output.

(1) If the predicted power of wind power and solar power is smaller than declaration planning output, as shown in following formula:

$$P_p^*(t) + P_w^*(t) < L(t) \tag{1}$$

Then wind power and solar power are connected to power grid:

$$P_w(t) + P_p(t) = P_w^*(t) + P_p^*(t) \tag{2}$$

Wherein: $P_w(t)$ and $P_p(t)$ is wind power and solar power grid electricity at time t.

Battery power plant is discharging to meet the energy state and the maximum power constraints:

$$P_x(t) \in (0, P_{rate}) \tag{3}$$

$$P_x(t)\Delta t \le E_{bat}(t) - E_{bat.\min} \tag{4}$$

Wherein: $P_x(t)$ is dispatching output of battery power plant at time t, P_{rate} is the rated power of battery plant, $E_{bat}(t)$ is the energy state of battery plant at time t, $E_{bat.\min}$ is the minimum energy state of battery plant, meeting the following formula:

$$(1-\eta)L(t) \le P_w(t) + P_p(t) + P_x(t) \le (1+\eta)L(t) \tag{5}$$

Wherein: η is the deviation parameter, its value equals 10%.

(2) If the predicted power of wind power and solar power is larger than declaration planning output, as shown in following formula:

$$P_p^*(t) + P_w^*(t) \ge L(t) \tag{6}$$

Then wind power and solar power are connected to power grid:

$$P_w(t) + P_p(t) = L(t) \tag{7}$$

When the remaining electricity of wind power and solar power is smaller than the maximum charging power of battery plant, as shown in the following formula:

$$(P_w^*(t) + P_p^*(t)) - (P_w(t) + P_p(t)) < 1.2P_{rate} \tag{8}$$

The charging power of battery plant is:

$$P_X(t) \in (0, (P_w^*(t) + P_p^*(t)) - (P_w(t) + P_p(t))) \tag{9}$$

When the remaining electricity of wind power and solar power is larger than the maximum charging power of battery plant, as shown in the following formula:

$$(P_w^*(t) + P_p^*(t)) - (P_w(t) + P_p(t)) \ge 1.2P_{rate} \tag{10}$$

The charging power of battery plant is: $P_x(t) = 1.2P_{rate}$. Meeting the following formula is $P_x(t)\Delta t \le E_{bat.\max} - E_{bat}(t)$.

Wherein: $E_{bat.\max}$ is the maximum energy state of battery plant.

It has to be noticed that during load peak, when the wind and solar power generation predicted power is larger than the declared plan, wind power and solar power generation grid power can be increased within the deviation of planning declaration output, maximizing the use of wind power and solar power generation.

3 Wind-solar-battery hybrid optimal dispatching model

3.1 Objective function

The paper considers the revenue of electricity sale under the TOU, the punishment costs of declaration planning output deviation in wind-solar-battery hybrid system. The amount of abandoned wind and the amount of abandoned light and other factors is reduced, the maximum expected revenue under the constraints of the system is set as objective. In addition, the variance of net load may reflect the degree of flatness of wind-solar-battery hybrid output, the smaller of net load variance, the more flat net load curve, on the one hand, thermal power depth peak shaving or shutdown can be avoided, on the other hand, hydro-thermal frequent adjustment times can be reduced, therefore, the minimum net load variance is set another objective.

Objective 1: The maximum revenue of wind-solar-battery hybrid system

$$\max f_1 = \sum_{t=1}^{96} \frac{1}{M} [\rho_{pri.t}(P_w(t) + P_p(t) + P_x(t)) - \rho_{pen.t} \left| P_w(t) + P_p(t) + P_x(t) - L(t) \right| - \rho_{dro.t}(P_{dro.w}(t) + P_{dro.p}(t))] \tag{11}$$

Wherein: M is 1h the number of time units,this article is 4; $\rho_{pri.t}$, $\rho_{pen.t}$, $\rho_{dro.t}$ is respectively joint system sell electricity prices,deviating from the plan output punishment prices, abandoned wind power and abandoned solar power punishment prices at time t ; $P_{dro.w}(t)$, $P_{dro.p}(t)$ is abandoned wind power and abandoned solar power at time t .

Objective 2:The minimum net load variance

$$\min f_2 = \frac{1}{96} \sum_{t=1}^{96} (P_j(t) - P_{jt.av})^2 \tag{12}$$

Wherein: $P_j(t)$ is net load variance value at time t , $P_{jt.av}$ is net load variance average at time t .

Net load value $P_j(t)$ can be represented as at time t :

$$P_j(t) = L_S(t) - P_w(t) - P_p(t) - P_x(t) \tag{13}$$

The average of the net load is $P_{jt.av} = \frac{1}{96} \sum_{t=1}^{96} P_j(t)$

3.2 Constraint condition

The wind farm output constraint is $0 \le P_w(t) \le P_w^*(t)$;The solar field output constraint is $0 \le P_p(t) \le P_p^*(t)$.

3.2.1 Na/S battery electric field characteristics and constraints

Because the Na/s battery has high specific energy, adaptation of wide and has realized the advantages of the batch production, this article selects Na/S battery energy storage system as the research object. This article discharge $u_{disch}(t)$ and recharge $u_{ch}(t)$ to Na/S battery energy storage system is two kinds of running state.

$$u_{disch}(t), u_{ch}(t) \in \{0,1\} \tag{14}$$

Na/S battery through power converter can control the charging and discharging. When Na/S battery converter capacity is large enough, the instantaneous charging and discharging power of the sodium sulfur batteries can reach 1 ~ 5 times the rated power, but based on the internal temperature, its output has certain limitation, this limit is called pulse limit Na/S battery N_{pulse}, based on the relationship between sustainable battery discharge time T_{dur} and N_{pulse} [3] :

$$T_{dur}(t) = -3.4497N_{pulse}^3(t) + 21.5962N_{pulse}^2(t) - 45.7961N_{pulse}(t) + 34.7117 \quad (15)$$

Na/S battery energy storage E_{bat} within changing over time, E_{bat} expression is as follows:

When charging:

$$E_{bat}(t+1) = E_{bat}(t) + \frac{1}{M}P_x(t)\Delta t \bullet \eta_c \quad (16)$$

When discharging:

$$E_{bat}(t+1) = E_{bat}(t) - \frac{1}{M}P_x(t)\Delta t / \eta_f \quad (17)$$

Wherein: η_f, η_c is Na/S Battery discharge and charging efficiency.

According to the operation characteristics of Na/S battery energy storage unit, as they are in the Wind-Solar-Battery system to satisfy the constraint conditions are as follows:

A)For running state constraints

$$u_{disch}(t) + u_{ch}(t) = 1 \quad (18)$$

Two kinds of state of a Na/S battery storage system is mutually exclusive .

B) For pulse factor constraints

$$0.8 \le N_{pulse}(t) \le 1 \quad (19)$$

$$N_{pulse}(t) = N_{pulse}(t+1) \quad (20)$$

C) For the charging and discharging power constraints

$$0 \le P_x(t) \le N_{pulse}(t)P_{rate} \quad (21)$$

$$-1.2P_{rate} \le P_x(t) \le 0 \quad (22)$$

Wherein: P_{rate} is Na/S battery power rating, for maximum power Na/S battery charging, the charging power of the selected generally slightly greater than the rated power, 20% higher than the rated power of the numerical value.

D) Status of Na/S battery energy constraints

$$E_{bat\min} \le E_{bat}(t) \le E_{bat\max} \quad (23)$$

E) A scheduling cycle of Na/S battery charge and discharge frequency constraints

$$Y_{dis} + Z_{ch} \le N \quad (24)$$

Wherein: Y_{dis}, Z_{ch} is Na/S Battery discharge total conversion and charging conversion plant.

4 Wind-solar-battery hybrid optimal dispatching model solving

The particle swarm algorithm is adopted to solve multi-objective optimization problem, the conventional method is transferring multi-objectives problem into single objective problem, but the non-dominant characteristic of various objectives determines that multiple objectives can't simply linear weighted. The Pareto optimal and particle swarm algorithm are combined in the paper, the optimal individual and optimal global are obtained through Pareto optimal mechanism, the flight direction of particles can be guided, the optimal solution can be searched concurrently. The above method is introduced to solve the wind-solar-battery hybrid optimal dispatching model, and the specific flow chart is shown as follows:

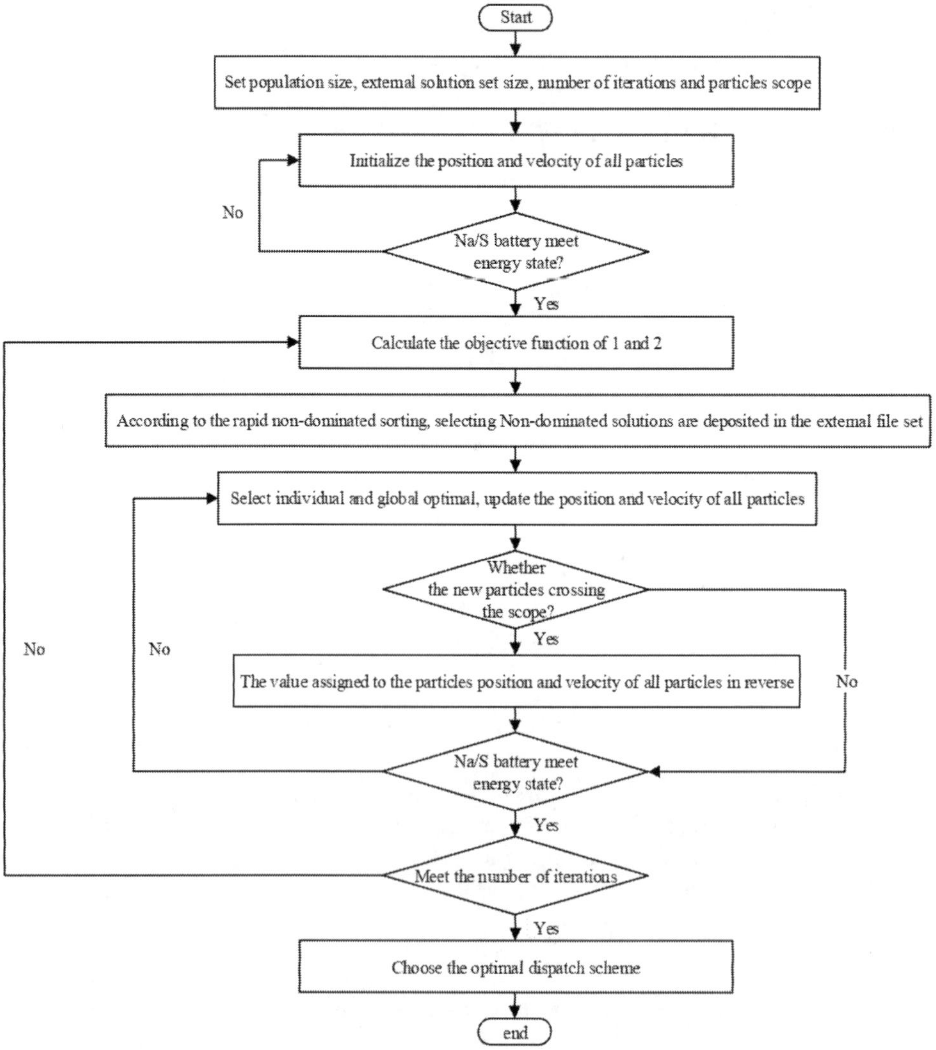

Fig. 1. The flow chart of Wind-Solar-Battery joint optimization scheduling model

5 Reliability assessment process

In this paper, non-sequential Monte Carlo method for system state selection.

This article uses the two state model. It is assumed that each component has only two states of failure and operation, and that the failure of the components is independent of each other. If the failure rate and repair rate of the components i are λ_i and μ_i, respectively, and the forcing-out rate of the components is $for_i = \frac{\lambda_i}{\lambda_i + \mu_i}$, then the status of the components is:

$$s_i = \begin{cases} 0 & (failure \quad state) \ r_i \le for_i \\ 1 & (normal \quad state) \ r_i > for_i \end{cases} \tag{25}$$

Where, r_i is the component i in the [0,1] interval evenly distributed random number.

Such a system state with d elements can be denoted as $s = (s_1, s_2, ..., s_i, ..., s_d)$.

Non-sequential Monte Carlo state of all components of the system after the election, the system may make a great change in the network topology, so the need for network topology analysis. In this paper, depth-first algorithm for network topology analysis to determine whether the system is unfolded, and then its power flow analysis, get the voltage of each node, the line active, reactive power value. Then cut the load calculation, the system reliability index calculation required data.

After the system state selection and state analysis, calculate the system reliability index.

(l) LOLP (Loss of load probability) is $LOLP = \frac{N_{fi}}{N_s}$, Where: N_{fi} said the number of power failures or nodes; said the number of samples.

(2) EPNS (Expected power of not supplied) is $EPNS = \left(\sum_{j=1}^{N_{fi}} P_{fij}\right) / N_{fi}$, Where: P_{fij} is the power failure power of node i in the jth sampling state of the system.

(3) EENS (Expected energy of not supplied) is $EENS = EPNS * t = \left(\sum_{j=1}^{N_{fi}} E_{fij}\right) / N_{fi}$, Where: E_{fij} is the node j in the system the first j sampling state of the power outage.

6 The result of example and analysis

6.1 Basic data and parameters

With IEEE-30 system simulation, the wind-solar-battery hybrid system and typical daily load predicted curve constructed system in a region in Northwest China was analyzed. Wherein: the installed capacity of wind power and solar is 150MW and 100MW respectively, the maximum discharge power of the Na/S battery energy storage system is 30MW, the rated power is 96MW • h, the initial energy state is 50%, the market price of electricity based on TOU is shown in Table 1, in order to reduce the deviation from the planning output, the output deviation punishment coefficient of the hybrid system is 1.5 times of electricity price, the punishment cost of abandoned wind and light is 0.05 yuan MW • h.

Table1. Market sale of electricity TOU

Period of time	**Time interval range**
Peak period 0.8yuan/ MW • h	11:00-15:00;19:00-21:00
Ordinary period 0.5yuan/ MW•h	8:00-10:00;16:00-18:00 ;22:00-23:00
Valley period 0.2 yuan/ MW • h	0:00-7:00

6.2 Result analysis of the wind-solar-battery storage system

When the battery is not added to power stations, the deviation curve of wind-solar-battery from planning output is shown in Figure2 (a), when the battery power station is added, the deviation curve of wind-solar-battery from planning output is shown in Figure2(b). Table 2 shows the comparative data before and after the battery power station is added.

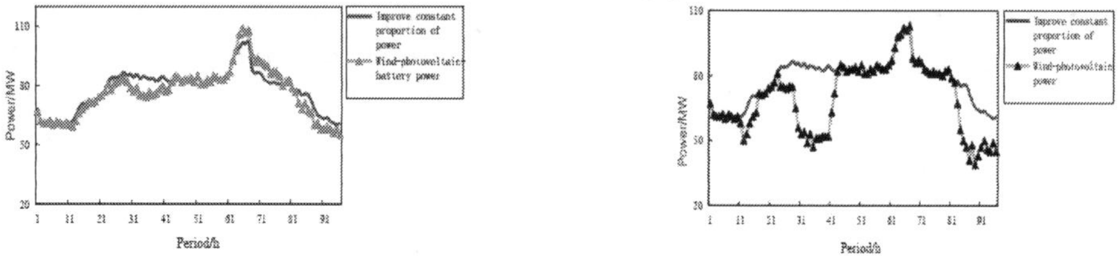

(a) (b)

Fig. 2 Join the deviating from the plan before and after the battery output curve

Table.2 Join the battery power station before and after the contrast data

Project	**Total revenue /10^4 yuan**	**Penalty cost/10^4 yuan**	**Total abandon energy of Wind-PV/MW.h**	**Relative to maximum offset/%**	**Net load variance**
Wind-PV	664.6	230.7	239	39.5	2493
Wind-PV-battery	796.4	83.4	52	6.2	1759

It can be concluded from Figure.2 and Table.2 that:

1) Before the battery power plant is added, the total revenue of wind-solar-battery is 6.646 million Yuan, and after the battery power plant is added, since the battery stores the wind power and solar power at low price, and feeds back to power grid at peak price, so the total revenue of wind-solar-battery has significantly increased, reaching 7.964 million Yuan.

2) Before the battery power plant is added, due to the uncontrollable output of wind-solar-battery, leading to the output curve of wind-solar-battery deviates significantly from the planning output curve, the punishment cost, maximum deviation, and the maximum relative deviation percentage is 2.307 million Yuan, 32MW, 39.5 % respectively. And after the battery power plant is added, the wind-solar-battery hybrid system becomes controllable, it can be found that the output power of the hybrid system is significantly consistent with the planning output curve, the punishment cost, the maximum deviation and the maximum relative deviation percentage has significantly reduced, which are 834 thousand Yuan, 5MW, 6.2% respectively. In addition, through rational control of the battery charge and discharge strategy, the wind power and solar power can be used to the maximum extent, the total amount of abandoned wind decreases from the original 239MW • h to 52MW • h.

3) After the battery power plant is added, wind-solar-battery hybrid system transfers into stable, adjustable power supply, obtaining smooth net load curves, the net load variance decreases from the original 2493 to 1759, thus ensuring the safe and stable operation of the system.

6.3 Reliability evaluation

Through the optimal system configuration obtained in Section 6.2, the amount of power generated by wind power, solar, energy storage and thermal power generation. This and the typical daily load curve quantity is brought into the IEEE-30 node system, and the reliability assessment is carried out to obtain the reliability index of the system.

Table.3 Reliability evaluation comparison

System reliability index	No new energy system	the wind-solar-system	the wind-solar-battery storage system
LOLP(10^{-2})	0.66390	0.66390	0.63233
EPNS(10^{-1})/MW	0.34491	0.34491	0.29881
EENS/(MW.h).a^{-1}	676.259	676.259	633.634

As can be seen from Table 3, the reliability of the power system without new energy is better. However, due to the random fluctuation of the scenery, the scenery becomes less accessible, the power shortage becomes larger and the reliability deteriorates after the scenery is connected to the system. The charge-discharge characteristics of the sodium flow battery, smooth access to the system after the net load curve, making the system reliability.

7 Conclusion

The paper combines wind power, solar power and battery power, through reasonable control of the battery charge and discharge strategy, the wind-solar-battery hybrid system turns into a stable and adjustable power supply. The constraint of Na/S battery storage system charge and discharge times and the deviation of wind-solar-battery hybrid system output from the planning power output constraint are considered in the paper. And the reliability of the model is evaluated. It can be concluded from the example that: wind-solar-battery hybrid system can stores surplus wind power and solar power during low load period and feeds back into peak load period lacking of electricity, the output power of the hybrid system is significantly consistent with the planning output curve, obtaining smooth net load curves, tracking the variation curve of load, improving the overall economic profit and system stability.According to the different new energy optimal allocation of the reliability of the power grid, to achieve the best reliability of the grid.

Acknowledgement: Supported by the Foundation of Xi'an Aeronautical University (2017KY1222).

References

1. Zhu Lingzhi, Chen Ning, Han Hualing. Wind power consumptive key problems and countermeasures analysis[J]. Automation of Electric Power Systems, **35(22)**: 29-34 (2011) .

2. Sheng Siqing, Sun Xiaoxia. An economic dispatching strategy of peak shifting by wind farm and pumped storage plant[J]. Power System Technology, **38 (9)**:2484-2489(2014).
3. Ding Ming, Wang Weisheng, Wang Xiuli, et al. A review of the effect of large-scale PV generation on power systems[J]. Proceedings of the CSEE, **34(1)**: 1-14(2014).
4. HU Xiaotong, LIU Tianqi, HE Chuan. Calculation method of storage capacity margin for standalone microgrid considering stochastic characteristics[J]. Electric Power Automation Equipment, **37(12)**: 80-85(2017).
5. TAN Xinguo, WANG Hui, ZHANG Li, et al. Multi-objective optimization of hybrid energy storage and assessment indices in microgrid[J]. Automation of Electrical Power Systems, **38(8)**: 7-14(2014).

An Improved Flooding Routing Protocol for Wireless Sensor Networks Based on Network-Coding

Churan Tang[1,*], and *Linghua* Zhang[2]

[1] Institute of Information Engineering, Chinese Academy of Sciences, Beijing, China
[2] Nanjing University of Posts and Telecommunications, Nanjing, China

Abstract. A central question in wireless sensor network research is how to reduce the consumption of the energy of the sensor nodes. Theoretically, the network coding technology proposed by Ahlswede *et al* (2000) can improve the network reliability and network throughput, increase the robustness and save energy. Based on the classic flooding routing protocol, the present study proposes a new flooding control protocol, i.e. NC-Flooding for wireless sensor networks. NC-Flooding protocol introduces five mechanisms to enhance the efficiency of wireless sensor networks. As shown by MATLAB simulation results, NC-Flooding protocol reduces the number of broadcasts of wireless sensor networks, increases the throughput of the network and increases the bandwidth utilization. We conclude that NC-Flooding protocol reduces data forwarding cost and node energy consumption and extends nodes' life cycle, thus increasing network utilization.

1 Introduction

In recent years, wireless sensor network research has been focusing on the problem of how to improve the node's energy consumption. Because the energy of the sensor node is limited, the key technology to extend the node's survival time lies in reducing the energy consumption of the node. Ahlswede *et al* proposed that the network coding (NC) technology has the potential to reduce the packet forwarding frequency of the node [1]. Since the energy of the node used for encoding computation is far less than the energy of the node sending packets, theoretically, the NC technology can reduce the node's energy loss. Thus, it is possible to enhance the routing protocol by applying network coding technology to the wireless sensor network.

It is generally agreed that the flooding protocol plays an important role in balancing the traffic distribution of the system [2]. Although the network coding technology brings a lot of research on wireless sensor networks[3], most of the research has focused on the LEACH, PEGASIS and DD protocols [4,5,6,7], and the research on flooding protocol is very rare. However, the flooding protocol is the basis of many routing protocols, since many parts of the above mentioned protocols are in the form of flooding protocols.

*Corresponding author: tangchuran@163.com

Therefore, the study of network coding for flooding protocols is of great significance to understanding protocols for the wireless sensor networks. The purpose of this study is to investigate whether the flooding protocol, when combined with NC, can reduce the number of packet forwarding and the energy loss of the sensor nodes, and whether it can increase the throughput of the network and thus extend the lifecycle of network nodes.

2 NC-flooding routing protocol design

2.1 NC-flooding protocol flow chart

We propose the following procedure for the working of NC-Flooding protocol.

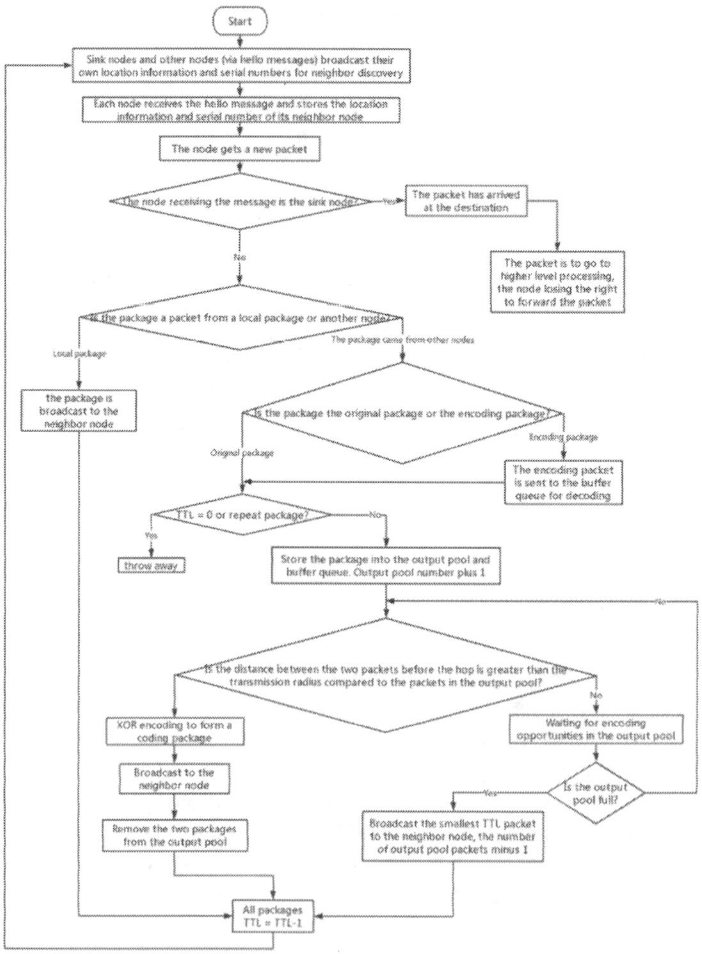

Fig.1. NC-Flooding protocol flow chart

2.2 NC-flooding protocol mechanisms

The NC-Flooding protocol introduces five mechanisms, as described below:

(1) active XOR coding mechanism

In order to increase the chances of network coding, a coding mechanism is used that makes active XOR encodes: when the intermediate node receives a packet, it does not broadcast the packet immediately, but waits for a period of time to actively seek coding chances until the output pool is full.

(2) preferentially broadcast the data packets generated by the local nodes.

This can take advantage of the short-term contact between nodes for packet transmission to improve transmission efficiency, and shorten the delay as much as possible.

(3) Each node stores the transmitted encoding packet for decoding

When the node needs to broadcast a packet out, the packet is removed from the output pool, but it is not immediately removed from the node cache. The node continues to store it in the buffer queue for decoding, so that in future the data package a $\oplus$ b can be decoded through a $\oplus$ (a $\oplus$ b) packet.

(4) discard duplicate packets

After the forwarding node receives a packet, the packet is judged as to whether it is a new packet. If it is not new, the node discards it and does not forward it. This, to some extent, eliminated the implosion phenomenon.

(5) nodes set up two kinds of storage space

Each node has two kinds of space for storage: output pool and buffer queue. The buffer queue follows the first-in first-out principle. If the buffer queue is full, the first packet is deleted and used for decoding.

3 NC-flooding protocol network simulations and analyses

3.1 Simulation Experiments and Performance Evaluations

The performances of the flooding protocol and NC-Flooding protocol in wireless sensor network communication are simulated by MATLAB platforms. The comparison between the two protocols is based on the remaining energy and the number of transmitted packets.

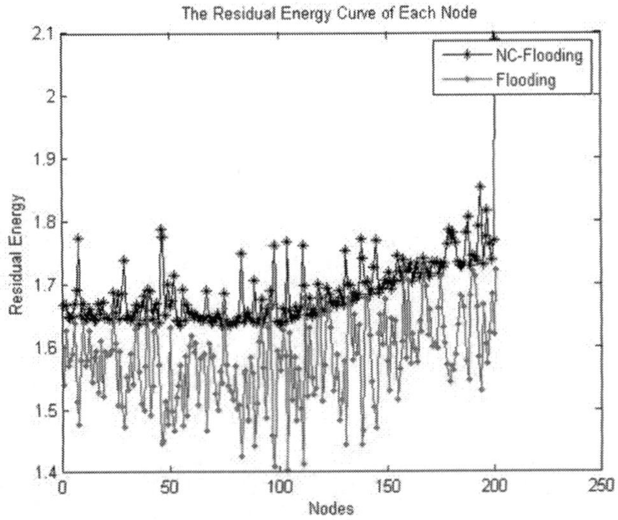

Fig. 2. Remaining energy in nodes (the number of nodes = 201, radius = 50)

Figure 2 shows the comparison of the remaining energy of 201 nodes using NC-Flooding and Flooding protocols. It can be seen that the residual energy of the NC-Flooding protocol is about 1.7 units, and the remaining energy of the Flooding protocol is about 1.55 units. The conclusion is that NC-Flooding protocol is more energy efficient than Flooding protocol, so that the lifetime of wireless sensor nodes in the network is extended in the case of NC-Flooding protocol.

3.2 Factors that affect network coding

The following three figures show the residual energy curves when the parameters vary.

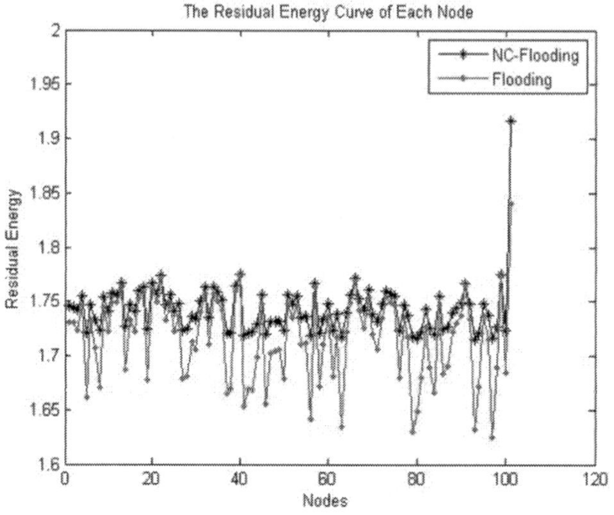

Fig. 3. Remaining energy in the node (the number of nodes = 101, radius = 45)

As can be seen from Figure 3, when the number of nodes = 101, transmission radius = 45, NC-Flooding saves about 0.05 measure more of energy than the Flooding protocol.

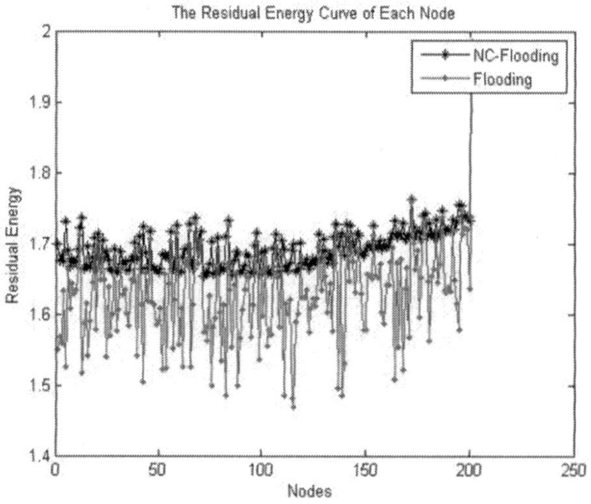

Fig. 4. Remaining energy in nodes (the number of nodes =201, radius = 45)

As can be seen from Figure 4, NC-Flooding saves about 0.1 measure more energy than the Flooding protocol when the number of nodes is 201 and the transmission radius is 45.

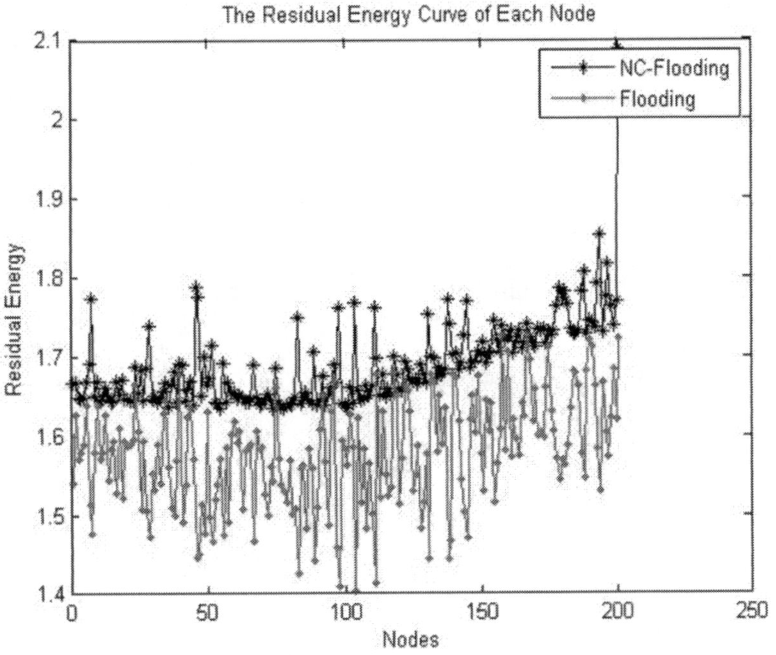

Fig. 5. Comparison of remaining energy in nodes (the number of nodes = 201, transmission radius = 50)

Again as can be seen from Figure 5, when the number of nodes =201, transmission radius = 50, NC-Flooding routing protocol is 0.15 measure more efficient than the Flooding routing protocol.

From the simulation results obtained we find that in terms of energy consumption, NC-Flooding protocol is better than the Flooding protocol. We also find that factors that affect network coding include the average density and transmission radius of wireless sensor nodes. The higher the average density and transmission radius of nodes in wireless sensor networks, the more opportunities for network coding, and the more advantages of network coding in saving network energy.

4. Discussions and conclusions

The key issue for wireless sensor network to solve is how to increase the network node's life cycle. In order to reduce the energy consumption of the nodes and prolong the service life of the nodes, we propose the NC-Flooding protocol and have made MATLAB simulations using NC-Flooding protocol to reduce the number of packets forwarded by nodes in the wireless sensor network. The simulations suggest that the network's communication efficiency is increased by the NC-Flooding protocol.

Thus, the NC-Flooding protocol, which is the combination of the network coding and the flooding protocol, has the potential to apply to various situations of wireless sensor networks. More efficient versions of the NC-Flooding protocol can be designed by considering the effects of relevant factors, including the specific flow of data structures and protocols used to cache packets, node information and residual energy at each node. It is believed that this approach to network coding will bring actual benefits to the research in wireless sensor networks.

The simulations we performed also show that there are some factors that affect the network coding. The main factors are the average density of wireless sensor nodes and transmission radius. The higher the average density and transmission radius of nodes in wireless sensor networks, the more opportunities for network coding, and the more advantages in saving network energy

In conclusion, this study has deepened the insight of the role of network coding in the routing protocols of wireless sensor networks. The originality of this study is that we apply the network coding technology to a common basic routing protocol: the Flooding routing protocol, and Ihas found the actual role of network coding in improving the performance of wireless sensor networks. The significance of the NC-Flooding protocol is that the flooding protocol is the basis of many planar routing protocols such as DD, SPIN and GEAR. Since the NC-Flooding protocol can reduce the amount of data sent over the network through network coding, other wireless sensor network routing protocols that contain the Flooding protocols can also improve the performance of the individual networks through network coding. The NC-Flooding protocol based on network coding can also be applied to these protocols.

References

1. R. Ahlswede, N. Cai, S.Y.R. Li, R.W. Yeung, Network information flow, J. IEEE Transactions on Information Theory. 46(2000) 1204-1216.
2. K. Ralf, M. Muriel, Beyond routing: An algebraic approach to network coding, J. IEEE INFOCOM. 1(2002) 122-130.
3. Y.N. Wu, P.A. Chou, S.Y. Kung, Minimum-energy multicast in mobile ad hoc networks using network coding, J. IEEE Trans. Communications 53(2005) 1906-1918.
4. C. Intanagonwiwat, R. Govindan, D. Estrin, J. Heidemann, Directed diffusion for wireless sensor networking, J. IEEE/ACM Transaction on Networking. 11(2003) 2-16.
5. N. Cai, R.W. Yeung, Network error correction, part I: Basic concepts and upper bounds, J. Communications in Information and Systems. 1(2006) 19-36.
6. Z. Liu, Z. Qiu, Ring based multi-hop clustering routing protocol for wireless sensor networks, J. Journal on Communications. 29(2008) 105-113.
7. D. Culler, D. Estrin, M. Srivastava, Introduction: Overview of sensor networks, J. IEEE Computer Society. 37(2004) 41-49.
8. X.G. Qiao, Y. Chen, A control algorithm based on double cluster-head for heterogeneous wireless sensor network, in 2nd, International Conference on Industrial and Information Systems, (2010) 541-544.

Mobile Application Identification based on Hidden Markov Model

Xinyan Yang[1,*], *Yunhui* Yi[1], *Xinguang* Xiao[1], and *Yanhong* Meng[1]

[1]State Key Laboratory of Integrated Services Networks, Xidian University, Xi'an, China

Abstract. With the increasing number of mobile applications, there has more challenging network management tasks to resolve. Users also face security issues of the mobile Internet application when enjoying the mobile network resources. Identifying applications that correspond to network traffic can help network operators effectively perform network management. The existing mobile application recognition technology presents new challenges in extensibility and applications with encryption protocols. For the existing mobile application recognition technology, there are two problems, they can not recognize the application which using the encryption protocol and their scalability is poor. In this paper, a mobile application identification method based on Hidden Markov Model(HMM) is proposed to extract the defined statistical characteristics from different network flows generated when each application starting. According to the time information of different network flows to get the corresponding time series, and then for each application to be identified separately to establish the corresponding HMM model. Then, we use 10 common applications to test the method proposed in this paper. The test results show that the mobile application recognition method proposed in this paper has a high accuracy and good generalization ability.

1 Introduction

Smart phones and other mobile devices has become an indispensable part of people's lives. Researches from the firm IDC statistics [1] and StatCounter [2] has proved that internet traffic of the mobile device has exceeded the traditional desktop device. The explosive growth of the number of mobile application has brought great challenge to network management, such as, security issues.

Mobile application identification has vital significance to network security and network management. Traditional applications (traffic) identification technology can be divided into three categories: port based methods, payloads based methods and statistical features based methods. Mobile application identification needs to consider applications number, layer protocol, Content Delivery Network, cloud service and so on. But for now the method have poor scalability and the speed of application identification can be improved.

Traditional traffic identification can be divided into two categories: payload features based and statistical features based. As most of the mobile applications using HTTP

* Corresponding author: 2523242271@qq.com

protocol for network communication, application-layer header fields are commonly used as payload features. Wei et al. [3] and Xu et al. [4] proposed method to analyze and identify Android application. However, this method is valid only for a limited application. [5~7] proposed methods extracts different traffic feature to analyze and identify the Android applications. Although these recognition methods for mobile applications can obtain better accuracy, encryption protocol communication mode and violation of user privacy are problems faced by these methods. So Wang et al. [8] studied more detailed identification of the different mobile applications and use Random Forests to train classifier. Similarly, Conti et al. [9, 11] proposed a system framework to infer which particular actions are executed in application on user's device, and gain 95% accuracy. Park et al. [10, 12] used the same method with Conti to identify online chat mobile application. They extract behavioral characteristic based on data packets and combined three kind of classification algorithms: *Naive Bayes*, *AdaBoost* and *Decision Tree* to build classifier.

Saltaformaggio et al. [13] proposed NetScope, identifying fine-grained user activity of different mobile applications, but the accuracy is only 78.04%. Fu et al. [14] focused on identifying various use types of instant messaging applications. They use *Hierarchical Clustering* and threshold heuristic methods to divide network traffic into session and dialogs type what they define. Then *Random Forests* is used to train classifier. As a result, the accuracy of classifier is 95%. Alan et al. [15] tries to use TCP header information, data packet length feature and three existing methods and gain 88% accuracy. Taylor et al. [16] focused on the identification of encrypted traffic, they use *SVM* and *Random Forests* to build classification model respectively with 18 statistical features and gain 98% accuracy.

Based on the existing research technology, this paper proposes a mobile application traffic identification based on hidden Markov model for the shortcomings of existing research. Our approach can handle encrypted network traffic by extracting the statistical characteristics of multiple network traffic. We combine the statistical and temporal characteristics of multiple network flows and establish the corresponding models for different mobile applications. When identifying new applications, we only need to write a new model for the new application.

The remainder of this paper is organized as follows. In the second part we discuss the definition of HMM. In the third part, we elaborate on the application identification process presented in this paper. In the fourth part, we present the performance evaluation of our method. Finally, we give brief conclusions.

2 Hidden markov model

Hidden Markov Model (HMM) [17, 18] is one of the basic models in natural language processing, which has wide range usage. HMM is a probabilistic graphical model for time series data modeling, which is consist of a sequence of hidden states has the Markov property and cannot be observed, an observing sequence corresponding to hidden sequence.

A HMM model can be described by a five-tuples (Q, V, π, A, B) corresponds to the Markov model of network traffic. Collection of hidden states Q represents all the hidden state. Collection of observation states V corresponding to Q, every observation state has a certain probability with different hidden states. State transition probability matrix A represents transference between hidden states. The observation probability matrix B represents probabilities of every observed value corresponding to every hidden state. The initial state probability vector π represents initial probability distribution of the hidden state.

3 Application identification

3.1 Model training

Mobile application identification method presented in this paper is based on the modeling of network traffic that is generated when the application starts. A combination of statistical and temporal features of multi-network flows is used in this paper. We divide network traffic within time generated by application starts into one group. After statistical analysis of different applications' network traffic within 60s after applications starting, we choose to extract first 20 network flows according to the start time of network flow and then extract flow characteristic information from each of the network flow. In order to reduce the influence of network noise data of connection failures and other problems, we ignore the network flow that packet number less than 7, because theoretically speaking, the smallest complete TCP network stream includes TCP three-way handshake packets (3 packets), request packets, response packets and ACK packets. Then, three characteristics are calculated for each network flow, the average bytes of packet (BYTES_PER_PKG), the average bytes of the upstream packet (BYTES_PER_UP_PKG), and the average bytes of the down packet (BYTES_PER_DOWN_PKG).

Network traffic characteristics Difference for different applications leads to the different number of hidden states for the HMM model. In this paper, the number of hidden states is determined by clustering analysis of the network flow of the application. Hierarchical clustering is designed to build hierarchical clusters. This clustering method has an obviously advantage, effective distance metric. We use a condensed hierarchical clustering [17], at the beginning, each sample is an initial cluster, and then find the nearest two clusters to merge, the hierarchy moves upwards. In order to determine which clusters should be merged, you need to specify the distance between the cluster and the link criteria. The key of hierarchical clustering is how to calculate the distance between clusters, that is, to specify the distance and the link criteria. In order to measure the time series distance, we use the dynamic time warping method [19] (DTW).

The HMM model corresponding to each mobile application can be uniquely determined by $\lambda \sim (A, B, \pi)$. We use Baum-Welch (BW) algorithm to learn these three parameters π, A and B. We obtain that:

$$Q(\lambda,\bar{\lambda}) = \sum_I \left(\ln P(O,I \mid \lambda)\right) P(O,I \mid \bar{\lambda}) = \sum_I \ln \pi_{i_1} P(O,I \mid \bar{\lambda}) + \sum_I \left(\sum_{t=1}^{T-1} \ln a_{i_t i_{t+1}} \right) P(O,I \mid \bar{\lambda}) + \sum_I \left(\sum_{t=1}^{T} \ln b_{i,o_t} \right) P(O,I \mid \bar{\lambda}) \quad (1)$$

By maximizing Q can obtain the parameters A, B and π. We get:

$$\pi_i = \gamma_1(i) \Big/ \sum_{i=1}^{N} \gamma_1(i), \quad a_{ij} = \sum_{t=1}^{T-1} \xi_t(i,j) \Big/ \sum_{t=1}^{T-1} \gamma_t(i), \quad b_{ik} = \sum_{t=1, o_t = v_k}^{T} \gamma_t(i) \Big/ \sum_{t=1}^{T} \gamma_t(i).$$

For the observation probability matrix B, the observed state is a continuous numerical variable that follows the three-dimensional normal distribution, so B is no longer represented by b_{ik} ,but by the mean variable $\mu_i = \sum_{t=1}^{T} \gamma_t(i) o_t \Big/ \sum_{t=1}^{T} \gamma_t(i)$ and the variance matrix

$$\delta_i = \sum_{t=1}^{T} \gamma_t(i)(o_t - \mu_i)(o_t - \mu_i)^T \Big/ \sum_{t=1}^{T} \gamma_t(i).$$

3.2 Traffic classification

When the mobile application is identified, the sample data (observation state sequence) to be recognized is input to the HMM model corresponding to each mobile application, and the posterior probability of the sample data in each HMM model corresponding to the mobile application is respectively measured. Then, the decision principle is chosen to select the recognition result of the mobile application corresponding to the HMM model with the highest probability of posterior probability, then obtain the corresponding mobile application recognition result. The forward algorithm or backward algorithm is used for posterior probability.

According to the Bayesian decision principle, the HMM model corresponding to the maximum probability of posterior probability is selected. As the application category of the sample to be identified, and the posterior probability of the HMM model corresponding to the mobile application is obtained by the forward algorithm or the backward algorithm. Assume that there are n HMM model corresponds to the mobile application, noted λ_i, $i = 1, 2, \cdots, n$. The sample to be identified is an observation sequence O^m with the length m, which is composed of m network streams.

$$\lambda_{best} = \underset{\lambda_i \in \{\lambda_1, \lambda_2, \ldots, \lambda_n\}}{\arg\max} P(O^m \mid \lambda_i) \tag{2}$$

4 Performance evaluation

We use three different Andrew smartphone devices as the mobile application platform and connect to the PC side to receive the ADB instructions for PC-side transmission.

Table 1. Sample Information

Number	Name	Number of eigenvector		
		$Device_1$	$Device_2$	$Device_3$
App1	com.baidu.BaiduMap	166	65	35
App2	com.eg.android.AlipayGphone	144	55	30
App3	com.netease.cloudmusic	141	51	33
App4	com.netease.newsreader.activity	150	50	30
App5	com.ss.android.article.news	150	57	30
App6	com.taobao.taobao	153	61	31
App7	com.tencent.mm	180	50	35
App8	com.tencent.mobileqq	148	50	33
App9	com.UCMobile	153	54	35
App10	com.youku.phone	150	58	34
Sum		1535	551	326

The PC devices install USB wireless network cards to provide network access services for mobile device. $Device_1$ is Nexus 4 with Android 4.4.4, $Device_2$ is Nexus 5 with Android 5.1.1, $Device_3$ is One Plus with Android 6.0.1. The PC runs Wireshark software to capture the real-time network traffic data from USB wireless network card. The resulting samples are shown in Table 1.

We used the package manager to import the HMMWeka provided in [20] into Weka. The HMM classifier can be used to classify the sequence data represented as a relational attribute in Weka. The data instance must have a nominal type attribute, and a relational sequence attribute. Since we extract the eigenvectors are multivariate numerical properties, we use the Gaussian HMM model.

Using the corresponding eigenvector of $Device_1$ as the training data set, using Ten-fold cross-validation, the final result is shown in Fig. 1.

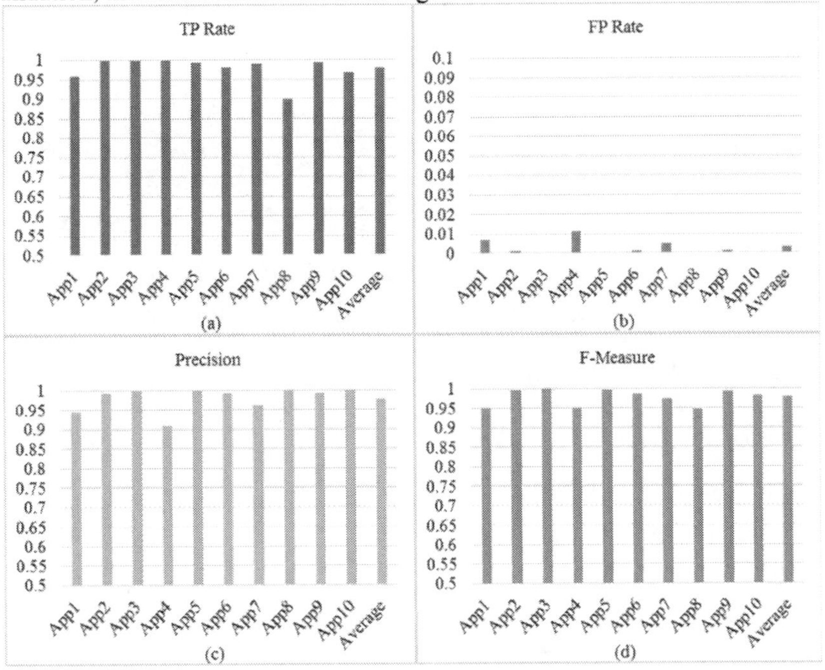

Fig. 1. Identify the accuracy rate results

In Fig. 1, the average accuracy of the classification recognition is 97.9 %, the average recall rate is 97.8%, F measure is 0.978, and all achieve good results. From the various categories of applications, the experiment of the application App4 (NetEase news) with the minimum accuracy that 90.9%, but the recall rate is 1.00. By observing the recognition results confused matrix display, NetEase news's 150 samples all correctly identified, however, 7 Baidu map samples, 4 excellent cool samples, 3 mobile QQ samples, one WeChat sample were wrongly classified as NetEase news.

In order to verify the generalization ability of the method, we use the eigenvector corresponding to $Device_1$ as the training data set, and the eigenvector corresponding to $Device_2$ and $Device_3$ as the test data set. The final result is shown in Fig. 2.

We test the network traffic of application on different devices, the average recall rate is 96.8%, the average recall rate is 96.6% and the F measure is 0.967. It can be seen that the method proposed in this paper has good generalization ability.

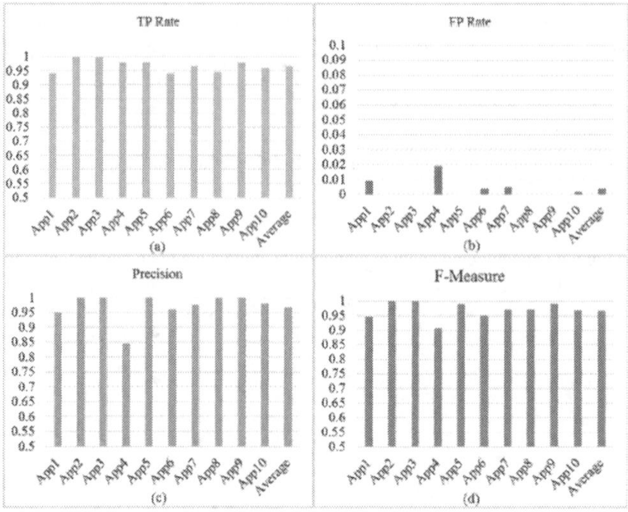

Fig. 2. Generalization ability test results

5 Summary

This paper introduces the process of mobile application recognition based on HMM model, and contains the data acquisition, feature extraction, model training, classification and identification. Finally, the proposed algorithm for mobile application recognition is 97.9%, and the generalization ability of the method is tested. The recognition accuracy is 96.8%. The experimental data used in this paper from a self-built wireless network with few users. The influence of different network on the accuracy of the method needs further verification.

Acknowledgment: This work was supported by the National Natural Science Foundation of China under Grant Nos 61372076 and 61301171, and the 111 Project under Grant No B08038.

References

1. Michael Shirer. Apple Tops Samsung in the Fourth Quarter to Close Out a Roller Coaster Year for the Smartphone Market[EB/OL]. http://www.idc.com/getdoc.jsp?containerId=prUS42268917. [2017-02-01].
2. Stat Counter Global Stats. Mobile and tablet internet usage exceeds desktop for first time worldwide[EB/OL]. http://gs.statcounter.com/press/mobile-and-tablet-internet-usage-exceeds-desktop-for-first-time-worldwide. [2016-11-01].
3. Wei X, Gomez L, Neamtiu I, et al. ProfileDroid: multi-layer profiling of android applications[C]//Proceedings of the 18th annual international conference on Mobile computing and networking. ACM, 2012: 137-148.
4. Xu Q, Erman J, Gerber A, et al. Identifying diverse usage behaviors of smartphone apps[C]//Proceedings of the 2011 ACM SIGCOMM conference on Internet measurement conference. ACM, 2011: 329-344.
5. Dai S, Tongaonkar A, Wang X, et al. Networkprofiler: Towards automatic fingerprinting of android apps[C]//INFOCOM, 2013 Proceedings IEEE. IEEE, 2013: 809-817.
6. Su X, Zhang D, Dai S, et al. Mobile traffic identification based on application's network signature[J]. International Journal of Embedded Systems, 2016, 8(2/3):217.

7. Chen Z, Yu B, Zhang Y, et al. Automatic Mobile Application Traffic Identification by Convolutional Neural Networks[C]//Trustcom/BigDataSE/I SPA, 2016 IEEE. IEEE, 2016: 301-307.
8. Wang Q, Yahyavi A, Kemme B, et al. I know what you did on your smartphone: Inferring app usage over encrypted data traffic[C]//Communications and Network Security (CNS), 2015 IEEE Conference on. IEEE, 2015: 433-441.
9. Conti M, Mancini L V, Spolaor R, et al. Can't you hear me knocking: Identification of user actions on android apps via traffic analysis[C]//Proceedings of the 5th ACM Conference on Data and Application Security and Privacy. ACM, 2015: 297-304.
10. Park K, Kim H. Encryption Is Not Enough: Inferring user activities on KakaoTalk with traffic analysis[C]//International Workshop on Information Security Applications. Springer International Publishing, 2015: 254-265.
11. Conti M, Mancini L V, Spolaor R, et al. Analyzing android encrypted network traffic to identify user actions[J]. IEEE Transactions on Information Forensics and Security, 2016, 11(1): 114-125.
12. Datta J, Kataria N, Hubballi N. Network traffic classification in encrypted environment: a case study of google hangout[C]//Communications (NCC), 2015 Twenty First National Conference on. IEEE, 2015: 1-6.
13. Saltaformaggio B, Choi H, Johnson K, et al. Eavesdropping on fine-grained user activities within smartphone apps over encrypted network traffic[C]//Proc. USENIX Workshop on Offensive Technologies (WOOT'16, in conjunction with Security'16). 2016.
14. Fu Y, Xiong H, Lu X, et al. Service Usage Classification with Encrypted Internet Traffic in Mobile Messaging Apps[J]. IEEE Transactions on Mobile Computing, 2016, 15(11): 2851-2864.
15. Alan H F, Kaur J. Can Android Applications Be Identified Using Only TCP/IP Headers of Their Launch Time Traffic?[C]//Proceedings of the 9th ACM Conference on Security & Privacy in Wireless and Mobile Networks. ACM, 2016: 61-66.
16. Taylor V F, Spolaor R, Conti M, et al. Appscanner: Automatic fingerprinting of smartphone apps from encrypted network traffic[C]//Security and Privacy (EuroS&P), 2016 IEEE European Symposium on. IEEE, 2016: 439-454.
17. Zhihua Zhou.Learning: Machine learning [M]. Tsinghua University Press, 2016.
18. Li Deng.Analytical Depth Learning --- Speech Recognition Practice [M]. Electronic Industry Press, 2016.
19. Müller M. Information retrieval for music and motion[M]. Heidelberg: Springer, 2007.
20. Marco Gillies. HMMWeka[CP]. http://www.doc.gold.ac.uk/~mas02mg/software/hmmweka/index.html. [Last accessed 2017-04-20].

Comparison of Three Different Styles of Submarine Sails on Electromagnetic Scattering under the Detection of Airborne Radar

Ji Liu[1], *Peilin* Huang[1], *Yaodong* Zhao[2], *Jinzu* Ji[1,*], and *Fengli* Xue[3]

[1]Scholl of Aeronautic Science and Engineering, Beihang University, Beijing, 100191, China
[2]Science and Technology on Electronic Information Control Laboratory, Chengdu, 610036, China
[3]Key Lab for Information Science of Electromagnetic Waves (MoE), Fudan University, Shanghai 200433, China

Abstract. This paper studies radar cross section of submarine sails on the water. Under the detection of the enemy's airborne radar, considering the motion of the submarine, the sail model of radar pitch angle incidence range analysis is established. By using CATIA software, the 3D models of AKULA sail, SUBOFF sail and VICTOR sail are built. On the basis of the physical optics method and the equivalent currents method, the scattering characteristics of sails RCS(radar cross section) are simulated under X radar band. Through the microwave anechoic chamber test, this paper verifies the accuracy of the combination of the physical optics method and the equivalent electromagnetic flow method. The influence of the distance from the airborne radar to the sail on the pitch angle of the electromagnetic wave is discussed, with the elevation angle of the radar antenna varies. Then, we illustrate the characteristics of circumferential direction RCS of the sail under different pitch angles. Finally, the mean RCS of the sail at a given pitch angle is simulated. The results show that the AKULA sail is considerably superior to SUBOFF sail and VICTOR sail on stealth performance with the pitch angle less than 4°. But when the pitch angle exceeds 10°, the SUBOFF sail can be given priority.

1 Introduction

A good stealth performance is significant for the submarines to survive. Most of the submarines, especially conventional submarines, often need to regularly surface and ventilate. Periscope, vent valve and other devices of the submarine are often exposed in the radar wave in the depth of cruising. These devices are mostly cylindrical that make radar screen appear stable and bright display. It can be seen that radar is still one of the important means of detecting submarines, which need to be considered its radar stealth performance.

The sail is mainly used for enclosing pressure command, lock chamber and various lifting devices, which is an important part of modern submarine to perform cruise, send and receive information, reach and leave the dock, observe and command [1, 2]. Exposed to the

* Corresponding author: jijinzu@buaa.edu.cn

surface of the sail, deck, bridge and outer walls of the lifting device, composing a large radar wave reflection source, can be discovered by the Army's synthetic aperture radar above sea level ranging from a few kilometers to 300km [3]. The sail will provide a clear signal to the radar in a navigational or semi-submersible state. Therefore, reducing the size of the sail and optimizing the contour line is the goal pursued by submarine designers, aimed at reducing the adverse effect of the sail [4].

Considering the military requirements of the underwater non-acoustic stealth technology, several non-acoustic stealth individual technologies are emphasized based on foreign non-acoustic detection technology in reference [5]. The sails of SUBOFF submarine model with different horizontal position, height and shape are calculated in different schemes. The optimal design scheme on power performance is obtained by comprehensive comparison, guaranteeing the grid similarity in different cases [6]. Reference [7] have introduced the development of submarine stealth technology, then have analyzed the factors that affected the submarine stealth and put forward the technical measures to improve the stealth ability of submarine and the stealth ability of non-acoustic radiation. In the reference [8], the numerical simulation method is used to calculate the resistance, flow field and pressure distribution of the outer shell of different sails. The new type of attack submarines tend to be low-lying and increase the smooth transition between the hull and the sail, reducing the submarine hydrodynamic noise [9]. The mechanism, characteristics, evaluation methods of the sail noise and low noise design techniques of the sail are analyzed by Hu Qiwang, targeting shrinkage ratio sail model as the research subject [10]. The Renault average Navier-Stokes (RANS) method is used to calculate three dimensional viscous flow field of the submarine, in which the influence of the sail size and relative position on the hydrodynamic performance of the submarine is analyzed [11].

Since the 1960s, there have been a number of submarines with low-lying profile and excellent streamlined submarines, such as the German 212, the Swedish 2000 and the former Soviet Union's "AKULA" nuclear submarine. Relevant research has been carried out in the new 3D sail both at home and abroad. Gorski has designed and studied the new 3D sail and conducted a wind tunnel test on its flow field [12]. Wang Zhibo compared the influence of different three-dimensional sails on the wake field and analyzed the relationship between the sail configure and the characteristics of the wake field [13]. The influence of the three-dimensional dune-shaped sail on the resistance and wake field was analyzed, which verified that changing configure of the sail can reduce the resistance and achieve the uniform wake field [14].

Sufficient researches have been conducted on the traditional straight-walled sails and the new three-dimensional sails, but they focused on the properties of flow field of the sails. In this paper, the effect of three designed sails referring to AKULA, SUBOFF, VICTOR submarines on radar stealth will be compared, aimed at obtaining configure of good stealth performance. The three different styles of submarines are shown in Fig. 1. Fig. 1(a), Fig. 1(b) and Fig. 1(c), respectively, show the AKULA, SUBOFF and VICTOR submarine configuration characteristics.

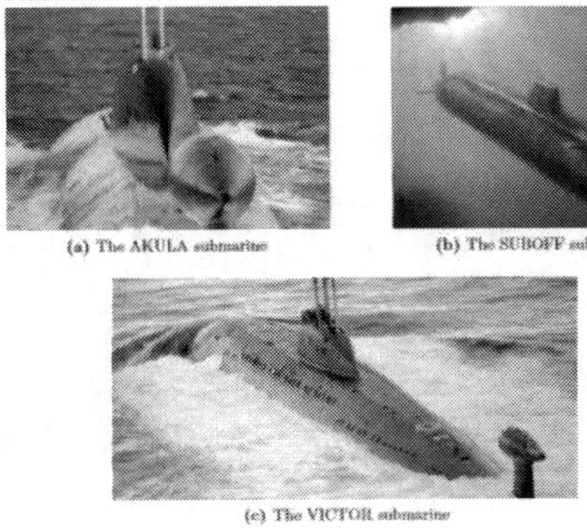

Fig. 1. Three different styles of submarines

2 Theoretical basis

The numerical simulation of a submarine sail's electromagnetic scattering characteristics includes the following two aspects: the pitch angle of the radar wave considering atmospheric refraction effect; the RCS calculation method.

2.1 The pitch angle of the radar wave considering atmospheric refraction effect

In the modern air-to-sea warfare, the largest radar threat to submarines is the enemy's airborne radar, compared to ground and sea based radar. Therefore, this paper assumes that the enemy radar is an airborne radar. And the electromagnetic scattering characteristics of the sail in various situations are discussed in this case. In calculating the target pitch angle, the radar wave in the Earth's atmospheric refraction effect is also taken into account. As is shown in Fig. 2, the target pitch angle is illustrated as follows:

$$\theta_1 = \arccos\left(\frac{a_1 + h_1}{a_1 + h_t}\cos\theta\right) \tag{1}$$

Where θ_1 is the target pitch angle, θ is the pitch angle of the airborne radar antenna, a_1 is the equivalent earth radius($a_1 = \frac{4}{3}a$) and a is the radius of the earth (a = 6370km), h_t is the height of the airborne radar from the sea level, h_1 is the sea level height of the submarine measured from the sea surface, in which the earth is defined as a spherical surface with a radius of 6370 km. The mentioned formula can be easily deduced using the sine theorem shown in Fig. 2

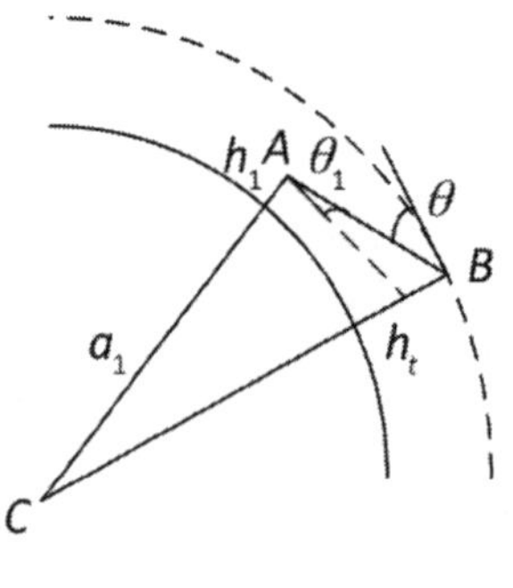

Fig. 2. The pitch angle of the sail relative to the radar wave

It can be seen that θ_1 has a minimum value θ_{min} in case that θ is infinitely close to zero. Whether a positive direction to increase or reduce in negative direction, the value of θ_1 is obviously greater than θ_{min}. Thus effective pitch angle of the submarine can be acquired in face with airborne radar.

2.2 RCS calculation method

In this paper, the physical optics method and the equivalent electromagnetic flow method are used to simulate the electromagnetic scattering characteristics of the sail. Specifically, the physical optics method is used to calculate the surface facet scattering, while the equivalent electromagnetic flow method is used to calculate the edge diffraction [15].

The formula calculating the facet scattering by physical optics is as follows

$$\sqrt{\sigma} = \frac{jk}{\sqrt{\pi}} \hat{n} \cdot \left(\hat{e}_s \times \hat{h}_i \right) \int_S e^{jk\left(\hat{s}-\hat{i}\right)\cdot \mathbf{r}'} dS \quad (2)$$

Where σ is the RCS of a single surface element, j is an imaginary unit, k is the wave number, $\hat{n}$ is the surface normal vector, $\hat{e}_s$ is the direction of the antenna polarization, $\hat{h}_i$ is the direction of the incident magnetic field, $\hat{s}$ is the far field radiation direction, $\hat{i}$ is the incident direction, $\mathbf{r}'$ is the source point coordinate, dS is the surface element.

In the mentioned physical optics method, shadowing test is interpreted as two steps. First, facets are judged whether in the illuminated portion of the body. One effective method is that multiplying the incident direction by the normal direction of the facet. That is to say, if $\hat{n}\cdot\hat{i} < 0$, the facet is illuminated. Second, in the illuminated region, one facet may be shadowed by another bright facet, which is taken into consideration in this paper. The idea is that when the center of a facet is shadowed by another facet, it is considered that the facet is shadowed [16, 17].

3 Electromagnetic test validation

This paper has researched the electromagnetic scattering characteristics of the radar cross section of the sails. According to the physical optics method and the equivalent electromagnetic flow method, the paper completes the simulation of the RCS characteristic of the sails. Before conducting the simulation, the accuracy and scientificity of the mentioned method should be validated by electromagnetic test.

3.1 Electromagnetic test experiment

In this paper, the 3D digital models of sails are created by CATIA software shown in Fig. 3. Then, the digital sail models are imported to the prepared program to simulate the sail's RCS obtaining the sail's electromagnetic scattering characteristics.

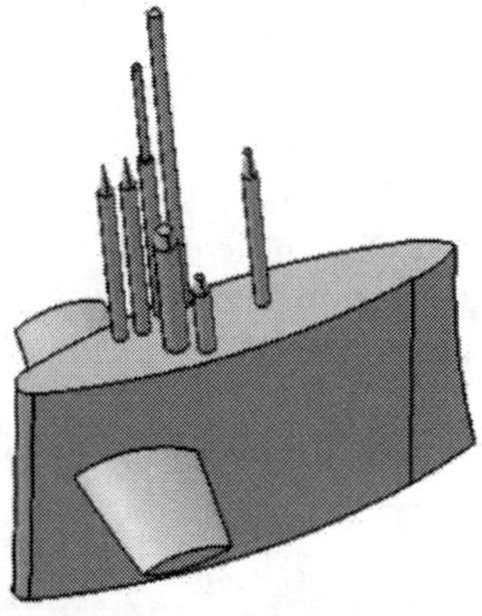

Fig. 3. 3D digital models of the submarine sail

The 3D scale entity model of the sail is made and tested in an anechoic chamber as is shown in Fig. 4. Finally, the sail RCS curve of the electromagnetic test is acquired compared to the simulation shown in Fig. 5.

(a)Entity model of sail

(b)The sail is tested

Fig. 4. Electromagnetic test of the sail in an anechoic chamber

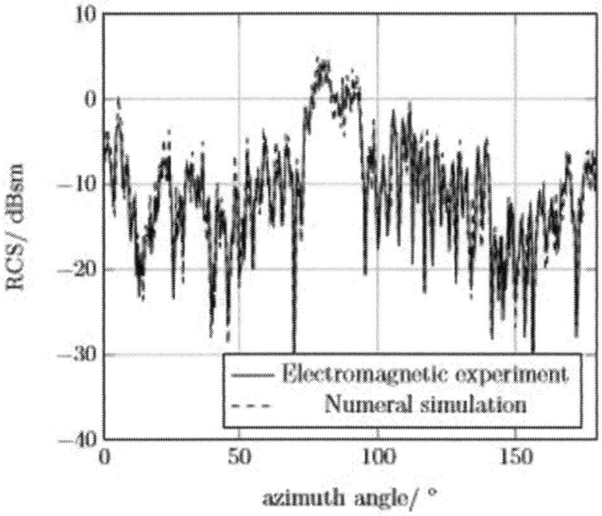

Fig. 5. RCS characteristics of the sail from simulation and electromagnetic test

3.2 Result of electromagnetic test

In this section, the program, based on the physical optics method and the equivalent electromagnetic method, is utilized to simulate the RCS of the 3D digital sail model. Then, the RCS characteristics of the electromagnetic test are compared with that obtained in the simulation program, as is shown in Fig. 5.

The initial conditions of the electromagnetic test and the numerical simulation remain the same. The incident radar wave is X band, that is to say, the wavelength is 3 cm. The incident wave pitch angle is 0° and the polarization direction is horizontal polarization. Taking into account the symmetry, the azimuth is selected as $0^{\circ} \sim 180^{\circ}$. It can be seen from the Fig. 5 that the simulation results are in line with the electromagnetic test experiment. The results show that the numerical simulation method is accurate and scientific, which can be used to model more complex and large targets for electromagnetic scattering.

4 Sail RCS characteristics simulation and analysis

4.1 3D models of sail

In this section, on the background of the AKULA submarine, SUBOFF submarine and VICTOR submarine, CATIA software is employed to establish the 3D sail digital models shown in Fig. 6. These three typical different styles of submarine sails are created labelled as model A, B, C respectively. For the model A, the AKULA concept adopts a ternary complex surface presenting as smooth streamline along the XY, XZ and YZ profile. The advantage of this configuration is to reduce the fluid resistance, improving the submarine's mobility, but the influence of stealth should be explored. For the model B, referring to SUBOFF submarine, it employs a conventional upright appearance, whose cross section is similar to the aircraft's airfoil. This is one of the most common and typical layouts, and most of the early submarine sails use this approach. The structural characteristics of Model B determine that it can accommodate more electronic and mechanical equipment. The model C can be simplified to be a combination of three simple rotating bodies (cone, cylinder and sphere), in line with the design idea of low-rise sails. Therefore, it can be regarded as a representative of the low-rise sails. Compared with Model B, Model A and Model C have a major advantage that the sail can be better fused with the hull.

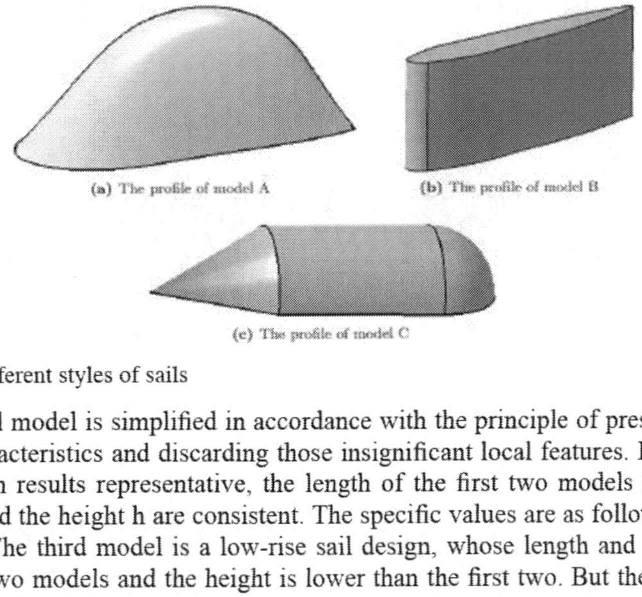

(a) The profile of model A (b) The profile of model B

(c) The profile of model C

Fig. 6. Three different styles of sails

The 3D sail model is simplified in accordance with the principle of preserving the main scattering characteristics and discarding those insignificant local features. In order to make the comparison results representative, the length of the first two models l, the maximum thickness b, and the height h are consistent. The specific values are as follows: l = 14m, b = 3m, h = 4m. The third model is a low-rise sail design, whose length and width are larger than the first two models and the height is lower than the first two. But the total volume is consistent with the first two sails.

4.2 Sail RCS numerical simulation and analysis

Based on the physical optics method and the equivalent electromagnetic flow method, the mentioned models are divided into multiple small triangular facets. When in calculation of the RCS of sails, the secondary reflection and shadowing need to be considered. It is generally believed that azimuth angle in the plane of the range of $0^\circ \sim 360^\circ$ belongs to the radar threat area of ships and submarines. Reference to the national naval airborne radar situation, the naval airborne radar frequency band is mostly X-band($8 \sim 12$GHz). Therefore, the RCS of sails are calculated at the middle value of the X band(10GHz) with the azimuth angle $0^{\circ} \sim 360^{\circ}$.

Taking into account the vertical polarization of the sea level scattering contribution is very large, the horizontal polarization is chosen in the simulation process. In this section, based on physical optics method and equivalent currents method, according to mentioned pitch angle range and radar band, MATLAB software is used to calculate the RCS of the previously established 3D sail models in Fig. 8. From the previous conclusion, the minimum pitch angle of the sail is 0.72° relative to the airborne radar. In Fig. 8, three curves represent the RCS of the three different styles of sails at the minimum pitch angle.

In Fig. 7, β is denoted as the pitch angle of the sail. Fig. 9 shows the variation of the RCS at different azimuth angles with the pitch angle swinging between $1^{\circ} \sim 4^{\circ}$. As seen from the figure, with the pitch angle over a range, the AKULA RCS curve fluctuates but the number of spikes is always two. Moreover, the locations of the two spikes are concentrated in the vicinity of 103° and 255°, almost without changing. The RCS curve is beneath 0dB at most other angles, which conforms to stealth design principles. However, the RCS spike width becomes widened with the increase of the pitch angle. Meanwhile, the height of the spike increases with the increase of the elevation angle and then decreases. At the elevation angle of 3°, the RCS is as high as 49.98dB, which is 53.4% higher than when it is 1°.

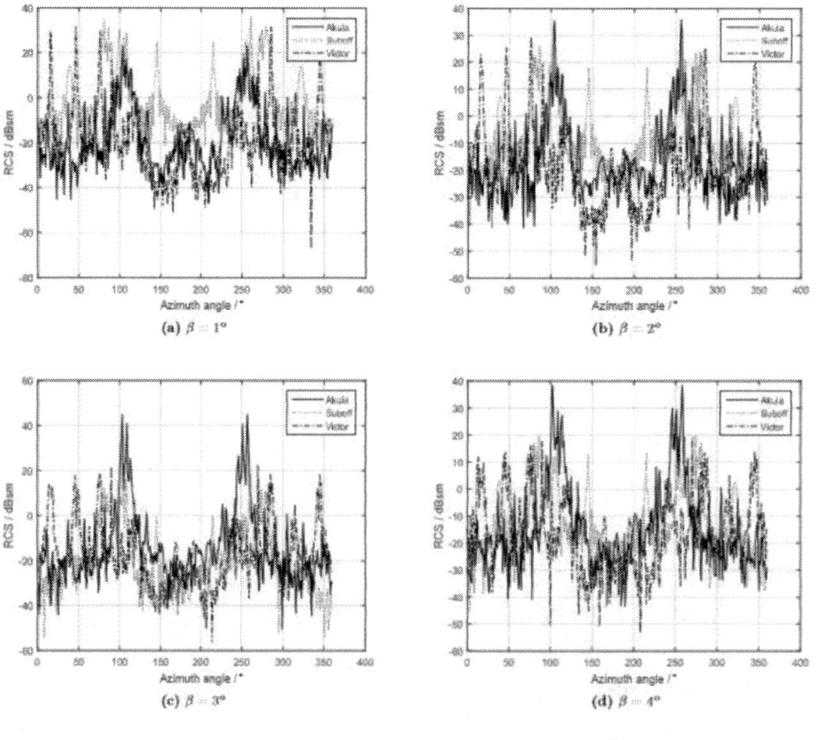

Fig. 7. The comparison of the RCS results of the sails when $\beta = 1 \sim 4^{\circ}$

With the variety of pitch angle, SUBOFF and VICTOR curves tend to remain essentially unchanged, but the heights of the curve spikes decrease. Compared with AKULA curve, the number of SUBOFF and VICTOR curve spikes is too much, whose peak values exceed 20dB when it is 1°. This configuration design features lead to electromagnetic wave diffusing very strongly in a number of directions, which greatly increases the probability that the submarine will be detected by hostile radar.

Fig. 8 shows the mean RCS of the sails at $0 \sim 20^{\circ}$ pitch angle. The three curves representing AKULA, SUBOFF and VICTOR sails respectively are compared. The significance of mean RCS lies in that the probability of the sail being detected in all directions is assumed identical, in the face of airborne radar. Under this assumption, the influence of the pitch angle on the mean RCS of the sail is discussed. It can be seen from the Fig. 8, with the increase of the pitch angle, the AKULA mean RCS decreases first in a small range. Then, the curve tends to be stable and fluctuates very little. This indicates that the pitch angle change has little effect on the AKULA mean RCS. SUBOFF mean RCS curve shows a monotonically decreasing trend, but the decrease amplitude is gradually reduced. VICTOR's mean RCS curve goes up first and then the trend goes down, whose spike appears at 15° pitch angle and its corresponding RCS is as high as 32.99dB.

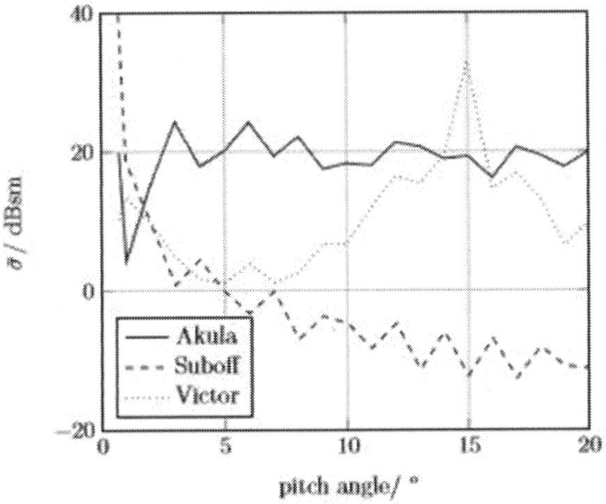

Fig. 8. The RCS mean curve of the sail with the pitch angle varies

5 Conclusions

The RCS characteristics of the AKULA sail, SUBOFF sail and VICTOR sail on the water have been calculated and analyzed in this paper. It is assumed that the threat to the sails is airborne radar. Based on the concept of the fusion of the sail and the hull, the AKULA model is created. Moreover, on the basis of the concept of low-lying sail designing, the VICTOR model is built. Both of them are compared with the SUBOFF model representing the traditional sails. Utilizing the physical optics method and the equivalent electromagnetic flow method, the RCS characteristics of three designed sails have been calculated under X band of radar in this paper. And the mean RCS of the sails are also investigated with the change of pitch angle. Then, a sail RCS reduction strategy on the stealth configuration of the subsequent modification is proposed. Through the mentioned research, the conclusions of this paper can be summarized as follows:

1. Under $0.7179^{\circ} \sim 4^{\circ}$ pitch angle, the AKULA RCS curve has only two spikes, whose spikes are concentrated in the vicinity of 103° and 255°. Furthermore, the scattering direction is non-major threat direction, which is highly advantageous for monostatic stealth. Compared to AKULA, the other two have too much spikes on RCS curves resulting in the probability of being detected by enemy radar increasing greatly.

Therefore, the AKULA sail is considerably superior to SUBOFF sail and VICTOR sail on stealth performance with the pitch angle less than 4°. According to the AKULA electromagnetic scattering characteristics, an effective measure to improve the stealth effect of the AKULA sail is to apply the absorbing material in the vicinity of 103° and 255° azimuth angle to consume the scattered energy of the position.

2. Observing the mean RCS curve, when the pitch angle exceeds 10°, the SUBOFF mean RCS is more than 50% lower than the other two. It is indicated that the SUBOFF sail can be given priority in the high pitch angle.

References

1. Roy Burcher, Louis Rydill, and C. W Bert. Concepts in submarine design. Journal of Applied Mechanics, 62(1), 1995.
2. Yu Cun Pan, Qi Dou Zhou, and Huai Xin Zhang. Numerical simulation of rotating arm test for prediction of submarine rotary derivatives. Journal of Hydrodynamics Ser B, 27(1):68–75, 2015.
3. Yang Jian, Wu Chao, and Gu Yang. Measures to improve the stealth capability of submarine. Shipbuilding Technology, (1):22–24, 2006.
4. Du Bo, Huang Jianwei, and Chen Yuan. Optimal design of the top form of submarine sail. Ship and ocean engineer, 36(2):107–110, 2007.
5. Peng Liang, Wang Jianxun, and Deng Haihua. Review of the non-acoustic detection and stealth technology. Ship Science and technology, 36(5):6–10, 2014.
6. Lv Minghe. Optimization design of submarine command platform enclosure. China water and transport, 14(1):1–4, 2014.
7. Jiao Fangjin. Development of submarine stealth technology. National defense science and technology, (4):35–37, 2003.
8. Huilan Yao, Huaixin Zhang, Hutao Liu, and Wencheng Jiang. Numerical study of flow-excited noise of a submarine with full appendages considering fluid structure interaction using the boundary element method. Engineering Analysis with Boundary Elements, 77:1–9, 2017.
9. Chen Feng and Qi Guoying. Research on technical characteristic of foreign new generation nuclear submarine. Ship science and technology, 36(9):153–157, 2014.
10. Hu Qiwang. Research of noise mechanisms of submarine sail model. PhD thesis, Harbin Engineering University, 2007.
11. Wu Fangliang, Wu Xiaoguang, and Ma Yunyi. The effect of submarine sail on the resistance and wake field. The Ocean Engineering, 27(3):91–99, 2009.
12. Joseph J. Gorski and Roderick M. Coleman. Use of rans calculations in the design of a submarine sail. 2003.
13. Zhibo Wang, Huizhi Yao, and Nan Zhang. Calculation and analysis of the effects of sail form on submarine wake. Journal of Ship Mechanics, 2009.
14. Longju Liu and Yong Xu. Numerical study about the effect of touradon shaped submarine sail on flow field. Journal of Sichuan Ordnance, 2014.
15. George T Ruck. Radar cross section handbook, volume 2. Plenum Publishing Corporation, 1970.
16. Jinzu Ji and Hongqian Wu. Shadowing algorithm of facets in physical optics (po) based on determinant. Optik - International Journal for Light and Electron Optics, 126(14):1366–1368, 2015.
17. Ji Jinzu and Liu Zhanhe. Electromagnetic occultation algorithm based on facets grouping and optimization. Journal of Beijing University of Aeronautics and Astronautics, 35(4):453–456, 2009.

Research on Dynamic Graph Target Tracking Method Fusing the Color Local Entropy

Junchang Zhang[1,2]*, *Chenyang* Xia[1], *Leili* Hu[2], and *Yanling* Zhou[1]

[1]School of Electronics and Information, Northwestern Polytechnical University, Xi'an 710072, China
[2]Department of Luoyang Institute of electro-optical devices, Luoyang Henan 471009, China

Abstract. Focusing on the problems of target deformation, occlusion, background interference and rotation, a robust video tracking method is proposed in this paper, which is based on the superpixels and dynamic graph matching. Firstly, to make the superpixels edge fit better and structure tighter, the local gradient feature is fused into the simple linear iterative clustering (SLIC) method. Secondly, the candidate target superpixels set is generated by Graph Cuts and to obtain more accurate foreground superpixels set, the LASVM classification results are fused into the Graph Cuts energy function. Thirdly, in order to make the proposed tracker more robust, the color local entropy is fused into the diagonal elements of the affinity matrix. Experiment results show that the proposed algorithm has strong robustness and better tracking accuracy.

1 Introduction

Video tracking has become an important research direction in the field of computer vision. It is used in the field of human-computer interaction, video surveillance and human behavior analysis widely and has important application value in civil and military fields. According to the tracking principle, the video tracking algorithms can be considered as three aspects: template matching algorithm, state estimation algorithm and classification problem algorithm.

The template matching algorithm locates the target by finding the similarity between the target model and the candidate model according to the criterions. The classic template matching algorithm is the Mean Shift algorithm 1. It has a better performance in a simple tracking scene. But the tracking performance becomes worse rapidly when target moves rapidly in complex scene. To reduce the background interference caused by the symmetric kernel, Chen1 construct the asymmetric nuclear according to the segmentation of the target character. It can reduce the background interference and improve the tracking efficiency. To solve the problem of severe occlusion and do not reduce the real time, Xu[3] combined the weight of the over-segmentation. To reduce the interference of similar background, Li3 introduced the target and the environment ratio coefficient to ensure the accurate update of the target model. The state estimation algorithm predicts the object state by using the state equation, and then extracts the real state information of the target. Particle filter is one of the typical algorithms, but the calculation is time-consuming, and is easy to occur the parti-

· Corresponding author: zhangjc@nwpu.edu.cn

cle degradation phenomenon. Then, Okuma4 proposed the Boosted particle filter algorithm. The classification tracking algorithm transforms the tracking problem into classification problem through training samples. It is common to estimate the target by the support vector machine. Then, Avidan proposed the support vector tracking and set tracking. Grabner5 fused the semi-supervised learning algorithm and boosting algorithm, and proposed the Semi-Boost tracking algorithm. It could solve the tracking drift problem. Babenko6 proposed multiple instance learning (MIL) algorithm, which is used to solve the problem that the training sample size is small or the sample is blur.

Only a few people have considered the occlusion and deformation problems at the same time. The performance of the mentioned algorithms would become poor when deal with the deformation and occlusion problem at the same time. However, Cai7 proposed the dynamic graph tracking (DGT) algorithm that has a good performance in dealing with deformation and occlusion problem. The classical SLIC method 8 is easy to generate the error segmentation at the edge pixels when the target is similar to the background in the DGT algorithm. Meanwhile, the color histogram is sensitive to similar background interference and illumination in the DGT algorithm. Therefore, the paper proposed an improved video tracking method to solve the above problems. It fuses the local gradient information into the SLIC method and combines the color local entropy 9 with the HSV color feature. The improved algorithm is more robust than the DGT algorithm.

2 DGT tracker

The DGT algorithm includes superpixels generation, image segmentation, graph model construction, graph matching and model update. The diagram is shown in Figure 1.

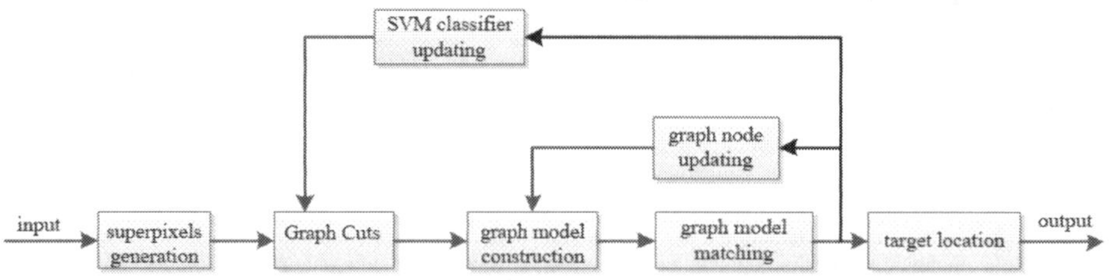

Fig. 1. The schematic diagram.

Firstly, the superpixels are generated by the SLIC algorithm which fuses the local gradient information. Then the superpixel is taken as a basic unit for the subsequent processing. Secondly, to obtain better segmentation results, the results of LASVM classification is fused into the Graph Cuts energy function. The DGT tracker takes the superpixels as foreground whose label value is 1 and the superpixels as background whose label value is 0 when the energy function is minimized. Thirdly, the target graph model and candidate graph model are constructed by ε-neighborhood way. Both structure information and appearance information can be exploited sufficiently in the affinity matrix. Fourthly, the matching result is achieved by spectral method. And then the target location is estimated according to the matching result. Finally, target graph model is updated according the matching result in real-time.

3 The improved SLIC algorithm

It is worth to notice that the SLIC method can generate superpixels according to the number of superpixels specified by users. And the pixel feature is expressed by the lab color space and the location information in the SLIC method. Then pixels will be classified as different superpixels according to the similarity of features, so the feature accuracy is crucial to the superpixel segmentation. When the target and background are similar, they are easy to be considered as the same area. Therefore, in order to improve the accuracy of the segmentation, we fused the 3×3 neighborhood gradient feature into the distance formula. Adding the local gradient can help the superpixels move slowly in the boundary, and the boundary fitter. So we can obtain more accurate superpixels boundary. The proposed method is better than the conventional SLIC method. The local gradient formula can be expressed as (1).

$$gredient = \frac{1}{N}\sum\nolimits_{q}\frac{(\mathrm{f(q)}-\mathrm{f(p)})^2}{dist(\mathrm{p,q})} \tag{1}$$

Where $\mathrm{f}(\cdot)$ is the pixel value, $dist(\mathrm{p,q})$ is the distance between center point p and pixel point q. N is normalization constant.

$$N=\sum\nolimits_{q}\frac{1}{dist(\mathrm{p,q})}.$$

The distance can be expressed as (2):

$$D_s=\sqrt{d_{lab}^2+\frac{m^2}{S^2}d_{xy}^2}+\lambda * gredient \tag{2}$$

Where λ is a weight parameter.

The set $\{T_i\}$ is obtained by the SLIC algorithm. Then the candidate object superpixels set $\{T_i\}_{i=1}^{n_Q}$ can be obtained by Graph Cuts algorithm. The energy function can be expressed as follows:

$$E(B)=\sum_{p\in S}D_p(b_p)+\sum_{p,q\in N}V_{p,q}(b_p,b_q) \tag{3}$$

Where $\mathrm{B}=\{b_p \mid b_p\in\{0,1\}, p\in S\}$ is the label of $\{T_p\}$. $\sum_{p\in S}D_p(b_p)$ is the regional energy function term. $V_{p,q}(b_p,b_q)$ is the boundary energy function term. The definition of $\sum_{p\in S}D_p(b_p)$ can be found in the DGT algorithm [11]. The definition of $V_{p,q}(b_p,b_q)$ can be redefined as follows:

$$V_{p,q}(b_p,b_q)=\exp(-2*sqrt(abs(H_p-H_q))) \tag{4}$$

Where, p and q are neighboring superpixels. H is the value of the superpixel color local entropy.

The boundary energy function shows the segmentation boundary information in the physical sense. The color local entropy is more effective than the color feature in capturing the discontinuity between the neighborhood superpixels. When the value of color local entropy of p and q are similar, the value of $V_{p,q}(b_p,b_q)$ is large. Otherwise, the value is close to zero. Adding the binary energy term could reflect the penalty of error distribution in the Graph Cuts energy function effectively. The candidate target superpixels set can be obtained by the Graph Cuts by minimizing the energy function.

4 Color local entropy

The color local entropy is introduced in this paper. The color local entropy not only reflects the local color information, but also contains the location information and the entropy information. So the tracking system has a better performance in approaching the challenges of occlusion and deformation, and it is more robust in dealing with the challenges of rotation and similar background interference.

In this paper, we take a superpixel as a local area, and calculate the value of color local entropy in the superpixel. Color local entropy is a kind of the color feature expressed by the form of entropy. Meanwhile, taking the distance as weight coefficient is more effective in expressing the color local entropy. The color local entropy is expressed as follows:

$$H_c = -\sum_{u=1}^{m} p_u \log p_u \tag{5}$$

$$p_c = C\sum_{i=1}^{n} k\left(\left\|\frac{x_i - x_0}{d}\right\|^2\right)\delta\left[b(x_i)-u\right] \tag{6}$$

Where x_i and x_0 are the pixel location and the center location in the superpixels area respectively. And d is the maximum distance from x_0 to any pixel point in the superpixel area. $\delta\left[b(x_i)-u\right]$ is a Dirac function, which is used to determine whether the pixel color value of the object area belongs to the u th bin. k is the location weight coefficient. C is the normalized factor. The formulation of k and C are as follows:

$$k(r) = \begin{cases} 1, 0 < r \le \alpha \\ 1-\left(\dfrac{r-\alpha}{1-\alpha}\right)^2, \alpha < r \le 1 \end{cases} \tag{7}$$

$$C = \left[\sum_{i=1}^{n} k\left(\left\|\frac{x_i - x_0}{d}\right\|^2\right)\right]^{-1} \tag{8}$$

Compared with the traditional color feature, the color local entropy is better in describing and expressing the appearance feature. On the one hand, color local entropy retains the advantages of the color feature which is stable in the challenges of deformation and occlusion. On the other hand, it has the features of image local entropy that resisting geometric distortion and stability to illumination and similar background interference. At the same time, introducing the location information as weights coefficient can reduce the influence of the symmetry of entropy. The color local entropy feature can be used in the graph matching. Graph matching is the matching between the target graph $G(V,E)$ and the candidate graph $G'(V',E')$. $G(V,E)$ is obtained by updating the target graph nodes in every frame. $G'(V',E')$ is the set of the candidate target superpixels. It is constructed by ξ-neighborhood way. The matching between $G(V,E)$ and $G'(V',E')$ is a process of constructing and solving the affinity matrix. The node information and edge information are combined together in the affinity matrix. Therefore, the graph model is robust in the challenges of occlusion and deformation. In the affinity matrix, we fuse the color local entropy into the diagonal element $\Omega_1(c_{ii'})$ instead of the simple color feature. The non-diagonal element $\Omega_2(c_{ii'}, c_{jj'})$ is the edge corresponding relationship between the candidate graph and the target graph. $\Omega_1(c_{ii'})$ and $\Omega_2(c_{ii'},c_{jj'})$ are as follows:

$$\Omega_1(c_{ii'}) = \exp\left\{-\frac{1}{\varepsilon_1^2}(D(f_i,f_{i'}))^2\right\} \tag{9}$$

$$\Omega_1'(c_{ii'}) = \exp\left\{-(H_i - H_{i'})^2 / H_i + H_{i'}\right\} \tag{10}$$

$$\Omega_1(c_{ii'}) = \min(\Omega_1(c_{ii'}), \Omega_1'(c_{ii'})) \tag{11}$$

Where $\varepsilon_1 = 1/\sqrt{2}$ is a constant, $\Omega_1(c_{ii'})$ is the χ^2 distance between superpixel i and i'. $\Omega_1'(c_{ii'})$ is the color local entropy distance between superpixel i and i'. The color local entropy is more holistic compared with the color feature. When the object is similar to the background, the color difference is small and the value of $\Omega_1(c_{ii'})$ is larger. It is easy to result in the error matching. While, the value of $\Omega_1'(c_{ii'})$ is smaller relatively because of the color local entropy including the location information and the entropy information. The possibility of matching the success is small. Therefore, the color local entropy can be used to reduce the error matching ratio, and the matching result is more robust.

$$\Omega_2(c_{ii'},c_{jj'}) = \exp\left\{-\frac{1}{\varepsilon_2^2}\left\|(l_i - l_j) - (l_{i'} - l_{j'})\right\|_2^2\right\} \tag{12}$$

Where, $\varepsilon_2 = r/\sqrt{2}, r = \sqrt{W \cdot H / N_s}$. $l_i - l_j$ is the distance where l_i and l_j are the node spatial location in the graph $G(V,E)$. Therefore, $\Omega_2(c_{ii'},c_{jj'})$ reflects the change of edges when the object is deformed. Hence, it is insensitive to deformation relatively.

The details of the target location and updating part can be found in [10]. In the process of location, the weight coefficient consists of $\Omega_1(c_{ii'})$ and $\Omega_2(c_{ii'},c_{jj'})$, as well as their neighborhood, thus it is more flexible. Concerning the value of the weight coefficient, there are two situations as follows: Firstly, if both the superpixels and it is neighborhood are the target, the weight value is relatively large. Secondly, if a superpixel is matched successfully, while the neighborhood superpixels are not matched successfully, the weight value is relatively small. The process of updating includes updating retraining the LASVM and updating the target graph nodes.

5 Experiments

The proposed algorithm is implemented in C++ code on a PC with 2.20 GHz CPU and 2 GB memory. The selected video sequence is mainly characterized by deformation, occlusion, background interference, rotation and illumination. Meanwhile, the proposed algorithm is compared with other tracking algorithms (CT algorithm, Frag algorithm, TLD algorithm, DFT algorithm, DGT algorithm, L1APG algorithm and SPT algorithm). The tracking performance is evaluated from the three aspect of qualitative analysis, quantitative analysis and the analysis of feature. We choose nine kinds of different video data (basketball, bolt, avatar, david3, football1, lemming, mountain-Bike, up, walking) to discuss the performance of some state-of-the-art trackers. We choose some data for the qualitative analysis. The tracking results can be seen in the Fig2.

5.1 Qualitative analysis

Deformation: Structure deformation is a great challenge for bounding box based trackers. For example in the sequences of basketball and bolt where the target changes structure quickly, the DGT algorithm and the improved algorithm have a better performance than other algorithm. But the bounding box of the improved algorithm is more accurate.

Occlusion: Sequences with target occlusion, such as basketball, bolt and lemming, brought difficulties to CT algorithm and TLD algorithm, because the lacking of the occlusion handling mechanisms. Meanwhile, the Frag algorithm and the SPT algorithm have an occlusion handling mechanisms, while they do not always have a good performance due to the interference of other challenges. The improved algorithm has a better performance in dealing with these challenges.

Illumination variations: Illumination variations have serious influence on the appearance features. The illumination variations sequence including avatar, basketball and lemming. It is obvious in the avatar sequence especially. In the avatar sequence, the other trackers had a drift. The improved algorithm has a better performance, because of fusing the color local entropy feature.

Rotation and Background interference: The most of sequence that we chose has the background interference and rotation on different degrees. It is typical in the bolt and lemming sequences. Many trackers have a poor performance in dealing with these challenges, including the DGT algorithm. While, the improved algorithm has a good performance because of the color local entropy feature. So, the improved algorithm is more robust than DGT algorithm.

avatar #0044 basketball #0660 bolt #0089 lemming #0364
—CT ····TLD —DFT —L1APG ····Frag —SPT ---DGT the proposed method

Fig. 2. Tracking results

5.2 The analysis of characteristics of performance

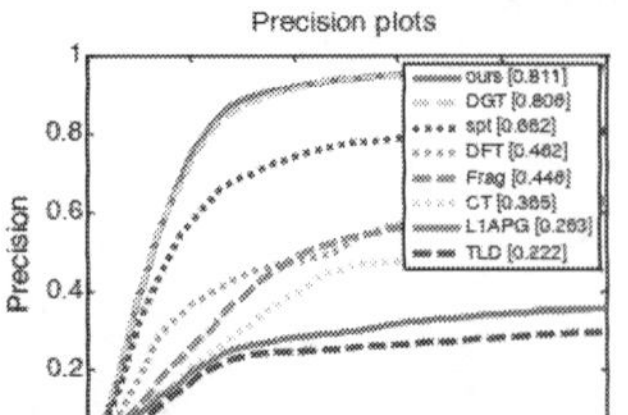

Fig. 3(a). The average ACEP.

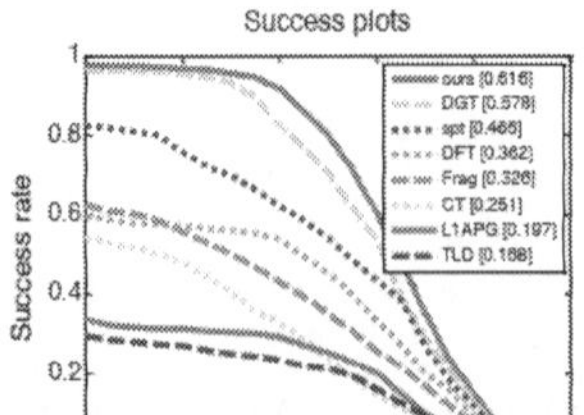

Fig. 3(b). The average SC.

The characteristics include deformation, occlusion, rotation, background interference and illumination. The Fig 3(a) shows the average ACEP value of the improved algorithm is more accurate than other trackers in these characteristics. Meanwhile, the Fig 3(b) shows the improved algorithm has a good performance than other trackers.

6 Conclusion

Due to only adopted the color feature to represent the object, the original DGT algorithm is sensitive to background interference and illumination, therefore, we take full use of the advantage of local gradient and color local entropy, and proposed an improved DGT algorithm. The proposed algorithm not only has a better performance in dealing with deformation and occlusion, but also is good in deal with background interference, rotation and illumination. The experiments results have shown that the improved algorithm is better than the DGT algorithm.

Reference

1. D. Comaniciu, et al, IEEE Trans. Pattern Anal. Mach. Intell, **5**, 564 (2003).
2. T. Liu, X P. Cheng, IEEE International Conference on Computer Engineering and Technology, 575(2010)
3. Y. Xu, Systems Process and Control, 224(2013)
4. N. Li, IEEE Conference on Electrical and Computer Engineering. Canadian, 3(2015)
5. K. Okuma, et al. Multitarget Detection and Tracking, **3021**, 28(2004)
6. H. Grabner, H. Bischof, IEEE Computer Society Conference on Computer Vision and Pattern Recognition, 260(2006)
7. B. Babenko, M H. Yang, S. Belongie, IEEE Trans Pattern Anal Mach Intell, 983(2009)
8. Z. Cai , L. Wen, Z. Lei, et al, IEEE Trans. Image Processing, **12**, 5497(2014)
9. R. Achanta, A. Shaji, K. Smith, et al, SLIC superpixels. Epfl, (2010)
10. W. Huan, W. Qinglin, W. Meng, et al, Third International Conference on Instrumentation, Measurement, Computer, Communication and Control, 114(2013)
11. A. Bordes, et al, Journal of Machine Learning Research, **6**, 1579(2012)

Suspended Microracetrack Resonator with Lateral Sub-wavelength-Grating Metamaterial Cladding for Mid-infrared Sensing Applications

Zecen Zhang[1,·], *Geok Ing* Ng[1], *Ting* Hu[1], *Haodong* Qiu[1], *Xin* Guo[1], *Wanjun* Wang[1], *Mohamed S.* Rouifed[1], *Chongyang* Liu[1], *Jiaxu* Sia[1], *Jin* Zhou[1], and *Hong* Wang[1]

[1]NOVITAS, Nanoelectronics Centre of Excellence, School of Electrical and Electronic Engineering, Nanyang Technological University, 639798 Singapore

Abstract. A one-time etching suspended microracetrack resonator with lateral sub-wavelength-grating (SWG) metamaterial cladding is theoretically and experimentally demonstrated on commercial 340 nm-thick-top-silicon silicon-on-insulator (SOI) platform for mid-infrared (MIR) bio-chemical sensing applications. The suspended structure can offer a larger exposed area of waveguides with the testing chemicals as well as a decent sensitivity. And the one-time etching process also eases the fabrication. The suspended waveguide is optimized with a balance between propagation loss and the sensitivity. The suspended microracetrack resonator is experimentally measured at 2 µm wavelength and well fitted with an extinction ratio (ER) of 12.3 dB and a full-width-at-half-maximum (FWHM) of 0.12 nm, which corresponds to a quality factor (Q factor) of 16600. With the equivalent refractive index method and a specially developed numerical model, the expected sensitivities of fundamental TE and TM mode were calculated as 58 nm/RIU and 303 nm/RIU respectively. This one-time etching suspended microracetrack resonator shows great potential in MIR optical bio-chemical sensing applications.

1 Introduction

Recently, silicon photonics based on silicon-on-insulator (SOI) platform has attracted a lot of research interest, since it can utilize the industrial mature fabrication process with lower cost. Many efforts have been invested on the SOI based bio-chemical sensing in the near-infrared (NIR) band, typically around 1.3-1.6 µm wavelength [1-6]. Various structures and methods have been utilized to achieve high sensitivity [7-18]. However, limited work has been reported on mid-infrared (MIR) sensors based on the SOI platform. One of the limitation of MIR sensing based on SOI platform is the large absorption in SiO_2 at the wavelengths longer than 4 µm. One solution is the suspended structures with the buried-oxide-layer removed, which can also increase the exposed area of waveguides with the testing material hence increase the sensitivity [19-22]. In 2012, a suspended membrane waveguide based microring resonator working at 2.75 µm was reported by Z. Cheng et al.

· Corresponding author: ZZHANG023@e.ntu.edu.sg

https://doi.org/10.1051/itmconf/20181702005

[23]. In 2013, Y. Xia et al. experimentally reported a suspended Si resonator working at 3.4 μm and 5.2 μm [24]. But for these two structures, multiple etching processes are needed, which include a partial etching of the rib waveguide and a full etching of the via holes for the following hydrofluoric acid (HF) etching. Furthermore, the wide and thin slabs beside the rib waveguide, which target to suppress the mode leakage, limit the mechanical stability of the system.

In this manuscript, for the first time, we theoretically and experimentally demonstrate a one-time etching suspended microracetrack resonator with lateral sub-wavelength-grating (SWG) metamaterial cladding on a commercial SOI platform for MIR bio-chemical sensing application. A quality factor (Q factor) of 16000 and an extinction ratio (ER) of 13.4 dB were measured at 2 μm wavelength. Furthermore, with the equivalent refractive index method and a specially developed numerical model, the expected sensitivities of fundamental TE and TM mode were calculated as 58 nm/RIU and 303 nm/RIU. This system shows great potential for the MIR band sensing applications.

2 Device designs, fabrication and characterization

The one-time etching suspended microracetrack resonator with lateral SWG metamaterial cladding are designed on a commercial SOI wafer with 340 nm-thick-top-silicon and 2 μm-thick buried SiO2 (BOX) layer. The cladding layer is air. At first, designing and optimizing the fundamental building block namely the suspended waveguide were carried out. Fig. 1 shows the schematic of the suspended waveguide.

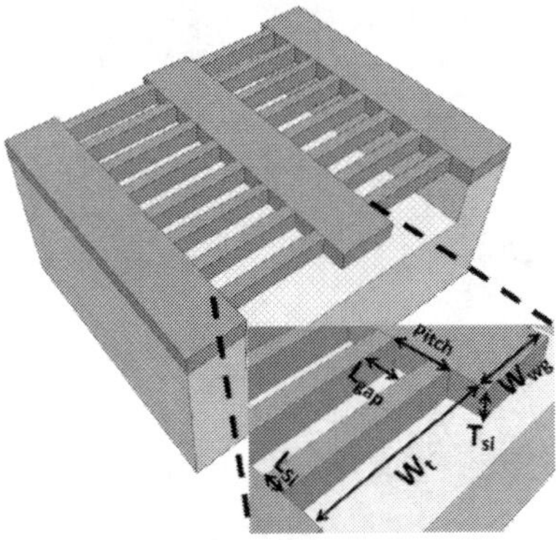

Fig. 1. The schematic of the one-time etching suspended waveguide with lateral SWG metamaterial cladding

For the optimization of the suspended waveguide, three crucial points need to be addressed: 1. Diffractive effects and back-reflections; 2. Mechanical stability; 3. Enhance the overlap between the evanescent field and the testing chemicals. First, in order to suppress the diffractive effect and back-reflections, the pitch of the sub-wavelength grating ($Pitch = L_{si} + L_{gap}$) needs to follow the Bragg condition [21]:

$$Pitch < Pitch_{Bg} = \frac{\lambda}{2n_{B-F}} \tag{1}$$

where $Pitch_{Bg}$ is the Bragg period; λ is the working wavelength; n_{B-F} is the effective index of the fundamental Bloch-Floquet mode propagating in the waveguide. Second, in order to obtain a robust structure to overcome the fluctuations caused by testing liquid or gas flows, we need to have wide silicon pillars. However, it is known that the sensitivity is determined by the overlap between the evanescent field and the testing chemicals [25]. The trade off is that while the duty-cycle ($DC = L_{si} / (L_{si} + L_{gap}) = L_{si} / Pitch$) increases with the pitch fixed, the exposed area of waveguide becomes smaller as well as the overlap between the evanescent field and the testing chemicals, which results in a degradation of sensitivity. Hence, a balance between the mechanical stability and the sensitivity needs be considered under the precondition of a small enough *Pitch* that can suppress diffractive effect and back-reflections. The width of the lattice is set as 2 μm to prevent the lateral energy leakage. Another two important influencing factors are the width and the thickness of the waveguide. The reduction of the waveguide cross-section area will compress the mode field. Consequently, more energy will gather at the surface of the waveguide thus bringing a higher overlap between the evanescent field and the testing chemicals but at the expense of a higher propagation loss. This is another trade-off which needs to be taken into account.

In order to test and verify the above discussions, one-time suspended waveguides with different dimensions were fabricated on a commercial SOI wafer with a 340 nm-thick-top-silicon layer and a 2 μm BOX layer. The waveguide and SWG cladding are defined with electron beam lithography (EBL) at the same time and subsequently fully etched to the BOX layer with deep reactive ion etching (DRIE) in order to have straight and smooth sidewalls. Then the BOX layer is etched away with buffered oxide etching (BOE).

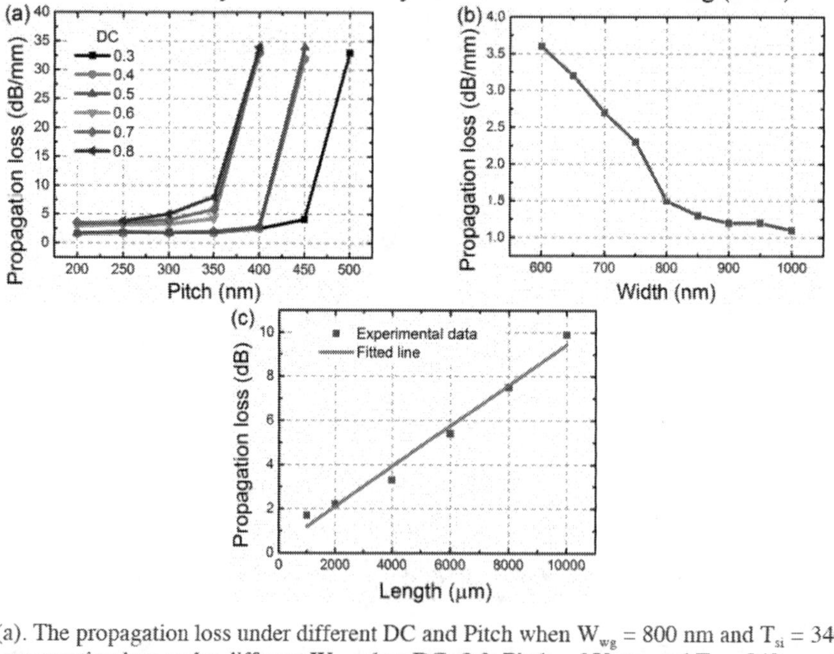

Fig. 2. (a). The propagation loss under different DC and Pitch when W_{wg} = 800 nm and T_{si} = 340 nm; (b) The propagation loss under different W_{wg} when DC=0.3, Pitch = 350 nm and T_{si} = 340 nm; (c) The experimental measured propagation loss and fitted line when DC=0.3, Pitch = 350 nm, W_{wg} = 800 nm and T_{si} = 340 nm.

All the characterization is conducted under room temperature with fundamental TE mode. As shown in Fig. 2(a), when *DC* = 0.3, *Pitch* > 450 nm, the propagation loss suddenly increases significantly and reaches the limitation of our detector (-32 dB) due to the serious diffractive effect and back reflections. With the increase of *DC* to 0.8, the cut-off point moves to smaller pitches, which is consistent with the reported simulation results [21]. In order to completely avoid the diffractive effect and back reflections while possess a large exposed area of waveguides and enough mechanical stability, we choose the dimensions as *Pitch* = 350 nm and *DC* = 0.3. Fig. 2(b) shows the influence of the waveguide width on the propagation loss with *Pitch* = 350 nm and *DC* = 0.3. As seen, with the increase of width from 600 nm to 800 nm, the propagation loss drops dramatically.

But when the width further increases, the decreasing rate of propagation loss becomes slower and then saturated. Although a much wider waveguide (W_{wg} > 800 nm) can offer a better confinement and a lower propagation loss, the sensitivity is degraded due to a less energy leakage and in turn a smaller overlap between the evanescent field and the testing chemicals. As a result, we set W_{wg} = 800 nm in order to have a balance between the propagation loss and the sensitivity. Due to the limitation of experimental setup, the impact of the thickness is not investigated in this work. The shrinking of thickness will put more compression to the mode field from vertical direction, which will result in a larger energy leakage of fundamental TM mode and a higher sensitivity. But this will also result in a higher propagation loss as a larger portion of energy is scattered by the roughness at the upper and lower surfaces. With all the above optimized parameters and T_{si} = 340 nm, the propagation loss has been plotted and fitted in Fig. 2(c). As seen, the propagation loss of the one-time suspended waveguide is about 9.2 dB/cm.

Based on the above suspended waveguide design ($Pitch$ = 350 nm, DC = 0.3, W_{wg} = 800 nm, and T_{si} = 340 nm), the suspended microracetrack resonator was fabricated and characterized. The scanning electron microscope (SEM) images of the fabricated device have been shown in Fig. 3. The coupling length (CL) and the gap width (W_g) between the bus waveguide and the microracetrack are set as 10 μm and 200 nm respectively. The radius of the bendings (R) is set as 50 μm.

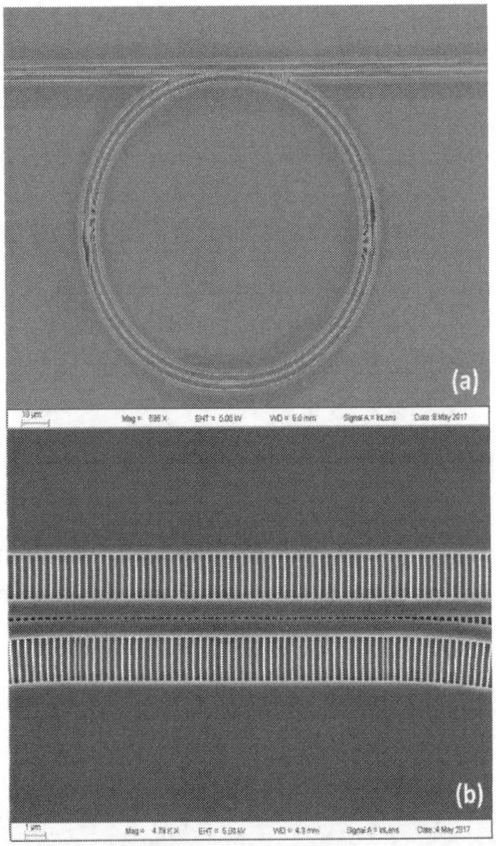

Fig. 3. (a). The overview SEM image of the one-time etching suspended microracetrack resonator; (b) The magnified SEM image of the coupling region.

The experimental and theoretical fitting results are shown in Fig. 4. The fitting numerical model is specially developed based on the equivalent refractive index method [14,15,26,27]. As *Pitch* = 350 nm is small enough, the equivalent refractive index of the lateral SWG metamaterial can be written as:

$$n_{eq} = n_{cladding} + DC*(n_{si} - n_{cladding}) \tag{2}$$

where $n_{cladding}$ is the refractive index of the cladding layer, such as air or testing chemicals; n_{si} is the refractive index of silicon. With this equivalent refractive index of the lateral cladding layer, the effective indices of the suspended waveguide at different wavelengths can be calculated with the BeamPROP module of Rsoft software by taking the dispersion into account. Then by substituting the effective indices into our numerical model and tuning the coupling coefficient k and round-trip power attenuation α^2, the fitted transmission spectrum can be obtained. The fitting parameters are: k = 0.375i, α^2 = 0.9116. From the measurements, the full-width-at-half-maximum (FWHM) is about 0.12 nm, which corresponds to a quality factor (Q factor) of 16600. The extinction ratio (ER) is about 12.3 dB.

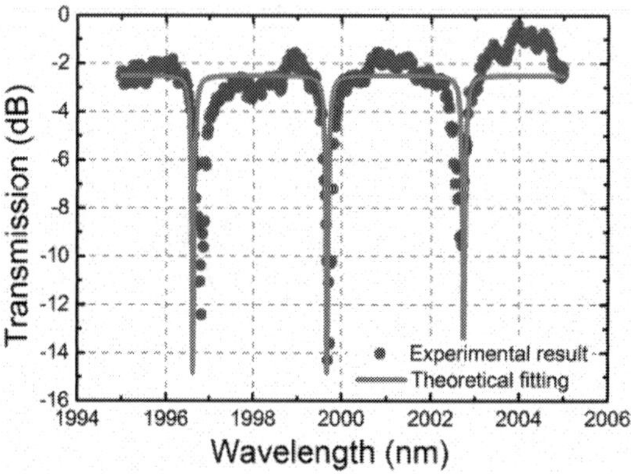

Fig.4. The experimental and theoretical fitting results of the one-time etching suspended microracetrack resonator with SWG metamaterial cladding under CL = 10 µm, W_g = 200 nm, and R = 50 µm.

Here we calculated the sensitivity with the ethanol-water solutions of different concentrations (0% ~ 4%). The refractive index of pure water is 1.306 at 2 µm wavelength. When the concentration of ethanol increases by 1%, the refractive index of the ethanol-water solution increases by 0.00047. As shown in Fig. 5, by substituting the fitted parameters and the different equivalent refractive indices of the cladding layer into our numerical model, the transmission spectra can be calculated. By measuring the wavelength shifting of the resonant dips, the sensitivities can be obtained as 58 nm/RIU and 303 nm/RIU for fundamental TE and TM mode, respectively. The moderate sensitivity of fundamental TE mode is due to the lattice structure at the two sides of waveguide, which covers the area at the connection point with the waveguide. And less exposed area of the waveguide results in smaller overlap between the evanescent field and the testing chemicals. If the BOX layer can be etched away with vapor HF to avoid the releasing stress, thinner silicon pillars can be fabricated and more exposed area can be obtained. Besides, by reducing the width of waveguide, the mode field is compressed and more energy will gather at the side walls, which also can improve the sensitivity but increase the propagation loss at the same time.

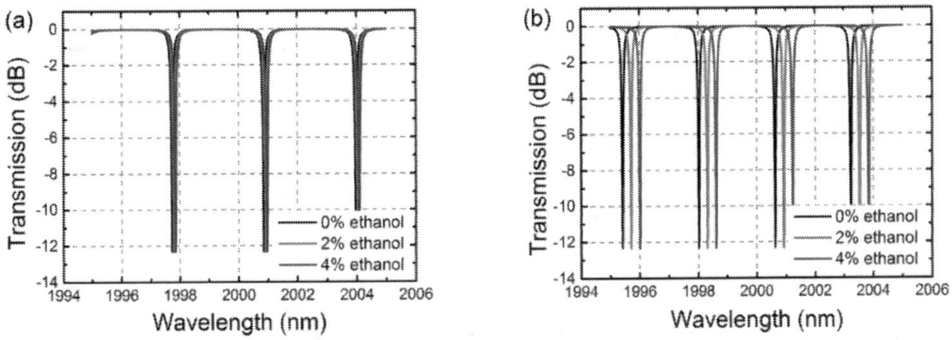

Fig. 5. (a) The normalized transmission spectra of fundamental TE mode under the ethanol-water solutions of different concentrations; (b) The normalized transmission spectra of fundamental TM mode under the ethanol-water solutions of different concentrations

3 Conclusion

In this manuscript, for the first time, we have theoretically and experimentally demonstrated a one-time etching suspended microracetrack resonator with lateral SWG metamaterial cladding for MIR bio-chemical sensing applications. With the advantage of suspended structure, the overlap between the evanescent field and the testing chemicals is greatly enhanced, which is helpful for improving the sensitivity. The one-time etching process also makes it easier to fabricate. Various one-time etching suspended waveguides with different dimensions were fabricated and characterized. The propagation loss of the optimized suspended waveguide is experimentally measured as ~9.2 dB/cm. Based on the optimized suspended waveguide, the one-time etching suspended microracetrack resonator was fabricated and tested. The experimental transmission spectrum is well fitted with our specially developed numerical model. The ER is ~12.3 dB. The FWHM is about 0.12 nm which corresponds to a Q factor of ~16600. With the equivalent refractive index method and our numerical model, the expected sensitivities of fundamental TE and TM mode were calculated as 58 nm/RIU and 303 nm/RIU respectively. The results presented in this manuscript show a great potential of the one-time etching suspended microracetrack resonator with SWG metamaterial cladding for MIR integrated optical bio-chemical sensing applications.

References

1. K. D. Vos, I. Bartolozzi, E. Schacht, P. Bienstman, and R. Baets, Opt. Express, **15**, 12, 7610-7615, (2007).
2. K. D. Vos, J. Girones, S. Popelka, E. Schacht, R. Baets, and P. Bienstman, Biosensors and Bioelectronics, **24**, 8, 2528–2533, (2009).
3. A. L. Washburn, L. C. Gunn, and R. C. Bailey, Anal. Chem., **81**, 22, 9499–9506, (2009).
4. A. L. Washburn, M. S. Luchansky, A. L. Bowman, and R. C. Bailey, Anal. Chem., **82**, 1, 69–72, (2010).
5. J. G. W.-Pérez, P. Cheben, A. Ortega-Moñux, C. A.-Ramos, D. P.-Galacho, R. Halir, I. M.-Fernández, D.-X. Xu, and J. H. Schmid, Opt. Lett., **39**, 15, 4442-4445, (2014).
6. X. Wang, J. Flueckiger, S. Schmidt, S. Grist, S. T. Fard, J. Kirk, M. Doerfler, K. C. Cheung, D. M. Ratner, and L. Chrostowski, J. Biophoton., **6**, 10, 821-828, (2013).

7. S. T. Fard, V. Donzella, S. A. Schmidt, J. Flueckiger, S. M. Grist, P. T. Fard, Y. Wu, R. J. Bojko, E. Kwok, N. A. F. Jaeger, D. M. Ratner, and L. Chrostowski, Opt. Express, **22**, 12, 14166-14179, (2014).
8. W. C. Jiang and Q. Lin, Proc. SPIE, **9367**, Silicon Photonics X; 936708, (2015).
9. T. Claes, J. G. Molera, K. D. Vos, E. Schacht, R. Baets. and P. Bienstman, IEEE Photonics J., **1**, 3, 197–204, (2009).
10. K. B. Gylfason, C. F. Carlborg, A. Kaźmierczak, F. Dortu, H. Sohlström, L. Vivien, C. A. Barrios, W. V. D. Wijngaart, and G. Stemme, Opt. Express, **18**, 4, 3226-3237, (2010).
11. P. J. Bock, P. Cheben, J. H. Schmid, J. Lapointe, A. Delâge, S. Janz, G. C. Aers, D.-X. Xu, A. Densmore, and T. J. Hall, Opt. Express, **18**, 19, 20251-20262, (2010).
12. J. Wang, I. Glesk, and L. R. Chen, Opt. Express, **22**, 13, 15335-15345, (2014).
13. V. Donzella, A. Sherwali, J. Flueckiger, S. T. Fard, S. M. Grist, and L. Chrostowski, Opt. Express, **22**, 17, 21037-21050, (2014).
14. V. Donzella, A. Sherwali, J. Flueckiger, S. M. Grist, S. T. Fard, and L. Chrostowski, Opt. Express, **23**, 4, 4791-4803, (2015).
15. J. Flueckiger, S. Schmidt, V. Donzella, A. Sherwali, D. M. Ratner, L. Chrostowski, and K. C. Cheung, Opt. Express, **24**, 14, 15672-15686, (2016).
16. K. Miyamoto, K. Ishibashi, K. Hiroi, Y. Kimura, H. Ishii, and M. Niwano, Appl. Phys. Lett., **86**, 053902, (2005).
17. F. K. Tittel, Y. Bakhirkin, A. Kosterev, R. Lewicki, S. So, G. Wysocki, and R. F. Curl, Proc. SPIE, **6900**, 69000Z, (2008).
18. M. Sieger and B. Mizaikoff, Anal. Chem., **88**, 11, 5562-5573, (2016).
19. R. Soref, Nat. Photonics, **4**, 495-497, (2010).
20. Z. Cheng, X. Chen, C. Y. Wong, K. Xu, C. K. Y. Fung, Y. M. Chen, and H. K. Tsang, Opt. Lett., **37**, 7, 1217-1219, (2012).
21. J. S. Penadés, C. A.-Ramos, A. Z. Khokhar, M. Nedeljkovic, L. A. Boodhoo, A. O.-Moñux, I. M.-Fernández, P. Cheben, and G. Z. Mashanovich, Opt. Lett., **39**, 19, 5661-5664, (2014).
22. J. S. Penades, A. O.-Moñux, M. Nedeljkovic, J. G. W.-Pérez, R. Halir, A. Z. Khokhar, C. A.-Ramos, Z. Qu, I. M.-Fernández, P. Cheben, and G. Z. Mashanovich, Opt. Express, **24**, 20, 22908-22916, (2016).
23. Z. Cheng, X. Chen, C. Y. Wong, K. Xu, and H. K. Tsang, IEEE Photon. J., **4**, 5, 1510-1519, (2012).
24. Y. Xia, C. Qiu, X. Zhang, W. Gao, J. Shu, and Q. Xu, Opt. Lett., **38**, 7, 1122-1124, (2013).

Band-modulation of MgZnO/ZnO Metal-semiconductor-metal Photodetectors

Jundar Hwang[1,]·, and *Junshou* Lin[1]

[1]Department of Electrophysics, National Chiayi University, Chiayi, Taiwan, China.

Abstract. Magnesium (Mg) diffusion behavior on the band modulation of MgxZn1-xO/ZnO metal-semiconductor-metal photodetectors (MSM-PDs) was studied. As the annealing temperature increases, Mg atoms diffuse from MgxZn1-xO into the underlying ZnO layer, which modulates the detection band of the fabricated MSM-PDs from two distinct bands into one band. For the annealing temperature lower than 900 °C, two detection bands were achieved located in the wavelength region of 280–320 nm and 360–400 nm, attributed to the absorption of the MgxZn1-xO and the ZnO layer, respectively. When the annealing temperature is raised to 900 °C, the MgxZn1-xO/ZnO bi- layer becomes homogenized into a single MgxZn1-xO layer, leading to only one detection band with a wavelength region of 280–340 nm. In the photoluminescence measurement, the as-deposited MgxZn1-xO/ZnO bi-layer demonstrates two distinct emission peaks located at about 340 and 400 nm for the absorption of the MgxZn1-xO and ZnO layers, whereas only one emission peak of 355 nm was observed in the 900 °C-annealed MgxZn1-xO/ZnO bi-layer.

1 Introduction

ZnO and $Mg_XZn_{1-X}O$-based ultraviolet (UV) photodetectors (PDs) have been continuously studied because the ZnO material has many advantages, including a wide band gap (3.37 eV), high transparency (>80%) in the visible wavelength region, high exciton binding energy (60 meV), and non-toxicity [1,8]. By mixing ZnO with another wide-direct-band-gap material, MgO (7.8 eV), the tunable bandgap material of $Mg_XZn_{1-X}O$, which can modulate the detection wavelength of PDs by varying Mg content, can be formed [9-11]. In addition, no significant lattice distortion is found in the $Mg_XZn_{1-X}O$ material because Mg^{+2} has a very similar ionic radius to that of Zn^{+2} [12].

Although GaN and $Al_XGa_{1-X}N$ materials have been employed in various PDs, expensive and high-temperature technology was required to grow the GaN and $Al_XGa_{1-X}N$ materials, including molecular beam epitaxy and metal organic chemical vapor deposition systems. In contrast, ZnO and $Mg_XZn_{1-X}O$ materials can be grown using low-cost and low-temperature techniques, including radio-frequency (RF) magnetron sputtering and hydrothermal methods [13,14]. As opposed to pure ZnO or $Mg_XZn_{1-X}O$ materials, the

· Corresponding author: jundar@mail.ncyu.edu.tw

$Mg_xZn_{1-x}O/ZnO$ bi- layer heterostructure is a promising technological platform as evidenced heterojunction field-effect transistor, multi-quantum-well (MQW) light-emitting diodes, MQW-PDs, and optoelectronic devices with superlattice, as well as two-dimensional electron gas (2DEG) structures [15].

Previously, many $Mg_xZn_{1-x}O/ZnO$ heterojunction UV-PDs were fabricated [16-120]. As compared to the MSM-PDs without the $Mg_xZn_{1-x}O$ capping layer, the PDs with the $Mg_xZn_{1-x}O/ZnO$ bi-layer presented higher dark current, photocurrent, and photoresponsivity due to the shielding of ambient oxygen, defect, and surface states passivation by the $Mg_xZn_{1-x}O$ capping layer [21]. The $Au/Mg_xZn_{1-x}O/ZnO$ PDs had larger responsivity than $Au/ZnO/Mg_xZn_{1-x}O$ PDs [22]. By varying the applied bias voltage, the detection wavelength of the $Mg_xZn_{1-x}O/ZnO$ MSM-PDs could be modulated from a single to a dual wavelength [23]. MgZnO/ZnO bi-layer with 2DEG behavior was investigated [24-26].

The photoluminescence (PL) was investigated by annealing the $Mg_xZn_{1-x}O/ZnO$ bi-layer, which tuned the Mg composition [27]. Dual-band $Mg_xZn_{1-x}O$ UV-PDs were fabricated by employing two $Mg_xZn_{1-x}O$ layers with different Mg compositions [28]. The Mg atomic reconstruction was observed in p-type interface (ZnO on Zn-polar MgZnO), but not in n-type interface (MgZnO on Zn-polar ZnO) due to the different polarity of the interface [29]. The Mg atomic reconstruction was not caused by thermal diffusion, instead by the asymmetry of energy scales.

In this work, the Mg thermal diffusion behavior on the MSM-PDs with the $Mg_xZn_{1-x}O/ZnO$ bi-layer was studied. We found that by increasing the annealing temperature of the $Mg_xZn_{1-x}O/ZnO$ bi-layer, one could modulate the detection band of the fabricated MSM-PDs from two bands into one band.

2 Experiments

ZnO and $Mg_xZn_{1-x}O$ layers with a thickness of 250 nm were deposited consecutively on a sapphire substrate using an RF magnetron sputtering system with a substrate temperature of 200 °C in a 10-mTorr Ar atmosphere. X-ray photoelectron spectroscopy showed the Mg content being 0.3 in the as-deposited $Mg_xZn_{1-x}O$ film. Then, the $Mg_xZn_{1-x}O/ZnO$ bi-layers were annealed at various temperatures between 700 and 900 °C for 2 h, which forced the Mg atom to diffuse from $Mg_xZn_{1-x}O$ to the underlying ZnO layer. The as-deposited (not annealed) $Mg_xZn_{1-x}O/ZnO$ bi-layer was also prepared for comparison. MSM-PDs were fabricated by evaporating Au electrodes on the $Mg_xZn_{1-x}O$ surface in an interdigitated pattern. Inter-diffusion behavior of Mg atoms was studied by absorption, PL, and secondary ion mass spectrometry (SIMS) measurements. Current–voltage (*I–V*) characteristics were recorded using a Keithley 2400 source meter, and the photoresponse was measured with a monochromator by illuminating the samples from the $Mg_xZn_{1-x}O$ side with a 300-W Xe arc lamp.

3 Results and discussions

Dark *I–V* characteristics of the fabricated MSM-PDs for the as-deposited and various-temperature-annealed $Mg_xZn_{1-x}O/ZnO$ bi-layer are shown in Fig. 1. Clearly, the current increases with annealed temperature because the sheet resistance of the $Mg_xZn_{1-x}O$ and ZnO layers was reduced by the thermal energy of the annealing process. With increasing annealing temperature, the sheet resistance of the ZnO and $Mg_xZn_{1-x}O$ layers decreased from 179 MΩ/□ and 189 MΩ/□ for the as-deposited films to 0.6 KΩ/□ and 100 KΩ/□ for the ones annealed at 900 °C.

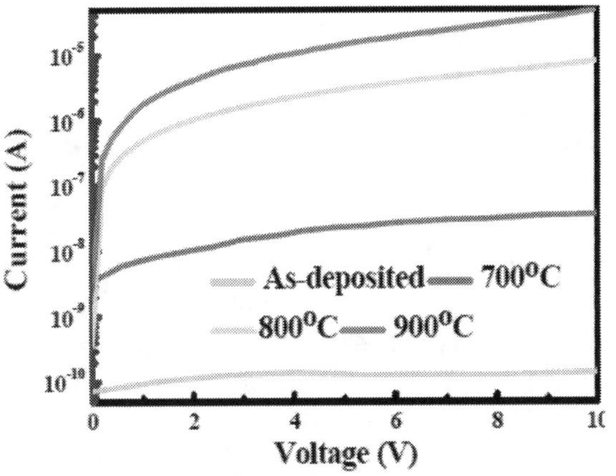

Fig. 1. Dark *I–V* characteristics of the fabricated MSM-PDs with as- deposited and various-temperature- annealed $Mg_xZn_{1-x}O/ZnO$ bi-layer

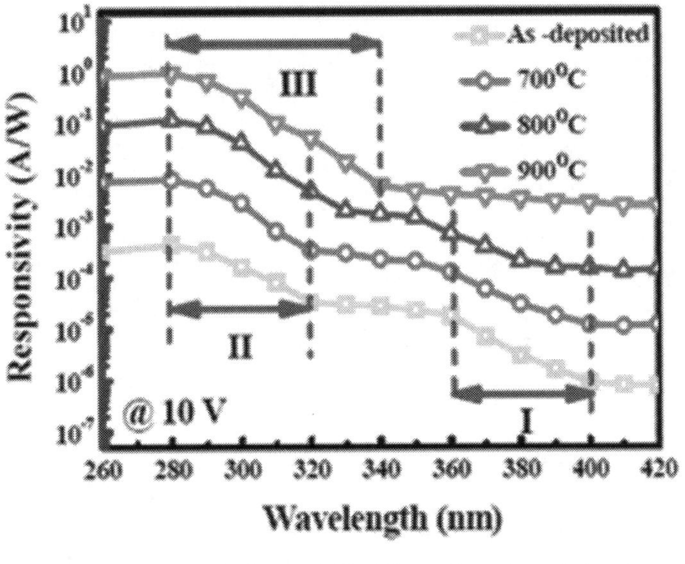

Fig. 2. Responsivity versus wavelengths for the MSM-PDs with as-deposited and various-temperature-annealed MgxZn1- xO/ZnO bi-layer biased at 10-V voltage

The plot of responsivity versus wavelength for the MSM-PDs with as-deposited and various-temperature-annealed $Mg_xZn_{1-x}O/ZnO$ bi-layer biased at 10 V is shown in Fig. 2. It is interesting that the MSM-PDs with as-deposited and 700–800 °C annealed $Mg_xZn_{1-x}O/ZnO$ bi-layer demonstrate two sharp increasing bands in responsivity, that is; the MSM-PDs have two detection bands, I and II. In contrast, only one sharp increasing band is observed in the MSM-PDs with 900 °C annealed $Mg_xZn_{1-x}O/ZnO$ bi-layer, meaning these MSM-PDs has only one detection band, III.

In the MSM-PDs with as-deposited and 700–800°C annealing, the sharp increasing band of region I, wavelength region of 360–400 nm, originated from the absorption of ZnO layer. However, the sharp increasing band of region II comes from the absorption of the $Mg_xZn_{1-x}O$ layer, having a wavelength region of 280–320 nm. In contrast, the absorption band of ZnO disappears and only one absorption band is observed in the MSM-PDs with 900 °C annealed $Mg_xZn_{1-x}O$/ZnO bi-layer. This absorption band has a wavelength region of 280–340 nm, which is shorter than the absorption region (360–400 nm) of ZnO. Thus, the one absorption band (280–340 nm) is an absorption result of the $Mg_xZn_{1-x}O$ layer with Mg content (x value) less than 0.3 for the as-deposited $Mg_xZn_{1-x}O$ [10,11, 30].

More evidence of Mg inter-diffusion can be observed in the SIMS depth profile of the as-deposited and various temperature annealed $Mg_xZn_{1-x}O$/ZnO bi-layers, shown in Fig. 3. It is clear that the top $Mg_xZn_{1-x}O$ and bottom ZnO layers are present in the as-deposited $Mg_xZn_{1-x}O$/ZnO bi-layer with Mg concentration of about 30%, shown in Fig. 3(a). The sharp interface between $Mg_xZn_{1-x}O$ and ZnO leads two detection bands in the MSM-PDs with the as-deposited $Mg_xZn_{1-x}O$/ZnO bi-layer, shown in Fig. 2. No significant Mg diffusion is seen in the 700 °C annealed $Mg_xZn_{1-x}O$/ZnO bi-layer, shown in Fig. 3(b), which causes a similar responsivity between the MSM- PDs with as-deposited and 700 °C annealed $Mg_xZn_{1-x}O$/ZnO bi-layer, also shown in Fig. 2.

Whereas a significant Mg diffusing, from top $Mg_xZn_{1-x}O$ into the underlying ZnO layer, is present in the 800 °C annealed $Mg_xZn_{1-x}O$/ZnO bi-layer, shown in Fig. 3(c). The Mgdiffusion results in decreased Mg concentration from ~30% for the as-deposited (Fig. 3(a)) to ~23% for the 800 °C annealed $Mg_xZn_{1-x}O$/ZnO bi-layer, shown in Fig. 3(c). The decrease in Mg concentration causes a red-shift of the $Mg_xZn_{1-x}O$ absorption edge; the Mg atom also diffuses into the underlying ZnO layer, generating a blue-shift of the ZnO absorption edge. On further increasing the annealing temperature to 900 °C, the $Mg_xZn_{1-x}O$/ZnO bi-layer gets homogenized into a single $Mg_xZn_{1-x}O$ layer with ~8% Mg distributed almost uniformly as shown in Fig. 3(d), leading to only one detection band in the 900 °C annealed MSM-PDs, shown in Fig. 2.

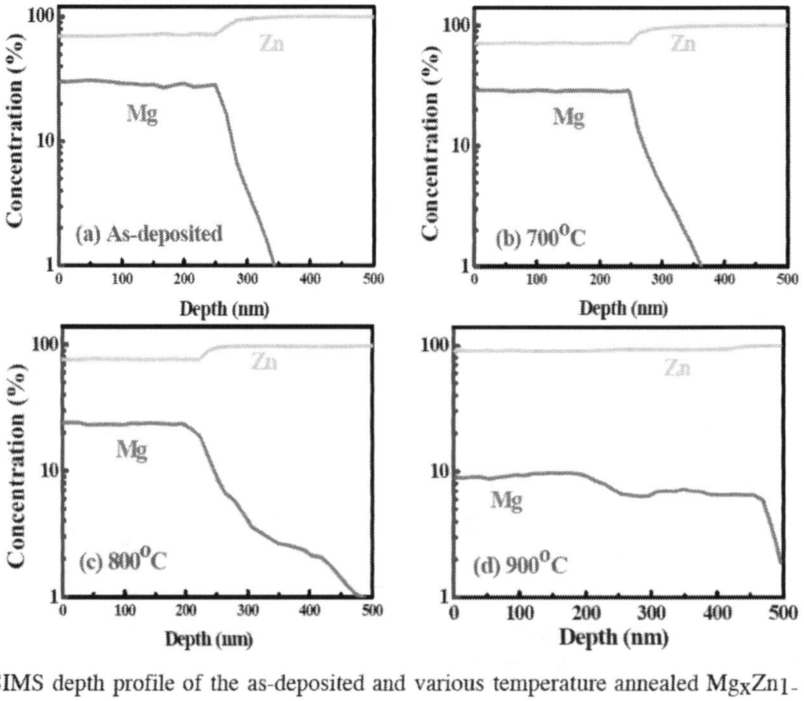

Fig. 3. SIMS depth profile of the as-deposited and various temperature annealed $Mg_xZn_{1-x}O$/ZnO bi-layer

The normalized PL spectra of the as-deposited and various-temperature-annealed $Mg_xZn_{1-x}O$/ZnO bi-layer are shown in Fig. 4. The as-deposited $Mg_xZn_{1-x}O$/ZnO bi-layer demonstrates two distinct peaks located at about 340 and 400 nm for the emissions of the $Mg_xZn_{1-x}O$ and ZnO layers, respectively, as shown in Fig. 4(a). PL is maintained at almost the same peak wavelengths in the 700 °C annealed $Mg_xZn_{1-x}O$/ZnO bi-layer, shown in Fig. 4(b). It is a fact that no significant Mg diffusion is observed in the SIMS depth profile of Fig. 4(b). However, compared to the as-deposited $Mg_xZn_{1-x}O$/ZnO bi-layer, the annealed $Mg_xZn_{1-x}O$/ZnO bi-layer reveals a larger emission peak in $Mg_xZn_{1-x}O$ than that in ZnO.

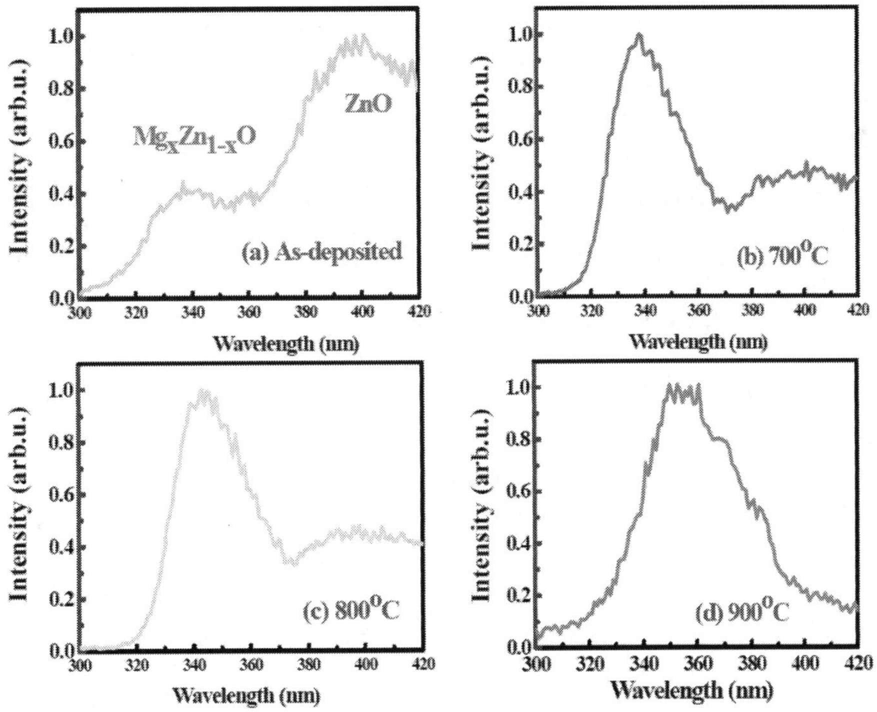

Fig. 4. Normalized PL spectra of the as-deposited and various-temperature-annealed $Mg_xZn_{x-1}O$ / ZnO bi-layer

This is because the crystalline property of the $Mg_xZn_{1-x}O$ film is largely improved after annealing due to the full width at half maximum being drastically reduced from 0.54^o to 0.36^o for the as-deposited and 700 °C annealed $Mg_xZn_{1-x}O$ layers, respectively. $Mg_xZn_{1-x}O$ is the top layer, and the incident light is illuminated from the $Mg_xZn_{1-x}O$ side in the PL measurement. When raising the annealing temperature to 800°C, the emission wavelength of $Mg_xZn_{1-x}O$ is red-shifted and that of the ZnO is blue-shifted, due to the Mg diffusing across $Mg_xZn_{1-x}O$/ZnO interface, shown in Fig. 4(c). On further increasing the annealing temperature to 900°C, only one PL peak occurs at about 355 nm, due to the completely homogenized $Mg_xZn_{1-x}O$ layer generated, as shown in Fig. 4(d).

4 Conclusions

The tunable detection band of MSM-PDs with $Mg_xZn_{1-x}O$/ZnO bi-layer was fabricated. By varying the annealing temperature from 700 to 900 °C during fabrication, we can modulate the detection band of the fabricated MSM-PDs from two bands into one band. When the annealing temperature is lower than 900 °C, two distinct detection bands were achieved due to the absorption of $Mg_xZn_{1-x}O$ and the underlying ZnO layers. When the annealing temperature was raised to 900 °C, only one detection band was observed in the NSM-PDs. This is because the $Mg_xZn_{1-x}O$/ZnO bi-layer is completely mixed into one $Mg_xZn_{1-x}O$ layer owing to the diffusion of Mg atoms from $Mg_xZn_{1-x}O$ to the underlying ZnO layer. PL measurement show that there are two emission peaks in the as-deposited and 700–800 °C annealed $Mg_xZn_{1-x}O$/ZnO bi-layer. However, only one emission peak was found in the 900°C annealed $Mg_xZn_{1-x}O$/ZnO bi-layer.Equations should be centred and should be numbered with the number on the right-hand side.

Acknowledgement: This work was supported by the Ministry of Science and Technology of the Republic of China, Taiwan, under Contract No. MOST 105-2112-M-415-001-MY3.

References

1. H. Endo, M. Sugibuchi, K. Takahashi, S. Goto, S. Sugimura, K. Hane, Y. Kashiwaba, Appl. Phys. Lett. 90, 121906 (2007)
2. J.D. Hwang, F.H. Wang, C.Y. Kung, M.C. Chan, IEEE Trans. Nanotechnology **14**, 318 (2015).
3. G. Cheng, X. Wu, B. Liu, B. Li, X. Zhang, Z. Du, ZnO nanowire Schottky barrier ultraviolet photodetector with high sensitivity and fast recovery speed, Appl. Phys. Lett. **99**, 203105 (2011)
4. G. Tabares, A. Hierro, J.M. Ulloa, A. Guzman, E. Muñoz, A. Nakamura, T. Hayashi, J. Temmyo, High responsivity and internal gain mechanisms in Au-ZnMgO Schottky photodiodes, Appl. Phys. Lett. **96**, 101112 (2010)
5. J.D. Hwang, J.S. Lin, S.B. Hwang, Annealing effects on MgZnO films and applications in Schottky-barrier photodetectors, J. Phys. D: Appl. Phys. **48**, 405103 (2015)
6. Y.K. Su, S.M. Peng, L.W. Ji, C.Z. Wu, W.B. Cheng, C.H. Liu, Ultraviolet ZnO Nanorod Photosensors, Langmuir 26, 603 (2010)
7. S.J. Young, L.W. Ji, S.J. Chang, X.L. Du, ZnO Metal-Semiconductor-Metal Ultraviolet Photodiodes with Au Contacts, J. Electrochem. Soc. **154**, H2**6** (2007)
8. L.K. Wang, Z.G. Ju, J.Y. Zhang, J.D. Zheng, Z. Shen, B. Yao, D.X. Zhao, Z.Z. Zhang, B.H. Li, C.X. Shan, Single-crystalline cubic MgZnO films and their application in deep-ultraviolet optoelectronic devices, Appl. Phys. Lett. **95**, 131113 (2009)
9. S. Han, Z. Zhang, J. Zhang, L. Wang, J. Zheng, H. Zhao, Y. Zhang, M. Jiang, S. Wang, D. Zhao, C. Shan, B. Li, D. Shen, Photoconductive gain in solar-blind ultraviolet photodetector based on Mg0.52Zn0.48O thin film, Appl. Phys. Lett. **99**, 242105 (2011)
10. L.K. Wang, Z.G. Ju, J.Y. Zhang, J.D. Zheng, Z. Shen, B. Yao, D.X. Zhao, Z.Z. Zhang, B.H. Li, C.X. Shan, Appl. Phys. Lett. **95**, 131113 (2009)
11. Q. Zheng, F. Huang, J. Huang, Q. Hu, D. Chen, K. Ding, IEEE Electron Dev. Lett. **33**, 1033 (2012).
12. J.D. Hwang, S.Y. Wang, S.B. Hwang, J. Alloy. compd. **656**, 618 (2016)
13. J.D. Hwang, J.S. Lin, S.B. Hwang, Annealing effects on MgZnO films and applications in Schottky-barrier photodetectors, J. Phys. D: Appl. Phys. **48**, 405103 (2015)
14. Q. Zheng, F. Huang, K. Ding, J. Huang, D. Chen, Z. Zhan, Z. Lin, MgZnO-based metal-semiconductor-metal solar-blind photodetectors on ZnO substrates, Appl. Phys. Lett. **98**, 221112 (2011).
15. J.D. Hwang, C.C. Yang, C.M. Chu, MgZnO/ZnO Two-Dimensional Electron Gas Photodetectors Fabricated by RF-Sputtering, ACS Appl. Mat. Interfaces **9** , 23904 (2017)
16. T.H. Wu, I.C. Cheng, C.C. Hsu, J.Z. Chen, J. Alloy. compd. **628**, 68 (2015)

17. R. Liu, D. Jiang, Q. Duan, L. Sun, C. Tian, Q. Liang, S. Gao, J. Qin, Appl. Phys. Lett. **5**, 043505 (2014)
18. J.D. Hwang, G.S. Lin, Nanotechnology **27**,375502 (2016)
19. L.K. Wang, Z.G. Ju, J.Y. Zhang, J.D. Zheng, Z. Shen, B. Yao, D.X. Zhao, Z.Z. Zhang, B.H. Li, C.X. Shan, Appl. Phys. Lett. **95**, 131113 (2009)
20. Q. Zheng, F. Huang, J. Huang, Q. Hu, D. Chen, K. Ding, IEEE Electron Dev. Lett. **33**, 1033 (2012)
21. T.H. Wu, I.C. Cheng, C.C. Hsu, J.Z. Chen, UV photocurrent responses of ZnO and MgZnO/ZnO processed by atmospheric pressure plasma jets, J. Alloy. compd. **628**, 68 (2015)
22. R. Liu, D. Jiang, Q. Duan, L. Sun, C. Tian, Q. Liang, S. Gao, J. Qin, Origin of the responsivity characteristics of Au/ZnO/MgZnO and Au/MgZnO/ZnO structured ultraviolet photodetectors, Appl. Phys. Lett. **105**, 043505 (2014)
23. J.D. Hwang, G.S. Lin, Single- and dual-wavelength photodetectors with MgZnO/ZnO metal-semiconductor-metal structure by varying the bias voltage, Nanotechnology **27**, 375502 (2016)
24. H.A. Chin, I.C. Cheng, C.I. Huang, Y.R. Wu, W.S. Lu, W.L. Lee, J.Z. Chen,; K.C. Chiu, T.S. Lin, Two dimensuonal electron gases in polycrystalline MgZnO/ZnO heterostructures grown by rf-sputtering process, J. Appl. Phys. **108**, 054503 (2010)
25. H. Tampo, H. Shibata, K. Matsubara, A. Yamada, P. Fons, S. Niki, Two-dimensional electron gas in Zn polar ZnMgO/ZnO heterostructures grown by radical sources molecular beam epitaxy, Appl. Phys. Lett. **89**, 132113 (2006)
26. M. Brandt, H.V. Wenckstern, G. Benndorf, H. Hochmuth, M. Lorenz, M. Grundmann, Formation of a two-dimensional electron gas in ZnO/MgZnO single heterostructures and quantum wells, Thin Solid Films **518**, 1048 (2009)
27. A.K. Das, P. Misra, R.S. Alimsha, A. Bose, S.C. Joshi, S. Porwal, T.K. Sharma, S.M. Oak, L.M. Kukreja, Ultraviolet/visible photodiode of nanostructure Sn–doped ZnO/Si heterojunction, J. Appl. Phys. **114**, 183103 (2013)
28. Y.N. Hou, Z.X. Mei, H.L. Liang, D.Q. Ye, C.Z. Gu, X.L. Du, Dual-band MgZnO ultraviolet photodetector integrated with Si, Appl. Phys. Lett. **102**, 153510 (2013)
29. K. Imasaka, J. Falson, Y. Kozuka, A. Tsukazaki, M. Kawasaki, Spontaneous polarization driven Mg concentration profile reconstruction in MgZnO/ZnO heterostructures, Appl. Phys. Lett. **104**, 242112 (2014)
30. P. Kumar, H. Malik, A. Ghosh, R. Thangavel, K. Asokan, Bandgap tuning in highly c-axis orinted Zn1-xMgxO thin films, Appl. Phys. Lett. **102**, 221903 (2013)

A New Data Fusion Method for Multi Terminal Fault Location Based on Sensor Networks

Qing-Sen Cai[1,*]

[1]Electrical engineering, Xi'an Aeronautical Institute, Lianhu District, Xi'an, Shaanxi, China

Abstract. Data fusion with different types of data that used for grid fault location can bring more accurate and clear results. Therefore, a new method for fault location which contains multi grid current and voltage, time and coordinate data information is proposed. Transient traveling wave is analyzed for determine the required data information in the first place, and then affirm the positioning principle and the selection rules of positioning network according to characteristics of multi fault traveling wave. Finally, Grid fault location will be precisely positioned by applying multiple data grid fault location algorithm. Simulation results shows that the proposed method is feasible, and the new algorithm has higher positioning accuracy.

1 Introduction

The existing fault location system adopts traveling wave information generally. There are two kinds of positioning principle: single-terminal location and double-terminal location. For single-terminal location, the information that needs to be identified include first arrival time of fault wave, arrival time of reflected wave from fault point and arrival time of reflected wave from opposite end bus etc. The process of identify is complicated so that the precision of location is low. Double-terminal location only needs to identify the first arrival time of fault wave form two terminal, it is easy to implement machine analysis and automation. Therefore, double-terminal location is widely used in practical positioning systems, single-terminal location as an auxiliary method [1].

Double-terminal location needs synchronization at both ends of the fault line. As long distance measurement and synchronization system has been widely used, the existing power grid monitoring technology is changing rapidly, and the synchronization problem of double-terminal positioning is solved. However, most of lines are single-circuit line so that huge amounts of resources need to be consumed in the process of fault location [2]. Multi-terminal location could integrate data from all the grid, so it is good at improve the accuracy of fault location and optimize the structure of networks [3]. It is an important research direction that built a network with multi-terminal sensors to locate the position of fault.

The research of multi-terminal location has achieved some results. References[4] presents the development and implementation in a computational routine of algorithms for

* Corresponding author: oddnewlife@126.com

fault location in multi-terminal transmission lines. References [5] proposed a new fault feeder selection scheme and choose the fault feeder by calculating the rank of every feeder's matrix and using the first transient traveling wave can realize fault location. References [6] proposed a traveling wave fault location method based on the multi measuring points. Detection device with Rogowski coil as the core was installed along the DC line long range.

Setting a main terminal in a fixed position is necessary under any existing fault location system, other terminals transmit data to the main terminal. The result of fault location is length between main terminal and fault position. Thera are some defects, for instance: 1. Traveling wave arrival time will be inaccurate because of the traveling wave speed varies on different lines. 2. Massive energy will be consumed during the long distance transmission. 3. Traveling wave attenuation will be very large when the fault point is far from the main terminal. 4. The main purpose of fault location is display the geographical position of fault but not the length from the main terminal.

In view of the above shortcomings, this paper presents the following characteristics: 1. Main terminal is not fixed, the terminal which traveling wave arrival time is shortest will be used as main terminal. 2. The result of fault location is in the form of plane coordinates, for the maintenance personnel, plane coordinates is a definite location information.

2 Location data extraction and analysis

When the power line short circuit to ground somewhere, there will be a transient traveling wave spread to the whole grid, this traveling wave will refract and reflect when the impedance of the line is discontinuous. Fault locating required extract data from this transient traveling wave and analyse the data in order to locate the fault point through the algorithm. For the single-terminal and double-terminal location, the data that arrival time of traveling wave needs to be extracted [7]. References [8] presents a new method for single-terminal traveling wave location with amended wave velocity by double-terminal asynchronous data. This method analyse the data that changes of polarity of the wave after catadioptric. References [9] presents a method of locating fault based on the calculation of the ratio of amplitudes of components at different frequencies. The wavelet modulus maxima of the travelling wave head at two different scales, the ratio of the wavelet modulus maxima at the two corresponding central frequencies can be obtained. References[10]extract the propagation path information of traveling wave to location the fault point.

2.1 Voltage and current traveling wave

When the power line occurs grounding fault, the situation equivalent to connect a power source to the grid, from the micro angle of the line, the distributed capacitance that close to the fault point will charge fast, and then discharge to the neighboring distributed capacitor, the neighboring distributed capacitance also charge and discharge. This process proceeds along the line to a distance, at the same time, the inductance of an electric current through a wire produces a magnetic field, this is the process of traveling wave of voltage and current. Fault location that use traveling wave should obtain the voltage and current traveling wave firstly. Sensors that could be used include CVT[11], CT, traveling wave data acquisition device[12] etc.

2.2 Aerial mode component of transient traveling wave

Power grid adopts three-phase circuit, electromagnetic coupling exists in each phase of the line, so the wave equations that established by the data from sensors immediately are not independent, this brings some difficulties to the calculation. According to the mode transmission theory, three phase voltage and current traveling wave could be transform to line module and zero module. Common method include symmetrical components transform, Clarke transform, Park transform, Karenbauer transform etc.[13]

Zero modulus component flows through the earth, it contact with the power system grounding closely. The situation is very complex, so line mode component is used in the fault location system usually and zero mode component is used rarely[14].

2.3 Maximum modulus of transient traveling wave

Transient traveling wave contains a lot of fault information such as fault distance, fault angle, fault frequency etc. The most important data that this paper need is arriving time of fault traveling wave, it could be extract from singularity characteristics of fault traveling wave.

Singularity characteristics of fault traveling wave could use the Lipschitz index to express. The transient traveling wave is transformed by wavelet. With the increase of the scale of wavelet transform, the data which Lipschitz index is non negative are the point that maximum modulus of transient traveling wave is increased or unchanged, in those data, the earliest time data will be used in this paper.

3 Location principle and location algorithm

In the two-dimensional space, the difference in the distance between the points on the hyperbola and the two focus is constant. Location principle and location algorithm in this paper use this feature, connect the difference in distance and the difference in arriving time of traveling wave.

3.1 Location principle

The pictorial representation of the location principle is shown in Fig.1. The fault is generated at point P, and the difference between arrival time of the main terminal O and the auxiliary terminal A is known, that P could be located in a hyperbola with the focus of O and A. In the same way, point P could be located in another hyperbola with the focus of O and B. The intersection of those two hyperbolas is the fault point P accurately.

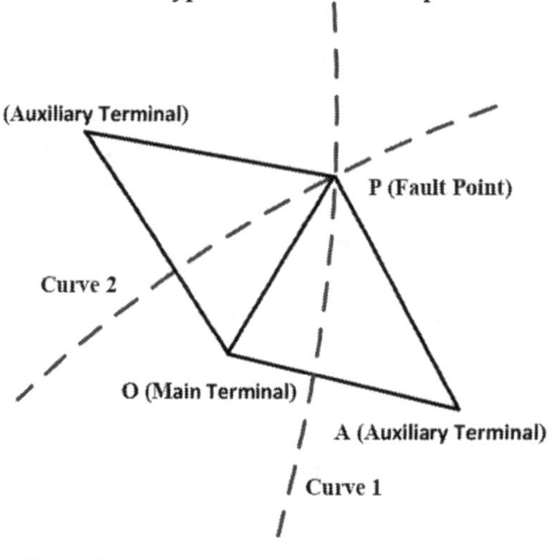

Fig.1. Schematic diagram of Location principle

3.2 Location network selection

From the aforementioned location principle, among the many sensors in the grid, three terminal sensor constitute a location network could locate the fault point. When fault occurs, transient traveling wave propagation to the whole network from the fault point and the closer the fault point is, the faster the sensor will receive the transient traveling wave data.

In order to avoid lower localization accuracy caused by traveling wave dispersion, the location network should contains the fault line ends terminal, so the data that traveling wave polarity is fused in the method in this paper. When the internal fault occurs, the traveling wave polarity of two line ends terminal is reversed, and when the external circuit fault occurs, the traveling wave polarity of two line ends terminal is same [15].

Selection rules of the location network and each terminal number are as follows:

1. In accordance with the order of arrival time of the transient traveling wave, the terminal is selected to constitute location network. The terminal which traveling wave arrival time is the first will be treated as 'main terminal', and will be numbered '0'. This terminal is responsible for receiving data, calculation of positioning and export the location result.
2. The terminal which traveling wave arrival time is the second will be add to location network, and then determine the current traveling wave polarity, if the polarity is contrary to terminal '0', this terminal will be treated as 'major auxiliary terminal', and will be numbered '1'. Or else, this terminal will be treated as 'minor auxiliary terminal', and will be numbered '2'.
3. The terminal which traveling wave arrival time is the third needs to be judged. If the location network already has terminal '1', this terminal will be add to the location work directly as terminal '2'. If there is no terminal '1' in the location work, the polarity of this terminal should be judged, if the polarity is contrary to terminal '0', this terminal will be treated as terminal '1', or else ,this terminal will be eliminated.
4. In accordance with the foregoing rules, select another terminal add to the location network and numbered '3'.

The purpose that add terminal '3' is in order to avoid the situation that three terminal of location network are in a straight line. In this special situation, positioning accuracy will be reduced greatly.

3.3 Location algorithm

In the location network, we assume $i = 0,1,2,3$ represent the number of terminal. The coordinates of terminal is (x_i, y_i). The traveling wave arrival time of each terminal is t_i. The distance between terminal and fault point is l_i. The velocity of traveling wave is v.

We can define a measurement matrix by subtracting arrival of 'main terminal' from arrival time of each 'auxiliary terminal':

$$\mathrm{T=[dt_1,dt_2,dt_3]^T} \tag{1}$$

The covariance matrix of measurement matrix is:

$$P = E[TT^T] = \sigma^2 \begin{bmatrix} 1 & 0.5 & \cdots & 0.5 \\ 0.5 & 1 & \cdots & 0.5 \\ \vdots & \vdots & \ddots & \vdots \\ 0.5 & 0.5 & \cdots & 1 \end{bmatrix} \tag{2}$$

Where "σ^2" is variance of measurement error.

The actual value matrix of the difference between arrival time of auxiliary terminal and main terminal is:

$$D = \frac{1}{v}[dr_1, dr_2, dr_3]^T = D(X) \tag{3}$$

Where"X" is a vector containing coordinates of fault point.

We can get the quadratic estimate of measurement and actual value:

$$J = [T - D]^T P^{-1} [T - D] \tag{4}$$

Set the gradient of "J"zero, we can get the minimum value of the error between the measured and actual values:

$$\frac{\partial J}{\partial X} = W\Lambda a = 0 \tag{5}$$

Where:

$$W = \left[\frac{\partial D(X)}{\partial X}\right]^T P^{-1} \tag{6}$$

$$\Lambda = diag\left[\frac{1}{l_0 + l_1 + v \cdot dt_1} \cdots \frac{1}{l_0 + l_3 + v \cdot dt_3}\right] \tag{7}$$

$$a = \left[l_1^2 - (l_0 + v \cdot dt_1)^2 \cdots l_3^2 - (l_0 + v \cdot dt_3)^2\right] \tag{8}$$

Substituting"a"into formula (5), we can get:

$$2AX = V_d + l_0\varphi \tag{9}$$

Where:

$$A = \begin{bmatrix} x_0 - x_1 & y_0 - y_1 \\ x_0 - x_2 & y_0 - y_2 \\ x_0 - x_3 & y_0 - y_3 \end{bmatrix} \tag{10}$$

$$V_d = [(v \cdot dt_1)^2 + K_0 - K_1 \text{L} \ (v \cdot dt_3)^2 + K_0 - K_3]^T \tag{11}$$

$$\varphi = 2[v \cdot dt_1, \text{L} \ , v \cdot dt_3]^T \tag{12}$$

The weighted least squares solution is:

$$X = \frac{1}{2}(A^T P^{-1} A)^{-1} A^T P^{-1} (V_d + l_0\varphi) \tag{13}$$

$$l_i = \sqrt{(x_i - x)^2 + (y_i - y)^2} \tag{14}$$

Substituting“ X ”into formula (14), we can get a quadratic equation with one unknown “ l_0 ”, solve this equation, then substituting “ l_0 ”into location equation (14), we can calculate the coordinates of the fault point.

4 Simulation implementation of localization method

Now, in this paper we made a simulation mold with 11 terminals system whose single-line diagram is depicted in Fig.2. Simulation analysis is performed using EMTDC and MATLAB.

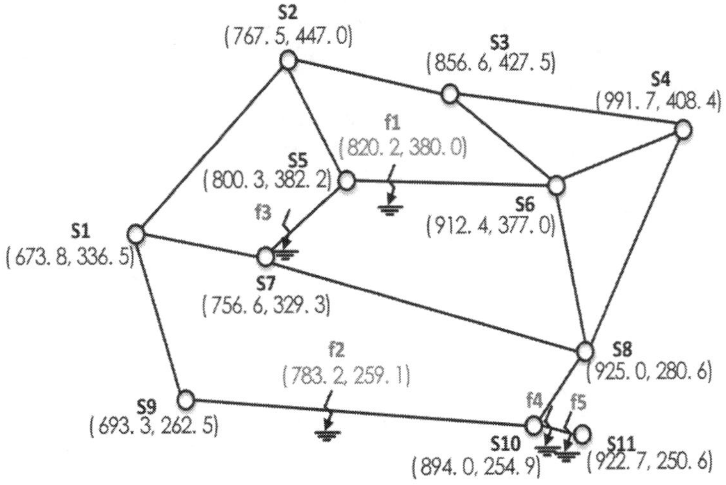

Fig.2. Simulation mold of power grid

4.1 Fault location process

Take the fault ‘f1’ in Fig.2 as an example, the simulation adopts single-phase grounding fault, fault location process as follows:

1. Analyze fault traveling wave data and select location network.

The fault occurs between terminal ‘S5’ and ‘S6’, transient traveling wave arrive at ‘S5’ first, so ‘S5’ is the ‘main terminal’-terminal ‘0’.

Then transient traveling wave reach at ‘S7’, by analyze the polarity of transient current traveling wave data we find that ‘S7’ and ‘S5’ have the same polarity, it means ‘S7’ and ‘S5’ are on the same side of the fault point, so add ‘S7’ into the location network as terminal ‘2’.

Arrival time of ‘S1’and ‘S6’is very close, in the actual grid, exist phenomenon of wave dispersion[16], transient traveling wave reach at ‘S6’ is earlier, and the polarity is contrary to the ‘S5’, it means ‘S6’ and ‘S5’ are on the different side of the fault point, so add ‘S6’into the location network as terminal ‘1’. ‘S1’ add into the location network as terminal ‘3’. Transient current traveling wave at each terminal is shown in Fig.A1.

From this, location network selection is complete, it consist of (S5,S6,S7,S2).

2. Analyze fault traveling wave at each terminal, extract arrival time of traveling wave.

Transform the forward (backward) traveling wave of each terminal by wavelet, increase scale of wavelet transform successively, and extract the time of point which arrival time is shortest and Lipschitz index is nonnegative.

Take 'S5'as an example, the transient forward traveling wave is subjected to 6 different scales of wavelet transform, as shown in Fig.A2, there is a maximum modulus point at 80ns, and its Lipschitz index is zero, so 80ns is treated as the arrival time of terminal '0'.
Arrival time of each terminal in the location network is shown in Table 1.
3. Extract coordinate data at each terminal of location network, as shown in Fig.2, the data format using two-dimensional coordinates, coordinates of terminal '0' is (800.3,382.2)km. Coordinates of each terminal in the location network is shown in Table 1.

Table 1 Data at each terminal of Location network

Component of Location network	Coordinate/km	Arrival time/ns
Terminal'0'(S5)	(800.3,382.2)	80
Terminal'1'(S6)	(912.4,377.0)	328
Terminal'2'(S7)	(756.6,329.3)	316
Terminal'3'(S2)	(767.5,447.0)	330

4. Substituting arrival time data and coordinate data into the location algorithms, we can obtain the coordinate of fault point (f1) is (820.1.380.3) km, and the actual coordinate of fault point is (820.2,380.0) km, the deviation is (0.1,0.3)km.

4.2 Influencing factors of positioning accuracy

The fault location method of this paper has some factors that affect the positioning accuracy, mainly including the following points:

1. Transient traveling wave velocity. In the simulation of this paper, the transient traveling wave is regarded as electromagnetic wave, but in the actual grid the velocity is related to frequency, so it is different in different lines. We will fuse line parameter data in next step.

2. Sampling frequency of traveling wave calculation. The sampling frequency in this paper is 109(1/s), the unit of time data obtained is nanosecond. If the sampling frequency is increased, the positioning error can be reduced.

3. Coordinate precision of each terminal. The location algorithm of this paper is directly related to the coordinates of each terminal, improve coordinate precision can effectively improve the positioning accuracy.

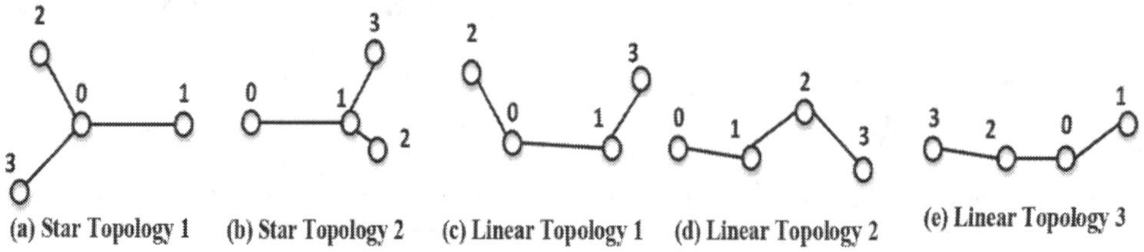

Fig. 3. Common location network topology

4. Topology of location network. Because the more lines the transient traveling wave crosses, the more distorted it will be, the topology of location network will affect the

accuracy of location. The location network usually has several topologies as shown in Fig.3, topology (a) and (b) is star. In topology (a) the location error is minimum because there is only one line between 'auxiliary terminal' and 'main terminal'. In topology (b), the location error is bigger than (a), because there are two lines between terminal '2' or '3' and 'main terminal'. Topology (c), (d), (e) is linear, the location error will be bigger, because always there are over two lines between 'auxiliary terminal' and 'main terminal'.

4.3 Special case analysis

The fault location method of this paper has some factors that affect the positioning accuracy, mainly including the following points:

According to the different topologies of location network in Fig.3, this paper proposes to add the data 'number of connected lines of each terminal' to reduce the positioning error.

1. For the topology (b) in Fig.3, after location network is selected, we can compare the number of connected lines of terminal '0' and '1', if this number of terminal '0' is bigger than terminal '1', the location network remain unchanged , if not, exchange terminal '0' and '1', create a new location network.

Take the fault 'f2' in the Fig.2 as an example, the location network selected by the aforementioned location process is (S9,S10,S11,S12), its topology as (b) in Fig.3, the actual coordinate of fault point is (783.2,259.1), Fault location coordinates that obtained by using method of this paper is (783.5,269.4), the deviation is (0.3,10.3.) Then we extract the number of connected lines of terminal '0' and '1', it is 1 and 3, so we exchange the terminal '0' and '1', new location network is (S10,S9,S11,S12), its topology as (a) in Fig.3, we obtain the coordinate by using method of this paper is (783.0,259.2), the deviation is (0.2,0.1).

2. For the three linear topology in Fig.3, there are severe lines between terminal '2' or '3' and 'main terminal', we some appropriate changes in the location network selected rules:

Firstly, same as the modification in topology (b), we extract the number of connected lines of terminal '0' and '1', set the terminal which this number is big as terminal '0'. Then delete the terminal '3' from the location network, seek a new terminal which is connect with terminal '0', set it as terminal '3', create a new location network.

Take 'f3', 'f4', 'f5' in Fig.2 as examples, adopt the above modification method then simulate, we obtain the results as shown in Table 2.

The method of fault location in this paper requires mutual communication between the terminals, after fuse the data of each terminal, select the location network, then locate the fault point. In this process, if some terminals failure to communicate with other terminals, some data will lose. Under this special situation, the location network perhaps contains some terminal that across multiple lines from fault point, this leads to a decrease in location accuracy.

Take the 'f1' fault in the Fig.1 as an example, we analyze the situation that one terminal is failure as follow:

1. According to the aforementioned positioning process, when 'f1' fault occur, the selected location network is (S5,S6,S7,S2), if one terminal that in addition to these four terminals is failure, the location network is unchanged, so the location result is unchanged.

2. Terminal '3' (S2) is failure, according to the aforementioned positioning process, the location network is (S5,S6,S7,S3), location result is (819.8,380.3), the deviation is (0.4,0.3)km.

3. Terminal '2' (S7) is failure, the location network is (S5,S6,S7,S3), location result is (819.7,380.5), the deviation is (0.5,0.5)km.

4. Terminal '1' (S6) is failure, the location network is (S5,S3,S7,S2), location result is (819.2,381.2), the deviation is (1.0,1.2)km.

5. Terminal '0' (S5) is failure, the location network is (S7,S6,S2,S1), location result is (823.7,378.3), the deviation is (3.5,1.7)km.

We can see from those results that when one terminal is failure, the location accuracy in this paper will be influence. Failure terminal more close to 'main terminal', the more location accuracy decrease.

5 Conclusion

This paper proposes a new method of fault location, data fusion a variety of data in power grid and the location results use the form of two-dimensional coordinates. Through simulation experiment we can see that this method has high location precision, adapt to the needs of intelligent grid, suitable for the development of fault location software.

In the matter of topology of location network, two kinds of topological relations of star type and linear type are analyzed respectively in five cases, obtained the topology with minimal location error, for other topology, we make appropriate changes of location network selection, the experiment results show that the location accuracy has been improved.

By analyzing the main factors that affect the location accuracy, it is found that the location accuracy has decreased under the special conditions. Therefore, the subsequent in-depth study is how to improve location accuracy measures under special circumstances

Table 2 Simulation results of linear topology

Topology	Fault Point	Location Network Before modification / After	Result Before modification / After	Deviation Before modification/ After
(c)	(769.3,344.7) f3	S7,S5,S1,S2/ S7,S5,S1,S8	(766.1,348.9)/ (769.5,344.1)	(3.2,4.2)/ (0.2,0.6)
(d)	(903.6,253.8) f4	S10,S11,S8,S6/ S10,S11,S8,S9	(873.7,279.5)/ (903.4,254.1)	(29.9,25.7)/ (0.2,0.3)
(e)	(913.1,252.7) f5	S11,S10,S8,S6/ S10,S11,S8,S9	(887.1,302.1)/ (913.2,252.8)	(26.0,50.2)/ (0.1,0.1)

Appendix A

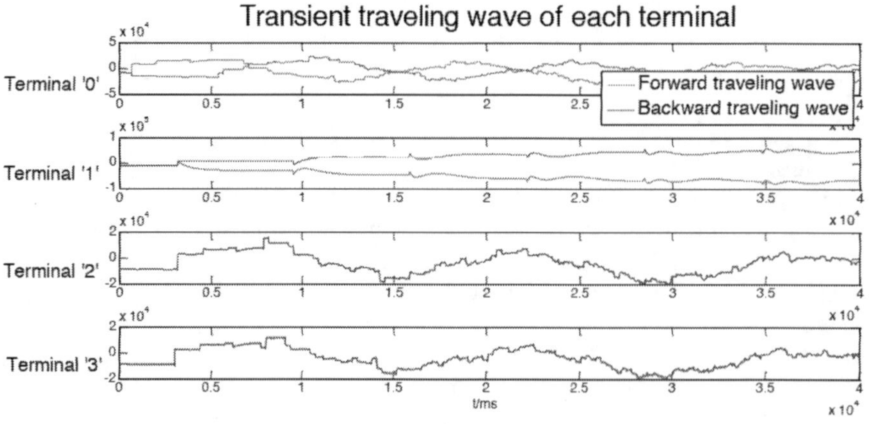

Fig. A1. Transient traveling wave of each terminal

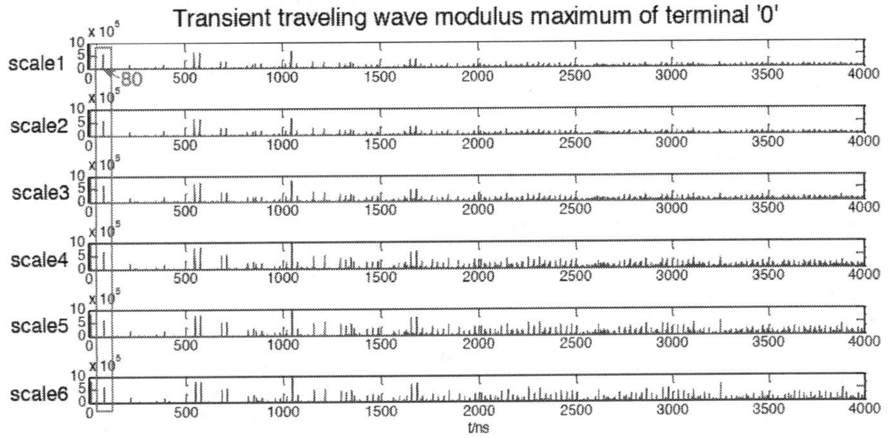

Fig. A2. Transient traveling wave modulus maximum of terminal '0'

References

1. Qin Jian, Study on Single Terminal Method and Double Terminal Method of Traveling Wave Fault Location in Transmission Line. J. Automation of Electric Power System 30(6):92-95(2006)
2. Mert Korkal, Traveling-Wave-Based Fault-Location Technique for Transmission Grids Via Wide-Area Synchronized Voltage Measurements. J. IEEE TRANSACTIONS ON POWER SYSTEMS 27(2):1003-1011(2012)
3. Li Zhenxing, Traveling Wave Fault Location Multi Point Measurement Information of Region Power Grid. J. Automation of Electric Power System 41(8):146-152(2017)
4. Giovanni Manassero, Fault-Location System for Multi terminal Transmission Lines. J. IEEE TRANSACTIONS ON POWER DELIVERY 25(3):1418-1426(2010)
5. Liang Rui, Fault Line Selection and Location in Distribution Power Network Based on Traveling Wave Time Difference of Arrival Relationships. J. High Voltage Engineering 40(11):3411-3417(2014)
6. Shu Hongchun, Fault Location for Traveling Wave Based on Multi Measuring Points for UHVDS Long Distance Transmission Line. J. High Voltage Engneeing 43(7):2105-2114(2017)
7. Xu Bingyin, Modern Fault Location Techniques Based on Fault Generated Travelling Waves and Their Applications. J. Automation of Electric Power System 62-65(2001)
8. Li Zhenxing, Single-terminal traveling wave location algorithm based on amending wave velocity.Power System Protection and Control 45(8):16-22(2017)
9. Xu Mingming, A Fault Location Method for the Single-phase-to-earth Fault in Distribution System Based on the Attenuation Characteristic of Zero-mode Traveling Wave. J. Transaction of China Electrotechnical Society 30(14):397-403(2015)
10. Zeng Xiangjun, Novel network based traveling wave location algorithm with information fusion. J. Journal of Electric Power Science and Technology 24(1):38-44(2009)
11. Wu Linyong, Frequency Domain Traveling Wave Fault Location Method Using CVTs Secondary Signals. J. Automation of Electric Power System 32(8):73-82(2008)
12. Fang Liqian, A High-Speed Traveling Wave Acquisition System Based on PCI Bus. J. Power System Technology,2006,30(3):80-84.

13. Song Guobing, A Novel Phase mode Transformation Matrix. J. Automation of Electric Power System 31(14):57-60(2007)
14. Ge Yaozhong, Principle and technology of new type relay protection and fault location. M. Xi'an Jiaotong University Press, (1996)
15. Dong Xingli, DIRECTIONAL PROTECTIVE RELAYING BASED ON POLARITY COMPARISON OF TRAVELLING WAVE BY USING WAVELET TRANSFORM. Automation of Electric Power System 11-15(2000)
16. Qin Jian, Study On dispersion of travelling wave in transmission line. J. Proceedings of the CSEE 19(9):27-36(1999)

Improvement of Ultrasonic Distance Measuring System

Yu Jiang[1], *Rui* Song[2,*], and *Mingting* Yuan[3]

[1]Qingdao University, College of automation and electrical engineering, 266071 Qingdao and Shangdong University,College of control science and engineering, 250000 Jinan, China
[2]Shangdong University,College of control science and engineering, 250000 Jinan, China
[3]Qingdao University, College of automation and electrical engineering, 266071 Qingdao, China

Abstract. This paper mainly introduces a kind of ultrasonic distance measuring system with AT89C51 single chip as the core component. The paper expounds the principle of ultrasonic sensor and ultrasonic ranging, hardware circuit and software program, and the results of experiment and analysis.The hardware circuit based on SCM, the software design adopts the advanced microcontroller programming language.The amplitude of the received signal and the time of ultrasonic propagation are regulated by closed loop control. [1,2]The double closed loop control technology for amplitude and time improves the measuring accuracy of the instrument. The experimental results show that greatly improves the measurement accuracy of the system.

1 Introduction

Ultrasonic is a kind of sound wave that frequency is higher than 2KHz. It has good directivity, strong penetration ability and easy to obtain more concentrated sound energy.[3]The use of ultrasonic detection is relatively fast, convenient, simple and easy to control in real time. And ultrasonic can meet the practical requirements of industry in terms of measurement accuracy. So it has been widely used in mobile robots, car safety, ocean measurement and so on. The design of the system mainly includes two parts, that is the hardware circuit and the software program. The hardware circuit mainly includes the single chip circuit, the transmitting circuit, the receiving circuit, the display circuit and the power supply circuit. This paper uses AT89C51 microcontroller as the core of the digital display ultrasonic range finder. The whole circuit is designed by modularization, which is composed of signal transmitting and receiving, power supply, display and so on. The received signal amplitude and the propagation time of ultrasonic extraction use double closed-loop control technology. The experimental results show that the system has high precision measurement level and can meet the range requirement in industry.

* Corresponding author: rsong@sucro.org

2 Ultrasonic sensor and the principle of ultrasonic distance measurement

2.1 Ultrasonic sensor

The ultrasonic sensor is a kind ofsensor that converts ultrasonic signals into other energy signals (usually electrical signals). It has the function of converting electrical signals into mechanical signals and converting mechanical signals into electrical signals. We chose the piezoelectric ultrasonic generator in the design.[4] The piezoelectric ultrasonic generator actually works by using the resonance of a piezoelectric crystal. This paper adopts HC-SR04 ultrasonic sensor. This module has stable performance, accurate measurement of the distance, module of high precision and small blind region. The ultrasonic time sequence diagram is shown in Fig. 1.

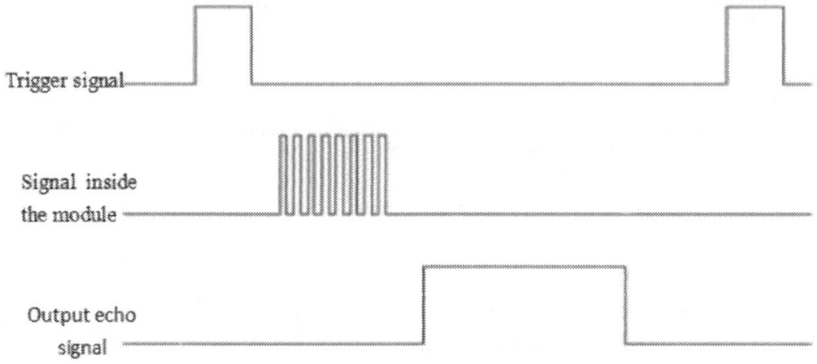

Fig. 1. The ultrasonic time sequence diagram

2.2 The principle of ultrasonic distance measurement

The principle of ultrasonic distance measurement is TOF (time of flight). [5]The emission circuit sends out the ultrasonic. The ultrasonic waves propagate in the air and is reflected back when it meets an obstacle. The receiving circuit receives the reflected ultrasonic wave, and the single chip microcomputer measures the time required for transmitting to receiving. The time for detecting the ultrasonic wave transmitted from the emitter to the receiving end is t, and the time is time of flight. The velocity of ultrasonic wave propagation in the air is C, and the distance between the emission point and the measured object is s. [6]The range formula is expressed as:

$$S = \frac{1}{2}ct \tag{1}$$

The wave velocity of ultrasonic wave is related to the propagating medium, which is the fastest in the solid and the slowest in the gas. Ultrasonic is a kind of sound wave, so its velocity is related to temperature. Table 1 lists the sound velocity at several different temperatures. When in use, if the temperature change is not big, it is considered that the velocity is basically unchanged. If the measurement accuracy is very high, it should be corrected through temperature compensation method. The relationship between the velocity of sound and the temperature in the air can be expressed as:

$$v = 331.41 + 0.6 (m/s) \tag{2}$$

Table 3. The sound velocity at several different temperatures

temperature(℃)	-30	-20	-10	0	10	20	30
Sound velocity(m/s)	313	319	325	333	338	344	349

In order to further improve the accuracy of the measurement, this design increases the angle compensation as shown in the diagram. Measuring distance is

$$d = \sqrt{s^2 - (\frac{h}{2})^2} \quad (3)$$

When s>>h, and c is the ultrasonic speed.

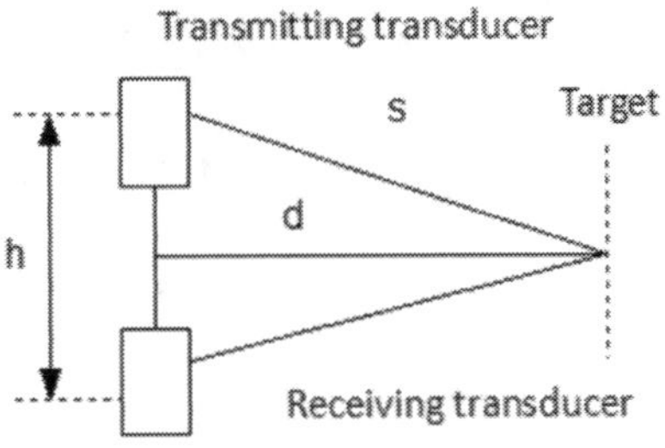

Fig. 2. Schematic diagram of ultrasonic ranging

3 System hardware design

The hardware design of the instruments include Ultrasonic transducer receiving and sending circuit, Remote data communication circuit, LCD display circuit, High frequency counting timing circuit, Monitor timer, Alarm and clock circuit, temperature compensation circuit, AT89C51 single chip microcomputer and memory circuit. The principle diagram of the hardware system is shown in Fig. 3.

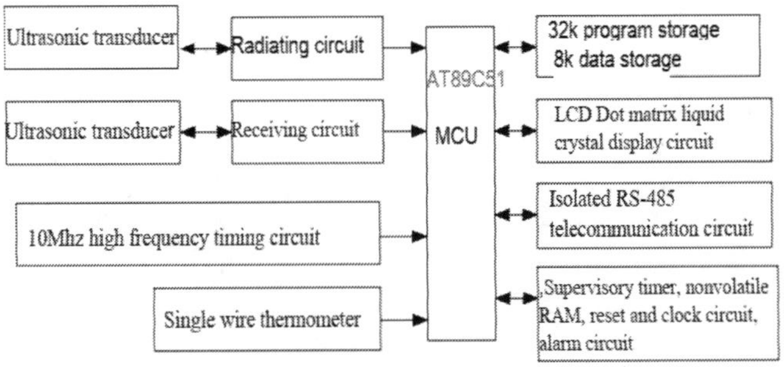

Fig. 3. Hardware system

3.1 Singlechip circuit

The AT89C51 singlechip is the core component of the instrument. The singlechip timer sends out the square wave pulse signal around 40KHz. The pulse is added to the ultrasonic sensor through the ultrasonic driving circuit, and the ultrasonic sensor sends out the ultrasonic. Because the output power of the MCU port is relatively small, it is difficult to meet the requirement of measuring distance. The ultrasonic transducer is output by the ultrasonic transducer after enlarging the amplifying circuit. The emitted ultrasonic wave is used as the input of the system. [7]The phase locked loop locks this signal, and produces a lock signal to start microcontroller interrupt program. The internal timer stops the timing, software system calculat and analyz the signal then. The corresponding calculation results are sent to the LED digital tube for display. The single ship sequence diagram is shown in figure 4.

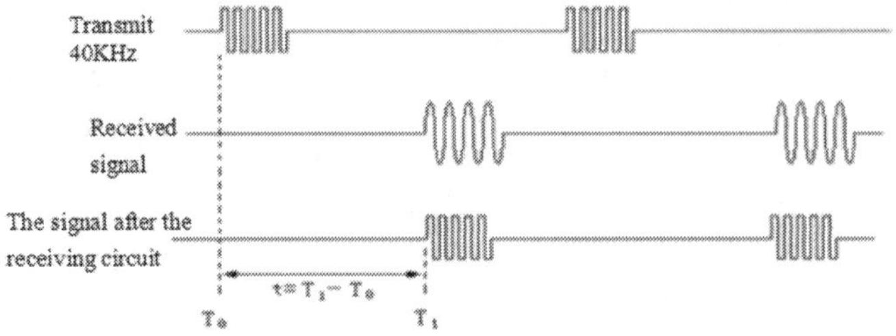

Fig.4 .SCM sequence diagram

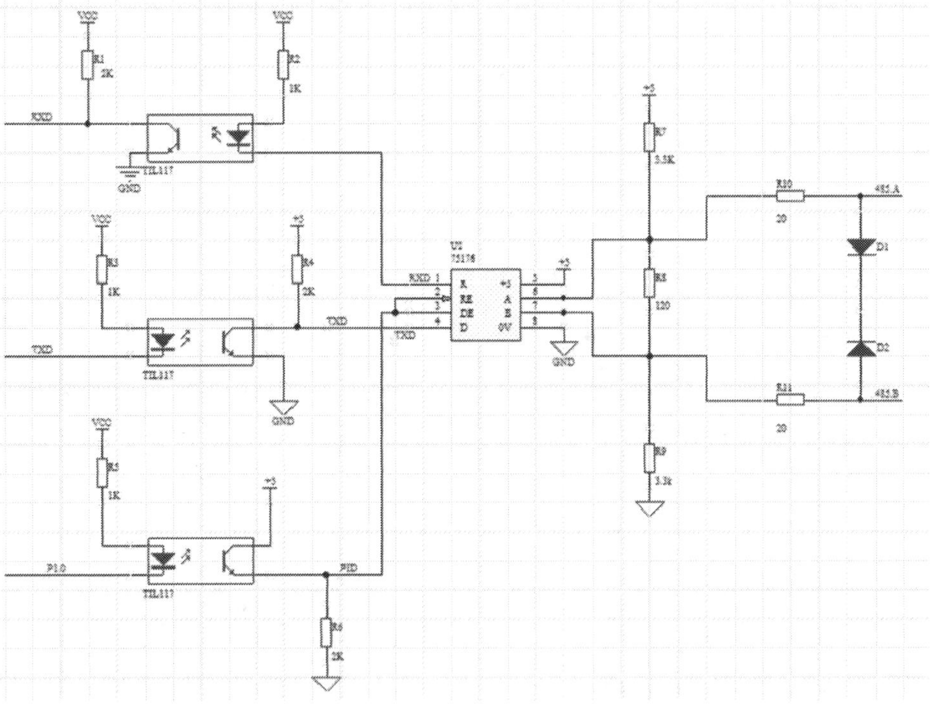

Fig.5. Isolated RS-485 telecommunication circuit

3.2 Transmitting circuit

The transmitting circuit uses square wave modulation pulse transmitting circuit. The principle is shown in Figure 3. The singlechip generates a control signal and this signal triggered monostable multivibrator generates a main control pulse. When the master pulse is in high level, square wave generator produces a square wave pulse, the frequency is same with frequency transmitting transducer. Through the drive switch, transformer coupled excites ultrasonic transducer to emit ultrasonic.

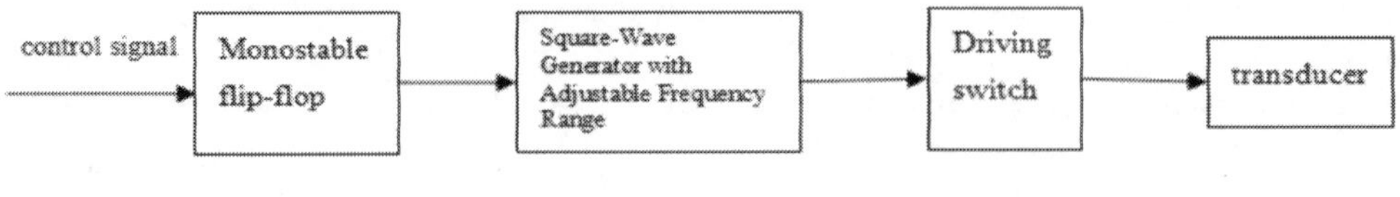

Fig. 6. Transmit circuit schematic

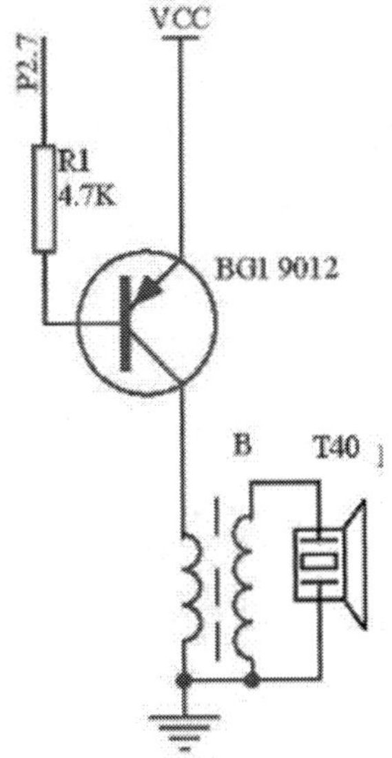

Fig. 7 Transmitting circuit

3.3 Receiving circuit

The receiving circuit filters the signal to form the echo envelope, and the high speed voltage comparator produces a receiving signal pulse and transmits it to the 51 single chip circuit.

In order to overcome the received signal amplitude changes caused by changes in the distance test.mber equations consecutively. In the hardware circuit design, using 4 point CMOS analog switch, based on the principle that the amplification of the inverting amplifier depends on the ratio of the resistance value, the resistors with 1, 1/2, 1/4 and 1/8 weights are in parallel in turn, and the logic level is used to control the resistance, and the synthetic resistance of 0~15 times is obtained.[8] In this way, a programmable amplifier with 0~15 times gain is obtained. As shown in Figure 9. In the system, programmable operational amplifier circuit, bandpass filter, absolute value circuit, π filter circuit, peak value holding circuit, voltage comparator and single chip microcomputer form the closed loop control loop with adjustable amplitude. The peak holding circuit extracts the maximum envelope of the received signal, and compares it with the preset threshold circuit.[9]When it is lower than the preset threshold, that the received signal is in the best received signal amplitude range, digital signal generated by the microcontroller control programmable amplifier, gain adjustment circuit, to achieve closed-loop gain control, the received signal amplitude changes in the vicinity of the threshold setting, so as to overcome the increase or decrease the amplitude of the signal caused by the change of the distance.

 https://doi.org/10.1051/itmconf/20181702008

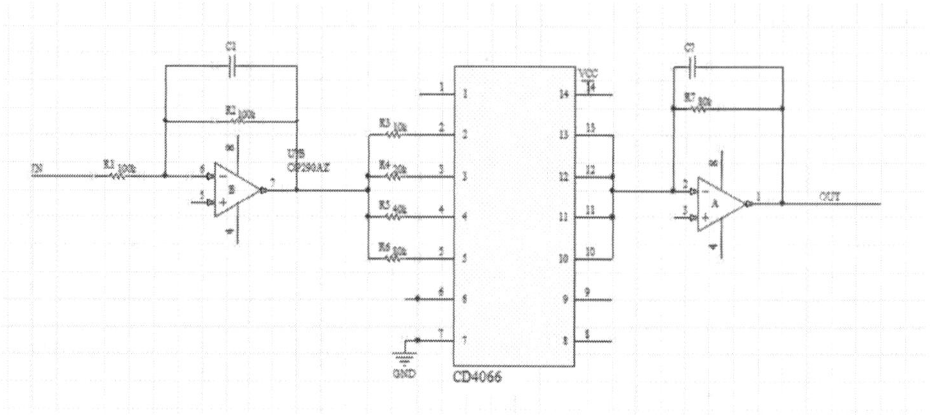

Fig.9. The circuit principle

The propagation time is extracted based on ultrasonic echo. When a fixed threshold is used to read the ultrasonic propagation time, the time error will be caused by the variation of the echo amplitude, which will greatly affect the accuracy of ranging. Therefore, in the system design, a programmable variable threshold generation circuit is designed by using digital potentiometer, and a time readable closed loop control circuit is formed by high-speed voltage comparator (reduced signal comparison delay), microcontroller and variable threshold circuit.For the same distance, the echo signal is adjusted from a gain adjustment loop to a reasonable range.[10] Its envelope passes through a high speed voltage comparator to form a receiving pulse, and the width of the receiving pulse is detected by a single chip microcomputer. When it is not within reasonable limits (the 990us 1000US), according to its value, the microcontroller output digital adjustment signal, control the digital potentiometer to produce a new threshold.[13,14] Thus the closed loop control of the received pulse width can be realized, and the timing error caused by the same distance is overcome by the amplitude change, and the measurement precision is improved.

3.4 Display circuit

The system uses a Trinity LED digital tube to display the measured distance, such as figure 10.

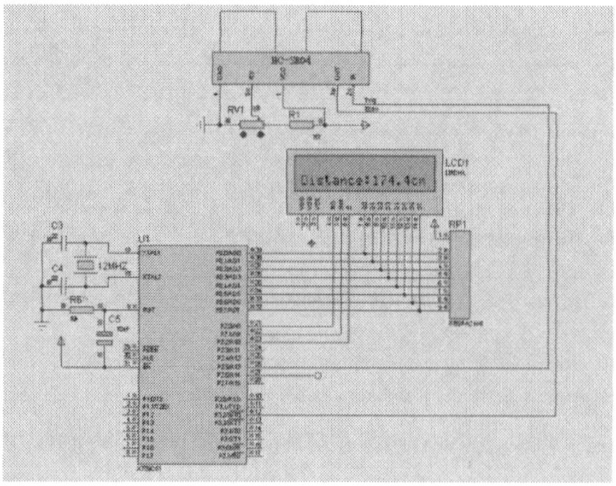

Fig.10. display circuit

3.5 Power circuit

The working current of the system is about 30-45mA. In order to ensure the system to work and debug the system for convenience, we use the USB port to supply the power directly to the computer.The 6V AC current is rectified by diode into a pulsating DC current, then it passes through the filter capacitor C1 to form the direct current. The voltage in the circuit passes through the integrated circuit transforms into 5 volt DC to supply to the whole system for electricity. In order to further improve the quality of power supply, the 5 volt DC power is filtered by C3 and C4 again.The power supply circuit is shown in Figure 11.

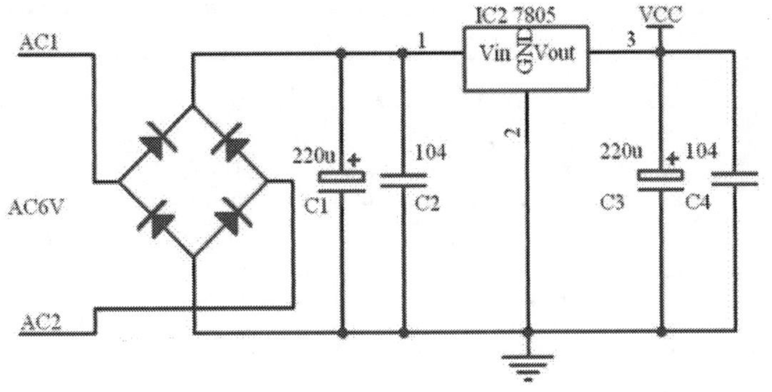

Fig. 11. power circuit

4 Software design

The instrument software design use advanced microcontroller programming language. It is convenient to carry out various mathematical operations.The main modules include ultrasonic transceiver module, automatic gain control module, receiving pulse width modulation module, temperature measurement module, data sorting and filtering module, remote communication module and so on. [11]The program flow is shown in Figure 13 .

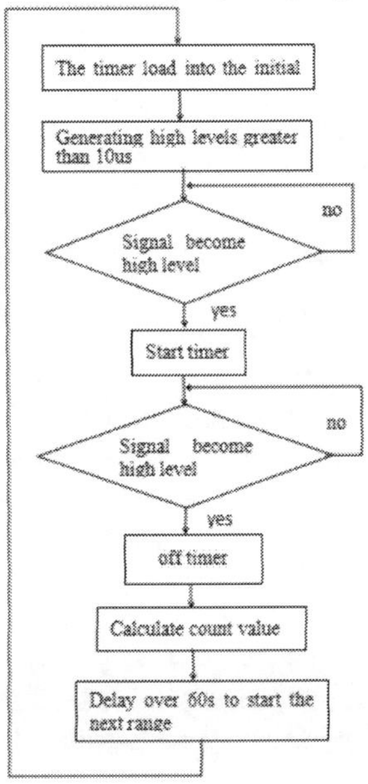

Fig. 13. Software design diagram

5 The result of the experiment

Double loop control receives a pulse width range for (990us ~ 1000US). The typical experimental data are shown in Table 2 and table 3.

Table 2 Experimental data of double closed loop control (Unit: mm)

Measurement times	*Actual distance*	*Measuring distance (double closed loop)*	*Deviation*	*Measuring distance (fixed threshold)*	*Deviation*
1	3000	2999.6	-0.4	3003.2	3.2
2	3000	3000.1	0.1	2997.4	-2.6
3	3000	3000.2	0.2	3004.1	4.1
4	3000	2999.8	-0.2	3003.9	3.9
5	3000	2999.6	-0.4	3005.3	5.3

Table 3 Typical experimental data of measured points (unit: mm)

Actual distance	1500	1700	1900	2500	3000	3050	3500	4500	5000
Ultrasonic distance	1500.3	1700.2	1899.7	2499.7	2999.8	3049.6	3500.3	4499.8	4999.5
Deviation	+0.3	+0.2	-0.3	-0.3	-0.2	-0.4	+0.3	-0.2	-0.5

Table 2 data is the average value of the 5 measured values at the same point. The data of Table 3 were obtained for the 3000mm test point. According to the Bessel formula,[12] the standard deviation of the double closed loop control is 0.32mm, and the standard deviation is 4.39mm when the fixed threshold is used. It can be seen that the measurement accuracy has been greatly improved when double closed loop control is adopted.

6 Conclusion

The experimental results show that in the closed loop control of amplitude, the control of automatic gain control circuit is avoided, and the amplitude variation caused by distance variation is overcome. For the time variable threshold control, variable threshold generation circui and time readable closed loop control loop overcome the timing error caused by the change of amplitude.

The results of laboratory studies show that the echo waveforms of different test distances are the same, but the echo amplitude is different. [15]For the same test distance, the echo waveform is almost the same, and the amplitude is still slightly changing. In the case of the same waveform, in the same distance and different distance, the wave amplitude of the wave should be changed because the sound wave is affected by the propagating medium. In the design of ultrasonic distance measuring system, the change of echo amplitude must be overcome so that the precision of distance measurement can be improved.

Acknowledgements: Thanks for Project Name:Key Technology Research and Application Demonstration of Robot Welding Production Line for Large Scale Structure of Coal Mine Engineering Machinery; Project Number:2015BAF01B02; Project Type: Nation Science and Technology Supporting Plan Program .

References

1. K. Imano, H. Kawazu, H. Inoue, Elec. & Comm. in Japan, **Volume 79, Issue 12,** (1996)
2. Holmes C, Drinkwater B W, Wilcox P D. Ndt & E International,**38(8)**, pp.701-711. (2005)
3. Y Mizutani, T Suzuki, H Ikeda, H Yoshida et al, IEEE, **vol.2.**983-986(1996)
4. J. K. Andersen,The Journal of the Acoustical Society of America **98(3)** September (1995)
5. Fukuoka I, Iida M, Morimatsu H, et al. *Ultrasonic wave transmitting system: US 4020446 A[P].* (1977)
6. Wheatley Iii, Charles E, and D. N. Punch, *High dynamic range closed loop automatic gain control circuit.US, US5283536US*,(1994)
7. A Bulavinov, Post-Print, **45(6)**,1141-1146(2012)
8. Z R Huang, H BQin, B Z Huang . Chinese Journal of Sensors & Actuators, (2006)
9. CY Chen, and T. P. Sun, 1794-1796, IEEE (2006)
10. M Lu, ICSICT .IEEE Beijing Section, April (2016)
11. W. Huang. IEEE International Conference on Electronic Measurement & Instruments,(2015)
12. A Velichko, PD Wilcox. AIP Conference Series American Institute of Physics, **137-144**, (2009)
13. B Bayram, O Oralkan, AS Ergun, E Haeggström, GG Yaralioglu, et al. IEEE Trans Ultrason Ferroelectr Freq Control, **52(2):**326.(2005)
14. Zhang, Jian Qiang, J. Zhang, and H. Y. Zhao.Applied Mechanics & Materials **563:199-202**(2014).
15. Wang Y J, Zhang L, Instrument Technique & Sensor, (2014)
16. Tisserand, E., and Y. Berviller,Electronics Letters, **52.22**, 1847-1849(2016)

Research and application of heat map system for resource allocation of flood control based on GIS

Weijian Li[1], *Long* Xie[1], *Yong* Lei[1], *Yu* Guo[1], *Xiaoqing* Zhou[1]

[1] The Pearl River Hydraulic Reserch Institute, Room 2305, Tianshou Building, Tianshou Road, Tianhe District, Guangzhou City, China
liweijianshmily@126.com

Abstract. Flood control resources are valuable resources for flood control and rescue, providing the flood relief work with the most direct rescue workers, tools as well as equipment. With the continuous development of society and economy, local governments at all levels, especially those of which are seriously affected by flood and waterlogging, have raised higher requirements for the allocation of flood control resources. When disasters such as flood and waterlogging happen, a reasonable allocation of flood control resources can quickly deploy relevant flood control resources for the disaster relief work and play an important role in reducing damage to personnel and property loss to a minimum, which stabilizes and promotes the socioeconomic development. Research of resource allocation of flood control based on GIS (Geographic Information System) is gradually becoming an important technical support for scientific resource allocation. This research focuses on the introduction of the characteristics and advantages of the heat map system based on GIS and its application in resource allocation of flood control. The important role the heat map system based on GIS plays in allocation and management of flood control resources is introduced in the applying case of Guangzhou.

1 Introduction

In the history of mankind, floods occur almost every year, causing countless losses of human, material and financial resources. Traditionally, flood is deemed to be an unavoidable natural disaster to human beings; however, with the progress of science and technology of modern society, people begin to gradually understand flood, using modern means to monitor the occurrence process of the disaster and giving guidance to relevant units to carry out disaster prevention and relief work in a timely manner. The losses of personnel and property can therefore be reduced to a maximum.

Valuable to flood control and disaster relief, flood control resources are also resources provided by local governments at all levels on demand according to time and space characteristics of flood, waterlogging and other disasters. In recent years, with the continuous socioeconomic development, urban flood control projects cannot gradually meet the requirements for flood control tasks in the new situation while problems such as hardening of cities' underlying surfaces become increasingly serious, bring more frequent floods and waterlogging. Before a disaster happens, it's management problem for social governors in terms of how to rationally deploy flood control resources in order to quickly organize professional rescue personnel as well as materials for relief work after a disaster.

In this paper, an urban storm water model is established by collecting materials including the relevant rainfall data, urban waterlogging point data and urban river data of the research area; combined with the current spatial distribution characteristic of flood control resources, GIS heat mapping technology is introduced to realize the visualization of flood disaster data and to make scientific suggestions for distribution and disposition of the planned flood control resources.

This research takes Guangzhou, China as an example to study the disposition of flood control resources in the jurisdiction of Guangzhou. Located in the south of China Pearl River estuary, Guangzhou is in the subtropical monsoon climate zone with the average annual rainfall being over 1600mm. The Pearl River Delta region where Guangzhou is located is covered with a dense drainage network and the rainfall is abundant, which easily leads to flood, waterblogging, etc. All of these bring make it difficult for the government administrative departments to manage flood control and the relief work.

1.1 A brief introduction of heat map technique based on GIS

GIS, Geographic Information System, is a specific and important spatial information system. Supported by computer hardware and software systems, GIS is a technical system which collects, stores, manages, calculates, analyzes, displays and describes the relevant geographical distribution data for the whole or part of space of the surface of the earth (including the atmosphere). GIS is not only a "tool" that expresses and simulates the realistic spatial world and performs spatial data processing as well as analysis, but also it can be deemed as "resources" dealing spatial problems.

Heat map technique based on GIS means to construct a heat map system with spatial information attributes. It is the research achievement formed by the combination of GIS technology and heat mapping technology, being able to provide drawing technique which shows two- and three-dimensional space and is divided according to ranks. Combining spatial distribution of the current flood control, this paper collects and researches data such as those of rainstorm runoff, storm tide and disaster points for waterlogging of Guangzhou city. Therefore, it generates a dynamic configuration map based on spatial information data including flood control rescue teams, flood control materials and flood control equipment to achieve a dynamic update of resources of flood control and an optimized configuration.

1.2 Characteristics of heat map based on GIS

Heat map technique based on GIS is a new technology integrating geographical information collection technology, remote sensing technology, computer graphics technology, software engineering technology and real-time data rendering technology. Its fundamental principles are as follows: to achieve a scientific storage and management of the basic information data of the research content through data collation and processing and to set up a data recording with geographical location information; to dynamically generate a heat map data layer through the position attributes and the hierarchical attributes of the data layer, which are put onto the GIS geographical data layer to form GIS heat map data including position information such as the map layer and the heat map layer. The main characteristics of GIS heat map technique are as follows:

First, there are visual effects of a distinct level. The heat map layer generated by information data is actually a data hierarchy map generated in the research scope area. The division of the hierarchy is showed by the changes of color shapes, which leads to an obvious change among different hierarchies to achieve a distinct display of the hierarchical division.

Second, there is real spatial location information. The traditional heat map display is based on non-spatial information images generated by graphic images, which is unfavorable to spatial overlay analysis and topology analysis in engineering. Heat map technique based on GIS is based on the spatial geographical coordinates, generating a layer with coordinate position information through attributes of the built-in hierarchical division of the data. This layer can be easily superimposed onto data with any geographical coordinate information to achieve a superimposing analysis for multi-source data and to provide great help to engineering research.

Third, there are characteristics of a dynamic generation. Heat map data is a data layer dynamically generated according to some scattered data in the research scope. There is a real-time dynamic update of the layer data according to the hierarchical attributes of the scattered data.

1.3 Problems of resource allocation of flood control

Flood control resources are related to a series of problems of safety issues of flood control, ecological environment protection, social sustainable development and so on. With China's rapid socioeconomic development, urban flood control projects seem to be particularly vulnerable in the construction of various projects, being unable to meet the requirements for flood control in the new situation; problems such as the increasingly expanding built-up areas, congestion of drainage network, hardening of cities' underlying surfaces, etc. are becoming more and more serious, which will cause disasters such as flood and waterlogging.

At present, most of China's resources of flood control in different areas are in a stage of labour management. The lack of a scientific and rational planning and management of resources including flood control rescue teams and emergency supplies usually leads to a situation where the relevant rescue teams and materials cannot arrive on the scene when a disaster happens. Based on the above information, it is necessary for management departments of three proofings at all levels to have a more comprehensive, more correct and more scientific management of resources of flood control in order to improve the efficiency and the standard of rescue and relief work of three proofings. The heat map system of resource allocation of flood control based on GIS which provides guidelines for the routine management work of management departments of three proofings is raised therefrom.

2 The application of heat map system based on GIS in resource allocation of flood control

The application of GIS heat map system in resource allocation of flood control refers a dynamic generation of a heat map layer according to the disaster class of the disaster type after having an in-depth research of flood types such as storm tide, waterlogging points, etc. in the research area by using spatial information technology and dividing the classes of all types of disasters. This heat map layer reflects the demand for resources of flood control in disaster points and the surrounding areas. According to the demand for resources of flood control , the system will evaluate whether the position for each flood control resource point, staffing and deployment of rescue materials are reasonable or not.

2.1 Mechanism research of rainstorm runoff

According to the historical data of vegetation, soil and intensity, distribution as well as time taken of rainstorm of Guangzhou, this paper researches the mechanism of rainstorm runoff in some feature areas such as business zones, old towns, residential areas with low density, mountainous and hilly regions and plain areas with drainage network after combining factors such as buildings of urbanization and the changing of underlying surfaces. Based on the above data, a research on the distribution of an urban disaster is conducted with a single factor being the rainstorm. As the basis of a superimposing working condition, this rainstorm runoff mechanism dynamically generates a disaster heat map under the influence of the rainstorm factor.

2.2 Research on flood and storm tide superimposed on rainstorm

Factors such as the relevant signals including blue, yellow, orange and red rainstorm warning signals issued by Meteorological Observatory and the region areas of the rainstorm warnings are used as a division of rainstorm's orders of magnitude. By using the rainstorm runoff mechanism of orders of magnitude and superimposing floods and storm tides in different frequencies, this paper analyzes the sphere and the degree of influence of rainstorm waterlogging, floods and storm tides under different stimulated working conditions and constructs the distribution of an urban disaster under the condition that flood and storm tide superimposed on rainstorm.

2.3 A superimposition of other relevant flood's types of factors

Guangzhou is located in Pearl River estuary in South China. Meanwhile, Nansha District and Panyu District which are all located in the southern area of Guangzhou are typical plain areas because they are covered with a dense drainage network. River dykes play an important role in resisting flood and storm tide. However, when there is a catastrophic flood, situations such as dyke-breaching and dyke-overflowing happen frequently, which makes plain areas suffer from flood disasters. Huadu District and Conghua District are located in the northern area which is a hilly region mainly of uplands. There are many pools of various sizes and around 200 reservoirs. Therefore, when under the conditions such as an extreme weather, lack of construction quality and other unusual factors, dyke-breaching and dyke-overflowing may happen and downstream regions of the reservoirs will suffer from flood.

By collecting the above relevant information of each water project, this paper establishes some possible factors causing disasters such as dyke-breaching, dyke-overflowing, breaching of reservoir dams and dam-overflowing. The distribution of an urban disaster based on all kinds of flood conditions is constructed after considering the possibility of each factor that causes disasters. As the basis of a superimposing working condition, this model of the mechanism research dynamically generates a disaster heat map within cities.

2.4 Code generation of heat map and analysis of spatial superimposition

With a synthesis of rainstorm runoff mechanism research, research on on flood and storm tide superimposed on rainstorm and research on other relevant factors of flood, this paper conducts a weighting division of the average disaster-suffering situation of Guangzhou these years and establishes some possible factors based on disaster influence within Guangzhou. These factors are important references for resource allocation of flood control.

The factor of possibility of flood impact is a research result based on a working condition of multi-disasters, which has an instructive impact on the frequency of flood occurrence. It is also an achievement of a scientific research on flood. By constructing a dynamic disaster-affected heat map based on the possible factors of a flood disaster, it is possible to visually show the possible disaster situations in each area within Guangzhou; based on data including the basic map data based on GIS, such as geographical basic map, road network layer and flood control resource distribution map, the spatial superposition analysis of dynamic disaster-affected heat map data, flood control resource data and data of road network accessibility are realized. According to the results of the superposition analysis, the data map based on the demand for resources of flood control is dynamically generated. The data heat map fully demonstrates the demand for resources of flood control of different areas within Guangzhou and it is an important reference for flood control rescue teams, flood control materials and flood control equipment configuration for management departments of three proofings.

2.5 Heat map system of resource allocation of flood control

Heat map system of flood resource allocation of flood control is a assistant decision system of resource allocation based on GIS technology. This system uses the B/S architecture model based on the data of possible disaster-affected factors within Guangzhou and the data of the resources of flood control, which facilitates the update and the maintenance of data in the future. The main functions of this system include: a simple map-mode browsing, a dynamic generation of heat map of rainstorm runoff mechanism research, a dynamic generation of research on flood and storm tide superimposed on rainstorm, a dynamic generation of heat map of other flood factors, a dynamic generation of comprehensive factors of disaster-affected possibility, a dynamic generation of heat map of the demand for resources of flood control and function modules including an assistant decision for resource allocation of flood control. The structure chart of the system's main functions is showed in figure 1. Through the research of this system, the paper constructs a function based on an analysis of possibility of being impacted by flood and provides an important reference for the allocation of resources of flood control in Guangzhou.

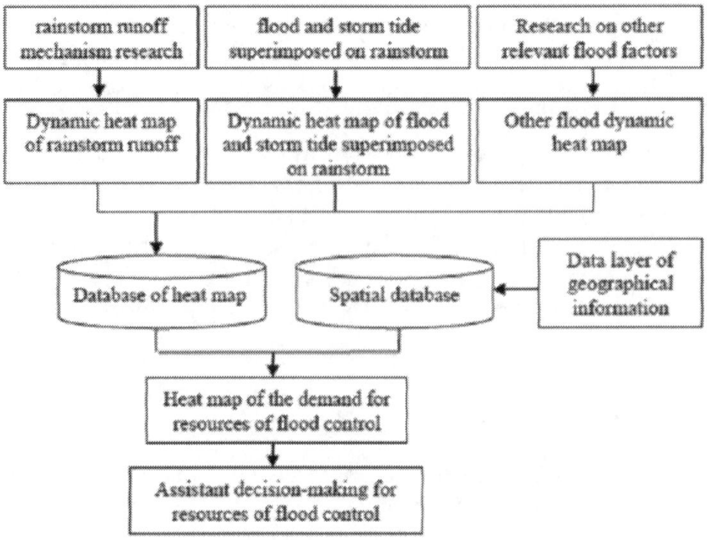

Figure. 1. The structure chart of functions of resource allocation of flood control chart of Guangzhou.

3 Conclusion

Through the practice, it is proved that the GIS heat map technique has a prospect of being used widely in the management of resources of flood control. And the relevant information of flood disaster, waterlogging disaster, rescue team, rescue tool and rescue equipment can be visualized by GIS heat map technique to achieve an automated evaluation of resources of flood control, the automated management, the scientific decision-making and other functions, which greatly improve standard of decision-making for managerial staff to manage resources of flood control and promote a comprehensive construction of disaster prevention and rescue work.

Acknowledgments.

Special fund for science and technology development in 2016 of Department of science and technology of Guangdong Province under Grant No. 2016A020223007.

References

1. Jia Zhong, Gang Lie.: Research on the Mode of Urban Flood Control Emergency Reserves(In Chinese). Yangtze River, 44(20), 102-106(2013)
2. Juan Li, Miaoyi Li, Ying Long Anrong Dang.: Analysis of multi center city in China based on Baidu thermal map(In Chinese). Data Augmented Design, 1673-8985, 30-36(2016)
3. Hongqi Chen, Jiancang Xie, Yirong Shen, Ni Wang.: Research on the Cooperative Inventory Models of Flood Prevention Materials (In Chinese). System engineering theory and Practice, 4, 91-98(2017)
4. Shangwen Xie.: Modernization analysis of storage management of flood control material storage (In Chinese). Heilongjiang Science and Technology of Water Conservancy, 39 (1), 189-190(2011)
5. Jingqi Han.: Modernization of management of storage and storage of flood control materials (In Chinese). Science and Technology Innovation Herald, 16, 116-117(2016)

Vehicle velocity estimation based on uncertainty theory for vehicle impact accidents

Haocun Dong[1] , *Jiaqi* Yuan[2], *Zhongguo* Nie[3]

[1] Automobile and Traffic College, Shenyang Ligong University, Shenyang 110159, China
[2] Shenyang Longchang Pipeline Survey Center, Shenyang, 110031,China
[3] Shenyang Jiashi Judicial Identification Office, Shenyang 110025, China
{Haocun Dong, Jiaqi Yuan, Zhongguo Nie. Donghaocun@163.com

Abstract. Based on the uncertainty theory, a corresponding uncertainty analysis method for speed calculation model for the road traffic accidents of vehicle impact is set up.

1 Introduction

To some extent, the severity of traffic accidents depends on the impacting characteristics of velocity of vehicle impact [1]. Determining vehicle impact velocity is an important basis for identification of road traffic accidents, however, the actual accident velocity estimation will use some physical accident parameters, whether it is the accident scene measurement parameters such as vehicle braking distance, or the experience parameters such as wheel and road surface adhesion coefficient, which all contain uncertain information, that is, the accident parameter has uncertainty [2,3,4], which inevitably leads to the uncertainty of estimation result of the traffic accident velocity. How to judge the random uncertainty of the accident velocity estimation result caused by the uncertainty of these parameters is a key problem [5].

The uncertainty of the parameters included in the vehicle impact traffic accidents is studied by the uncertainty theory, the range of the velocity before impact is deduced according to the uncertainty of these parameters, and the accuracy and confidence of the calculation results are analyzed to improve the reliability of the calculation results, and to make a scientific and impartial analysis of road traffic accidents [6,7].

2 Brief description of the basic theory of uncertainty

For a certain measurement parameter, because the real value is not an ideal concept of the concrete value, it is impossible to give the error size, but only the range of error value can be given, and use the uncertainty to describe the uncertainty of the parameters. Measurement of uncertainty is used to represent the dispersion of the measured value, which is an estimate of the true value of the measured value in a certain value range. Measurement of uncertainty usually contains several components, and all the uncertainty components are characterized by standard deviation. The categories of uncertainty can be divided into standard uncertainty, synthetic standard uncertainty and extension uncertainty (also known as expanded uncertainty). The uncertainty characterized by standard deviation is the standard uncertainty. The uncertainty of the synthesis of the standard uncertainty of each component is the synthesis uncertainty. The extension uncertainty gives the range of the measurement results where the measured value is located in a high confidence probability [8].

2.1 Source of uncertainty

The mathematical model of the measured parameter y is multivariate function $y = f(x_1, x_2, x_3, \cdots x_n)$, and the value of y depends on the uncertainty of other n input quantity $x_i (i = 1,2,3,...n)$, that is

$$Y = F(X_1, X_2, X_3 ... X_N) \quad . \tag{1}$$

From the best value $x_i (i = 1,2,3,...n)$ of each input X_i, the best value y of Y can be obtained, that is, the calculation result

$$y = f(x_1, x_2, x_3, \cdots x_n) \quad . \tag{2}$$

Therefore, the uncertainty of the calculation result y is derived from $x_i (i = 1,2,3,...n)$, that is, the uncertainty u_y of y depends on the uncertainty u_{xi} of each input amount x_i.

The true value of each direct measured value x_i is recorded as x_z, the uncertainty u_{xi} of x_i is expressed with absolute error Δ_{xi}, and the uncertainty u_{xi} of input quantity x_i is

$$u_{xi} > |\Delta_{xi}| = |x_i - x_z| \quad . \tag{3}$$

For the uncertainty of the measured parameter y, the calculation process is as follows.

2.2 Calculate the standard uncertainty u_{xi} of the input x_i

The evaluation of standard uncertainty is divided into two categories which are evaluation of category A and evaluation of category B: category A is evaluated by statistical analysis of the observed columns, and calculate the standard uncertainty of the best estimation value, category B is evaluated by analyzing the distribution characteristics of the measurement columns to evaluate the standard deviation and the standard uncertainty, evaluation of category B plays an important role in the uncertainty evaluation. In view of the actual situation of the current road traffic accident scene investigation and the repeatability of the relevant data measurement, the velocity identification in the accident reconstruction model is suitable for the evaluation result of the evaluation method of category B [9,10].

By using the half width a_i of the change interval of the input quantity x_i to divide the inclusion factor k_i, the standard uncertainty u_{xi} of the x_i can be obtained

$$u_{xi} = \frac{a_i}{k_i} . \tag{4}$$

Inclusion factor k is also known as a range factor. If the input quantity x_i obeys the normal distribution, the inclusion factor is obtained by querying the normal distribution integral table; If the input quantity x_i is uniformly distributed, the inclusion factor is $\sqrt{3}$ [8].

2.3 Calculate the synthetic standard uncertainty u_y

The standard uncertainty of the measured parameter y caused by the standard uncertainty u_{xi} from a single x_i is:

$$u_{yi} = \left|\frac{\partial y}{\partial x_i}\right| u_{xi} . \tag{5}$$

The relative change $\frac{\partial y}{\partial x_i}$ of the function y corresponding to u_{xi} is called the uncertainty transfer coefficient.

According to the theory of error synthesis, when each input quantity is independent, each input quantity will introduce a uncertainty factor, under their joint influence, the uncertainty of output y shall be the synthesis of all uncertainty components, so the synthetic standard uncertainty u_y of function y is calculated from the following formula:

$$u_y = \sqrt{\sum_{i=1}^{n} u_{yi}^2} = \sqrt{\sum_{i=1}^{n} \left(\frac{\partial y}{\partial x_i}\right)^2 u_{xi}^2} . \tag{6}$$

2.4 Calculate the extension uncertainty U

The extension uncertainty is also called extended uncertainty, and the extension uncertainty U can be obtained by multiplying the synthetic standard uncertainty u_y with the inclusion factor k multiplied by the function y .

$$U = ku_y . \tag{7}$$

Using the extension uncertainty as the uncertainty of the measured parameter y , the function y is expressed as

$$Y = y \pm U . \tag{8}$$

This means that the best value given to the measured parameter Y is y, which contain most of the value of Y in the interval from $y-U$ to $y+U$, so the value range of the function value can be determined.

3 The basic algorithm and uncertainty evaluation of vehicle velocity in vehicle impact accidents

3.1 The basic algorithm of vehicle velocity in vehicle scratch accidents

The sides of the two cars scratch, or the contact surface of the impact head between the two cars is narrow, or the contact surfaces of the impact between the head of rear vehicle and the tail of the front vehicle is narrow, and the common velocity of the two vehicles is not existed in the compression process of the impact, so the impact pattern belongs to the scratch accident. In the process of vehicle' overtaking the center line or returning to the its lane, the scratch accident occurs more. The nature of the vehicle scratch accident is still a impact accident.

According to the law of conservation of energy, for an impact system composed of two impacting vehicles, the kinetic energy of a vehicle before impact in normal driving, and the energy transformation before and during the impact, are dissipated in the braking, sliding and deformation of the vehicle, etc. respectively. According to the braking or sliding distance after the vehicle impact, the deformation amount can be converted to the equivalent velocity component corresponding to a vehicle, and then synthesize the velocity of each part, and the driving velocity before the collision can be obtained [11].Therefore, the velocity of the impacting vehicle and the impacted vehicle before the scratch is equal to the velocity of the respective sliding after the impact of the two vehicles, plus their respective velocity changes in the course of the impact, that is

$$v_{i0} = v_i + v_{bi} \quad . \tag{9}$$

In the formula, v_{i0} is the instantaneous velocity of the vehicle before the scratch, v_i is the instantaneous velocity of the vehicle after the scratch, v_{bi} is the change of the velocity in the vehicle scratching process.

According to the law of conservation of energy, the kinetic energy of the vehicle is converted into friction work, and the instantaneous velocity v_i can be calculated according to the vehicle sliding distance

$$v_i = \sqrt{2g\varphi_i s_i} \quad . \tag{10}$$

In the formula, g is the acceleration of gravity, φ_i is the adhesion coefficient of the vehicle, s_i is the sliding distance after the vehicle scratch.

According to the law of conservation of energy, the velocity variation of the vehicle before and after the scratch is v_b, the corresponding equivalent velocity of which can be calculated by the empirical formula obtained from the test according to the deformation D of the part of the impact

$$v_{bi} = hD_i \quad . \tag{11}$$

In the formula, D_i is the deformation of the vehicle impact parts, h is the ratio constant between the velocity and deformation, and is generally obtained by empirical formula.

The formula (10) and the formula (11) are brought into the formula (9) to obtain the instantaneous driving velocity v_{i0} of the vehicle before the scratch which is:

$$v_{i0} = v_i + v_{bi} = \sqrt{2g\varphi_i s_i} + hD_i \quad . \tag{12}$$

3.2 Uncertainty evaluation of instantaneous velocity of vehicle before scratch

The parameters of the uncertainty associated with the instantaneous velocity of the vehicle are removed, excluding the gravity acceleration g, including φ_i, s_i and D_i, where the second order uncertainty is introduced by φ_i and s_i. The relationship between the velocity of the vehicle and its uncertainty can be expressed as

$$v_{i0} = f_i(\varphi_i, s_i, D_i) \quad . \tag{13}$$

When evaluating the uncertainty of the instantaneous velocity before the vehicle scratch, the standard uncertainty u_{xi} of each input quantity $x_i(\varphi_i, s_i, D_i)$ shall be calculated first

$$u_{\varphi i} = \frac{a_{\varphi i}}{k_{\varphi i}} \quad . \tag{14}$$

$$u_{si} = \frac{a_{si}}{k_{si}} \quad . \tag{15}$$

$$u_{Di} = \frac{a_{Di}}{k_{Di}} \quad . \tag{16}$$

Secondly, the standard uncertainty component $u_{vi0.xi}$ of each input quantity $x_i(\varphi_i, s_i, D_i)$ is determined

$$u_{vi0.\varphi i} = \left|\frac{\partial v_{i0}}{\partial \varphi_i}\right| u_{\varphi i} = \sqrt{\frac{g s_i}{2\varphi_i}} \cdot u_{\varphi i} \quad . \tag{17}$$

$$u_{vi0.si} = \left|\frac{\partial v_{i0}}{\partial s_i}\right| u_{si} = \sqrt{\frac{g\varphi_i}{2 s_i}} \cdot u_{si} \quad . \tag{18}$$

$$u_{vi0.Di} = \left|\frac{\partial v_{i0}}{\partial D_i}\right| u_{Di} = h \cdot u_{Di} \quad . \tag{19}$$

Evaluate the synthetic standard uncertainty u_{vi0} of the velocity of the identified vehicle v_{i0} before scratch and impact

$$u_{vi0} = \sqrt{\sum_{i=1}^{n} u_{vi0.xi}^2} = \sqrt{u_{vi0.\varphi i}^2 + u_{vi0.si}^2 + u_{vi0.Di}^2} \quad . \tag{20}$$

By multiplying the synthetic standard uncertainty u_{vi0} of the function v_{i0} with the inclusion factor k, the extension uncertainty U_{vi0} of the function v_{i0} can be obtained.

$$U_{vi0} = ku_{vi0} \quad . \tag{21}$$

Using the extension uncertainty as the uncertainty of the measured parameter v_{i0}, the measured driving velocity v_{i0} before the vehicle impact is expressed as

$$V_{i0} = v_{i0} \pm U_{vi0} \quad . \tag{22}$$

This means that the optimum value of the measured parameter is v_{i0}, which can contain most of the V_{i0} in the range of $v_{i0} - U_{vi0}$ to $v_{i0} + U_{vi0}$, and can determine the range of driving velocity before the vehicle scratch.

4 Case analysis of actual accidents

The passenger car is driving from west to east, its left front wheels cross the yellow line in the middle of the road which is in the early overtaking stage, the truck is driving from east to west, its left front wheels press the yellow line in the middle of the road which is in the late overtaking stage, and is returning to its own lane, and the impact occur at the left front corner when the two vehicles are overtaking across the middle line. The key content of accident identification is the velocity before the impact of the passenger car.

The passenger car in the accident is driving opposite to the truck, there is no common velocity in the impact, the impact form is the reverse scratch, and the driving velocity v_{10} before the impact of the passenger car shall be equal to the sliding velocity after its impact v_{10} plus the change of its velocity in the impact v_{b1}.

$$v_{10} = v_1 + v_{b1} \quad . \tag{23}$$

4.1 The instantaneous driving velocity v_{10} of the passenger car before scratch

According to the accident scene picture, after impact, the distance between the passenger car on the road is $s_1 = 34.1 \pm 0.10\text{m}$, the angle between the longitudinal axis and the longitudinal axis is 53.5^o, considering that the passenger car is not braking and has irregular rotation and sideslip, the comprehensive estimate of [12,13,14] has its adhesion coefficient $\varphi_1 = 0.26 \pm 0.02$, and the average deformation is $D_1 = 0.32 \pm 0.02\text{m}$ if the head of the bus is calculated on a double curved surface, and the total mass of the truck is more than 17000kg, so the ratio constant between the velocity of the passenger car and deformation is $h = 67$ [15], according to the law of conservation of energy, the instantaneous velocity v_{10} of the passenger car before the scratch is obtained

$$v_{10} = v_1 + v_{bi} = \sqrt{2g\varphi_1 s_1} + hD_1 = 68.863 \pm 3.236\text{km/h} \quad (24)$$

4.2 Evaluation of uncertainty of driving velocity v_{10} of the passenger car before scratch

The vehicle velocity identification of road traffic accidents is evaluated by the B-type evaluation method. According to the uncertainty theory, take the value of the inclusion factor corresponding to the confidence probability 0. 95 as $k = 2$, calculate according to formula (14)~(22), and the standard uncertainties of the parameters φ_1, s_1 and D_1, which are related to the driving velocity v_{10} before the passenger car scratch with the uncertainty, are $u_{\varphi 1} = 0.01$, $u_{s1} = 0.05\text{m}$ and $u_{D1} = 0.01\text{m}$, respectively, and the standard uncertainty components are $u_{v10.\varphi 1} = 0.913$, $u_{v10.s1} = 0.0348\text{m}$, $u_{v10.D1} = 0.67\text{m}$, where the uncertainty coefficient of the adhesion coefficient φ_1 and the deformation amount D_1 of the collision site is large, which has a significant effect on the calculation results of the velocity before the impact, in contrast, the uncertainty of the sliding distance s_1 after the vehicle scratch is very small. After comprehensive calculation, the synthetic standard uncertainty is $u_{v10} = 1.133\text{km/h}$ and the extension uncertainty is $U_{v10} = 2.266\text{km/h}$, then what can be obtained is that the interval of the velocity value of the passenger car before the scratch is

$$v_{10} = 68.863 \pm 2.266\text{km/h} = 66.597 \sim 71.129\text{km/h} \quad (25)$$

The conclusion of this case is that the velocity of the passenger car is 69km/h before the impact.

5 Conclusion

Without considering the error of geometric parameters in the field, in this paper, the uncertainty of the parameters such as the adhesion coefficient of vehicle and road surface, the sliding distance after scratch and the deformation of the vehicle impacting part are analyzed in the road traffic accident under the condition of scratch form of vehicles. The uncertainty of the degree of deformation introduced by the adhesion coefficient and the impact site has significant influence on the calculation results of the vehicle velocity before impact, and the uncertainty calculation method for the velocity identification is obtained, so as to determine the range of the driving velocity before the vehicle impact.

References

1. Yuan Q., Chen H.Y., Li Y.B.: Using Injury Severity Data to Determine the Impact Speed of Traffic Accidents between Vehicle and Vulnerable Road User. J. Chinese Journal of Forensic Sciences. V86 (3), 32-39 (2016)
2. Chen T., Wei L., Gong B., Zhou W.X.: Parameter Sensitivity Analysis of Reconstruction System for Vehicle-Vehicle Collision Accidents. J. Automotive Engineering. 34(9), 771-776 (2012)
3. Zhang J., Zhang X., Li J., Ni X. D., Gao J. G.: Sensitivity Analysis on the Selected Parameters in Typical Vehicle Collision Models. J. Automotive Engineering. 34(10), 905-908 (2012)
4. Hu N., Lu G.Q., Li T., Li Y.B.: Calibration Precision Experiments Analysis of Photogrammetry in Traffic Accident Scene Based on Separately-calibrate Method. J. Automotive Engineering. 30(7), 557-560 (2008)
5. Liu Z.Q., Wang P., Zhang J.H., Wang Y., Gong B.: Review of Traffic Accident Reproduction Technology and Its Developing Trend. J. China Safety Science Journal. 17(4), 16-20 (2007)
6. Yuan Q., Zhang G. Q., Guo R., Li Y.B.: Research Evolution on the Theory Methods of Vehicle-speed Analysis of Traffic Accidents. J. Journal of Transportation Engineering and Information. 7(2), 21-27 (2009)
7. Yuan Q., Li Y.B.: Influence of Parametrical Uncertainties on Traffic Accident Reappearance of Vehicle Side Impact. J. Transactions of the Chinese Society for Agricultural Machinery. 36(5), 16-19 (2005)
8. Fei Y.T., Error theory and data processing. M. China Machine Press. (2015)
9. Tan D. R., Yin P.: Speed Estimation for Vehicle-Bicycle Side Impact Accident Based on the Uncertainty Theory. J. Automotive Engineering. 32(3), 220-222 (2010)
10. Deng H.Y., Mo Y.Z., Jiang S.X., Han Z.G.: Application of the Uncertainty Evaluation Algorithm to Automobile Accident Recurrence. J. Journal of Central South University of Forestry & Technology. 26(4), 96-100 (2006)
11. Yuan Q., Li Y.B.: Uncertainty Evaluation on the Energy Method of Vehicle Traffic Accident Reconstruction. J. China Journal of Highway and Transport. 15 (1), 110-112 (2002)
12. Li C. C., Liu X. M., Rong J.: Experimental Study on Effect of Road Condition on Pavement Friction Coefficient. J. Journal of Highway and Transportation Research and Development. 27(12), 27-32 (2010)
13. Sui B.: Research on the Traffic Accidents Vehicle-Speed Reproduction Methods. D. Harbin Institute of Technology. (2012)
14. Yu Z. P., Zuo J. L., Zhang L.J.: A Summary on the Development Status Quo of Tire-Road Friction Coefficient Estimation Techniques. J. Automotive Engineering. 28 (6), 546-549 (2006)

15. General Administration of Quality Supervision, Inspection and Quarantine of P. R. C., Standardization Administration of P. R. C.: Identification for the Speed of Vehicle Involved in Road Traffic Accidents. S. China Standard Press. GA/T 33195-2016 (2016)

The best marketing plan of photographing for money deduced by extensible mind mapping

Bifeng Guo, *Rui* Fan ,*Chong-wen* Huang,*Fuyu* Ma,*Zihao* Li, *Qiubin* Liu,*Penghui* Liu,*Weitao* He

Faculty of Software,Guangdong Ocean University,Zhanjiang,China
1037486652@qq.com,fanrui@gdou.edu.cn,972606984@qq.com
452388727@qq.com,1018690570@qq.com,952167400@qq.com
liupenghui@outlook.com,1305190319@qq.com

Abstract. With the development of society and economy, there is a new way of marketing research by people's taking photos of the respondents. They can get paid after finishing the survey tasks by taking photos. However, the contradictory problem is that, as for the project leader, the well pay makes him spend too much money while the poor pay causes low task completion rate. The solution to the problem is to put forward a way to find the best marketing plan of the project, which can both meet the demands of marketing research and reduce the budget. By means of Extenics in combination with extensible mind mapping, we find the best marketing plan for it.

1 Introduction

Photographing for money is a kind of self-service model of Internet. Users can apply for VIP after downloading the cell phone application. The VIP of it can get the research task they want. The tasks are usually photographing some information like shelves of goods that can't be searched from the Internet. The VIP of the application can get paid after finishing the task of photographing. This kind of way of marketing research not only provides companies with merchandise check and useful information but also it takes less time compared with conventional marketing research. Besides, it guarantees the authenticity of the data.

As for the research manager, he or she should make the price of each task according to different situations. However, there is a deadly problem in the promising way of marketing research. That is, if the price is high, the project manager may spend much money to complete the marketing research, in contrast, the project won't be finished.

In this case, finding the best price of each task becomes the key question of it.

Photographing for money is a contradictory problem and it is the best way to solve the contradictory problem by means of Extenics [1]. The discipline provides us with formalized model to explore the possibility of objects and methods of extensive innovation [2], which is used to address problems in various fields. Our team devoted ourselves to develop computer-aided software based on Extenics. We have done some research about innovative software architecture and developed an innovative mobile software. We developed an Extensive mobile software [3], did some research on web service-based Extensive system

 https://doi.org/10.1051/itmconf/20181703003

[4], worked for modeling Extenics innovation software [5] and explored a method for self-adapted software[6]. The way of mind mapping [7] was put forward long time ago and some developed software based on mind mapping can intuitively activate our divergent thinking [8], enlarging the mindscape of us. However, the software has no convergence mechanism and it can't direct our thinking to success. Extenics offers us both way and procedure of innovative thinking. Besides, it provides a way to evaluate superority values for each step of innovative thinking in combination with quantitative and qualitative mathematical model, creating reference for next-step thinking direction. Nevertheless, Extenics is a mathematical way [9] after all. It can't clearly reflect the deduced thinking of people. Therefore, it is a new innovative way, namely, to solve problems based on mind mapping in combination with Extensive procedures and methods so that people can deduce problems intuitively and regularly, hence the thinking deductive architecture of Extenics with mind mapping (see Figure 1). From Figure1 we can see there is an original problem breaks down into a subproblem which can be the kernel problem if it can't break down. As for the kernel problem, we can make a modeling setting its conditional element, goal element and dependent function. Each of them can change itself to another and finally change it into a best one. Then we make Extensive transformation and superiority evaluation. This is the whole procedure of Extensive solution printed on the mind mapping. Not only can it reflects our thinking intuitively but it leads us to a right thinking to solve problems.

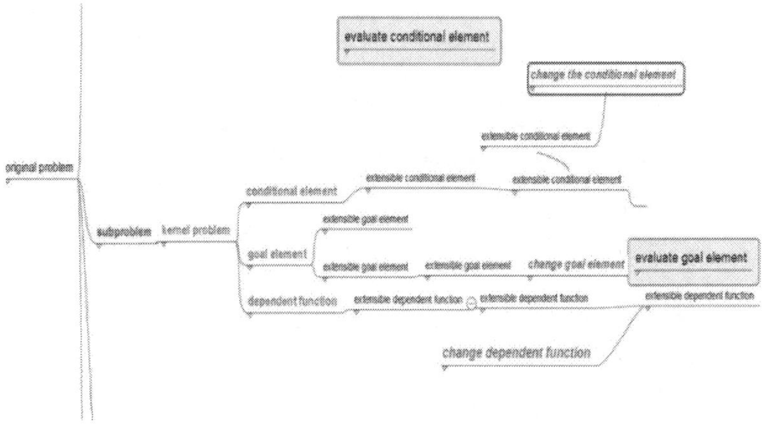

Figure1 Extenics Mind Mapping

2. Procedures of solving the problem

2.1 Data preprocessing

To find a completed project for analysis, we found the data from a Chinese mathematical modeling contest. The project consists of 835 sets of data including each set of task number, task latitude, task longitude, price and its completion. We processed the data with Excel trying to look for the relationship among each task's geographical situation, price and completion.

By comparing Figure 2 with map of Guangdong Province, China, we find that most prices of these tasks are between 60 and 70 and they are located in traffic developed places. Our analysis to related papers proved that the train station of each city is the center of the city. Then we select 5 positions of the relevant train stations in order to explore which district each task belongs to i.e., Guangzhou Station, Foshan Station, Dongguan Station, Shenzhen Station and Huizhou Station. To find which city these tasks belong to, we calculate the distance between each task position to the 4 stations, judging them by the shortest distance. Then we analyze the task amount, completed task and completion rate of each district. The table (Table 1) is shown below.

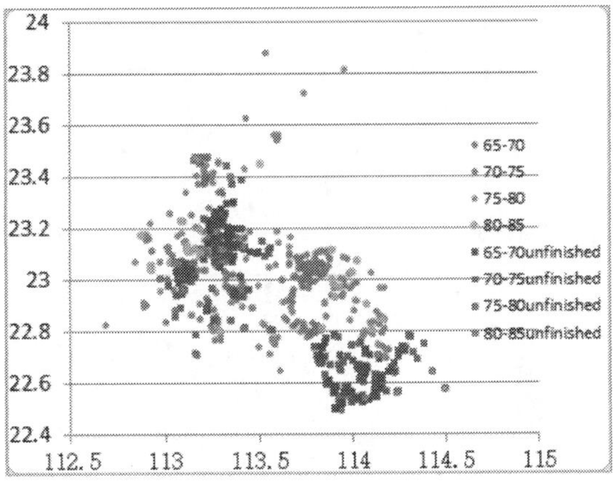

Figure2 Task Distribution

Table 1 District-completion Statistics

District	Total tasks	Completed tasks	Completion Rate
All	835	522	62.51%
Guangzhou	313	191	61.02%
Shenzhen	188	64	34.04%
Foshan	161	101	62.73%
Dongguan	172	165	95.93%
Huizhou	1	1	100%

We exclude the data in Position Huizhou for there is only a set of data. Next we analyze the data to find out the factors influencing the completion rate. By consulting some papers, we eventually ensure that the economic development level of each district greatly influences the completion rate. Consequently, we look up the data of the economy in these districts. They are shown below.

Table 2 District Economy Level

District	Annual GDP per capita
Guangzhou	21868.09
Shenzhen	25789.98
Foshan	17485.11
Dongguan	12453.30

For the sake of convenient calculation, we define Variable E to describe the economy level. According to the data above, Egz=22.0,Esz=26.0,Efs=17.5,Edg=12.5. Also, we define another variable Local Value Rate to describe whether each task is worth completing, which is defined as Formula 1.

$$LocalValueRate = \frac{Marked\ Price}{E} \qquad (1)$$

We calculate the Local Value Rate and compare it with completion rate to explore the relationship between them. Table3 below shows the data.

Table 3 Value Rate and Completion

Local Value Rate	Task Completion
2.9-3.2	0.4892
3.2-3.5	0.6029
3.5-3.8	0.4285
3.8-4.1	0.4861
4.1-4.4	0.6923
4.4-4.7	nil
4.7-5.0	0.9333
5.0-5.3	0.9091
5.3-5.6	0.9259
5.6-5.9	0.9811
5.9-6.2	0.9429
6.2-6.5	0.9545
6.5-6.8	1
6.8-7.1	1

We analyze the data above with software called SPSS, reflecting the relevance of Local Value Rate and Task Completion is 85.8%. So we draw a conclusion that local economy level also influences the completion besides the price.

2.2 The advantages to using freeplane

We solve the problem by deducing a tree in the software called Freeplane[10] in combination with Extenics.

The software Freeplane provides us with a visible mind mapping, from which we can draw figures and profiles according man's thoughts. We can draw a part of mapping whenever we think of the problem and it can carve human's procedure of addressing problem in the software shown as a mapping that is easy to understand. The software fits mind for Extenics innovation well. Mind mapping without Extenics innovation can't control minds' thinking, causing the mess of human's innovative direction. Consequently, we solve the problem by using Freeplane in combination with Extenics means.

2.3 Problem modeling

In this problem, what we are concerned about is whether we can increase the completion without spending more money. There is no doubt that without taking any action, the completion is a fixed value. The task completion now is 62.5% and we should make it greater than 62.5%. Through analyzing, there are 2 kernel problems to be found. They are finding out other marketing plans and changing the local economy level.

According to the Extensive innovation first we set up the goal element and conditional element, defining a discrete dependent function in the mind mapping. The mind mapping is shown in Figure3.

After the model set, we manage to think of the plans where there are more positive elements in order to increase the dependent function value by means of Extensive innovation. As for another kernel problem changing the local economy level, it seems that it is not our ability to change the economy level of each district and it is a ridiculous thought. So we don't refer to it in the following.

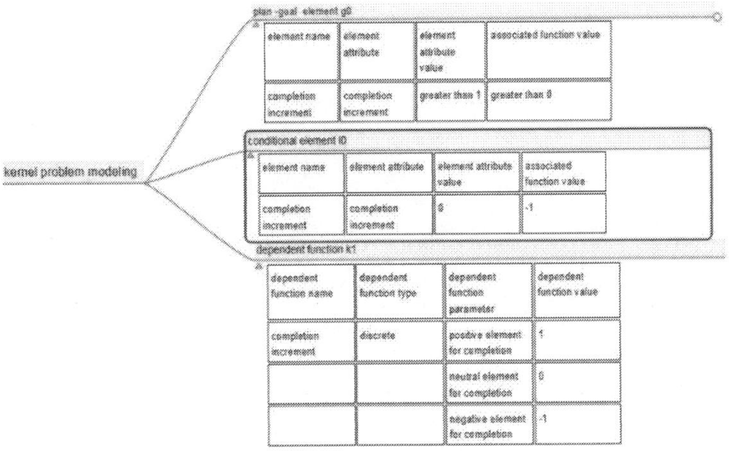

Figure3 Problem Modeling

2.4 Extensible transformation

Heading for the goal element, we find out three marketing plans that can meet the requirement. They are distance-changed plan, price-accumulated plan and package plan. We think of 3elements aimed at the 3 marketing plans including distance factor, difficulty factor and human factor. The details of the 3 marketing plans are shown below.

Distance-changed plan: First the manager hands out a part of tasks close to the center of a district where the traffic is developed. After most of the handed-out tasks are completed, the manager hands out some tasks a little farther from the center of a district to increase the complement. As for the plan, at the beginning of the project without changing the price, more people will be willing to finish the tasks. Then after the next tasks are handed out, people would like to go to the place to get more payment and they can complete more tasks without changing places, which is positive to distance factor. The difficulty of the task is fixed in the plan, which is neutral difficulty factor. As for the task catchers, they prefer this plan for the reason that they can get more earnings in a trip, which is positive to human factor. Consequently, the element attribute value is 2.

Price-accumulated plan: At a certain time, task catchers get less payment of each task when completing fewer tasks. As they completed more tasks, each payment of each task increases according to their completion quantity. The plan doesn't make a constraint of distance to them compared with the original plan, which is neutral to distance factor. The difficulty of the plan is fixed too, which is neutral to difficulty factor. As for the task catchers who catch fewer tasks in a certain time, it is disadvantageous for them. However, it is beneficial for those who catch more tasks, which is neutral to human factor. The element attribute value is 0.

Package plan: The manager makes some of the closed tasks cascade so that many catchers will not argue for the same task and they get paid after completing a cascade of tasks. This is neutral to distance factor. The tasks that are easier to be completed will be completed more quickly. However, the harder's one's completion may decrease causing other easier tasks unfinished in the same cascade, which is negative to difficulty factor. The thought of package is a comparison to salary system, people prefer annual salary system than monthly salary system, which is positive to human factor. Consequently the dependent attribute value is 0.

We place the innovative procedure to the mind mapping, showing the mind of human while having an innovative thought.

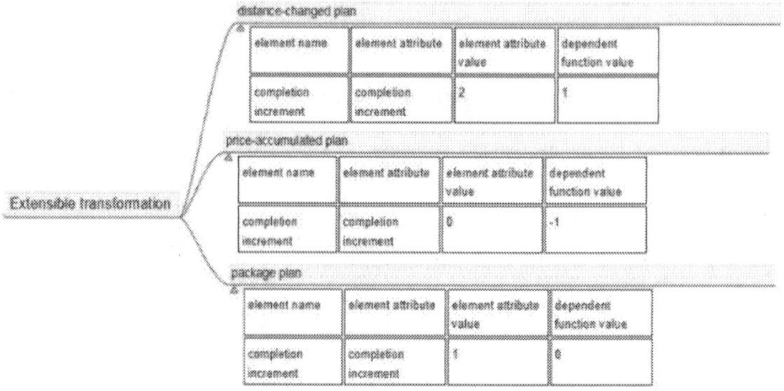

Figure4 Extensible Transformation

2.5 Superiority evaluation

From 3 marketing plans above, we select a best marketing plan for the problem for its attribute dependent function value is 1.0 and it is greater than the other two, reflecting that distance-changed plan is the best mathematical model among the three plans and it is more likely to solve the contradictory problem in this case. Consequently, we select it as the best marketing plan. The whole procedure of the innovative mind in combination with Extenics is shown in Figure5.

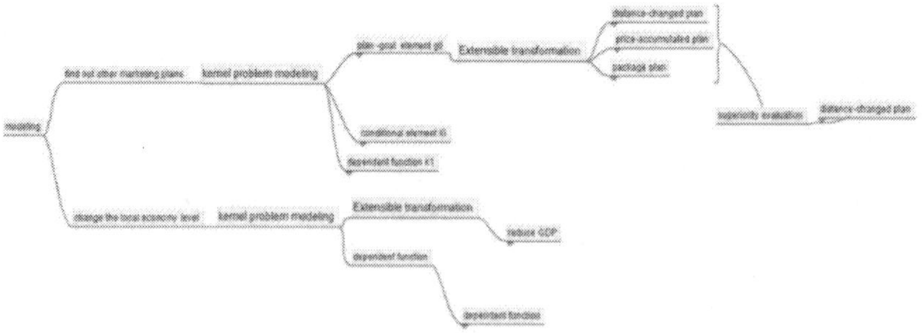

Figure 5. Whole Procedure of Innovation Mind

3. Conclusion

In order to make the marketing research effectively, the idea of photographing for money was put forward. However, the problem is that well pay makes the company spend too much money while the poor pay causes low task completion rate. We create a new way to solve the problem by the methods of Extenics in combination with mind mapping, and it solves the contradictory problem to some extent. We draw a conclusion that distance-changed plan is the best marketing plan in this issue. The manager can start a marketing research in this way and improve the plan in practice. Besides, the marketing plan can also be used in the issue of Taxi Problem and Dining Problem. What we are going to research is that developing a new software in combination with both Extenics and mind mapping so that we can solve problems in the correct direction and make the mind mapping more intuitively.

Acknowledgements.

The research is supported by Guangdong Provincial Science and Technology Project (2014A040402010) and Guangdong Province Innovation and Entrepreneurship Training Program for College Students (201710566036).

References

1. Wen C, Yang C. Basic theory and methodology on Extenics [J]. Chinese Journal, 2013, 58(13):1190.
2. Li X, Li L, Chen Z. toward Extenics-Based Innovation Model on Intelligent Knowledge Management [J]. Annals of Data Science, 2014, 1(1):127-148.Association A M. Journal of Marketing Research [J]. Journal of Marketing Research, 2004, 17(6):900-909.
3. Yan S, Fan R, Chen Y, et al. Developing Mobile Software for Extenics Innovation [J]. 2016.Cai W, Yang C Y, Bin H E. Several Problems on the Research of Extenics [J]. Journal of Guangdong University of Technology, 2001.
4. Yan S, Fan R, Chen Y, et al. Research on Web services-based Extenics Aided Innovation System [J]. Procedia Computer Science, 2017, 107(C):103-110.
5. Rui Fan. Modelling Extenics Innovation Software by Intelligent Service Components. The open Cybernetics and Systemics Journal, Volume 8, 2014:1-7.
6. FAN Rui, PENG Yinqiao, CHEN Yuefeng,etc.A method for self-adaptive software formal modeling by Extenics. CAAI Transactions on Intelligent Systems, 2015, 10(6): 901-911.
7. Helen Kershaw. Mind mapping [J]. Bereavement Care, 1998, 17(3):44-44.
8. Mccrae R R. Creativity, divergent thinking, and openness to experience [J]. Journal of Personality & Social Psychology, 1987, 52(6):1258-1265.
9. Li X, Li L, Chen Z. toward Extenics-Based Innovation Model on Intelligent Knowledge Management [J]. Annals of Data Science, 2014, 1(1):127-148.
10. Surhone L M, Tennoe M T, Henssonow S F. Freeplane [J]. Milwaukee Journal Sentinel, 2010, 65(1):93-95.

The solution of excess ingredients in hotels deduced by extensible mind mapping

Fuyu Ma , *Rui* Fan, *Chongwen* Huang, *Bifeng* Guo, *Zihao* Li, *Qiubin* Liu,*Penghui* Liu,*Weitao* He

Faculty of Software,Guangdong Ocean University,Zhanjiang,China
452388727@qq.com, fanrui_nc@126.com, 972606984@qq.com,
1037486652@qq.com, 1018690570@qq.com, 952167400@qq.com,
liupenghui@outlook.com, 1305190319@qq.com

Abstract. Aiming at the contradictory problem that the hotels' daily excess ingredient causes a lot of losses, which is contradictory to the profit purpose of ingredient, this paper establishes kernel model and Extensible model through Extensible theory methods combined with mind mapping. Through evaluating the characteristics of alike relative matter-element, making up comprehensive dependent functions and using Extensible transformation, we can get various solutions. And then, taking the matter-element characteristics as evaluation criteria, we can carry out the superiority evaluation to the solutions and finally get the superior solution.

1 Introduction

The ingredient of the hotel must ensure the freshness and quality of the ingredient every day. The daily excess ingredient is either sold to dealers at a discount, or thrown away. In any way, which causes a lot of losses, which is contradictory to the profit purpose of ingredient. The ingredient is not enough to meet the needs of daily operations, influencing hotel's normal running and makes a lot of losses. In order to keep daily operations, the hotel will purchase overmuch ingredient, but it will cause the waste of ingredient.

Extenics [3] is a new discipline based on the study of contradiction. Extenics method is used to analyze the contradiction, and find the superior solution. People continually study and discuss the using of Extenics from the various aspects of life. For examples, paper [4] studies the application of Extenics in self-service tourism. Paper [5] studies the application of Extenics in renting. Paper [6] studies the application of Extenics in job hunting. Besides, our team has developed a innovative software based on Extenics and has done some researches on innovative software architecture. We modeled Extenics Innovation Software by intelligent Service Components [7], developed Mobile Software for Extenics Innovation[8], did a research on web services-based Extenics Aided Innovation System[9] and came up with a method for self-adaptive software formal modeling by Extenics[10]. Extenics mainly uses Extensible transformation and comprehensive dependent function to generate the superiority evaluation and finally get the superior solution. These thinking and methods can correctly guide people to carry out innovative thinking activities in an effective direction. Extenics can effectively guide people to carry out innovative thinking activities, and this advantage makes up for the shortcomings of mind mapping. However,

Extenics is so abstruse and abstract to understand for normal people, so we should combine mind mapping and Extenics theory to solve contradictory problems.

Mind mapping [1], as a tool of creative thinking, has been widely used; Mind mapping can help people to analyze the problems in a hierarchical way. It can refine the problems and find the key factors to solve the problems. The establishment of mind mapping is beneficial for people to solve the problems in Systematic analysis and deep thinking, which is helpful to people's creative thinking. However, because its scope of thinking is too wide without any guidance and constraints, it causes the thinking process excessive divergence. Therefore, Mind mapping can't effectively control the innovation process in the direction of effective deduction. Freeplane [2] software is a visual tool of mind mapping. It can clearly show the whole thinking process of people. Whenever, as long as people have a new idea of thinking about their problems, they can record it on the software by themselves. Therefore, the software can make our thinking more convenient, clear and effective.

In order to solve the contradiction of hotels' excess ingredient, this paper will combine the theory of Extenics in Freeplane platform to model, transform and evaluate. In the end, according to the superiority evaluation, we will select the superior solution. The correct and effective combination of the Extenics and mind mapping will make our innovative thinking activities more convenient and efficient.

2 The steps of solving problem by extensible mind mapping

We solve problems by using the knowledge of Extenics to deduce a thinking tree on the Freeplane software platform.

2.1 Problem modeling

After a normal daily operation, the hotel had about 20 kg ingredients remains. per kg of the ingredient cost 6￥.The hotel can get 60% of the cost for refund if they return the remains ingredient to the supplier, which is not healthy for the development of the hotel. To make a profit, the weight of excess ingredient should control lower than 25kg and the profits made by the selling of the food should be controlled form the same as the cost to twice of the cost . In this situation, the promotion effect to the hotel is fine. Obviously, there is a question that the subjective desire is incompatible with the objective conditions. To solve this question, first step is to extend the contradictory problem to two kernel question, as it is shown in the picture.

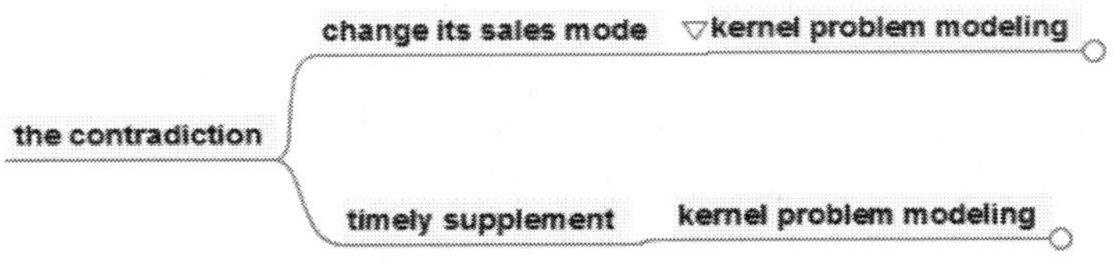

Figure1. Two Kernel Problems

We consider how to extend the shelf life of ingredient or other treatment to increase profit. For another kernel problem that the supplier timely supply supplement when the ingredient is not enough. Few suppliers can do that, so we don't refer to it in the following.

Furthermore, we extendedly analyze the kernel problem and establish the kernel problem modeling. According to the theory of Extenics, we will set up the goal element, the conditional element and the dependent function. As shown in the following picture:

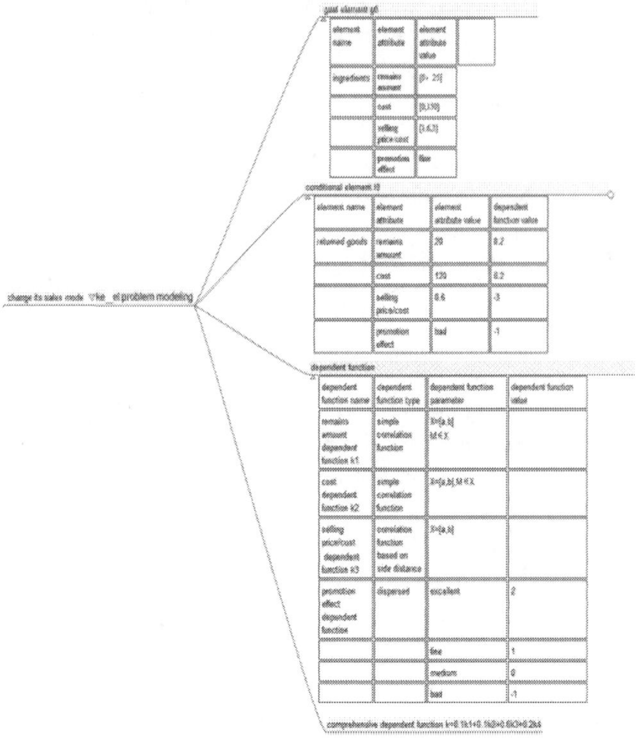

Figure2. Target Element, the Conditional Element and the Associated **Function**

It can be seen from the picture that the extensible modeling of kernel problem is P0=g0l0. Both of goal element and conditional element has some attributes. Set c1= remains amount,c2=cost,c3= selling price/cost,c4= promotion effect, X1=[0 , 25], X2=[0,150], X3=[2 [f1] *fator,2], X4=fine. The factor is c3's factor. We use it to form the satisfaction section so that we can screen out the strategy which has lower effect on the profit when we are forming final strategy. For now, we amuse factor is 0.6 which means X3=[1.2,2].

2.2 Establishment of dependent function

2.2.1 Establishment of dependent function about remains amount and cost

Generally, both of the remains amount and cost are as low as possible(0⩽remains amount ⩽25, 0⩽cost⩽150) when others factors meet demand. Thus, we need to create simple dependent function between remains amount and cost whose positive region is finite interval. According to paper[10] 2.7.6 session ,when the positive region is that X is <a, b> and M∈X, the simple dependent function is:

$$K(x) = \begin{cases} \frac{x-a}{M-a} & x \le M \\ \frac{b-x}{b-M} & x > M \end{cases} \qquad (1)$$

set x=20,a=0,b=25,M=0,the result of the dependent function about remains amount is k=0.2; set x=120,a=0,b=150,M=0,the result of the dependent function about cost is k=0.2

2.2.2 Establishment of dependent function about selling price/cost

According to the paper [11], set X3=[1.2,2] and the best value is x3=2, and it obtains the right distance .

$$\rho(x,2,X3)=\begin{cases}1.2-x & x<2\\ -0.8 & x=2\\ x-2 & x>2\end{cases} \quad (2)$$

According to the paper [11], the other formulas are as follows:

$$\rho(x,X)=\left|x-\frac{a+b}{2}\right|-\frac{b-a}{2} \quad (3)$$

set X3=[a, b] and X=[1, 2].

$$D(x,X3,X)=\begin{cases}\rho(x,X)-\rho(x,X3) & \rho(x,X)\neq\rho(x,X3)\text{and } x\notin X3\\ \rho(x,X)-\rho(x,X3)+a-b & \rho(x,X)\neq\rho(x,X3)\text{and } x\in X3\\ a-b & \rho(x,X)=\rho(x,X3)\end{cases} \quad (4)$$

$$k(x)=\begin{cases}\frac{\rho(x,x_3,X3)}{D(x,X3,X)} & \text{other}\\ \frac{\rho(x,x_3,X3)}{D(x,X3,X)}-1 & \rho(x,X)=\rho(x,X3)\text{and } x\notin X3\end{cases} \quad (5)$$

Combining (2), (3), (4) and (5), the result is k=-3

2.2.3 Establishment of dependent Function about promotion effect

In this paper, we give grade descriptions of the promotion effect which are excellent, fine, medium and bad. The values are 2, 1, 0and -1.The established discrete function is as follows.

$$k(x)=\begin{cases}2 & x=\text{excellent}\\ 1 & x=\text{fine}\\ 0 & x=\text{medium}\\ -1 & x=\text{bad}\end{cases} \quad (6)$$

When the excess ingredient is returned to the supplier, the value of promotion effect is -1.

2.3 Establishment of comprehensive dependent function

By establishing the comprehensive dependent function, we can judge the solution more accurately and find the root of the contradiction better. According to the above statement, the comprehensive dependent function is as follows:

$$K_P=ek_a+fk_b+gk_c+hk_d \quad (7)$$

k a, k b, k c and k d are the function values of each function. And e and f are the weight of remains amount and cost, because they are easily affected by objective conditions, such as weather, customers' favorite and so on , so their weight is 0.1. The g is the weight of selling price/cost, because The starting point of our solution is to increase profit,so the weight is 0.6.The h is the weight of promotion effect, it has a certain importance for the hotel, so the weight is 0.2.Therefore , Draw the following formula:

$$K_P = 0.1 \times 0.2 + 0.1 \times 0.2 + 0.6 \times (-3) + 0.2 \times (-0.1) < 0$$

It is shown that the above problem is incompatible, so it is necessary to carry out extensible transformation. The following paper will give the Extensible transformation of the contradictory problem.

2.4 Extensible transformation

From the above statement, the reason of the comprehensive dependent function less than 0 is that the function values of selling price/cost and promotion effect are less than 0. In order to change the value of the two functions into positive values, the extensible transformation of the conditional element is carried out. The following is the condition extensible transformation strategy given in this paper:

Conditional element can be replaced with network good. With the rapid development of networking, online sale become more and more popular. The excess ingredients also can be sold in this way.

Conditional element can be replaced with bundling products, bundling means bundling other products together and selling them together. For most consumers' psychology, this strategy can bring more guests to the hotel.

Conditional element can be replaced with Promotional products, the ingredient as free promotional products for promotion can greatly enhance the promotion of the hotel.

Conditional element can be replaced with food which has longer storage time. Ingredients can be made into meatballs, cakes and so on, as long as the treatment is great, not only did not the hotel make the loss, but also the profits are not low.

The extensible transformation session are shown as follows through the Freeplane software.

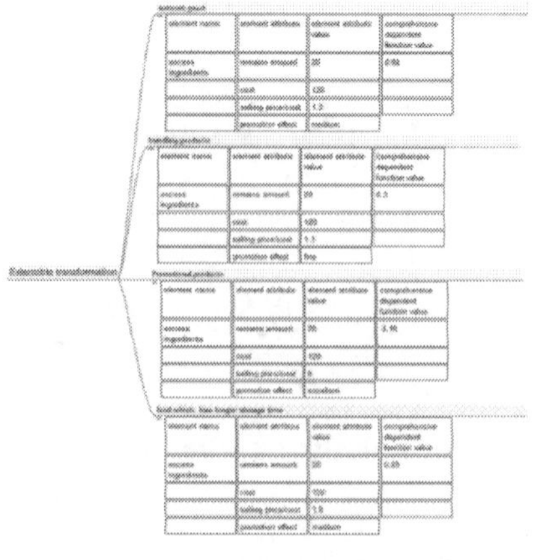

Figure3. Extensible Transformation

2.5 Superiority evaluation

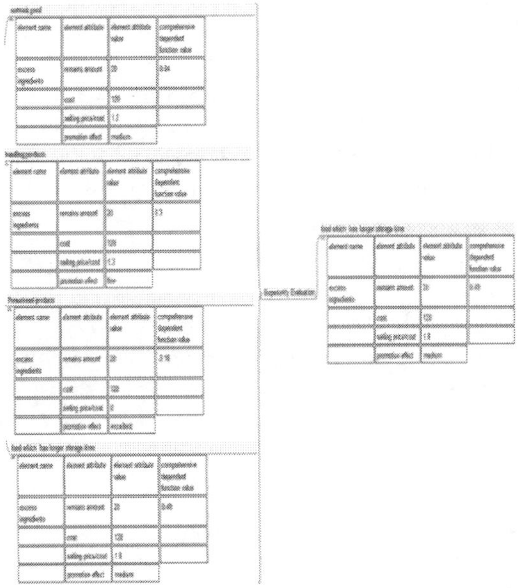

Figure4. Superiority Evaluation

After extensible transformation, the four strategies can be evaluated according to the comprehensive dependent function. The comprehensive dependent function value of the forth solution is 0.49 and are greater than the comprehensive dependent function value of the other three solutions, so we choose the forth solution as the superior solution. Therefore, we can increase the profit of excess ingredients through the way.

Through the complete extensible thinking routes, we can see more clearly how the superior solution is deduced, and the routes are shown in the following figure.

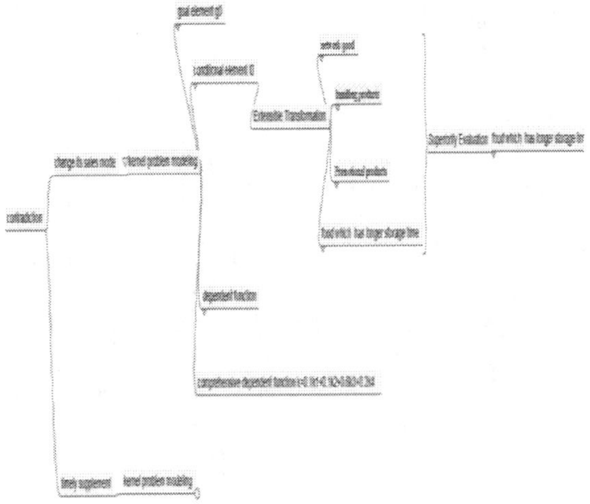

Figure5. The Complete Extensible Thinking Routes

3 Conclusion

This paper focuses on the contradictory problem of excess ingredient that the excess ingredient causes a lot of losses, which is contradictory to the profit purpose of ingredient. For this problem, we use Extenics theory combined with the mind mapping to solve it By the steps that are problem Modeling, Extensible transformation and superiority evaluation, finally we screen out the forth solution as the superior one. In conclusion, Extenics can correctly guide me to think in an effective direction. And the mind mapping can clearly show my thinking route, which make my thinking more efficient and more convenient. In the future, we can research how to combine Extenics and mind mapping to make a new Extensible mind mapping software which can solve most of the daily contradictory problems.

4 Especially thanks

This paper is supported by Guangdong science and technology project (2014A040402010) and Guangdong college students' innovation and entrepreneurship project (201710566036).

5 References

1. Helen Kershaw. Mind mapping [J]. Bereavement Care, 1998, 17(3):44-44.
2. Surhone L M, Tennoe M T, Henssonow S F. Freeplane [J]. Milwaukee Journal Sentinel, 2010, 65(1):93-95.
3. Wen C, Yang C. Basic theory and methodology on Extenics [J]. Chinese Journal, 2013, 58(13):1190.
4. Fang Zhuojun, Li Weihua Li Chengxiao. Research and implementation of extensible strategy generation system for self-service travel [J]. Journal of Guangdong University of Technology, 2009, 26(2): 83-89.
5. Li Chengxiao, Li Weihua. Rental extensible strategy generation system [J]. Journal of Guangdong University of Technology, 2011, 6(3):274-278.
6. Chen Yanan, Li Weihua. Research and implementation of extensible strategy generation system for job hunting problem [J]. Journal of Guangdong University of Technology, 2012, 29 (1): 88-93.
7. Rui Fun. Modeling Extenics Innovation Software by intelligent Service Components. The open Cybernetics and Systemic Journal, Volume 8, 2014: 1-7.
8. Yan S, Fan R, Chen Y, et al. Developing Mobile Software for Extenics Innovation [J].2016. Cai W, Yang C Y, Bin H E. Several Problems on the Research of Extenics [J]. Journal of Guangdong University of Technology, 2001.
9. Yan S, Fan R, Chen Y, et al. Research on web services-based Extenics Aided Innovation System [J]. Procedia Computer Science, 2017, 107(C):103-110.
10. FAN Rui, PENG Yinqiao, Chen Yuefeng, etc. A method for self-adaptive software formal modeling by Extenics. CAAI Transactions on Intelligent System, 2015, 10, (6): 901-911.
11. Wen C, Yang C. Matter element model and its application [M] Chinese Journal, 1 994.

Lecture notes in computer science: research on hybrid grid algorithm of voronoi diagram

Binjun Wang [1], *Qiushi* Wang [2], *Jingying* Li [1]

[1]Department of Information Technology and Cybersecurity, People's Public Security University of China, Beijing: 100240, China
[2]Department of IOT, First Research Institute of the Ministry of Public Security of PRC, Beijing: 100048, China
{ Bin-jun Wang 1, Department of Information Technology and Cybersecurity, People's Public Security University of China, 100240. 2-3-602#, No. 29, Leyuan load, Daxing Dstrict, Beijing, China. wangbinjun@ppsuc.edu.cn

Abstract. Characteristics and performance of two grid methods, which include the growth method and the point by point scanning method of Voronoi diagram, are analyzed qualitatively and quantitatively. The theoretical analysis and experimental results show that the growth method is faster, but the boundary of Voronoi diagram generated by the point by point scanning method is more accurate. By combining the advantages of these two grid methods, the hybrid grid algorithm is proposed: the growth method is used firstly to extend a large step, and then the point by point scanning method is used to color the remaining blank pixel. The theoretical analysis and experimental results show that the speed of the hybrid grid algorithm is close to the fastest growth algorithm, and the accuracy is as well as the point by point scanning algorithm.

1 Introduction

Voronoi diagram [1, 2]is an important topic in computational geometry field, which is often used to solve problems of location optimization, space division and path planning in the fields of geography, meteorology and mobile communication. It has important theoretical and practical value.

The key issues of Voronoi diagram is the generating algorithm. At present, Voronoi diagram generating algorithms can be classified as the vector methods and grid methods. The vector methods have the advantage of high precision, but its data structure and calculation are more complex, and only applicable to the case of simple Voronoi diagram. The typical vector methods include incremental method [3], divided method [4] and indirect method [5]. The grid method has no limitation on the generator which can be a point, a line or a surface with different partitions and weights, but it is time-consuming and the result has lower accuracy. The typical grid methods are point by point scanning method [6] and growth method which includes distance table algorithm [7] and discrete construction algorithm [8].

The divisional weighted Voronoi diagram is the most complex situation when generator is a point, and the weighted Voronoi diagram is a special case when the diagram just has one sector. And the normal Voronoi diagram is a special case when the generators in the weighted Voronoi diagram have the same weight. Therefore, the algorithm of divisional weighted Voronoi diagram also can be used to generate normal Voronoi and weighted voronoi diagrams. The existing grid methods of divisional weighted Voronoi diagram include growth method and point by point scanning method. In this paper, the advantages and disadvantages of two algorithms are analyzed. A hybrid grid algorithm of divisional weighted Voronoi diagram is proposed. The spatial complexity of the algorithm is equivalent to that of the two algorithms, and the time complexity is close to the fastest growth algorithm, but the resulting Voronoi diagram is as accurate as the point by point scanning algorithm.

2 The relative research and analysis

2.1 Qualitative analysis

The main idea of point by point scanning method: the weighted distance between any pixel on the plane and all sectors of all generators is calculated in turn, and the generator with the nearest weighted distance is the generator that the pixel belongs to. In reference [6], weighted Voronoi diagram is generated by point by point scanning method. This idea can also be used to generate the divisional weighted Voronoi diagram by calculating the nearest generator's sector. This algorithm needs to calculate the weighted distance between any pixel on the plane and all generators. Therefore, the time complexity is constrained by the number of generators and sectors.

However, the discrete construction algorithm proposed in reference [8] has the following problems:

Problem 1: The rough boundary problem. The formation of the boundary is approximated by the "collision" of the generator synchronization extension process, and the final resulted edge is related to the order of the generators expansion process. Fig.1 (a) and Fig.1 (b) are the simulation results of the same generator in different order, and there are some differences in the boundary. Fig. 1 (c) is a comparison result of the point by point scanning method. In fact, there are inherently imprecise of the growth method on the boundary, both of the existing algorithm [7, 8] have this boundary imprecision problem.

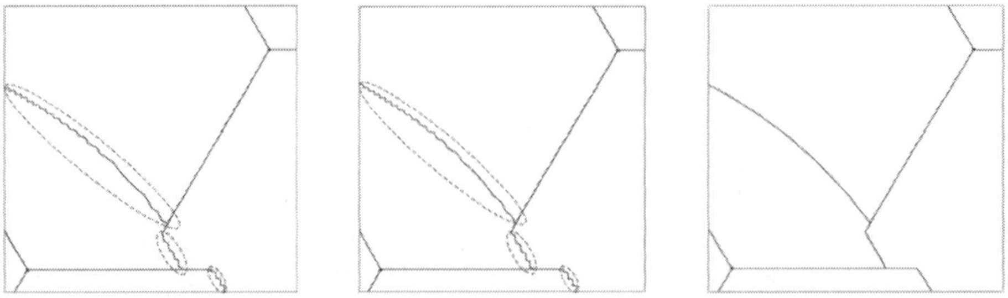

(a) Result 1 of DCA (b) Result 2 of DCA (c) Result of PPSA

Figure.1 the results of the rough boundary problem

Problem 2: The angular increment problem. In order to scan and color pixels on extended arc with all radii, the original algorithm sets a sufficiently small and fixed angular increment in order to color the arc with large radius correctly, which means that the angular increment for small radius arcs and large radius arcs are the same. This results in the slow coloring speed of the original algorithm in the early (when the radius is small) stage. The improved method is to set the angular increment as a dynamic value that decreases as the radius increases, see (2). It can satisfy the correctness of the algorithm with both small and large radius, and the efficiency of the algorithm is obviously higher.

Problem 3: The zebra stripe problem. It does not take into consideration of the large weight situation in original algorithm. For the generator with large weights, if the actual value of the radius (step) increment is greater than 1, it will result in some area that is not colored due to the large step. The principle is shown in Fig.2 (a). Fig.2 (b) is an example of the results, in which there are two generators with relatively large weights, one in the lower left corner and the other in the upper right corner. The result is an error.

On the other hand, when the weight of the generator is too small, the original algorithm has to compute the extended arc repeatedly, which affects the efficiency of the algorithm.

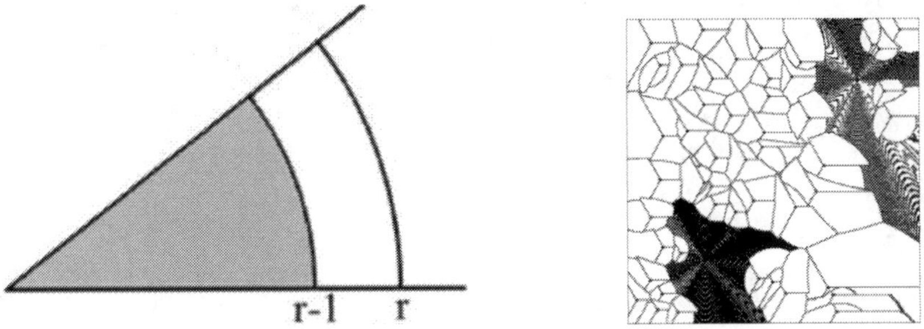

(a)The principle diagram (b) Example diagram

Figure 2. The zebra stripes problem

Problem 4: The discontinuous region problem. The more important problem of this algorithm is that it does not consider the case of discontinuous Voronoi diagram (property Ⅳ of reference [2]). The algorithm is only correct in the situation when the discontinuous region is absent in the Voronoi diagram! The problem is discussed in reference [9], but the termination condition is not analyzed in detail. In order to clarify the termination condition of the growth method, the theorem 1 is given firstly.

Theorem **1:** For the growth method, during the algorithm process, if a certain pixel in the drawing area is first covered by a generator, the color of the pixel will not be changed during the following process.

Proof: (omitted).

Inference **1:** For the growth method, when the maximum weight generator covers all pixels on the panel, the algorithm ends.

Proof: The general situation is proved firstly. For any of the generator, if all the pixels on the panel can be covered by its extension area, then the color of any pixel in the drawing area is determined by the extension process or previous algorithm process. According to Theorem 1, the algorithm ends.

Therefore, the conclusion is also true for the maximum generator.

Inference **2:** For the growth method, the algorithm ends when all pixels of the drawing area are colored.

Proof: (omitted).

Inference 1 sets the termination condition of the algorithm from the perspective of the generator, while inference 2 sets the termination condition from the perspective of the panel. According to the inference 1, when the situation in Fig.3 occurs (the maximum weight generator is close to a corner and another relatively larger weight generator is close to another corner), although the panel has been completely covered and the color of each pixel on the panel is determined, the algorithm still needs to continue. Thus the efficiency is relatively low. According to inference 2, the algorithm would be more efficient with a counter. When the total numbers of pixels on the panel are all colored, the algorithm ends.

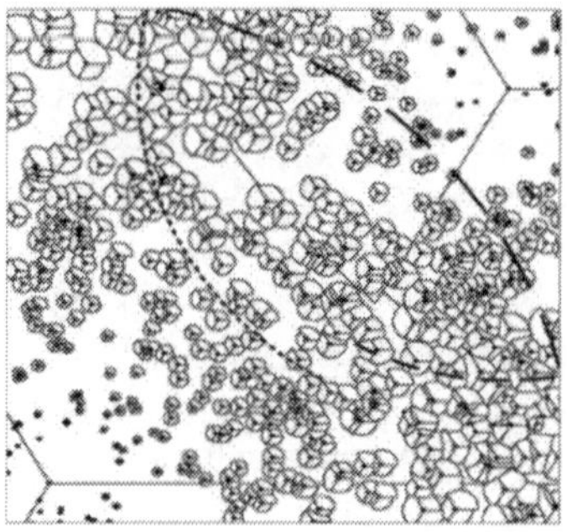

Figure 3. Cover the drawing area with the largest generator as the termination condition

It should be noted that the reference [7] also has problem 1 and 4. Problem 1 is the common problem of the growth method. Unless the parallel algorithm is used, any conventional algorithm of the growth method will have problem 1. Problem 4 is caused by the irrational design of the distance table algorithm [7] and the discrete construction algorithm [8].

In addition, according to the growth method, when the generator distribution is uneven or there is a super large weight generator, the boundaries of the majority of generators have been determined, but some individual generator expansion is not yet ended, because the algorithm needs to expand synchronously before it ends. It means that all generators still need to be calculated, which seriously affect the efficiency of the algorithm, as shown in Fig.4.

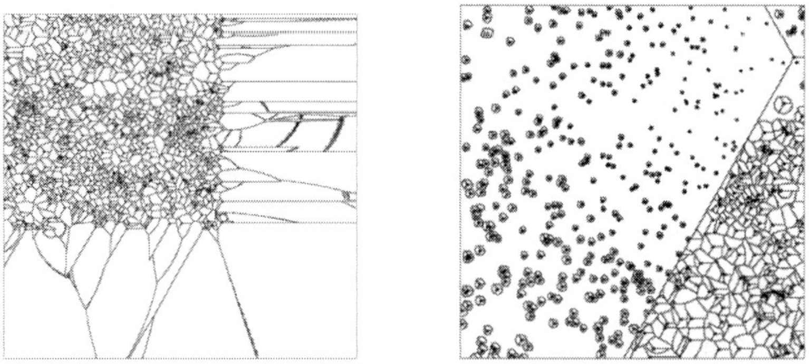

(a) Generator distribution is uneven (b) exists of super large weight generator

Figure 4. The influence problem of the growth method later steps

2.2 Quantitative analysis

Discrete construction algorithm [8] is that each pixel on the expansion arc of each generator is colored with the law of radius increment and the angle increment. Each pixel is calculated according to Eq. 1, in which (x0, y0) is the coordinate of the generator, r is the current expansion step of a sector of the generator, w is the weight of a sector of the generator, α is the initial angle, k is the scanned kth pixel on the extended arc, θ is the angular increment. It requires 6 times of multiplication to determine the color of each pixel in discrete construction algorithm. In particular, it also requires a sin function and a cos function as well, so the efficiency is low.

$$(x0+w*r*\cos(\alpha+k*\theta),\ y0+w*r*\sin(\alpha+k*\theta)) \quad \textbf{(1)}$$

In the original discrete construction algorithm [8], the angular increment is fixed. In order to meet the accuracy requirements with large radius, the fixed angular increment must be small enough, these results in a very large repetitive workload to calculate the extended arc when the radius is small. In fact, the angular increment should be the corresponding angle of the adjacent two pixels on the extended arc. The minimum distance between two pixels on the panel is 1, and the corresponding minor arc will be slightly larger. According to the calculation relationship of radius, minor arc and angle, the angular increment should be calculated with Eq. 2 which can satisfy the correctness of the algorithm, and the efficiency of the algorithm is improved as well.

$$\Theta = 1/r \tag{2}$$

Correspondingly, according to the point by point scanning method, if there are n generators, to determine the color of any pixel on the space, it need to calculate the weighted distance between (x, y) and all the generator (xi, yi) in order to get the minimum weighted distance, as shown in Eq. 3. Where w_i (i=1, 2,···, k) is the weight of each generator (divisional weighted Voronoi diagram is similar to this). The point by point scanning method requires k times of 2 times multiplications, 1 times division and 1times square root to determine the color of each pixel.

$$\min \{ \sqrt{(x_i - x)*(x_i - x) + (y_i - y)*(y_i - y)} / w_i \mid i=1,2,\cdots,n\} \tag{3}$$

We estimate the calculation amount of Eq. 1 and Eq. 3. Eq. 4 and Eq. 5 are Taylor's expansion of sin and sqrt functions respectively.

$$\sin x = \sum_{i=0}^{n} \frac{(-1)^i}{(2i+1)!} x^{2i+1} + \sin^{(2n+3)}(\xi) \frac{x^{2n+3}}{(2n+3)!} \tag{4}$$

$$\sqrt{x} = 1 + \sum_{i=2}^{n} \frac{(-1)^{n-1}}{n!} \frac{(2n-3)!}{(n-2)!} (x-1)^n + \frac{(-1)^n}{(n+1)!} \frac{(2n-1)!}{(n-1)!} \xi^{(\frac{1}{2}-n)} (x-1)^n \tag{5}$$

If the accuracy is required as 10-9, Lagrange remainder of Eq. 4 is $\left| \sin^{(2n+3)}(\xi) \frac{x^{2n+3}}{(2n+3)!} \right| \le 10^{-9}$, Consider extreme conditions $\left| \frac{(\frac{\pi}{2})^{2n+3}}{(2n+3)!} \right| \le 10^{-9}$, we could get n=5. In other words, if Taylor expansion of sin function iterates 5 times, its accuracy can reach 10-9. At this point, the total calculation amount of multiplication and division in Eq. 4 is 1+4*n, which is 21. The calculation amount of cos function is the same as sin function, which is 21, too. Lagrange remainder of Eq. 5 is $\left| \frac{(-1)^n}{(n+1)!} \frac{(2n-1)!}{(n-1)!} \xi^{(\frac{1}{2}-n)} (x-1)^n \right| \le 10^{-9}$, consider extreme conditions $\left| \frac{1}{(n+1)!} \frac{(2n-1)!}{(n-1)!} 2^{(\frac{1}{2}-n)} \right| \le 10^{-9}$,we could get n=8. At this point, the total calculation amount of multiplication and division in Eq. 5 is 1+7n, which are 57.

Therefore, according to Eq. 1 based on the discrete construction algorithm, it needs 48 times of multiplication and division to determine the color of a pixel. According to Eq. 3 based on the point by point scanning method, it needs 60*k times of multiplication and division to determine the color of a pixel. So, on the whole, the efficiency of the discrete construction algorithm is better than the point by point scanning method.

3 Hybrid algorithm design

Based on the above analysis, it can be seen that the point by point scanning method is more accurate, and the time complexity of the algorithm is not related to the distribution of the generator. The boundary of the growth method is inherently imprecise, and the algorithm has high computational efficiency at early stage while it has low computational efficiency at later stage. In general, the efficiency of discrete construction algorithm is theoretically superior to point by point scanning method, but the discrete construction algorithm becomes slower, especially in the late stage, when the generator distribution is uneven or there is a super large weight generator.

Therefore, the idea of the hybrid algorithm we proposed is: firstly, according to the basic idea of discrete construction algorithm, all generators are preprocessed simultaneously to extend a large step (proportional to the weight of each generator) to the situation where most of the generators are in contact with each other, and the sector filling algorithm we proposed is used to fill the sectors of a generators efficiently, in which the overlapping pixel is set into black color. Secondly, turn all the black pixels in the first step into white color. Thirdly, the remaining white pixels are filling color by point by point scanning method. Finally, the boundary of the Voronoi diagram is extracted. The hybrid algorithm not only guarantees the efficiency, but also improves the accuracy of the Voronoi diagram.

3.1 The data structure design

The major data structure of the algorithm is the data structure of the generator. Each generator consists of two-dimensional coordinates, the weight, the angle, the color of each sector, and so on. Among them, the angular range is [0, 360], the weight range is [0,∞].

```
struct Generator
{
   public int x;             //x coordinate
   public int y;             //y coordinate
   public float w[];         //Sector weight array
   public int a[];           //Sector angle array
   public int RGB[][3];      //Sector color array
}AllGen[];
```

3.2 The algorithm design

```
Algorithm 1: hybrid grid algorithm of Voronoi diagram
   S1:                                  //Initialization stage
   All the pixels on the panel are set to white.
   S2:                                  // Preprocessing stage
   S2.1: set the value of k.  //reference Eq. 6
   S2.2: for(each sector j of each generator i){
   S2.2.1:  R=k*AllGen[i]->w[j];      //calculate radius
   S2.2.2:  algorithm2(AllGen[i]->x, AllGen[i] >y, AllGen[i]->a[j], AllGen[i]->a[j+1], R,
AllGen[i]. RGB);
            }
   S3:                                  //deal with overlap stage
   turn all blank pixels to white;
   S4:                              // Calculate residue pixels stage
   for (all pixel on the panel){
```

if (the pixel is white){
according to the point by point scanning method, calculate the color of pixel, and set the pixel with the color;
}
}
S5: //calculate the boundary stage
Scanning the panel, and extracting boundaries of the divisional weighted Voronoi diagram.
S6：end.

Algorithm 2 is used to color a sector of a generator. Since the initial coverage area of each generator may overlap, the algorithm will set the pixel to black if it is in the overlapped area during the progressive scanning and filling. Filling algorithm is relatively mature, such as the seed algorithm [10] and the progressive scan algorithm [11], and so on. A sector colored with filling algorithm is more special, we proposed a more efficient algorithm to do so.

Algorithm 2: (omitted).

4 Hybrid algorithm performance analysis and correctness proof

4.1 The performance analysis of the algorithm

The preprocessing stage of algorithm 1 calculates the color of each sector of each generator by a large step with weight r synchronously using algorithm 2 in which the main calculation is the boundary of a sector. Obviously, from the macroscopic point of view, this algorithm is faster than the discrete construction algorithm which calculates the extended arc pixel by pixel, and also faster than the point by point scanning method.

In addition, due to the use of the point by point scanning method in the later stage of hybrid grid algorithm, it solves the repetitive calculation problem in the later stage of growth method when the generator distribution is uneven or there is a super large weight generator, and the inherently imprecise of growth method (problem 1) are solved as well.

One of the key issues affecting the efficiency of this algorithm is the design of the initial step size. If the initial step is too large, the overlap area in preprocessing will be large, which means requiring more recalculation of the overlapping area color by the point by point scanning method; On the other hand, if the initial step is too small, there will be too many blank areas, the advantages of the preprocessing stage of this algorithm will be loosed. Ideally, the coverage area of all sector of each generator is just a balance between the blank area and the overlap area.

Without loss of the generality, we assume that the generators are equidistribution (Uneven distribution means that there are more generators in some space, and less generators in the other, which does not affect the correctness of the algorithm). Assuming that the total area is m, then the maximum value of k which meet Eq. 6 is basically the requirement for first step in algorithm 1.

错误!未找到引用源。 **(6)**

4.2 The correctness proof of the algorithm

In the preprocessing stage, firstly, each sector of generators extends in a large step, according to the principle of discrete construction algorithm, the area which is not overlapped has already determines the color, the area which is not yet processed will be colored according to point by point scanning method in late stage, in which the accuracy of the hybrid grid algorithm is the same as the point by point scanning method.

How about the correctness of the overlapped area? Because the algorithm 2 sets the overlapped area to black, and S3 in algorithm 1 replace all the black pixels to white. In S4 of the algorithm 1, the color of each pixel in the overlapped area is determined by the point by point scanning method. So, the accuracy of the overlapped area is the same as the point by point scanning method.

5 The experimental results and analysis

The experiment environment is the software of Visual Studio 2010 C#, the hardware of Intel ®Core (TM) i5 with CPU 2.4GHz and 2.0GB RAM. We reproduce the original discrete construction algorithm [6] (ODCA) and point by point scanning method [7] (PPSM) respectively, and implement the improved discrete construction algorithm (IDCA) and the proposed hybrid grid algorithm (HGA).

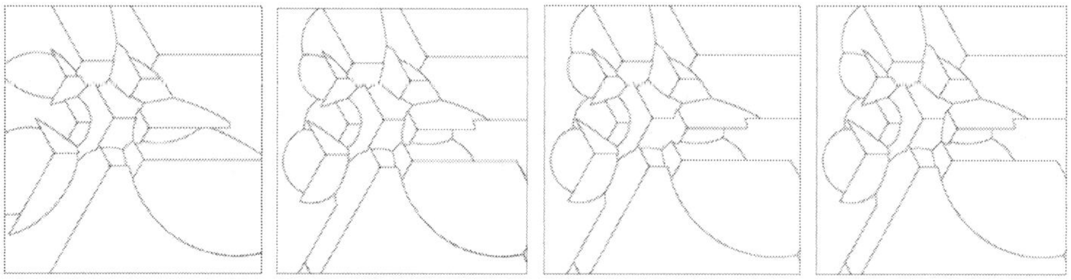

(a) ODCA (b) IDCA (c) PPSM (d) HGA

Figure 5. The result contrast of four algorithms

Fig.5 is the result of the ODCA, IDCA, PPSM and HGA with 800 * 800 grid size and 10 generators.

Table 1 the time efficiency of these methods with different panel size and number of generators.

panel size	number of generators	ODCA	IDCA	PPSM	HGA
300*300	10	0.9	2.4	1	1.2
	50	8.8	4.6	1.9	1.6
	100	11.9	4.6	3.4	2.1
	200	16.3	2.4	6.4	3.1
	500	26.8	2.5	8.5	7.3
500*500	10	9.8	4.1	2.8	3.2
	50	25.1	11.3	5.3	4.5
	100	32.5	6.6	7.2	5.8
	200	44.9	7.3	15.1	8.5
	500	71.2	11.4	24.9	17.2
800*800	10	27.3	9.8	7.6	8.2
	50	57.8	15.4	10.8	11.1
	100	88.6	23.3	16.5	15.5
	200	113.2	17.8	27.6	21.1
	500	178.9	20.6	58.9	42.7

It can be seen from the experimental results in Fig.5, Table 1 and Fig.5 that the original discrete construction algorithm is not correct and the efficiency is not high. The improved discrete construction algorithm is ideal implementation of the growth method, in which the result is correct and algorithm is more efficient, but the result of Voronoi diagram boundary is not accurate. The hybrid grid algorithm is faster than the point by point scanning method, and quite the same as the improved discrete construction algorithm. The trend is that the improved discrete construction algorithm is better.

When those algorithms are in application, if the accuracy requirement for Voronoi diagram boundary is not high, the improved discrete construction algorithm can be used, otherwise, the hybrid grid algorithm is a better choice.

6 Summary

In this paper, the properties and performance of growth method and point by point scanning method are analyzed from qualitative and quantitative aspects. A hybrid grid algorithm is proposed, which combines the advantages of growth method and point by point scanning method. At the same time, a special algorithm is proposed to improve the efficiency of filling the sector color of generators, which further improves the generation efficiency of the hybrid grid algorithm while processing divisional weighted Voronoi diagram.

The problems need further research is as follows: Firstly, the determination of the initial step k can be further refined. Secondly, the overlapped area determined color according to the point by point scanning method only related to the generators that overlaps each other. Thirdly, after a color of a pixel is defined by point by point scanning method, all pixels on the line between the pixel and a generator maybe can easily calculate. These studies can further improve the performance of the hybrid grid algorithm.

References

1. Voronoi G. Nouvelles applications des paramètres continus à la théorie des formes quadratiques. Premier mémoire. Sur quelques propriétés des formes quadratiques

positives parfaites[J]. Journal für die reine und angewandte Mathematik, 133, 97-178(1908).
2. B.N. Boots. Weighting thiessen polygons. Economic Geography, 56(3), 248-259(1980).
3. Ohya T. Improvements of the Incremental Method for the Voronoi Diagram with Computational Comparison of Various Algotithms [J]. Journal of the Operations Research Society of Japan, 27(4), 69-97(1984).
4. Shamos M I. and Hoey D. Closest-point Problems,In: Proceedings of the 16th Annual Symposium on the Foundations of Computer Science, 151-162(1975).
5. Fortune S. Voronoi diagrams and Delaunay triangulations [J]. Computing in Euclidean geometry, 1, 193-233(1992).
6. Youhui Zhang. A Study on the Weighted Voronoi Diagrams [D]. Beijing University of Aeronautics and Astronautics, 1998.
7. Watanabe T, Murashima S. A Method to Construct a Voronoi Diagram on 2-D Digitized Space in O (1)Computing Time[J]. Transactions of the Institute of Electronics Information & Communication Engineers, 79(1996).
8. iling Ma. The Construction of Divisional Weighted Voronoi Diagrams and Count of Area [D]. Hebei Normal University, 2004.
9. Jingying Li, Binjun Wang. A Study on the Correctness of Discrete Construction Method [J]. Journal of People's Public Security University of China (Science and Technology), 22(3), 94-97(2016)
10. Lieberman H. How to Color A Coloring Book. computer graphics. 12, 111-116(1978)
11. Theo Pavlidis. Filling Algorithms for Raser Graphics [J]. computer graphics and image processing, 10, 126-141(1979)

Impact of nitrate ammonium and calcium (CAN27%) on the environment.

Fares Redouane[1], *Bouadi* Abed[2], *Lounis* Mourad[1]

[1]LAAR, University of Science and Technology - Mohammed Boudiaf - BP 1505 - Oran – Algeria
[2]Centre universitaire Ahmed ZABANA RELIZANE, Algeria
E-mail: fares-redouane@hotmail.com

Abstract: In this research, a detailed study for energy consumption levels evaluation and environmental impacts assessment in the fertilizers production sector in Algeria was achieved. An analysis of the various inputs and outputs to the process to identify different sources of pollution throughout the life cycle of fertilizer was used. One product is making the subject in this study; CAN 27% N. The flows of material and energy for each phase of the life cycle were counted and the associated environmental problems were identified. The analysis was conducted according to the LCA standards ISO (International Standard Organization) 14040 series and the impacts categories studied are Global Warming Potential, Acidification Potential, Troposphere Ozone Precursor Potential, and Resources use. The results show that Cumulative Energies Requirement and GHG emission in Algerian fertilizers production process are significant. Ammonia plant use 82% of total natural gas that is consumed by fertilizer manufactory. Production of ammonia per year requires 4,506.107MJ of electricity and 2,059.108of natural gas and generates 1.82 T CO2 eq. (equivalent).

1. Introduction

The fertilizer industry is characterized by its high energy demand and the extensive greenhouse gas (GHG) emissions [1]. The European Commission estimates that fertilizer production consumes between 2% and 3% of global energy [2], and accounts for about 1.2% of global GHG emissions [3].

Such impacts can occur at the local, regional or global level inducing adverse or even dangerous effects on human health and its environment. Thus, an environmental assessment as well quantitative as qualitative is imperative and requires, an identification of the root causes of this degradation, a diagnosis establishment on the territory as vast and diversified as of Algeria. For this, a permanent follow-up is necessary to predict the trend of the receiving environment and recommend the appropriate remedies. These threats remain serious and generalize to deterioration of our living environment, Pollution of water, depletion of forest resources, extinction of plant and animal species, accumulation of chemicals that poison soils, desertification gaining more ground every day and fumes of toxic gases seriously altering the air we breathe.

The concentration of human activities in areas in close seas proximity, like the Mediterranean Sea, has always had a long-term, high environmental impact resulting in degradation of the marine environment [4].

Modern civilization and the human activities are undeniably the main causes of the contamination of the atmosphere, hence the pollution of the air generated mainly by the discharges of industrial installations. This constantly growing pollution contributes to an imbalance of the ecosystem to bring about profound changes in the global climate. It should be noted that a large part of the domestic and industrial energy responsible for this pollution is produced by fossil fuel combustion processes, the result of which is obviously highly polluting pollutant species, such as carbon oxides (COx), nitrogen oxides (NOx), sulfur oxides (SO_2) and aerosols. [5]

However, coastal areas are exposed to enormous risks of pollution, the demographic pressure where the majority of the world's population is located near the coast, the growth of urban areas, coupled with a rapid expansion of industry and tourism, and a flared exploitation of marine resources [6]. Humanity has become sensitive of the fragility of this environment, especially since biological resources are often threatened, from where a large part of the economic resources (tourism, fishing, port activities) come from coastal areas [4].

ALGERIA is a traditionally agricultural country, and is resolutely committed from its independence in a process of industrialization aimed at getting the country out of the underdeveloped world and into the ranks of the industrialized nations. Most of the factories produced were indeed poorly established [6] and the criteria established at the time were obedient, most often to political considerations which in any case did not take into account environmental concerns.

Many industrial units have been established on the most fertile land and on water bodies and are now seriously threatened by pollution.

Indeed, the Algerian coast is relatively polluted. This pollution is the combination of several factors, but discharges of untreated industrial wastewater are the most important factor. Several authors [7], [8] have shown increasing pollution throughout the Algerian coastline, especially in the coastal areas of major cities.

On a global scale, the problem of climate change is much more complex to analyze and understand, mainly because of feedbacks, sources and sinks of non-identifiable greenhouse gases. It must be possible to supply the quantity needed for domestic and industrial consumption, to recycle wastewater as much as possible and to limit polluting discharges into the natural environment.

Better production and less polluting are the challenges facing industry in all sectors by politicians in charge of the environment and public opinion.

The constraints in legislative and normative form are more and more drastic. Industries as diverse as chemistry, petrochemicals, agribusiness, tanneries, metal waste industries or paper mills produce a wide variety of effluents that require new investigations and process development.

The fertilizer production sector has been the subject of several studies around the world aimed at assessing environmental impacts [9], and energy performance in their production processes [10], [11]. Fertilization has a significant impact on soil than on groundwater [12]. Soil salinity [13], heavy metal accumulation [14], water eutrophication [15], nitrate accumulation, and GHG emissions [16] are impacts caused by the excessive and uncontrolled use of fertilizers [17].

Nowadays, ammonia contributes significantly to the nutritional needs of terrestrial organisms by acting as a precursor to fertilizers, which is very accommodating to increase crop yields [19]. Ammonia is also a building block for the synthesis of many chemicals (nitric acid, ammonium chloride ...) and is used in many commercial cleaning products (in the form of salts, solutions or anhydrous) . There are several manufacturers in the world producing 157 million tonnes of ammonia per year [20], of which Algeria provides 0.4% [4].

Worldwide, ammonia production is mainly synthesized by the Haber-Bosch process [9]. Natural gas is the main raw material for ammonia production, accounting for nearly 80% of global ammonia production [10]. However, it is a process of energy discharge and mainly causes the production of greenhouse gases (GHG). In fact, ammonia production is responsible for about 0.93% of global GHG emissions [19]. About 1.5 tonnes of CO_2 are emitted into the atmosphere during the production of 1 tonne of ammonia [21]. Greenhouse gas emissions from fertilizer production are expected to increase before stabilizing due to growing demand for sustainable food supplies for a growing world population [21]. The increase in greenhouse gases (GHG) in the atmosphere is one of the major environmental problems affecting the world's population during this century [22].

Recently, the fertilizer production (ammonia production) sector has been addressed by several authors ([23], [3], [24]). Based on the results of these studies, [1] concluded that the production of one ton of ammonia requires an average energy consumption of $25x10^3$ to 35.10^3 MJ. In 2007, [25] exploited an average global energy consumption of $36,9x10^3$ MJ/T. [26] estimated average energy consumption for ammonia production in Europe of around 34.7 GJ/T. These studies have focused on GHG emissions assessment and primary resource needs. In addition, inventories of inputs used in these studies are based on bibliographic data or simple estimates [1].

Life cycle assessment assesses the environmental impacts generated by a production process or service. The primary benefit of LCA is its ability to account for all product-related inputs and emissions in a particular function throughout its "cradle to grave" lifecycle. It is commonly used to perform a complete emission assessment (standardized method for the ISO series international standards system).

2. Methodology

This investigation presents a LCA of liquid ammonia produced in Algeria (Arzew fertilizer production complex). It is based on an inventory with primary data and aims to assess the environmental impacts associated with the product life cycle compared to previous studies. Several impact categories that have been studied in this study are: resource use, global warming potential, acidification potential, and the precursor potential of troposphere ozone. As noted above, all studies have been devoted to GHG emissions assessment and, due to the lack of results of the impact of the troposphere ozone impact in the bibliography; the results comparison will be summarized in the comparison of GHG emissions and energy needs. This will enable us to assess the extent of the environmental impact of the Algerian ammonia production process and determine its environmental position relative to other plants around the world.

An LCA has been developed and implemented from the ISO 14040 standard. ISO 14040: 2006 specifies the principles and framework for performing the life cycle assessment. ISO 14044: 2006 establishes the requirements and provides guidelines for performing an LCA. The latter consists of four phases: the definition of the objectives and scope of the study, the life cycle inventory, the life cycle impact assessment and the life cycle interpretation [27], (ISO, 2006a, 2006b).

3. Selection and description of study area

The complex Fertial (Arzew) specialized in the production of ammonia, nitric acid, ammonium nitrate, and urea, is located on the Arzew industrial platform 40 km west of

Oran, 3 km east of Arzew, and 4 km west of Bethioua and is close to the sea. This region is one of the most polluted areas of the Algerian coast. [4]

The region of Arzew is characterized by a moderate climate. Generally, the minimum air temperature does not fall below 0 °C and the maximum does not exceed 40°C The average annual temperature is 18.5°C, with average monthly extremes of 28.8 °C in August [28]. The winds on Arzew blow from West to Southwest. In December southwest winds from 7h to 18h: west and south winds at 13h. The same remarks can be noted for the months of January, November, March, April and May. Nevertheless, for the last three months, Northeast winds have been recorded [28]. According to the months of drought are the predominantly north-easterly months. There are, moreover, warm winds from the South and Southwest. These are hot and dry winds from 09 to 16 days a year.

In addition, wind is one of the forces governing currents and swells. The latter constitute a very important ecological factor along the Algerian coastline in the absence of permanent currents and tides since they are the only active ones in the bays and gulfs of the offshore coast.

4. Results and Interpretation

4.1. Resources use

4.1.1 Ammonia

The production of one ton of ammonia requires cumulative material demand and cumulative energy demand which are shown in both tables below:

Cumulative Material Request

Table 1. Cumulative material Requirement (CMR) for one tone of ammonia

	resources	*Qnt*	*Unit*	*%*
primary resources	natural gas	0,518	T	27,34%
	water	1,06	T	49,30%
	N2	0,5	T	23,25%
	Total	2,07	T	

Cumulative Energy Request

Table 2. Cumulative Energy Requirement (CER) for one tone of ammonia

resources	*Qnt*	*Unit*	*%*
natural gas	26,349	GJ	50,72%
combustible gas	25,596	GJ	49,27%
process fuel	20,608	GJ	39,67%
HP (High Pressure)	0,167	GJ	0,32%
electricity generation	4,82	GJ	9,27%

https://doi.org/10.1051/itmconf/20181703006

4.1.2 Nitric acid

The production of one tone of nitric acid requires 7.47 t of primary natural resources.

Table 3: Cumulative material Requirement (CMR) for one ton of nitric acid

	resources	Unité	Qnt	%
primary resources	natural gas	T	0,166	2,22%
	HP	T	2,1	28,11%
	air (O2)	T	5,2	69,61%
	Total	T	7.47	

The energy requirement in the nitric acid production process is of the order of 20.42 GJ/T of acid nitric acid, 36.43% of which is 7.44 GJ is used as raw material; the rest is consumed as fuel in production processes. Gas is the main source of energy used by 20.41 GJ or 99.95%.

4.1.3 Calcium ammonium nitrate CAN (27% N)

Production of one tone of CAN 27% requires 6.07 t of primary natural resources

Table4. Cumulative Demand for Materials (CCD) for one tone of CAN 27%

resources	*renewable*	*water*	*1,86*	*T*
		air(O2)	3,77	T
	Non-renewable	natural gas	0,01	T
		calcium carbonate	0,21	T
		$CaCo_3$	0,22	T

The cumulative energy Requirement (DER) is 23.12 GJ/T of CAN 27%, this quantity is mainly used to supply energy to the system (electricity generation, steam production), energy non-renewable (natural gas) have 99.99% of DER, the consumed amount of natural gas is 23.09 GJ or 99.87% of total DER.

The quantities of the main pollutants and their percentages emitted during the production of each unit are illustrated in the following table

Table 5. Quantities and percentages of major pollutants emitted from each unit

Units		Ammonia (t/t)		Acid nitric (t/t)		CAN (t/t)	
pollutants		Qnt	%	Qnt	%	Qnt	%
Greenhouse gases	CO_2eq	1,89		2,78		2,22	
	CO_2	1,75	92,85%	0.71	25,21%	0,839	37,80%
	CH_4	0,11	5,80%	2,00	72,08%	1,31	59,11%
	N_2O	0,02	1,30%	7,26 10^{-2}	2,61%	6,68 10^{-2}	3,01%
Acidification	SO_2eq	3,40 10^{-4}		4,929 10^{-3}		5,64 10^{-3}	
	NOx	3,34 10^{-4}	98,10%	4,551 10^{-3}	92,33%	5,23 10^{-3}	92,70%
	SO_2	6,392 10^{-6}	1,88%	2,61 10^{-4}	5,29%	7,33 10^{-5}	1,30%
	NH_3	1,22 10^{-13}	0,00%	1,13 10^{-4}	2,30%	3,33 10^{-4}	5,90%
Tropospherezoneprecursor	TOPP eq	5,75 10^{-3}		5,53 10^{-3}		5,24 10^{-3}	
	CH_4	7,06 10^{-4}	12,27%	1,09 10^{-4}	1,97%	5,14 10^{-5}	0,98%
	NOx	4,68$10^{-3}$	81,34%	5,28 10^{-3}	95,40%	5,00 10^{-3}	95,50%
	CO	2,27 10^{-4}	3,95%	8,02 10^{-5}	1,45%	1,21 10^{-4}	2,30%
	NMVOC	1,35$10^{-4}$	2,35%	6,36 10^{-5}	1,15%	6,29 10^{-5}	1,20%

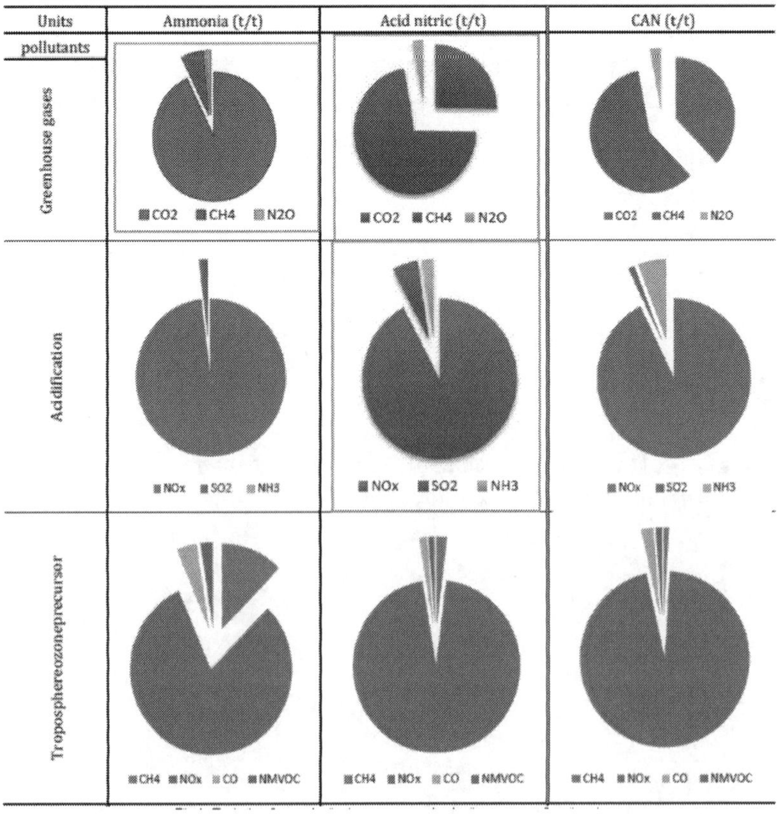

Figure.1. Emission factors in the impact categories in the process of each unit

Table 6 below shows the CO2eq emission rate for the production of one ton of ammonia in some previous studies, and compared it with the result obtained by our investigation.

Table 6. Comparison of CO_2eq emissions with previous studies

Region	Value	Unit	Reference
World average	2,07	T CO_2eq/T of ammoniac	[25]
Europe	1,95		[26]
USA	1,26		[29]
Canada	1,6		[30]
Australia	1,8		[11]
Netherlands	2,16		[32]
Fertial-Arzew	1,89		

Table 7 illustrate the rate of N_2O emission for production the production of one ton of nitric acid for different previous study and compare it with our investigation. We find that the emission of 72.6 Kg of N_2O on the production of 1 ton of nitric acid and significantly higher than the global standard which appears in the following table.

Table 7. Comparison of N_2Oéq emission with previous studies

Region	Value	Unit	Reference
World	9	kg N_2O/T HNO_3	[30]
Europe	21.6		[26]
USA	9		[10]
Fertial-Arzew	72.6		

In present study, we determined an emission average of 2.22 tones of CO_2eq for one tone of CAN, and refer to a study by [9] where they calculated the carbon dioxide footprint for several places; most of the results are shown in Table 8 below

Table 8. Eq CO2 emission for the production of one tone of CAN [9]

Region	Value	Unit
World average	2,567	CO_2eq/T CAN 27%
Europe	2,208	
Russia	2,565	
North America	2,285	
China	3,261	
Rest of the world	2,249	
Fertial-Arzew	2.22	

5. Conclusion

The objective of this study is to evaluate the degree of pollution in the gaseous effluents of the FERTIAL-ARZEW complex known by its diversity in mineral fertilizer manufacturing processes.

The fertilizer industry occupies an important place in the development of local economies through its essential role as a producer of the basic elements for the development of the agricultural sector. This work provides an overview of the environmental issue in the fertilizer production sector. It has been realized to enrich the theoretical and practical knowledge on the evaluation of environmental problems of sector. Knowledge of the nature and quantities of raw materials used and substances emitted into the environment by the fertilizer industry in Algeria.

The space-temporal monitoring of several physicochemical factors has given us the image of a relatively intense pollution which results in a significant organic and mineral load. The results of the various analyzes carried out revealed the presence of a large high concentration of N_2O in the exhaust gas was noted at the level of the evacuated gases.

The need to use a credible environmental assessment tool and especially to take into account all the production processes used by the sector seems essential. The use of Life Cycle Analysis is the most appropriate method of the moment for such an objective. Its global vision enables it to analyze the inputs and outputs of a production process, to take into account input data from upstream processes and to add the impact related to its processes during the evaluation.

The application of LCA on the production of fertilizers and chemicals "Fertial-Arzew" attests to the use of conventional production processes, with a high consumption of raw materials. This results in overconsumption of non-renewable energy (natural gas) main fuel for the production of HP (High Pressure) steam and ammonia.

In order to address these industrial pollution problems, the development of sound remediation processes downstream of the fertilizer manufacturing process should be a priority for this industry. In addition, an information and warning system on pollution peaks must be set up in the FERTIAL complex's environmental management program. As a result of this study, it appears that the production of fertilizers consumes large amounts of fossil energy and therefore generates GHGs.

The ammonia unit accounts for 75% of Fertial-Arzew's total production, and consumes 78% of the company's natural gas. Ammonia is therefore the main product of the company. The production of one tonne of ammonia contributes mainly to global warming by the emission of about 1.89 t CO2 eq of GHGs, and to the depletion of resources by the consumption of 51.94 GJ of natural gas. The latter is 25.16% higher than the world average of 41.5 GJ/T of ammonia. In light of these results, it can be considered that the ammonia unit is the main source of environmental impact in terms of GHG emissions and natural resource use.

The reasons for this overconsumption of energy lie in two factors; the first is related to the dilapidated facilities since 1982, which forces the unit has restarted following frequent breakdowns. A second factor relates to gas reforming operations, operations that contribute mainly to the depletion of natural resources on one side and GHG emissions on the other side. This may be due to the low efficiency of the catalytic reaction, in which the catalysts are used for more than 10 years.

In the light of the results we have obtained and studies previously carried out, certain aspects should be developed and deepened:

The upgrading of industrial equipment and its regular maintenance and the replacement of catalysts in the production units (particularly in the ammonia and nitric acid unit) are two links in the chain of the cycle which will ensure a better performance of production units and contribute to the reduction of natural gas consumption and consequently the reduction of GHG emissions.

6. References

1. Wood S, Cowie .A., A review of greenhouse gas emission factors for fertilizer production. Cooperative Research Centre for Greenhouse Accounting, for IEA

Bioenergy Task 38,2004. On line at: http://www.ieabioenergy task38.org/publications/GHG_Emission_Fertil-izer%20Production_July2004.pdf,
2. IPPC, Intergovernmental Panel on Climate Change (IPCC). Reference Document on Best Available Techniques for the Manufacture of Large Volume Inorganic Chemicals – Ammonia, Acids and Fertilizers. BREF 08.07. Integrated Pollution Prevention and Control, under the European Commission. 2007.
3. Kongshaug G., Energy consumption and greenhouse gas emissions in fertilizer production.Proceedings on IFA Technical Conference, Marrakech, Morocco. 28-09 to 01-10, 1998.
4. FARES R., LOUNS M., Pollution characterization of liquid wastes of the factory complex fertial (Arzew, Algeria): J Air Wast Manage Assoc,2016, 66: 260-266
5. FARES R., Aissa A., Characterization of Gaseous Pollutants from the Fertilizer Complex Fertial (Arzew-Algeria) Environ SciInd J. 2017; 13(5):151.
6. FARES R., LOUNS M., Determination of the Sea Waters Quality of Arzew-Algeria Gulf. J Pollut Eff Cont 5: 188. 2017, doi: 10.4176/2375-4397.1000188
7. BAKALEM A., GRIMES S., La pollution en milieu portuaire : les peuplements macrobenthiques du port de Skikda (Algérie). Workshop « Circulation des eaux et pollution des côtes méditerranéennes des pays du Maghreb ». Rabat 9-11 Nov. 1992, Eds INOC Izmir (Turquie), 1993,195- 202.
8. GRIMES S., Peuplements benthiques des substrats meubles de la côte algérienne : taxonomie, structure et statut écologique. Thèse Doctorat, Univ. Oran ; Département de Biologie. 2010, 360p.
9. Kool A, Marinussen M, Blonk H., LCI data for the calculation tool Feed print for greenhousegas emissions of feed production and utilization. GHG Emissions of N, P and K fertilizer production. GravinBeatrixstraat 34, 2805 PJ Gouda, Netherlands: Blonk Consul-tants; 2012.
10. IEA (International Energy Agency), Tracking industrial energy efficiency and CO2 emissions. 2007,p. 324.
11. EFMA, (European Fertilizer Manufacturers' Association), Production of Ammonia. Booklet No. 1 of 8: Best Available Techniques for Pollution Control in the European FertilizerIndustry. B-1160 Brussels, Belgium: Ave. E van Nieuwenhuyse. 2000.
12. Barros R, Isidoro D, Aragüés R.,. Irrigation management, nitrogen fertilization and nitrogen losses in the return flows of La Violada irrigation district (Spain). Agriculture, Ecosystems &Environment: 2012, 155(15): 161-171
13. Ammari T.G, Tahhan R, Abubaker S, Al-zubi Y, Tahboub A, Taany R, Abu-Romman S, Al-Manaseer N, Stieiya M.H., Soil Salinity Changes in the Jordan Valley Potentially Threaten Sustainable Irrigated Agriculture. Pedosphere. 2013: 23(3): 376-384.
14. Gupsa D.K, Chatterjee S, Datta V, Walther C., Role of phosphate fertilizers in heavy metal uptake and detoxification of toxic metals. Chemosphere: 2014, 108: 134-144.
15. Smith V.H., Reference Module in Earth Systems and Environmental Sciences. Eutrophication: 2009, 61-73.
16. Kahrl F, Yunju L, Yufang S, Tennigkeit T, Wilkes A, Jianchu X., Greenhouse gas emissions from nitrogen fertilizer use in China. Environmental science & policy: 2010, 13: 688-694.
17. Savci S., Investigation of Effect of Chemical Fertilizers on Environment. Procedia APCBEE: 2012, 1: 287-292.
18. Gilbert P, Thornley P., Energy and carbon balance of ammonia production from biomass gasification, Bio-ten., Holiday Inn, Birmingham, 2010. On line at: https://www.escholar.manchester.ac.uk/api/datastream?publicationPid=uk-ac-man-scw:91274&datastreamId=FULL-TEXT.PDF.

19. IFA, International Fertilizer Industry Association (IFA)., Production and international trade committee. world pa statistics by country in '000 tones product. Potash public. 2014c. On line at: http://www.fertilizer.org/en/doc_library/Statistics/PIT/Potash_public.xlsx
20. Anderson K, Bows A, Mander S., From long-term targets to cumulative emission pathways: reframing UK climate policy. Energy Polic, 2008, 36(10): 3714-3722.
21. Gilbert P, Alexander S, Thornley P, Brammer J. Assessing economically viable carbon re-ductions for the production of ammonia from biomass gasification. J Clean Prod 2014;64 :581–9.
22. De Morais RF, Boddey RM, Urquiaga S, Jantalia CP, Alves BJR., Ammonia volatilization and nitrous oxide emissions during soil preparation and N fertilization of elephant grass (PennisetumpurpureumSchum.). Soil BiolBiochem, 2013, 64: 80–8.
23. Davis J, Haglund C., Life Cycle Inventory (LCI) of Fertiliser Production. Fertiliser Products Used in Sweden and Western Europe.. Master's Thesis, Chalmers University of Technology. SIK-Report No. 654. 1999.
24. Patyk A., Balance of Energy Consumption and Emissions of Fertilizer Production and Supply. Reprints from the International Conference of life cycle assessment in agriculture, food and non-food agro-industry and forestry: achievements and prospects, Brussels, Belgium. 1996.
25. Williams G, Al-Ansari F., IFA Benchmarking of Global Energy Efficiency in Ammonia Production. Workshop on Energy Efficiency and CO2 Reduction Prospects in Ammonia Production, In. Ho Chi Minh City, Vietnam: IFA Technical Committee Meeting, 2007.
26. Haas MJGde, van Dijk TA., Inventarisatieklimaatvriendelijkekunstmest. Wageningen: Nutriënten Management Instituut NMI, 2010.
27. FinnvedenG,Michael Z, HauschildM, Ekvall T, Guinée J, Heijungs R., Recent developments in life cycle assessment. J Environ Manag, 2009, 91(1):01–21.
28. TAGHEZOUT Fatima, Impact Environnemental Des Rejets D'eau Le Long Du Littoral Occidental Algérien, mémoire de magister, Université d'Oran. Faculté des Sciences de la Nature et de la Vie Département de Biologie. 2015,170p
29. EPA (US Environmental Protection Agency). Synthetic Ammonia, AP-42. 5th ed. vol. 1. Chapter 8: Inorganic chemical industry; 1993.
30. IPPC, Intergovernmental Panel on Climate Change (IPCC). Reference Document on Best Available Techniques for the Manufacture of Large Volume Inorganic Chemicals – Ammonia, Acids and Fertilizers. BREF 08.07. Integrated Pollution Prevention and Control, under the European Commission. 2007.
31. Kramer KJ, Moll HC, Nonhebel S., Total Greenhouse Gas Emissions Related to the Dutch Crop Production System. AgricEcosyst Environ, 1999.

Analysis on stress state of box-girder web under prestressing effect

Haijun Yin [1,2], *Ziqing* Li[1], *Xianwu* Hao [1], *Baojun* Zhao [3]

[1]School of highway Engineering, Chang'an University, Xi'an 710064, China;
[2] Xi'an Architecture & Technology University, Xi'an 710055,China;
[3] Shaanxi Provincial Communication Construction Group, Xi'an 710075,China

Abstract: In order to study the effect of prestressed box girder webs stresss state, determining the stress distribution within a web, research and analysis of vertical prestressed box girder, curved beam prestressed sensitivity under the web. Establishing the finite element model of the box girder web vertical prestressing effect is analyzed, results show that the principal tensile stress of the web is sensitive to the vertical prestress, applying the vertical prestress can effectively reduce the principal tensile stress of the web; with the decrease of the effective vertical prestress, the neutral axis above the principal compressive stress decreases rapidly, while below the neutral axis decreases relatively slow; Under the same vertical preloading stress level, the roots of cross section of the compressive stress of web reserves than L / 4 section of the web. Calculation and analysis of curved beam under bending point, different bending angles and bending radius of principal stress effect on the web, Results show that the set of curved beam web when the curved beam bending stress concentration easily, appear the main tensile stress; Increase the bending radius can effectively reduce beam cross-section of web principal tensile stress, along with the rising of the next corner, principal tensile stress peak value increases gradually, thus setting bending beam, should try to reduce the bending angle.

1 Analysis of the vertical prestress influence

Vertical prestress can effectively resist the main tensile stress and shear stress of the box girder. But some of the bridge cracks are still common even though the web has vertical prestress. One of the main causes of this problem is the loss of vertical prestress. The vertical prestress of some bridges may even lose more than half [6], which is very detrimental to the force of the box. In order to explore the impact of vertical prestress on the fracture of the peritoneal plate of the box girder, ANSYS, a finite element software, was used to analyze the sensitivity of the vertical prestress effect of the girder. Due to the structure and load symmetry, take a quarter of the real bridge modeling, SOLID45 unit are adopted to simulate the concrete and LINK8 element to simulate prestressed reinforcement, the prestress effect is included in the equivalent load, and the calculation model is shown in figure 1.There are four kinds of calculation conditions:

Working condition 1: the effective vertical prestress is accounted for 100% of tension control;

Working condition 2: the effective vertical prestress is accounted for 60% of tension control;

Working condition 3: effective vertical prestress is accounted for 30% of tension control;
Working condition 4: excluding vertical prestress.

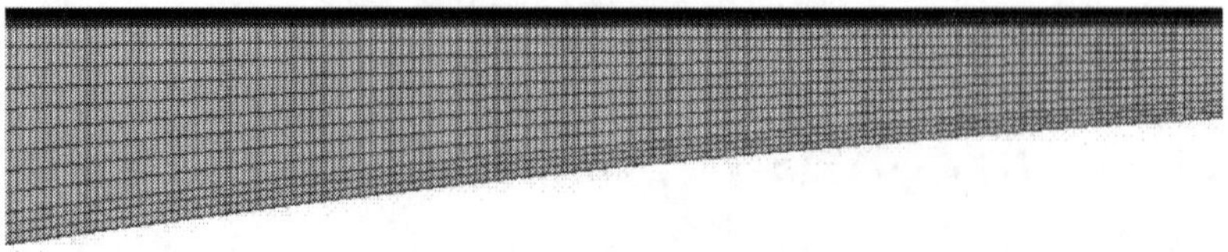

Figure .1 Local Calculation Model

The main stress of the two sections of the box girder section 2 of the root and the 1/4 sections are drawn in figure 2.Figure 3 shows the main stress vector diagram of the box girder in the area near the L/4 cross section of the bridge under different working conditions.

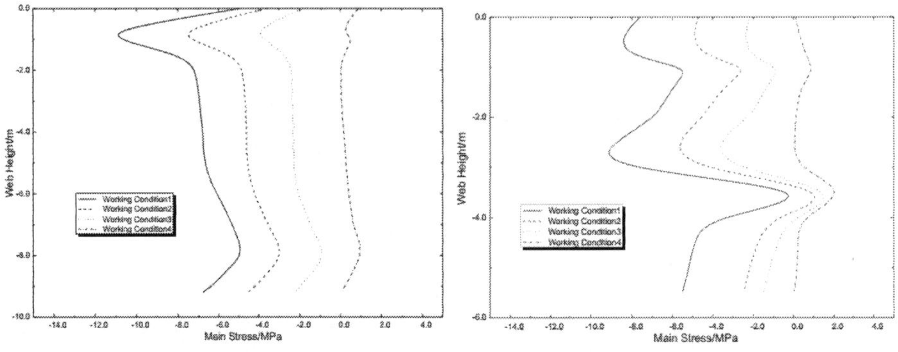

(a) Section 2 of the Root **(b)** 1/4 Cross Section

Figure .2 Comparison of Principal Stress in Each Working Condition

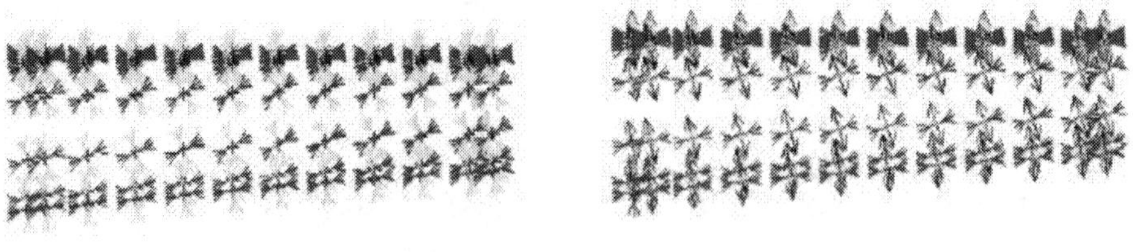

(a) Working Condition 1-3 **(b)** Working Condition 4

Figure .3 Main Stress Vector Diagram of Vertical Web under Different Working conditions

The calculation results show that: (1) The main tensile stress of the web is more sensitive to the vertical prestress, and the vertical stress can be applied to reduce the tensile stress. (2) When the effective vertical prestress is kept at more than 60%, the minimum principal stress is basically above 2.0 Mpa, so the calculation formula of vertical prestress in the specification is reasonable by multiplying the reduction factor of 0.6. (3) With the decrease of the effective vertical prestress, the main compressive stress above the neutral axis of the abdominal plate decreases faster, while the lower part of the neutral axis decreases slower. (4) In the condition of excluding vertical prestress, The main tensile stress is generated along the entire cross-section of the abdominal plate, If the stress loss of prestressed tendon and the shrinkage creep effect of concrete are considered, the main tensile stress may exceed the limit, which will cause the web to crack. Therefore, the vertical prestress setting is necessary.(5) In contrast, under the same vertical preloading stress level, the root section of the web compressive stress reserves bigger than L/4 section of the web. In other words, L/4 section web easier to crack, the box girder web plate cracking phenomenon is consistent with engineering practice [7] [8].

2 Analysis of the influence of downward bending beams of the web

2.1 The stress of web sensitivity analysis of the downward bending beams

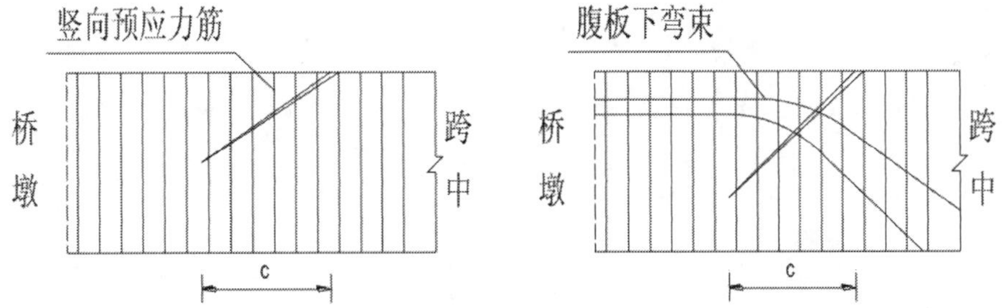

(a) Without Downward Hending Beam **(b)** Set Downward Bending Beam

Figure 4 A Diagram of the Layout of Prestressed Tendons in Continuous Rigid Frame Bridges

In the way of prestressed reinforcement arrangement in the large span PC box girder bridge, there are two kinds of fabric reinforcement (see Figure 4) under which the bending beam is set and the bending beam is not set. It is easy to construct the rigid frame bridge with the longitudinal prestressing and vertical prestressing to overcome the main tensile stress. The box girder with bending beam can effectively improve the stress state of the web and overcome the fracture of the abdominal plate caused by the main tensile stress[9].

Taking the background bridge as an example, two kinds of bridge models are established, which are to cancel the downward bending beams and to set the downward bending beams. In order to analyze the influence degree of the downward bending beam to the web stress, we choose the A section of control section 141 main pier to calculate (see Figure 5), and analyze the stress change of two schemes along the box girder in the finished state.

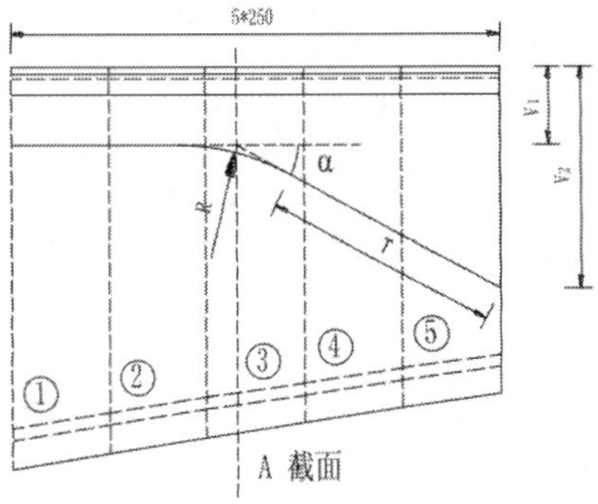

Figure 5 The Calculated Section

Figure 6 is the contrast diagram of the height stress variation along the box girder at the A section of the 141 main pier with two kinds of reinforcement. The longitudinal coordinates in the diagram represent a change along the height of the web, the unit is m; the negative value of the abscissa represents the compressive stress, and the positive value represents the tensile stress, and the unit is MPa.

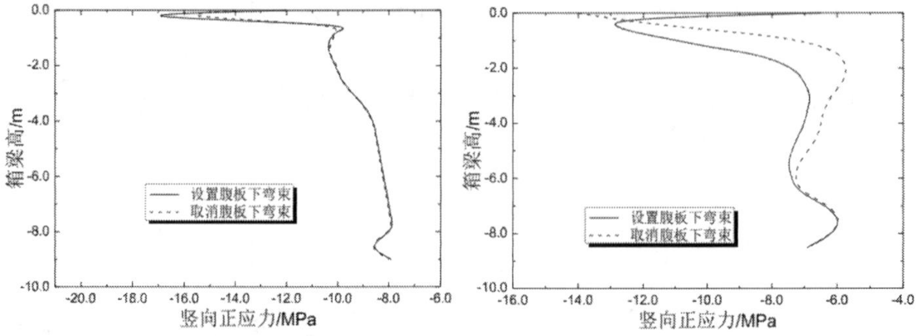

(a) Longitudinal positive stress (b) Vertical positive stress

The results show that: (1) Bending beam has less influence on longitudinal normal stress of box girder, but the peak of stress changes sharply in the roof straight-beam anchorage. The reason is that the horizontal component of bending beam strengthens the longitudinal stress of box beam; (2) The influence of the bending beam on the vertical normal stress of the box girder decreases from the upper part to the lower part of the box girder; (3) The adown bending beam can effectively reduce the main tensile stress of the web, The main tensile stress is greatly reduced, less impact on the part below the centroid of the web.

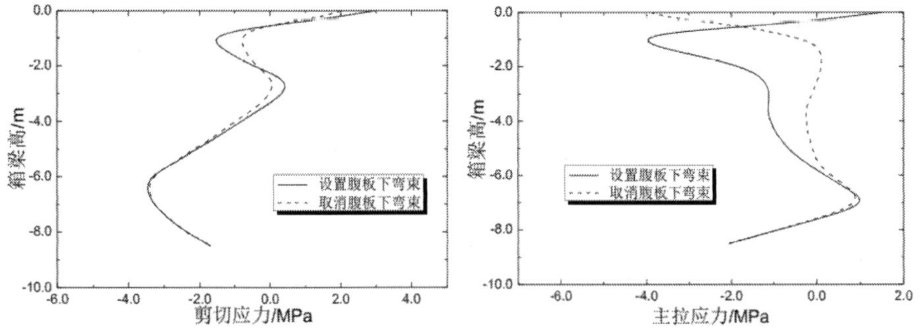

(c) Shear Stress (d) Principal Stress

Figure. 6 Comparison of the stress of A cross section of the Box Girder in Two kinds of Reinforcement

Therefore,compared with the set of Web bending beam with beam scheme, cancellation of web bending beam, in the A section near the root of the box girder, box girder along the height direction of the principal compressive stress decreases, and in the area above the center of the web, the principal tensile stress increases obviously and easily overrun, cause cracking in webs[11].

2.2 Analysis of the influence of downward bending beam on the slanting cracks of box girder web

In the cantilever construction of PC box girder webs, oblique cracks parallelled to the bending beam are usually appeared. The laws of fracture crack mechanism, location, direction and distribution reflect that the cracks are generated during the bending of the lower bending beam Caused by the radial force [6] (Figure 7)

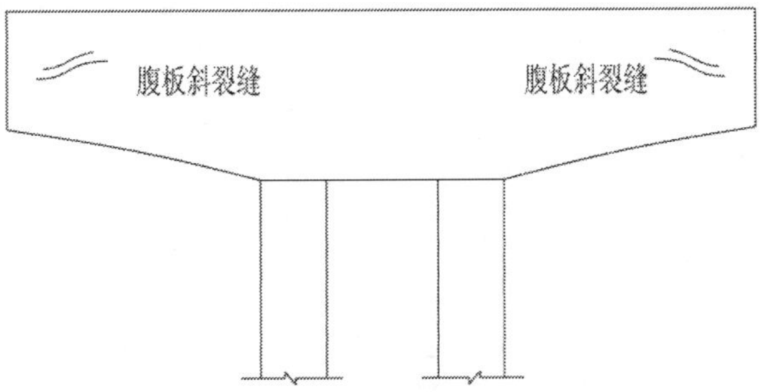

Figure. 7 The Slanting Cracks of Box Girder Web

(1) Analytic solution

The radial distribution force of the radial core to the concrete is generated within the curve range after the adown bending beams of the web are stretched. (Fig. 8),q=P/R,the effective preload is P , the radius of the web beams is R [12].

Set,

$$\begin{cases} X = \cos\alpha \\ Y = \sin\alpha \end{cases} \tag{1}$$

According to the balance of vertical force on the curve $\sum Y = 0$,it is obtained,

$$\int_S q\cos\alpha ds = \Delta F_y \tag{2}$$

That is,

$$\int_{\theta_1}^{\theta_2} qR\cos\alpha d\alpha = P_2\sin\theta_2 - P_1\sin\theta_1 \tag{3}$$

$$q = \frac{P_2\sin\theta_2 - P_1\sin\theta_1}{R(\sin\theta_2 - \sin\theta_1)} \tag{4}$$

Where, P is radial force; T is tension of prestressed tendons; θ is bending angle of prestressed tendons;R is radius of curvature.

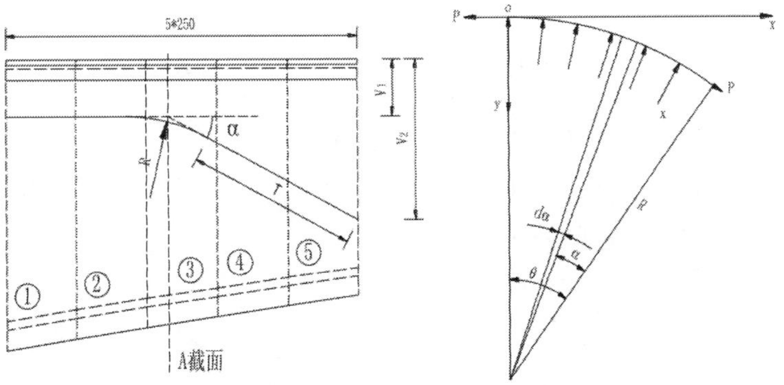

Figure 8 The Radial Force Caused by Downward Bending Beam

(2) Numerical solution

In this paper, ANSYS finite element software is used to calculate the influence of different downward bending beams on the main stress of the web. In the calculation analysis, the influence of bending point, bending angle and bending radius of the downward bending beam in the web is considered, and a total of 6 calculation models are given, and the calculation parameters are shown in Table 1.

Table 1 The Calculation Parameters

Model	$R(m)$	α°	$T(m)$	$V_1(m)$	$V_2(m)$
1	6.0	27.98°	6.113	4.73	1.37
2	8.0	27.98°	5.615	4.73	1.37
3	10.0	27.98°	5.117	4.73	1.37
4	12.0	27.98°	4.618	4.73	1.37
5	10.0	17.43°	5.509	4.06	1.37
6	10.0	36.81°	5.064	6.978	1.37

The concrete of the web is simulated by SOLID45 element, in which elastic modulus is $E=3.35\times10^4 MPa$, the downward bending beam in the web is chosen to simulate with LINK8 element, the Poisson's ratio is 0.3, the bending curve of the lower beam is simulated according to the actual line shape, without considering the role of transverse prestress and the vertical prestress. The finite element model and the calculation results are shown in Figure 10 to 12.

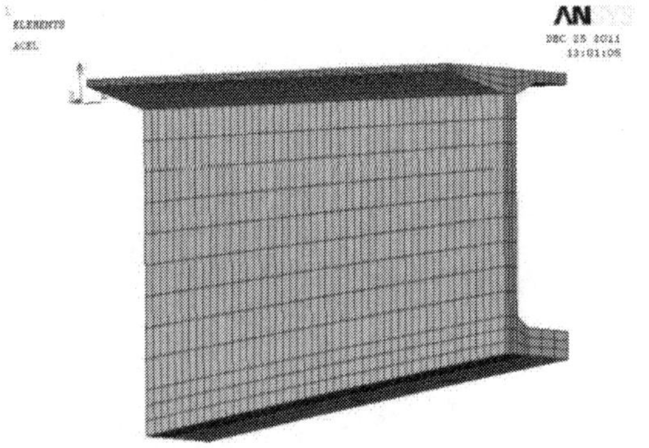

Figure10 Finite element Model

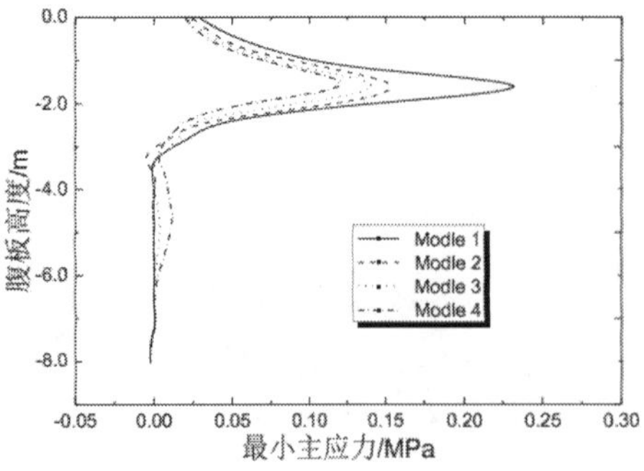

(a) Different bending radius

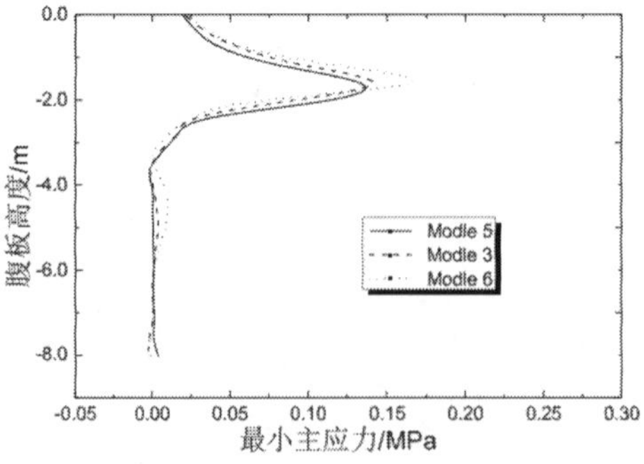

(b) Different bending angle

Figure 11 Comparison of minimum principal stress (principal tensile stress) of section A of web under different conditions

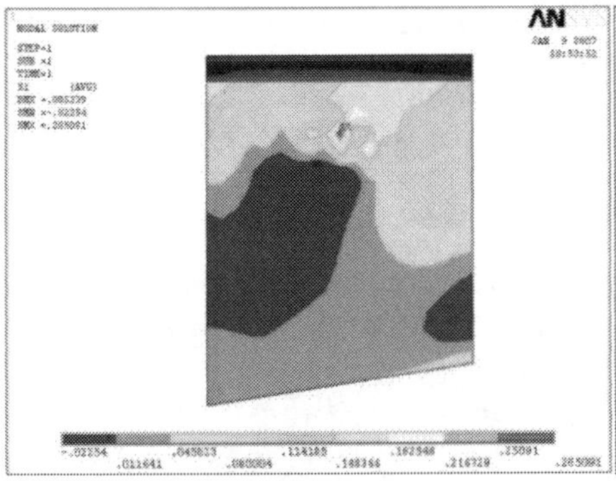

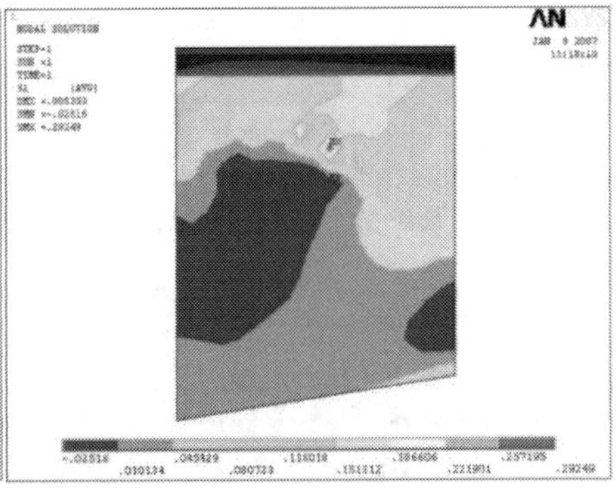

(a) Principal stress cloud diagram of Model 1 (b) Principal stress cloud diagram of Model 2

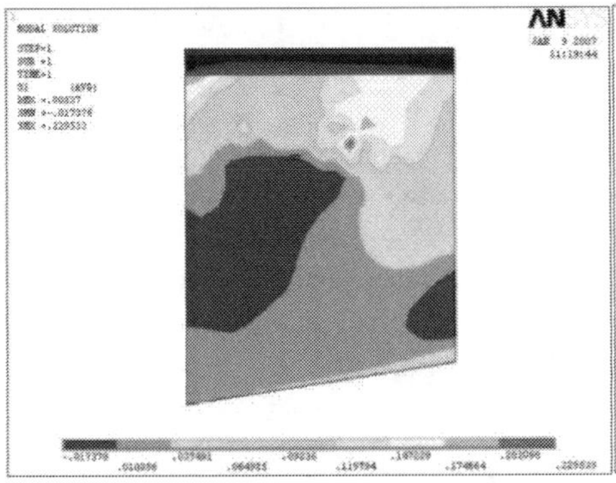

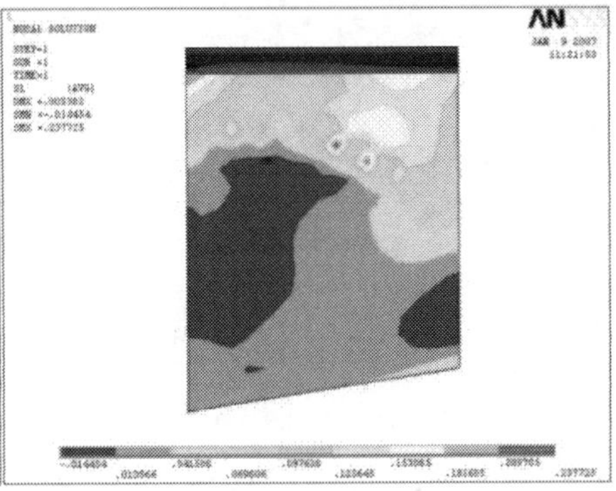

(a) Principal stress cloud diagram of Model 3 (b) **Principal** stress cloud diagram of Model 4

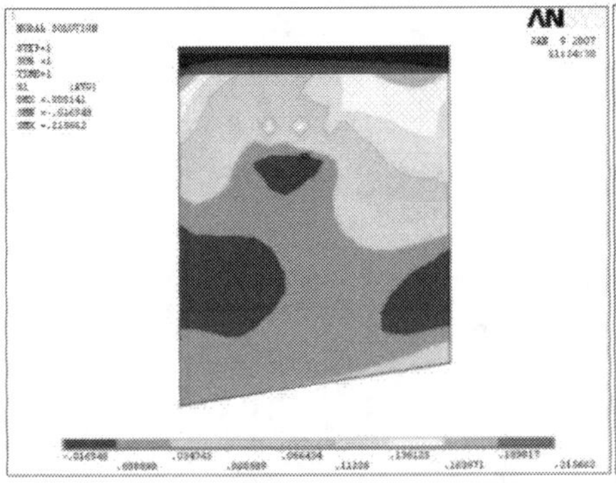

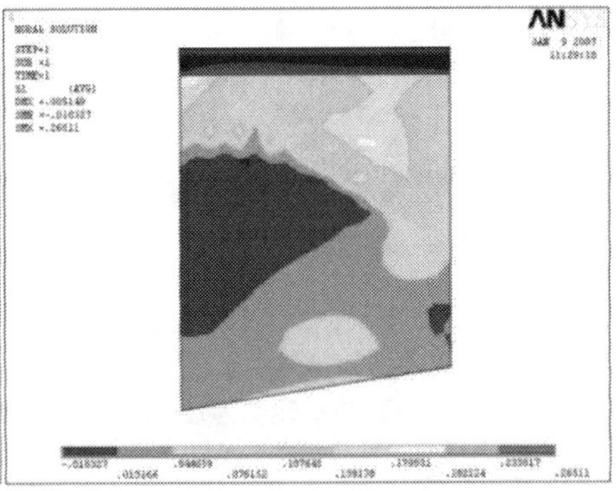

(a) Principal stress cloud diagram of Model 5 (b) Principal stress cloud diagram of Model 6

Figure 12 The main stress of the **web** under each condition cloud diagram

The calculation results show that: (1) when the downwards bending beam is set in the web, the stress concentration is easy to occur at the bend of the bending beam and the main tensile stress appears. (2) Compared with Modle1 to Modle4, the main tensile stress decreases from 0.28MPa to 0.14MPa. Increasing the bending radius can effectively reduce the principal tensile stress at the web beam cross section. From Modle5, Modle3 and Modle6, it can be seen that as the lower corner increases, the peak value of the main tensile stress increases from 0.13 MPa to 0.20 MPa. Therefore, when setting the lower corner beam, the cornering angle should be minimized. (3) The diagonal cracks appearing along the direction of the web beam layout have a limited impact on the bridge structure and will be automatically closed during the bridge's operation. Therefore, it is only necessary to seal the diagonal cracks [6] [13].

3 Conclusion

(1) The main tensile stress of the abdominal plate is more sensitive to the vertical prestress, and the vertical prestress can be applied to reduce the stress of the main plate.

(2) When the effective vertical prestress is kept at more than 60%, the minimum principal stress is basically above 2.0 Mpa, so the calculation formula of vertical prestress in the specification is reasonable by multiplying the reduction factor of 0.6.

(3) With the decrease of the effective vertical prestress, the main compressive stress above the neutral axis of the abdominal plate decreases faster, while the lower part of the neutral axis decreases slower.

(4)In contrast, under the same vertical preloading stress level, the root section of the web compressive stress reserves bigger than L/4 section of the web. In other words, L/4 section web easier to crack, the box girder web plate cracking phenomenon is consistent with engineering practice.

(5) When the bending beam is set under the web, the stress concentration is easy to be concentrated in the bending bend at the next bend. Increasing the bending radius can effectively reduce the principal tensile stress at the web beam cross section. As the lower corner increases, the peak value of the main tensile stress increases. Therefore, when setting the lower corner beam, the cornering angle should be minimized.

(6) The diagonal cracks appearing along the direction of the web beam layout have a limited impact on the bridge structure and will be automatically closed during the bridge's operation. Therefore, it is only necessary to seal the diagonal cracks.

References

1 .Lou zhuang hong. The fracture of prestressed beam bridge [J]. Highway traffic technology, 2000, 12 (6):49-52.
2 .Lu jianming, Chen ke. Analysis of the main stress of prestressed concrete box girder web [J]. Highway traffic technology, 2005, 22(10): 51-55.
3. Peng wei, hongyan, ke shangang et al. Research on fracture control of PC continuous box girder bridge [J]. Journal of zhejiang university of technology, 2003, 1: 22-27.
4. Zhao baojun, Yin hai-jun, hao xianwu, meng jiang. Test analysis of vertical prestress diffusion effect of PC box girder web. [J]. Civil architecture and environmental engineering.
5. Li bin. A study on the vertical prestress of the web of the box girder with the secondary tensioning of steel wire. [D]. Master's thesis. Hunan University. 2009.
6. Xiao xing. Analysis of the causes of the oblique fracture of the web in the construction of prestressed concrete box girder Bridges [J]. Modern transportation technology, 2007, 4 (1):43-47.
7. Yan fanghua. The setting analysis of bending beam under the web of continuous box girder with cantilevered cantilever [J]. Northern traffic, 2007, 12 (12)
8. Christopher J Waldron.Investigation of Long-term Prestress Losses in Pretensioned High Performance Concrete Girders [D].American: The Virginia Polytechnic Institute and State University, 2004, 1-206.

9. Zhong xingu, li feng, zou jianmin et al. Analysis of the stress of the abdominal plate under the vertical prestress of concrete box girder Bridges [J]. Journal of hunan university of science and technology, 2005, 20 (2): 48-52.
10. Shao xudong, li bin, zeng tiansheng. The calculation and measurement of the stress field of the prestressed steel strand of the low retraction prestressed steel wires applied to the vertical prestress of the web [J]. Highway traffic technology. 2009, 9(9).
11. Tadros M.K.,Al-Omaishi,N.,Seguirant,S.J.Prestress Losses in Pretensioned High-Strength Concrete Bridge Girders. National Cooperative Highway Research Program Report [J], Transportation Research Board, National Research Council, 2003.
12. Yan donghuang, Lin Ming, yuan Ming. Analysis on the elastic compression loss of the vertical prestressed tendon of concrete box girder.
13. H.Broo,Lundgren,B.Engstrom. Shear and torsion interaetion in prestressed hollow core unit s [J].Magazine of Conerete Researeh, 2005, 57(9):521-533.

Research on structural dynamic characteristics of continuous steel box girder-bridge with lager ratio of wide-span

Haijun Yin[1,2], *Ziqing* Li[1], *Xianwu* Hao[1]

[1] School of highway Engineering, Chang' an University, Xi' an 710064, China
[2] Xi' an Architecture & Technology University, Xi'an 710055,China;

Abstract. Structure natural frequency and mode of vibration can not only reflect the structure modal parameters of dynamic properties, but also incarnate the dynamic evaluation characteristics of bridge structure. This paper applies ANSYS to establish the finite element model based on a continuous steel box girder bridge in order to obtain the corresponding modal analysis parameters. Through the environmental stimulation test, The results show that height of the steel box girder and the setting of diaphragm plate is reasonable, transverse space of piers not merely provide enough support but also ensure lateral stability of the bridge, as well as offering aside the maximum lateral clearance of the existing road. Meanwhile, the calculation results have important engineering practical values. which can provide basic data for the design, construction and maintenance of similar Bridges.

1. Introduction

Box-shaped cross-section has good structural properties and greater torsional stiffness, and be widely used in large-scale bridge structures [1]. Steel bridge with box section is especially satisfied with structure and construction requirements. Steel box girder has merits of high intensity, large bending torsional stiffness, good overall performance, light weight, high degree of factory operation, quick construction progress, and structures with box girders in the process of construction and service all have a good stability. Hence, this girder is used in large, long span bridges [2]. Steel girder with a long cantilever belt can reduce the self-weight of the bridges, the piers structural dimensions and bridge cost. However, steel box girder cantilever panels and stiffeners due to long-term exposure to the atmosphere, prone to steel box wall corrosion. In addition, closed of the steel box girder can improve the corrosion resistance of the steel structure. Therefore, a curved thin steel plate is added on the outside of the cantilever plate, and the stiffening rib of the cantilever plate is completely closed, which can avoid the corrosion problems caused by the stiffening rib of the steel box girder, especially the streamline shape design, which has superior wind resistant performance and concise appearance, smoothness and beauty. Ouyang Yongjin and Liu Shizhong et al [3-7] did a lot of works on the shear lag effect of steel box girder. The author and Chen Huifa did a lot of works on the dynamic response of continuous box girder under earthquake load [8-11], and obtained more accurate calculation results. After reviewing a large amount of data, the author found that there is little data on the research of natural vibration characteristics of large-span-to-span bridges. However, the research on the vibration problem of continuous steel box girder with large span and span ratio to obtain the maximum space under the existing municipal roads has very few reference values. In this paper, a three-dimensional finite element model of plate and shell considering the pile-soil interaction is established for a large-span, single-span, multi-compartment continuous steel box girder in Xiamen city. The vibration characteristics of the structure are analyzed. Incentive test comparative analysis of the test results. At the same time, the calculation results can also provide basic data for the design, construction and maintenance of the bridge and similar bridges, which has important engineering practical value.

2 Project overview

The length of a rapid trunk road in Xiamen City is 1080 meters, of which the length of steel box girder is 252 meters. The span of continuous steel box girder of equal height is arranged in two forms of (40+55+40) meters and (35+45+35) meters, where the design load is city A level and the clearance height is more than 5.0 meters. The continuous steel box girder adopts the single box multi-chamber section and the streamline shape design. The full width of the steel box girder top is 25.0 meters, the floor width is 13.5 meters, the length of the cantilever on both sides are 5.75 meters, the height of the steel box girder is 2.0 meters, Side of the welded steel beam, the lower flange design streamlined.

Bridge deck structure using orthotropic board, roof section thickness are 14 mm, in order to adapt to the smooth curve of the plane curve, longitudinal rib section are used inverted T-type welding, transverse ribs general spacing 2.0 m, diaphragm thickness 12mm ~ 36mm, floor thickness of 14mm ~ 36mm, the general board thickness 14mm ~20mm. Bridge pier is slightly open at the top of the double-rectangular portal pier, near the road with semi-elliptical softening. The rectangular column of bridge pier is 2×1.6m with a thickness of 1.6m on the side. The pier top of the connecting pier is locally thickened to meet the need of arranging two supports, and the pier in the pier spacing of the pier adopts 6.5m. Abutment reinforced concrete U-abutment. The basis of pile foundation, pile diameter Φ1.6m. In this paper, a large span ratio of 0.45 three-span continuous steel box girder (40+55+40) m as the research object, its natural vibration characteristics of a special study. Continuous steel box girder bridge cross section shown in Figure 1.

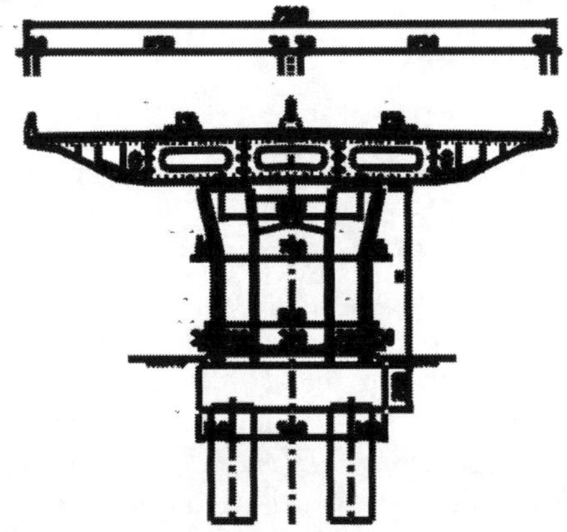

Figure. 1 Cross-section of Steel Box Girder (Unit:cm)

3 Finite element model

The vibration characteristics of the structure are mainly determined by the stiffness and quality of the structure, thus accurately simulating the stiffness and mass of the structural members [13-14]. A three-dimensional finite element model of continuous steel box girder was established with the help of the large-scale finite element structural analysis software ANSYS. The shell63 elemnt was used to simulate the pier and steel box girder. In the simulation process, in order to avoid or reduce the appearance of morbid units as much as possible, a custom meshing unit is adopted, which can faithfully reflect the change of structure shape and detail.

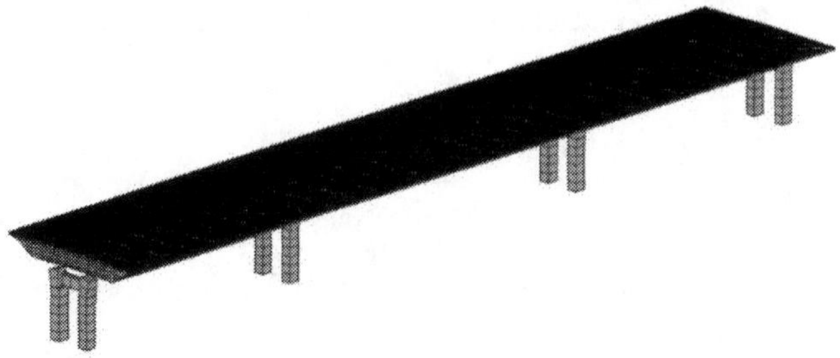

Figure. 2 Finit Elemet Model of the Continuous Steel Box Girder-bridge

The three-span continuous steel box girder adopts the isolation rubber bearing, with four unidirectional movable supports, three bidirectional movable supports and a fixed support. The support and the box girder bottom plate are connected by the support plate. In the finite element model, the support type is constrained and simulated according to the corresponding line displacement. For the steel box girder, the rigidity of the shell element is the rigidity of the box girder itself, and the quality is the quality of the steel box girder. The deck pavement, railings, sidewalks, lamp posts, etc. are all calculated in the form of linear density. According to the consolidation simulation, the bridge piers and cap are included in the joint action of pile-soil-structure. The bridge deck pavement is calculated according to the additional mass unit, and its dynamic characteristics are analyzed in the spatial analysis model. The finite element model of continuous steel box girder is shown in Fig.2.

4 Analysis of structural vibration characteristics

4.1 Structural calculation theory

Solving the structure of the natural frequency (period) is essentially the problem of solving a generalized eigenvalue. There are many ways to solve the eigenvalue problem, such as inverse iteration method, Rayleigh-Leeds method, Ritz vector method, subspace iteration method, Lanczos vector method [15]. At present, the subspace iteration method is widely used, and it can be applied to solve some eigenvalue problems. It is the most commonly used and effective method for solving large matrix eigenvalue problems. In keeping the orthogonal condition, assuming that n initial vectors and repeating iterations until the number of iterations is big enough to satisfy the convergence condition, can get first $k(k<n)$ of the matrix eigenvalue and characteristic vector .Therefore, in this paper, the method of subspace iteration is used to calculate the self - vibration characteristics of large - width span - span steel box girder.

Vibration mode and frequency of structural free vibration are important dynamical characteristic parameters of structural system, which play an important role in solving the dynamic response of structural system [16].

The finite element free vibration equation of the structural system is:

$$[K]\{x\} = \omega^2[M]\{x\} \tag{1}$$

In the formula: $[K]$ is total stiffness matrix; $[M]$ means total mass matrix; $\{x\}$ for the mode vector; ω Is the circular frequency.

From formula (1), we can get the Rayleigh quotient:

$$\omega^2 = \frac{\{x\}^T[K]\{x\}}{\{x\}^T[M]\{x\}} \tag{2}$$

Pulsating method is also called the environment random excitation method. The structure under the action of environmental incentive, such as disturbances caused by ground pulsation, natural wind, vehicle, machine etc. Although the amplitude of structure is minuscule, but the frequency of the pulse response contains quite rich. Without any excitation equipment, it can apply to the whole structural natural vibration characteristics of the test. The ambient vibration response of large and wide span of continuous steel box girders was picked up by ultra-low frequency acceleration sensor. For accurate steel box girder vibration response, In this paper, the environmental vibration data of each measuring point is filtered to high and low frequency signal components. Then the data were analyzed by power spectrum analysis and mutual power spectrum, In the end, we can obtain the coherence function and phase difference function of the signal power spectral density function of each measurement point and the reference point signal, the power spectral density and coherence function determine the frequency of each mode, and the power spectral density and phase difference function determine the modes of each mode.

4.2 Comparison of dynamic analysis and measured results

4.2.1 Analysis of self-vibration characteristics

In structural dynamic characteristics, the self-oscillation frequency reflects the stiffness of the structure to a large extent, and the first few steps have the control effect on the dynamic characteristics. Therefore, in the analysis of the dynamic characteristics of the bridge, it is necessary to accurately calculate self-vibration frequency and corresponding vibration mode of the bridge, and analyze the mode characteristics. In order to calculate the necessary self-vibration frequency and the corresponding mode of vibration, the bridge adopts sub-space iterative method to calculate the bridge mode. Due to the limited space, this paper only lists the results and modes of the first 10 self-vibration characteristics, as shown in table 1 and FIG. 3 respectively.

Based on the above calculation model, the necessary self-oscillation frequency and corresponding mode vector are determined by subspace iterative method. The first 10 vibration characteristics and frequency are listed in table 1.

Table. 1 Comparison of Natural Frequency and Vibration Type in First 10 Steps

Order	Feature	Frequenc (Hz)	Order	Feature	Frequency(Hz)
1	Pier2 vertical bending+ Longitudinal vibration of the beam	1.817	6	Beam first-order anti-symmetry twist	3.316
2	Longitudinal vibration of pier2 + Beam vertical bending	2.025	7	Beam first-order symmetry twist	3.514
3	First-order symmetrical beam torsion	2.52	8	Beam second-order symmetry twist	4.109
4	Second-order beam anti-symmetrical vertical bending	3.072	9	Pier longitudinal vibration + anti-symmetrical beam torsion	4.590
5	Second-order beam symmetrical vertical bending	3.309	10	Main span first antisymmetric vertical bending + torsion	5.655

The 1st order vibration mode

The 2nd order vibration mode

The 3rd order vibration mode

The 4th order vibration mode

The 5th order vibration mode

The 6th order vibration mode

The 7th order vibration mode

The 8th order vibration mode

The 9th order vibration mode

The 10th order vibration mode

Figure. 3 Structure Mode of Vibration in First 10 Steps

As can be seen from figure 3, the self-vibration characteristics of the bridge show the following characteristics:

The bridge pier belongs to the low-fat structure, and only one fixed support (2 # pier top) is set in the three-span continuous bridge, and the longitudinal stiffness of the bridge is weaker than the horizontal and vertical direction of the bridge. Therefore, the first mode of the bridge shows that the whole bridge has the vertical vibration of the whole bridge and the bending vibration of the bridge pier, with the characteristics of two and a half wave vertical vibrations of the main span (L = 55m).

The second order vibration shows the vertical half-wave vibration of the main span, the vibration frequency of 2.025Hz is 11.43% higher than the first order frequency of the longitudinal vibration of the bridge.

The third order vibration mode is given priority to span structure first-order symmetric torsional vibration, the vibration frequency of 2.52 Hz, in spite of bridge deck width is 25.0 m, but the bridge lateral support spacing is only 6.5 m, its vibration frequency is 38.6% higher than the vertical bending. It is shown that the bridge lateral support 6.5 m in maximum limit to ensure lateral stability of the bridge to set aside the maximum lateral clearance at the same time.

The 4th and 5th order vibration frequency were 3.072 Hz and 3.309 Hz, vertical symmetric and antisymmetric vibration modes respectively, showed a double root vibration characteristics, respectively for the two sides across the vertical half wave bending vibration, on both sides of the bridge structure in the cross is symmetrical layout, the characteristics of vibration frequency and the corresponding appear heavy root. It is shown that the finite element model of the bridge is correct and reflects the dynamic characteristics of the bridge.

The 6th order for antisymmetric vibration torsional vibration, but also reflect the characteristics of this bridge transverse bearing set only 6.5 m, the vibration frequency of 3.316 Hz and on both sides of the bridge across the vertical vibration frequency of 3.072 Hz and 3.309 Hz close to that bridge transverse span width of 6.5 m is a better support.

Span structures of the 7th order vibration mode is given priority to the first order torsional vibration, the vibration frequency of 3.514 Hz, even though the deck width is 25.0 m, and the lateral support of bridge middle span of only 6.5 m. It is suggestted that bridge lateral support 6.5 m can maximally ensure lateral stability while left transverse bridge to the world's largest net.

The 8th order vibration is the high order of the whole bridge, which is called torsional vibration, and the vibration frequency is 4.109 Hz.

The 9th vibration is the span of the bridge and the longitudinal vibration frequency of the 2# piers is 4.59Hz respectively. The vibration characteristics of transverse symmetry of bridge structure are reflected.

The 10th order vibration is the high order resistance of the bridge. The vibration frequency is 5.655 Hz. The frequency of vibration is 23.2% higher than that of the ninth stage, and there is a jump in frequency.

From the bridge the first ten order vibration frequency and vibration model, bridge longitudinal, vertical and torsional vibration frequency is smaller, vertical and torsional vibration of beam body appear alternately, showed that the height of the steel box girder structure, the density of diaphragm plate set reasonable, pier transverse spacing Settings to ensure the premise of bridge piers can provide enough support ability and can ensure the lateral stability of the continuous steel box girder, and also to allow maximum lateral clearance of the existing road.

In the first ten steps, there is no single horizontal vibration of the bridge, indicating that the transverse stiffness of the bridge is far greater than that of vertical and torsional rigidity.

4.2.2 Comparison between the calculated results and the measured results

The finite element program ANSYS is used to analyze the dynamic characteristics of steel box girder with large width to span ratio. The results of natural vibration of bridge structure are compared with the results of ambient excitation test. For limited space only the first 10 order comparison results and mode shapes are given, as shown in table 2.

From table 2, it is shown that the first vibration mode of the bridge is the vertical vibration of the 2 pier and the longitudinal vibration of the beam. The measured frequency is 1.99Hz, and the theoretical self - vibration frequency is 1.817Hz. The second order mode is the longitudinal vibration of the 2 pier and the vertical bending of the beam. The measured frequency is 2.79Hz, and the theoretical self - vibration frequency is 2.025Hz. The third order mode is the first symmetric torsion of the beam. The measured frequency is 2.93Hz, and the theoretical self - vibration frequency is 2.520Hz. The fourth order mode of vibration is the two order anti-symmetric vertical bending of the beam. The measured frequency is 3.12Hz, and the theoretical self - vibration frequency is 3.072Hz. The fifth order mode is the second order symmetrical vertical bending of the beam. The measured frequency is 3.71Hz, and the theoretical self - vibration frequency is 3.309Hz. The calculation results show that the measured frequency of self-vibration is greater than the theoretical calculation. The minimum value of the measured damping ratio is 2.32% and the maximum value is 6.86%.

Table. 2 Comparison of Natural Frequency and the Environmental Stimulation

Order	Measured self-vibration frequency (Hz)	Damping Ratio (%)	Theoretical self-vibration frequency (Hz)	Vibration mode
1	1.99	5.55	1.817	Pier2 vertical bending + Longitudinal vibration of the beam
2	2.79	2.32	2.025	Longitudinal vibration of pier2 + Beam vertical bending
3	2.93	6.86	2.520	First-order symmetrical beam torsion
4	3.12	3.49	3.072	Second-order beam anti-symmetrical vertical bending
5	3.71	6.00	3.309	Second-order beam symmetrical vertical bending
6	/	/	3.316	Beam first-order anti-symmetry twist
7	/	/	3.514	Beam first-order symmetry twist
8	4.49	4.27	4.109	Beam second-order symmetry twist
9	/	/	4.591	Pier longitudinal vibration + anti-symmetrical beam torsion
10	/	/	5.655	Main span first antisymmetric vertical bending + torsion

The measured vertical bending fundamental frequency of steel box girder is 2.79Hz, the theoretical fundamental frequency is 2.025Hz. The measured fundamental frequency of symmetrical torsion is 2.93Hz and the theoretical fundamental frequency is 2.520Hz. The theoretical calculated value and the measured natural vibration characteristic of the steel box girder are similar. The measured frequency is greater than the theoretical value. It indicated that the actual stiffness of the joint is greater than the theoretical stiffness and the quality of the bridge is good. In addition, it shows that the dynamic calculation model of the bridge is reasonable and the calculation method is correct. The measured the first eight order main damping ratio is 2.32% ~ 6.86%, which is close to the general bridge damping ratio of 0.01 ~ 0.10, belonging to the normal range. It shows that the bridge has good dynamic performance.

5 Conclusion

(1) In the design of steel box girder-bridge, a curved thin steel plate is built on the outside of the cantilever plate to avoid the corrosion of the steel box girder cantilevered ribs. The shape design of streamline shape is designed, the bridge type is beautiful, it is more advantageous to enhance the bridge structure's anti-wind ability.

(2) Through discrete analysis and accurate simulation of steel box girder-bridge, ANSYS software is used to analyze the structure and use the environmental excitation to test the bridge.

(3) The results show that, from the first ten stages of the bridge vibration frequency and vibration mode, the bridge longitudinal, vertical and torsional vibration frequency difference is small. The vertical and torsional vibrations of the girder alternately appear, which shows that the height of the steel box girder structure and the density of the diaphragm are reasonable and feasible. The lateral spacing of bridge piers can ensure the lateral stability of continuous steel box girders and provide the maximum horizontal clearance to the existing roads under the premise of ensuring sufficient pier supporting capacity.

(4) The calculation results of the bridge can also provide basic data for the design, construction and maintenance of similar bridges. It is of great practical value for engineering.

References

1. Guo Jin-qiong, Fang Zhen-zheng, Zheng Zhen. Design Theory of Box girder [M]. Beijing : China Communications Press,2008
2. Xiang Hai-fan. Advanced Theory of Bridge Structures [M].Beijing: China Communications Press, 2008
3. Liu Shi-zhong. Non-uniform thin wall box analysis of considering both shear lag and shear deformation [J].China Journal of Highway and Transport, 2002,15 (3);61-63.
4. OUYANG Yong-jin. Investigation of Shear Lag Effect of Continuous Steel Box Girder Bridge with Great Width-to-Span Ratio [J].World Bridges, 2009, 14 0(1); 29-32.
5. Zhang Yuan-hai, Wang Lai-lin, Li Qiao. One-dimensional finite element method and its application for the analysis of shear lag effect in box girders [J]. CH INA CIVIL ENG INEERING JOURNAL, 2010, 40(80):44-50
6. ZHOU Sh-i jun, YANG Z-i jiang. Finite Beam Element for Analysis of Effect of Concentrated Bending Moments on Shear Lag in Box Girders [J]. JOURNAL OF THE CHINA RAILWAY SOCIETY, 2010, 32(03):90-94
7. ZHOU Mao-ding, LI Li-yuan, ZHANG Yuan-hai. Research on Shear-lag Warping Displacement Function of Thin-walled Box Girders [J]. China Journal of Highway and Transport, 2015, 28(6): 67-73.
8.Yin Haijun, Xu Lei, Shen Yuekui, Lin Qingning, Yan Wen Study of Seismic damages of Bridges in Wenchuan Earthquake[J].J.Xi'an Univ. of Arch. & Tech.(Natural Science Edition),2008,40(5):672-677.
9. YIN Hai-jun. Static and dynamical analysis of Fu rong-jiang Extra-Long Bridge [D]. Gansu: Lanzhou Jiao tong University, 2007.
10. YIN Hai-jun,LI Zi-qing ,GUO Qi, YAN Wen, HAN Fei. Study on the dynamic characteristics of long span continuous rigid frame bridge with high wall piers [J].J. Xi'an Univ. of Arch. & Tech. (Natural Science Edition), 2010, 42(5):663-668.
11 .Chen Huifa (U.S) Duan Lian (U.S), Translated by Cai Zhongmin and Wu Jun. Aseismatic Design of Bridges [M]. Beijing: China Machine Press, 2008
12 .LIU Yan-hui, TAN Ping, ZHOU Fu-lin, WENLIUHAN Heisha, MERCAN O. Shaking Table Test for Seismic Simulation of Continuous Isolation Girder Bridge with High Piers[J]. China Journal of Highway and Transport, 2015, 28(2): 60-68, 94.
13. Zhang Li-ming. Application method and example of algor and ansys on bridge engineering [M]. Beijing: People Communication Publishing House, 2003
14. Fan Li-chu,Hu Shi-de, Ye Ai-jun . Seismic design of long-span bridges [M]. Beijing:People Communication Publishing House,2001.
15 .Wu Hong-qing, Ren Xia. Structural finite element analysis [M]. Beijing:China railway publishing house,2000.

16 .Zhu Ledong. Modal Identification of Bridges [J]. JOURNAL OF TONGJI UNIVERSITY, 1999, 27(2):179-183.

Work orders management based on XML file in printing

Peipei Ran[1],*, *Wenjie* Yang[1], *Zhongyue* Da[1], and *Yuke* Huo[1]

[1]School of Printing and Packing Engineering, Beijing Institute of Graphic Communication, Beijing, China

Abstract. The Extensible Markup Language (XML) technology is increasingly used in various field, if it's used to express the information of work orders will improve efficiency for management and production. According to the features, we introduce the technology of management for work orders and get a XML file through the Document Object Model (DOM) technology in the paper. When we need the information to conduct production, parsing the XML file and save the information in database, this is beneficial to the preserve and modify for information.

1 Introduction

Extensible Markup Language, short for XML, announced in 1998 by the W3C, become a universal format for EDI (Electronic Data Interchange) and replace the Standard Generalized Markup Language (SGML) and Hyper Text Mark-up Language (HTML) due to the advantages such as easily used, strong expansibility, data and expression separated, simple data exchange. XML is a versatile and well-operational data exchange technology that enables heterogeneous compatibility with information systems and ensures efficient transfer, exchange, sharing and integration of data between data modules [1]. The role of XML file is: the first is application' configuration file, the second is used to exchange data between different language, the third is as a database to save data [2]. The work orders management is core module of Enterprise Resource Planning (ERP) in printing industry. In actual production, we can import the XML file that from other enterprises into the local ERP system to conduct production, or send the work order information to other enterprises in the form of XML files.

2 Management of work orders

The system of work orders management is development on the foundation of technology such as Java, DOM, XML and database, the framework for development technology is shown as figure 1.

1 Corresponding author: 376007414@qq.com

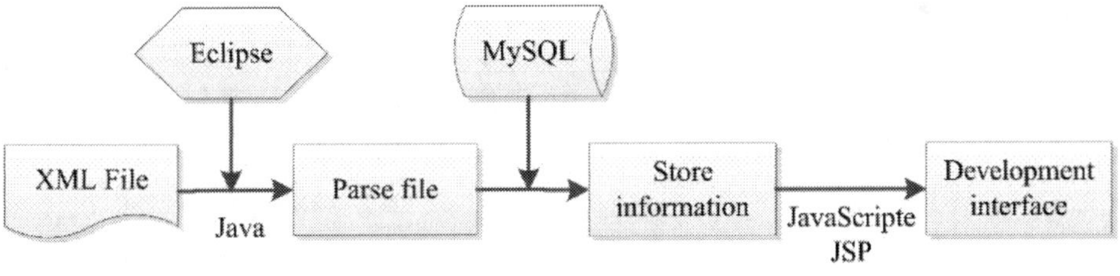

Fig.1. The framework for development technology

First, the client can provide a XML file which contains the product structure, printing effect and contact information to printing industry. Second, the industry receive the XML file and start to parse the file and save the basic information for jobs and description information for process in database. Third, the system store the work orders information through MySQL database, including the basic information of work orders, parts, process and description.

3 The parsing technology

3.1 The execution rote for XML file parsing

The XML file is a kind of tree structure consisting of different type nodes. The top nodes is usually used to describe the purpose and requirements that the entire production achieves, also said product information description. The center nodes, also said process group nodes, refer to the process of center production, for example, the printing of hardcover book includes the process of platemaking, printing, book-cover making and post-press finishing, each process can be regarded as an center node. Each center node contains nodes, also said process nodes, which represent a specific, single, simple process that required to complete an intermediate product [3].

There are two methods for parsing of XML file: the first is to read or modify the information according to the DOM tree structure that composed of relationship between different type nodes. The second is to read the information of XML file in order, also read the needed data. The paper mainly introduces how to create, modify, query the XML file through the first method (as shown in figure 2), beginning with the root node to parse different types nodes that constitute the entire production process, including the nodes describing the product information and process.

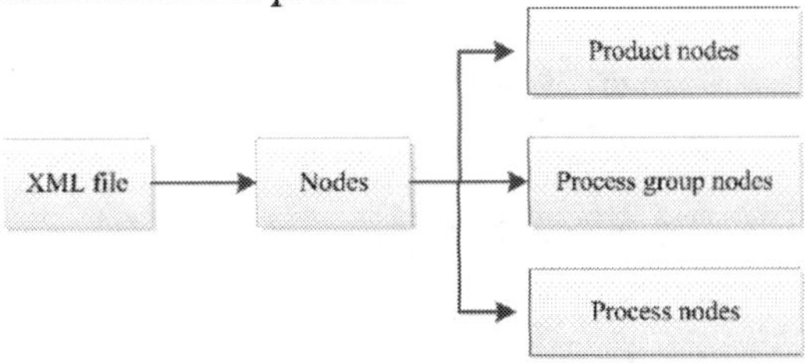

Fig.2. The execution rote for XML file parsing

3.2 The technology of DOM

Document Object Model, short for DOM, is a standard independent to language and platform and developed by W3C, this standard provides an interface that can be used in a variety of programming languages, operating systems and platforms, it also defines the logical structures of document and the methods to preserve and modify document [4].

DOM technology can transfer XML file into a document object model of tree structure, the user can dynamically create document and traverse the structure of document through interviewing the object model [5]. The data in document can be modified, deleted and added. Its working principle is shown in figure 3.

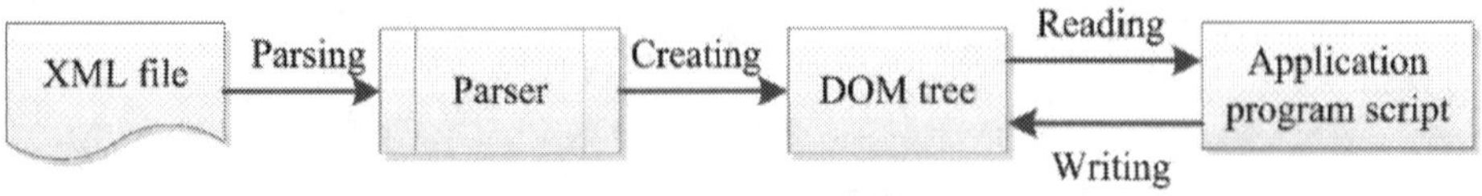

Fig.3. The working principle of DOM

4 The creating and parsing for XML file

First, in order to expediently share information between different ERP systems, based on security of information transfer, using DOM technology to create XML file according to information of work orders, as shown in Figure 2.

The XML file for work orders:

```
<? Xml version="1.0" encoding="UTF-8"?>
<Book-Printing>
    <plan planNo="17-11-0012">
        <Client>the Bookshops in Beijing</Client>
        <Product>
            <Name>Software Engineering</Name>
            <Numb>1000< /Numb>
            <Style>books</Style>
            <Units>book</Units>
        </Product>
        <Salesman>Mr. Wang</Salesman>
        <Print>The cover is four colors printing, text is single color
            printing</print>
        <Post-press>
        Wireless binding, cover sub membrane, local UV, plastic seal.</post-press>
        <Remark>******</Remark>
    </plan>
    <part planNo="17-11-0012">
        <cover part-ID="17-11-0815">
            <Paper>
                <Name>250g Space shuttle paper </Name>
                <Pages>1.8</Pages>
                <Over-plus>0.2</Over-plus>
                <Units>ling</Units>
                <Color-Numb-front>4</Color-Numb-front>
                <Color-Numb-reverse>0</Color-Numb-reverse>
                <Size>840*540</Size>
            </Paper>
        </cover>
    </part>
    <Process    planNo="17-11-0012">
        <Plate process-ID="17-11-0815_2">
            <Name>CTP</Name>
            <Numb>4</Numb>
        </Plate>
```

<Process_1 process-ID ="17-11-0815_21">
Single surface optical film </Process_1>
<Process_2 process-ID ="17-11-0815_22>
Bronzing</Process_2>
</Process>
</Book-Printing>

This file contains four parts: basic information of work orders, part information, process information and description of printing information, these parts are linked by ID. The "plan" node and its child nodes include basic information of work orders, for example the information of client and product. The "part" node and its child nodes refer to the basic part information for production, such as the name, specification, number of paper in the printing of cover. The "process" node and its child nodes consist refer to the process information consisting of process of part production, such as plate and the process in post-press.

Second, the data in the file is obtained through the parsing technology, the process is shown in figure 4.

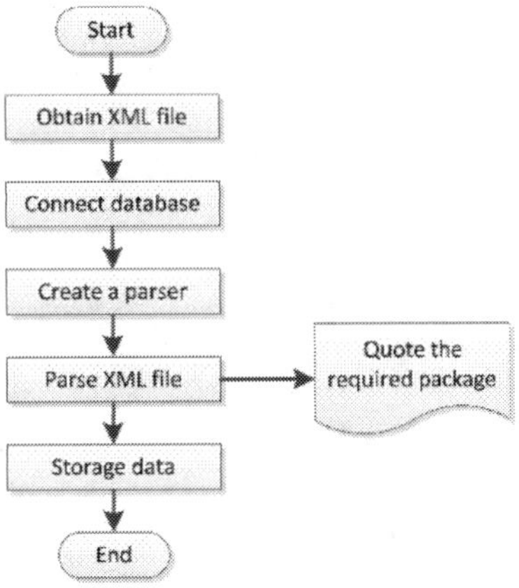

Fig.4. The process of parsing XML file

Third, the data obtained from the XML file is stored in database, it can be browsed by user in the interface of work orders management system, as shown in figure5.

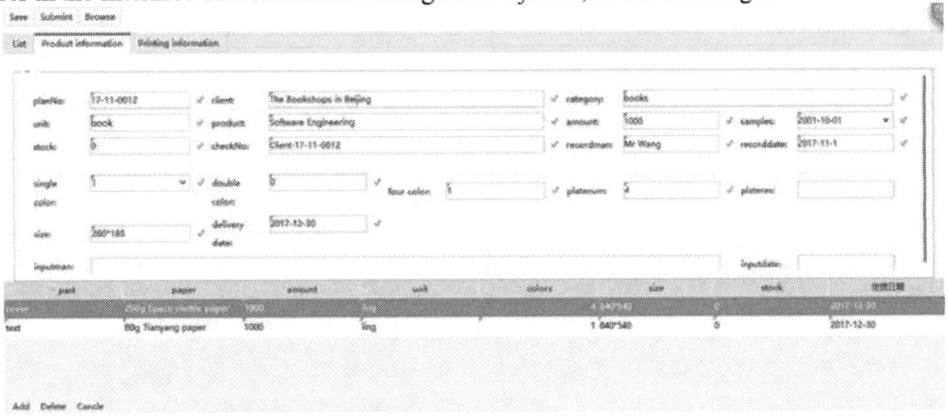

Fig.5. The interface of work orders management

The figure 5 display the interface of work orders management, including the detail information for client, product and printing process. Users can directly add or modify information on this interface, or make changes through the XML file.

5 Conclusion

Printing production is composed of a series of independent processes, which rely on a variety of data to contact for each other. In different stages of production, various types of information in order to pass from receiving the order to production to logistics and distribution, the production process become more complicated due to exchange of information, which directly leads to the production of low efficiency and high consumption. The work orders management, as core module of ERP in printing industry, in order to facilitate the exchange of information between the production departments or enterprises, using DOM technology to transfer woke orders information into XML files, the XML file can be encrypted, compared with the traditional word file, the information is safer and hard to leak. It can be transmitted between different systems in companies, the production sectors or enterprises only need to resolve the information they need to carry out production guidance, this can reduce the waste of the time, but also can improve the efficiency of production and management.

Acknowledgment: The study is supported by the National Key Scientific Instrument and Equipment Development Project (No.2013YQ140517).

Reference

1. Feifei Chen. The Research and Application of XML Document Resolution Technology Based on DOM4J [J]. Software Guide, 2016, 15(3).
2. Yi Sun. The development and research of XML ıntegrated edıtıng and analysis environment [D]. Wuhan: Wuhan University of Technology, 2003.
3. Jie Shi. The design of printing industry orders management system for supporting JDF [D]. Beijing: Beijing Institute of graphic communication, 2011.
4. Shuyi Fan, Yan Li, Chen Meng. Application of SAX and DOM in XML file parsing [J]. Microcomputer Applications, 2011, 12 (27).
5. JingYang, ShuangeZhou. A conversion method forunstructured data based on XML [J]. Computer Science, 2017, 11 (44).

https://doi.org/10.1051/itmconf/20181703010

Development of cost management and aided decision system for casting enterprises based on ERP

Hailin Zhang [1]

Shandong Jianzhu University, School of Computer Science and Technology, Jinan 250101, Shandong, China, 10086

Abstract. The present situation of production management and the application status of ERP in small and medium sized foundry enterpriseswere analyzed in this paper and a set of cost management and aided decision system based on ERP for foundry enterprises was developed. Application of the system can help managers regulate the production process, reduce production costs and improve economic efficiency.

1 Introduction

In the past two decades, the infrastructure of domestic foundry enterprises has been greatly developed. However, with the deepening of market economy and economic globalization, the focus of casting enterprises has shifted from the original single safety production to All-round development of economic efficiency as the center. Competitiveness of casting enterprises will be directly reflected in the safe production, low-cost operation and rapid response to customer needs.However, according to the study for foundry enterprises found that the domestic casting enterprises generally have poor information exchange, the data format between the enterprise sector is not uniform, the data is not concentrated, there is no decision support system, material planning is not strict and inventory control is not scientific and other questions[1-5].

Process flexible method of casting enterprise ERP was studied in literature[1]. The application status of China's foundry ERP wasstudiedand the application of HZERP was mainly introduced in Literature [2]. The cost accounting of various production processes was studiedin literature [3]. The construction of casting defect database was studiedin Document [4].The integration of foundry production and financial supply chain was studiedin literature [5].The advantages and disadvantages of the foundry enterprise ERP in the above documentswere comprehensively analyzed and the cost management and aided decision system for the foundry enterprise was developed in this paper.

[1] Corresponding author: lynn963@163.com

2 System requirememts analysis

With the development of market economy, foundry enterprises are facing more and more intense competitive environment, ERP is being favored by all walks of lifebecause it has a richer function.

At present, the understanding of the principle of ERP of the domestic foundry industryis not enough, and the importance for ERP implementation is not high, many casting enterprises still believe that ERP implementation isthe installation of simple reportsoftware and purchase of computer equipment, this will lead to that ERPcannot play the desired effect.

The cost management and aided decision-making system of foundry enterprises based on ERP developed in this paper can solve these problems in a targeted way.

The system is divided into five subsystems, which are include casting parameter subsystem, production process subsystem, cost accounting subsystem, equipment management subsystem and system maintenance subsystem. System function block diagram is shown in Figure 1.

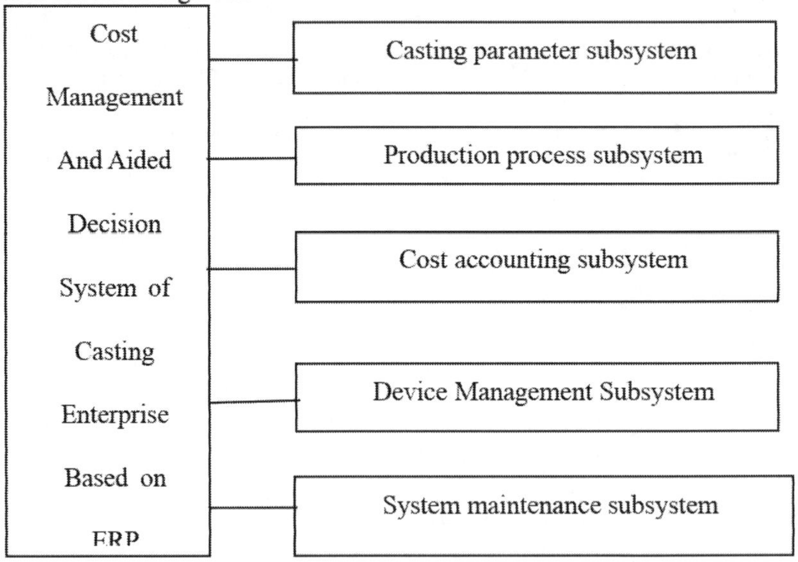

Fig. 1. System function module diagram

3 Pringcples of cost calculation

Cost is a comprehensive economic indicator; all aspects of work performance of business management can be directly or indirectly reflected in the cost, so the cost control is an important part of the work of the enterprise.

Enterprises through the cost of planning, control, supervision, assessment and analysis to promote the management of various departments, and constantly optimize the use of resources, and strive to reduce costs and improve economic efficiency.Enterprises will promote the management of various departments, constantly optimize the use of resources, strive to reduce costs and improve economic efficiency through the planning, control, supervision, assessment and analysis of cost.

Cost management is the core of the ERP system, the fundamental purpose of the enterprise selected ERP system is scientific reduction of operating costs and making decisions according to the actual data.

3.1 The cost type in ERP

The cost accounting in the ERP system uses the standard cost system, which has standard costs, target costs and actual costs. As a tool for management control standard costcan simplify the cost accounting procedures, be conducive to cost analysis, and adjust business strategy in the face of rapidly changing market; target cost is the need for cost control; actual costs are used to reflect the actual production situation.

The system calculates the actual cost by calculating the production cost of each subsystem and carries out the cost budget and then find out the problems in the actual production to provide the data support for making the rational decision through comparing the cost of the actual cost and the forecast cost.

3.2 Principles of cost calculation in ERP

In ERP, the cost is calculated through the bill of materials BOM (Bill of Material). BOM is a complete, formal, structured list of components that lists the hierarchical membership and quantity relationships from raw materials to parts, components up to the end product.BOM is the basis for cost accounting, but also the basis for the preparation of material procurement and production planning.The cost calculation method in ERP is called the cost rolling method, which usually used to calculatethe standard cost and the actual cost.The BOM structure of a product is shown in Figure 2, which is a three-tier structure, the first layer is the final product A, the second layer is its direct component and the third layer is the direct subordinate partsof the second layer.The leaf nodes of the product tree are non-subdivided parts, standard parts or purchased parts.

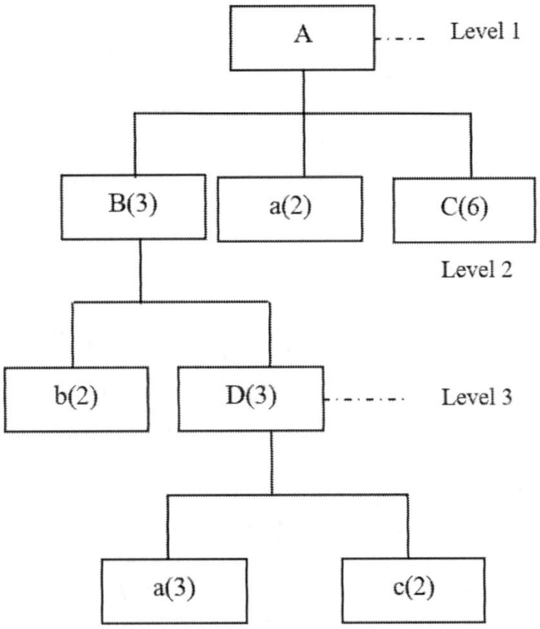

Fig.2. BOM structure diagram

According to the characteristics of the process of casting production, the step-by-step method in the cost calculation method is selected as the cost calculation method, that is, the actual cost calculation is carried out as the individual production module according to the order of the casting production process, and finally the cost is accumulated.

4 Implemation of the system

The system was developedbased on Windows7 by the use of C # as the development language, the use of Visual Studio 2015 as a development platform and the use of SQL Server 2015 as a back-end database. System design features are as follows:

ERP cost management was introduced into the casting production process. Casting material cost management was carried out by the use of advanced concepts of ERP cost management andcombination with the actual situation of casting production to provide accurate cost information for the cost of management and decision-making of enterprise.

Using the method of comparative analysis as the method of material cost analysis, qualitative analysis method was used as the method of casting material cost decision-making, which can provide a complete set of cost information management and decision-making system for casting materials for enterprises. So that enterprises can find the problem of the production, better control productions costs and improve business efficiency through comparing the predicted cost of materials with the actual cost.

5 Application of the system

After the system was developed, it was also adjusted according to the actual needs, and now has been stable operationfor some time. Then take the cost accounting system as an example to illustrate the application of the system.

The costing subsystem can find the problems in the production by comparing the cost and the actual cost reduce the production cost and improve the enterprise's efficiency by modifying the ratio of the raw materials or improving the production process.

The cost accounting subsystem is divided into three modules: raw material demand cost summary and cost analysis.

Among them, the raw material demand module is divided into two parts: raw material demand and raw material supply.

According to the production process, the cost summary module can record the productions cost of the various modules and calculate the final total cost starting from the sand production.

The total cost and the production costs of each module can be found when querying, which will help decision-makers to keep abreast of the entire production process dynamic information.

Table 1. Comparison of before and after the implementation of this system in Shandong Chang Lin

business project	before the implementation of the system	after the implementation of the system
raw material management	the cost of business was affected by price fluctuatingof scrap, coal and other raw material	reducing raw material costsby the cost accounting
production management	production plans rely on personal experience, easily lead to inventory backlog	make plans scientifically ,reduce inventory
device management	maintenance,scrapping, updatingand maintenance of device was not timely	timely maintenance of equipment to improve production efficiency

In accordance with the various labor departments of production process subsystems, cost analysis module can compare the actual cost and forecast coststo determine whether the production process and material ratio is to meet the requirements. If the requirements are met then proceed to the next step, if the requirements are not met, you need to find the cause of the problem, improve the process or material ratio, make it more perfect, and ultimately achieve the expected cost, achieve the purpose of cost control and supporting decision-making.

The system is often used in Shandong ChangLin Machinery Co., Ltdfor some time and has achieved good results, the specific comparison shown in Table 1 above.

6 Conclusions

The system has the friendly interfaceeasy to operate and has a stable operation in Shandong Province for some time. The system can help managers quickly and accurately understand the progress of real-time production, accurately calculate the cost and the total cost of the ministry, compare with the predicted cost, detect and correctthe various problems in the Ministry of Industry and achieve the purpose of reducing production costs.

References

1. Xiao-Wei FAN, Xiao-Yuan JI and Jian-Xin ZHOU.2016.Research on Process Flexibility Method and Application of ERPSystem to Foundry Enterprises. FOUNDRY.165,11(November,2016),1089-1094.
2. Jian-Xin ZHOU,Xiao-Yuan Ji and Dun-Ming Liao.2013.Research andapplication of ERP system for foundry enterprise. China Foundry.10,1(Janury,2013), 8-17.
3. Jing-Wen QIAO.2015.Analysis on Cost Analysis and Control Measures of Foundry Enterprises. Automation and Instrumentation,190(August,2015), 79—80.
4. Zeng-Li LI, Zhong-De SHAN and Ke-RuiLI.2017.Construction and Application of Casting Defects Database.FOUNDRY.66,2(February,2017), 150—154.
5. Ting-Yong Ming, Xiao-Yuan Ji and Jian-Xin Zhou.2016.A Feasibility Analysis of the Integrationand the Financial Supply Chain Systemof the Manufacturing Systemin the Foundry Enterprise.Special Casting and Nonferrous Alloys.36,6(June,2016), 594—597.

Codebook metrics evaluation for millimeter wave communications by antenna array response and signal to noise ratio

Adam Mohamed Ahmed Abdo[1,*], *Xiongwen* Zhao[1*], *Rui* Zhang[2], and *Yu* Zhang[1]

[1]School of Electrical and Electronic Engineering, North China Electric Power University, Beijing 102206, China

[2]National Key Laboratory of Electromagnetic Environment, China Research Institute of Radiowave Propagation, Qingdao 266107, China

Abstract. Codebook design is a key point in beam-forming which is necessary for millimeter Wave (mmWave) communications to compensate its huge path loss. In our study, we demonstrate the benefits of the number of antenna elements for beamforming; we focus on the number of required beams to cover the whole circle with considering the available number of antenna elements. In addition to, we propose a new codebook structure based on unique phase states. Based on the Array Factor (AF) and Signal-to-Noise Ratio (SNR), the proposed codebook is compared and evaluated with the uniform weighting codebook, circular array codebook, and IEEE802.15.3c standard codebook. The results show that the proposed codebook achieves SNR values and side-lobes cancel a bit better than IEEE802.15.3c, but higher peak and wider dynamic range of SNR and better array directivity compared with the uniform weighting and circular antenna codebooks. Thus, the proposed codebook is expected to improve signal quality and increases user throughput significantly.

1 Introduction

The demand growth for wideband data transmission, mmW communication band, is getting considerable attention in wireless local area networks (WLANs) and wireless personal area networks (W-PANs), and in dense user scenarios for fifth generation (5G) radio systems. mmWavesystem is used in short rangeand high data rate communication system with huge unlicensed bandwidth, significant capacity and flexibility. Also, it allows high transmit power and less interference effect. Moreover, it can be applied in large file transfer and uncompressed high-definition video streaming [1]. Further improving transmission range of mmW band also enhances spatial efficiency [2], [3].

However, the mmWave band faces many impairments such as high free space path loss level, high attenuation, and oxygen absorption compared with low-frequency communication band [1], [3]. To compensate the significant path loss, the directional

[1] Corresponding author:adam_ma83@yahoo.com, zhaoxw@ncepu.edu.cn

antenna is used to generate narrow directional beams, which provides significant gain [4], [5].

Beam-forming techniques help to investigate many benefits including the system throughput enhancement, spatial reuse, and minimal interference. Moreover, as the antenna size is directly proportional to wavelength, the mmWave antenna is tiny compared with other low-frequency communication. Therefore, the beam-forming technology can be used to improve the link quality as well as angle information distribution. All these factors motivate the researchers to focus on mmW communication [4], [5]. Analog beam-forming is much less hardware complexity and power consumption constraint so that it preferred in 60GHz indoor mmWave communication [2], [5]. The main purpose of the array antenna is to improve the SNR by adding correlated signals and uncorrelated noise. This improvement measures regarding array gain or array response [8]. The mmWave communication uses two techniques. The first is codebook based beam steering to solve energy constraint. The second one has phased array antennas with fixed amplitude beam weighting vector to solve complexity problem. In phased array antenna, to generate the beam pattern by shifting each antenna element a single radio frequency (RF)signal [9]. Moreover, the codebook has several ways to set antenna weight coefficients. Training is the way to find the best beam pair between transmitter and receiver [10]. Taking IEEE802.15.3c as a reference codebook, there are many studies conducted in different ways to construct codebooks. In [10], uniform weighting based codebook is designed by simple weighting window function and a weighting vector constituting a conjugate number. The circular antenna codebook weight vector is constructed by circularly shifting each column [1].

In this paper, we propose a new form of codebook design based on the number of phase states. Additionally, we compare the proposed codebook with the reference codebooks using SNR and AF as performance evaluation factors. Furthermore, we demonstrate the effect of the number of antenna elements on the generated beams, and how to make the beam wide or narrow, as well as the compressing the beam to cover narrow-angle with high gain and directivity.Weprovide some results and conclusions about the codebooks design and its evaluation, regarding AF and SNR. In addition, we demonstrate the effect of the number of antenna element on the generated beam.

2 System model

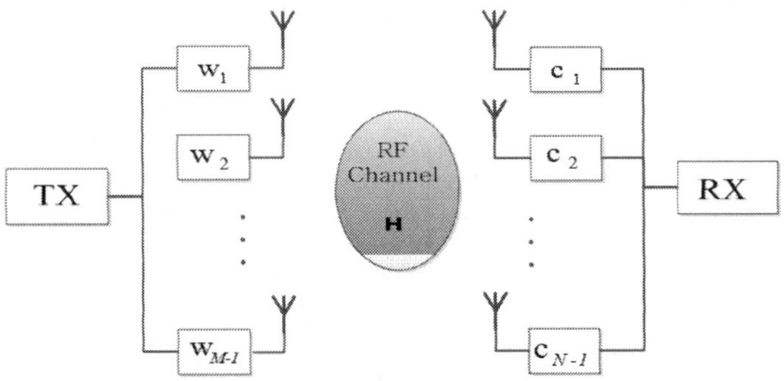

Fig. 1. MIMO System Model

The MIMO system model is shown in Figure 1 The device 1 (DEV1) is equipped with a linear array of M transmit antennas, the device 2 (DEV2) has N receive antenna. Data transmission between the two devices involves the following: at the transmitter side, the signal after baseband processing is upconverted to RF band, then multiplied by transmitter code vector w. On the receiver side, then the received RF signal is down-converted to abaseband signal, and then multiplied by receiver code vector c; both weight vectors satisfy

$|w_i| = |c_i| = 1$ .We can generate beams by shifting each antenna element RF signal, each column (beam) is circularly generated by shifting a previous beam by angle $2\pi/N$ [1], [7].

2.1 Codebook design and principles

The followings are fundamental codebooks design principles [11]: First, the codebook designed for the phased antenna, each column of codebook matrix determine the phase shift of each element. Second, the IEEE802.15.3c codebook constructed with $\pi/2$ phase resolution without changing in amplitude. Third, codebooks support different antenna configurations and available for multi-antenna elements. Fourth, the columns in the codebook are orthogonal. Therefore multiple beams can be generated simultaneously with minimum interference [3], [10].

2.2 IEEE802.15.3c codebook design

Let's consider a linear array antenna with uniform spacing of half wavelength, the system with M antenna elements and K is the required number ofbeam patterns generated by the codebook, then when $K \geq M$, each element of the codebook matrix is given by:

$$w(m,k) = j^{\,fix\left(\frac{m\times \mathrm{mod}(k+(k/2),K)}{K/4}\right)} \quad (1)$$

where $m = 0,1,\ldots,M-1$, $k = 0,1,\ldots,K-1$, also the same definition for all codebooks.

The function *fix(x)* returns the biggest integer, which is smaller or equal to its value, this codebook is called IEEE 802.15.3c codebook with four discrete phases [10]. From (1) we can express N-phase's codebook as follow:

$$w(m,k) = e^{j\frac{2\pi}{N} fix\left(m\times \mathrm{mod}\left(k+(K/2),\, K\right)\right)} \quad (2)$$

where N indicates the number of discrete phases.

2.3 Uniform weighting based codebook

Uniform weighting is a simple window weighting function scheme; the weights are selected to generate beam patterns in a given directions according to the direction of main response axis.When the main response axis (MRA) in the direction of θ_k, where θ_k is the direction ofthe k^{th} beam, if the normal-line is 1-D array antenna, and the uniform antenna element spacing is $d\,(d = \lambda/2)$, then the codebook weighting vector elements is given by:

$$w(m,k) = e^{jm\pi d.\sin(\theta_k)} \quad (3)$$

2.4 Proposed codebook

The 2-bit discrete resolution codebook, for M antenna elements of theuniform phasearray, is similar as described in (1), this codebook matrix each column is corresponding to the phase rotation of antenna elements. The 2-bit resolution codebook in (1) generates patterns with different gain along the main axis because 2-bit resolution limits the phase quantization, it is clear that the beam patterns generated by (1) as mentioned in[10] have anunequal gain. We propose a different codebook weighting element construction, compared with other reviewed codebooks, the main difference is the phase state, which follows $\varphi = 2^n$, where n is integer positive number. The expression of the entire codebook weighting elements is given as:

$$w(m,k) = j^{\left(\frac{(m-1)(k-1)-K/2}{\varphi/4}\right)} . \tag{4}$$

The $n-bit$ codebook as expressed in (4) is reasonable to improve the phase resolution and achieves equal gain along the main response axis.

The codebooks in (1), (3), and (4) consider as auniform spacing linear array antenna. Therefore 1-D AF can be written as (5):

$$AF_k(\theta) = \sum_{m=0}^{M-1} w(m,k) e^{j\frac{2\pi md}{\lambda}\cos(\theta)} . \tag{5}$$

The transmitter weight vector can bewritten as $\mathrm{w}_k = [w_0\ w_1\ ...w_{M-1}]^{\mathrm{T}}$, where θ is thepolar angle of the direction of arrival (DOA), d is the spacing between elements; λ, K, and M are signal wavelength, required beam patterns and a number of antenna elements respectively [4].Similarly, we can obtain 2-D AF and codebook weight vector from corresponding 1-D AF and codebook in a given direction. Assume, we have$M$ number of antenna elements are located in an$x$-y plane. Then the polar angle in the x-direction is θ, the azimuth angle in the z-direction is ϕ. Similarly, d_x and d_y are the spacing between elements. Moreover, M_x and M_y represent the number of antenna elements in agiven directions.

Therefore,the2-DAF resulting in AF in x-direction multiplied by AF in the$y$-direction as: $AF(\theta,\phi) = AF_x(\theta,\phi) * AF_y(\theta,\phi)$, by using the summation we will have [11]:

$$AF(\theta,\phi) = \sum_{m_1}^{M_x-1}\sum_{m_2}^{M_y-1} w_{m_1,m_2} e^{j2\pi\left[\frac{m_1 d_x}{\lambda}\cos\theta\sin\phi + \frac{m_2 d_y}{\lambda}\sin\theta\sin\phi\right]} . \tag{6}$$

2.5 Circular antenna codebook design

Suppose the circular array antenna consists of two layers, the outer circle with radius $r_1(r_1 = M\lambda/16)$, where M is the number of antenna elements in multiple of 8,the inner circle radius is $r_2(r_2 = \lambda/2)$, for more information about inner and outer layers referredin [1]. In this study, we focus on the outer circle to design codebook of circular array antenna which is used mainly to produce the beam patterns, the weight vector for this codebook as follows:

$$w(m,k) = e^{-j2\pi\frac{r_1}{\lambda}\cos\left(\frac{2\pi\times\mathrm{mod}((m-k),M)}{M}\right)} . \tag{7}$$

1-D Antenna array response of circular codebook is given by:

$$AF_k(\theta) = \sum_{m=0}^{M-1} w(m,k) e^{j2\pi\frac{r}{\lambda}\cos\left(\theta-\frac{2\pi m}{M}\right)} . \tag{8}$$

Similarly, 2-D array response expression as follow:

$$AF_k(\theta,\phi)=\sum_{m=0}^{M-1} w(m,k)e^{j2\pi\frac{r}{\lambda}\left[\sin\theta\cos(\phi-\phi_m)-\sin\theta_0\cos(\phi_0-\phi_m)\right]} . \quad (9)$$

We can rewrite(9) as:

$$AF_k(\theta)=\sum_{m=0}^{M-1} w(m,k)e^{j\left[2\pi\frac{r}{\lambda}\sin\theta\cos(\phi_0-\phi_m)+\alpha_m\right]} . \quad (10)$$

The maximum AF occurs when all phases equal to unity or $2\pi\lambda^{-1}r\sin\theta.\cos(\phi-\phi_m)+\alpha_m=2\pi i$ where $i=0,\pm1,\pm2$; $\forall m$; the principal of maximum pattern direction when $i=0$ *is* defined by (θ_0,ϕ_0), where $\alpha_m=-2\pi\frac{r}{\lambda}\sin\theta\cos(\phi-\phi_m)$, $\phi_m=\frac{2\pi m}{M}$.

2.6 SNR expression

At the beginning of transmission, the RF signal **s** weighted at DEV1 by applying weighting vector $\mathrm{w}=\left[w_1\ w_2\ \ldots\ w_{N_t}\right]^{\mathrm{T}}$ at the transmitter side. Then the $N_t\times1$ signal vector will be produced and transmitted. The transmitted signal will be received by DEV2, by applying receiver weight vector $\mathrm{c}=\left[c_1\ c_2\ \ldots\ c_{N_r}\right]^{\mathrm{T}}$, which is predefined code vector at the receiver side, the combined received signal and noise in [13] as:

$$\mathbf{r}=\mathrm{c}^{\mathrm{H}}\mathbf{H}\,\mathrm{w}\,\mathbf{s}+\mathrm{c}^{\mathrm{H}}\mathbf{n} . \quad (11)$$

where c^{H} is conjugate transpose matrix of DEV2codebook vector c, $\mathbf{H}$ is $N_t\times N_r$ channel matrix which constructed as in [14], $\mathbf{s}$ is $N_t\times1$ transmitted signal and $\mathbf{n}$ is $N_r\times1$ additive white Gaussian noise with variance σ. The normalizedtotal power of all transmit antennas is:

$$\mathrm{E}\left[|\mathbf{s}|^2\right]=\frac{1}{N_t} . \quad (12)$$

The weight vector follows the relation: $\mathrm{w}^{\mathrm{H}}\mathrm{w}=N_t$ and $\mathrm{c}^{\mathrm{H}}\mathrm{c}=N_r$, from (11), the output SNR can be derived as:

$$\gamma=\mathrm{E}\left[\left|\mathrm{c}^{\mathrm{H}}\mathbf{H}\mathrm{w}\mathbf{s}\right|^2\right]\Big/\mathrm{E}\left[\left|\mathrm{c}^{\mathrm{H}}\mathbf{n}\right|^2\right] . \quad (13)$$

Consequently, from (12) the expression in (13) can be rewritten as:

$$\begin{aligned}\gamma&=\mathrm{E}\left[\left|\mathrm{c}^{\mathrm{H}}\mathbf{H}\mathrm{w}\right|^2\right]*\mathrm{E}\left[|\mathbf{s}|^2\right]\Big/N_r\sigma^2\\&=\left|\mathrm{c}^{\mathrm{H}}\mathbf{H}\mathrm{w}\right|^2\Big/N_tN_r\sigma^2\end{aligned} . \quad (14)$$

Expression (14) explains the received SNR.

3 Results and discussion

In this section, we evaluate the performance of the proposed codebook with the reference codebooks through simulation.

3.1 SNR Evaluation

We obtainthe results by assuming the number of beams $K = 64$, and we calculate the SNR at different noise variances. In Figure 2(a), we suppose the noise variance $\sigma = 0.5$, the proposed codebook achieves a higher dynamic range of SNR than the conventional codebooks, almost 30dB. Although, in some codebook indices the proposed codebook gets the highest SNR among the rest of the codebooks. The main reason behind these variations is due to the geometric arrangement of the weight elements, which mainly depend on the steering weighting function of each codebook.

By taking $\sigma = 1$, as shown in Figure 2(b), the comparison trends look the same as $\sigma = 0.5$. However, the effect of noise dramatically degrades the absolute value of SNR for all codebooks by about 15dB. Itis verified in equation (14), in which more noise is gained by the factor number of receiver antenna elements. The results show that the proposed codebook has a higher peak and dynamic range than the reference codebooks.In Figures 3 and 4, we obtain the CDF and PDF of SNR respectively. From Figure 3, the SNR distribution of the uniform codebook is very narrow compared with the other three codebooks because this codebook has a small dynamic range. On the other hand, the probability of CDF of the proposed codebook has a higher value than other codebooks with higher dynamic range. From Figure4, the proposed codebook and the IEEE802.3c have wide SNR and comparable PDF values, unlike the uniform and circular codebooks which have narrow SNR values.

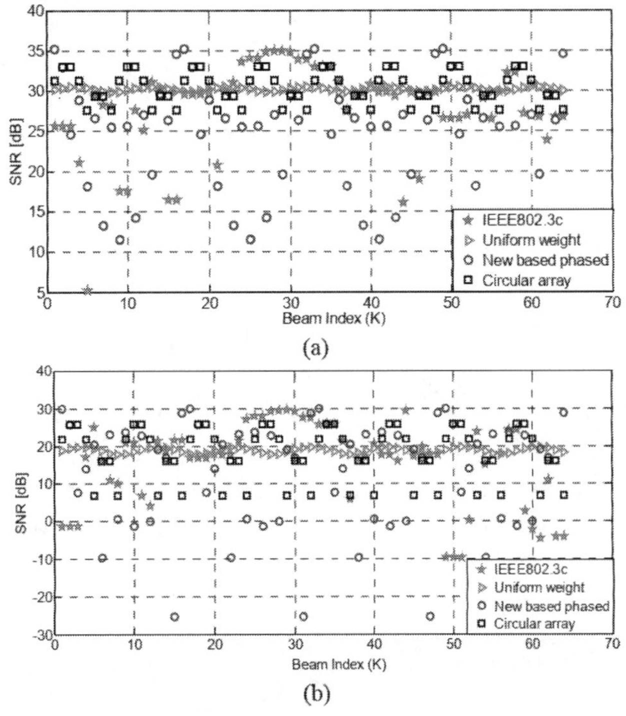

Fig. 2. SNR versus beam index: (a) $\sigma = 0.5$; (b) $\sigma = 1$

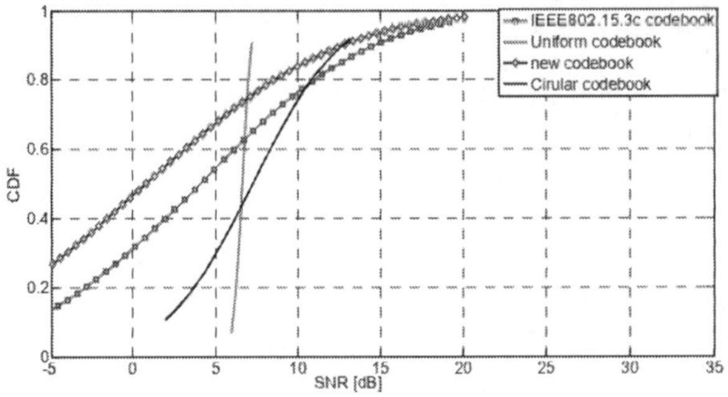

Fig.3. CDF for SNR of codebooks with respect to $\sigma = 0.5$

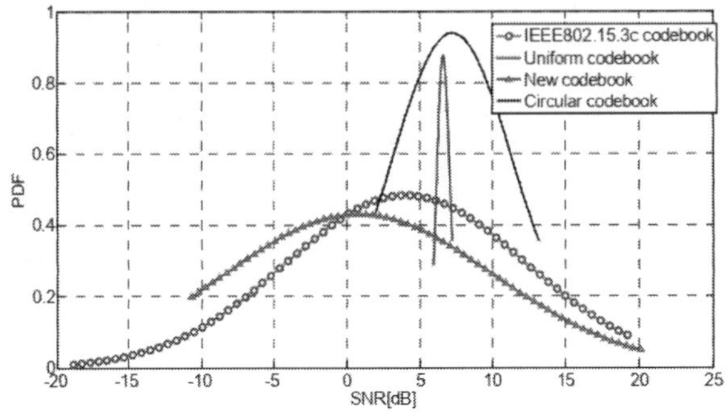

(b)

Fig. 4. PDF for SNR of codebooks: with respect to $\sigma = 1$

3.2 Array factor evaluation

In this paper, we compute AF as a function of 2-D angles to get the 3-D plot as shown in Figures5, 6, 7, and 8. Elevation and azimuth angles are considered for linear array antenna in the range $[0,\pi]$, and for circular array antenna in the range $[-\pi,\pi]$. By increasing with selected step angle α, i.e. $[\theta+\alpha,\phi+\alpha]$, the proposed and the IEEE802.15.3c codebooks have maximum responses from $(0,\pi/4)$ to $(5\pi/6,\pi)$ as shown in Figure5 and Figure 6. However, IEEE802.15.3c has more peak sidelobes than the proposed codebook. In Figure7 the uniform codebook has maximum AF at $(\pi/2,\pi/2)$ with small side lobes at $(\pi/2,\pi/4)$ and $(\pi/2,3\pi/2)$. From Figure8, the circular codebook has maximum values at $(\pi,-\pi/2)$ and $(-\pi,\pi)$ with small minor side lobes. Thus, in terms of coverage, the circular codebook is desirable. On the other hand, regarding theratio of peak to minor side lobes, the proposed codebook is the choice. However, the ratio of peak-to-side lobes gives more emphasis than the coverage in mmW communication. Hence, the proposed codebook is preferably better than others.

https://doi.org/10.1051/itmconf/20181703011

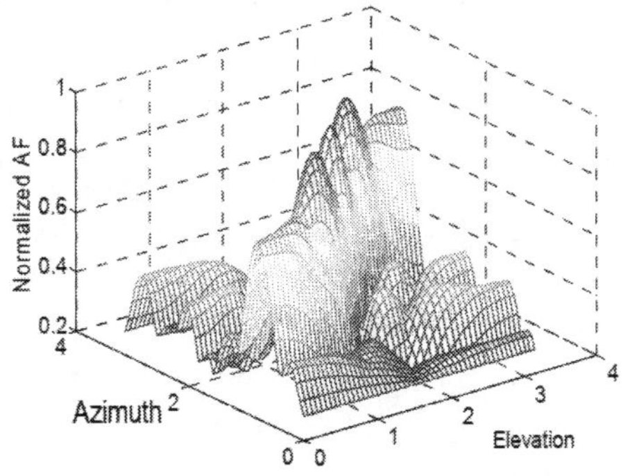

Fig. 5.3-D Array Factor for IEEE802.3c codebook

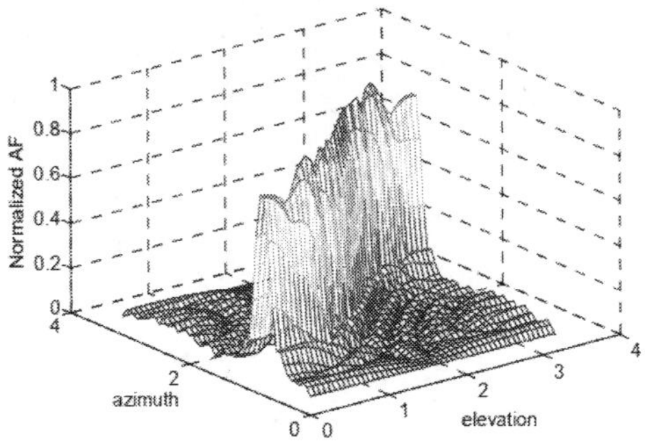

Fig. 6.3-D Array Factor for the proposed codebook

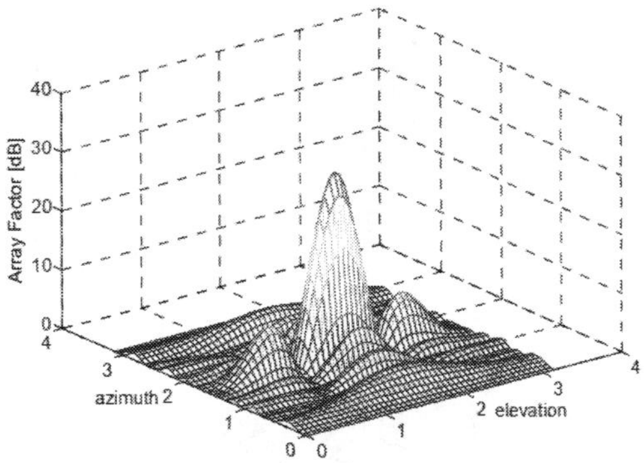

Fig. 7.3-D Array Factor for the Uniform weight codebook

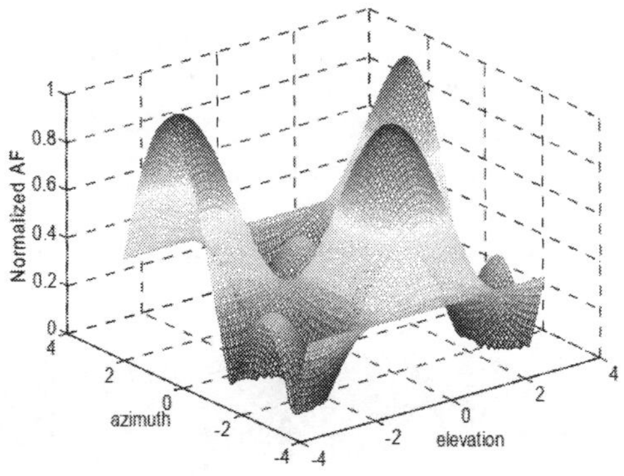

(d)

Fig. 8.3-D Array Factor for Circular array codebook

3.3 Effect of the number of antenna elements

The number of antenna elements hasan excellent contribution on the designed beams as shown in Figures9, 10, 11, and 12. The beam width of each generated and the beam-gain fully depends on the number of antenna elements, as illustrated in Figure9 the number of antenna elements (M) equal to 32 and the number of beams (K) equal to 16. The beams interferewith each other, and the beam width is wide relatively. Consequently, Figure10 $M = 100$ and $K = 16$ with a narrow beam and reduces the beams interfere. Refer to the results in Figure11 and Figure12. Meanwhile, by increasing the number of antenna elements, we can cover the area of all direction (Omni-direction) without beams interference.

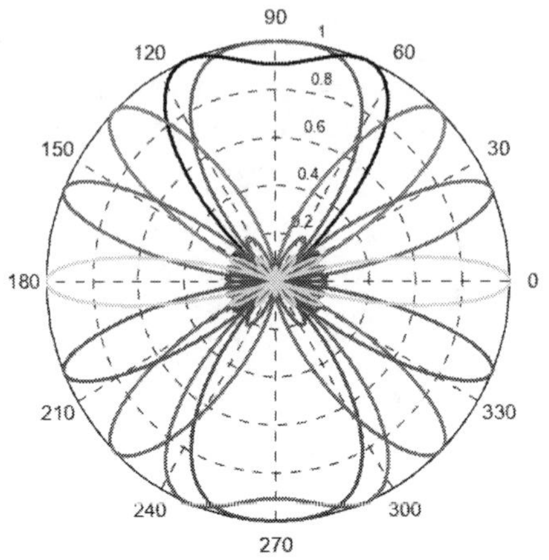

Fig. 9. Effects of the number of antenna elements on the generated beams when $M = 32$ and $K = 16$

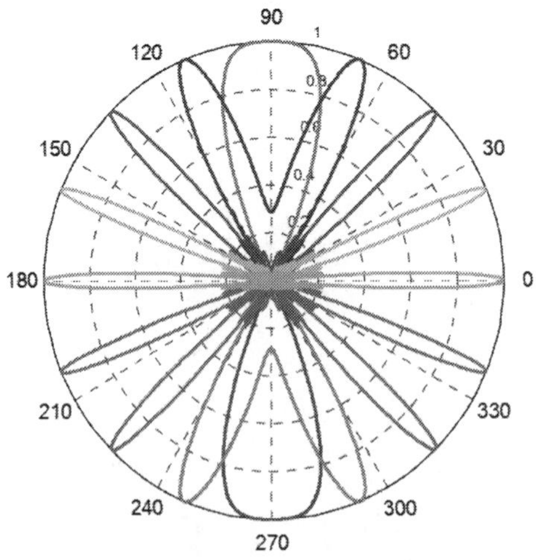

Fig. 10. Effects of the number of antenna elements on the generated beams when $M = 100$ and $K = 16$

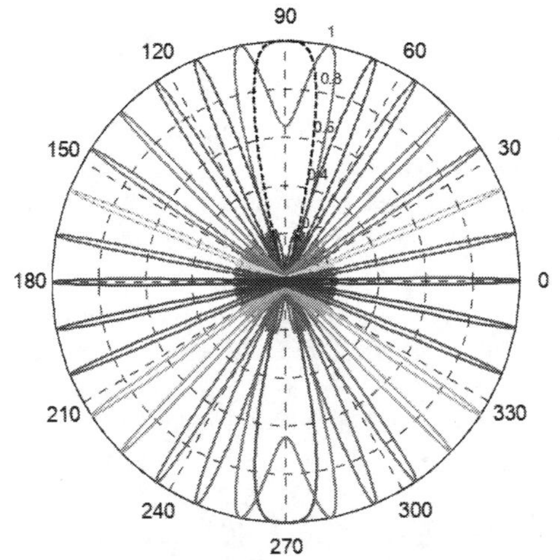

Fig. 11. Effects of the number of antenna elements on the generated beams when $M = 256$ and $K = 32$

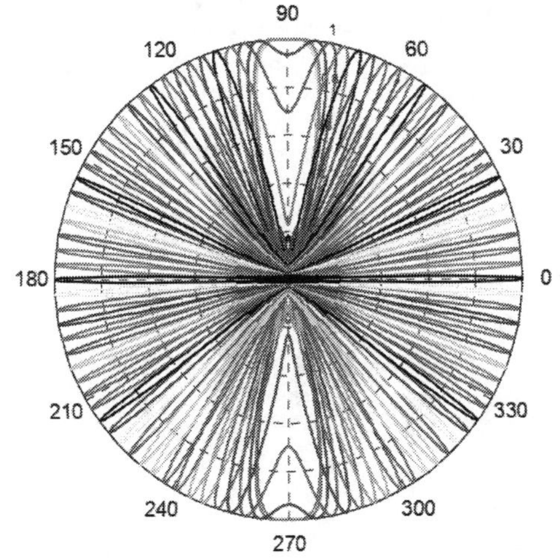

(d)

Fig. 12. Effects of the number of antenna elements on the generated beams when $M = 256$ and $K = 100$

4 Conclusion

In this paper, a new codebook is proposed and compared with the IEEE 802.15.3c, uniform weighting, and circular array antenna codebooks. The results show that the proposed codebook achieves better SNR, array directivity as well as small side lobes, compared with the IEEE 802.15.3c, but higher peak and wider dynamic range of SNR and better array directivity compared with the uniform weighting and circular antenna codebooks. Generally, the proposed codebook has much smaller side lobes and wide main response angle regarding the conventional codebooks. Thus, the proposed codebook is expected to improve signal quality and increase user throughput significantly.

Acknowledgment: This work was supported by National Key Laboratory of Electromagnetic Environment, China Research Institute of Radiowave Propagation under grant No. 201600012

References

1. Feng, W., Xiao, Z., Jin, D., Zeng, L.: Circular-antenna-array-based codebook design and training method for 60GHz beamforming. IEEE Wirel. Commun. Netw. Conf. WCNC, pp. 4140--4145 (2013).
2. Wang, J.: Beam codebook based beamforming protocol for multi-Gbps millimeter-wave WPAN systems. IEEE J. Sel. Areas Commun, vol. 27, no. 8, pp. 1390--1399 (2009)
3. Xiao, Z., He, T., Xia, P., Xia, X.: Hierarchical Codebook Design for Beamforming Training in Millimeter-Wave Communication. IEEE Trans. Wireless Commun, vol. 15, no. 5, pp. 3380--3392 (2016)
4. Kutty, S.,Sen, D.: An improved numerical optimization method for efficient beam search in 60 GHz indoor millimeter wave wireless networks. Int. Symp. Adv. Networks Telecommun. Syst. ANTS, vol. 2016–Febru, pp. 1--6 (2016)
5. Lee, H., Ko, Y.: Low Complexity Codebook-Based Beamforming for MIMO-OFDM Systems in Millimeter-Wave WPAN. IEEE Trans. Wireless Commun, vol. 10, no. 11, pp. 3607--3612 (2011)
6. Zou, W., Wang, L., Guo, C.: 3D-beamforming codebook design based on directly search for millimeter-wave communications. Proc. - IEEE INFOCOM, vol. 2016–Septe, pp. 1003--1008 (2016)
7. Hosoya, K., Prasad, N., Ramachandran, K., Orihashi, N., Kishimoto, S., Rangarajan, S., Maruhashi, K.: Multiple sector ID capture (MIDC): A novel beamforming technique for 60-GHz band multi-Gbps WLAN/PAN systems. IEEE Trans. Antennas Propag., vol. 63, no. 1, pp. 81--86 (2015)
8. Harry, L., Trees, V.: Optimum Array Processing. Part IV of Detection, Estimation, and Modulation Theory, (2002)
9. Weixia, Z., Chao, G., Guanglong, D., Zhenyu, W., Ying, G.: A new codebook design scheme for fast beam searching in millimeter-wave communications. vol. 11, no. 6, pp. 12--22 (2014)
10. Zou, W., Cui, Z., Li, B., Zhou, Z., Hu, Y.: Beamforming codebook design and performance evaluation for 60GHz wireless communication," 11th Int. Symp. Commun. Inf. Technol. Isc. 2011, no. Iscit, pp. 30--35 (2011)
11. Wang, J., Lan, Z., Sum, C., Pyo, C., Gao, J., Baykas, T., Rahman, A., Funada, R., Kojima, F., Lakkis, I., Harada, H., Kato, S.: Beamforming codebook design and performance evaluation for 60GHz wideband WPANs. IEEE Veh. Technol. Conf, pp. 0--5 (2009)
12. Zou, W., Du, G., Li, B., Zhou, Z.: A unified codebook for fast beam searching in millimeter-wave communications. 2012 Int. Conf. Comput. Probl. ICCP 2012, no. 61171104, pp. 218--223 (2012)
13. Zhang, H., Wu, C., Cui, X., Gulliver, T., A., Zhang, H.: Low complexity codebook-based beam switching for 60 GHz anti-blockage communication. J. Commun., vol. 8, no. 7, pp. 428--439 (2013)
14. He, T., Xiao, Z.: Suboptimal Beam Search Algorithm and Codebook Design for Millimeter-Wave Communications. Mob. Networks Appl., vol. 20, no. 1, pp. 86--97, (2015)

Research on single carrier frequency domain equalization system based on FQPSK modulation

Meng Zhang[1,*] and *Zhisong* Bie[1,a]

[1]Beijing University of Posts and Telecommunications, Xitucheng Road 10#, Haidian District, Beijing, P.R.China.

[2] zhisongbie@bupt.edu.cn

Abstract. Feher-patented quadrature phase shift keying (fqpsk) modulation is proposed for single-carrier frequency domain equalization (sc-fde). this paper puts forward a new method modulation called cc-bcd-fqpsk. the fqpsk signal is oversampled to make that the discrete fourier transform (dft)/ inverse dft (idft) processing of it can be applied for sc-fde. the methodology for maintaining waveform continuity with a cyclic prefix (cp) is presented. wrap-around viterbi algorithm (wava) is suggested for demodulation after equalization at the receiver. simulation results show that sc-fde system based on cc-bcd-fqpsk modulation has higher spectral efficiency than linear modulation qpsk and is an effective approach for eliminating isi and using nonlinear high power amplifier.

1 Introduction

In recent years, high-speed data communication system such as aircraft-to-earth communications have been developing continuously, and the transmission of high-speed data has become the focus of research. The wireless channel environment changes at any time and is very complex, and multipath fading through wireless channel leads to frequency selective fading and inter symbol interference (ISI). As a kind of equalization technology to effectively eliminate ISI, single carrier frequency domain equalization (SC-FDE) has lower peak to average ratio (PAPR) and sensitivity to frequency offset, which makes it more popular than orthogonal frequency division multiplexing (OFDM) in the case of using high power nonlinear power amplifier.

At present, some linear modulation schemes have been applied to SC-FDE, but one of the obvious drawbacks of linear modulation is that the envelope jitter of the signal is very serious and very sensitive to nonlinear distortion, which leads to high requirement for power amplifier. The aircraft-to-earth communication system often requires high power efficiency, so efficient nonlinear modulation is considered to solve this drawback.

FQPSK was first proposed by Kato and Feher in 1983 and belongs to IJF-OQPSK [3, 4]. FQPSK signal has quasi constant envelope characteristics, which is insensitive to nonlinear

[*] Corresponding author: zhangmeng4113@163.com

distortion and can be used in nonlinear power amplifiers without considering the power back-off problem to achieve high power efficiency. At the same time, the FQPSK signal is continuous without mutation, which makes the FQPSK signal spectrum more compact, less high frequency components, and higher frequency band utilization. Due to its excellent spectral efficiency, power efficiency and low bit error rate, FQPSK has received extensive attention in the field of deep space communications and space telemetry.

Therefore, this paper studies the SC-FDE system based on FQPSK modulation, so that the high-speed data communication system such as aircraft-to-earth communications can not only achieve low complexity against ISI in the frequency domain, but also can play the spectrum advantages of FQPSK to attain higher power efficiency. But there are two issues need to be considered. Firstly, FQPSK signal is changing continuously, so discrete Fourier transform (DFT)/ inverse DFT (IDFT) cannot be directly applied to the received samples. Secondly, FQPSK signal needs to be added a cyclic prefix, because it cannot be directly used for SC-FDE as a non-linear modulation. When the cyclic prefix is added, the phase continuity of the signal needs to be maintained. Hence, this paper discusses how to add a cyclic prefix for applying FQPSK modulation to SC-FDE system.

The remainder of this paper is as follow. Section 2 reviews FQPSK modulation and introduces a new CC-BCD-FQPSK modulation. Section 3 constructs the SC-FDE system based on CC-BCD-FQPSK modulation. Section 4 gives the performance simulation results over the spatial channel model (SCM) channel.

2 CC-BCD-FQPSK modulation

A block diagram of FQPSK modulator is shown as follow Figure 1, where a cross-correlator unit is added after the IJF encoder unit, which reduces the 3-dB envelop fluctuation of IJF-FQPSK nearly to 0-dB to make the signal appears constant envelope.

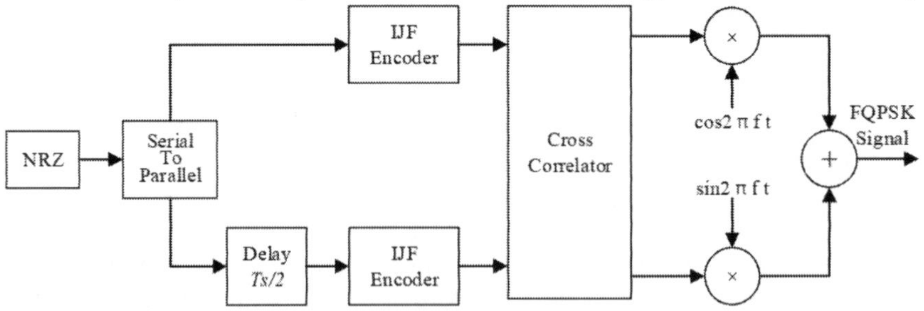

Fig. 1. The diagram of FQPSK modulation

Simon, M.K. and Yan, T.Y. proposed a symbol-by-symbol cross-correlator mapping method for FQPSK and implemented it with trellis code [3]. Define 16 basic waveforms, $s_i(t);\ -T_s/2 \le t \le T_s/2;\ i = 0,1,2,\cdots,15$ as Eq. (1), which together form the transmitted signal set of the I and Q path.

$$
\begin{aligned}
&s_0(t) = A,\quad -\frac{T_s}{2} \le t \le \frac{T_s}{2}, && s_8(t) = -s_0(t)\\
&s_1(t) = \begin{cases} A, & -\frac{T_s}{2} \le t \le 0 \\ 1-(1-A)\cos^2\frac{\pi t}{T_s}, & 0 \le t \le \frac{T_s}{2} \end{cases} && s_9(t) = -s_1(t)\\
&s_2(t) = \begin{cases} 1-(1-A)\cos^2\frac{\pi t}{T_s}, & -\frac{T_s}{2} \le t \le 0 \\ A, & 0 \le t \le \frac{T_s}{2} \end{cases} && s_{10}(t) = -s_2(t)\\
&s_3(t) = 1-(1-A)\cos^2\frac{\pi t}{T_s},\quad -\frac{T_s}{2} \le t \le \frac{T_s}{2} && s_{11}(t) = -s_3(t)\\
&s_4(t) = A\sin\frac{\pi t}{T_s},\quad -\frac{T_s}{2} \le t \le \frac{T_s}{2} && s_{12}(t) = -s_4(t)\\
&s_5(t) = \begin{cases} \sin\frac{\pi t}{T_s} + (1-A)\sin^2\frac{\pi t}{T_s}, & -\frac{T_s}{2} \le t \le 0 \\ \sin\frac{\pi t}{T_s}, & 0 \le t \le \frac{T_s}{2} \end{cases} && s_{13}(t) = -s_5(t)\\
&s_6(t) = \begin{cases} \sin\frac{\pi t}{T_s}, & -\frac{T_s}{2} \le t \le 0 \\ \sin\frac{\pi t}{T_s} - (1-A)\sin^2\frac{\pi t}{T_s}, & 0 \le t \le \frac{T_s}{2} \end{cases} && s_{14}(t) = -s_6(t)\\
&s_7(t) = \sin\frac{\pi t}{T_s},\quad -\frac{T_s}{2} \le t \le \frac{T_s}{2} && s_{15}(t) = -s_7(t)
\end{aligned} \tag{1}
$$

All 16 waveforms have continuous slope throughout the defining intervals, and have zero slope at the end points, so that the FQPSK signal has no slope discontinuity anywhere regardless of the value of A. The waveforms are shown in Figure 2, and the envelope fluctuation of the FQPSK signal is 0dB in the case $A = 1/\sqrt{2}$.

Define d_{In} , d_{Qn} as I, Q path data symbols respectively in the interval $[(n-[1/2])T_s, (n+[1/2])T_s]$. And the corresponding mapping symbols D_{In} , D_{Qn} , which both range over the set (0,1), are defined as follow Eq. (2).

$$
\left.\begin{aligned} D_{In} &\triangleq \frac{1-d_{In}}{2} \\ D_{Qn} &\triangleq \frac{1-d_{Qn}}{2} \end{aligned}\right\} \tag{2}
$$

Then, define the binary-coded decimal (BCD) representation of the indices i , j by

$$
\left.\begin{aligned} i &= I_3 \times 2^3 + I_2 \times 2^2 + I_1 \times 2^1 + I_0 \times 2^0 \\ j &= Q_3 \times 2^3 + Q_2 \times 2^2 + Q_1 \times 2^1 + Q_0 \times 2^0 \end{aligned}\right\} \tag{3}
$$

with

$$\left.\begin{aligned} I_0 &= D_{Qn} \oplus D_{Q,n-1}, & Q_0 &= D_{I,n+1} \oplus D_{In} \\ I_1 &= D_{Q,n-1} \oplus D_{Q,n-2}, & Q_1 &= D_{In} \oplus D_{I,n-1} = I_2 \\ I_2 &= D_{In} \oplus D_{I,n-1}, & Q_2 &= D_{Qn} \oplus D_{Q,n-1} = I_0 \\ I_3 &= D_{In}, & Q_3 &= D_{Qn} \end{aligned}\right\} \tag{4}$$

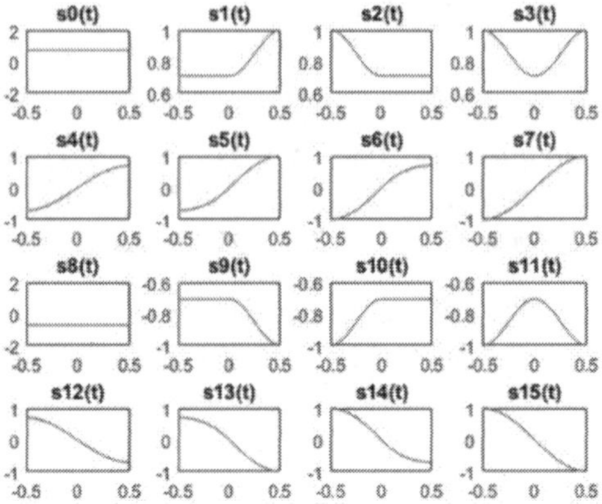

Fig. 2. 16 basic waveforms ($T_s = 1$, $A = 1/\sqrt{2}$)

The implementation of FQPSK modulation via convolutional code cascaded with binary-coded decimal (CC-BCD) is shown as Figure 3, which can be recognized as a two-parallel-level convolutional encoder cascaded with a BCD mapping unit. The convolutional encoder (6, 2, [3 3]) has two parallel levels with 2 inputs D_{In}, D_{Qn} and 6 outputs I_3, $I_2 = Q_1$, Q_0, Q_3, I_1, $I_0 = Q_2$, and each level has 2 shift registers. The outputs of the convolutional encoder are mapped by the BCD mapping unit to generate i and j, which are the indices used to select waveforms from the 16 basic waveforms to form the transmitted signals of the I, Q path at the corresponding time.

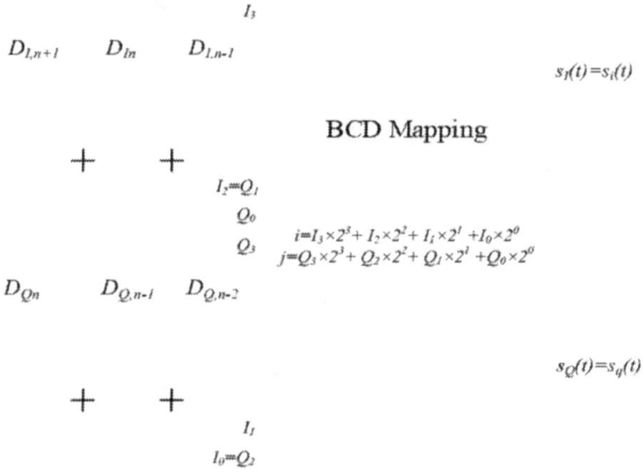

Fig. 3. The diagram of CC-BCD-FQPSK modulation

The state transitions and outputs of CC-BCD code mapping are shown as Table 1. The first row indicates current two-level registers state ($D_{Q,n-1}\ D_{Q,n-2}\ D_{In}\ D_{I,n-1}$), the first column indicates current input ($D_{I,n+1}\ D_{Qn}$), and the results indicate next state of the convolutional encoder and indices (i , j) of I and Q paths transmitted signals outputted by BCD mapping under current state and current input.

Table 1. State transitions and outputs of CC-BCD code mapping

	0	1	2	3
0	0/(0,0)	8/(1,12)	2/(0,1)	10/(1,13)
1	0/(4,2)	8/(5,14)	2/(4,3)	10/(5,15)
2	1/(12,3)	9/(13,15)	3/(12,2)	11/(13,14)
3	1/(8,1)	9/(9,13)	3/(8,0)	11/(9,12)
4	0/(2,0)	8/(3,12)	2/(2,1)	10/(3,13)
5	0/(6,2)	8/(7,14)	2/(6,3)	10/(7,15)
6	1/(14,3)	9/(15,15)	3/(14,2)	11/(15,14)
7	1/(10,1)	9/(11,13)	3/(10,0)	11/(11,12)
8	4/(3,4)	12/(2,8)	6/(3,5)	14/(2,9)
9	4/(7,6)	12/(6,10)	6/(7,7)	14/(6,11)
10	5/(15,7)	13/(14,11)	7/(15,6)	15/(14,10)
11	5/(11,5)	13/(10,9)	7/(11,4)	15/(10,8)
12	4/(1,4)	12/(0,8)	6/(1,5)	14/(0,9)
13	4/(5,6)	12/(4,10)	6/(5,7)	14/(4,11)
14	5/(13,7)	13/(12,11)	7/(13,6)	15/(12,10)
15	5/(9,5)	13/(8,9)	7/(9,4)	15/(8,8)

3 SC-FDE system based on CC-BCD-FQPSK modulation

As mentioned in the introduction, there aretwo problems to consider when applying FQPSK signal to SC-FDE. According to section 2, the CC-BCD-FQPSK signal is composed of the 16 basic waveforms, which are all continuous in the interval $-T_s/2 \le t \le T_s/2$ without mutation point, so the transmitted signal is continuous. To ensure that the received samples can be applied with DFT/IDFTand fully recovered, the CC-BCD-FQPSK signal needs to be oversampledat the transmitter, so that the discrete CC-BCD-FQPSK signal can be applied for SC-FDE.

Therefore, the SC-FDE system model based on CC-BCD-FQPSK modulation is built and illustrated as Figure 4, which involves cyclic prefix design, frequency domain equalization, and demodulation and so on. The binary source inputs are modulated by CC-BCD-FQPSK modulation after adding cyclic prefix, then sent to channel. At the receiver, after the received signal is synchronized, cyclic prefix is removed, block DFT is carried out, and equalization is carried out in the frequency domain, the signal is converted back to the time domain for demodulation to recover the received binary symbols.

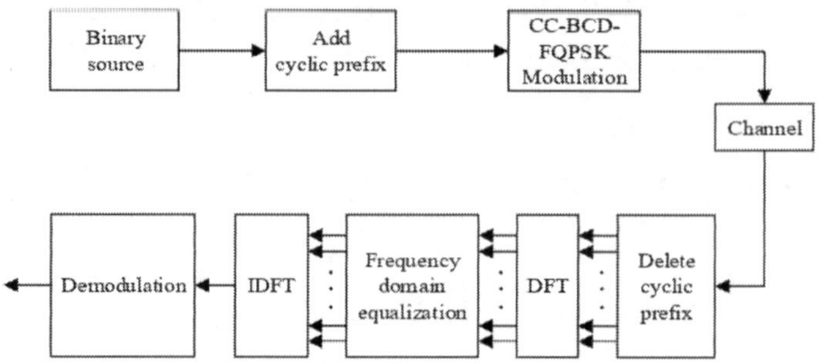

Fig.4. The basic structure of SC-FDE system based on CC-BCD-FQPSK modulation

3.1 Frame structure Design

For the purpose of the waveform continuity of the transmitted signal to obtain high spectral efficiency and eliminating ISI, a length-G cyclic prefixis designed to be appended to the transmitted FQPSK signal, and G equals or exceeds the maximum channel multipath delay.By removing the cyclic prefix at the receiver and detecting the signal in the frequency domain, the ISI will be removed.

Addition of the cyclic prefix is not straightforward forFQPSK signal, because waveform continuity mustalways be maintained.

Assume that FQPSK signal $s(t)$ is modulated by the binary sequence $\{x_n\}$, $n=0,1,\ldots,N-1$. Because the transmitted signal is composed of many data block, to maintain waveform continuity between two adjacent blocks when a cyclic prefix is added, it is essential that a cyclic prefix is added to the binary sequence firstly and then FQPSK modulation is implemented.This is done by simply copying l_t tail symbols $x_{N-l_t+1}, x_{N-l_t+2}, \cdots, x_N$ and appending them to the beginning of $\{x_n\}$ firstly. The newly formed symbol sequence donated as $\{\overline{x}_n\}$, is

$$\overline{x}_n = x_{(n)_N}, \quad n=-l_t,-l_t+1,\ldots,-1,0,1,\ldots,N-1 \qquad (5)$$

where $(n)_N$ is the residue of n modulo- N .The length-$(N+l_t)$ sequence $\{\overline{x}_n\}$ is applied to FQPSK modulator to form the corresponding signal $\overline{s}(t)$.

Given that the oversample multiple is p , then modulated samples length of the binary sequence $\{x_n\}$ is $M=p\times N$, and $\overline{s}(t)$ samples length is $L=p\times(N+l_t)$. Because the FQPSK modulation is a memory-modulated method andthe first 4 symbols of the $\{\overline{x}_n\}$ are affected with the previous block, actual cyclic prefix length is $G=p\times(l_t-4)$, which must equal or exceed the maximum channel multipath delay. The illustration is shown as Figure 5.Though this method of cyclic prefix design has some redundant samples, it can maintain waveform continuity of each data block.

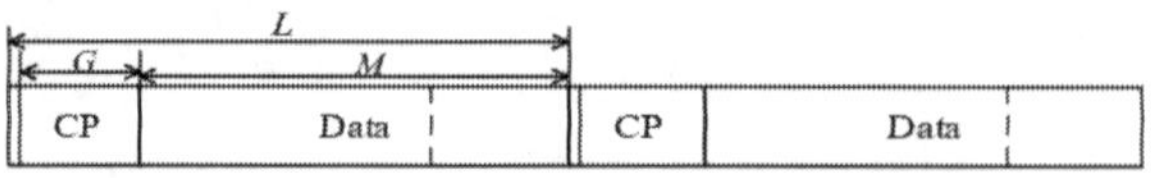

Fig. 5. Cyclic prefix design

Given that the initial state of CC-BCD-FQPSK modulation of the first data block is 0, record the final state, which is used to be the initial state of next data block, so that waveform continuity of the transmitted signal is maintained.It is worthily noted that initial state and final state of the binary source sequence $\{x_n\}$ are same, which leads thatthe convolutional coding is actually tail-biting convolutional coding (TBCC).

At the receiver, cyclic prefix is removed to eliminate ISI. After frequency domain equalization, data blocks are transferred back to time domain, Viterbi algorithm is suggested for demodulation.

3.2 Frequency Domain Equalization

Frequency domain equalization means that the equalization is done in frequency domain rather than in time domain. The basic concept is to compensate the frequency characteristics of the baseband system via the frequency characteristics of the tunable filter, so that the features of the baseband system including tunable filters can meet the requirements of no distortion transmission. As shown in Figure 4, the received signal is equalized in the frequency-domain after the DFT unit to estimate the channel parameters and make compensation of the frequency characteristics.

There are some common methods of frequency domain equalization, such as zero-forcing (ZF) equalization, minimum mean square error (MMSE) equalization and least squares (LS) equalization [6]. In this paper, MMSE equalization is applied to compensate the frequency characteristic, which can greatly reduce computation complexity compared to time domain equalization for channels having long impulse response.

3.3 Demodulation

The equalized signal is transferred back into the time domain by using IDFT to be demodulated. As described in section 3.1, the transmitted data blocks are actually modulated by TBCC. Frequency domain equalization and DFT/IDFT don't change the character of initial state same with final state of data block, so demodulating algorithms for TBCC can be used, which are mostly based on Viterbi Algorithm (VA) [7].

In this paper, wrap-around Viterbi algorithm (WAVA) is used to demodulate the received samples to recover the binary symbols, which is one of the circular Viterbi Algorithm (CVA) and uses the loopback characteristics of the convolutional code to repeat the received data blocks several times to form a long sequence for Viterbi decoding until the stop condition is satisfied.

4 Simulation results

As illustrated as figure 6, compared to linear modulation QPSK, the spectrum of FQPSK modulation is more compact and has less high frequency components and higher frequency band utilization.

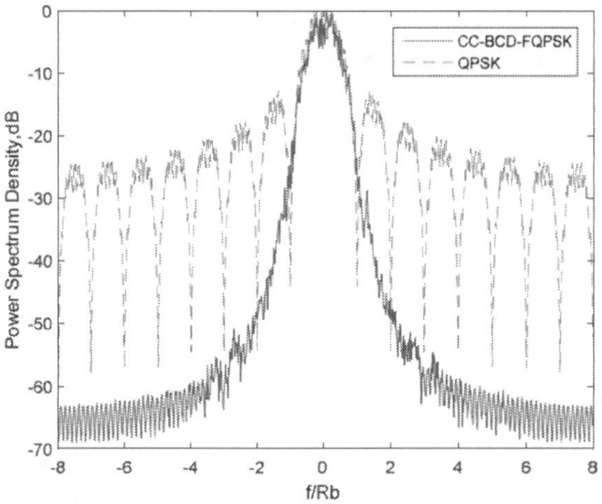

Fig.6. The power spectrum destiny of CC-BCD-FQPSK modulation and QPSK modulation

According to the structure of SC-FDE system based on CC-BCD-FQPSK modulation, simulation platform is built. Spatial channel model (SCM) is set as channel model. Binary data block length of I, Q paths is $N = 1024$, tail symbols length is $l_t = 80$, oversample multiple is $p = 16$, so the actual cyclic prefix length is $G = (80-2)*16 = 1248$. The modulated signals get through SCM channel and be recovered to binary symbols at the receiver. The bit error ratio (BER) performance is shown as Figure 7.

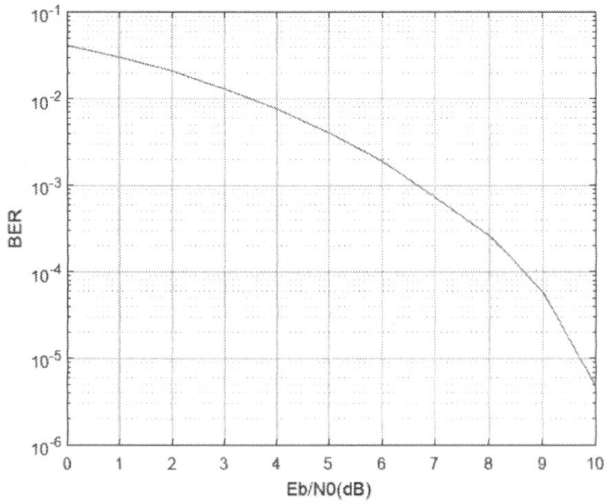

Fig. 7. BER performance of SC-FDE system based on CC-BCD-FQPSK modulation.

5 Conclusions

This paper considers applying FQPSK modulation for SC-FDE system. Firstly, this paper puts forward a new modulation method called CC-BCD-FQPSK modulation. To apply a DFT/IDFT on FQPSK signal, oversampling is used to generate a discrete representation for the FQPSK signal. Secondly, to maintain the waveform continuity of FQPSK signal, cyclic prefix is designed. Adding cyclic prefix first and then implementing FQPSK modulation is necessary for waveform continuity, which is different from implementing modulation first and then adding cyclic prefix of conventional SC-FDE. The simulation results demonstrate that on the basic of providing good BER performance, SC-FDE system based on CC-BCD-FQPSK modulation attains excellent spectrum efficiency for multipath channel.

However, the work of this paper still has lots of deficiencies and defects, remaining to be further improved and perfected.

References

1. Feher, K. 1982. Filter: U.S. Patent 4339,724.
2. Kato, S. and Feher, K. 1986. Correlated signal processor: U.S. Patent 4567,602.
3. Leung, P. S. K. and Feher, K.1993.F-QPSK - A Superior Modulation Technique for Mobile and Personal Communications. IEEE Transactions on Broadcasting, 39(2): 288-294.
4. Kato, S. and Feher, K. 1983. XPSK: A New Cross-Correlated Phase-Shift Keying Modulation Technique. IEEE Transactions on Communications, 31: 701-707.
5. Mehdi, H. and Feher, K. 1994. FQPSK, power and spectral efficient family of modulations for wireless communication systems. Vehicular Technology Conference, 1994 IEEE 44th. IEEE: 1562-1566.
6. Simon, M. K. and Yan, T. Y. 1999. Performance Evaluation and Interpretation of Unfiltered Feher-Patented Quadrature Phase-Shift Keying (FQPSK). TMO Progress Report, 42-137.
7. Tan, J. and Stuber, G.L.2005. Frequency-domain equalization for continuous phase modulation. IEEE Transactions on Wireless Communications, 4(5): 2479-2490.
8. Nakao, M., Ishihara, T. and Sugiura, S. 2017. Single-Carrier Frequency-Domain Equalization with Index Modulation. IEEE Communication Letters, 21(2):298-301.
9. Pancaldi, F. and Vitetta, G. M. 2006. Equalization Algorithms in the Frequency Domain for Continuous Phase Modulations. IEEE Transactions on Communications, 54(4): 648-658.
10. Van, T. W., Nsenga, J., et al. 2008. Applying Frequency Domain Equalization to Precoded CPM. IEEE International Conference onAcoustics, Speech and Signal Processing (ICASSP): 2901-2904.
11. Thillo, W. V., Nsenga, J., et al. 2009. Low-complexity Frequency Domain Equalization for Continuous Phase Modulation. IEEE Transactions on Wireless Communications, 8(3):1435-1445.
12. Hassan, E. S., Zhu Xu, et al. 2009. A Continuous Phase Modulation Single-carrier Wireless System with Frequency Domain Equalization. IEEE International Conference on Computer Engineering and Systems.
13. Shao, R., Lin. S., Fossorier, M. P., et al. 2003. Two Decoding Algorithms for Tail biting Codes. IEEE Transactions on Communications, 51(10): 1658-1665.
14. Pai, H.R., Han, Y.S., et al. 2008. Low-Complexity ML Decoding for Convolutional Tail-Biting Codes. IEEE Communications Letters, 12(12): 883-885.

Researches about factor market distortions on the impacting factors of international technology spillover

Xiaoyang Jia[1*], *Xiaoyu* Liu[2], *and Xiaofei* Liu[1]

[1] Shandong Foreign Trade Vocational Collage, No.201, Jufeng Road, Licang District, Qingdao, 266000

[2] Qingdao University of Technology, No.236, Fuzhou South Road, Jiaozhou City, 61785377@qq.com

Abstract. In this paper, we selected 1999-2015 Provincial Panel Data in China statistical yearbook. The effects of factor market distortions on international technology spillovers are discussed. In the factor market distorted elements of the market to promote the rapid growth of the economy in the short term, it may inhibit the international technology spillover effect, but the move is beneficial to realize the sustainability of high quality economic growth. The results showed that the technology spillover effects of the import trade, FDI and patent applications presented different feature in different stages. The article from the perspective of the development of technology breakthrough summarizes factors price distortions on the international technology spillover mechanism and study with the policy changes, elements of the market to improve dynamic changes, the factor price distortion effect of international technology spillovers stage effect.

1 Introduction

The technological progress is the power and source of a country's economic growth, but also reflects the quality of economic development. The international technology spillover is one of the most important ways of technological progress. In previous years, China in the economic development of most importance to economic growth rate, local government introduced various policies, through the elements of market pricing, distribution rights to control the distortion factor markets, in order to provide preferential government policies, attract domestic and foreign enterprises to invest and set up factories, the ultimate objective is to boost GDP. Worth noting is that China is in the process of economic restructuring, the elements of the market distortions become a widespread phenomenon (Lu, Wen-Min etc., 2006), its performance as the factor market segmentation, factor price of underestimating (Zhang Jie, 2011; Chen Yongwei, Wei Min Hu, 2011; Bing Zhan Shi, 2016). Factor market distortion in a certain extent stimulates the local government investment at the price of resources. The distorted elements modes should be given. Chinese economy development rely on distorted elements of the market price, the extensive growth mode not only cannot

[*]Corresponding author: jiaxyqd@163.com

achieve the sustainable growth of high quality material resources consumption, and may be required for international technology spillover of market of soil loss, but cannot reach a convergence technology, catch up with and surpass the developed countries (Banerjee, 2005; Guner, 2016) [1]. This paper starts from the perspective of the Chinese factor market distortions in the, considering the shortcomings of existing research into phases of ideas, examines national policy guidance before and after the transformation, the elements of the market distortion phase influence on international technology spillover effect[2]. This article mainly includes the following aspects: one is to enrich the existing literature on the theory of factor price and will distort international technology spillovers associated, and its model, clarifies the theoretical relationship between; two is the construction of capital and labor factor price distortion index, improve the existing methods which were quantified, and investigate the changes of capital, the labor factor price distortion before and after the change of national policy guidance, and stage division; three is the use of empirical test, 2SLS OLS price and GMM methods distorted different effects in different phases of international technology spillover effect, the effect of the stage characteristics significantly depends on the policy oriented transformation and factor price distortion, so this paper focuses on stage characteristics analysis. Arrangement of the structure of the rest of the paper is as follows: the second section is the theoretical model; in the third part, econometric model design, index construction and data source; the fourth part of the sample is divided into two sub intervals, capital, labor factor prices distorted effect of international technology spillovers empirical testing and result analysis; finally is the conclusion of this paper.

2 The model design, indicators and data sources

In an open economy, factor price distortion technology spillover effect on international trade, FDI and patent applications will affect. This paper chooses 1999-2015 provincial panel data. It measures the variables as follows:

2.1 Factor price distortion measure

The basic idea is to estimate the production function to calculate the marginal output elements, i.e. elements should be paid, then do the ratio of elements and the actual reward is obtained, factor price distortion index. Set the production function for the following form. In the process of estimation β_{Kit} and β_{Lit}, for the selection of the regression equation, panel data regression, sub annual, sub provinces etc [3]. Respectively. Regression, the regression shows the various regression methods measure results are basically the same, equation 1 is the overall regression the simplest method.

$$Y_{it} = \mathrm{TFP}_{it} K_{it}^{\beta_{Kit}} L_{it}^{\beta_{Lit}} \qquad \text{Eq(1)}$$

The elements of the marginal output and TFP respectively:

$$MP_{Kit} = TFP_{it} \beta_{Kit} K_{it}^{\beta_{Kit}-1} L_{it}^{\beta_{Lit}} = \beta_{Kit} Y_{it} / K_{it} \qquad \text{Eq(2)}$$

$$MP_{Lit} = TFP_{it} \beta_{Lit} K_{it}^{\beta_{Kit}} L_{it}^{\beta L_{it}-1} = \beta_{Lit} Y_{it} / \mathrm{L}_{it} \qquad \text{Eq(3)}$$

$$lnTFP_{it} = \ln Y_{it} - \beta_{Kit} \ln K_{it} - \beta_{Lit} \ln L_{it} \qquad \text{Eq(4)}$$

In the process of equation 2 and equation 3, estimation β_{Kit} and β_{Lit} , for the selection of the regression equation, panel data regression, sub annual, sub provinces etc. Regression, the regression shows the various regression methods measure results are basically the same, here is the overall regression the simplest method. In the marginal output to obtain elements MP_{Kit} , MP_{Lit} , the price of capital r_{it} , the price of labor w_{it} , the price distortion and total distortion calculation of various elements. In the equation4, individual economy workers and employees is in the same in hypothesis.

2.2 Data sources

This paper selects Chinese 1999-2015 provincial panel data analysis. Among them, the area of GDP, CPI index, the number of patent applications, labor remuneration, the price index of investment in fixed assets and total investment in fixed assets from the "China statistical yearbook". Each year the loan interest rate from the people's Bank of China. The area over the patent application authorization from the Ministry of science and technology, science and technology statistics database Chinese. Chinese technology overflow amount, to go abroad to import technology overflow abroad direct investment in China and the application amount of total authorized patents in China are derived from the "China Statistical Yearbook" and "national intellectual property rights Bureau statistics yearbook".

3 The analysis of the test results and the mechanism

3.1 Statistical analysis of factor price distortions

Do the ratio of payments due and the elements of the real reward, by factor price distortion index. If the ratio is greater than 1, that is greater than the actual income factors deserve elements, factor prices showed the reverse distortion, whereas the positive factor price distortion. Since 2007, labor factor price distortion index decreases, distortion factor improved significantly, reflecting the reform of China's price system is better to implement the elements. Is total factor twist, distortion degree decreased from 6.8 in 2006 to 2007 5.6, decline range is the biggest, twist after amplitude average value is about 5.4, which shows that the degree of marketization of our country gradually deepened, especially in 2007 as a turning point, policy oriented changes the factor market distortion levels decreased significantly, before and after the change of the more prominent.

3.2 The analysis of the test results and the mechanism

The statistical analysis of factor price distortions results showed that variables are for the same order integration variables, further co-integration test found that variables there is a long-term equilibrium relationship, so as to avoid the spurious regression. In the model, capital and labor factor twist term, factor and the overall distortion and import and export volume and foreign capital introduction and technical achievements of the interactive item may be a multicollinearity problem and influence the results of the regression significantly [4]. Therefore, the reduced polynomial or interaction effect model reduces the degree of collinearity between variables. The mechanism of inhibition of factor price distortion technology spillover effect can be summarized as resource trap effect. Want to import competing sectors through competition incentive and imitation effect and improve the variety and quality of the production of intermediate goods and capital goods, thus reversing the import of foreign domestic enterprises situation, is an extremely slow process

[5].Factor price distortions has no inhibiting effect on technology spillovers, the resource trap effect can better solve the problems. In the multi-national corporation, master advanced technology, using new knowledge, management, accounting and marketing techniques or production line organization may have a demonstration effect and human capital flow effect on the local competitors, but more foreign owned enterprises will tend to enter the effect is suppressed[6]. Obviously, this phase factor market distortion is serious, the inhibition of FDI technology spillover effect. The coefficient of labor factor variable is distorted significantly negative, and the so-called demographic dividend government and enterprises by lowering the wages of workers. Compared with the results of the first stage of the method of instrumental variables regression, capital element distortion coefficients by a significant negative variable is significantly positive, suggesting that policy oriented transformation, factor market distortions reduce, bring about significant technology spillover effects of FDI through competition incentive effect, demonstration imitation effect, way to the east country. Similarly, labor distortion coefficients by a significant negative variable is significantly positive, indicating that the change in policy, elements of the degree of marketization progress make FDI through the effect of human capital, skill talent flow effect and so on ways to promote the technology spillover.

Table 1. Factor price distortions stage test results on international trade technology spillover effect

Explain Variable	2SLS	FE	2SLS
S_{it}^{d-rdk}	-0.140 (-0.89)	-0.112 (-1.34)	0.085 (1.02)
S_{it}^{d-rdl}	0.086 (1.64)*	0.159 (0.77)	0.163 (2.01) **
$DistK_{it}$	-0.078 (-3.12) ***	0.379 (1.46) *	0.062 (2.17) **
$DistL_{it}$	-0.049 (-1.89) **	-0.154 (-1.23)	0.106 (1.64) *
lnY_{it}	1.915 (4.04) ***	2.367 (3.94) ***	2.528 (4.53) ***
$ln K_{it}$	0.149 (0.86)	0.578 (1.48) *	0.234 (1.74) *
$ln L_{it}$	0.121 (1.96) **	0.206 (2.05) **	0.171 (2.37) **
$Dist_{it} * tr_{it}$	-0.045 (-2.83) **	0.056 (2.62) **	0.084 (2.99) ***
C_{it}	7.255 (24.40) ***	6.872 (20.26) ***	6.560 (25.50) ***
R^2	0.705	0.674	0.753

Note: The numbers in parentheses in Table t Statistics symbol***, **, *respectively at the 1% level, 5% and 10% of the significant variables.

From Table 1 shows in the first stage, capital, labor factor price distortion coefficients are negative and overall factors price distortions and foreign capital to introduce the degree coefficient for the interaction term is also negative, and the coefficient through the test of significance of 5%, which indicates that the factor price distortion inhibited the technology spillover of FDI in China. Secondly, the use of factor price distortion make enterprises more inclined to rely on cheap elements to profit, and investment will tend to be more funds for investment in fixed assets, the industrial structure, curing technology spillover is blocked. Thirdly, capital, labor and other factors underestimated the price will stimulate domestic enterprises and entrepreneurs in the intensive use of tangible elements, and have less pressure and power investment in independent innovation, technology spillover is difficult to effectively undertake and internalization of multi-national corporation.

4 Conclusion

Depends on its own R&D capability and the absorption of foreign technology spillovers to improve the technology progress level of a country or region, the international technology diffusion as a technology spillover is the important channel, is an important source of technological innovation capability is weak developing countries and regions in the technological progress[7]. Theoretically speaking, in the market under the condition of complete, the mechanism can play their respective roles. But China's market-oriented reform process of marketization degree lag in the asymmetric phenomenon in the product market and factor price formation mechanism by administrative monopoly and government regulation of the distortions, mainly for distortion directly, such as land, capital and labor prices low estimate; distorts overhead, tariffs, import quotas, and exchange rate policy influence[8]. Because the market is not perfect, non optimal allocation of factors of production resources in the national economy, the factor price of opportunity cost deviation or departure. This will cause the regression results of the first three parts technology spillover model test in the first stage. And after the government's adjustment of the policy, promote to the elements of the market process, and the survival environment of the enterprise in the market regulation and factor market distortions can be solved to a great extent, the related theories of the role play, international technology spillover effect improved significantly.

At present, the world of scientific inventions and technological achievements mainly from developed countries, the global R&D investment is mainly from developed countries. In general, the developed countries are the leading country scientific invention and technological innovation, while the developing countries and regions in the country to follow and imitate technology belong to. Technology progress of developing countries and regions not only need research and innovation in China, largely reliant on foreign sources of technology. While the international technology spillover is one of the main ways of developing countries of technological progress, has a significant effect on the host countries to enhance the quality of economic development. In the original phase (1999-2007), local governments controlled the resource elements' pricing power leading to factor market distortions, thus weakening and barraging the international spillover effects. In policy orientation phase (2008-2015), government payed more attention to the quality of economic development, the degree of market distortion factors significantly reduced and the role of market mechanism played, international technology spillover got an increase gradually. This article from the perspective of the development of technology breakthrough summarizes factors price distortions on the international technology spillover mechanism and study with the policy changes, elements of the market to improve dynamic changes, the factor price distortion effect of international technology spillovers stage effect.

Acknowledgments: This work is supported by Shandong Higher School Humanities And Social Science Program Project(J17RB149) .

References

1. Banerjee, A., and Duflo, E., 2005 .Growth Theory through the Lens of Development Economics.

2. Banerjee, A., and Munshi, K., "How Efficiently is Capital Allocated? Evidence from the Knitted Garment Industry in Tirupur", Review of Economic Studies (Jan. 2004) , 19-42
3. Buera, F., Kaboski, J., and Shin, Y., "Finance and Development: A Tale of Two Sectors", American Economic Review (May 2011) , 1964-2002.
4. Coe, D. T, Helpman, E., "International R&D Spillovers", European Economic Review (May 2005), 859-887.
5. Lu, Wen-Min, Liu, John S. , "The Marginal Efficiency Of Capital: Reply To Fuller's Rejoinder" , Quarterly Journal of Austrian Economics(Jan. 2015) , 61-67.
6. Galindo, A., Schiantarelli, F., and Weiss, A., "Does Financial Liberalization Improve the Allocation of Investment?" Journal of International Economics (Feb. 2016) ,562-587.
7. Gill, I. S., Kharas, H. J., Bhattasali, D., "An East Asian Renaissance: Ideas for Economic Growth", World Bank Publications, 2007.
8. Guner, N., Ventura, G., and Xu, Y., "Macroeconomic Implications of Size-Dependent Policies", Review of Economic Dynamics (Apr. 2016), 721-744.

Research on AO/FO batch management technology in aircraft production

Haijun Yin[1,a*], *Yuning* Wang[1,b], and *Yingji* Shan[1c]

1Shenyang Aircraft Industry (Group) Co., Ltd. No.1 Lingbei St HuangGu district, Shenyang, China

[a]yin_hj2010@163.com, [b]wyn20090101@163.com, [c]skyjz@163.com

Abstract. Based on the analysis of the characteristics and significance of AO/FO in the process of aircraft production, this paper analyzes the format rules of AO/FO batch management from the perspective of technology realization, and details the AO/FO The change of the query and the change status tracking, introduces the AO/FO single-stand status display in the batch management, increases the structure definition of the attribute table in the batch management, and designs the relevant algorithm to store and calculate the batch information. Finally, based on the above theory support AO/FO batch management system successfully used in the production of a machine.

1 Introduction

Influenced by the small batch and the variety of production methods, the aircraft product production organization is put into production by batch, and the assembly process is organized according to the production. The technical state of the production is concentrated in assembly, and the main basis of product assembly is the assembly outline, namely AO. AO is an instructional process document which is written by the technical department according to the requirements of assembly technique, process level and quality assurance[1]. MBOM is based on separation process surface based on product batch of vehicles management of manufacturing product structure view[10], some different types of aircraft sorties of MBOM may not be the same, before generated by the product code and batch of vehicles to find suitable for the vehicles of AO/FO[2-3]. It also requires effective management of all kinds of data in the aircraft's batch production[3-4].

The development of early aircraft products is mainly based on single configuration, and simultaneously is affected by the first generation of CAPP software architecture. The aircraft manufacturers mainly manage AO/FO through the latest version of valid form. With the promotion of serialized and configured development mode of aircraft manufacturing, the traditional AO/FO management mode is no longer suitable for the management and control of aircraft technical state. From the technical realization perspective, this paper discusses the realization mode of AO/FO management from valid management of latest version to valid management of multiple versions based on shipset,

* Corresponding author: yin_hj2010@163.com

and successfully applies this mode in the production process of a certain type of batch-produced aircraft.

2 AO/FO batch management and its rules

2.1 Meaning of batch management

In a traditional CAPP system, there are multiple versions of AOs/FOs under the same component number, but the latest version is valid. If the aircraft from different shipset are produced simultaneously in a development process, the valid shipset management is required to be performed on different versions of AOs/FOs to realize the association of revision with batch and the simultaneously-valid multiple versions, thereby effectively guiding the production and assembly of parts from different batch, to guarantee the correctness and uniqueness of production data.

When AO/FO is required to be changed, the compiler has mastered the information about aircraft batch concerned with this change, and the corresponding valid AO/FO requires to be solved by means of the logical operation of batch validity management module of CAPP system. Because the multiple versions of AOs/FOs may be concerned in each change, this is a complicated recording process, and therefore, it is required that a change process must be traceable, which enables users to master the change process, functioning as prevention of change missing.

AO/FO batch management is also the management of aircraft configuration, and in the aircraft configuration, the principle that the latest revision is valid [4] is adopted, that is, when different batch of AOs/FOs are changed, the highest version of AO/FO of components in this shipset is the valid one. Reasonable management of AO/FO batch validity will aid in the improvement of the ability to manage and control aircraft state, such that the problem of design and manufacturing is disposed more accurately and effectively [5-6].

2.2 Batch management format rules

When inputting validity, necessary batch format rules must be agreed, to realize unified data rules, which functions as calculation and query. Table 1 lists several batch management forms.

Table 1. Several AO/FO Batch Management Forms

No.	Batch Form	Batch Format Writing Rules.
1	Only	According to configured bits, formatted in figures.
2	From	According to configured bits, formatted in figures and English symbol "-".
3	Segment	According to configured bits, formatted in figures and English symbol "-".

"Only" indicates this AO/FO is only applicable to the production or assembly of the batch components;

"From" indicates this AO/FO is applicable to the production or assembly of this batch and its subsequent components;

"Segment" indicates this AO/FO is applicable to the production or assembly of the batch components within a range.

Batch information may be any one of the above three conditions to represent the only meaning, and may be any combination of the above three conditions to represent multiple meanings.

3 Changing and tracking of AO/FO batch information

3.1 Change

The query of AO/FO of a CAPP system component may be performed by the operator according to number localization or changing basis. According to different product processing states, the searched result may be divided into three conditions:

(1) When a product belongs to a manufactured product from its processing state, the system displays all query results of the product, the compiler identifies the corresponding shipset (version) of AO/FO, works out the rework and repair AO/FO, and assigns the batch information to it;

(2) When a product belongs to an in-process product from its processing state, the system displays all query results of the product, the compiler identifies the corresponding shipset (version) of AO/FO, creates a temporary amendment sheet, and assigns the batch information to it;

(3) When a product belongs to a product to be manufactured from its processing state, the system displays all query results of the product, the compiler identifies the corresponding shipset (version) of AO/FO, needs to update the original AO/FO, computes the recommended batch according to logical algorithm, and assigns the batch information to it[7-8].

3.2 Tracking of change state

The compiler can look up the change state and the change process by locating AO/FO number and version, and gives a feedback for updating condition of a component's AO/FO to the compiler, including unchanged batch, changed batch, time of change, and changed version.

4 Single sortie state displaying

By displaying the single sortie state, the directory information display that AOs/FOs of a certain model of aircraft in a shipset are all effective is realized, mainly including two aspects of content.

(1) When displaying the single sortie state, the aircraft model, compilation unit and compiler corresponding to AO/FO are involved, and the authority of AO/FO department is divided and positioned;

(2) The single sortie state may also be inquired and displayed by taking other process documents as input conditions, such as temporary amendment sheet, matching card, technical sheet, rework and repair AO/FO, as well as by means of AO/FO type (general, important and critical).

4.1 Query condition setting of single sortie state

The set query conditions mainly include model, batch, compilation department, compiler, type of process document, basis of compilation, etc., wherein the model is automatically loaded by the system, and is not editable in general; the batch is input by the operator, with the format rule automatically judged by the system. the department and the compiler are usually constant, and can be selectively input by the operator; process documents may include part number, matching card, temporary amendment sheet, technical sheet, rework and repair AO/FO, etc., one or more of which can be selected by the operator. The basis of compilation may be divided into process documents, process improved contents or other documents, one or more of which can be selected by the operator[9-10].

4.2 Query result of single sortie state

The system performs logical operations based on the set query condition to query out AO/FO and process documents for this batch within the range of the condition. The results of querying a directory mainly include AO/FO number, AO/FO version, document type and document name.

5 Structural definition and logical algorithm of attribute table

5.1 Structural definition of database

In this paper, it is recommended that oracle database be used for defining and storing batch management data, AO/FO data be structured, and table structural definition be added in the database, in order to record the generation, change and final result display of all batch information and for translation display of AO/FO batch management information. Refer to Table 2 for the structural definition of attribute table.

Table 2. Structural Definition of attribute table

No.	Field Definition	Field Value Type	Field Meaning	Remarks
1	ID	Integer (32)	Internal Sequence	Auto-increment Sequence
2	PLANNO	String (64)	Number	Structured Data Value
3	MODI	Integer (8)	Internal Change Times	Auto-increment Sequence
4	JC	String (128)	Batch Change Requirement	Interface Value
5	VER_FROM	String (16)	Unchanged Version	Structured Data Value
6	VER_NOW	String (16)	Changed Version	Computation Value
7	VER_NO	String (16)	Internal Version Sequence	Auto-increment Sequence
8	JC_FROM	String (128)	Unchanged Batch	Structured Data Value
9	JC_TO	String (128)	Changed Batch	Computation Value

5.2 Logical algorithm

5.2.1 Variable definition

The number INPUT_PLANNO, minimum shipset INPUTJC_MIN and maximum shipset INPUTJC_MAX are the data input by the operator;

shipset change MODI will automatically increase with shipset change; the corresponding revision VER_FROM is from the structured data of the system; the variables

ORA_MIN, ORA_MAX and VER_NOW are computed by system design logical algorithm.

Table 3. Attribute Table of Logical Algorithm Variable Definition of Batch Management

No.	Data Source	Variable Meaning	Variable Name	Remarks
1.	Input Dialog Box	Procedure Number	INPUT_PLANNO	Interface Value
2.	Input Dialog Box	Minimum Batch	INPUTJC_MIN	Interface Value
3.	Input Dialog Box	Maximum Batch	INPUTJC_MAX	Interface Value
4.	Database	Batch Change	MODI	Auto-increme nt Sequence
5.	Database	Historical shipset is less than the maximum value of INPUT_MIN.	ORA_MIN	Computation Value
6.	Database	Historical shipset is more than the minimum value of INPUT_MIN.	ORA_MAX	Computation Value
7	Database	Corresponding Revision	VER_FROM	Structured Data Value
8	Database	New Revision	VER_NOW	Computation Value

5.2.2 Algorithm Flow

Within the scope of the same number and batch change, if the changed batch (JC_TO) is less than the minimum batch (INPUTJC_MIN) or the unchanged batch (JC_FROM) is more than the maximum batch (INPUTJC_MAX), indicating no eligible batch record, it is unnecessary to upgrade the original AO/FO, but it is necessary to establish new AO/FO with the steps as shown in Algorithm 1; if the unchanged batch (JC_FROM) is less than or equal to the minimum batch (INPUTJC_MIN), it is necessary to upgrade the original AO/FO as well as compute and store the corresponding batch information, and specific steps are shown in Algorithm 2. This section provides batch solving algorithms in two conditions:

Algorithm 1: Establishment of New AO/FO

Step1: Assign 0 to the AO/FO revision (VER_FROM) corresponding to the current batch;

Step2: Increase the new AO/FO revision (VER_NOW) by 1;

Step3: Assign the minimum shipset (INPUTJC_MIN) to the unchanged batch (JC_FROM);

Step4: Assign the maximum shipset (INPUTJC_MAX) to the changed batch (JC_TO);

Algorithm 2: Solving of Revision and Batch

Step1: Record AO/FO where the unchanged batch is as R1;

Step2: Regard new AO/FO revision (R1. VER_NOW) as the current AO/FO revision (VER_FROM);

Step3: Increase the new AO/FO revision (VER_NOW) by 1;

Step4: Assign the minimum shipset (INPUTJC_MIN) to the unchanged batch (JC_FROM);

Step5: Compare the changed batch of R1 (R1.JC_TO) with the maximum shipset (INPUTJC_MAX); if the changed batch of R1 (R1.JC_TO) is less than the maximum shipset (INPUTJC_MAX), assign the changed batch of R1 (R1.JC_TO) to the newly recorded batch (JC_TO), and assign the changed batch of R1 (R1.JC_TO) by 1 to the minimum shipset (INPUTJC_MIN);

Step6:Compare the minimum shipset (INPUTJC_MIN) with the maximum shipset (INPUTJC_MAX); if the former is less than the latter, then do Step 1 to Step 5;

Step7: Compare the changed batch of R1 (R1.JC_TO) with the maximum shipset (INPUTJC_MAX); if the former is more than the latter, then do Step 8 to Step 12;

Step8: Assign the maximum shipset (INPUTJC_MAX) to the changed batch (JC_TO);

Step9: Assign the AO/FO revision of R1 (R1.VER_FROM) to the current AO/FO revision (VER_FROM);

Step10: Assign the new AO/FO revision of R1 (R1.VER_NOW) to the new AO/FO revision (VER_NOW);

Step11: Assign the maximum shipset (INPUTJC_MAX) increased by 1 to the unchanged batch (JC_FROM);

Step12: Assign the changed batch of R1 (R1.JC_TO) to the changed batch (JC_TO).

6 Necessary constraints on batch change

When the batch is changed, it is required to add the following necessary constraints on batch change to ensure change logic accuracy and data integrity:

(1) Before completion of some change, it is unable to perform next change;

(2) During some change, the leading strategy is computed by the above mentioned logical algorithm, and the change process to be performed is recorded by a method of making change identification.

7 Conclusions

In this paper, through the use of the above rules and algorithms, the software functions were improved, and successfully applied to the manufacture of a certain type of aircraft, to achieve the sorting and version of the match. For the same AO/FO, the latest version of AO/FO is a valid version; for different versions of AO/FO, it may correspond to different batches, which can exist as both valid AO/FO. The implementation of this AO/FO batch planning to achieve the same batch of production sites, different parts of the production line at the same time production, and can be part of the production status of the effective tracking. This batch management method has been in a batch of aircraft production process to achieve the engineering application, improve the management of aircraft technology status, which has great technical promotion value.

References

1. Yan Yijun, Ye Wenhua, and Yang Yutu. Research and Development of Aircraft Batch Management System Based on AO [J]. China Manufacturing Informatization, 2000, 21(6): 703-706.
2. Shan Linqing. Research and Realization of Aircraft Manufacturing BOM Management Method [D]. Xi'an: Northwestern Polytechnical University. 2005.
3. Yan Yijun. Research and Development of Aircraft Assembly Batch Management System Based on AO [D]. Nanjing: Nanjing University of Aeronautics and Astronautics. 2007.
4. Li Rong, SunYan, and Jiang Haokang. Product Data Batch Validity Management [J]. Business Research, 2014, 16: 53-54.

5. Wang Shuang. Technical Research of Aircraft Manufacturing Process Information System [D]. Xi'an: Northwestern Polytechnical University. 2006.
6. Jia Xiaoliang. Development of Process Information Integration Platform for Manufacturing Enterprises and Research of its Key Technologies [D]. Xi'an: Northwestern Polytechnical University. 2004.
7. Guo W. A Method of Dispatch Reliability Distribution and Prediction for Civil Aircraft in Development Phase[J]. Civil Aircarft Design & Research, 2012.
8. Dongqi W U, Zhu W, Wang C, et al. Research on the Three-dimensional AO Technology for Airplane[J]. Modern Machinery, 2010.
9. Wu M C, Hsu Y K. Design of BOM configuration for reducing spare parts logistic costs[J]. Expert Systems with Applications, 2008, 34(4):2417-2423.
10. Li Y, Zhao L. Heuristic Assembly Order Design of Aircraft Based on Semantics Association[J]. Lecture Notes in Electrical Engineering, 2013, 227:263-268.

Energy consumption index minimized resource allocation in hybrid energy multiuser OFDM system with distributed antennas

Huanhuan MAO[1], *Pengcheng* Zhu[1,*], and *Jiamin* Li[1]

[1] National Mobile Communications Research Laboratory, Southeast University, Nanjing, 210096, P. R. China

Abstract. Energy harvesting is one of the promising option for realization of green communication and has been a growing concern recently. In this paper, we address the downlink resource allocation in OFDM system with distributed antennas with hybrid power supply base station, where energy harvesting and non-renewable power sources are used complementarily. A joint subcarrier and power allocation problem is formulated for minimizing the net Energy Consumption Index (ECI) with system Quality of Service (QoS) and bit error rates constraint. The problem is a 0-1 mixed integer nonlinear programming problem due to the binary subcarrier allocation variable. To solve the problem, we design an algorithm based on Lagrange relaxation method and fraction programming which optimizes the power allocation and subcarrier allocation iteratively in two nests. Simulation results show that the proposed algorithm converges in a small number of iterations and can improve net ECI of system greatly.

1 Introduction

In the past decade, green communication has become an unignorable and urgent topic because of the enormous energy consumption in mobile communication systems. Only for radio frequency energy, it is up to 27GW in 2015 [1] and will continuously increase. This trend has stimulated growing interest of researchers on innovative energy supply schemes, such as energy harvesting. With energy harvesting, renewable energy such as wind, solar and thermal replaces the conventional nonrenewable energy sources, which in turn reduces the emissions of carbon dioxide and other toxic gas. However, due to the intermittent and random nature of energy harvesting, it is instable and is usually used as an auxiliary of non-renewable energy sources such as power grids and diesel engines. The nature of energy harvesting makes it challenging to derive transmission schemes in existing systems [2]. Various aspects of resource allocation scheme have been studied in energy harvesting. In a multi-picocell downlink network [3], power allocation for maximizing the energy efficient was studied and an offline scheme which needs the non-causal CSI was proposed. For cellular network, there have been significant research progress in resource allocation of various types. In [4], energy efficient resource allocation for OFDMA systems with hybrid

* Corresponding author: p.zhu@seu.edu.cn

power supply base station was studied. An offline scheme with non-causal CSI and a suboptimal online scheme were proposed to jointly allocate the power and subcarrier. In [5], an OFDM-based cellular system was studied, and a low complexity suboptimal resource allocation algorithm was proposed. The algorithm assigns subcarrier based on channel power gain and performs power allocation separately.

Distributed antenna system (DAS), has been proposed as a promising solution for future mobile communications due to its advantages of improving the spectral efficiency and power efficiency [6]. Resource allocation in cellular DAS system has been investigated by many researchers [7] [8]. The authors in [7] investigated energy efficient resource allocation considering proportional fairness for a downlink multiuser OFDM system with distributed antennas. A low complexity suboptimal algorithm which separate the subcarrier and power allocations was proposed. In [8], maximize rate-sum capacity resource allocation problem was derived in OFDM distributed antenna systems and the performances was compared between co-located systems (CAS) and DAS.

In this paper, we focus on a OFDM system with distributed antennas with a hybrid power supply base station. Assuming perfect CSI at base station, we define the ratio of non-renewable power and sun rate a net Energy Consumption Index(ECI) and minimize it under the system Quality of Service(QoS) and bit error rates constraints by jointly optimizing the subcarrier and power allocation. The problem is a 0-1 mixed integer nonlinear programming problem. In order to solve this problem, we propose a two nesting iterative algorithm based on fraction programming and Lagrangian relaxation method. For the outer nest, Dinkelbach method is adopted to ensure the convergent net ECI. And the inner nest derives a resource allocation policy. First, the subcarrier allocation variable is relaxed and the original problem becomes a convex problem. Then the Lagrange dual function of the relaxed problem and the optimal power allocation policy are derived. Simulation results show the proposed algorithm converges quickly and significant improvements on system net ECI is derived.

2 System model

2.1 Channel model

Consider the downlink of an OFDM-DAS system with M remote antenna units (RAUs) with single antenna, N subcarriers and K single antenna users, as illustrated in Fig.1. The central RAU is a base station with a hybrid renewable and non-renewable power supply which connecting other RAUs via fiber-optical and plays a central processing unit role. The signal received by user k at subcarrier n from RAU m can be expressed as

$$y_{k,n,m} = \xi_{k,n,m} h_{k,n,m} \sqrt{p_{k,n,m}} x_{k,n,m} + z_{k,n,m}, \tag{1}$$

where $h_{k,n,m}$ is the channel fading from RAU m to user k on subcarrier n, $z_{k,n,m} \sim \mathcal{CN}(0, \sigma_z^2)$ refers to the additive Gaussian white noise (AGWN), $x_{k,n,m}$ and $p_{k,n,m}$ represent the information symbol and transmit power on subcarrier n to user k from RAU m, and $\xi_{k,n,m}$ stands for a binary subcarrier assignment indicator. If subcarrier n is allocated to user k at RAU m, then $\xi_{k,n,m} = 1$, else $\xi_{k,n,m} = 0$.

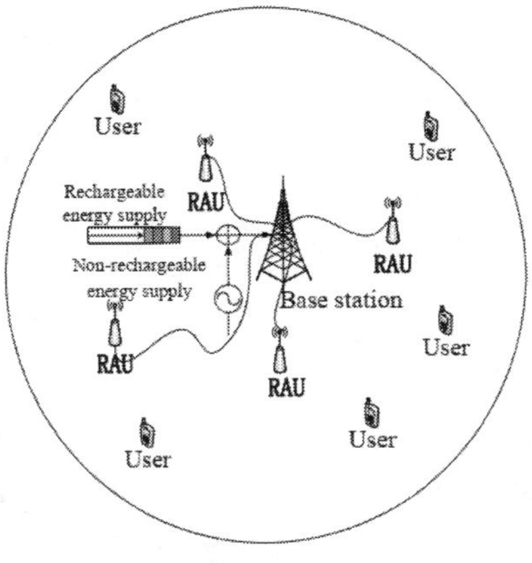

Fig. 1. A hybrid energy OFDM system with distributed antennas

To derive maximum rate-sum capacity, we assume a subcarrier is limitedly allocated to one user from one RAU [8], that is $\sum_k \sum_m \xi_{k,n,m} = 1, \forall n$.

In this paper, we consider a composite channel model

$$h_{k,n,m} = \sqrt{g_{k,m}} v_{k,n,m}, \tag{2}$$

where $g_{k,m}$ denotes the large scale fading coefficient that consists of path loss and shadowing between user k and RAU m, and $v_{k,n,m}$ stands for the small scale fading between user k and RAU m on subcarrier n. We assume perfect CSI is available at the central RAU.

The large scale fading can be calculated as

$$g_{k,m} = c s_{k,m} / d_{k,m}^{\alpha} \tag{3}$$

where c refers to a path gain constant at reference distance, α stands for path loss coefficient, $d_{k,m}$ is the distance between RAU m and user k and $s_{k,m}$ denotes is a shadow fading variable, which follows logarithmic normal distribution. The received SNR of user k on subchannel n from RAU m is

$$\gamma_{k,n,m} = p_{k,n,m} \left| h_{k,n,m} \right|^2 / \sigma_z^2, \ if \ \xi_{k,n,m} = 1 \tag{4}$$

2.2 Hybrid power supply model

As shown in Fig.1, there are two type of energy sources in the base station: the renewable energy from energy harvesting battery and the non-renewable energy of power grid or diesel engine. There are three parts of energy consumption at the base station: the power amplifier, the fiber-optical dissipation and the circuit processing including filtering, modulation, channel coding and so on. For the circuit processing and fiber-optical dissipation are also powered by the two energy resource, i.e. $P_C = P_C^R + P_C^N$, and $(M-1)P_F = P_F^N + P_F^R$,where P_C^R and P_C^N refer to the circuit processing power supplied by renewable energy and non-renewable energy, respectively, P_F^R and P_F^N refer to the fiber-optical power supplied by renewable energy and non-renewable energy, respectively.

Similarly, for the power amplifier the transmit power is written as $\sum_{k=1}^{K}\sum_{n=1}^{N}\sum_{m=1}^{M}\xi_{k,n,m}p_{k,n,m} = P_A^R + P_A^N$, where $P_A^N = \sum_{k=1}^{K}\sum_{n=1}^{N}\sum_{m=1}^{M}\xi_{k,n,m}p_{k,n,m} - P_A^R$ and P_A^R is the power supplied by non-renewable energy and renewable energy respectively.

3 Resource allocation

3.1 Problem Formulation

Suppose the system operates in slotted time. The channel is non-time-varying during each slot, and resource allocation is performed at every slot. If continuous-rate adaptation is used, the overall date rate or the SE of user k at the current time slot is given by [7],

$$R_k = \frac{1}{N}\sum_{n=1}^{N}\sum_{m=1}^{M}\xi_{k,n,m}\log_2\left(1+\beta\gamma_{k,n,m}\right), \tag{5}$$

where $\beta = -1.5/\ln(5BER)$, $1/\beta$ is SNR gap and BER is required bit error rate.

And we assume the weighted sum rate of the system R can be calculated as

$$R = \sum_{k=1}^{K}\theta_k R_k, \tag{6}$$

where θ_k stands for different user priority given by upper layer, and $0 \le \theta_k \le 1$.

The total non-renewable power consumption of the system is

$$P_{\text{total}}^{N} = \left(\sum_{k=1}^{K}\sum_{n=1}^{N}\sum_{m=1}^{M}\xi_{k,n,m}p_{k,n,m} - P_A^R\right)/\eta + P_C^N + P_F^N, \tag{7}$$

where η denotes the efficiency of the power amplifier.

And in this paper, we define net ECI (J/bit) [9] of the system as

$$W_{\text{nECI}} = \frac{P_{\text{total}}^{N}}{R} \tag{8}$$

where the numerator is the non-renewable power of the system which costs in later utilization. Whereas, the renewable power is renewable and self-sustainable and need no extra pay.

Let $p_m^{\max}$ and $P_{\max}^{R}$ denote the maximum output power of the power amplifier at RAU m and the maximal power that the energy harvesting battery can supply. Note that $P_{\max}^{R}$ is determined by both the battery capacity and the remained energy of the last time slot. We would like to minimize net ECI under the system QoS constraint. The corresponding optimization problem is formulated as

$$\begin{aligned}
&\min_{\mathrm{P},\Xi}\ W_{\mathrm{nECI}}=\frac{P_{\mathrm{total}}^{\mathrm{N}}}{R}\\
&s.t.\ \ \mathrm{C1}:\sum_{k}\sum_{m}\xi_{k,n,m}=1,\forall n \qquad \mathrm{C2}:P_{\mathrm{C}}=P_{\mathrm{C}}^{\mathrm{R}}+P_{\mathrm{C}}^{\mathrm{N}}\\
&\qquad \mathrm{C3}:(M-1)P_{F}=P_{\mathrm{F}}^{\mathrm{N}}+P_{\mathrm{F}}^{\mathrm{R}} \qquad \mathrm{C4}:P_{\mathrm{A}}^{\mathrm{R}}/\eta+P_{\mathrm{F}}^{\mathrm{R}}+P_{\mathrm{C}}^{\mathrm{R}}\le P_{\mathrm{max}}^{\mathrm{R}}\\
&\qquad \mathrm{C5}:\xi_{k,n,m}=\{0,1\},\forall k,n,m \qquad \mathrm{C6}:\sum_{k=1}^{K}\sum_{n=1}^{N}\xi_{k,n,m}p_{k,n,m}\le p_{m}^{\max},\forall m\\
&\qquad \mathrm{C7}:R\ge R_{\min} \qquad \mathrm{C8}:p_{k,n,m},P_{\mathrm{A}}^{\mathrm{R}},P_{\mathrm{F}}^{\mathrm{R}},P_{\mathrm{C}}^{\mathrm{R}},p^{\mathrm{R}},P_{\mathrm{C}}^{\mathrm{N}},P_{\mathrm{C}}^{\mathrm{R}}\ge 0,\forall k,n,m
\end{aligned} \tag{9}$$

where the optimization variables are the power allocation policy $\mathrm{P}=\left\{P_{\mathrm{A}}^{\mathrm{R}},P_{\mathrm{F}}^{\mathrm{R}},P_{\mathrm{C}}^{\mathrm{R}},p^{\mathrm{R}},P_{\mathrm{C}}^{\mathrm{N}},P_{\mathrm{C}}^{\mathrm{R}},p_{k,n,m},\forall k,n,m\right\}$ and the subcarrier assignment policy $\Xi=\{\xi_{k,n,m},\forall k,n,m\}$, and $R_{\min}$ is the system minimum rate requirement.

The constraint C4 indicates that consumed renewable power should be no more than that the energy harvesting battery can supply. C6 ensures that transmit power at RAU m is no more than the maximum output power of the power amplifier at RAU m. C1 and C5 are constraints on the subcarrier assignment, and C1 indicates that each subcarrier can only be allocated to one user from one RAU. C7 specifies the QoS constraints. There is a binary variable $\xi_{k,n,m}$ in (10), thus it is a 0-1 mixed integer nonlinear problem. This kind of problem is known as NP-complete. And the objective function is a fraction and is non-convex. The exhaustive search algorithm needs to search $(KM)^{N}$ subcarrier allocation policies to solve (10). The computational complexity increases exponentially with the number of subcarriers.

3.2 Transformation of the optimal problem and fractional programming

There are two steps of transformation to solve (10). First, we set $\varepsilon=\frac{P_{\mathrm{total}}^{\mathrm{N}}}{R}$ and define

$$y(\mathrm{P},\Xi,\varepsilon)=P_{\mathrm{total}}^{\mathrm{N}}-\varepsilon R. \tag{10}$$

And we define $Y(\varepsilon)=\min_{\mathrm{P},\Xi}y(\mathrm{P},\Xi,\varepsilon)$ and $\varepsilon^{*}=\min_{\mathrm{P},\Xi}\frac{P_{\mathrm{total}}^{\mathrm{N}}}{R}$. It has been proved in [10] that $Y(\varepsilon)$ is equivalent to the original objective function in (10) if and only if $Y(\varepsilon^{*})=\min_{\mathrm{P},\Xi}y(\mathrm{P},\Xi,\varepsilon^{*})=y(\mathrm{P}^{*},\Xi^{*},\varepsilon^{*})=0$.

And then we relax the binary variable $\xi_{k,n,m}$ to a continuous variable between 0 and 1 and C5 is transformed to

$$0\le\xi_{k,n,m}\le 1 \tag{11}$$

In this paper, we solve the problem in two nest iterative algorithm. for the outer iteration, we adopt the Dinkelbach method and propose Algorithm 1 shown at Table 1. The convergence is proved in [12] if the inner iterative algorithm solves the (10).

$$\min_{\mathrm{P},\Xi} P^{\mathrm{N}}_{\mathrm{total}} - \varepsilon R \\ s.t.\ \text{C1-C4,(11),C7-C8} \tag{12}$$

Table 1. Proposed Algorithm1 based on iterative Dinkelbach method

Algorithm 1 Outer Iterative Algorithm	
1:	**Initialization:** Set the maximize number of iteration $IterNum_{\max}$, the tolerance Δ, the initial value of $\varepsilon(0)$, $convergence = 0$.
2:	**Repeat**
3:	Solve the problem (12) by the inner iterative algorithm listed in Table 2 for a given ε and obtain the $P^{\mathrm{N}}_{\mathrm{total}}$ and R
4:	**If** $\left\|P^{\mathrm{N}}_{\mathrm{total}} - \varepsilon(iter)R\right\| \le \Delta$
5:	$convergence = 1$, $\varepsilon^* = P^{\mathrm{N}}_{\mathrm{total}}(iter)/R(iter)$
6:	**else**
7:	**Update** $\varepsilon(iter) = \dfrac{P^{\mathrm{N}}_{\mathrm{total}}(iter)}{R(iter)}$.
8:	**End if**
9:	**Until** $iter > IterNum_{max}$ or $convergence = 1$

3.3 Lagrange slack method and subgradient method

To solve (12), we derive the Lagrange function by introducing non-negative Lagrange multipliers [11],

$$\begin{aligned} L(\mathrm{P},\Xi,\rho,\psi,\lambda,\boldsymbol{\mu},\phi) &= \left(\sum_{k=1}^{K}\sum_{n=1}^{N}\sum_{m=1}^{M}\xi_{k,n,m}p_{k,n,m} - P^{\mathrm{R}}_{\mathrm{A}}\right)/\eta + P^{\mathrm{N}}_{\mathrm{C}} + P^{\mathrm{N}}_{\mathrm{F}} - \varepsilon R \\ &+\rho\left(P^{\mathrm{N}}_{\mathrm{C}} + P^{\mathrm{R}}_{\mathrm{C}} - P_{\mathrm{C}}\right) + \lambda\left(P^{\mathrm{R}}_{\mathrm{A}}/\eta + P^{\mathrm{R}}_{\mathrm{F}} + P^{\mathrm{R}}_{\mathrm{C}} - P^{\mathrm{R}}_{\max}\right) - \phi\left(R - R_{\min}\right) \\ &+\psi\left(P^{\mathrm{N}}_{\mathrm{F}} + P^{\mathrm{R}}_{\mathrm{F}} - (M-1)P_{\mathrm{F}}\right) + \sum_{m=1}^{M}\mu_m\left(\sum_{k=1}^{K}\sum_{n=1}^{N}\xi_{k,n,m}p_{k,n,m} - p^{\max}_m\right) \end{aligned} \tag{13}$$

where $\rho,\psi,\lambda,\boldsymbol{\mu},\phi$ are the Lagrange multipliers of C2-C4 and C6-C7, respectively. Note that (12), C1 and C8 are used for later derivation for the optimal solution. The corresponding Dual problem of (13) is omitted due to spacing limit. With the KKT conditions, we can obtain

$$p^*_{k,n,m} = \left[\frac{\theta_k(\varepsilon+\phi)}{N\ln 2\left(1/\eta+\mu_m\right)} - \frac{\sigma_z^2}{\beta\left|h_{k,n,m}\right|^2}\right]^+ \tag{14}$$

where the notation $[x]^+$ represents $[x]^+ = \max\{0,x\}$.

To determine the subcarrier assignment scheme, we differentiate the Lagrange function with respect to $\xi_{k,n,m}$, we can obtain

$$\partial L(\ldots)/\partial\xi_{k,n,m} = \left(1/\eta+\mu_m\right)p_{k,n,m} - \theta_k(\varepsilon+\phi)\log_2\left(1+\beta p_{k,n,m}\left|h_{k,n,m}\right|^2/\sigma_z^2\right)/N \tag{15}$$

It can be observed from (16) that $L(\mathrm{P},\Xi,\rho,\psi,\lambda,\boldsymbol{\mu},\mathbf{v},\phi)$ is an affine function in $\xi_{k,n,m}$. Hence to obtain the minimum value of $L(\mathrm{P},\Xi,\rho,\psi,\lambda,\boldsymbol{\mu},\phi)$ with given Lagrange multipliers and in consideration of C5, the optimal $\xi^*_{k,n,m}$ is given as

$$\xi^*_{i,n,j} = \begin{cases} 1, \text{ if } (i,j) = \arg\min\limits_{(k,m)} \partial L(\mathrm{P},\Xi,\alpha,\beta,\gamma,\lambda,\boldsymbol{\mu}) / \partial \xi_{k,n,m} \\ 0, \ else. \end{cases} \tag{16}$$

Similarly, it can be derived that $L(\mathrm{P},\Xi,\rho,\psi,\lambda,\boldsymbol{\mu},\mathbf{v},\phi)$ is an affine function in $P_{\mathrm{A}}^{\mathrm{R}}, P_{\mathrm{F}}^{\mathrm{R}}, P_{\mathrm{C}}^{\mathrm{R}}, p^{\mathrm{R}}, P_{\mathrm{C}}^{\mathrm{N}}, P_{\mathrm{C}}^{\mathrm{R}}$. And to minimize the consumption of non-renewable energy, we allocate the power as

$$P_{\mathrm{A}}^{\mathrm{R}} = \min\left(\sum_{k=1}^{K}\sum_{n=1}^{N}\sum_{m=1}^{M} \xi_{k,n,m} p_{k,n,m}, \left[\eta P_{\max}^{\mathrm{R}}\right]^{+} \right) \tag{17}$$

$$P_{\mathrm{C}}^{\mathrm{R}} = \min\left(P_{\mathrm{C}}, \left[P_{\max}^{\mathrm{R}} - P_{\mathrm{A}}^{\mathrm{R}} / \eta \right]^{+} \right) \tag{18}$$

$$P_{\mathrm{C}}^{\mathrm{N}} = \left[P_{\mathrm{C}} - P_{\mathrm{C}}^{\mathrm{R}} \right]^{+} \tag{19}$$

$$P_{\mathrm{F}}^{\mathrm{R}} = \min\left((M-1) P_{\mathrm{F}}, \left[P_{\max}^{\mathrm{R}} - P_{\mathrm{A}}^{\mathrm{R}} / \eta - P_{\mathrm{C}}^{\mathrm{R}} \right]^{+} \right) \tag{20}$$

$$P_{\mathrm{F}}^{\mathrm{N}} = \left[(M-1) P_{\mathrm{F}} - P_{\mathrm{F}}^{\mathrm{R}} \right]^{+} \tag{21}$$

After allocating the power and subcarrier, we update the Lagrange multipliers using the subgradient method to guarantee convergence. The update equations are given by

$$\lambda^{i+1} = \left[\lambda^{i} + \varsigma_1^{i} \left(P_{\mathrm{A}}^{\mathrm{R}} / \eta + P_{\mathrm{F}}^{\mathrm{R}} + P_{\mathrm{C}}^{\mathrm{R}} - P_{\max}^{\mathrm{R}} \right) \right]^{+} \tag{22}$$

$$\mu_m^{i+1} = \left[\mu_m^{i} + \varsigma_2^{i} \left(\sum_{k=1}^{K}\sum_{n=1}^{N} \xi_{k,n,m} p_{k,n,m} - p_m^{\max} \right) \right]^{+} \tag{23}$$

$$\phi^{i+1} = \left[\phi^{i} - \varsigma_3^{i} \left(R - R_{\min} \right) \right]^{+} \tag{24}$$

where i represents the iteration number, and ς are the positive iterative step size.

Note that there is no need to update ρ and ψ since C2 and C4 are equality constraints. If the step size satisfies the infinite travel condition [12], the above update equations guarantee the convergence of optimal solution. Based on the analysis, we propose Algorithm 2 to solve the problem (13), which is shown at Table 2.

Table 2. Proposed Algorithm 2

Algorithm 2 Inner Iterative Algorithm
Initialization: Set the maximize number of iteration I_{max}, the tolerance Δ, the initial value of Lagrange multipliers, $convergence = 0$.
Repeat
Calculate $p_{k,n,m}, \forall k,n,m$ according to (14).
Calculate $\partial L(\mathrm{P}, \Xi, \rho, \psi, \lambda, \boldsymbol{\mu}, \phi) / \partial \xi_{k,n,m}, \forall k,m$ according to (15).
Obtain subcarrier assignment $\xi_{k,n,m}$ according to (16).
Allocate power $P_{\mathrm{A}}^{\mathrm{R}}, P_{\mathrm{F}}^{\mathrm{R}}, P_{\mathrm{C}}^{\mathrm{R}}, p^{\mathrm{R}}, P_{\mathrm{C}}^{\mathrm{N}}, P_{\mathrm{C}}^{\mathrm{R}}$ according to (17-21).
Update: Lagrange multipliers $\psi(i), \lambda(i)$, $\boldsymbol{\mu}(i)$, according to (22-24).
Calculate $P_{\mathrm{total}}^{\mathrm{N}}(i) - \varepsilon R(i)$
If $\left|\left((P_{\mathrm{total}}^{\mathrm{N}}(i) - \varepsilon R(i)\right) - \left(P_{\mathrm{total}}^{\mathrm{N}}(i-1) - \varepsilon R(i-1)\right)\right| \le \Delta$
$convergence = 1$.
End if
Until $i > I_{max}$ or $convergence = 1$

4 Simulation results and discussion

In this section, we evaluate the performance of the proposed algorithm. The OFDM system has $N = 128$ subcarrier, K users and M RAUs. Users are located within a radius $D = 1000$ meters from the base station, and the locations is generated randomly obeying uniformly distributed during the simulation.

There are three locations of RAUs, $\{(0,0)\}$, $\{(0,0),(0,D/2),(0,-D/2)\}$, $\{(0,0),(0,D/2),(0,-D/2),(D/2,0),(-D/2,0)\}$. The path loss exponent $\alpha = 4$ and a 8 dB shadowing fading coefficient is used. The small scale fading is assumed to be independent and identical distributed (i.i.d.) Reyleigh random variables. The noise variance is $\sigma_z^2 = 104$ dBm. The circuit power of the base station is $P_{\mathrm{C}} = 40$ dBm and the fiber optical power is $P_{\mathrm{F}} = -0.6$ dBm. The maximum power of power amplifier of RAU m is $p_{\max}^{\mathrm{m}} = 30$ dBm, $\forall m$. The minimum rate requirement of system is $R_{\min} = 1$ bit/s/Hz. And $\theta_k = 1$, $\forall k$. The efficiency of power amplifier is $\eta = 0.38$. Because channel fading and locations of users are changing, all results are an average of 2000 simulations.

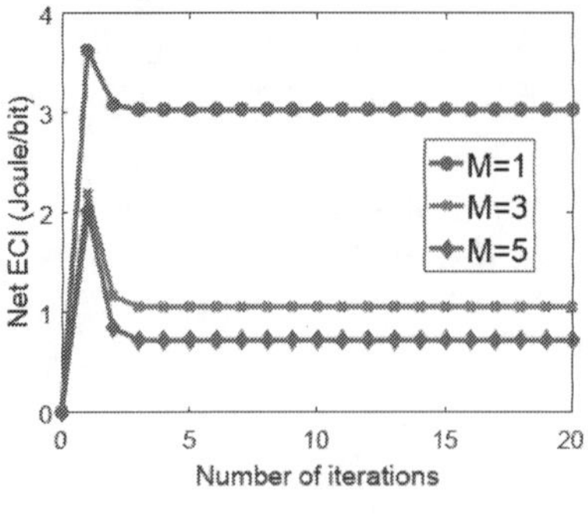

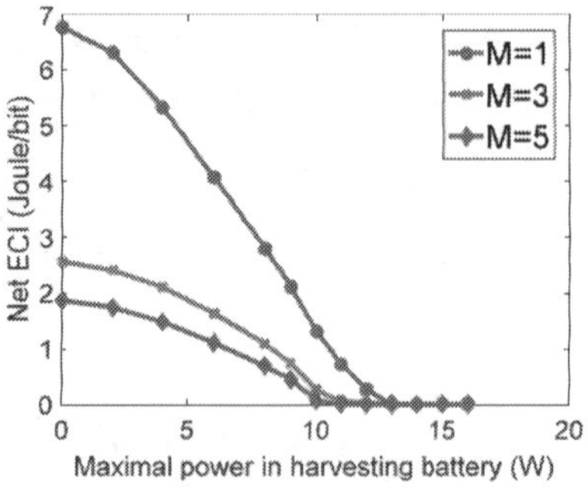

Fig. 2. Convergence of Algorithm 1 (PE=8 W, N=128, K=5)

Fig. 3. Net ECI versus maximum renewable power (K=5, N=128)

Fig. 2 shows the convergence of the proposed algorithm via the number of iterations. We choose three number of RAUs, and $M = 1$ refers to the OFDM-CAS system. As shown in Fig.2, the algorithm obtains a convergent solution within 4 iterations in all three scenarios. Moreover, the net ECI gets smaller in OFDMA-DAS than OFDMA-CAS system.

Fig. 3 shows the system net ECI with different value of maximum renewable power. It is reasonable that net ECI decreases as the value of maximum renewable power increases with different number of RAUs. This phenomenon shows net ECI is improved with the energy harvesting supply.

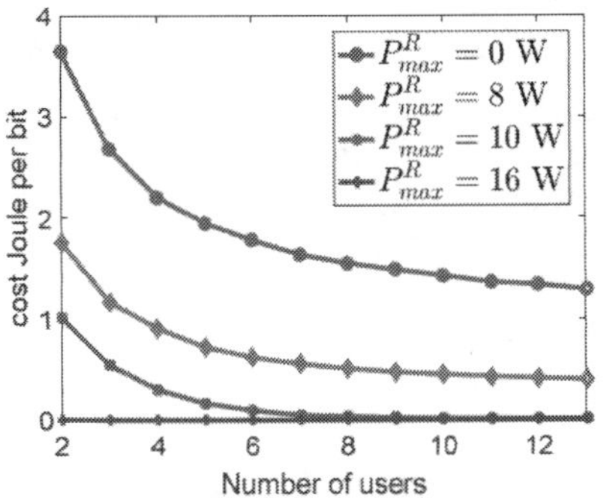

Fig. 4. Net ECI with different number of users, M=5

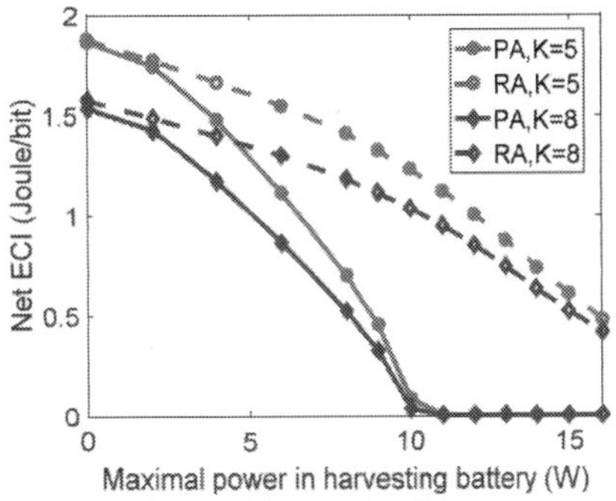

Fig. 5. Comparison with RA algorithm in system net ECI

Fig. 4 shows the system net ECI with different number of users. We choose three scenarios, no renewable energy scenario, lacking renewable energy scenario and sufficient renewable energy scenario. Interestingly, the net ECI decreases with the number of users increases. And as the number of users increasing larger, the decline of net ECI gets flat. With more users, RAUs have larger probability to access subcarriers in good channel state with the fix system QoS constraint, resulting in better performance.

Fig. 5 illustrates the comparison of the proposed algorithm(PA) and the rate adaptive (RA) algorithm in system net ECI. The RA algorithm which maximize the sum rate of the system can be adopted by traditional water-filling algorithm. The proposed algorithm can achieve better performance than the RA algorithm and the improvement increases as the value of maximum renewable power increases.

5 Conclusion

We studied the resource allocation in a downlink OFDM DAS system with hybrid power supply. To minimize net ECI of the system with system QoS and BER requirement constraints, we proposed two nested algorithm based on fractional programming and Lagrange relaxation method. Through simulation studies, net ECI of the system under the proposed scheme was investigated and the results showed that the proposed algorithm converges quickly and improves the system net ECI significantly. Interests for future work include the transmit scheme with imperfect CSI, as well as optimization algorithm with low computational complexity.

Acknowledgments: This work was supported in part by National Natural Science Foundation of China (NSFC) (Grant Nos. 61571120, 61501113), and by Natural Science Foundation of Jiangsu Province (Grant Nos. BK20151415, BK20150630).

References

1. Klein T E, Richard P.: ICT Energy Challenges, Impact and Solutions[C] In:19th International ICIN Conference-Innovations in Clouds, Internet and Networks (2016)
2. Ku, M. L., Li, W., Chen, Y., Liu, K. R.: Advances in Energy Harvesting Communications: Past, Present, and Future Challenges. IEEE Communications Surveys and Tutorials 18(2): 1384--1412 (2016)
3. Ni, X., Yuan, D., Teng, Y., Song, M.: Energy efficient power allocation scheme for multi-cell with hybrid energy sources. In: Personal, Indoor, and Mobile Radio Communications (PIMRC), 2015 IEEE 26th Annual International Symposium on, pp. 1611--1616. IEEE. (2015)
4. Ng, D. W. K., Lo, E. S., Schober, R.: Energy-efficient resource allocation in OFDMA systems with hybrid energy harvesting base station. IEEE Transactions on Wireless Communications, 12(7), 3412--3427 (2013)
5. Yu, B., Ma, P., Ma, Y.: Resource allocation and energy management in ofdm-based cellular systems. In: Communication Systems (ICCS), 2016 IEEE International Conference on. IEEE, pp. 1--6. IEEE. (2016)
6. Li, J., Wang, D., Zhu, P., You, X.: Spectral efficiency analysis of single-cell multi-user large-scale distributed antenna system. IET Communications, 8(12), 2213-2221 (2014)
7. He, C., Li, G. Y., Zheng, F. C., You, X.: Energy-efficient resource allocation in OFDM systems with distributed antennas. IEEE Transactions on Vehicular Technology, 63(3), 1223-1231 (2014)
8. Xu, W., Niu, K., He, Z., Wu, W.: Resource allocation in multiuser OFDM distributed antenna systems. In: Vehicular Technology Conference, 2007. VTC-2007 Fall. 2007 IEEE 66th, pp. 1797-1801. IEEE. (2007)
9. Auer, G., Blume, O., Giannini, V., Godor, I., Imran, M., Jading, Y., ... Wajda, W.: D2. 3: Energy efficiency analysis of the reference systems, areas of improvements and target breakdown. EARTH, 20(10). (2010)
10. Dinkelbach, W.: On nonlinear fractional programming. Management science, 13(7), 492-498 (1967)
11. Boyd, S., Vandenberghe, L.: Convex optimization. Cambridge university press (2004)
12. Boyd, S., Mutapcic, A.: Subgradient methods. Lecture notes of EE364b, Stanford University, Winter Quarter, 2007 (2006)

The research on collaborative optimization of emergency human resource allocation

Qilin Li[1,*,a], *Chuanliang* Jia[1,b], and *Jiu* Su[1,c]
[1]School of Management Science and Engineering, Central University of Finance and Economics, Beijing
[a]cdliqilin@163.com, [b]cnbjjcl@163.com, [c]sujiesu@126.com

Abstract. On aglobal scale, the occurrence of different types of emergencies has had a tremendous impact on the economies and people's lives. The optimization of emergency human resource allocation is increasingly important. This paper gives full consideration to the control targets of each fire rescue points and the demands of both demand points and potential demand points. We build an emergency human resource allocation model and optimize it through the collaborative optimization. This paper finally carried on the case analysis to verify the feasibility of the model. The model better simulates the reality and can be referred by some government officials in some emergency cases.

1 Introduction

With the process of globalization and modernization entering into a period of generalization and deepening, human society has not only acquired countless opportunities, but also has undergone numerous risks and tests. The trend of social pluralism has caused the occurrence of mass incidents in modern society, and the emergency management has become a hot topic in the world. The demand for materials and human resource is explosive in emergency management, and a large amount of demand has raised higher requirements for human resource allocation. Whether the allocation of human resources is effective is the core key of the emergency management.

Emergency human resource allocation plays an important role in emergency management. Mohsen A. Jafari (2008) considered the configuration of medical personnel in emergency situations and proposed a solution to the allocation of limited human resources. Peng Yi and Xu Jianghong (2010) analyzed the current situation and shortage of emergency human resources in China, emphasized the importance of human resources in the emergency management and put forward corresponding solutions. Cao Jie(2011) studied emergency human resource management from the resource support, guarantee system and emergency human resource classification.

This paper takes the actual situation of the work of emergency management into consideration. Taking fire disaster as an example, we suppose the location of the demand points have been confirmed within a certain range of a city. Under the situation of limited human resource, the location of the emergency incidents requires multiple fire points to

[*]Corresponding author: cdliqilin@163.com

send emergency personnel to rescue together. However, it is necessary to study the optimization of emergency human resource with the consideration of the potential possibility for similar emergencies in other regions. To make the rescue work convenient and fast, fire points should be fixed and should not be relocated. In this paper, we study the human resource allocation of fire stations and the suggestion of the optimization is of significant reference value to similar incidents.

2 The theoretical basis of emergency human resource allocation

2.1 The problem description

Taking a city as the study area, we divide it into several small areas which need rescue service. In order to simplify the problem, we further consider the small areas as demand points and assume an area broke out a fire at a time. The fire stations that can participate in the rescue are fixed and known.

For any fire incident, the demand for fire personnel is related to the situation of the fire. If the fire had not yet developed into a larger fire, the fewer firefighters needed to be deployed. But the firefighters are limited, a certain amount of fire fighting force need to be sent to a small fire. With the spread of fire, he demand for personnel will rise as the disaster worsens. In this paper, we assume that the demand for personnel will exceed the lower limit. The fire points need to save some fire fighters in response to the demand of other potential demand points when allocating human resource.

So the fire points need a certain amount of human resources for potential demand points. This part of the staff can arrive at the scene to rescue in time, and to stop the fire as soon as possible. Therefore, in the face of major emergencies, rescue work often requires the cooperation of multiple fire points to complete control targets successfully. In the study of this problem, the time of emergency personnel's arrival is preferred consideration. For the other areas of potential fire, we can determine occurrence probabilities, and consider the potential demand of various areas according to historical data.

2.2 The description of collaborative optimization method

Assuming that the system design problem can be decomposed into Nsub-subjects, the optimization process of collaborativeoptimization method can be described in the following mathematical expressions:

The system level is defined as:

$$\min F(Z): \tag{1}$$

$$s.t.\ J_i^*(z) = \sum_{j=1}^{s_i} (Z_j - X_{ij}^*)^2 = 0 \tag{2}$$

$$i = 1, 2, \ldots n \tag{3}$$

Z is the system-level optimization design vector; Z_j represents the j-th system design variable; S_i is the number of design variables for the discipline i ; X_{ij}^* represents the optimization result of the j-th design variable for the discipline i .

The discipline level is defined as:

$$\min J_i(x_i) = \sum_{j=1}^{s_i} (x_{ij} - z_j^*)^2 \tag{4}$$

$$s.t.\ c_i(x_i) \leq 0 \tag{5}$$

x_i is design vector of discipline i ; S_i is the number of design variables for the discipline i ; x_{ij} represents the j-th design vector of discipline i ; z_j^* represents the expectation of the j-th design vector that system level allocated to the discipline level. c_i (x_i)is the constraint of subject level.

3 The collaborative optimization model of emergency human resource allocation

Suppose there are N urban areas, one of which has a fire, and the rest of the N-1 areas are likely to be in fire at any time.The human resource layout of the fire points in a city has been determined and firefighters need to be deployed to respond to the rescue work.At the same time, the fire points need to consider the fire probability in the other N - 1 area and save some human resource to ensure the timely rescue of the potential area.

To build the model, we firstly set the parameters as follows:

- There are m fire points where $i = 1, 2, \ldots m$;
- There are n areas where $j = 1, 2, \ldots n$; To make the model simple, we assume the on-fire location j=1 and other potential location $j = 2, \ldots n$;
- Fire stations i own q_i emergency personnel where $i = 1, 2, \ldots m$;
- The area of fire needs r_1 firefighters;
- The fire station i has sent x_{i1} firefighters to the scene of the fire;
- The fire station i sent x_{ij} firefighters to the potential fire sites where $j = 2, \ldots n$;
- y_{i1} is0-1 variable. If the fire point sends emergency personnel to the place where the fire has occurred, the value is 1, otherwise it is 0;
- y_{ij} is 0-1 variable. If the fire point sends emergency personnel to the potential place where the fire is likely occurred, the value is 1, otherwise it is 0;
- t_{i1} means the time that firefighters need from the fire point i to the place where the fire has occurred
- t_{ij} means the time that firefighters need from the fire point i to the potential place where the fire is likely occurred where $j = 2, \ldots n$
- U_j represents the amount of human resource that is not met in each area
- D_j means the latest time for each area j to request for support. After that, the fire spread quickly, causing even greater losses and bringing more casualties to life

• δ_{ij} represents the delaying time from the fire point to the area of demand. If the emergency fire personnel can reach the demand point before, then $\delta_{ij}=0$; Otherwise, there will be a delay and $\delta_{ij} > 0$

• p_j represents the probability of fire in each potential place. It can be obtained by historical data and the study of fire. It is in [0, 1]

We build collaborative optimization model as follows.

The system level:

$$min\, U_1 + \delta_1 + \sum_{j=2}^{n} p_j \left(U_j + \delta_j\right) \tag{6}$$

$$s.t. \sum_{i=1}^{m} x_{i1} + U_1 \geq r_1 \tag{7}$$

$$\sum_{i=1}^{m} y_{i1} \geq 1 \tag{8}$$

$$\sum_{i=1}^{m} y_{ij} \geq 1 \ \left(j = 2,3,\cdots,n\right) \tag{9}$$

$$0 \leq t_{ij} - \delta_{ij} \leq D_j \sum_{i=1}^{m} y_{ij} \tag{10}$$

$$x_{ij}, U_j, \delta_{ij} \geq 0 \tag{11}$$

The discipline level:

$$j = 1,2,\ldots n \tag{12}$$

$$\sum_{i=1}^{m} x_{ij} + U_j \geq p_j r_j \ \left(j = 1,2,3,\cdots,n\right) \tag{13}$$

$$\sum_{j=1}^{m} x_{ij} \leq q_i \tag{14}$$

$$\delta_{ij} \leq \sum_{i=1}^{m} y_{ij} M \tag{15}$$

$$y_{ij} \in \{0,1\},\ \left(i, j = 1,2,\cdots,n\right) \tag{16}$$

$$x_{ij}, U_j, \delta_{ij} \geq 0 \tag{17}$$

Formula (6) is the objective function of the system level of emergency model. It minimum the sum of the delaying time that firefighters need from fire points to demand points under certain possibility and the sum of emergency rescue resource which could not meet the demands. Formula (7) means the human resource of all fire points should meet the demand of the fire area. Formula (8) and (9) ensure at least one fire station sent or saves emergency personnel for the demand or potential demand points. Formula (10) means, if the deadline is missed, the needed time from fire station i to demand point j, the delaying time and the deadline should meet certain requirements. Formula (12) represents the target function of each fire point. Each fire point has its own human resource demand and the minimum delay time (fire effectiveness). Formula (13) and (14) represent the sum of the emergency personnel reserved for fire points should be as much as possible to meet the demand of the potential occurrence. Formula (15) is the constraint that the emergency personnel can provide the maximum demand human resource. Equation (16) means that the value can only be 0 or 1.

4 An application example

We use an example to illustrate the feasibility of the collaborative optimization model of emergency human resource. Suppose that there are 4 fire points in a region, respectively I_1, I_2, I_3, I_4.And three crowded public places may be in fire, which are demand points J_1, J_2, J_3.There has been a fire in public place J_1. And two other public places will fire with different probabilities at the same time or not.
We will consider the deployment plan of emergency human resource. The distribution of fire points and demand points is shown in figure 1

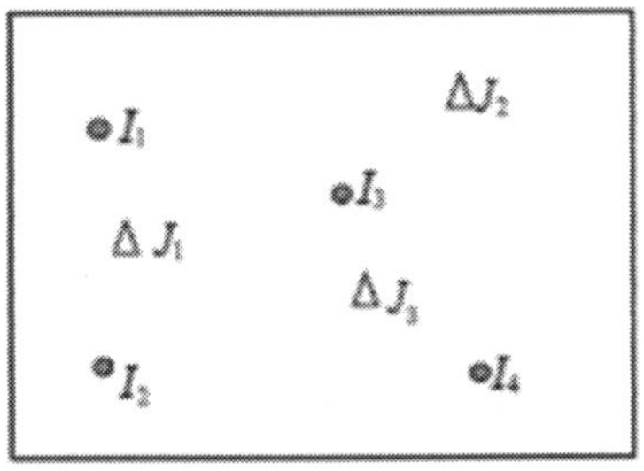

Fig.1. The distribution of fire points and demand points

The personnel quantity q_i of each fire point is randomly generated four integer values between 20 and 40. The demand r_j of each demand point is randomly generated three integer values between 20 and 40. The fire possibility of demand point J_2 and J_3 is randomly generated two decimal numbers between 0 and 1. The needed time and the latest arrival time from each fire point to each demand point is respectively determined by [10, 90] and [30, 50] as an integer. The parameters are set as shown in table 1

The parameters are taken into the model, and table 2 is obtained through MATLAB

Table 2 shows the fire points needs to allocate the number of personnel, and the fire points save some emergency human resource for the potential demand with certain probability. According to table 2 and setting parameters, we can draw deployment diagram which is shown in figure 2.

As we can see from figure 2, fire points I_1, I_2, I_3 can meet the human resource requirements of the demand point J_1,which has been a fire. And fire points I_1, I_3 can meet the human resource requirements of the demand point J_2,which is likely to fire. fire points I_3, I_4 can meet the human resource requirements of the demand point J_3, which is likely to fire.

Table1. The parameters setting

(t_{ij})	J_1	J_2	J_3	q_i
I_1	20	50	70	20
I_2	30	75	60	25
I_3	35	40	20	36
I_4	75	55	35	26
D_j	35	50	45	
r_j	28	20	35	
p_h	1	0.05	0.02	

Table 2. The basic model results

(x_{ij})	J_1	J_2	J_3
I_1	10	2	0
I_2	12	0	0
I_3	6	8	18
I_4	0	0	10

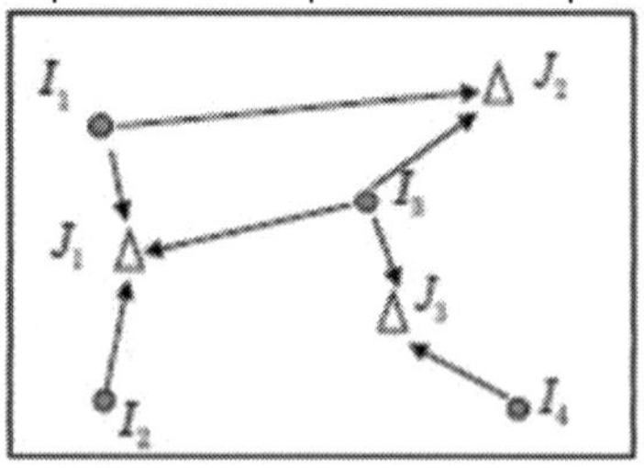

s

Fig 2. The relationship map of the deployment

5 Conclusion

In the case of emergency rescue, a reasonable allocation of human resources should be required to respond to emergencies. In this paper, we optimize the human resource allocation through the collaborative optimization method by considering the fire target of the whole area and each fire point.We make a full consideration to the control targets of each fire rescue points and the demands of both demand points and potential demand points. We build an emergency human resource allocation model and optimize it through the collaborative optimization.Research shows that using collaborative optimization can meet both current and potential fire targets and save human resources. The conclusion canbe referred by some government officials in some emergency cases.

As for the future scope, without considering the evolution of the fire situation, we should deeply modify the model in the future work. Also the number of fire points and demand points are less than the real situation.This limits the widespread use of the model.Further research can make the model more realistic.We should improve this model by considering more fire points and demand points and the multifarious change of the fire disaster.

Acknowledgment: This paper is supported by Program for Innovation Research in Central University of Finance and Economics

References

1. B. Balcik, B. M. Beamon. Facility location in humanitarian relief[J]. International Journal of Logistics Research and Applications, 2008, 11(2):101-121
2. Jiang Jingui, Liang Jingguo. Research on emergency management mechanism based on grid management [J]. Intelligence journal, 2008, 27 (6) : 26-28
3. Liang Xianyan, Wu Shuxian. Analysis on human resources in emergency management [J]. Management observation, 2008 (9) : 14-15.
4. Lu Na. Research on human resource allocation in crisis management organization [J]. Management, 2011 (1) : 102-102.
5. Ronald Klingler. Human Rights Management in Public Sector: System and Strategy [M]. Renmin University of China Press, 2001.
6. Peng Yi, Xu Jianghong. Research on human resource management in emergency management [J]. Journal of Taiyuan urban vocational and technical college, 2010 (3) : 50-52
7. Sun Ying. Research on resource distribution and scheduling model in emergency management of emergencies [D]. Graduate school of Chinese academy of sciences, 2008.
8. Wu Yufeng. Research on emergency human resource management in the context of public crisis [J]. Human resource management, 2014 (9) : 85-85
9. Chen Y L, Emergency D O. Emergency management of nursing human resourcedeployment when emergency department crowding[J]. China Modern Medicine, 2013
10. Chu W H J, Lee C C. Strategic information sharing in a supply chain[J]. European Journal of Operational Research, 2006, 174(3):1567-1579..
11. Jafari M A, Golmohammadi D, Seyed K. Staff Management in Emergency Evacuation Preparedness and Response[J]. Journal of Homeland Security & Emergency Management, 2008, 5(1):1254-1265
12. Lämmel G, Grether D, Kai N. The representation and implementation of time-dependent inundation in large-scale microscopic evacuation simulations[J]. Transportation Research Part C Emerging Technologies, 2010, 18(1):84-98
13. Mete H O, Zabinsky Z B. Stochastic optimization of medical supply location and distribution in disaster management[J]. International Journal of Production Economics, 2010, 126(1):76-84
14. Wang F X, Ren J. Human Resources Optimization Allocation Model Based on Human Matching for Position[J]. Technology & Innovation Management, 2011.
15. Yang Q, He G, Li L. Application of Genetic Algorithm on Human Resources Optimization[C]// International Conference on Computer and Communication Technologies in Agriculture Engineering(cctae 2010) (volume. 2010:160-163.

Design of fresh food sensory perceptual system for cold chain logistics

Ying Zhang[1,*] , *Ruqi* Cheng[1], and *Shaohui* Chen[2]

[1]College of Electronic Information and Optical Engineering, Tianjin, 300071,China,

[2]National Engineering and Technology Research Center for Preservation of Agriculture Products, Tianjin, 300384, China

Abstract. According to the present stage low-level information of China's cold chain preservation, designed a kind of fresh food sensory perceptual system for cold chain logistics based on Internet of things. This system highly integrated applied many technologies such as the Internet of things technology, forecasting technology for fruits and vegetables preservation period, RFID and Planar bar code technology, big data and cloud computing technology and so on.Designed as a four-layer structure including sensing layer, network layer, control layer and user layer. The system can implement the real-time temperature and humidity environment parameters monitoring and early warning of the whole cold chain logistics for fresh agricultural products from picking, storage, transportation and processing link. It greatly improved the information level of cold chain circulation in our country and has a strong marketing value.

1 Introduction

Cold chain logistics refers to all kinds of special supply chain systems which can make fresh agricultural products remains in the low temperature environment in the nodes of the product processing, storage, transportation, distribution, retail and other various supply chain and furthest extent possible to ensure product quality and safety, reduce the loss after the origin of harvest of fresh agricultural products such as meat, eggs, poultry, the aquatic products, fruit and vegetables [1]-[3]. At present, the development of cold chain logistics in our country is still in the start-up stage, and the large-scale, systematic, intelligent cold chain logistics system has not formed, which still has a gap compared with the demand of the modern agriculture development, the residents' consumption improvement and the agricultural export expansion. fruits and vegetable products in our country loss as high as 20% ~ 35% due to the storage, transportation and sales under the natural environment condition, the annual loss as 180 billion yuan, while only 1% ~ 5% in developed countries. Therefore, it is urgent to establish the perfect cold chain technology system and perfect cold chain information management technology system in our country [4]-[7].

Cold-chain information will gather various elements in the cold-chain to the database, for in-depth development and rational utilization of cold chain resources using modern

* Corresponding author: caroline_zy@nankai.edu.cn

sensor technology, communication technology, network technology and database technology[8]-[10]. Cold-chain information technology is the combination of cold chain logistics and information technology, which is a kind of solution of cold chain logistics cost reduction, and at the same time is an important guarantee of food quality and safety. Many developed countries have set up virtual agricultural cold chain logistics supply management system, to achieve the all-the-way tracking, dynamic monitoring of all kinds of goods, at the same time connect the demand information and product information through the network and improve the operational efficiency of the cold chain logistics. The informatization process of the whole logistics industry in China starts late, which has not high overall level, especially specific to cold chain logistics. This paper designed a kind of fresh food sensory perceptual system for cold chain logistics based on Internet of things, RFID and Planar bar code technology, big data and cloud computing technology, which mainly includes three parts that the front information awareness, information embedded real-time monitoring and data collection, information sharing center. It realized real-time dynamic information collection, analysis, transmission and intelligent early warning for the agricultural products from warehousing, transportation, sales and other links of the remote monitoring. It greatly improves the modern cold chain logistics information level and the operational efficiency of the cold chain logistics.

2 Fresh food sensory perceptual system design

The block diagram of fresh food sensory perceptual system is shown in figure 1. In order to achieve the whole seamless real-time monitoring of the cold chain, the system uses a four-layer structure: sensor layer, network layer, control layer and user layer.

The sensor layer is mainly responsible for acquisition and processing of environmental parameters such as the temperature and humidity, carbon dioxide, oxygen, etc. in cold storage or refrigerated trucks. Applying RFID electronic tag technology, the system combines the RFID card information with the monitored fresh goods, which is used for the input and processing of agricultural products information and identity identification. At the same time, through RFID and two-dimensional code binding, so that consumers in the market can be traced back to the whole situation of fresh food safety.

The network layer is mainly responsible for collecting and uploading real-time environmental information. The network connection adopts the wired link mode of TCP/IP for the refrigeration house, which has the advantages of mature technology, fast link speed and stable network. For the refrigerator car, the remote real-time information monitoring, collection, analysis, transmission and intelligent warning of agricultural products from warehousing, transportation, sales and other links are realized, by using 4G/3G network transmission and GPS technology.

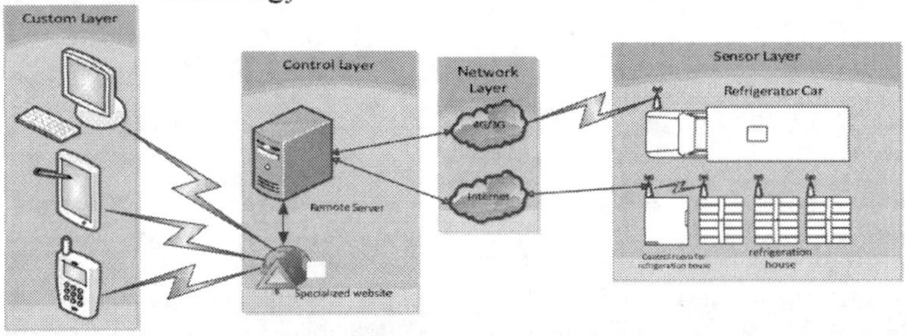

Fig. 1. The block diagram of fresh food sensory perceptual system

The control layer collects the identity of agricultural products, real time environment and other information, combined with the preservation model of vegetables, fruits and other agricultural products, to forecast, sharing and intelligent warning of important information as fresh keeping period of agricultural products. Achieve the centralized analysis, query, management and online sales of information.

The user layer is designed with a special website and mobile phone special APP for different information terminal, through the user interface, the user can carry on fresh food whenever and wherever possible online information query, full traceability, network consumption etc.

3 Sensor layer and network layer design

In order to realize the real-time monitoring of the whole cold chain circulation process of fresh products, cold storage and transportation links as an important part of the whole chain of cold chain is the key. Therefore, the sensor layer and network layer of Fresh Food Sensory Perceptual System is designed which combines with RFID, the two dimensional code recognition technology, 4G/3G network transmission technology, and has the function of GPS, provides technical support for the realization of seamless real-time monitoring throughout the cold chain. In the design of sensor network layer, Fresh Food Sensory Perceptual System uses 4G/3G network and remote server for real time data exchange. The block diagram is shown in Figure 2.

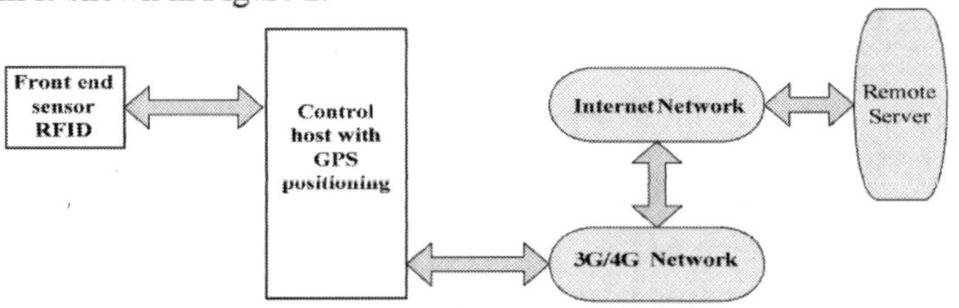

Fig. 2. The block diagram of sensing network layer

4 Control layer and user layer design

The control layer is responsible for receiving the transmission information from the control host and achieves intelligent forecasting and early warning based on the received information. In order to achieve effective data transmission and storage, a dedicated transmission data structure is designed. The structure diagram is shown in Figure 3. In order to ensure the uninterrupted transmission of information, the link structure parameter information is also designed in the data structure. The parameter information records the real-time link, disconnection and other information and when the disconnection information reaches the warning value, the intelligent host can be disconnected or restarted, thus ensures the continuity of communication.

Start code	RFID information code	Temperature and humidity information	Oxygen and carbon dioxide information	Cold storage / vehicle identification information	Shelf life prediction information	Link parameter information	End code

Fig.3. Transmission data structure diagram

The user layer is the information exchange interface of the user and the system. Two main user interfaces are designed according to the different terminal. For the end computer user special information website is designed, which has a multi-level user management system and can query and record real-time data according to user permissions. The website can also carry out the whole process of fresh goods traceability and shelf life prediction inquiry, which provides certain basis for consumers to buy fresh products. Furthermore, in order to adapt to more and more demands of all kinds of smart terminals such as the mobile phone and tablet computer this system designs a special APP software Cooperating with the website, so that users can query possible information online and achieve online payment and other operations through mobile phone and other portable terminal browsing.

5 Monitoring and early warning process design

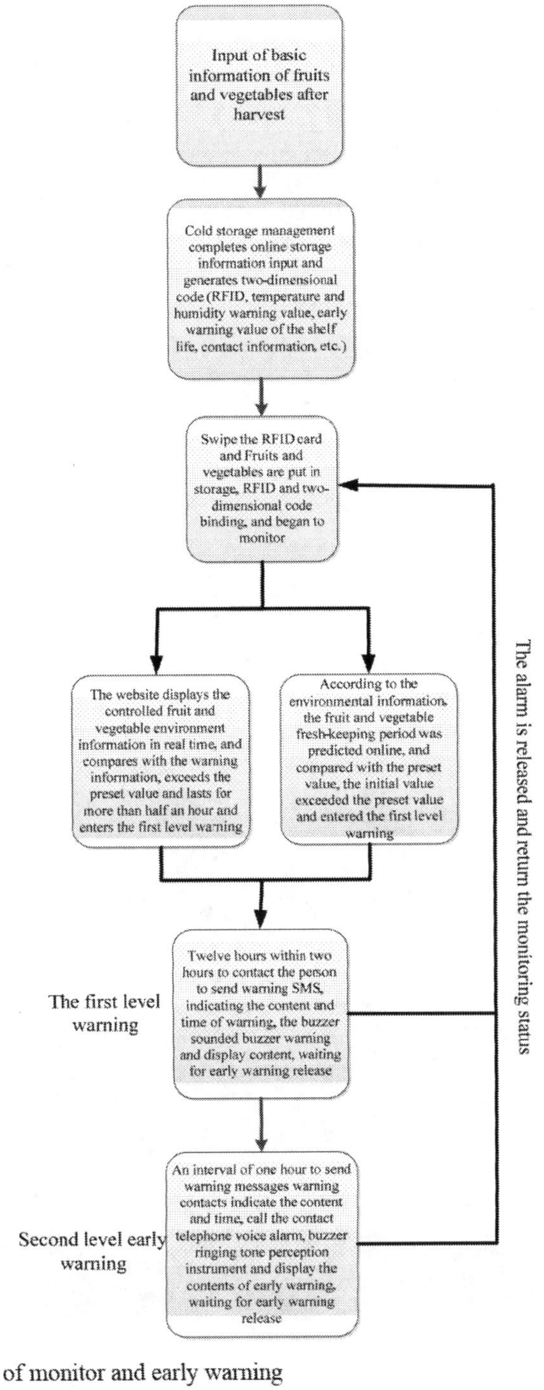

Fig. 4. The flow chart of monitor and early warning

In order to realize the full time and space online monitoring and early warning of fruits and vegetables, on the basis of Internet of things perception instrument hardware, it also established a special data management center and special website, and designed a complete monitoring and early warning process. The process from the fruits and vegetables after the information input to storage information filling, RFID and two-dimensional code binding storage, monitoring and early warning level and content are introduced in detail, as shown in figure 4.

6 System implementation and technical parameters

According to the above design, we build a complete perception system of fresh products by using STM32F103VCT6 as the main chip and combining the sensors of temperature and humidity, oxygen and carbon dioxide concentration, RFID and 3G/4G modules.The system consists of a Fresh Food Sensory Perceptual System(as shown in Figure 5 and a dedicated web site (as shown in Figure6.The system has realized the monitoring of the uninterrupted environmental parameters of the whole cold chain of fresh products. The specific technical parameters of the system are shown as table 1.

Table 1. The system specific technical parameters

Parameters	Values
external temperature	-40~100°C
built-in temperature	-20~60°C
humidity	0~100%RH
temperature accuracy	±0.5°C
humidity accuracy	±3%RH
Record interval	2 seconds ~24 hours
specification of power supply	DC12V 1A
The power consumption	less than 0.24W
Applicable environment	-20~60°C

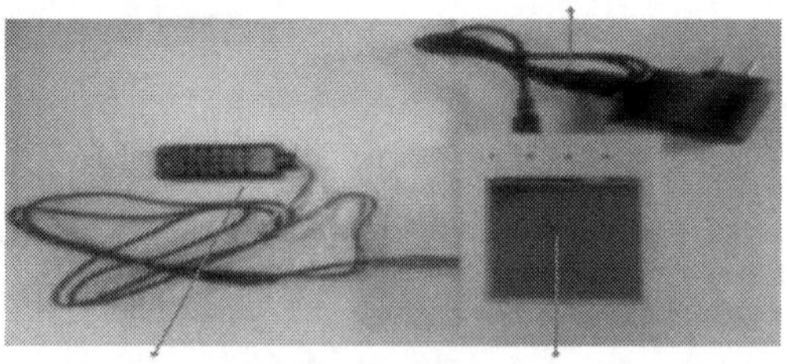

Fig. 5. Fresh food sensory perceptual system

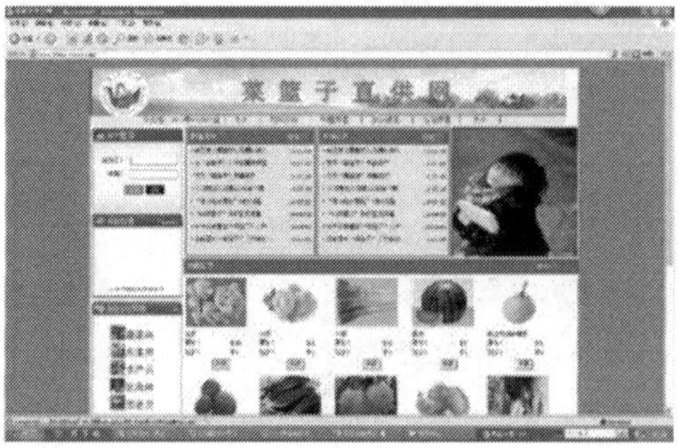

Fig.6. Special website for fresh food sensory perceptual system

7 Conclusion

Aiming at the problem of low information level of cold chain preservation in China, a kind of fresh food sensory perceptual system for cold chain logistics based on Internet of things is designed. This system highly integrated applied many technologies such as the Internet of things technology, forecasting technology of fruits and vegetables length for preservation, RFID and Planar bar code technology, Big data and cloud computing technology and so on, which has four layer structures including sensing layer, network layer, control layer and user layer .The system can implement the real-time temperature and humidity environment parameters monitoring and early warning of the whole cold chain logistics for fresh food from its picking, storage, transportation and processing link, which greatly improving the information level of cold chain circulation in our country and has a strong marketing value.

Acknowledgments: Supported by Key Projects of Tianjin Science and Technology Support Plan: Research and development of fruit and vegetable cold chain circulation support technology of Internet of things(No. 15ZCZDNC00240)

References

1. Wang Ying, Ma, Xianping, Sun Ying. Present situation and development strategies of food cold-chain logistics in China. 4th Asian Conference on Refrigeration and Air-Conditioning, ACRA, pp. 263-266(2009)
2. CHEN Ning. The Current situation and the Countermeasures of China's cold chain logistics development. Logistics engineering and management. 39(01), 14-15(2017).
3. Lin, Hui Dan; Gao, Geng Jun .Transportation safety countermeasure analysis on cold-chain logistics of fresh agricultural products. Advanced Materials Research, 860-863, 3123-3127, 2014, Energy Development.
4. GUO Hong-xia1, SHAO Ming. Process Reengineering of Cold Chain Logistics of Agricultural Products Based on Low-carbon Economy. Asian Agricultural Research, 4(2), 59-62(2012).
5. REN Wei-zhe, WANG Lin-lin. The analysis of typical mode of domestic and foreign food cold-chain logistics. Guangdong Agricultural Sciences, 2, 212-214(2013).
6. R.D. Heap. Cold Chain Performance Issues Now and in the Future. Bulletin of the IIR, 223-236(2006).
7. B Commère. Controlling the Cold Chain to ensure Food Hygiene and Quality. Bulletin of the IIR, 2, 182-188(2003).
8. R. D. Heap. Cold Chain Performance Issues Now Future. Bulletin of the 1IR ,4, 223-236(2006).
9. Li Jie. Issues of food-related cold-chain logistics management in China. 2010 International Conference on Logistics Systems and Intelligent Management, ICLSIM 2010, v 3, p 1319-1322
10. Xiao Jun,Wang, Zhongwei. The construction of symbiotic synergistic mode of forest fruit industry and cold chain logistics in China, ICLEM 2010: Logistics for Sustained Economic Development - Infrastructure, Information, Integration - Proceedings of the 2010 International Conference of Logistics Engineering and Management, v 387, p 487-494, 2010

Research on the development of scientific and technological intelligence in big data environment

Qiong Wu[1,* a], *Chensheng* Wu[1,b], and *Yanjun* Liu[1,c]

[1]No.140, Xizhimenwai Street, Xicheng District, Beijing, 100044 P R CHINA.

[a]wwqqppdd@163.com, [b]wu1082@163.com, [c]65415643@qq.com

Abstract. This paper describes the features of Internet data from the perspective of the development of scientific and technological intelligence in the era of big data. It has discussed the main problems that affect the construction of scientific and technological intelligence system and the specific technical problems in the process of construction. What's more, it has clarified that in the big data environment, the basic features of the development of scientific and technological intelligence and problems faced by the big data intelligence system. Finally, the author has predicted the opportunities and challenges for scientific and technological intelligence service agency posed by the big data.

1 Basic features of the big data environment

The scientific and technological intelligence has gone through the era of intelligence scarcity and intelligence popularization, and is moving towards the age of intelligence holography. Only the big data can complete the holographic description of the service object. Now the big data era has gradually shifted to the "artificial intelligence era," and also has made a profound impact on the enormous changes brought about by the external environment in the field of scientific and technological intelligence. For scientific and technological intelligence, how much data is called big data? It does not really matter whether the measurement standard is in TB, ZB, or PB, and what's important is that we can see the panorama of the intelligence service, also known as holography. For this reason, we have to change the way of thinking about data processing, and the mistaken concept of big data that its data and data structure obtained by technological means [1].

1.1 Distributed data and un-structured data

The data is usually divided into two categories in the industry: structured data and unstructured data. However, in the context of big data, the traditional means of processing structured data has all but failed due to the millions of data sources. As a result, we have to process the structured data we search by using the means of processing unstructured data.

* Corresponding author: wwqqppdd@163.com

That is, when we process hundreds of structured data sources, we can process them according to their structural features. However, if the quantity increases, thousands or even tens of thousands of disorder structured data cannot be processed according to their structural features and must be dealt with by unstructured means.

1.2 The Internet is big and comprehensive "database"

There is no denying the fact that the Internet is the largest and most comprehensive database. In the traditional sense, the scientific and technological community is desired to find the largest and most authoritative database, thus obtaining the most needed information content. With the development of the Internet, the traditional structured database content can often be retrieved on the Internet[2]. However, the information on the Internet cannot be compared with the structured data that has gone through secondary processing in terms of quantity, coverage, comprehensiveness and speed of response.

2 Core issues of big data intelligence system

The core issues of big data scientific and technological intelligence system are the intelligence search capabilities and human reading ability. Identifying and obtaining the vast amount of information (also known as big data) from the largest "database" - the Internet – serve as the foundation of big data scientific and technological intelligence system. How to convert big data information into information with tens of thousands of words that are suitable for people to read is a problem that must be solved in processing big data.

2.1 basic features of scientific and technological intelligence system

The intelligence collection of the intelligence system requires All-Source Intelligence, which requires collecting all information sources on the Internet and multivariate & heterogeneous data from toll database and internal enterprise information, which is the reason of creating big data. In fact, only big data can fully reflect the full range of intelligence objects, so we must make network-wide collection when we collect information. Otherwise, it is very difficult to collect the order parameter that reflects the essential changes of intelligence objects. According to the theory of H.Haken, the order parameters are the decisive factors in the transformation of old and new systems, where the order parameters will change. Therefore, the so-called intelligence system tracking only a few dozen or hundreds of websites cannot actually track the key order parameters of the intelligence system, and is also difficult to give a prediction and warning of the revolutionary system changes with the greatest intelligence value. This is one of the most urgent tasks that the construction is actually going to accomplish.

2.2 The core driving force of scientific and technological intelligence system under big data

The capability of identifying and judging demand and applying big data processing systems to identify data associations and making judgments is a big change in the importance of scientific and technological intelligence in the era of big data. First, intelligence points' position discrimination capability in the global. This will answer whether all your intelligence information covers all of the key points (or points of knowledge) in the field, and coverage of manually processed intelligence in the global. Second, classification capability. The classification of the search information through mathematics method, models and tools is essential in the era of big data. This capability has turned from general capability to one of the core capabilities in the age of manual processing data. Third, concentrating capability. The concentrating capability that can concentrate big data with little intelligence information into "high concentration" information and match with human reading ability serves as the foundation of human reading ability. Information visualization is also an important step in human reading ability. Fourth, associating capability. The basic feature of big data is data association, but how to identify the data association and its logical relationship through mathematical, psychology, sociology and other means is the capability that the scientific and technological intelligence should identify beyond IT's data association. Fifth, interpretation auxiliary capability. Intelligence interpretation is the core content of intelligence. The intelligence interpretation is traditionally based on personal knowledge, perception, sensitivity on the information and data. In the era of big data, the interpretation of information data must be related to the data. While interpreting the data information, the auxiliary system provides the related knowledge of data information, i.e. the related links, which will help the readers (usually technical experts) make more comprehensive and profound understanding of the content behind the information data, inspire and assist readers to understand the objects, so that they can make a more comprehensive and systematic interpretation, which is also known as "interpretation supporting system or identification supporting system." Sixth, report assisted generation. After interpreting scientific and technological intelligence, it is usually necessary to provide a consultation report with the demander. The writing of the report often occupies a large amount of time of the researchers. In fact, this report requires the scholars to re-summarize the knowledge in relevant fields[3]. The big data intelligence system can provide similar contents that are contained in the big data based on experts' outline or paradigm, and then the experts can modify them accordingly, thus quickly completing the scientific consultation report. Seventh, capability of identifying industry experts. Scientific and technological intelligence is interpreted and determined by the human brain, and possessor of domain knowledge – experts, how to choose them is the key to the interpretation of scientific and technological intelligence. In order to find the competent experts to perform right thing, intelligence agencies required to establish a comprehensive network that contains huge expert information, structure and relationships.

2.3 Intelligence system integrated workshop hall's core capability feature

With the model that is built based on the mathematic, social simulation knowledge, it can use the "science" mode of thinking to help solve the qualitative problems of "liberal arts", and quantitatively give accurate explanation, and achieve changes from quantity to quality on this basis. In fact, this is the concept of the integrated workshop hall proposed by Mr. Qian Xuesen in the early nineties. This concept has laid a solid theoretical foundation for the intelligence community to meet the era of big data and also has pointed out the direction for the construction of scientific and technological intelligence system in the era of artificial intelligence. On this basis, the mathematical model analysis of practical engineering is of great significance in the quantitative analysis under qualitative guidance. On the basis of this engineering model and tool, the identification of correlation supply of knowledge and opinion behind it and digging of more valuable information from the data are the correct understanding of intelligence interpretation. The development process from factual data to process-based data is a change based on the understanding of the data, which has changed the data from "dead" to "live" and changed from the happened facts to the ongoing facts. That is: with various means such as data mining in the IT industry, under the guidance of the system of science, it will identify its association and laws, and help make the intelligent, scientific decision, which is the basic path for the development of big data.

3 Problems faced by scientific and technological intelligence system in the big data environment

3.1 Problems faced by professional intelligence agencies

In order to truly and clearly understand the needs of scientific and technological intelligence, and interpret the intelligence needs with more accurate language, the professional intelligence agencies should possess over 10 years of intelligence research experience and obtain background knowledge in terms of IT and mathematical modeling, thus jointly completing the research and development of intelligence system. Since the intelligence is a discipline that studies complex systems, the development of information systems cannot solely rely on computer technicians, which requires systematic and scientific thought, foundations of mathematical modeling, concepts of complex social systems, awareness of social sciences and long-term experience. It is precisely because of this, Professor Shen Guchao of Nanjing University has put forward: the academic circles feature lack of verification and poor operability due to the emphasis on analysis of various models of theory, methods and tools; business circles feature strong universality, insufficient individualization, different from the description of academia and failing to meet demand for intelligence in the market competition due to the perspective of quantitative analysis of business intelligence; the industry circle accepts the concept proposed by the academic circles and uses the information system developed by the "business circle", which has caused many questions in the big data products[4].

3.2 Dilemma of professional and technical layer

First, capacity of the database. At present, the "small" common database can only accommodate millions of records, and tens of millions, hundreds of millions of data will encounter when we operate big data system. The "big" database is inconvenient to use. Second, Windows program installation. Big data processing system will operate dozens of applications simultaneously. However, Windows will drastically reduce its operational efficiency after installing multiple software programs, and even cannot function properly. Sometimes, the system will crash. Third, disk file format. The file format in the original Windows XP only supports 2G, which has made restrictions for the big data files with over 10 G. Other problems exist in the Win7 operating system. Excel2003 can only process 60,000 rows of records, while Excel 2007 and 2010 can only process one million rows of records, which have not taken the big data demand into consideration. Fourth, I/O capacity. When processing big data, the cache of disk system actually does not work, and the disk reads and writes data at mechanical speed, which is one millionth of processing speed of CPU cache and other electronic transmission. It has formed a bottleneck in the big data processing. Even Hadoop cannot solve the problem, unless large-scale data center can provide services at any time. The best way to process I/O at this point is the SSDs, the solution of using laptops + SSDs can perform better than that of data center + disk arrays. Fifth, memory problem. No matter how much memory windows can manage, they cannot keep up with the expected memory for big data processing. Although Hadoop can manage larger memory, it cannot solve the problem of transferring data between memories in different machine (the transmission speed of the network cable is one thousandth of the memory speed). The operating system of parallel computing system has not fully supported the big data system. Sixth, Hadoop problem. The parallel processing cannot be cross-calculated[5],see Figure 1.

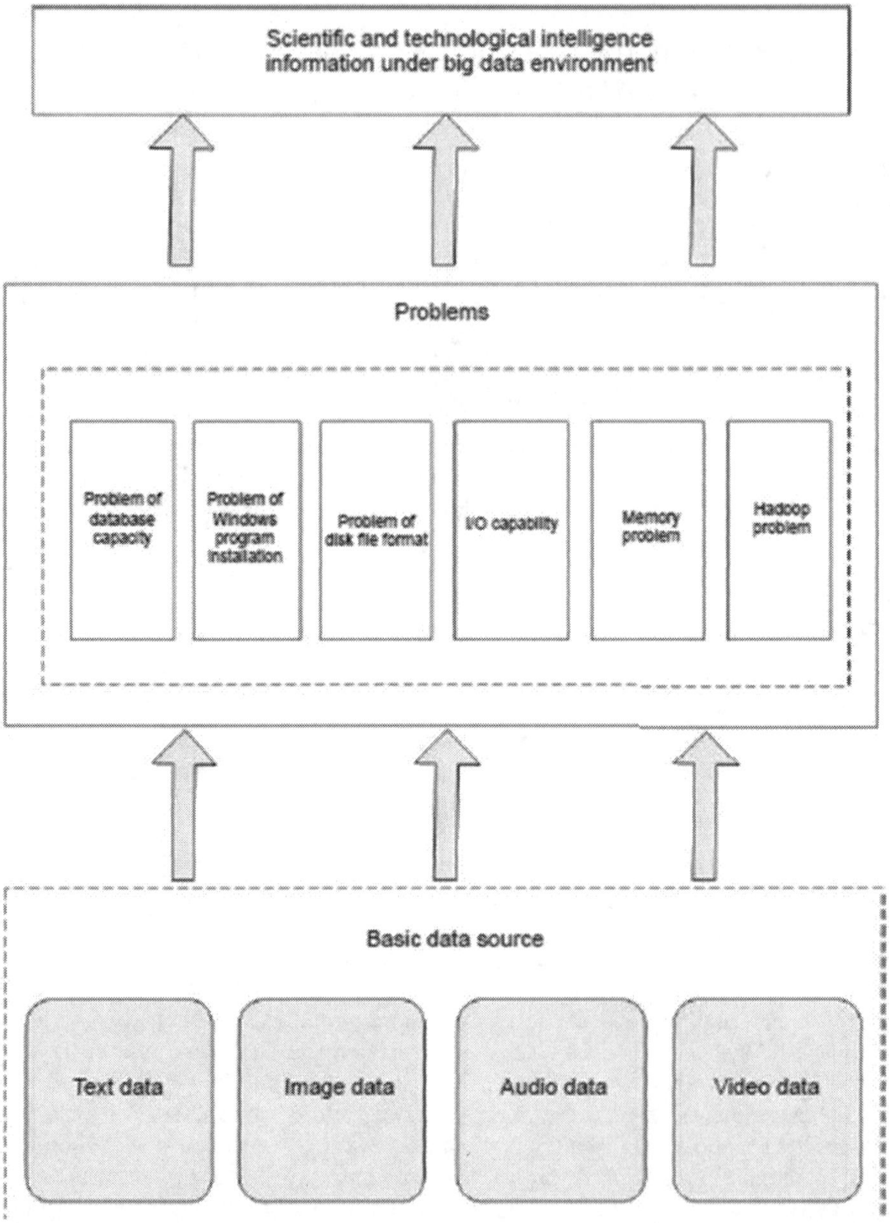

Fig. 1. Problems of professional and technical layer

At present, in the context of artificial intelligence, the IT industry is still exploring the true meaning of big data. For example: the debate on unstructured databases, C++ and Java are suitable for processing big data, but the scientific and technological intelligence industry has changed from the urgent desire to obtain intelligence information in big data to instruct service objects "what to do and how to do". Therefore, the current intelligence industry should use existing IT means to "summarize" large amount of disorganized original "data", then extract the content with core values and organize them into the content that the demand side strongly needs, thus extracting valuable core information. On this basis, it will complete the extraction of relevant intelligence information, apply in practice, and ultimately complete the countermeasures and suggestions report under the support of big data, which is the framework of the intelligence system services in big data environment.

4 Opportunities and challenges for scientific and technological intelligence service agencies presented by big data

The storage, analysis and processing of intelligence information in the era of big data is an important means of acquiring knowledge and also the key content of intelligence research. With the rapid development of digital technology and network, massive unstructured and rapidly growing data continue to emerge, causing a great impact on intelligence research. Intelligence studies will inevitably face a technological revolution. From the date of the birth of scientific and technological intelligence, it has never been a comprehensive grasp of intelligence objects. This possibility is realized for the first time in the context of the big data era. The scientific and technological intelligence that historically relies on the exclusive source of information as the feature, the ability to interpret intelligence as the core competitiveness, has developed and enabled the scientific and technological agencies to empower unique ability to serve through the application of unique big data tools as a means, safeguarding the interpretation of intelligence as the goal and using semi-automatic intelligence as the core capability under the guidance of unique intelligence thinking. The big data helps scientific intelligence agencies accomplish its mission and provides the theoretical and practical basis of identifying differences and existence between intelligence agencies and general soft science agencies [6] .

References

1. Herman Haken [M]. Germany: Shanghai Translation Publishing House, 2001.
2. Qian Xuesen, Yu Jingyuan, Dai Ruwei. A New Scientific Field - An Open and Complicated Giant System (Including Social Systems) and Its Methodology [J] .Journal of Nature, 1990 (1).
3. Qian Xuesen, Open Complex Giant System [J]. Pattern Recognition and Artificial Intelligence, 1991 (1)
4. Dai Ru-wei. Metasynthesis from qualitative to quantitative [J]. Pattern Recognition and Artificial Intelligence, 1991 (1).
5. Dai Ruwei. Metasynthesis Method from qualitative to quantitative (Met synthesis) - Open complex giant system methodology [M] Beijing: Tsinghua University Press, 1996.
6. Dai Ruwei. The Proposal and Recent Development of Metasynthetic Method (M) from Qualitative to Quantitative [J]. Natural Science, 2009, 31 (6).

ITM Web of Conferences **17**, 03019 (2018) https://doi.org/10.1051/itmconf/20181703019
WCSN 2017

An overview of current situations of robot industry development

Qiong Wu[1,*,a], *Yanjun* Liu[1,b], and *Chensheng* Wu[1,c]

[1]No.140, Xizhimenwai Street, Xicheng District, Beijing, 100044 P R CHINA.

[a]wwqqppdd@163.com, [b]65415643@qq.com, [c]wu1082@163.com

Abstract. As an industry of emerging technology, robot industry has become one of important signs to evaluate a country's level in science and technology innovation and high-end manufacturing, and an important strategic field to take the preemptive opportunities in development of intelligent society. Developed countries such as the USA, Germany, France and Japan have formulated their robot R&D strategies and planning in succession. China boasts good industrial foundation and has made encouraging progress in the course of development of robot technology. This paper briefly discusses the application type of robot industry and current situations of robot industry development in countries around the world, and makes detailed explanation of current situations of robot industry development in China.

1 Introduction

Robot is a kind of automation equipment combining advanced technologies of multiple disciplines such as machinery, electronics, control, computer, sensor and artificial intelligence [1]. It is an automation technology and can execute some tasks under unmanned situation by programming. That is to say, robot can receive operator's instruction and then execute the instruction independently. In addition, robot is one of the forms of artificial intelligence (AI). HubSpot's market analyst Mimi An describes it as the "technology able to do things as human being can — regardless of conversation, vision and learning, or social contact and inference" , just as AI applications in iPhone-based Siri and Google Assistant. Therefore, robot industry, as an industry of emerging technology, has become one of important signs to evaluate a country's level in science and technology innovation and high-end manufacturing, and an important strategic field to take the preemptive opportunities in development of intelligent society. Developed countries and regions such as the USA, Japan, the UK and the European Union have formulated their robot R&D strategies and planning in succession. China boasts good industrial foundation and has made encouraging progress in the course of development of robot technology.

* Corresponding author: wwqqppdd@163.com

2 Current situations of robot industry development

2.1 Development history of robot

2.1.1 Infancy stage (1910-1960)

First, the word of "Robot" was created by Karel Capek, a writer of Czechoslovakia, in 1910. In his science fiction, he first used the word "Robot" on the basis of Robota for "Hard Labor and Manual Work" and Robotnik for "Worker". The New York World's Fair 1911 in the USA displayed the home robot Elektro made by Westinghouse Electric Corporation. Elektro was controlled by cable and could walk, speak 77 words and even have a cigarette, making people's dream for home robot more specific. In 1914, American George Devol manufactured the world's first programmable robot (namely the first real robot in the world) and registered the patent. Such mechanical hand was equipped with versatility and flexibility, so it could do different jobs according to different programs. In 1959, Devol and American inventor Joseph Engelberger jointly manufactured the first industrial robot. Later, they established the first robot manufacturing factory Unimation in the world. In memory of Engelberger's contributions to R&D of and publicity to industrial robot, he was called the "Father of Robotics"[2].

2.1.2 Mid-term development stage (1961-1989)

In 1962, American AMF Company produced "VERSTRAN" (meaning "Universal Handling"), which was a commercialized industrial robot in real sense and exported to many countries in the world, thus setting off a race of robot research around the world. Since the mid-1960s, American Massachusetts Institute of Technology and Stanford University and the British University of Edinburgh had established robot labs in succession, and the USA started an upsurge of research of 2G robot with sensor and "Feeling", and set out for AI. In 1968, Stanford Institute announced its successful robot Shakey. With visual sensor, able to find and grab blocks according to operator's instruction, Shakey could be taken as the first intelligent robot in the world, but the computer controlling it was as large as a room. In 1969, Kato Ichiro Lab of Waseda University, Japan researched and developed the first robot walking on two feet, for which Kato Ichiro was reputed as the "Father of Manlike Robot". In 1973, robot was firstly combined with minicomputer, promoting birth of Robot T3 by American Cincinnati Milacron Company. In 1978, American Unimation Company offered general-purpose industrial robot PUMA, marking that industrial robot technology had become mature completely. Today, PUMA is still serving production lines in factories. In 1984, Eagleburger further marketed Robot Helpmate able to deliver food, medicine and mails to patients in hospitals.

2.1.3 Rapid development stage (since 1990)

In 1998, Denmark Lego presented robot (Mind-storms) kits, making robot manufacturing as easy as building block, relatively simple and able to be realized through free piece-up assembly. Since then, robot began to enter individual world. In 1999, Japanese Sony marketed its dog-like robot AIBO, which was sold out at once. After that, entertainment robot became one of the ways for robot to enter common families. In 2002, American iRobot Company presented dust-extractor robot Roomba, which can avoid obstacles, automatically design advancement route and automatically drive to the charger if the power is insufficient. Roomba is the home robot with the highest sales and most commercialized in the world at present. In June 2006, Microsoft marketed Microsoft Robotics Studio, making robot more and more modular and uniform platform-based. Bill Gates predicted that home robot will sweep over the world very soon.

2.2 Classification of robot applications

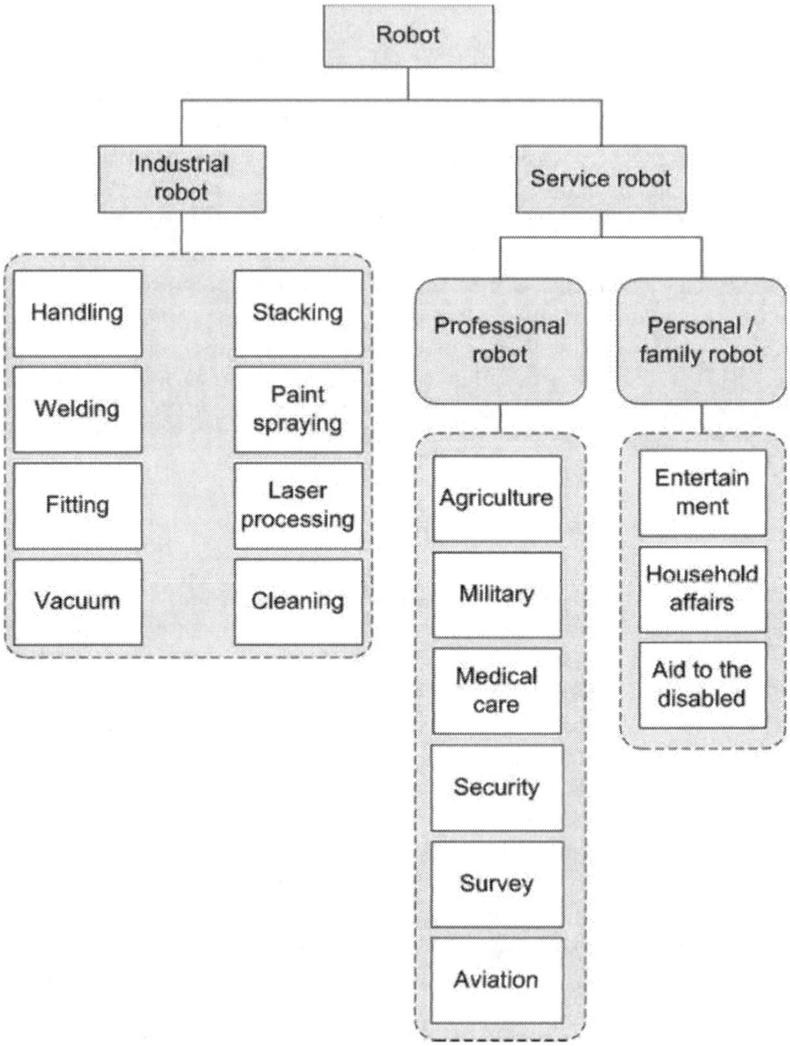

Fig. 1. Classification of Robot Applications

In terms of application fields, robot can be classified into industrial robot and service robot. The industrial robot means the multi-joint mechanical hand or multi-degree-of-freedom robot for industrial field, with typical applications including welding, handling, assembly, fitting, vacuum, spraying, stacking, laser processing and cleaning. The service robot consists of semi-automatic or fully automatic robot except for those in industrial production, including professional robot and family personal robot, of which, the professional robot includes exclusive robot for agriculture, military, medical care, security, survey and aviation (also called special robot) and the home robot for household affairs, entertainment and aid to the disabled[3].

2.3 Current situations of robot industry development in countries around the world

Currently, at least one third of countries in the world are in R&D of robot. In the field of service robot, leading Western countries are represented by the USA, Germany and France and leading Asian countries are represented by Japan and ROK. Each of the countries has its own specialty in robot R&D field and application type. For example, the USA focuses more on R&D of military robot, while some EU countries have launched the biggest civilian robot R&D project in the world.

The USA is the birthplace of robot, and its robot technology keeps leading in the world, is complete, all-round, advanced and highly adaptable, and dominates in military, medical care and home service robot industry, with the market share of about 60%; Germany is leading in service robot application research around the world, and its robot housekeeper Care-O-Bot3 is equipped with sensor, 3D color camera, laser scanner and 3D stereo camera. In addition, Care-O-Bot3 also boasts the abilities of sound control or gesture control, self-learning and understanding voice order and gesture order; the Government of France attached importance to robot technology from the beginning, greatly supports service robot research plan, and has established a complete science and technology system, with the key in robot application research particularly; Japan is a major power in robot production, R&D and use, and has always taken robot as a strategic industry and made great efforts to support the industry from technology and funds, with the R&D mainly centering on service robot. In recent years, demands for robot products in old people nursing market promote enterprises to race in R&D of mini home robot; ROK also takes service robot technology as 10 major "Engine" industries for its development in the future, considers service robot as a new economic growth point, and gives key supports to robot technology[4].

3 Current situations of robot industry development in China

China's service robot market began to take initial shape in 2005 or so. Compared with Japan, the USA and other developed countries, China started late and has a big gap in R&D of service robot, but has witnessed rapid and violent development in recent years. Many traditional robot user enterprises have entered robot industry through independent R&D, investment and M&A one after another and comprehensively applied technologies such as AI to develop service robot, and some innovative leading enterprises have emerged. For example, DJI-Innovations, Siasun Robot & Automation Co., Ltd. and Shanghai STEP Robotics Co., Ltd. as well as other enterprises in the field have won their market share.

3.1 Industrial robot

Since 2013, industrial robot technology has developed vary fast in China under promotion of national policy guarantee and technology development. New technology will promote further development of robot technology. Technologically, China is now at the period of rapid development. By 2025 or so, industrial robot technology will realize a great progress in China. The Chinese Government attaches very high importance to R&D of key components in speed reducer, servo and controller, as the three key components account for over 70% of the cost of industrial robot. Previously such components were mainly relied on foreign technology, but now they are made in China gradually.

By 2016, China had reported nearly 50 industrial parks for industrial robot completed or in progress and about 800 influential robot companies. At present, local governments have also recognized importance of robot and taken active measures to develop robot-related industries, with representative Chinese industrial robot enterprises including: Siasun Robot

& Automation Co., Ltd., Harbin Boshi Automation Co., Ltd. and Nanjing Estun Automation Co., Ltd[5].

3.2 Service robot

Intelligent service robot has become an emerging growth point of robot industry in China. In recent years, development of AI technology has further fueled R&D of service robot, and voice interaction, face identification, automatic positioning and navigation as well as other AI technologies have been further integrated with traditional products, and innovative products have been presented continuously, for example, intelligent sound box marketed by Linglong Tech and Alibaba in succession and intelligent interaction robot built by Xiaomi Robot. In terms of policy, China has mapped out relevant policies in succession, which serve as the strategic power for priority to development of service robot. With great supports of the policies, 25 robot industrial parks have been built in China, which are mainly in the Yangtze River Delta, the Pearl River Delta and Beijing-Tianjin-Hebei region. There are 1393 relevant enterprises in Jiangsu, Zhejiang and Shanghai as well as Anhui Province in the Yangtze River Delta region, 784 relevant enterprises in Bohai-Rim Beijing-Tianjin-Hebei region, Shandong and Liaoning, and 747 relevant enterprises in the Pearl River Delta area including Guangdong Province.

At present, in robot products with initial shape such as cleaning robot and educational and entertainment robot, a batch of enterprises with good combination of production, study and research have emerged. According to the information released by relevant departments, Top 5 service robot enterprises in China in 2016 are: Guangzhou Joinmax Digital Technology Co., Ltd., Shenyang Unecox Robot Co., Ltd., Shenyang Siasun Robot Automation Co., Ltd., Mirle Automation Technology (Shanghai) Co., Ltd. and Shanghai PartnerX Robotics Co., Ltd.[6].

3.3 Special robot

The Chinese Government attaches high importance to research and development of special robot technology, and supports the development through 863 Program, theme projects of key technologies for robot operating under special service environment and deep-sea key technology and equipment, promoting continuous progress of special robot technology. By far, China has conquered multiple core technologies including Ti-alloy manned cabin spherical shell manufacturing, high-depth buoyancy material preparation and deep-sea impeller, helping China make remarkable progress in domestic production of core deep-sea equipment. In addition, China is now leading globally in research and development of special UAV and underwater robot, and has initially developed series products of special UAV, underwater robot, search and rescue/explosive-removal robot in special robot field and advantages in some fields. For example, China Electronics Technology Group Corporation has researched and developed fixed-wing UAV intelligent swarming system and successfully completed 119-set fixed-wing UAV swarming flight test; CRRC Times Electric Co., Ltd. has developed the highest-tonnage deep-water trenching plough in the world, filling a gap of China in deep-sea robot equipment manufacturing field; the cable-controlled ROV “Discovery” and the autonomous underwater robot "Exploration" on the new-generation ocean comprehensive scientific research vessel “Science” have realized the first deep-sea shooting by intersection in the north of the South China Sea.

4 Conclusion

With development of technology and the advent of "Manpower Substitution" times, robot industry is extending from manufacturing industry to service industry, and countries in the world have taken robot industry as their development strategy one after another. Service robot, as an emerging field of robot industry, highly integrates intelligence, sensing, network, cloud computing and other innovative technologies and is combined with new mode of mobile Internet, providing a new window for promoting smart life and fueling industrial transformation.

References

1 Shi, M. China's Robot Industry Faces Severe Challenge in Development[J].Science & Technology Review. 2014(32):9.
2 Li, J. Et al. Greatly Develop Robot Industry to Promote Industrial Transformation and Upgrading in our Province [R]. Hangzhou: Zhejiang Province Economic and Information Commission.2013.
3 Robot Development Strategies of Countries in the World [EB/OL].[2014-12-08].
4 IFR.World Robotics 2014 Industrial Robots [EB/OL]. [2014-12-08].
5 Liu, S. Influences of Intelligent Robot on our Life[J].Market Weekly.Disquisition Edition, 2015(3):114-116.
6 Huang, Y. Et al. Current Situations of Intelligent Robot Application and the Development Trend[J]. International Academic Developments. 2009(4):38-39.

Analysis of character network heat based on web retrieval technology

Minglei Wu[1,a] *and Jingchang Pan*[2,b,*]

[1]School of Mechanical, Electrical & Information Engineering, Shan Dong University, Weihai; School of Rong Cheng, Harbin University of Science and Technology, Wei Hai, China
[2]School of Mechanical, Electrical & Information Engineering, Shan Dong University, Wei Hai, China
[a]wuming8511@126.com; [b]pjc@sdu.edu.cn

Abstract. Information technology is now developing rapidly, the Internet has also obtained widespread popularization. The amount of information on the network is increasing exponentially, whose information sources are widely distributed and varied. If the information can't be managed in an orderly manner, it will be difficult for the user to extract the information they need from such a massive amount of information. Although the current search engine give people a lot of convenience in searching for information, but the search engine can't reflect the user's personalized information demand with facing a wide variety of users with different information needs, knowledge background and interest. In this paper, a recommendation method based on search results with java as a technology is implemented. This method takes Baidu hot people ranking as an example for verifying.

1 Introduction

In the 1970s, research and application of personalized recommendation systems began to emerge. Grundy is universally recognized as the first personalized recommendation system that is put into use, and this system recommends relevant books for each user by creating a user interest model [1]. By the 1990s, the theoretical framework of the personalized recommendation system had been mature [2-4]. Tapestry mail processing system calculates the similarity between users for recommending [5]. GroupLens to establish user information group, the group of users can publish information, through the social information filtering system to calculate the similarity between users, and then to other users within the group to recommend [6]. Ringo uses the same social information filtering method to recommend music to users [7]. Other recommended systems include Amazon's book recommendation system, Jester's jokes recommendation system, Phoaks' page recommendation system [8-10]. Since the beginning of the 21st century, under the great data age, the individual demand for information has become more and more intense, and more and more personalized recommendation systems have been developed. The system of this paper mainly meet the user's personalized information needs through the second search analysis of the current search engine result.

---

*Jingchang Pan: pjc@sdu.edu.cn

2 Basic principles of search engine

Search engine is not a search for the Internet, it searches for pre-organized index database. Similarly, the search engine also can't understand the content on the page, it can only match the text on the page. Search engine workflow is shown in Fig. 1.

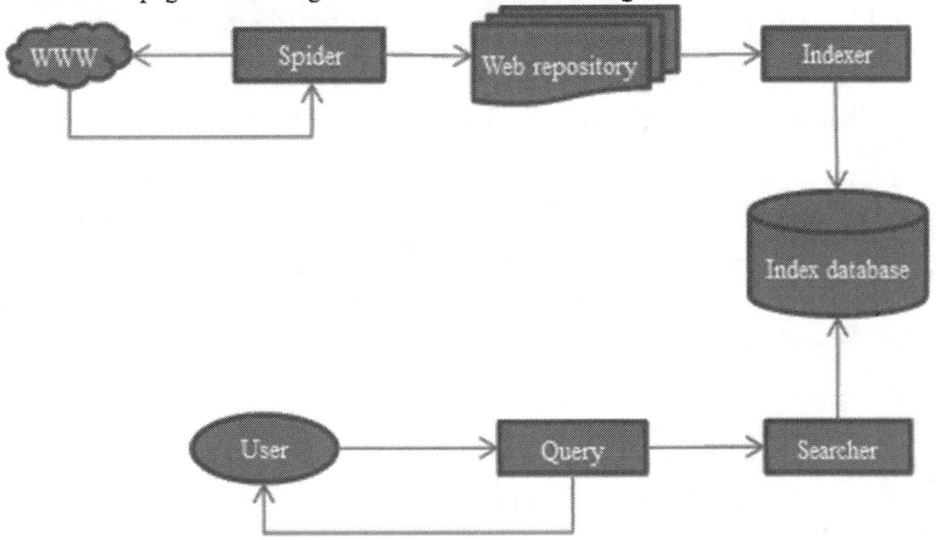

Fig. 1. Search Engine Workflow

Search engine workflow can be divided into four steps: Firstly, the web crawler crawls the page from the Internet according to the relevant algorithm (depth first, breadth first priority); secondly, the information on the page is processed after crawling the page ; thirdly, after the post-processing information will be saved in the index database; fourthly, the search result is sorted by the search engine and displayed to the user when the user searches the index information about the query in the index database.

In 1990, Alan Emtage of the University of Montreal used Archie engine for related information retrieval in a specific network, thus creating a new field of modern search engines. At present, the Internet search engine can be divided into three types according to the information collection methods and services provided by different ways.

(1) Director Search Engineer. The search engine is build based on manual or semi-automatic way, and the Internet page is browsed by a lot of manpower which will be compiled into HTML files, classified and arranged by a certain order in order to enable users to refer look up the index.

(2) Crawler-Based Search Engineer. The data source is automatically searched and indexed in a certain strategy by a spider robot program.

(3) Meta Search Engineer. There is actually no search engine in itself, but it relies on other original engine index or search interface to complete the task, that is, it doesn't have its own data, but submits the query request to more than one search engine at the same time. Then these results with repeated exclusion, rearrangement and other processing as a result of their own return to the user.

3 Principles of the proposed method

Although the current search engine brings a lot of convenience for searching information resources, but search engines fail to meet the user's personalized information demand due to a wide variety of users with different information needs, knowledge background and interest. The search engine can’t analyze the user's search intent by interaction, the user's preferences and interests can’t be tracked by capturing the user's records, and the user's feedback can,t be used , etc. Furthermore, the engine returns too much useless information and too little personalized results, so it is difficult to find interesting documents in a simple way. Personalization recommendation is a valid method for lightening the user's burden on information retrieval.

This paper takes Baidu hot people sorting as an example, and this proposed method with JAVA technology based on the Baidu search result for specific keywords of user’s interests. The concrete steps are as follows:

(1) To enter the interested content in the txt file;

(2)To automatically transmit the interested content one by one to the Baidu search engine to search by this proposed method;

(3) To return the Baidu search result to the txt file one by one by this proposed method;

(4) To copy the result to excel for analysis. (Processing results shown in Fig. 3, 4) .

The method flow is shown in Fig. 2.

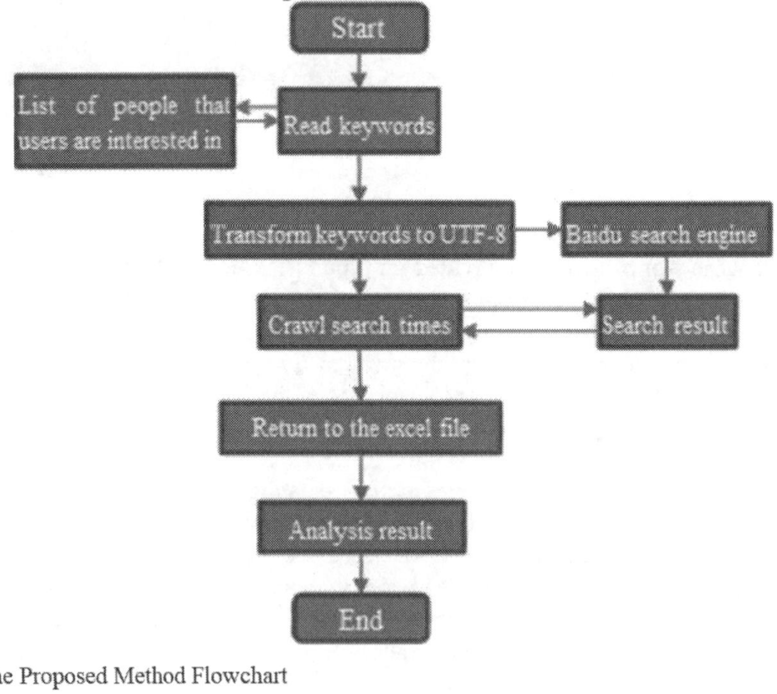

Fig. 2. The Proposed Method Flowchart

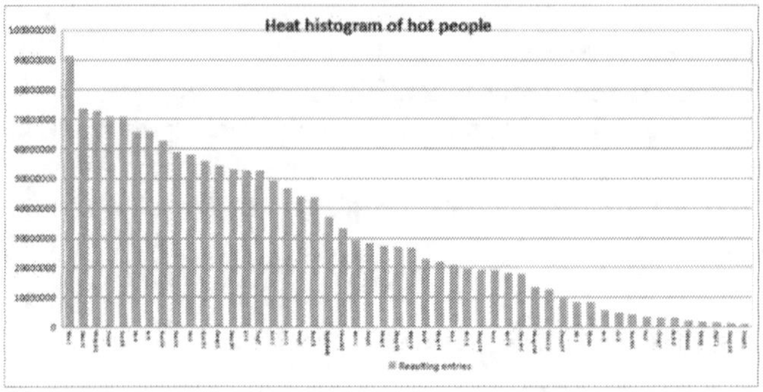

Fig. 3. Heat Histogram of Hot People

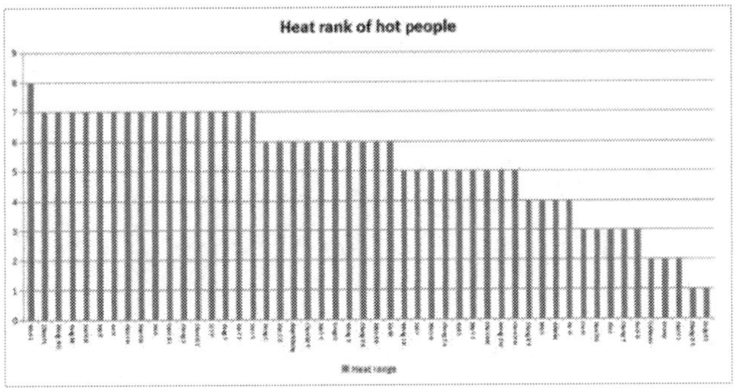

Fig. 4. Heat Rank of Hot People

4 Summary

In summary, this paper proposes a personalized retrieval method based on JAVA according to the personalized problem in Web retrieval, and this method can accurately grasp the corresponding Baidu resulting entry according to the user's interest. This method could not only be applied to the analysis of hot people, but also could be applied to such as Taobao, Jingdong and other large shopping sites to analyze and predict the behavior of consumers.

This research was financially supported by the National Natural Science Foundation of China (U1431102).

References

[1] E. Rich, User Modeling via stereotypes, Cognitive Science. 4(3) 329-354.
[2] P. Resnick, N. Iacovou, et al, Grouplens: An open architecture for collaborative filtering of netnews, in Proc 1994 Computer Supported Cooperative Work Conf, Chapel Hill, 1994, pp. 175-186.
[3] W. Hill, L. Stead, et al, Recommending and evaluating choices in a virtual community of use, in Proc. Conf Human Factors in Computing System, Denver, 1995, pp. 194-201.
[4] U. Mochio, Webu shinkaron : hontō no daihenka wa korekara hajimaru, Tokyo, 2006.
[5] D. Goldberg, D. Nichols, et al, Using collaborative filtering to weave an information tapestry, Comm ACM, 35(12) 61-70.
[6] J. A. Konstan, B. N. Miller, et al, Gouplens: Applying collaborative filtering to usenet news, Comm ACM, 40(3) 77-87.
[7] U. Shardanand, P. Maes, Social information filtering: Algorithms for automating 'Word of Mouth', in Proc Conf Human Factors in Computing Systems, Denver, 1995, pp.201-217.
[8] G. Linden, B. Smith, York J. Amazon.com recommendations: Item-to-item collaborative filtering, IEEE Internet Computing, 7(1) 76-80.
[9] K. Goldberg, T. Roeder, et al, Eigentaste: A constant time collaborative filtering algorithm, Information Retrieval J, 4(2) 133-151.
[10] L. Terveen, W. Hill, et al, PHOAKS: A system for sharing recommendations, Comm ACM, 40(3) 59-62.

Research on Monte Carlo application based on Hadoop

Minglei Wu[1,a] *and Jingchang Pan*[2,b,*]

[1]School of Mechanical, Electrical & Information Engineering, Shan Dong University, Weihai; School of Rong Cheng, Harbin University of Science and Technology, Wei Hai, China
[2]School of Mechanical, Electrical & Information Engineering, Shan Dong University, Wei Hai, China
[a]wuming8511@126.com; [b]pjc@sdu.edu.cn

Abstract. Monte Carlo method is also known as random simulation method. The more the number of experiments, the more accurate the results obtained. Therefore, a large number of random simulation is required in order to obtain a higher degree of accuracy, but the traditional stand-alone algorithm has been difficult to meet the needs of a large number of simulation. Hadoop platform is a distributed computing platform built on a large data background and an open source software under Apache. It is easier to write and run applications for processing massive amounts of data as an open source software platform. Therefore, this paper takes π value calculation as an example to realize the Monte Carlo algorithm based on Hadoop platform, and get the exact π value with the advantage of Hadoop platform in distributed processing.

1 Introduction

Monte Carlo method is also known as random simulation method and statistical test method, which is a technical methods based on statistical simulation or random simulation for solving the problem [1-3]. "Monte Carlo" is named after Monaco's famous casino - Monte Carlo, which is proposed by Metropolis, Ulam and Von Neumann who studied nuclear weapons during World War II. The basic idea of the Monte Carlo is to establish a probabilistic model or stochastic process, and calculate statistical characteristics of required parameters by observing the process or sampling test, and then use the arithmetic mean as the approximation of the solution [4-5]. In theory, the Monte Carlo method requires a lot of experiments. The more the number of experiments, the more accurate the results obtained. Therefore, a large number of random simulations is required in order to obtain a higher degree of accuracy, but the traditional stand-alone algorithm has been difficult to meet the needs of a large number of simulation.

Hadoop platform is a distributed computing platform built on a large data background and an open source software under Apache [6-9]. It is easier to write and run applications for processing massive amounts of data as an open source software platform. Therefore, Monte Carlo Method is put at the Hadoop platform, which makes it possible to use Monte Carlo

[*] Jingchang Pan: pjc@sdu.edu.cn

Method to deal with big data. At the same time, it is meaningful to improve the accuracy of the algorithm by using the advantages of Hadoop platform in distributed processing. Organization of the Text

2 Basic principle of Hadoop

The core idea of the Hadoop framework is Map / Reduce. Map / Reduce is a programming model for the calculation of large data volume. It is also an efficient task scheduling model. It divides a task into many fine-grained subtasks, which can be scheduled among idle processing nodes, so that the node with high-speed processing deals with more tasks, so as to avoid extending the completion of the entire task in that slow-speed processing node.

Calculative steps of Map/Reduce are as follows:

(1) The user program calls the MapReduce library, and the input large data set is divided into M data fragments;

(2) There are M Map tasks and R Reduce tasks to be assigned, and master assigns a Map task or Reduce task to an idle work site;

(3) The work site which is assigned a map task reads a data fragment to parse out key/value pairs. The user-defined Map function accepts an input key/value, and then produce a collection of middle key/value;

(4) MapReduce library brings together all intermediate 'value' values of the same intermediate key value I, and then transfer them to the reduce function;

(5) The user-defined Reduce function accepts a set of an intermediate key value I and a related value. The Reduce function combines these 'value' values into a set of smaller 'value' values. It normally outputs only 0 or 1 after calling the Reduce function each time. An intermediate 'value' value is supplied to the Reduce function through an iterator so that the collection of large amounts of 'value' values that can't be fully placed in memory is handled.

The MapReduce workflow is shown in Fig. 1.

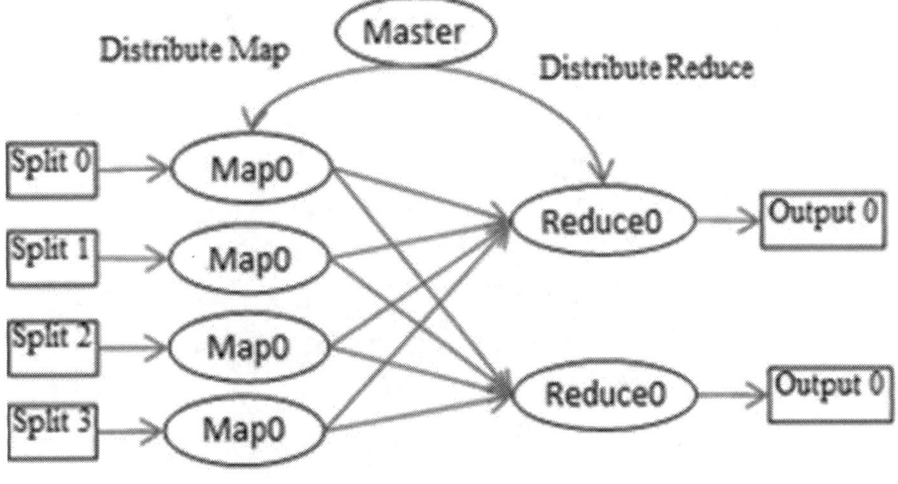

Fig. 1. The MapReduce Workflow

3 The proposed Algorithm

Monte Carlo has a high application value. Of course, it is also very significant in the field of mathematics research. The prototype of Monte Carlo method can be traced back to Buffon's needle problem in the late 19th century, which is an important problem in the classical probability that the value of π is determined by calculating the frequency of the needle onto the ground and combining the known exact relational expression. The Monte Carlo method is used to reproduce the value of π through imitating the idea of the ancients.

3.1 Basic idea

A circle B is got based on a square A (As is shown in Fig. 2). The area of A is given, so the area of B could be got by calculating the ratio of area (k=SB/SB). Then the value of π could be got by the formula (SB=πR2). Therefore, the value of k is the most critical.

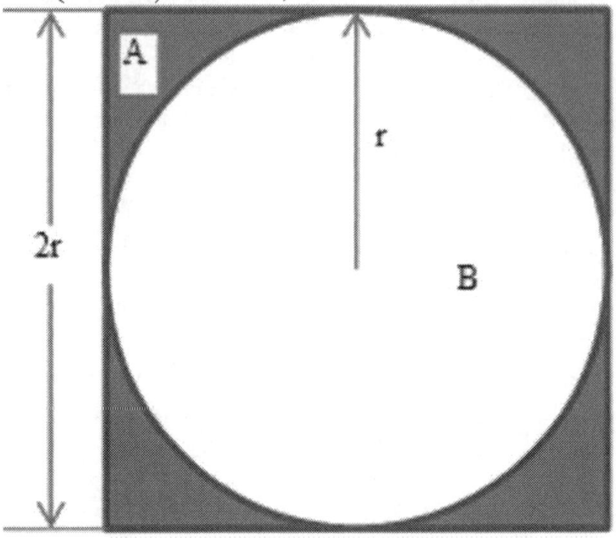

Fig. 3. Monte Carlo Simulation

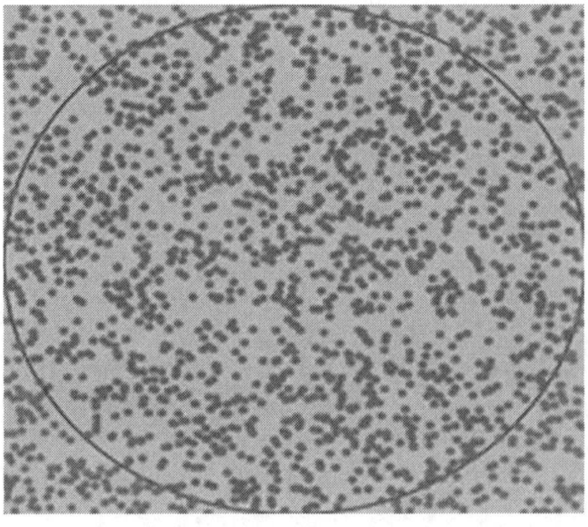

Fig. 2. The Square and The Inscribed Circle

A and B can be seen as an infinite number of points, and all points within B are within A. n points are randomly generated. If there are m points in B (The side length of A is assumed to be 10, and the center of A acts as the origin of the coordinate system. It falls in the B as long as the vertical and horizontal coordinates of the random point meet $x^2+y^2\leq100$), you can approximate the value of k (As is shown in Fig. 3), that is, the value of π can be obtained by k=m/n.

3.2 Algorithm flow

(1) 30 million between the 10 random points are generated with using the random function, and stored in three txt file;

(2) The point of the first step is read with using the map function, and the right point is found to output to the intermediate file;

(3) The intermediate file of the second step is read with using the reduce function, and the number of points within the circle is counted to calculate the value of π. (The algorithm flow is shown in Fig. 4)

3.3 Test environment and result

This experiment is mainly carried out on the Hadoop platform, and the configuration is as follows:

Hadoop cluster is composed of four computers, one of which is as a master node, and three other are as slave nodes. The operating system of node is centos7. The version of Hadoop is 2.7.2, 64 bit. The computer environment configuration is Intel (R) Core (TM) i7-3770 CPU 3.4GHZ, the memory is 8GB, and the operating system is 64-bit. Development tools: eclipse.

In this paper, 30 million between the 10 random points are generated with using the Monte Carlo random simulation. 3 nodes 30 million points (10 million points per node) are calculated respectively on 3 nodes with using Hadoop model, and the result is $\pi = 3.14130944$. The running time is 65000ms, and running time will have a certain difference in each run due to Hadoop's current situation. The more accurate of the value of π is seen from the data, but the time has no advantage. The reason of this result is relatively small experimental data, and the master node takes some time to distribute the task. Therefore, the advantage of cluster can't be reflected when the data set is too small. The time of distribution can be ignored when the data set is relatively large, so the advantage of the cluster will be very obvious.

4 Summary

In this paper, the classical Monte Carlo stochastic algorithm is used to calculate the value of πunder the parallel environment of Hadoop. This parallelization and cluster environment can effectively deal with massive amounts of data, and it can be widely used to analyze in a variety of large data environment.

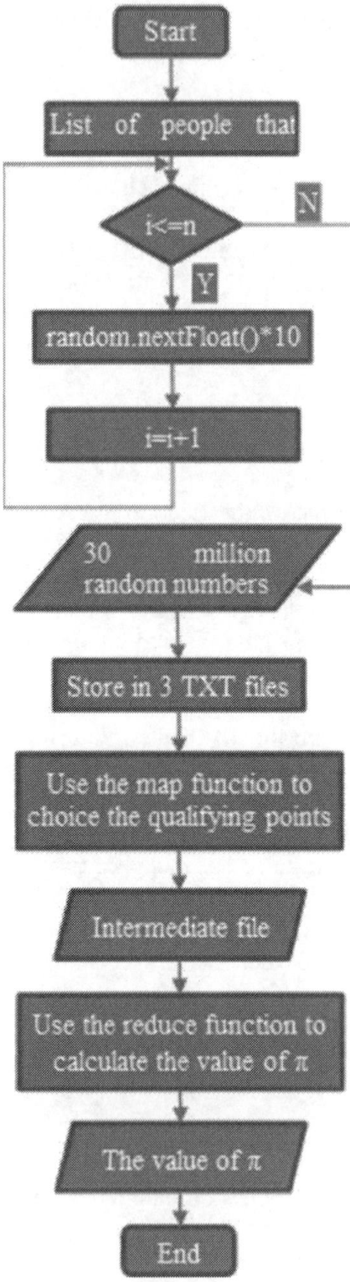

Fig. 4. Algorithm Flow

This research was financially supported by the the National Natural Science Foundation of China (U1431102).

References

[1]H. S. Liang, L. Cheng, et al, Monte Carlo simulation based reliability evaluation of distribution system containing microgrids, Power System Technology. 35(10) 76-81.

[2]R .Billinton, W. Li, Reliability assessment of electric power systems using Monte Carlo methods, USA, 1994.

[3]D. Lieber, A.Nemirovskii, et al, A fast Monte Carlo method for evaluating reliability indexes, IEEE Transactions on Reliability, 48(3) 256-261.

[4]G. Y. Sun, Study on Monte Carlo method for the physical process of neutron photon transport, He Fei, 2015, pp.10-59.

[5]X. Y. Zhang, Y. N. Zhu, et al, Monte Carlo simulation of radiation field, High Power Laser and Particle Beams, 25(1) 223-226.

[6]L. Yan, Large Data Application, Science Grand View Garden, 12(2) 75-76.

[7]Yan. X. F, Zhang. D. X, Big Data Research, Computer Technology and Development, 23(4) 168-172.

[8]F. T. Chi, C. L. Wei, et al, Big data mining with parallel computing: a comparison of distributed and MapReduce methodologies, The Journal of Systems & Software, 22(8) 16-22.

[9]W. X. Zhi, Y. Bao, et al, Beyond Hadoop:recent directions in data computing for internet services, Database Trends and Applications, 1(1) 45-61.

An intelligent LED landscape lighting system

Lei Zhang[1,2,*], *Jie Fang*[1,2] *and Ping Yu*[1,2]

[1] School of electrical and photoelectrical Engineering. West Anhui University, Lu'an, Anhui, 237012
[2] Intelligent Lighting and Display Technology Engineering center, West Anhui University, Lu'an, Anhui, 237012

Abstract. This paper introduces a kind of landscape lighting control system is composed of the monitoring center and intelligent controller. The intelligent controller realizes the control of the LED landscape lamp, and the monitoring center realizes the monitoring management of the system. The monitoring center and the intelligent controller communicate with each other through ZigBee net. This distributed LED landscape lighting system based on ZigBee network, can achieve the dimming, equipment monitoring, mode setting and fault alarm function, can effective management of landscape lighting system is composed of a large number of LED, solve the problems of large landscape lighting system lighting effects, monotonous monitoring management function is not perfect, the realization of LED landscape lighting system is difficult large scale problem.

1 Introduction

With the development of city and the improvement of people's living standard, more and more applications of various types of environmental lighting landscape lighting in the city, become a propaganda city, an important infrastructure to beautify the environment. Landscape lighting not only to illuminate the ground, creating a pleasant and comfortable atmosphere, but also pay attention to environmental protection and energy saving. Landscape lighting control system can fully reflect the advantages of LED used in landscape lighting, the color performance, strong light and color changing characteristics of LED with the most incisive play out, with appropriate control strategies, in accordance with the overall requirements of the environment, the programmed control of LED, through the LED color coordination, can produce the overall art the effect of landscape, showing a gorgeous scene. As landscape lighting facilities are mostly outdoors, the landscape control system combining intelligent control and monitoring is more in line with the needs of the modern people.

* Lei Zhang: leizh0326@wxc.edu.cn

2 LED landscape lighting system overall design

2.1 System composition

The system adopts the distributed system structure, and the system structure diagram is shown in Figure 1. It consists of the control center, the ZigBee gateway and the distributed controller.

The wireless communication is realized between the control center and the controller through the ZigBee gateway. The system uses PC as the control center, and the administrator can realize the remote monitoring and management of the equipment by operating the PC the control software. The controller receives the command of the control center through the ZigBee network, performs the operation according to the command request, realizes the pattern dimming and supplies the equipment information back to the monitoring center.

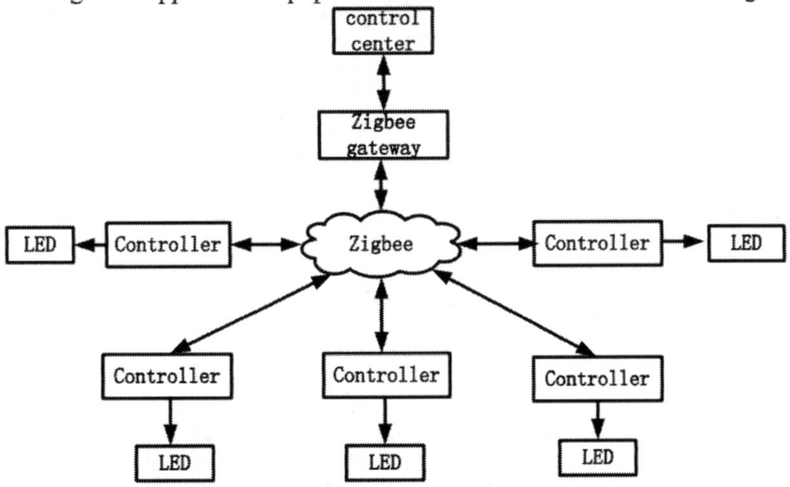

Fig. 1. System Structure Diagram

2.2 Function of Each Part

2.2.1 The functions of the control computer

(1) Provide human-computer interface for remote management and control

Through the control computer, a region LED lamps or a certain LED lamp can be controlled;

(2) Data monitoring and statistics

The control computer displays the running state of the LED device (real time current, voltage, etc.) in real time, collects and processes all the LED running data, and stores the data in the database server;

(3) Fault information management

When the LED lamp fails, an alarm signal is generated to facilitate the timely, accurate and convenient detection of the fault LED lamp, and the failure information is managed and monitored;

(4) Energy-saving control

LED landscape lighting system can automatically switch light and light according to the preset time or the time of sunrise and sunset.

2.2.2 ZigBee gateway

It is composed of two modules, ZigBee coordinator and serial communication, which is the communication hub of the system. ZigBee is an emerging wireless network technology, mainly used for short-range wireless network connections. It uses IEEE802.15.4 as standard to communicate between a large number of tiny sensors. These sensors require very low energy to relay data from one sensor to another in a relay mode to achieve efficient communication. ZigBee network has many advantages, such as low power consumption, low cost, high capacity (up to 65536 nodes), and it can solve the difficult problems of implementation and construction quickly and conveniently. Also use 2.4GHz free wireless frequency without charge for use. The serial communication module adopts RS232/485 standard interface technology, which can effectively solve the problem of wireless data communication and wired data communication network access.

2.2.3 The controller

As the terminal control equipment of the system, the dimmer is connected with the LED lamp and its main function.

(1) Detecting LED lamp input voltage, current, temperature and other operating conditions;

(2) According to the control commands sent by the monitoring center, the operation is carried out, and the functions of lighting adjustment, equipment and lighting information feedback are realized;

(3) Controlling the LED switch and brightness regulation.

2.2.4 LED lamp

The RGB LED, which is packaged as 5050, is built with opposing red LED (R), green LED (G) and blue LED (B). R, G, B produces red, green, blue three colors, for RGB LED, realizes each kind of color to provide the foundation. Among them, the red LED power supply range is 2.2V~2.6V, green LED power supply range is 3.2V~3.6V, blue LED power supply range is 3.2V~3.6V. Three built-in LED operating currents are 25mA.

3 Hardware design of led landscare lighting controller

The controller is composed of C8051F020 microcontroller, serial clock chip DS1307, LED driver PT4115, ZigBee communication module CC2530 and LED detection circuit. The block diagram is shown in figure 2.

3.1 C8051F020 microcontroller

C8051F020 microcontroller reads the clock, according to the time to achieve the LED landscape lighting on and off. At the same time receive the host computer through the ZigBee network instructions, to achieve the LED switch and brightness adjustment. If the host does not have instructions, it opens the landscape lighting in default mode, detects the status of LED in the LED lighting state, implements LED protection, and reports the LED status through the ZigBee network.

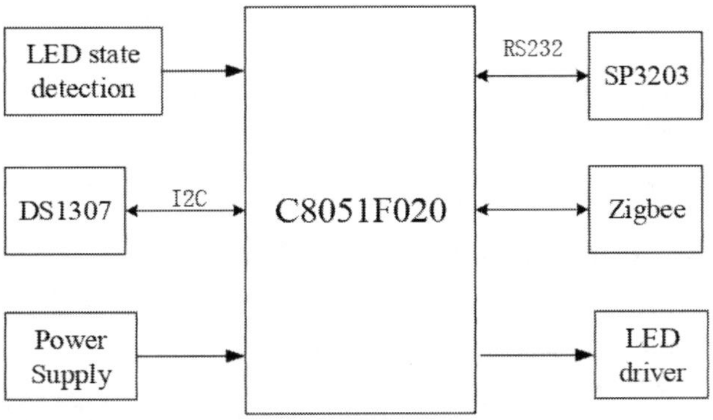

Fig. 2. Controller Structure Diagram

3.2 LED status detection circuit

1. Temperature detection circuit
LED has a negative temperature effect, positive current increases will cause a rise in junction temperature, temperature rise and further lead to the current increases, when the temperature exceeds LED bearing temperature will make the LED luminous efficiency is reduced, causing LED damage. Therefore, the system should have LED temperature detection function. To prevent the LED temperature is too high, to prevent decay, prolong the service life of the lamp. The digital temperature sensor DS18B20 is directly contacted with the LED board to measure the working temperature of the LED.

The light detecting circuit is used for detecting whether the LED works normally, and the light detecting circuit adopts a photosensitive diode, and the photosensitive junction of the photosensitive diode has a photosensitive property, and has a single guiding electric property.

2. Illumination detection circuit

The light detecting circuit is used for detecting whether the LED works normally. The light detecting circuit adopts a photosensitive diode, and the photosensitive junction of the photosensitive diode has a photosensitive property, and has a single guiding electric property. If the photodiode does not accept the light, the reverse leakage current is smaller, the circuit is not switched on, and when the circuit receives the light, the current is greatly increased, and the circuit is turned on. Because the current system of LED lighting needs is relatively low, only 30mA, the current sensor must use high precision, using ACS712 linear current sensor of Allergro company, built-in high precision linear hall sensor circuit, voltage current detection which can be loaded and the corresponding voltage value, and then read the current conversion of microprocessor through the A/D.

3.3 Dimming isolation circuit

In order to avoid the influence of LED constant current drive circuit on the control circuit, the photoelectric isolation method is used to isolate the strong current and the weak current. The PWM signal of the microcontroller is sent to the dimming pin of the PT4115 driver chip through the photoelectric isolator PC817. When the PWM is high, the driver chip works normally and the LED flows through the rated current. When the PWM is low, the LED driver cuts off the current on the LED light string. The brightness adjustment of LED is realized by adjusting the duty ratio of PWM.

3.4 LED drive circuit

According to the host computer instruction or the default mode, the MCU generates three PWM signals, controls the LED driver PT4115 current output, and controls the three color LED brightness of LED, G, B and R respectively, and realizes the color control of LED.

4 Software design of control system

4.1 Gateway program design

Because the ZigBee protocol stack is a semi open source protocol stack, the protocol stack architecture provided by TI company has written the physical layer, media access layer, network layer and the underlying code, as long as the realization of communication protocol module can meet the corresponding.

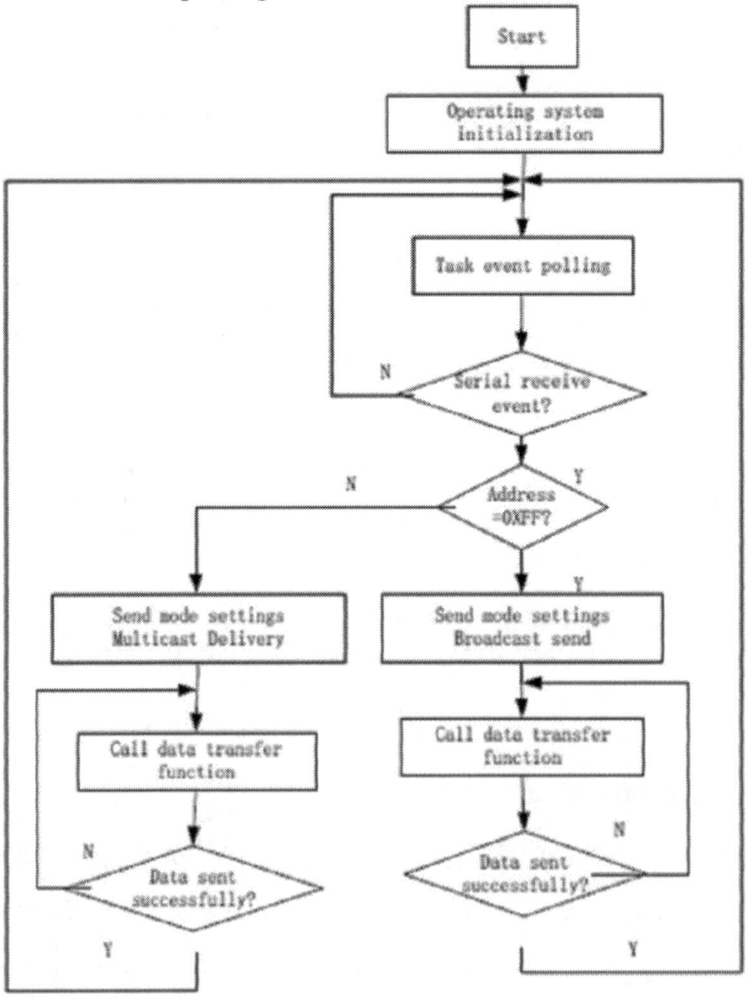

Fig. 3. Gateway Flowchart

The ZigBee gateway application flow diagram is shown in figure 3. After the ZigBee module is powered on, the system is initialized first, then the network is set up and started, and the system events are polled after the network is successfully set up. This paper is mainly

 https://doi.org/10.1051/itmconf/20181703022

applied to join the gateway node network, serial data reception event poll on whether, if a serial data reception, call the serial receiver function, remove the address information and control information is transmitted to the PC to read from the register, and to estimate the address information, if the address is 0xFF, then the transmission mode is set to broadcast, and sends control information to the ZigBee network in the all terminal lamp node; if the address is not 0xFF, it will send the multicast mode to send, and sends control information to the designated terminal lights all nodes within the group. In order to reduce the packet loss rate of data, the data sent out should also confirm whether the data is sent successfully, if not sent successfully, you need to resend.

4.2 Program design of controller node

After the control node device is powered on, the ZigBee module should first apply to join the network after initialization, and then access the operating system polling after obtaining the network access from the ZigBee gateway. The terminal equipment is mainly to check whether the data receiving event, if the data is received, then call the data receiving function, and will receive the data assigned to the PWM module register, output PWM dimming signal waveform, the data is successfully received at the same time, the terminal node sending data to coordinator should also receive success in order to inform the signal, the coordinator has successfully received data; if no data is received, according to the default mode controller PWM control LED light.

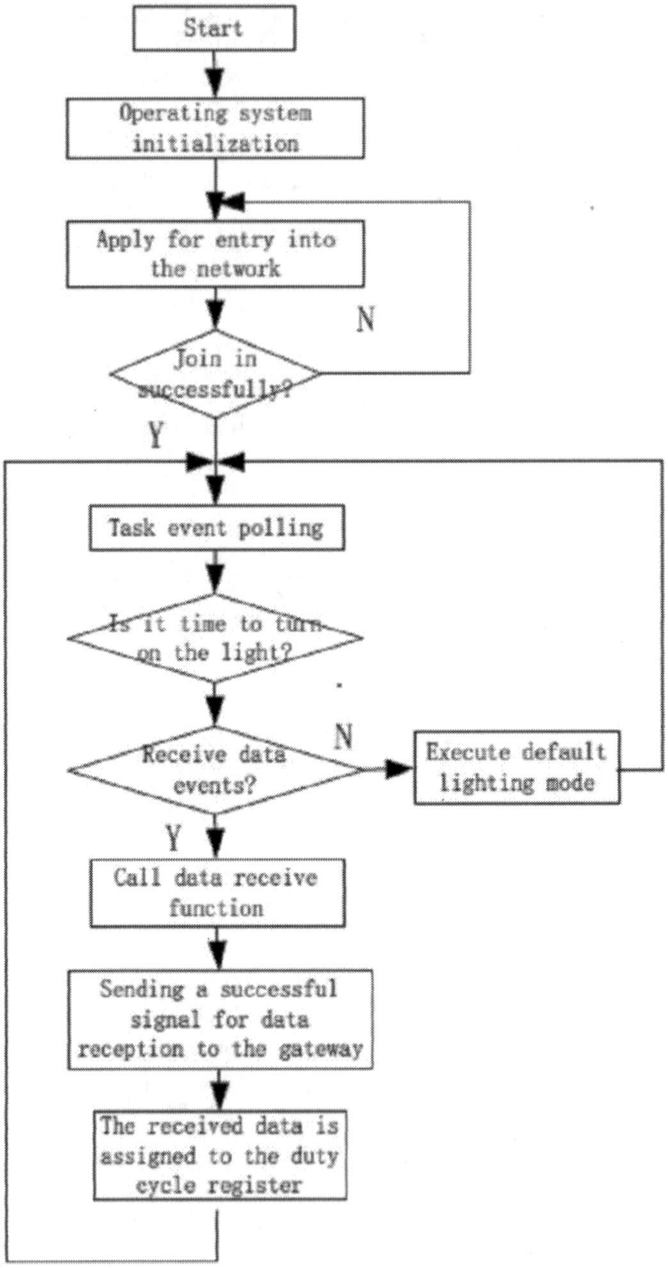

Fig. 4. Flow chart of controller program

4.3 Control center program

Intelligent landscape lamp control system, the upper computer interface uses Forcecontrol 7.1 development, mainly has control draw, monitoring draw, alarm draw, reports draw. switch light control, mode selection, area switch control and single light switch control. Control draw, switch light control, mode selection, area switch control and single light switch control. The monitoring draw monitors the status of the landscape lamp in real time, and displays the switch status, current, voltage, mode, etc. of the landscape lamp. Alarm draw to achieve fault alarm, when the current is too large, too large voltage, high temperature alarm.

5 Conclusion

In this paper, designed a LED landscape lighting control system based on configuration software and ZigBee network, introduces the overall architecture of the system and the working principle and realization method of hardware circuit and software, and verified by experiment. The system can provide various control functions and real-time monitoring functions for LED through wireless network communication on the PC, so as to meet the needs of different landscape lighting. To some extent, the problems such as monotonous lighting effects, imperfect monitoring and management functions and great difficulty in the expansion of large-scale landscape lighting systems are solved.

This work is supported by NFSC61302179, WXZR201620.

References

[1] Hangfeng Ji, Qiong Zhao, Xiaodong Wang, et al. Zig Bee-based LED intelligent lighting control system // 10th China International Forum on Solid State Lighting (China SSL). 2013.
[2] Faheem Ijaz, Adeel A. Siddiqui, Byung Kwan Im, Chankil Lee. Remote management and control system for LED based Plant Factory using ZigBee and Internet // 14th International Conference on Advanced Communication Technology (ICACT). 2012:942-946.
[3] He Sai, Chen Xiaoping. Application of Zig Bee technology in urban lighting monitoring system [J]. Computer system applications, 2011, 20(11):135-138.
[4] CaiYu. The Design and Implementation of LED Landscape Lighting Control System. Zhejiang University. 2015.
[5] Li Zhihua, Zhou Feng, Wang Yuanzhang, Yan Gang. LED intelligent lighting control system based on ZigBee. Modern building electrical. No. 6.Vol4.9-13.

A large data processing algorithm for energy efficiency in a heterogeneous cluster

Lei Wang[1,*], *Weichun Ge*[1], *Zhao Li*[1], *Zhenjiang Lei*[1] *and Shuo Chen*[1]

ICT Department, State Grid Liaoning Electric Power Co., Ltd, Shenyang, China
wl@ln.sgcc.com.cn; gwc@ln.sgcc.com.cn; lz@ln.sgcc.com.cn; leizj@ln.sgcc.com.cn; cs@ln.sgcc.com.cn.

Abstract. It is reported[i] that the electricity cost to operate a cluster may well exceed its acquisition cost, and the processing of big data requires large scale cluster and long period. Therefore, energy efficient processing of big data is essential for the data owners and users. In this paper, we propose a novel algorithm MinBalance to processing I/O intensive big data tasks energy efficiently in heterogeneous cluster. In the former step, four greedy policies are used to select the proper nodes considering heterogeneity of the cluster. While in the latter step, the workloads of the selected nodes will be well balanced to avoid the energy wastes caused by waiting. MinBalance is a universal algorithm and cannot be affected by the data storage strategies. Experimental results indicate that MinBalance can achieve over 60% energy reduction for large sets over the traditional methods of powering down partial nodes.

1 Introduction

With the development and application of information technology, the data produced is presented. How to store, manage, and apply these data to become an explosive growth. A general concern of the business community and academia. You know, there is great value in big data, so research based on big data is also very much. Many scholars call it the fourth paradigm of scientific research [1]-[2]. Cloud computing as a kind of Emerging economies based on economies of scale have become big data the first platform for storage and processing. The open source cloud meter is the platform Hadoop, HBase, and HadoopDB have been widely studied and the application. More and more businesses are building their own big data points the platform deals with growing business data and even offers Various services based on big data [3]. A lot of hardware resources are required to handle big data. Include servers, PCS, and even mobile devices. The making of these devices takes a lot of energy, mainly electricity, to be used globally electricity is generated mainly by thermal power so the big data also has great challenges to energy and environment [4]. In 2005, show that a server is within the lifetime of its use the total amount of electricity consumed has exceeded the purchase cost. And research show that, in 2008, the world's 4400 servers consumed electricity 0.8% percent, if you go like that, at that rate By 2020, that proportion

* Lei Wang: wl@ln.sgcc.com.cn

will be 3.2%. Epa (US Environmental Protection Agency) issued a report statement in 2006, the total electricity consumption of American IT agencies was 61 billion KWh, the electricity bill alone is $4.5 billion [5]-[7]. So that's a concern Big data storage and processing performance must also be used for energy consumption Give enough attention [8].

This paper mainly discusses the large data processing tasks of I/O intensive. The computationally intensive tasks are affected by the real-time running state of the processor large, and different hardware and operating system provided processor control machines. There are differences in system, so this paper does not consider computationally intensive large Numbers According to the task. Because of the data-intensive task for the processor with a small dependency, for a server, the processing of each data block is reduced the time and power consumed can be regarded as basically the same. A cluster consisting of n heterogeneous nodes processes a Map-Reduce tasks, assume that the nodes involved in task processing are C, the total energy consumed during task processing is

$$Toal\cos t = \max_{n_i \in C}\{T_i\}\sum_{n_i \in C} P_i \quad (1)$$

The Ti and pi represent the processing time of the I node Power consumption. By type (1) the total energy is mainly affected by two factors: use the nodes that perform the tasks and the maximum processing time of the nodes. Type (1) The two kinds of high-efficiency data processing methods:

1) To select

Some suitable nodes perform tasks to reduce total power consumption;

2) Equilibrium

The load of a node reduces the maximum execution time.

According to the actual situation of the node, determine which tasks each node performs, namely Equalize the load of each node, reduce task execution time, and further Reduces total energy consumption of the system. The method has three distinct advantages:

1) Fully consider the heterogeneity of the nodes;

2) There is no copy storage strategy shut;

3) Comprehensively consider the total number of nodes and load balance the factor of consumption.

2 Problem description

I/O intensive large data processing tasks for heterogeneous clusters. Energy efficient processing problems can be formalized as follows: given a set, the group is composed of h isomeric nodes and N = {n1, n2, n3, ..., nh}, of which A node ni (1≤i≤h) takes the time and work required to process a block of data. The consumption is Ti and pi. Given an I/ O intensive big data processing Task J, the data set that it needs to process contains m standard data blocks D = {d1, d2, ..., dm}, each block has r copies stored in h on a heterogeneous node. The actual storage location of each data block can be passed the metadata of the cluster is obtained, and the actual storage situation of the data set is L ={(n1.1,...,n1.r),(n2.1,..., n2.r),...,(nm.1,..., nm.r), }, ni.j $\in N(1 \le i \le m, 1 \le j \le r)$, which represents the j of data block di a copy is stored on the node without loss of generality, assuming ni.1 < ni.2<...< ni.r (1 ≤i≤ m), which can be known to be stored on node ni. The set of data blocks can be represented as Di= {dj | ni $\in$ (nj.1, ..., nj.r),1≤i≤m}. The solution of this problem is from node set N, select part of the nodes to handle task J and make these nodes work, the total energy consumed during processing is the least. Clearly, data set D a data block must have at least one copy stored on the selected node, the sample task can be successfully executed.

3 Processing algorithm

Through formula (1) and the analysis of the aforementioned issues shown the optimal target of high energy efficient data processing under the construction node is two:

1) Select the appropriate coverage node, i.e. the work in reduction (1) Part of the consumption $\sum_{n_i \in NS} P_i$;

2) Reduce the actual processing time of critical nodes, reduction type (1) time $\max_{n_i \in NS}\{|VC(n_i)|t_i\}$.

The analysis of the problem description section can find the exact solution to the problem is difficult, and it's hard to find the complexity in polynomial time solution.

In this paper, the approximate solution method is adopted to optimize the target decompose the problem into two relatively independent sub-problems: first find the appropriate coverage node and then allow the selected coverage node distribution, namely, load balancing each node to reduce critical nodes point processing time, finally achieve energy efficient target. The traditional way to achieve energy efficiency is by closing some nodes. The method, in fact, is the question of finding suitable coverage nodes after decomposition the topic. But the traditional approach does not take into account the heterogeneity of the nodes, therefore can be classified as hypergraph coverage problem or classic collection coverage problem to solve.

The problem with the node selection phase is that it is a given isomerism select the appropriate node in the node set as the overlay node performing I/O intensive large data tasks. In this question, by

the processing time of each node is determined by the number of new data blocks, the number of new data blocks is affected by the order of node selection the traditional WSCP solution does not apply to this problem.

In this section, we present a selection of selected cases based on the thinking of the greedy mind Greedy, as shown in algorithm 1.

3. 1 Algorithm

3.1.1 Greedy algorithm

Input: N = {n1, n2,..., nh}, D = {d1, d2,..., dm}, {t1, t2,...th}, {p1, p2,..., ph}, L = {(n1.1,..., n1.r), (n2.1,..., n2.r), …, (nm.1,..., nm.r)};

Output: overlay node set NS;

(1) Initialization: NS = DS = Ø;

(2) For each node ni $\notin$ NS do

(3) The weight of weight (ni) of each node is calculated;

(4) The maximum value of the option value is the coverage node;

(5) Update: DS = DS union NC (ni), NS = NS union {ni};

(6) If the DS then go Step (2);

(7) Else Return NS.

The selection of each node in algorithm 1 is based on a certain standard, at the current optimal node, the node may not be globally optimal, so, the solution is an approximate solution. The concrete choice idea is to calculate currently, the weight of each non-overridden node Weight (), the option value is the most. The large node ACTS as the new coverage node, and then updates the coverage node set. And its stored data set, continue the next calculation of weight and select nodes point, until the coverage node contains the entire dataset.

If the heterogeneity of the node is not considered at all, you only need to select the nodes that currently contain the new data blocks.

Overwrite the node so that the final selection can be approximated

The minimum number of cap nodes reduces energy consumption to a certain extent. But for heterogeneous nodes, the nodes that may be selected are inefficient and lead to eventual results, the energy expenditure is very high. The weight of each node in this scheme can be tabled shown for $Weight(n_i) = \frac{|NC(n_i)|}{t_i \times p_i}$

3. 2 Algorithm

3.2.1 MinBalance algorithm

Specific load balancing methods: MinBalance as algorithm 2, The node selected by algorithm 1 is shown to load balancing to determine each what data is actually processed by the node to enable the task to process the energy consumed the least. The main idea of the MinBalance method is to find the current covering all the key nodes in the node, as described in algorithm 2, these key nodes are then loaded with other coverage nodes balance, then proceed to the next iteration, looking for key nodes again load balancing until all the key nodes are currently unavailable and other nodes are balanced by load, as shown in algorithm 2.

Input: N = {n1, n2,..., nh}, D = {d1, d2,..., dm}, {t1, t2,...th}, {p1, p2,..., ph}, L = {(n1.1,..., n1.r), (n2.1,..., n2.r), …, (nm.1,..., nm.r)};

Output: total energy consumption TotalCost.

(1)Find the overlay node set NS;

(2)all key node KN in NS;

(3)For each key node kni do {

(4)For each cover node nj do {

(5)Calculates kij;}

(6)If max {kij} > 0 then Rebalance (kni, nj);

(7)Remove kni form KN;;

(8)If KN= Ø then break;}

(9)TotalCost= $\max_{n_i \in NS} \{|VC(n_i)| t_i\} \sum_{n_i \in NS} p_i$;

(10) Return TotalCost;

(11) Else go Step (2).

Rebalance(na,nb)

(12) Calculates kab;

(13) count=0;

(14) For each data chunk di $\in$ VC(na) do {

(15) If di $\in$ Db then {

(16) Remove di from VC (na) and add di to VC (nb);

(17) count+=1;}

(18) If count=kab then Return.}

3. 3 The energy consumption of MinBalance algorithm

This section focuses on the energy consumed by the MinBalance algorithm in handling big data tasks. In order to be easy to identify in the experimental results diagram, 4 kinds of implementation MinBalance algorithm are used in BMNF, BHPF,BLPF, BLEF. Figure 1 shows the energy consumed by the algorithm in dealing with small tasks when the data is randomly distributed. It can be seen that in the same situation, MinBalance can reduce energy consumption by about 10% when |D | = 100, and | D | = 1000, MinBalance can reduce energy consumption by about 60%.

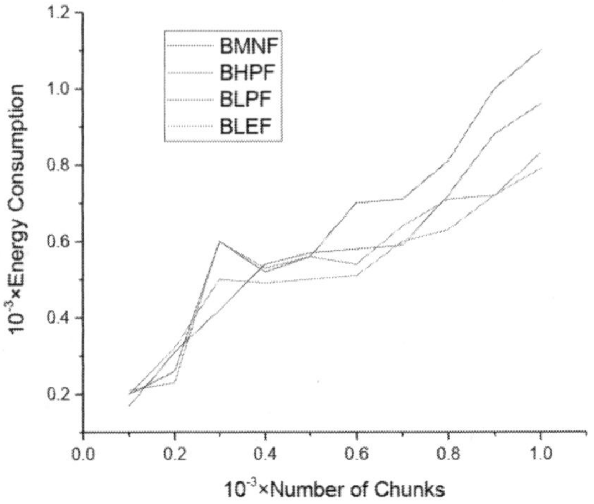

Fig. 1. MinBalance methods

4 Conclusion

This article addresses the I/O intensive large data points in heterogeneous clusters. In order to make a good calculation of the high efficiency MinBalance, this method is not subject to the shadow of the storage strategy. MinBalance decomposes complex problems into node selection and load. The equilibrium two steps are solved respectively, and the solution of the node selection is solved four different greedy strategies were adopted to fully consider the differences of the nodes Construct, select a small number of suitable nodes for task processing.

In the load balancing process focuses on the key section of the longest handling time point, as much as possible without increasing the maximum processing time. Its load is migrated to nodes with short processing time. The algorithm is in place when the data set is large, it is more than traditional closing node. The method reduces energy consumption by up to 60%. From the experimental results it can be seen that the MNF method with node-heterogeneity is the least energy efficient.

But the algorithm proposed in this paper is based on the idea of greed as an algorithm, it has not proved its exact approximate degree and above theoretically lower bound. The experiment in this paper is simulated, but the actual cluster is different time that nodes consume when processing big data is unpredictable and the property of the storage medium itself affects the same node. The power of data consumption of sample size may differ. So The next step will be to consider platforms such as real Hadoop conduct performance testing and analysis.

References

[1] Zhang L, Li K, Xu Y, et al. Maximizing reliability with energy conservation for parallel task scheduling in a heterogeneous cluster[J]. Information Sciences An International Journal, 2015, 319(C):113-131.
[2] Pati S, Mehta M A. Job aware scheduling in Hadoop for heterogeneous cluster[C]// Advance Computing Conference. IEEE, 2015:778-783.
[3] Botta A, Donato W D, Persico V. Integration of Cloud computing and Internet of Things [J]. Future Generation Computer Systems, 2016, 56(C):684-700.
[4] Kumar S, Kumar S, Kumar S, et al. Security, Privacy Issues and challenges In Cloud Computing: A Survey[C]// International Conference on Information and Communication Technology for Competitive Strategies. ACM, 2016:47.
[5] Zhang H, Li B, Jiang H, et al. A framework for truthful online auctions in cloud computing with heterogeneous user demands[C]// INFOCOM, 2013 Proceedings IEEE. IEEE, 2016:1510-1518.
[6] Hu H, Wen Y, Chua T S, et al. Toward Scalable Systems for Big Data Analytics: A Technology Tutorial [J]. Access IEEE, 2017, 2(1):652-687.
[7] Feller E, Ramakrishnan L, Morin C. Performance and energy efficiency of big data applications in cloud environments: A Hadoop case study [J]. Journal of Parallel & Distributed Computing, 2015, s 79–80(C):80-89.
[8] Majeed A, Shah M A. Energy efficiency in big data complex systems: a comprehensive survey of modern energy saving techniques [J]. Complex Adaptive Systems Modeling, 2015, 3(1):6.

The design of clothing washable labels based on NFC

Zhengdong Liu[1,*] *and Tianyu Ma*[1]

Beijing Institute of Fashion Technology, No. A2, East Yinghua Street, Chaoyang District, Beijing, P.R. China
+86 10 64288182, jsjlzd@bift.edu.cn; 615934441@qq.com

Abstract. In this paper, With the rapid development of NFC (Near Field Communication) technology and the digital advancement of clothing industry, a kind of clothing washable labels based on NFC is proposed and designed in this paper. It can be used to compose a clothing information system together with NFC mobile phones, mobile Internet, enterprise information centers, etc. By experiment, consumers can read and write NFC washable labels through their mobile phones, which can be quicker and more convenient to obtain clothing washing and maintenance information. Moreover, the NFC washable labels conform to the washing requirements of washable labels. The emergence of the NFC washable labels provides a physical basis for smart matching recommendations and precise directional push of clothing advertising information for consumers.

1 Introduction

Ordinary clothing washable labels only contain clothing washing and maintenance information, while NFC washable labels are a contact medium for clothing and consumers, clothing and enterprises, as well as consumers and enterprises.

Along with the digitalization process of clothing industry, Tao et al. [1] proposed a kind of RFID technology scheme for the raw material warehouse management of garment enterprises in 2007, which makes the raw material inventory quantity and inventory structure of garment enterprises more reasonable, improves the informatization of warehouse management, and reduces the cost of production and management of garment enterprises. In 2014, Zheng et al. [2] mentioned that the Central Bank supports NFC payment in the paper titled Promotion Strategies of NFC Mobile Payment Service for Telecommunication Operators, so NFC technology has obtained a relatively favorable opportunity for development and NFC mobile phones have begun to become popular. In addition to the rise of NFC payment, other NFC labels are also gradually used by the public. Ahsan et al. [3] indicated that, among intelligent wearable devices, compared with other short-range wireless communication technologies, NFC technology is more suitable for data communication and information sharing between intelligent wearable users, intelligent wearable devices and other portable electronic devices.

[*] Zhengdong Liu: jsjlzd@bift.edu.cn

Based on the above literature analysis and the related research on the digitization of clothing washable labels, existing RFID labels can be well used for clothing fabric storage management, clothing production process, store inventory theft and other aspects. However, consumers cannot build a relationship with garment enterprises through RFID labels due to lack of the means of directly reading RFID labels. In view of this situation, a kind of NFC washable labels is proposed and designed in this paper. Consumers can directly read clothing information parameters and washing instructions on clothing NFC washable labels by their mobile phones, and these labels can also record their clothing consumption habits. Therefore, clothing enterprises can receive and analyze their information so as to carry out accurate information push for them. Moreover, these labels reserve NFC payment interfaces for fast payment.

2 System framework

Evolved from radio frequency identification devices (RFID), NFC (Near Field Communication) technology is mainly used in entrance guard, bus cards, mobile payment, etc. In recent years, Apple, Samsung, MIUI and other mobile phone manufacturers have introduced a variety of NFC-enabled smart phones, which has brought great convenience for the promotion and application of NFC technology.

This system is composed of NFC-enabled mobile phone, NFC washable label, customized APP, enterprise information center, and mobile communication network, as shown in Figure.1. The customized APP is designed and produced according to the requirements of clothing enterprises, and consumers can download it to their NFC-enabled phones through Android or IOS system.

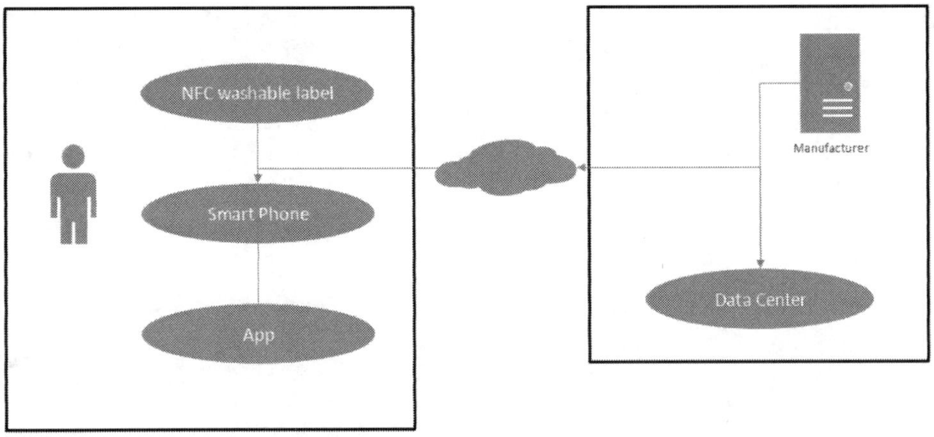

Fig. 1. Clothing information system based on NFC washable labels

The working procedures of the whole system are:

1. Starting with fabric tailoring, a globally unique identifier will be compiled on the basis of each NFC label, thus the entire garment production can be tracked;

2. When clothes are completed and turned into the inventory for management, they will be delivered to the stores in different quantities, or be directly sold online according to the actual situation of production and sales;

3. As soon as consumers buy the clothes and read NFC washable labels with NFC mobile phones, the consumption location, consumption time, and the information of purchased clothes will be recorded;

 https://doi.org/10.1051/itmconf/20181703024

4. After purchasing the clothes, during their daily use, open the APP before wearing them every time, and then put it close to NFC washable labels to record the frequency of wearing. The clothing maintenance information will be pushed in the evening;

5. Consumers' information is recorded and uploaded to enterprise information centers through the APP. According to each user's feedback, combined with popular trends and the analysis of large data, users' dress collocation recommendation and advertising information push are conducted through a specific recommendation algorithm.

3 Introduction of NFC labels and their partition

The type of NFC washable labels is NLABEL216 developed by NXP Semiconductors with non-contact data transmission and power supply; its operating frequency is 13.56 MHz, data transmission 106 kb/s. Its data integrity includes 16-bit CRC, odd-even check, bit coding and bit count; its maximum working distance is 100 mm (depending on different parameters such as field strength and physical dimension of antenna). The size of the EEPROM is 924 bytes, organized with 231 pages, 4 bytes per page, in which there are 888 bytes for users to freely read / write in the area (222 pages); the first 16 pages have a field-programmable read-only lock function in every page; after the first 16 pages, there's the field-programmable read-only lock function at every 16 pages. The configurable password protection has an optional failure attempt limit function; the anti-modification function supports the functional containers (CC) and lock bits; the original inspection supports ECC. The data retention period is 10 years; the tolerance of write operation is 100,000 cycles.

The details of partition are shown in Figure 2:

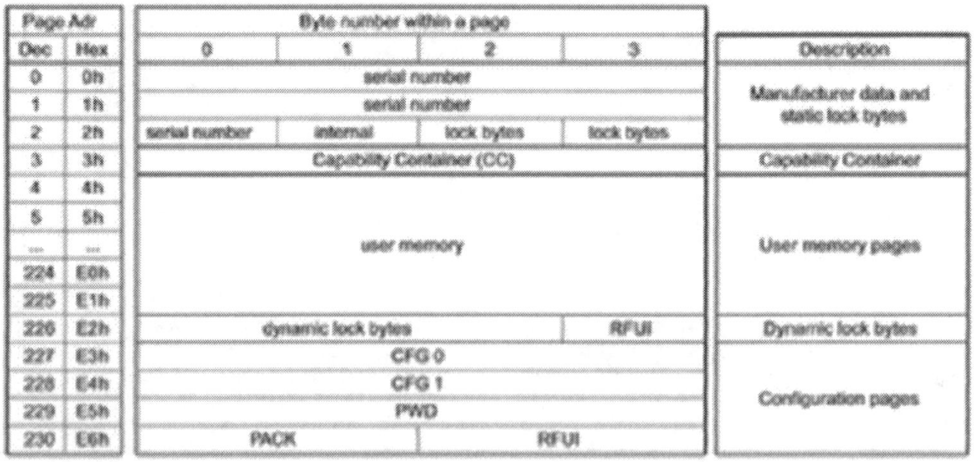

Fig. 2. NLABEL216 basic partition map

User Memory occupies a total of 888 bytes, which is a developable and designable part of NFC labels, and is divided into read-only information and changeable information for users. The read-only information provided by clothing enterprises includes: product name, reference price, model, clothing style, product composition, company profile, introduction of the brand culture, washing instructions, product production tracking, etc. The specific requirements can be set according to different enterprise requirements. The changeable information for users includes: evaluation of the clothes, self-designed collocation and choice, etc.

4 Design of digital washable labels based on NFC

There are mainly two different designing schemes — packaged type and post-paste type. From the aspect of used materials, the former gives priority to non-woven fabrics, the later polyester. From the appearance, NFC washable labels are nearly the same as ordinary washable labels in size, material, color, design and other aspects, with the width of 2-3 cm and the length of 4-8 cm in general; the difference comes in the combination mode between the NFC labels and the washable labels, and different combination has a small impact on the physical properties of the washable labels, and the design can still be conducted in accordance with that of the ordinary washable labels, only in which the combination of the NFC labels and the washable labels is added. Merchants choose the matching washable label according to different types of clothing; for example, clothes for autumn and winter are relatively thick, and the packaged type is generally a better choice; clothes for spring and autumn is relatively light and thin, and the post-paste type is a better choice.

The packaged-type NFC label adopts the Wet inlay technology to form an integral part with a width of 18 mm and a length of 43 mm, as shown in Side A and B of Figure 3. The identification of washable label printed in the frontage such as style number, color, size, washing instructions and others, has the width of 30 mm, length 75 mm, as shown in Side C and D of the Figure. Side B and D are combined by waterproof glue, then goes to the combination state of a washable label and a NFC label shown in Side E. Side E and C are combined again by waterproof glue to form a whole body.

The design of NFC label in post-paste type also adopts Wet inlay technology to form an integral part with a width of 15mm and a length of 35mm, as shown in Side A and B of Figure 3. The material of washable labels is polyester fiber; the dotted line in the middle is the crease. Side D is the frontage of the washable label, on which washing instructions are printed as ordinary labels do with the width of 25mm and the length of 100mm (50mm after folded according to the dotted line); NFC label is directly bonded with reverse side of the washable label; the result is shown in Side E.

5 Waterproof design for washable labels

According to the waterproof requirements on the electronic products of IEC 529-598, GB 4208-2008 and other standards [4], NFC washable labels need to match the IPX7 waterproof grade requirements: if the electrical equipment is immersed in water for a certain time or water pressure below a certain standard, it is ensured that they cannot be damaged due to immersion.

In order to make the designed and produced NFC washable labels achieve the required waterproofness, the Wet Inlay technology is adopted in the production of NFC labels, as shown in Figure 3. Firstly, two pieces of aluminum foil and PVC material are hot-pressed and composited to form antenna; after point DELO glue onto the solely-produced chip, it is aligned to the antenna bonding pad. The chip is fixed to the antenna bonding pad by hot pressing; the glue is solidified at the high temperature of over 200 ℃, so the complete Dry Inlay is formed, that is, the medium material of the NFC label is formed. Both sides of the medium material are coated with glue; with a waterproof, wear-resistant surface base material and the backing paper, the glue is solidified by hot pressing finally. So the formed Wet Inlay NFC label has waterproof and wear-resistant characteristics.

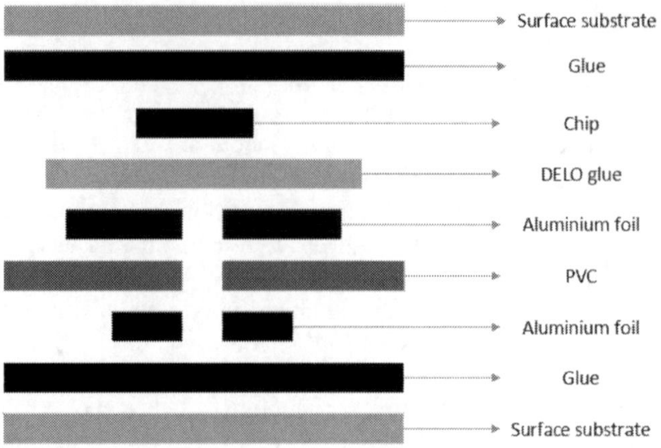

Fig. 3. Wet Inlay technology

6 Experimental results and analysis

In order to detect the waterproofness of NFC washable labels and the number of NFC washable labels used in actual, the IPX7 experiment on NFC washable labels was carried out. The standard experimental requirements of IPX7 are: Under the standard atmospheric pressure, the sample is placed into the immersion tank. The distance from the bottom of the sample to the water surface is at least 1 m. The distance from top of the sample to the water surface is at least 0.15 m. With the time duration of 30 minutes, the sample can still work properly.

According to the actual situation, some changes are made to the IPX7 experiment: Under the standard atmospheric pressure, 10 copies of the same NFC washable labels with numbering 1-10 were sewed in the same piece of cloth, then being placed into the ordinary washing machine for immersion; and neutral detergent was added. After they were washed for 30 minutes and dried at low temperature, the information on the washable label was read with a NFC mobile phone, and the printed surface was observed.

The process of NFC mobile phone reading and writing NFC washable labels is: compiling the APP that can read NFC labels by HBuilder, then packaging and installing it in the NFC phone; opening the APP, the distance between mobile phone and NFC sewed-in labels shall be less than 10 cm. If the phone can quickly read the content in the NFC label through the APP, the experimental results shall be recorded as successful, otherwise failed.

The experimental results are as shown in Table 1 and Figure 4.

Table 1. Number of water washing damage

	Label 1	Label 2	Label 3	Label 4	Label 5	Label 6	Label 7	Label 8	Label 9	Label 10	Mean
Number	135	120	156	200	163	200	189	145	200	166	167.4

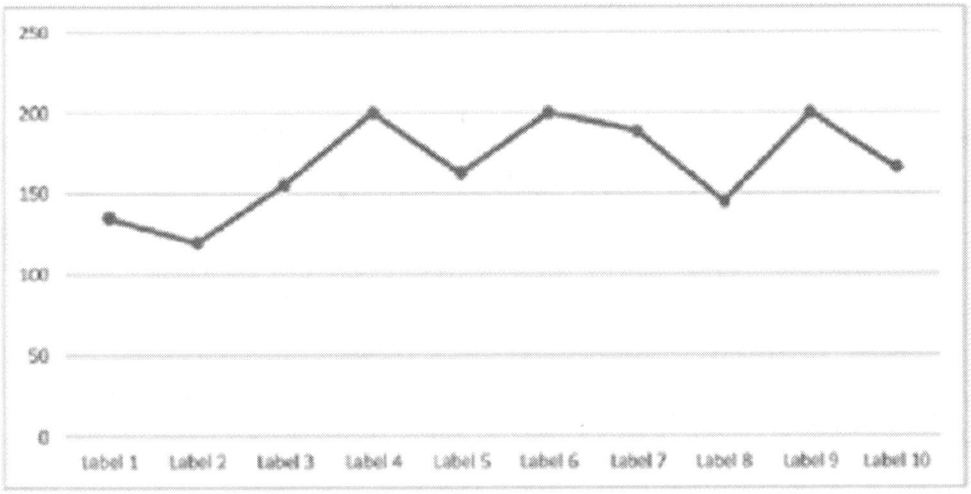

Note: The experiment was carried out for 200 times, those undamaged with the number of more than 200 were marked with 200.

Fig. 4. Number of water washing damage

The results showed that the number of water washing for NFC labels over 150 accounted for 70%, which is in accordance with the consulted number of water washing of RFID sewed-in labels in the market — 150-200, and no significant fading was observed on the surface. All above meet the washing requirements of washable labels.

7 Summary

With the rapid development of NFC mobile phones, the use of NFC labels has begun to affect all aspects of people's lives. The NFC washable labels proposed in this paper give the design of NFC washable labels and the detection of waterproof performance. It provides an interactive way for consumers to easily read clothing feedback information. Consumers can read NFC washable labels to get washing instructions and related information about clothes. Moreover, APP records and consumers' tracks provide a physical basis for intelligent collocation recommendation and accurate directional push of consumer clothing advertising information.

Our thanks to support of Beijing Education Commission scientific research Support Program (KYJH02150201) and major projects plan of Beijing science and Technology Committee.

References

[1] Tao Wei-wei, Chen Zhan-sheng, Yao Ming-hai, LI Meng-yuan. Design and implementation of clothing anti-counterfeiting system based on RFID. Journal of Mechanical & Electrical Engineering, 2012, 29(10), 1235-1238.

[2] Zheng B J. The design of interactive garment system. Industrial & Science Tribune, 2017, 16(15), 72-73.

[3] Ahsan K, Shan H, Kingston P. RFID applications: an introductory and exploratory study. IJCSI International Journal of Computer Science Issues, 2010, 7(1): 1-7.

[4] GB/T 14312-1993. The general specifications for water-proof clothing.

[5] Kwok S K, Tsang A H C, Ting J S L. An Intelligent RFID-based Electronic Anti-Counterfeit System (InRECS) for the Manufacturing Industry. Proceedings of the 17th World Congress The International Federation of Automatic Control. Seoul, Korea: [s.n.], 2008: 5482-5487.
[6] Zhang Yan. Application and Prospects of the internet of things technology in clothing industry. Advances in textile technology, 2015, 4: 80-84. DOI: 10.19507/j.cnki.1673-0356.2015.04.023
[7] Zhang Zhibin, Li Peng, Chen Shang. Preliminary study on the intelligent manufacturing innovation project of clothing manufacturing enterprises. Wool Textile Journal, 2016, 44(5): 62-65. DOI:10.19333/j.mfkj.2016.05.015

ITM Web of Conferences **17**, 03025 (2018) https://doi.org/10.1051/itmconf/20181703025
WCSN 2017

Data lake: a new ideology in big data era

Pwint Phyu Khine[1,a,b,*] *and Zhao Shun Wang*[1,c]

[1]Department of Computer Science and Technology, School of Computer and Communication Engineering, University of Science and Technology Beijing (USTB), 10083, Beijing, China
13051513579, [a]pwintphyukhinecs@gmail.com; [b]pwintphyukhinecs@outlook.com;
[c]zhswang@sohu.com

Abstract. Data Lake is one of the arguable concepts appeared in the era of big data. Data Lake original idea is originated from business field instead of academic field. As Data Lake is a newly conceived idea with revolutionized concepts, it brings many challenges for its adoption. However, the potential to change the data landscape makes the research of Data Lake worthwhile.

1 Introduction

In the era of big data, a new term called "Data Lake" came into view of the digital universe. The simplest intention of data lake is to munge every data produced by an organization to give more valuable insight in finer granularity. Big Data technologies are sometimes considered as destructive technologies as they revolutionized the traditional ways of doing things in this data intensive era. Concepts from distributed and parallel system are reapplied as the foundation of big data such as MapReduce paradigms for handling the big Vs characteristics – volume, velocity, variety, value and value. The incumbent SQL databases with ACID characteristics are challenged (and sometimes even replaced) by NoSQL databases with BASE characteristics. Now, Data Lake concept is trying to challenge the reliable, traditional data warehouses for storing heterogeneous complex data.

The idea of Data Lake was first initiated by Pentaho CEO Jame Dixon [9]. If a data warehouse or data mart is seem as a bottle of water cleaned and ready for consumption, then "Data Lake" is whole lake of data which is cleaned for ready use. Ref [16] added more in-depth definition for Data Lake as "a Data Lake stores disparate information while ignoring almost everything". Some believe that new data architecture is required [5] in the age of big data as this computational intensive era requests for new ideas and techniques for storing and processing voluminous, diverse, changing and evolving data. All data generated by an organization regardless of types, structures, or formats will be stored in Hadoop clusters or other similar framework in their original forms. When parts of the organizations need to use the data, that stored data will be loaded and transformed as required by that organization parts. Due to these, concepts in "Data Lake" seem to be challenging to the traditional ways of storing data i.e. data warehouse and data marts.

This paper is organized as follow. Introduction about data lake in big data era is described Section 1. Section 2 introduce about Data Lake concepts, describe the current data landscape and data lake architectural implementation. Comparison of data lake and data warehouse is explained in section 3. Section 4 describe the primary concerns and challenges imposed by Data Lake. Section 5 discuss the overview about data lake and conclude the paper.

---

* Pwint Phyu Khine: pwintphyukhinecs@gmail.com; pwintphyukhinecs@outlook.com;

2 Data lake concepts

As Data Lake is a relatively new concept, there are only a few academic literatures which are targeted to Data Lake. Ref [8] defines Data Lake as *"a methodology enabled by a massive data repository based on low cost technologies that improves the capture, refinement, archival, and exploration of raw data within an enterprise."* A data lake may contain raw, unstructured or multi-structured data where most part of these data may have unrecognized value for the organization.

The basic idea of Data Lake is simple, all data emitted by the organization will be stored in a single data structure called Data Lake. Data will be stored in the lake in their original format. Complex preprocessing and transformation of loading data into data warehouses will be eliminated. The upfront costs of data ingestion can also be reduced. Once data are placed in the lake, it's available for analysis by everyone in the organization [6].

Ref [3] suggested more specifications for Data Lake especially from the viewpoint of business domain instead of research community.

- All data are loaded from source systems.
- No data is turned away.
- Data are stored at the leaf level in an untransformed or nearly untransformed state.

The distinct characteristic of Data Lake is that it attracts more attention from business fields instead of academic research fields. Data Lake is a relatively new concept even for big data domain. Therefore, its definitions and characteristics, architecture, creation (implementation) and usage are far more prevalent in web articles and practitioner blogs than academic papers.

Different data lake concepts from the opinion about data lake is reviewed in [12] from "*Yesterday's unified storage is today's enterprise data lake*" to "*a massively scalable storage data repository that holds vast amount of raw data in its native format which is ingested by processing system (engine) without compromising the data structure.*"

2.1 Today data landscape

When comes to core, there are only two operations in data processing – Transactional and Analytical. Daily operations such as Online Transactional Processing (OLTP) are mostly work with CRUD-Create, Replicate, Update, Delete operations of the data for daily routines. Data will be structured and stored in SQL databases. In big data era, not only structured data but also semi-structured and unstructured data will be stored in NoSQL databases. Nonetheless, data in these databases will also be selected, cleaned, integrated, summarized, and transformed according the structure of the data warehouse schema for the analytical purpose. Currently, data warehouses are the dominant approach for providing analytical data. Only transformed data will be stored in the data warehouse.

Data warehouse is created based on fact table with simple W questions - "who, what, when, where" [11]. Then, dimension tables are supplemented based on the fields from the databases. Data are extracted, transformed to conform to data warehouse schema, and loaded into the Data Warehouse (ETL operations). Enterprise gather data from multiple operational databases into a single data warehouse storage to run ad-hoc queries. The query run on the consolidated data can help retrieve business intelligence conveniently.

This cause the separation of concerns for the two important concepts. Daily transactions will be performed by systems such as OLTP (Online Transaction processing). Analytical process such as data analysis, reviewing historical data and correlate data will be performed by analytical system such as OLAP (online analytical processing). Transactions data remain in operational databases whereas complex ad-hoc queries will run on data warehouses which serve for analytical purpose (thus they will not degrade the performance e.g. response time of transactions query). As DW are intended to build for analytical purpose, data are loaded into batch mode with the defined regular intervals. Data analytical process is performed on the data stored in the data warehouse to support the decision making of the enterprise and to obtain the valuable business insight.

However, as Data warehouses are very large and take time to create, "Data Marts" can be created. "Data Marts" are smaller than data warehouses, and intended to store the data of a part of the organization (i.e. a department in the enterprise). Data warehouse will store data of the whole enterprise. These data marts can be built separately. Or a part of the data warehouse intended for specific functionality or department can be extracted to create a data mart.

There are two famous definitions of Data Warehouse which come from their physical implementation. Inmon defined data warehouse is a subject-oriented (represent real-time object), integrated (data from different databases must be consolidated for showing a unified view), time-variant (data are loaded in time-interval and stored with appropriate timestamps for comparison and analysis), and non-volatile (i.e. instead of currently transition data, data will be collected and loaded into data warehouse in a point of time for analysis), thus no-update collection of data in support of management decision making. Data are stable and are not changed or deleted once are loaded [11]. Inmon approach, a top-down approach for implementation, makes the creation of data warehouse as a first step. In his approach, "data mart", targeted for departmental use, in a way a smaller portion of data warehouse, is created after the establishment of the main data warehouse. Kimball approach is different as it encourages the creation of data mart first. Then these departmental data marts are combined to create an organizational data warehouse. Therefore, Kimball approach is called bottom-up approach.

Data warehouses work better with bit-map indexes, applied materialized view for better optimization [11]. From bird's eye view, DWs are intentionally built for answering ad-hoc queries including historical data (and fall under the category of Analytical systems) which cannot be handled by transactional systems for daily operations. Data warehouses need to use operations like aggregate, join, etc. in one word – need to compute intensive query load. Therefore, most of the data warehouses are built as a single consolidated storage structure, highly summarized, ETLed data various transactional databases.

2.2 Data lake (architectural implementation)

Ref [7] give the explicit explanation of Data Lake from architectural view. "*A data lake uses a flat architecture to store data in their raw format. Each data entity in the lake is associated with a unique identifier and a set of extended metadata, and consumers can use purpose-built schemas to query relevant data, which will result in a smaller set of data that can be analyzed to help answer a consumer's question*". In essence, Data Lake is a data respiratory where all data in an enterprise i.e. structured, semi-structured, unstructured data + binary data are stored altogether regardless of types, format, or structure. The understanding of the data nature is delegated to the data consumer at the time of data retrieval (i.e. query time). When data are retrieved, user will transform that data according to the parts of the enterprise to acquire business insight.

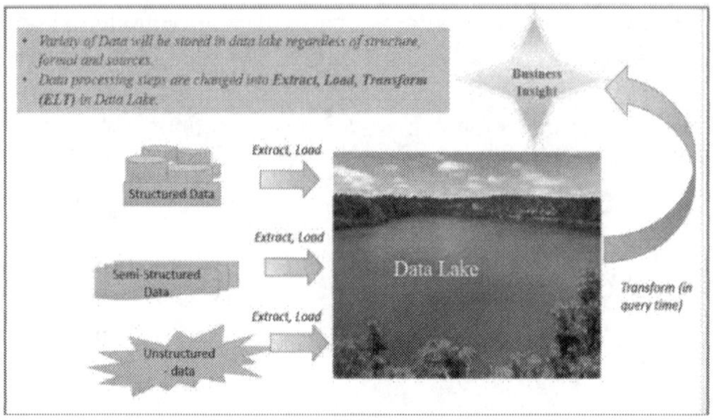

Fig. 1. A Simplified View of Data Lake

Many implementation of Data Lake are originally based on Apache Hadoop. Variety of data from heterogeneous data stores will be extracted to be stored in the Hadoop Cluster. HADOOP (Highly Available Object Oriented Data Platform) is a widely popular big data tool especially suitable for batch processing workload of big data. Hadoop have two main components – HDFS (Hadoop Distributed File System) and MapReduce engine. HDFS File System [17] handle the single point of failure and scalability by replicating multiple copies of data blocks in different nodes of the cluster. All data stored in these data block will be processed in MapReduce approach [10]. Data will be retrieved as a list of key-value pairs i.e. Map phase. The same keys of data will be shuffled, sorted and listed into groups to perform necessary operations i.e. Reduce phase. All data produced by an enterprise will be dumped into the Data Lake Hadoop Cluster [2].

For the real-time load, later data lakes are using stream processing framework such as Apache Spark, Apache Flink. The required data will be transformed according to the need of the analytics systems on the fly in the query time. Saving data with various format and structures from heterogeneous sources, and handling different data velocity (i.e. different processing speed of big data) request the careful consideration in building data pipe for carrying data into the lake [4]. Data Lake can often include a semantic DB, a conceptual model and add a layer of context to define the meaning of data its interrelationship with other data [12]. It can be said that Data Lake strategy includes storing all types of data (data variety) from SQL and NoSQL databases as well as combining the concepts of OLTP with OLAP. SQL databases are used to store structured data. NoSQL databases (Key-value, Columnar, Document, and Graph Stores) are used to store semi-structured and unstructured data. However, they can also be used to store structured data. All the transactional data from these databases (**Extract** - **E**) will be stored (**Load** - **L**) into the data lake without changing their format. When data are required (query time), data in the lake will be transformed (**Transform – T**) according to the parts of the enterprise system. Necessary works for query operations have to perform at the application level.

2.3 Suggestion for data lake improvement

As data lake use a flat architecture, each data element has a unique identifier and metadata tags. Although data lakes do not need to follow the strict pre-built schema for manipulation of different types and shapes of data, the order of data arrival time must be maintained. Because a range of data - from historical data to new data generated in near real time with different structure are stored in one place. Data and schema requirement are not predefined in advance until data are queried. This is the schema-on-read property of Data Lake [12].

Ref [12] also suggestion that the separation of data lake tier can be handled in two ways. The first approach is grounded on data structure, and another is centered on time lifetime. Based on data structure, Data Lake can be divided into three tiers - raw data, augmented daily datasets and third-party information respectively. Based on data lifetime, data can be categorized into data which has lifetime less than 6 months, older but still active data, and archived data that need to be retained although they are no longer used (suggested to move and maintain in slower, less expensive media) [12]. Metadata management is an important aspect in Data Lake. As Data Lakes do not have pre-defined schema like data warehouses, they have to rely on metadata during the query time for the analysis process. Metadata are added when data are stored. Ref [1] suggests a content metadata management framework for alignment in data lake construction using openML Data Lake with a prototype. Keys for creating a successful data lake are suggested in [4] as follow.

1. Align innovation initiative with corporate strategy. The priority of the enterprise strategy are Business Acceleration, Operational Efficiency, Security and Risk. Data Lake implementation should focus on the key priority of the corporate strategy.

2. Apply solid data integration strategy. The technology for data integration may be changing overtime in big data. The first Data Lake solutions are based on Hadoop. To handle real-time and streaming data, many DL solutions are now using Streaming framework such as Spark, Flink. Data Lakes need to keep track of evolving best-practices for metadata management. Data analytic pipeline need to automate the process of data extracting, loading, cleaning, transforming, and performing analytics.

3. Establish a modern onboarding strategy. Data Lake can get filled in batch load or in trickle feed. Simplify the process for loading data (regardless of types, sources or complexity) into the lake by enabling and establishing repeatable processes. Meanwhile maintain the appropriate level of data governance. Pay attention to the process of on the fly metadata injection.

4. Embrace new data management strategies by adopting of early ingestion and adaptive execution processing such as MapReduce, Spark, or Flink that allow for flexibility. Derive Metadata at onboarding (loading) time. Create the analytical model on the fly (automate the creation process). Extend data management processing and strategies to all data. Data analytics should be able to apply at anywhere in the data pipeline. Modernize the data integration infrastructure.

5. Apply Machine learning algorithms to drive real business value. The workflow for applying Machine learning algorithms should be repeatable. Data flow should go along with data preparation, engineering data feature, and manipulation of data sets.

3 Differention of data lake and data warehouse

Both data warehouse and data lake are data repositories. However, they are different in many aspects from concepts, structures, and implementation. Data warehouses have well-defined regulatory functions and storage capacity. In theory, Data Lakes have no limit for storage capacity. Any kind of data with any amount can be loaded into the data lake storage repository. "Data Lakes enable enterprises to look past the type and structure of data, giving them the chance to collect as much data as they desire" [15]. Ref [12] gives the data lake distinctions in contrast to data warehouse's processing of highly structured data, pre-built design before query time, slowly changing data as follows.

- Rapid arrival of unstructured data volumes
- Use of dynamic analytical applications (for query),
- Data become accessible as soon as it is created (as data are transformed based on query operation and application domain).

The detail of differentiation between data lake and data warehouse is explained in next sub sections.

3.1 Deviation of data lake from data warehouse

Data Lake concepts obviously deviate from data warehouse by means of processing of data in the "E-L-T" order and utilizing "Schema-on-Read" approach. Data warehouse approaches follow the traditional ETL process. First, data from operational databases are extracted (E). Then, the data are processed, cleaned and transformed (T) before loading (L) them into the data warehouses or data marts. Data warehouse are especially designed to handle read-heavy workload for analytics. Data warehouse need to define their schema in advance before data are loaded. Therefore, they are considered as "Schema-On-Write" approach.

Different from the traditional idea of ETL of data warehouses, Data Lakes make the different ordering in processing data. The data will be stored in its original format. The preprocessing step will not be handled until the data are required by the application or in query time. Therefore, it breaks the traditional ETL rules of data warehouse. Instead, DL promote the new idea of ELT (Extract, Load, Transform) the change of order for data processing **(ELT)**. There is no predefined data schema in DL. When data are extracted from the source to the data lake, the required metadata are especially added in the data. In this way, Data Lake can handle both write-heavy workload and read-heavy workload (transaction and analytics) recombining two separation of concerns (write and read). The data are not transformed until the applications call them. Only when the data are required and called by the application for query, the data are transformed into appropriate form using the metadata which is added earlier on. In this way, expensive data pre-transformation can be avoided in Data Lake. The transform operations will only be performed when data are read from the data lake. Therefore, Data Lake approach is called "Schema-on-Read" approach.

3.2 Comparison for data lake and data warehouse

From business domain, enthusiasts of data lake concepts [14] provide the summarization for the difference between Data Lake and data warehouse as in Table [9]. They can be further can be explained as follow.

Table 1. Comparison of Data warehouse and Data Lake

Comparison	Data Warehouse	Data Lake
Data	Structured, processed data	Structured/semi-structured, unstructured data, raw data, unprocessed data
Processing	Schema-on-write	Schema-on-read
Storage	Expensive, reliable	Low cost storage
Agility	Less agile, fixed configuration	High agility, flexible configuration
Security	Matured	Maturing
Users	Business professional	Data Scientists (especially those familiar with domain)

1. **Data** – A popular say in business domain is only 20% of the data are structured. Data warehouse is the cream of the crop as it only accepted ETL-ed and consolidated extremely summarized structured data. The other 80% of the semi-structured and unstructured data

(there is no exact suggestion how many % each of them take place - only largest portion is unstructured, and semi-structured portion is larger than structured data. Other experts predict as 70% of unstructured+ semi-structured data.) As DL store data in unstructured and unorganized way, they can be more easily manipulated and handled in a variety of ways which is surprisely more suitable for big data.

2. **Processing** – As mentioned before, data stored in data warehouse are carefully selected through Extract-Transform-Load process. They are intended to use only for analytical purpose – especially for the decision maker level. They passed through the Extract-Transform-Load order of data processing with Schema-on-Write approach. However, data warehouses are limited by their very summarized and structured nature. They are not able to answer out-of-box questions of decision makers or questions that need to extract transactions data and/or combined with unstructured data. User query can only performed limitedly on highly defined structured data. However, Data Lake can handle these kind of user query. Only when user query the data, the data will be transformed according to the user applications for the analytics level in the order of (Extract-Load-Transform) processing applying "Schema-on-read" approach. This gives more flexibility for data scientist who are familiar with domain to retrieve value from previously untapped or unexplored data such as raw or binary data combining with structured data. It is also a reason why data scientists are able to tolerate the imperfections of Data Lake and want to adopt and refine Data Lake.

3. **Cost** – Many data lake solutions are implemented in open-source framework and designed for commodity servers. Therefore, compared to the high-licensing fees of data warehouse storage, it is relatively much cheaper. According to [11], the cost of Data warehouse can be recovered within a year. However, the cost of Data Lake and its ROI is still a questionable debate.

4. **Agility** - Data warehouse design is made in advance before data are loaded (schema-on-write). By definition, it is a highly-structured definition with highly governed data management. Although it is possible to change the data warehouse design, it is very time consuming and require enormous effort as it is tied to many business processes. Sometimes, the whole design reconsideration is required leading to significant maintenance cost. Moreover, Data warehouse cannot handle the request of enterprises that want to analyze a wide variety of data. If they are forcibly enforced, data already loaded into the data warehouse may be corrupted or the Warehouse design may be damaged. Data Lake lacks the explicitly defined structure of data warehouse. Therefore, they are more flexible and agile. It gives the developers and data scientists the ability to easily configure the models, queries, and apps on-the-fly [14] [15]. Because of Data Lake agility and flexibility (as mentioned before), Data Lakes are worth to explore.

5. **Security** - Data warehouses have been there for decades and have well-defined security. However, data lakes are still lacking the answer to the complete security "when" question. Security of data in Data Lake are still left as open research area.

6. **Users** - Until now, Data Lake is still the most suitable for data analysts and data scientists, not analytics for everyone due to the reasons as mentioned above. Many experts in current market are more familiar with data warehouse procedures and consider Data Lake as incompetent and cumbersome. However, data scientists who are interested in the concepts of Data Lake are researching and building the data lake (especially test building of Data Lake in small and medium size enterprises, or building as sample prototypes). They are the main resources which has been providing feedbacks for data lake improvement.

4 Concerns and challenges of data lake

4.1 Data lake concerns

There are two primary concerns for Data Lake. From business point of view, Data Lake may be another marketing hype for Hadoop. From Technical point of view, Data Lake can easily be changed into data swamps [18].

Marketing Hype: Adversary argument is that Data Lake in reality is just a Hadoop's marketing hype of the Business Intelligence solution developers. Gartner point out that Data lake concepts is emerged from Agility and accessibility need of data analysis. Data Lake can definitely provide value to various parts of organization, but they are not the solution ready for enterprise-wide data management [6]. However, the accuse of "Hadoop marketing hype concept" has been slowly evaporating as current data lake solutions are implementing using other frameworks like streaming engines such as Spark, Flink, etc.

Data Swamp: Even for the supporter of data lake noticed the pitfalls of Data Lake. One of the biggest one is becoming a data swamp [7]. No one knows what will be put into the lake. Moreover, there is no procedures from preventing them such as entering wrong data, repeated data, or incorrect data [18]. Data feed into the data lake do not guarantee the veracity since their extraction. If no one knows what kind of data resides in the lake, they might not be able to find out that some data in the lake are corrupted until it's too late. As organizations have started using this technology without sophisticated security measures, these shortcomings become important. Moreover, security compromises are yet to be addressed [16]. Data Lake might have a tendency to data pollution and chances of becoming a data swamp are high. For data lake advocates, how to prevent a data lake from becoming a data swamp turn out to be an interesting topic.

4.2 Challenges of data lake

Data warehouse can guarantee governance, performance, security and access controls. They also have defined semantic consistency. None of these can be guaranteed by Data Lake. Data Lakes lack satisfactory guarantee in areas such as Security, Metadata management, and performance. As data are vaguely structured and most technologies are open-sourced, sensitive data may be compromised, and security can easily be compromised. Many users lack the ability to manage the metadata as Data Lakes do not provide specific mechanism for handling them [15]. Data extractor needs to start from scratch even when other analytics have been found value from these data as there is no metadata maintained or category classified to trace them back. Gaining value from Data Lake is particularly difficult. There are no unique identifiers in Data Lake for advanced searching of large data volume [16]. Unlike data warehouses, "Performance" of Data Lakes have not been benchmarked or proved. These lack of guarantee come from the fact that current Data lakes focus on storing disparate data and ignore how or why data are used, governed, defined and secured.
Based on [6], data lake challenges can be considered as follow.

1. Data lack the ability to determine data quality or the lineage of findings. Other data analysts have found out them in the same data lake but cannot provide for later analysts.
2. Data Lake accepts any data without oversight and governance.
3. There is no descriptive metadata or a mechanism to maintain metadata leading to data swamp.
4. Data need to analyze from scratch every time.
5. Performance cannot be guaranteed.
6. Security (privacy and regulatory requirements) and Access control (weakness of metadata management) as data in the lake can be replaced without oversight of the contents.

5 Discussion and conclusion

Data Lakes try to solve two problems – data silos (old problem) and challenges imposed by big data initiatives (new problem) [6]. Instead of having independently data collections, all data to be stored are collected in Data Lake to handle the old silos problem. The new problem is handling the challenges of big data era i.e. data lakes try to solve the challenges imposed by big data V's characteristics – volume, velocity, verity, variety and value.

If data generated or produced from different departments within an organization are stocked only in their data stores, the chances of becoming data silos are very likely. Data Lake tries to integrate data from these different stores in a single place attempting to end the possibility of data silos. Traditional data warehouse with structured format cannot handle variety of data with different latency need. In big data context, Data Lake may be able to tackle volume and variety if aforementioned challenges were handled.

Conceptually, Data Lake accepts any data structure and volume of data. Every data can simply store into the data lake. Data Lake considers that all required necessary data can be added into the lake as much as necessary (e.g. more nodes will be added in the Hadoop solution ensuring scalability). When data are retrieved from Data Lake, stored metadata and extra stored data can be used as a support for data transformation process and data analytic process.

Retrieving variety of data from heterogeneous sources and the need for handling different velocity processing speed request the careful construction of data pipelines. The data pipelines for feeding data into the lake have to paid attention for handling these Vs' requests when they are built. They need to carry not only all data generated and/or extracted, but also metadata of them and extra data for later use.

Data Lake may suffer by due to data velocity of big data. Data warehouses have definite specification in their operations. They will be loaded in batch at predefined time. Instead, there is no definite processing speed specification for Data Lake. Data Velocity is the speed of data needed to be extracted, cleaned, stored, transformed, loaded or processed. Data velocity can be differentiated into batch, near real-time, real-time and streaming. Since Data Lake tries to replicate the functionality of data warehouse, batch loading is possible for Data Lake. However, undefined flow of stream processing and the need of precise response in near-real time and real time system will ask for definite specification in handling in Data Lake. As security and metadata management are weak in Data Lake, data veracity cannot be assured.

However, Data Lake can provide unique value (untapped, unexplored and surplus) as data for profit which are important for organization. There are optimistic supporters of DL even when turning into data swamp. They argue that even data retrieved from data swamp can still be used to a point in applications and query where all data correctness is not necessary for instance analyzing customer shopping cards abandoning. Fraction of data extracted from Data Lake (even a swamp) can provide unique insights.

As mentioned before, Data Lake has one very important mission i.e. reconciliation of concerns. Analytical and Transactions are separated in the current data landscape. Daily operational data are stored in databases and handled by transactional systems for performing basic CRUD operations and simple query. Data from these transactional data systems are still need to be extracted, transformed, and loaded into highly summarized and consolidated data warehouses to perform ad-hoc analytical queries. The noble mission of data lake is to combine these transaction and analytic into one mechanism. Expected Scenario is that DL will store all transaction data in their naïve format, and allow extracting data on the fly necessary for analysis. Query and Transforms will be performed based on the need of application domain.

A Data Lake may need to pass through five maturity levels [2]. They are - 1. Consolidated and categorized raw data, 2. Attribute-level metadata tagging and linking such as joins, 3. Data set extraction and analysis, 4. Business-specific tagging, synonym identification, and links, and 5. Convergence of meaning within context. As data lake maturity level increases, the usage of Data Lake across enterprise and value of analytics will increase.

Data lakes are also increasing in popularity because of IoTs (Internet of Things) boom [16]. However, currently Data Lakes are not threatening to replace data warehouses as they have not handled the mentioned problems and challenges yet. Ref [16] also gives very interesting opinions of Data Lake. If the methods were discovered that will make ensure data lake solutions are worth replacing in place of warehouse, then the answer would be the evolution of the big data warehouses. It also coincide the opinion for tableau big data forecast [13]. The forecast predicts that Data Warehouse and Data Lake concepts may be combined in near future i.e. totally, Data Warehouse and Data Lake can become only one concept once again by enhancing and adding each other's capabilities. If Data Lake can successfully handle the challenges caused by big data and end the problems of data silos, the whole landscape of data storage architecture may change again in coming future.

Author expresses her gratitude to her supervisor Professor Wang Zhao Shun for providing encouragement in completing this paper. Author thanks to persons (both anonymous and entitled) who provided many good advices in completing this paper. The work is performed under the grant No 2017YFB0202303, National Key Research and Development plan 2017 for High Performance Computing.

References

[1] Ayman Alserafi, Alberto Abell´o, Oscar Romero, Toon Calders,Towards Information Profiling: Data Lake Content: Metadata Management, 2016 IEEE 16th International Conference on Data Mining Workshops.

[2] Brian Stein, Alan Morrison," The enterprise data lake: Better integration and deeper analytics, Technology Forecast: Rethinking integration", Issue 1, 2014, Retrieved 25, Aug. 2017: www.pwc.com/us/en/technology-forecast/2014/cloud-computing/assets/pdf/pwc-technology-forecast-data-lakes.pdf.

[3] Chris Campbell, Top five difference between data lakes and data warehouses, JAN 26, 2015, Blue Granite, Retrieved Aug 25, 2017. https://www.blue-granite.com/blog/bid/402596/top-five-differences-between-data-lakes-and-data-warehouses.

[4] Chuck Yarbrough, 5 Keys creating killer data lake, Retrieved July 21, 2017. http://www.pentaho.com/blog/5-keys-creating-killer-data-lake.

[5] Dan Wood, Big data requires a big new architecture, Forbes, Retrieved Aug 8, 2017. https://www.forbes.com/sites/ciocentral/2011/07/21/big-data-requires-a-big-new-architecture/#66609cb61157.

[6] Gartner.Inc, Gartner Says Beware of the Data Lake Fallacy, STAMFORD, Conn., July 28, 2014, Retrieved 29 Aug, 2017. http://www.gartner.com/newsroom/id/2809117.

[7] Hassan Alrehamy Coral Walker, Personal Data Lake With Data Gravity Pull, 2015 IEEE Fifth International Conference on Big Data and Cloud Computing, 26-28 Aug. 2015, Dalian, China.

[8] Huang Fang, Managing Data Lakes in Big Data Era: What's a data lake and why has it became popular in data management ecosystem, The 5th Annual IEEE International Conference on Cyber Technology in Automation, Control and Intelligent Systems, June 8-12, 2015, Shenyang, China.

[9] James Dixon, Pentaho, Hadoop and Data Lakes, Retrieved 10 Aug 2017. https://jamesdixon.wordpress.com/2010/10/14/pentaho-hadoop-and-data-lakes/
[10] Jeffrey Dean, Sanjay Ghemawat, MapReduce: Simplified Processing on large cluster, Communication of the ACM, Vol. 51, No. 1, Jan 2008.
[11] Michael Stonebraker, Uğur Çetintemel, One Size Fits All: An Idea Whose Time Has Come and Gone, Proceedings. 21st International Conference on Data Engineering, April, 2005. ICDE 2005, Tokyo, Japan.
[12] Natalia Miloslavskaya, Alexander Tolstoy, Application of Big Data, Fast Data and Data Lake Concepts to Information Security Issues, 2016 4th International Conference on Future Internet of Things and Cloud Workshops.
[13] Tableau, Top 10 Big Data Trends for 2017, Retrieved 30, Aug.2017: https://www.tableau.com/resource/top-10-big-data-trends-2017.
[14] Tamara Dull, Data Lake Vs Data Warehouse: Key Differences, Retrieved Sep 26, 2017 http://www.kdnuggets.com/2015/09/data-lake-vs-data-warehouse-key-differences.html.
[15] Timothy King in Best Practices, Data Warehouse vs. Data Lake; What's the Difference? June 9, 2016, Retrieved Sep 10, 2017: https://solutionsreview.com/data-management/data-warehouse-vs-data-lake-whats-the-difference/.
[16] Timothy King "The Emergence of Data Lake: Pros and Cons", March 3, 2016, Retrieved Sep 15, 2017: https://solutionsreview.com/data-integration/the-emergence-of-data-lake-pros-and-cons/
[17] Tom White, Hadoop: The Definitive Guide, 4th ed., Storage and Analysis at Internet Scale, O'Reilly Media, Inc., 1005 Gravenstein Highway North, Sebastopol, USA, 2015.
[18] Kumar Srivastava, Four Common Mistakes That Can Make For A Toxic Data Lake, Forbes, Nov 25, 2014, Retrieved Aug 24, 2017: https://www.forbes.com/sites/ciocentral/2014/11/25/four-common-mistakes-that-make-for-toxic-data-lakes/

Formal verification of dynamic hybrid systems: a NuSMV-based model checking approach

Zhi Xu[1,a,*], *Deming Zhong*[1,b], *Weigang Li*[2,c], *Hao Huang*[2,d] *And Yigang Sun*[3,e]

[1]Beihang University, XueYuan Road No.37,HaiDian District, BeiJing, China
[2]Hangfa Control System Research Institute of China, LiangXi Road No.37, BinHu District, WuXi, China
[3]Civil Aviation University Of China, North Way of Road, Dong Li District,Tian Jin,China
[a]332999245@qq.com; [b]zhongdeming@buaa.edu.cn; [c]bailingke@vip.sina.com; [d]1316247928@qq.com; [e]caucsyg@163.com

Abstract. Software security is an important and challenging research topic in developing dynamic hybrid embedded software systems. Ensuring the correct behavior of these systems is particularly difficult due to the interactions between the continuous subsystem and the discrete subsystem. Currently available security analysis methods for system risks have been limited, as they rely on manual inspections of the individual subsystems under simplifying assumptions. To improve this situation, a new approach is proposed that is based on the symbolic model checking tool NuSMV. A dual PID system is used as an example system, for which the logical part and the computational part of the system are modeled in a unified manner. Constraints are constructed on the controlled object, and a counter-example path is ultimately generated, indicating that the hybrid system can be analyzed by the model checking tool.

1 Introduction

Hybrid systems [1], also known as hybrid dynamic systems, are designed using interactions between the continuous subsystem and the discrete subsystem. The dynamic characteristics of continuous subsystems evolve with time, while the dynamic evolution of discrete subsystems is driven by events. Hybrid systems are found in a wide range of embedded system applications, including complex industrial control systems. In such systems, the dynamic evolution of the physical layer is described by the continuous computation of successive variables and the high-level coordination optimization process is characterized by symbolic operations and discrete monitoring decisions.

There are numerous challenges involved with the security analysis of dynamic hybrid systems [2]. First, the security attributes of such systems need analysis that combines comprehensive knowledge of control disciplines, computer science, mathematics, as well as security. Second, the interaction of the continuous and discrete subsystems adds complexity to the analysis problem. When a system is relatively simple, such as risk factors including only a single category, or a single system component without heterogeneous composition,

* Zhi Xu: 332999245@qq.com

or a linear time-invariant system, it is relatively straightforward to find and analyze the system risks. However, when analyzing the security of a complex system, due to heterogeneous component coupling, multi-class risk factors coexistence, nonlinear dynamic operation, and system state explosion, the existing security analysis techniques have been inadequate. The reason is that, when the two components of the hybrid system are analyzed separately, while ignoring the interaction of the two components, or the analysis of the interaction is only manually analyzed by experience, then the important system risks must be left out.

This work proposes a new approach to analyzing the security of dynamic hybrid systems that is based on a formal method. Formal methods are an effective means of logical consistency verification of the system, which can ensure the adequacy of verification. Formal methods include theorem proving and symbolic model checking. Model checking is a state traversal-based verification technique, iterating through all the system states to determine if the system meets the desired characteristics. In general, the inputs to a model checking tool include two parts: the finite state machine model, and the system features constrained by temporal logic expressions.

In this paper, the logical part and the computational part of a dual PID system are modeled in NuSMV [3]. Constraints are constructed on the controlled object, and a counter-example path is ultimately generated, indicating that the hybrid system can be analyzed by the model checking tool.

2 Case study

2.1 Preliminary

2.1.1 NuSMV

The research on model checking is mainly embodied in the development of model checking tools. At present, there are many open source model detection tools, among which NuSMV and SPIN [4] are the most widely used ones. NuSMV was developed by Dr. McMillan from Carnegie Mellon University, primarily through the reconstruction and performance optimization of SMV (symbolic model verifier) [5]. The NuSMV kernel is based on binary decision diagrams (BDDs) and is the first model detection tool based on a binary decision graph. NuSMV is completely open sourced and has good scalability; consequently numerous customized tools based on NuSMV have been presented. NuSMV is often used for reliability and security verification of industrial designs, and the NuSMV core is often used as a core component of other tools because of its powerful core capabilities and good scalability. NuSMV has many features, including interactive, call operations, variable analysis, partition, system characteristics test, as well as SAT (Boolean Satisfiability Problem). NuSMV is not only compatible with the SMV batch task, but also provides a set of textual interactive interfaces. Users can type a variety of instructions to perform relevant operations and calculations. NuSMV can support computational tree logic (CTL) and linear temporal logic (LTL). . When validating system features, the users can specify the path they are interested in and check the value of the associated variable on that path. When NuSMV discovers that the system has a path conflicting with the characteristics, the counter-example path will be fed back to the user.

2.1.2 Overview of PID control system

PID control is one of the earliest developed control strategies, and is widely used in industrial control due to its simplicity, robustness, as well as high reliability. A typical single PID closed-loop control system is shown in Figure 1.

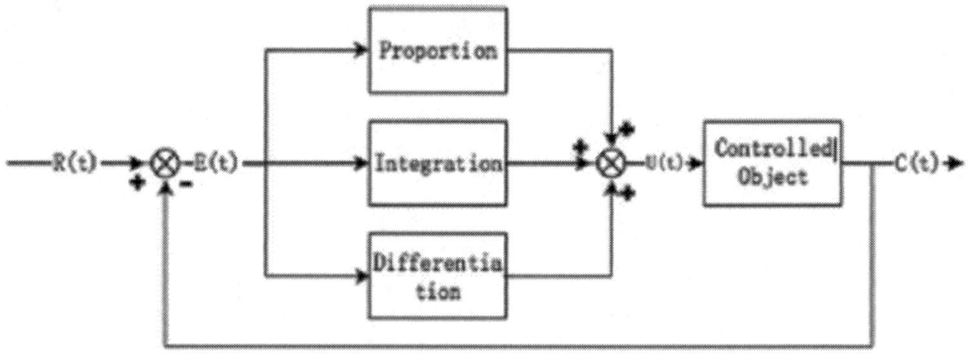

Fig. 1. Typical single PID closed-loop control system

According to the control deviation of the given value r(t) and the actual output value c(t), the PID controller computes the control value using the linear combination of Proportion (P), Integration (I) and Differentiation (D) to control the object. Its control rule obeys Equation 1:

$$u(t) = K_P\left[e(t) + \frac{1}{T_I}\int_0^t e(t)dt + T_D\frac{de(t)}{dt}\right] \quad (1)$$

where K_P the proportional coefficient, T_I is the integral time constant and T_D is derivative time constant.

2.2 Model construction

2.2.1 Models and parameters setting

To illustrate that hybrid systems can be analyzed using model checking tools, we select a double PID control system as an example to model and analyze. The specific model is shown in Figure 2. In this system, the two PID controller switching is the logical part, while the proportional, integral and differential calculation parts in each PID are the continuous part.

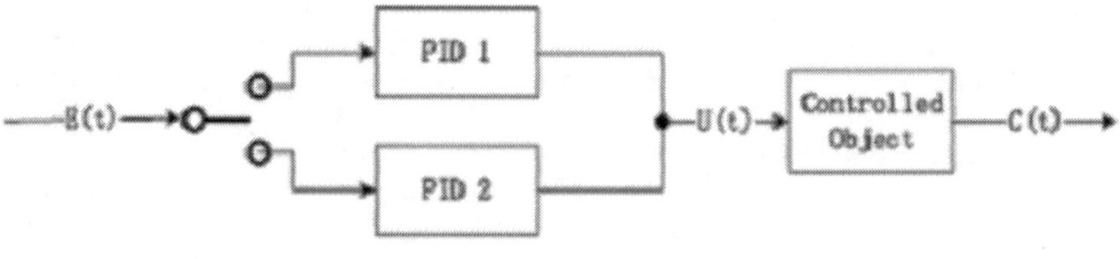

Fig. 2. Typical single PID closed-loop control system

Because the focus of this paper is on the logic and calculation part of the hybrid system, for a more direct and effective problem description, as well as to avoid unnecessary interference, ideal processing parameters are assumed. The time t is set as follows: when the time is in 0-3 seconds, the first PID controller is used; when the time is in 4-6 seconds, the second PID controller is used (Equation 2).

$$u(t) = \begin{cases} K_{P1}\left[e(t) + \frac{1}{T_{I1}}\int_0^t e(t)dt + T_{D1}\frac{de(t)}{dt}\right] & (0 \le t \le 3) \\ K_{P2}\left[e(t) + \frac{1}{T_{I2}}\int_0^t e(t)dt + T_{D2}\frac{de(t)}{dt}\right] & (4 \le t \le 6) \end{cases} \quad (2)$$

where $e(t) = 3t^2$, $K_{P1} = 1/3$, $T_{I1} = 1/3$, $T_{D1} = 1/2$, $K_{P2} = 1/3$, $T_{I2} = 1/3$, and $T_{D2} = 1$.

2.2.2 Model transformation

Based on the above description of the simplified models, the NuSMV representation is defined. The following transformation result as well as the transformation process description: some key script are shown in Table 1. (comments are the transformation process description).

Table 1. Key script about the model transformation

```
MODULE main
VAR
t : 0..6; -- running time of the whole system is 6s, and the step is 1s
P1 : 0..9; -- the value range of the proportional part of the first PID controller
I1 : 0..27; -- the value range of the integral part of the first PID controller
D1: 0..6; -- the value range of the differential part of the first PID controller
P2 : 0..36; -- the value range of the proportional part of the second PID controller
I2 : 0..216; -- the value range of the integral part of the second PID controller
D2: 0..6; -- the value range of the differential part of the second PID controller
u : 0..258; -- the output value range of the controller
y : Boolean; -- controlled object is set to Boolean
......
next(t) := case  -- the state transition paths of time
 (t >= 0) & (t <= 5) : t + 1 ;
 t = 6 : 0;
TRUE : t;
......
next(u) := case -- the state transition paths of output u
(t >= 0) & (t < 3) : next(p1) + next(i1) + next(d1);
(t >= 3) & (t <= 6) : next(p2) + next(i2) + next(d2) mod 259 ;
 u = 258 : 258;
TRUE : u;
esac;
next(y) := case -- the state transition paths of controlled object y
next(u) = 258 : TRUE;
next(u) < 258 : FALSE;
esac;
```

The constraints are constructed as follows.

CTLSPEC ! EF (y = TRUE)

Where y is the control object, which is a Boolean logic value.

The NuSMV model can be interpreted as a switch: when the state is TRUE, the switch is open; otherwise the switch is closed. Therefore, the above constraints on the model can be explained as follows: there is no state transition path, such that the switch is open.

2.2.3 Implementation verification

The output obtained after the NuSMV terminal loading the model script is shown in Figure 3.

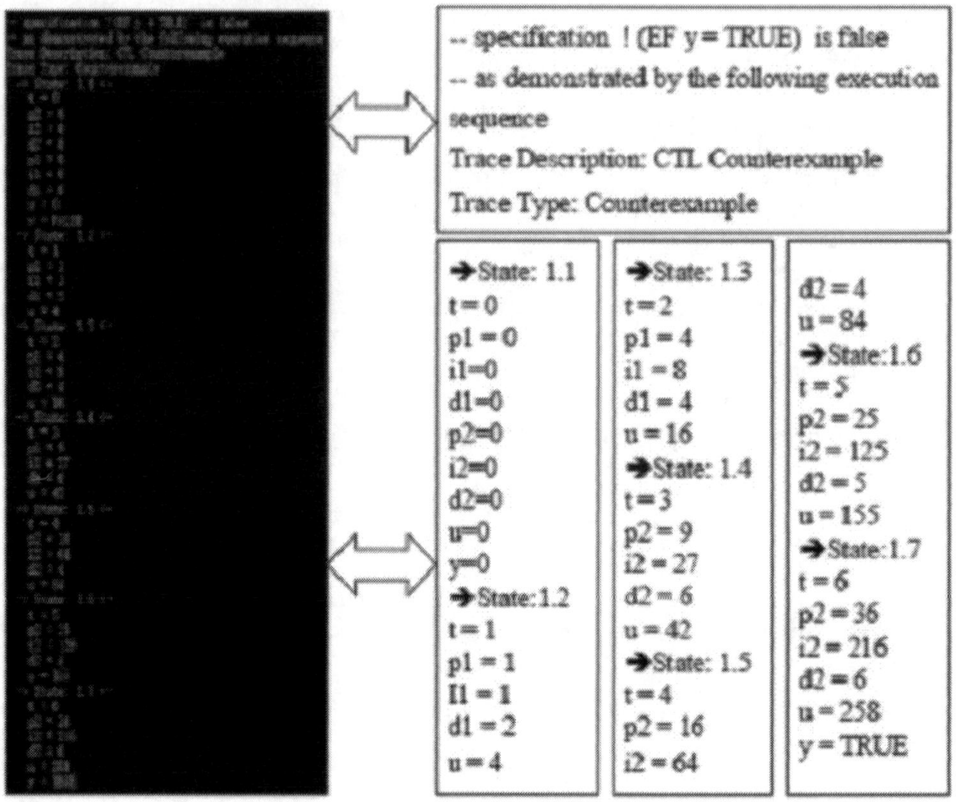

Fig. 3. The output after the NuSMV terminal loading the model script

Because NuSMV can support CTL/LTL logic, when the system characteristics are verified, the path that the users are interested in can be specified and the value of the associated variable on that path can be checked. When NuSMV discovers that the system has a path that conflicts with the characteristics, these counter-example paths are fed back to the users.

The results demonstrate that the system eventually leads to y=TRUE, i.e., the switch is opened, and a counter-example path is given to explain how each part of the state changes will lead to the final results of switch being opened.

3 Conclusion

In this paper, a model checking method is proposed to unify the logical part and the computational part of a dynamic hybrid system model. This provides a formal approach to the analysis of such systems, enabling their adoption into security critical embedded systems. A dual PID system is used as an example. The final results show that the two parts of the original separated process can be modeled together and the desired results can be obtained.

In the future, more complex hybrid systems need to be further explored, so that the proposed method can be more applicable, and the model expression can be more complete.

This research was supported by grants from Civil Aviation Joint Funds Established by National Nature Science Foundation of China and Civil Aviation Administration of China(No.U1533201), from a project of Ministry of Industry and Information Technology of China (No.JSZL2015601C008) and from the Major State Basic Research Development Program of China (973 Program) (No. 2014CB744904).

References

[1] KONG, S., GAO, S., CHEN, W., and CLARKE, E., 2015. dReach: δ-Reachability Analysis for Hybrid Systems. In International Conference on TOOLS and Algorithms for the Construction and Analysis of Systems, 200-205.
[2] YAN, Q., YU, F.R., GONG, Q., and LI, J., 2016. Software-defined networking (SDN) and distributed denial of service (DDoS) attacks in cloud computing environments: A survey, some research issues, and challenges. IEEE Communications Surveys & Tutorials 18, 1, 602-622.
[3] CIMATTI, A., CLARKE, E., GIUNCHIGLIA, F., and ROVERI, M., 2000. NUSMV: a new symbolic model checker. International Journal on Software Tools for Technology Transfer 2, 4, 410-425.
[4] HOLZMANN, G.J., 1997. The model checker SPIN. IEEE Transactions on Software Engineering 23, 5, 279-295.
[5] MCMILLAN, K.L., 1992. The SMV system. Symbolic Model Checking 38, 4, 161–165.

Research on wireless communication technology based on automatic logistics system of welder

Xuan Sun[1,a,*], *Zhi-yong Wang*[1,b] *and Zhe-dong Ma*[1,c]

[1]School of Mechanical Engineering, University of Jinan, Jinan, China
[a]me_sunx@ujn.edu.cn; [b]971917165@qq.com; [c]394396041@qq.com

Abstract. In order to meet the requirements of high real-time and high stability of data transmission in automatic welding system, RTU data format and real-time communication mechanism are adopted in this system. In the automatic logistics system through the Ethernet and wireless WIFI technology will palletizer, stacker, AGV car organically together to complete the palletizer automatic crawling the goods, AGV car automatic delivery, stacking machine automatically out of the Dimensional warehouse. .

1 Introduction

With the continuous development of China's economy, the advantage of lower cost of human resources has gradually disappeared [1]. Higher and higher cost of human resources, more and more Chinese enterprises lost the advantage of market competition, these enterprises urgently need to introduce automated production equipment to replace manpower, reduce costs [2]. The automatic logistics system can not only completely replace manpower, but also greatly increase the efficiency of production [3]. However, for automated logistics systems, wireless communication is the technical difficulty in this automation system. It requires the communication between the system to have higher real-time and higher stability [4]. Therefore, it is urgent to study a wireless communication network environment which can adapt to complex industrial environment, and has higher real-time and stability [5].

2 Application environment analysis of automatic logistics system for welding machine

Automated warehouse mainly uses high-level shelves, standard pallets, storage of goods, mainly in three-dimensional warehouse stacker, combined with automated logistics equipment to automate warehouse operations. The supporting equipment mainly includes palletizing equipment, AGV car and so on. The stacker will be responsible for the

* Xuan Sun: me_sunx@ujn.edu.cn

production line of packaging machine according to the rules to the stacking goods, AGV to carry the goods put the goods tray to the entrance of the three-dimensional warehouse, warehousing operations by stacking machine. At the same time stacker can manually send out or receive management computer instructions for outbound operations. The overall layout of the system is shown in Figure 1.

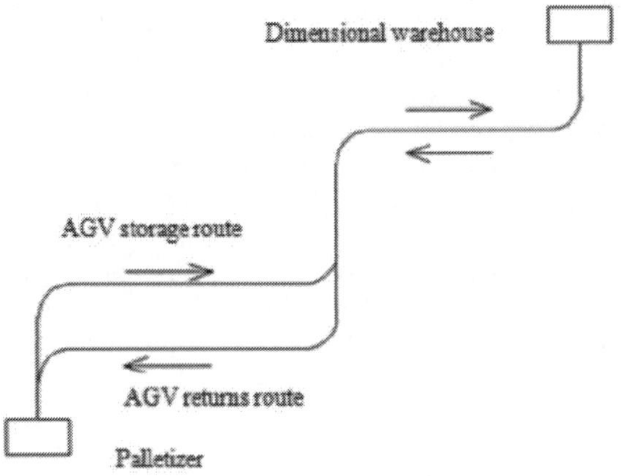

Fig. 1. Layout of automated warehouse system

As the production line of the welder needs to be transported to the distance of more than 300 meters in the three-dimensional warehouse, and in order to reduce the impact of the system on the original production environment, AGV car must run on a specific path. Path in figure 1. Through the AGV car running path, production requirements and cost analysis. Finally, we will use two AGV for welding machine transport operations. As the communication distance is long, and AGV and stacker are in motion state, the traditional RS232, RS485 and other wired communication cannot meet the system communication requirements, so this system is adopted Ethernet communication, the specific method is: using industrial WiFi signal router to cover the entire plant. Connect the management PC (server), stacker controller, palletizer controller, AGV car and other equipment to the router.

3 Network structure

Through the analysis of the on - site environment, the final communication structure of the system is shown in Figure 2.

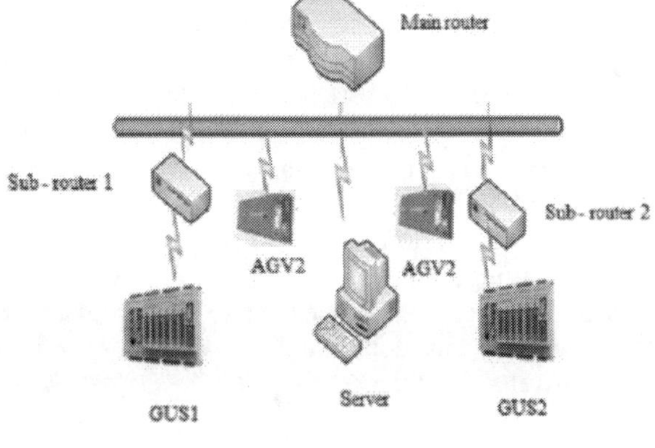

Fig. 2. Communication network diagram of stereoscopic warehouse system

In Figure 2, with PC as the management system of TCP communication server. Stacking machine, palletizing machine, AGV carrier through their respective Internet access module to access the local area network, real-time management PC to send status, request and other information; management PC to accept the connection of each device, Stacking machine, palletizer, AGV transporter through their respective Internet access module to access the local area network, real-time management PC to send status, request and other information; management PC to accept the connection of various devices, and verify, explain the equipment upload Of the data, so as to obtain the current state of each device. And the corresponding control instructions are sent according to the current system state, so that the other devices can be unified and managed according to the current state of each device. The stacker and palletizer are powered by a motion controller that communicates with the server via an RS232 serial port to the wireless WIFI module. AGV also uses the RS232 serial port to connect to the wireless WIFI module. And the server is directly connected to the Sub - router 2 LAN port, because the server is relatively close to the location of the Sub - router 2[6]. And wired data transmission than wireless WIFI transmission faster and more stable, so that other equipment can make a variety of information more quickly and accurately transmitted to the server.

4 Application of wireless Wifi technology

WIFI full name Wireless Fidelit, in essence, is a commercial certification, with Wi-Fi certified products in line with IEEE802.11a / b / g / n wireless network specifications, it is currently using a more extensive WLAN standard, the usual working frequency is 2.4GHz [7].

The automatic welding logistics system adopts wireless WIFI technology mainly because of the following aspects:

(1) Construction is convenient and quick. Because WIFI is a wireless technology. So in the construction of a wide range of network eliminates the need for a large number of cabling work, only a certain number of routers, using wireless bridging technology to meet the automatic logistics system requirements of the local area network.

(2) Radio waves transmit farther. At present, the wireless WIFI in the market can be transmitted over 100 to 300 meters without obstacles. However, the transmission distance of wireless Bluetooth is only about 15 meters. But the obstruction of the obstacle greatly reduces the quality of the wireless WIFI signal.

(3) The transmission speed is very fast. At present, routers in the market can reach 37.5Mbit/s, which can fully meet the needs of the data transmission of the automatic logistics system.

Due to obstruction of industrial equipment, the intensity of the wireless WIFI signal will be greatly reduced and the quality of the data transmission will be affected. Therefore, in a very complex factory environment, a single router has been unable to achieve high efficiency and high quality data transmission. In order to achieve high quality data transmission, we use wireless bridging technology to build a wireless communication environment with large signal intensity and wide coverage. At present, the wireless bridging technology mainly has the following three kinds:

1) Point to point wireless bridging;

Point to point wireless bridging mode can be used to transmit data far from the signal. It is bridged by two wireless routers, thus doubling the distance of data transmission.

2) Point to multipoint wireless bridging;

The point to multipoint wireless bridging mode enables the decentralized wireless network to be integrated into one entity, and one of the routers acts as the primary router to communicate with all other secondary routers.

3) Bridge relay

Bridge relay is the application of two LAN, there is a certain obstacle to block the transmission of data.

In Automatic Logistics System of Welder, we use a point to multipoint wireless bridging mode, the palletizer, stacker, AGV timely communication with the server, through the analysis of the site environment and AGV trajectory, we use a main router and two sub-router connection mode, the router placed in Figure 3.

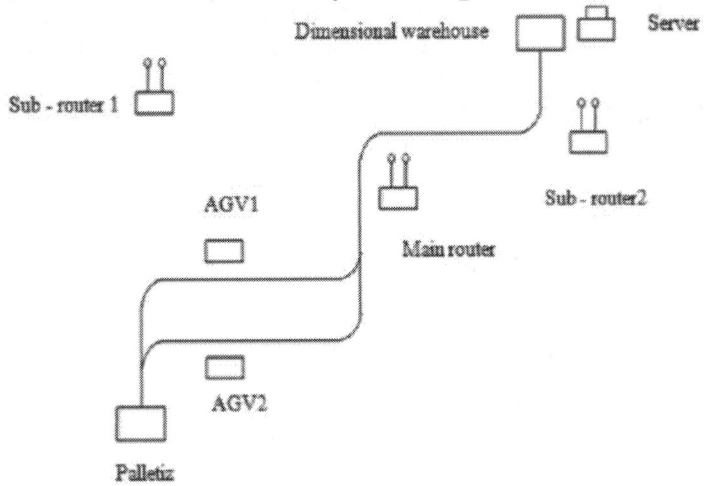

Fig. 3. Location map of router

The three routers shown in the diagram are all installed in the higher position of the factory to reduce the impact of the plant equipment on the signal. In order to enhance the stability of data transmission, all routers have fixed IP addresses, and in order to reduce other foreign equipment to snatch IP addresses, we set up a specific device is allowed to access specific routers. The stacker is closest to the sub router 1, so it is allowed to access, and the AGV trolley will also pass through the coverage of the sub router1, and also allow it to access. So we have to bind the MAC address of the access device to prevent the access of other devices, so as not to affect the stability of the system. The sub router 2 allows only AGV vehicles to access, but the master router is responsible for bridging the other two sub routers and connecting our servers. Thus, in the process of running, AGV car can choose which router to access according to its own needs, so as to ensure that the AGV car will transmit its status information to the server in time.

5 Selection of communication protocols

The network transport protocol mainly includes TCP protocol and UDP protocol, in which the UDP protocol is based on connectionless, which requires lower system resource and high transmission efficiency. However, the UDP protocol sends the information from the Send terminal to the Receiving terminal, but whether the receiver has received the information, it will not be verified, so the disadvantage of the UDP protocol is poor reliability and prone to loss of data packets.

TCP uses connection oriented communication. In the process of communication, it needs to complete the three handshake connection. This three-way handshake is between the Receiving terminal and the sender to receive and send data. The three handshake is as follows:

(1)First, establish a connection between Receiving terminal and send terminal. When the sender needs to send data, the sender will send a SYN packet to the receiver, indicating that they will be communication, and then wait for the response of the receiver.

(2)When the receiver receives the SYN packet sent by the sender, it will analyze the packet and send an ACK + SYN packet to the sender according to its own state, indicating that it has received the information and able to communicate.

(3) Finally, when the sender receives the ACK + SYN packet from the receiver, it sends an ACK packet to the receiver. After the packet is sent, the whole connection process is completed. And then the data can be transmitted between the receiver and the sender.

By using the TCP communication protocol, the reliability of data communication is greatly improved. Therefore, communication has been established before sending valid data. For the formal transmission of data laid a reliable foundation. And, TCP has a timeout retransmission mechanism and data validation mechanism, can guarantee the reliability of data transmission.

In the welder logistics system, because less transmission data, but the data reliability requirements are higher, so the choice of TCP transmission protocol. Through the analysis of the communication information between the equipment of the automatic logistics system of the welder, the response protocol is adopted, and the RTU data format is adopted on the basis of ensuring the convenience of programming. The data structure is shown in Table1.

Table 1. Communication protocol

Byte	1	2	3	4	5	6	7
Data name	Start	Start	Source device	Data length	Control command	Control parameter	check
Data	0x5A	0xA5		0x03			5 and 6 bytes XOR

The data is parsed as follows:

Start: 0x5A, 0xA5, Because WIFI wireless communication, the first two bytes of data often error, so the first two bytes of data transmission are 0x5A, 0xA5, used to avoid data transmission errors.

Source Device Number: Used to indicate the device that is transmitting information. 0x01 indicates the palletizer controller (GUS1), 0x02 represents the three-dimensional warehouse controller (GUS2), 0x03 represents the three-dimensional warehouse controller (turntable 3), 0x04 stands for AGV1, 0x05 means AGV2, 0x06 indicates the incoming PC (server).

Data length: there are 3 bytes after 0x03 bytes, for the server to verify the data.

Control command: 0x01 indicates that the request to enter the turntable instructions, 0x02 indicates AGV reach the specified location of the instructions.

Control parameters: When the control instruction is 0x01, the control parameter is 0x01, said the request to enter the No. 1 turntable instructions.

Check: XOR of control command and control parameter.

Because the control instruction segment and the control parameter segment are the parameters and commands that the server and the lower computer need to execute, it is necessary to ensure the correctness of the data, and the other data has little effect on the execution of the program.

When the sender sends data, the control instruction and the control parameter are XORed, and then the operation result is put into the check byte. When the receiving end receives data, the control instruction and the control parameter are XORed and the operation result is compared with the accepted check byte. If the data is the same, the receiver will then parse the data and send the response data to the sender. If the data is different, the receiver will not parse the data and will not send the response data. After a certain period of time, if the receiver cannot receive the response data will be re-sent to the receiver the same data. If the sender retransmits 5 times the data still does not receive the response data will be alarm, but the sender will continue to retransmit the data. If you re-issued 1000 times, still cannot receive the answer to stop sending, waiting for processing. After receiving the response will automatically terminate the alarm and perform the next action. Through this data verification to ensure the accuracy of the data, making the whole system more secure and reliable.

When the server receives the following data: 0x5A, 0xA5, 0x04, 0x03, 0x01, 0x02, 0x03, Indicates that AGV1 requests access to turntable 2.

Using this data format, the sender and the receiver duplicate check data ensure the correctness of the data. 7 bytes of data length not only to complete the welding automatic logistics system of various information transmission needs, and as much as possible to shorten the length of the data to improve the efficiency of data transmission, and meet the system requirements of high real-time.

6 Message transfer mechanism

According to the welding machine production rate analysis, the production process must be two AGV work at the same time to meet the production requirements. In order to prevent two AGV collision, AGV operation must be unified planning by the server. This requires the server to be able to understand the specific location of each AGV. After analyzing the running path of AGV, six important positions are finally determined, as shown in Figure 4. In these six positions, the IC card is fixed as the logo of the six positions. When the AGV arrives at each card, the location information is sent to the server. The server obtains AGV location information to accurately control the operation of AGV, palletizer, stacker, thus making the whole system safe and efficient operation.

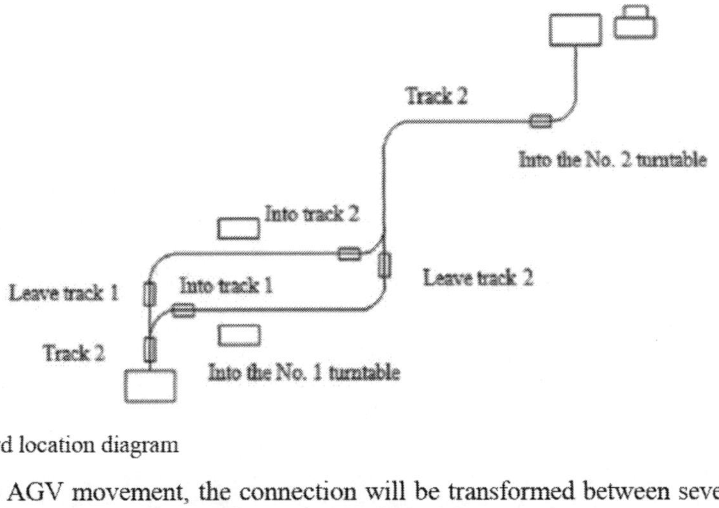

Fig. 4. IC card location diagram

With the AGV movement, the connection will be transformed between several routers. Making the connection time longer. Location information cannot be sent to the server in a timely manner. And in the complex environment, some wireless signal interference will temporarily interrupt communication of AGV, palletizer, stacker with server. So when AGV and server communication is interrupted, AGV will stop and wait, and will continue to send information to the server, the AGV was not restarted until the server received the information. If the server has not answered successfully after sending a certain number of messages, the system will alarm, so that the whole system is more secure operation.

Among them, two AGV through the wireless serial port conversion device to achieve serial signal conversion to wireless Ethernet signals, palletizer and three-dimensional warehouse through the wireless WIFI module will be wired Ethernet signal into wireless Ethernet signal. The management computer obtains the wireless Ethernet signal through the wireless network card. The device is simultaneously connected to the same network node. And then through the response mechanism to establish a connection. In order to achieve the system scheduling and monitoring.

In the communication network, there are five devices, namely, management computer, AGV1, AGV2, three-dimensional warehouse stacker, palletizer, the basic communication requirements are as follows: Among them, in order to achieve storage control, AGV1, AGV2, three-dimensional warehouse Stacking machines, palletizing machines communicate with the server. PC communicate with the warehouse stacker, and to complete the operation of the product into the warehouse.

In order to achieve communication requirements, there are two basic programs, one is not unified management between the equipment. Each device only establishes a connection when it is needed to send a message. Communication is complete, and close the connection. When AGV1 reaches the station of request to enter the turntable 2 will send a request to the server. Then the server issues a query command to the stacker controller. The stacker sends instructions to the server according to its own status. When the server receives the stacker information and then decide whether to allow AGV1 into the No. 2 turntable and send information. AGV1 performs the action after receiving the server's information. The advantage of this transmission mechanism is a small amount of data and the devices are independent of each other. Because data is sent when data is needed, and resulting in real-time poor, inconvenient unified monitoring of the state. Second, through the wireless WIFI built LAN, each device continually sends status information to the server, called a real-time communication mechanism. When the AGV sends a variety of request information, the server sends instructions directly to the AGV based on the received information. When AGV1 issues 0x5A 0xA5 0x04 0x03 0x01 0x02 0x03 (AGV1 requests to enter the No. 2 turntable) information, the server replies directly according to the received information.

When the AGV1 arrives at the request of the No. 2 turntable station, the server sends a direct command to allow AGV1 to enter the No. 2 turntable based on the palletizer status information that has been received. At the same time in order to be able to real-time monitoring of each device and server connection, the device will send an online information to the server every 5 seconds, indicating good communication with the server. When the server cannot receive the equipment online information will alarm, improve the reliability of the entire system. The advantage of this communication mechanism is a small amount of data. convenient unified management, monitoring, and good real-time.

In order to improve the system's real-time and easy management, the communication system using the second program. That is, the management of the computer as a LAN server, the rest of the equipment as a client, and the management of the computer to establish a connection. In order to reduce the number of inquiries, improve communication efficiency. Each device immediately uploads status to the server after the status changes. To facilitate the server to accurately determine the system status, issued the correct order.

7 Conclusion

Welding automatic logistics system using wireless WIFI technology to build a local area network, and to complete the data transmission between the various devices. Through the field test, the system, that uses RTU data format and real-time communication mechanism, fully able to meet the high real-time and high stability of the data transmission requirements.

References

[1] Xiaohui Wei, Meizhen Yang. Wireless WiFi technology application analysis. Modern commerce industry. 2013 (18): 26-32. In Chinese.
[2] Yang Li. WiFi technology principle and application research. Science and Technology Information. 2010 (06):56-62.
[3] Chunfei Zhang. WiFi technology principles and future trends. Digital Community & Smart Home. 2008 (11):182-186.
[4] Tao Wang, Introduction to Wireless Network Technology. Qinghua University Press, 2008.
[5] Qingjiang Jin,Wireless network technology and application. Shanghai Jiaotong University Press, 2003.
[6] Kyung-Chang Lee,Hyun-Hee Kim.Communication Delay Properties in Performance Model of Profibus Token Passing Protocol. Proceding of the 7th Korea-Russia International Symposium 2003.24:234-242.
[7] Y. F Wang, C. H Wang, X Huang. Guaranteed cost control with random communication delays via jump linear system approach. The 8th International Conferenceon Control, Automation, Robotics and Vision. 2004.23:180-186.

Data security and risk assessment in cloud computing

Jing Li [*] *and Qinyuan Li* [b]

State Grid Zhejiang Electric Power Research Institute, Hangzhou, China
[b]+86 13819177903, liqinyuan@zj.sgcc.com.cn

Abstract. Cloud computing has attracted more and more attention as it reduces the cost of IT infrastructure of organizations. In our country, business Cloud services, such as Alibaba Cloud, Huawei Cloud, QingCloud, UCloud and so on are gaining more and more uses, especially small or median organizations. In the cloud service scenario, the program and data are migrating into cloud, resulting the lack of trust between customers and cloud service providers. However, the recent study on Cloud computing is mainly focused on the service side, while the data security and trust have not been sufficiently studied yet. This paper investigates into the data security issues from data life cycle which includes five steps when an organization uses Cloud computing. A data management framework is given out, including not only the data classification but also the risk management framework. Concretely, the data is divided into two varieties, business and personal information. And then, four classification levels (high, medium, low, normal) according to the different extent of the potential adverse effect is introduced. With the help of classification, the administrators can identify the application or data to implement corresponding security controls. At last, the administrators conduct the risk assessment to alleviate the risk of data security. The trust between customers and cloud service providers will be strengthen through this way.

1 Introduction

Cloud computing is growing more and more attraction in recent years, as it has transformed the way organizations approach IT, reducing the IT cost by the novel service models. Nowadays, many organizations are increasingly transferring their application and data on the cloud, though losing the control of the application and data [1]. By the transforming of control of the application and data, organizations can gain the benefits in both efficiency and effectiveness, as well as reduce the expenses in purchasing and sustaining the infrastructure, especially for the acceptance of the public cloud computing. Many reports show that the cloud computing market continues to grow explosively. According to reports from Gartner [2], in 2017, the worldwide public cloud services market grows 18 percent to

* Jing Li: 18606830186@163.com

overall $246.8 billion, in contrast with $209.2 billion in 2016. Projected to grow 36.8 percent in 2017 to reach $34.6 billion, IaaS (Infrastructure as a Service) will be the highest growth. However, the SaaS (Software as a Service) is anticipated to grow 20.1 percent to reach $46.3 billion (see Table 1.)

Table 1. Worldwide Public Cloud Services Forecast (Millions of Dollars)

	2016	*2017*	*2018*	*2019*	*2020*
Cloud Business Process Services (BPaaS)	40,812	43,772	47,556	51,652	56,176
Cloud Application Infrastructure Services (PaaS)	7,169	8,851	10,616	12,580	14,798
Cloud Application Services (SaaS)	38,567	46,331	55,143	64,870	75,734
Cloud Management and Security Services	7,150	8,768	10,427	12,159	14,004
Cloud System Infrastructure Services (IaaS)	25,290	34,603	45,559	57,897	71,552
Cloud Advertising	90,257	104,516	118,520	133,566	151,091
Total Market	211,261	248,858	289,839	334,743	385,375

[a] Source: Gartner (February 2017)

As SaaS products become more sophisticated, including HCM and CRM, the SaaS market will show a slight slowdown in development during the years to come. Despite this, SaaS will still be the second largest section of the global cloud services market.

But for security experts, the cloud has a big dilemma. How do you use the benefits of the cloud while maintaining security control over your organization's applications and data? Determining whether increased risk is really worth agility and economic benefit is a matter of balance. Maintaining data management is the most important for the success of the cloud. Ten years ago, enterprise data typically resides on its own server within the organization's physical infrastructure, enterprise data center, and was able to separate confidential data into individual physical servers. Nowadays, in the cloud and virtualization, data may be under logical control of the institution, but physically it resides in the infrastructure belonged to and maintained by another organization.

NIST SP 800-145[3] defines four deployment models: private, community, public and hybrid cloud. Private cloud and public cloud are the most important and popular deployment models. In private cloud, the infrastructure is provided for dedicated use by a single organization offering service to multiple consumers. However, in public cloud, the infrastructure is designed to provide open use for the public. Different with private cloud, the infrastructure in public cloud is owned, managed, and operated by other cloud service provider, or a third party, but not the organization itself [4]. From the perspective of the network perimeter, public cloud is available and open to the public—is accessible via the internet. On the other hand, the private cloud is only open limitedly, behind the firewall which is under control by the organization. Besides, the private cloud is operated by organization itself. How to secure the application and data without direct control in public cloud is paramount for large-scale application.

Due to the lack of trust between users of the cloud service and cloud service providers, it is important that customers evaluate the security of the data. Risk evaluation is a standard practice that allows organizations to identify, demonstrate and follow other strategies to avoid data loss in the cloud. In this article, we first analyze the data security issues that cloud computing uses from the life cycle of the data. Data security issues are inherent as the lack of trust between cloud service users and cloud service provider. And then, we will give the data classification for reference on the data security. At last, a risk assessment framework will be described.

2 Data security in life cycle

Security content in the cloud resembles traditional security issue and is embodied in all stages of the life cycle. However, as a result of cloud virtualization and multi-tenancy, the content of data security in the cloud has its own unique features.

This section analyzes data security problems in the data life cycle [5] [6]. The data lifecycle represents the whole procedure from data production to dumping. The data life cycle is divided into five segments, as shown in Figure 1.

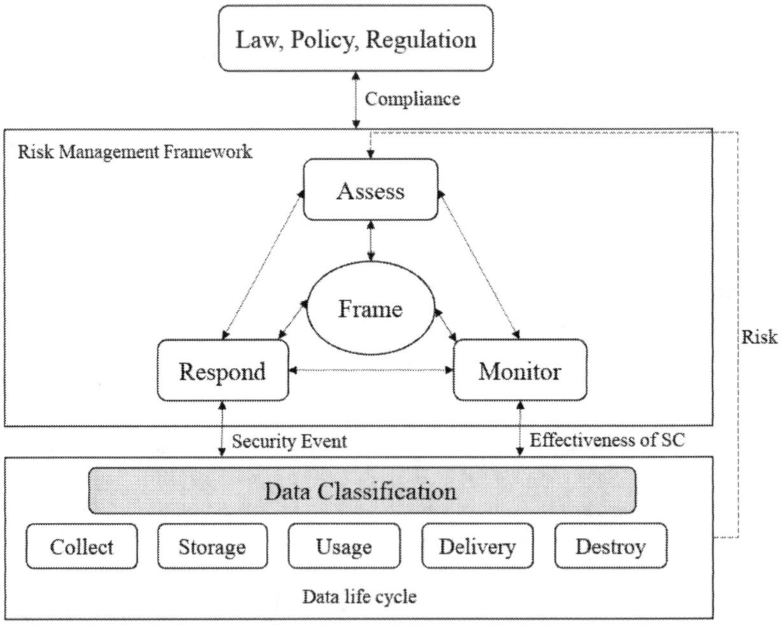

Figure 1. Data Management Framework

2.1 Collect

There are three security concerns in data collection phase: ownership, categorization and quality.

Ownership: In the traditional IT models, the data is stored in the local memory, organizations have the ownership. However, But in cloud models, the data ownership becomes a problem as the fact that the data is migrated Especially, for the personally identifiable information(PII), In particular, the data owner has the right to know what information of personally identifiable information is collected.

Categorization: Categorization will help organizations allocate their resources, prioritize the selection and placement of security controls, and ensure that sensitive systems meet baseline security standards.

Quality: Data may be collected from different sources with different format and quality. From a security perspective, securing the data should start from the collection phase and ensure the raw data is trusted and accurate.

2.2 Storage

Three aspects of information security must be considered in the data that stored in the cloud: confidentiality, integrity, and accessibility (CIA). Data encryption is a usual way to ensure data security. Besides, encryption algorithms and key management should be considered for the validity of encryption.

Data integrity should also be taken into account besides data confidentiality. If users place some GB (or more) data on cloud storage, how can they control the integrity of the data? As a fast and flexible particularity of cloud computing resources, users do not know the location where data is stored. Outbound or cloud storage requires users to use bandwidth and time. Some cloud venders, for example, Amazon, a fee is required for the data transfer. A method to directly certify the consistency of data in cloud storage with no uploading data after downloading data is a big issue. In the traditional IT models, the external attacks become the major threat to availability of data. But for the cloud models, other aspects that threat availability of data arise: (1) The availability of cloud computing services; (2) Cloud providers will always be stably operating? (3) Will the backup be provided in the cloud storage services?

2.3 Usage

Data encryption can be performed on static data using uncomplicated data storage services, such as Amazon S3. But for static data used in cloud applications such as PaaS or SaaS models, it is often unsuitable to encrypt data. Static data used in cloud applications is often not encrypted because data encryption can cause problems with index creation and queries. Almost all processed data is not encrypted in the cloud as well as in traditional IT environments. Because of the multi-party nature of cloud computing models, information processed by cloud applications and data from other users are stored jointly. A serious threat to data security can be posed by unencrypted data in this process. The utilization of personal data is more difficult. Owners of private data must know and be sure that the use of private information is consistent with the objective for which it was collected and if the personal data can be disclosed to third parties such as cloud service providers.

2.4 Delivery

The dissemination of data expands the use of data and complicates data rights. A data owner can transmit data in general, and other organizations can access data with no ratification of the data owner. So once data is delivered, the data owner must consider whether the user retains the original protection and usage restrictions. As for the distribution of private data, besides data authorization, the fineness of data distribution and transformation is also important. The granularity of the distribution is determined by the content strategy and the granularity of the segmentation. Data conversion refers to the separation of confidential information from the original data, which makes the data independent of the owner of the data.

2.5 Destroy

Because of the physical features of storage medium, the deleted data still exists and can be regained, which leads to unintentional disclosure of confidential information. Therefore, if the storage medium is not used any more, the information stored on the medium must be completely deleted.

3 Data classification

Data classification is a very efficient method to protect the data according to its importance and sensitivity. Document NIST Special Publication 800-60 (Guide for Mapping Types of Information and Information Systems to Security Categories) provides a guide for organizations to conduct data classification early in the design of information systems. With the help of the classification, the administrators can identify the application or data to implement corresponding security controls.

In this section, we introduce four classification levels (high, medium, low, normal) according to the different extent of the potential side influence on organizational operations, institutional assets, or individuals.

- Confidentiality: A scarcity of confidentiality is the **unauthorized leak** of data.
- Integrity: A scarcity of integrity is the **unauthorized alteration or damage** of data
- Availability: A scarcity of availability is the **commotion of access** to or use of data.

Table 2. Data Classification

No.	Classification	
	Business Information	***Personal Information***
High Sensitivity	Mid-long term development programs and special plans etc.	Identification card number, passport number etc.
Medium Sensitivity	Important indicator of marketing operations etc.	Email address or contents etc.
Low Sensitity	Company address book etc.	Payment recodes, etc.
Normal Sensitity	Public information (could be found from library or internet)	

3.1 High sensitivity

If the missing of CIA of data is anticipated to have a severe or destructive side effect, the classification of data is high sensitivity. Serious or destructive results indicate, for instance: (i) The severe decrease or loss of mission abilities results in the organization losing its ability to fulfill its primary function. (ii) Serious damage to plan assets. (iii) Significant financial loss. or (iv) r Serious or catastrophic damage to individuals.

Examples of high sensitivity data includes but not limited:

1) Core business information: Core business information is the distinctly important information for organization, the loss of which is very important on the mission, financial, reputation and so on. For example:

a) The mid-long term development programs and special plans

b) Safety protection scheme

c) key information for important infrastructure

d) core network topology

2) Personal sensitive information: Personal sensitive information is closely related to personal rights or interests, the disclosure or abuse of which may endanger property safety and life, adverse impact on personal reputation, leading to discriminatory treatment and other sensitive information. For example:

a) Identification card number, passport number, etc.

b) Credit/debit card information and bank account information

c) Protected Health Information

d) Electronic signatures, biometric information, password information, and private encryption keys

e) Criminal background

3) Industry-specific sensitive information: From perspective of national security, some Industry-specific sensitive information such as oil, gas, coal and power plant related information, should be protected strickly. For example:

a) Oil and gas production information

b) Petrochemical industry important production materials import plan and foreign exchange amount

c) Distribution of Urban Power Network Pipeline

d) Power transmission and transformation equipment reliability paremeter

3.2 Medium sensitity

When the loss of data of CIA is anticipated to have a serious side effect, the classification of data is medium sensitivity. A severe side effect indicates that, for instance : (i) The significant decrease of mission abilities to fulfill its primary function and the effectiveness of the functions is reduced (ii) substantial damage to institutional assets; (iii) substantial financial loss; or (iv) huge damage to individuals that involves nether mortality nor fatal injuries.

Examples of medium sensitivity data includes but not limited:

1) Important business information: Important business information is the information the loss of which will result in serious adverse impact on the mission, financial, reputation and so on. For example:

a) important indicator of marketing operations

b) operation monitoring core indicators and operational data

c) computer software source code

d) Important business agreements or contracts and the relevant information

2) Personal normal information: Personal information b(Personal information is information that is recorded electronically or otherwise, which can be used alone or in combination with other information to identify citizens, including but not limited to citizens' names, birth dates, identity document numbers, personal biometric information, telephone number and so on.) is divided into personal sensitive information and personal normal information. Thus, if personal information is not sensitive, it may be normal information. Generally, personal normal information cannot identify a person alone, but in combination with other information togather.

a) Email address or contents

b) phone number, home address

c) Information used to validate identity, such as name, date of birth, mother's name, etc.

d) other information not labeled as sensitive information (network user accout, race, ethnicity, marital status).

3.3 Low sensitity

When the loss of data of CIA is anticipated to have a limited side effect, the classification of data is low sensitivity. A limited side effect indicates that, for instance:(i)a decline in the capability of carrying out tasks to an extent and interval that the organization has the ability to fulfill its foremost functions, as well as noticeably reduce the effectiveness of the functions (ii) negligible damage to institutional assets; (iii) trivial financial loss; or (iv) minor damage to individuals.

1) Normal business information: Normal business information is the information the loss of which will result in limited adverse impact on the mission, financial, reputation and so on. For example:

a) Company address book

b) final accounts and audit report computer of projects

c) Important business agreements or contracts and the relevant information

d) employee performance review information

2) Personal service information: Personal service information is the data and content information that the organization collects in the service process with personal privacy attributes. For example:

a) payment recodes, such as gas, electricity, mobile phone bill, etc.

b) device information, such as Meter, electricity collection terminal

c) service content inforamtion, such as business charges, user price program, user price strategy, etc.

3.4Normal sensitity

If data is expected to be public, the classification of data is normal sensitivity. Most of the information from the internet is normal sensitive information.

4 Risk assessment framework

Risk management activity is carried out to address risk throughout the organization as a comprehensive and organization-wide activity. Risk evaluation is one of the pivotal components in the organization-wide risk management process (RMP), which is defined in NIST Special Publication 800-39, Managing Information Security Risk: Organization, Mission, and Information System View [8]. In [8], RMP includes four components: (a) framework risk; (b) evaluating risk; (c) Responding to risk; and (d) Monitoring risk. Fig.1 demonstrates the risk evaluation framework among the four components.

Risk framework is the principal step to evaluate risk, accentuating how organizations mount risks or build risk settings. And the "settings" portrays the environment of cloud or any other information system. It is truly onerous to set up a practical and high-efficiency framework, since the organizations not only make appropriate evaluations but also identify the risk limits.

Table 3. Components in RMF

Components	*Introduction/Purpose*
Framework	(1)To establish a risk context. (2)To engender a risk management scheme
Evaluating	(1) To identify the threats and vulnerabilities; (2) To identify the harm
Responding	To develop alternative countermeasures
Monitoring	To certify that risk response measures are put in to practice effectively

Risk evaluation is the secondary step after risk framing, which addresses the risk evaluation problems. It consists of two aspects: one is identifying the imperilments and vulnerabilities; the other is identifying the damage. The imperilments include both internal and external factors. And the damage means the adverse event when the adversaries manipulate some vulnerability successfully. In [9], risk is a function illustrating the probability of a imperilment event's incidence and potential side influence should the event take place. Generally speaking, risk evaluation process consists of four steps: (a) preparing for the evaluation; (b) conducting the evaluation; (c) communicating evaluation results; and (d) maintaining the evaluation.

Built upon the result of risk evaluation, risk responding components will respond to the risk to solve the problems and mediate the side effect as soon as possible. Organizations will carry out risk responses according to strategies and controls properly.

Nevertheless, risk cannot be eradicated absolutely and may change over time. The two ways that organizations monitor risk over time and evaluate the risk on ongoing foundations are the two key components of risk monitoring. The objective of surveillance is to certify that risk response measures are put into use. Consistent surveillance can classify configuration-related variations to cloud and the environments of operation. After that whether the risk response measures are effectual of not can be determinate. Through this method, the risk could be upheld at a comparatively low level all through.

5 Conclusion

In this paper, we analyze the data security issues of utilizing cloud computing from data life cycle. As the characteristics of service hosting, data security issues are inherent as the lack of trust between cloud service users and cloud service provider. We give the data classification for reference from business Information and personal information. The rank of data is divided into four levels (high, medium, low, normal). At last, we give out a risk management framework to guide the data security management.

References

[1] V. Chang and M. Ramachandran, "Towards Achieving Data Security with the Cloud Computing Adoption Framework," in IEEE Transactions on Services Computing, vol. 9, no. 1, pp. 138-151, Jan.-Feb. 1 2016.
[2] Gartner Says Worldwide Public Cloud Services Market to Grow 18 Percent in 2017. https://www.gartner.com/newsroom/id/3616417
[3] SP 800-145, "The NIST Definition of Cloud Computing," NIST Special Publications, Sept. 2011.
[4] M. Henze, J. Hiller, O. Hohlfeld and K. Wehrle, "Moving Privacy-Sensitive Services from Public Clouds to Decentralized Private Clouds," 2016 IEEE International Conference on Cloud Engineering Workshop (IC2EW), Berlin, 2016, pp. 130-135.
[5] T. V. Sathyanarayana and L. M. I. Sheela, "Data security in cloud computing," 2013 International Conference on Green Computing, Communication and Conservation of Energy (ICGCE), Chennai, 2013, pp. 822-827.
[6] X. Yu and Q. Wen, "A View about Cloud Data Security from Data Life Cycle," 2010 International Conference on Computational Intelligence and Software Engineering, Wuhan, 2010, pp. 1-4.
[7] SP 800-60, "Volume I: Guide for Mapping Types of Information and Information Systems to Security Categories", NIST Special Publications, Aug. 2008.

[8] SP 800-39, "Managing information security risk organization, mission, and information system view," NIST Special Publications, Mar. 2010.
[9] SP 800-30 revision 1, "Guide for conducting risk assessments," NIST Special Publications, Sept. 2012.

Mathematical model for crane scheduling in mixed yard

Huihui Han[1], Liying Mi[2], Tao Yang[,3] , and Xin Luo[4]*

[1]School of Computer Science & Technology, Donghua University, Shanghai, 201620, P.R. China,+8618302166037, E-mail: 18790507445@163.com
[2]Country School of Foreign Studies, University of Finance and Economics, Shanghai, 200433, P.R.China. E-mail: mi.liying@mail.shufe.edu.cn
[3]Donghua University Shanghai, 201620, P.R. China. E-mail: yangtao@dhu.edu.cn
[4]School of Computer Science & Technology, Donghua University, Shanghai, 201620, P.R. China. Email: xluo@dhu.edu.cn

Abstract. In mixed yards, the stacking status of the container is not in the order of the shipment, causing the efficiency of the process of loading and unloading decreased. Therefore, it is very important to come up with a method using the existing facilities to improve the efficiency and reduce the cost. In this paper(Produces the permission block, and copyright information Permission to make digital or hard copies of part or all of this work for personal or classroom use is granted without fee provided that copies are not made or distributed for profit or commercial advantage and that copies bear this notice and the full citation on the first page. Copyrights for third-party components of this work must be honored. For all other uses, contact the owner/author(s).) We propose a method that sets a buffer in the yard to minimize the duration of the shifting process. To implement this method, the integer programming model is founded and the small scale accurate solution is used to implement the crane scheduling in the shifting process. The results showed that the model mentioned earlier can solve the problem of crane scheduling in the process of shifting with efficiency and provide strategic support for the management of yard.

1 Introduction

With the development of modern port logistics, the logistics activities continue to be dense, the container transport become continuous popularization, and the growth of the throughput of ports, the problem of insufficient resources has begun to surface in the space of yards has become increasingly prominent. To solve this very problem, the mixed model prevails, which means there are import and export containers in the same container terminal, at the same period of time. In mixed yards, management and scheduling of the cranes is of great importance. It is linked to the efficiency of container gate in and out, even the operation of the whole port.

* Tao Yang: yangtao@dhu.edu.cn

Due to the inconsistency of the container storage status and shipping sequence, the efficiency of the loading process. This problem can be solved by taking the spare time before entering the yard to check the containers. This solution will not only improve the efficiency of stacking operations, but also reduce cost and improve satisfaction. In this paper, we are going to introduce the buffer area of the yards, take the minimum time to finish all requests as the goal, then discuss and optimize the yard crane scheduling problem in mixed yard.

2 Literature review

Many researchers have studied the stacking operations and crane scheduling in mixed yard. Liang et al. [1] studied multiple cranes working on containers loading and discharging operations in mixed yards. Taking the safe distance among yard cranes, equipment interference and the continuity into consideration, and then established a mixed integer mathematical model, to minimize the job completion time and reduce delay. Shao et al. [2] divided the yard crane scheduling problem into moving path and relocation scheduling. They developed a polynomial algorithm to get an optimal solution of the yard crane moving path model, and a bi-level heuristic algorithm based on memory simulated annealing to obtain satisfying solutions of the relocation optimization model. Zheng et al. [3] studied the crane scheduling in mixed yards, aiming at minimizing the cost of all tasks and the non-load and non-unload cost of all operating yard cranes during the fixed span, through non-linear mathematical planning model, and solve it with mixed genetic algorithm and tabu searching algorithm. Zheng et al. [4] studied the optimization of crane scheduling in mixed yard, taking the priorities and deadlines of both external and internal trucks into account, aiming at minimizing the operational cost and relocation amount. A genetic algorithm integrated the solution space cutting function and constructed tactics are proposed to solve the problem. Amir et al. [5] studied the effect of a handshake area on the performance of twin automated stacking cranes. They set up a model to minimize the completing time and blocking time, and then set 4 decision variables for the heuristic scheduling algorithm, despite the final result not being so idea.

Many scholars did some deep research on the shifting operations in mixed yards. To solve the problem of relocation, Zhu et al. [6] constructed a searching strategy with minimum number of basic relocation, yard crane cost and number of relocation times, then the beam search algorithm was used as well. Dong et al. [7] studied the optimum scheduling problem of container yard relocation among multiple bays. They established a mathematical model based on the balance between utilization rate and the relocating rate, and then solved the problem with mixed heuristic algorithm. Bian et al. [8] studied the problem of container preloading in the exporting area. A two-staged algorithm consists of a neighborhood searching algorithm and an integer programming model is proposed to develop a pre-marshalling plan to improve the layout of containers in a bay. Zhou et al [9] established a simulation model of the reshuffling process based on analyzing the actual reshuffles of import containers in the container yard. The heuristic algorithm is designed basing on the total least-reshuffles-estimate rule.

3 Yard crane scheduling model

3.1 Description

In mixed yards, to improve the efficiency of the containers' loading and unloading process, usually the containers are shifted before the arrival of a ship. Different from the traditional container yards, there are import and export containers in the yard at the same time, which means crane scheduling process will get harder. The problem will be described as follows. Two cranes in the same container terminal with a buffer in the middle of it. Shifting requests are completed by two yard cranes. The cranes do not go through the buffer zone. When a shifting request spans the buffer, the container is transported from the starting position to the buffer by a crane, and the other crane moves it from the buffer to the targeting position.

The optimization goal is to minimize the completing time of all requests, which assumes that: (1) the shifting is carried out only in the container sector, the storage status and the shifting demand are already known; (2) the container properties are all the same, special containers are not taken into consideration; (3) no new container entering the yard during the shifting process; (4) assuming the buffer is in the middle of the container terminal, which occupies one bay.

3.2 Model construction

3.2.1. Parameters and variables.

(1) indicator set
i, j: request indicators;
k: yard crane indicators;
m: number of yard crane;
(2) parameters
M: number of yard cranes;
N: number of requested containers;
n: number of requested containers which need to be split;
nl: number of request which completed by the land side yard crane;
ns: number of request which completed by the sea side yard crane;
Ω: number of requested containers, N task containers matching the natural number of (1-N);
H: maximum number of secure stacks;
ρ: spreader landing and grab (or put down and lift) a container's time consuming;
D: minimum safe distances between yard cranes;
K_m: number of shifting request which completed by yard crane m;
l: the length of a single bay;
v: the processing speed of the yard crane;
(3) decision variables
X_{im}: number of the containers which were handled by the bridge m Nth;
$a(X_{im})$: moving path of the extraction of container X_{im};
$H[a(X_{im})]$: maximum stacking height that occurs during the execution of $a(X_{im})$;
P_{kt}: yard crane's position k at time t;
T_l: completing time of land side yard crane;
T_s: completing time of sea side yard crane.

3.2.2. Model building.

Mark the coordinates of the container respectively (b_i, s_i, t_i) and (b'_i, s'_i, t'_i) before and after shifting. According to the analysis above, the mathematical model of shifting crane scheduling problem is constructed as follows:

Objective function:

$$T=\{TL,TS\} \quad (1)$$

Constraint condition:

$$B_i \geq (b'_i - b_i)+ (b_{i+1} - b'_i),1 \leq \mathrm{i} \leq \mathrm{N}(2)$$
$$B_i \geq (b_i - b'_i)+ (b'_i - b_{i+1}),1 \leq \mathrm{i} \leq \mathrm{N}(3)$$
$$B_i \geq (b'_i - b_i)+ (b'_i - b_{i+1}),1 \leq \mathrm{i} \leq \mathrm{N}(4)$$
$$B_i \geq (b_i - b'_i)+ (b_{i+1} - b'_i),1 \leq \mathrm{i} \leq \mathrm{N}\ (5)$$
$$T_l \geq \sum_{i=1}^{nl+n} B_i * l \div v + 4\rho,1 \leq \mathrm{i} \leq \mathrm{N}, 1 \leq \mathrm{nl}, \mathrm{n} \leq \mathrm{N}(6)$$
$$T_s \geq \sum_{i=1}^{ns+n} B_i * l \div v + 4\rho,1 \leq \mathrm{j} \leq \mathrm{N}, 1 \leq \mathrm{ns}, \mathrm{n} \leq \mathrm{N}(7)$$
$$\mathrm{N} = \mathrm{nl} + \mathrm{ns} + \mathrm{n},1 \leq \mathrm{nl}, \mathrm{ns}, \mathrm{n} \leq \mathrm{N} \quad (8)$$
$$P_{kt} \leq P_{(k+1)t} - D,1 \leq \mathrm{k} \leq \mathrm{M}\ (9)$$
$$\mathrm{h}[\mathrm{a}(X_{im})] \leq \mathrm{H},1 \leq \mathrm{i} \leq \mathrm{N}, 1 \leq \mathrm{k} \leq \mathrm{M}\ (10)$$
$$\sum_{m=1}^{M} K_m = N,1 \leq \mathrm{k} \leq \mathrm{M}\ (11)$$
$$X_{im} \in \Omega, 1 \leq \mathrm{i} \leq \mathrm{N}, 1 \leq \mathrm{m} \leq \mathrm{M}\ (12)$$
$$\mathrm{a}(X_{im}) \in \mathrm{A}(X_{im}), 1 \leq \mathrm{i} \leq \mathrm{N}, 1 \leq \mathrm{m} \leq \mathrm{M}\ (13)$$
$$K_m \leq N - 1, 1 \leq \mathrm{m} \leq \mathrm{M}\ (14)$$

The objective function (1) indicates that when two cranes complete the same one request together, the completing time of the request is set by the larger one; Constraints (2) - (5) indicate the bays that crane completing one single shifting request of a container and then moves to the next position; Constraints (6) and (7) represent the time that cranes on land and at sea need to complete all the requests; Constraints (8) represent the relationship between the number of requests completed by the sea side crane alone, the number of requests completed by the land side crane alone and the number of requests which need to be split and completed by two cranes; Constraints (9) represent the safe distance between two cranes and ensure the safety of operations; Constraints (10) makes sure that the stack height during each operation is less than the maximum stack height; Constraint (11) to ensure that all tasks completed; Constraints (12) - (14) specify the range of values for each variable.

3.3 Case study

To verify the feasibility of the model, we will solve an example as the following one. In the given example, there are six requests, which are completed by two cranes, as shown in Table 1. For the sake of simplicity, assuming the travel duration in bay (Y-direction) is longer than the ones in stack (X-direction), so only the movement time in bay is taken into consideration.

We simplified the shifting movement into four steps:

(1) The crane moves to the starting position of a request;

(2) The spreader goes down and grabs the container, then raise to the safe height;

(3) The crane moves to the target position requested;

(4) The spreader puts the container to destination and rises.

Repeat steps (1) - (4) until all shifting requests are completed. According to the actual cranes' working data, 10 seconds will be consumed when a crane goes through a single bay. One single going down and grabbing (or releasing) the container would consume 30 seconds. Figure 1 shows the moving path of the crane both with and without buffer zone.

 https://doi.org/10.1051/itmconf/20181703029

Table 1. Shifting requests' sequence

without buffer zone			with buffer zone		
start position	target position	number of crane	start position	target position	number of crane
32	10	2	32	16	2
			16	10	1
1	5	1	1	5	1
28	32	2	28	32	2
25	32	2	25	32	2
6	1	1	6	1	1
1	20	1	1	16	1
			16	20	2

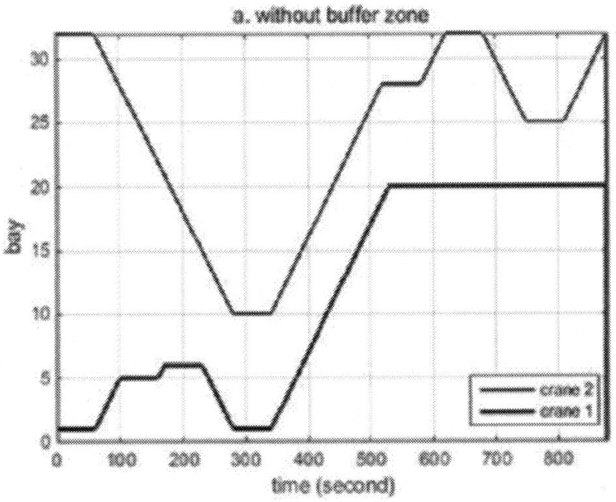

Fig.1 (a): Move path of cranes without buffer zone

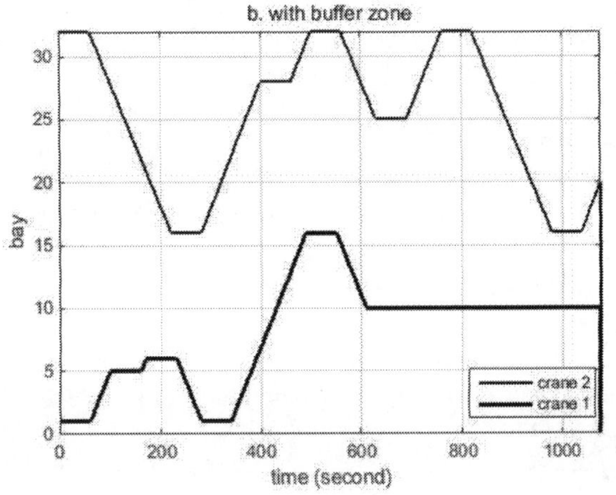

Fig.1 (b): Move path of cranes with buffer zone

The moving path of the cranes without buffer zone is shown in Fig. 1 (a). Both land side crane and sea side crane are moving in the entire yard space, and crane 1 would have to wait for a long time after completing its requests, requests of the cranes are imbalance, this is wasting the resources of crane yards. The moving path of cranes with buffer zones is shown in Fig. 1 (b). The cranes are only working on one side of the yard or buffer zone. The probability of generating interferences is relatively small. Although there is also waiting time, the probability of waiting time is reduced than the former one.

4 Conclusion

In this paper, we would be focused on a crane yard with buffer. Through the analysis of the paper, we get the shifting request sequence through the nearest neighbor equation, and the cranes' priority is determined by the longest remaining time. However, this article mentioned that the yard working condition is static and there is no new container entering the yard in the case of any shifting operation, so the next step is to solve the shifting problem with a dynamic situation.

Acknowledgments: The authors would like to thank Guangdong Province collaborative innovation and platform Environmental Science build of special funds (2014B090908004); Dongguan City professional town innovation service platform construction project" Dongguan City Humen garment Collaborative Innovation Center", whose constructive comments and suggestions helps us to improve the quality of this paper.

References

[1] Liang Chengji, Zhai diandian, and Wang dandan. 2016. Dynamic Scheduling Model Research for Multiple Yard Crane in Container Terminal. J. Computer Simulation. 33, 3 (Mar. 2016), 363-366.(in Chinese)

[2] Shao Qianqian, Xu Tingting, Yang Huiyun, and Jin Zhihong. 2016. Scheduling Optimization of Yard Crane for Import Conrainers Based on Truck Batch Arrival Pattern. J. Control and Decision. 31, 9 (Sep. 2016), 1654-1662. (in Chinese)

[3] Zheng Hongxing, and Yu Kai. 2013. Yard Crane Scheduling in the Mixture Storage Block Based on Hybrid Genetic Algorithm. J. Journal of Transportation Systems Engineering and Information Technology. 13, 5 (Oct. 2013), 150-158. (in Chinese)

[4] Zheng Hongxing, Dong Yiwen, Kuang Haibo, and Yu Kai. 2016. Yard Cranes Scheduling with Relocation at a Mixed Storage Block for Ship Loading. J. Systems Engineering – Theory & Practice. 36, 9 (Sep. 2016), 2362-2373. (in Chinese)

[5] Amir Hossein Gharehgozli, Floris Gerardus Vernooij, and Nima Zaerpour. 2017. A simulation study of the performance of twin automated stacking cranes at a seaport container terminal. J. European Journal of Operational Research. (Feb. 2017), 108-128.

[6] Zhu Minghua, Cheng Huanchong, and Fan Xiumin. 2012. Blocks Relocation problem with filter based beam search algotithm. J. Computer Integrated Manufacturing Systems. 18, 3 (Mar. 2012), 639-644. (in Chinese)

[7] Dong Xiaomei, Pan Yu, Xu Xiaoyong, and Ding Yanyan. 2012. Mathematical Model and Hybrid Heuristic Optimization Algorithm of Container Rehandling Among Different Bay Locations. J. Operation Research and Management Science. 21, 6 (Dec. 2012), 112-118. (in Chinese)

[8] Bian Zhan, Li Na, Li Xiangjun, and Jin Zhihong. 2014. Hybrid Optimization Algorithm for Pre-marshalling Export Containers. J. Control and Decision. 29, 2 (Feb. 2014), 373-378. (in Chinese)

[9] Zhou Pengfei, and Li Pian. 2013. Simulation Analysis and Heuristic Algorithm for Reshuffle Optimazation of Import Containers in Container Terminal. J. Systems Engineering – Theory & Practice. 33, 12 (Dec.2013), 3145-3155. (in Chinese)

Petri net methodology for solving healthcare management issues

Abdul Rauf Khushk[1] and Xiaozhong Li[2,*]

[1]College of Economics and Management, Tianjin University of Science and Technology, Tianjin 300222, China. Phone no: +86-13902000485, E-mail: arkhushk@gmail.com
[2]College of Computer Science and Information Engineering, Tianjin University of Science and Technology, Tianjin 300222, China, E-mail: lixz@tust.edu.cn

Abstract. Various approaches of Petri nets can be achieved as system security and information flow in the healthcare recording system inside any medical or health-related business. Petri net system formal modeling is essential as well as important to track down the records and secure information inside a preformed health organization. In this paper, we mainly focused on the formal model Petri net which security mechanism is controlled by public key encryption where PN based modeling is preferred. This Petri net is a mathematical modeling to solve graphical notation for step by step processes that include choice, repetition, and circumstantial execution. Petri nets offer widely mathematical applications of discrete and continuous event execution semiotics, with an efficient mathematical analysis processing theory. We sure that our formal model will lay a solid foundation to minimize the risks and overcome the security risks in the healthcare industry.

1 Introduction

The healthcare management system is one of the most important and necessary systems which maintains various kinds of information and records of casualties or patients as well as medicinal related personnel daily [1]. However, the information of every patient with corresponding departments should be regulated properly inside the hospital or the related organization as well as must be flexible for convenience. [2] There are lots of models proposed regarding the security as well as for the purpose of flexibility and reliability for information flow and data management such as [3] a discrete-event simulation system to model antibiotic distribution centers and suggest optimal staffing levels, spreadsheet-based software known as Flu Surge for Pandemic influenza is also a concern, An agent-based model known as PHIMs (Public Health Interactive Model & simulation) is described in as an interactive simulation environment, etc.

---

* Xiaozhong Li: lixz@tust.edu.cn

However, [4] the application of Petri net theory to the problem of healthcare modeling is not common but only five instances of research on the topic could be located. The different redesigned methodology is applied to the problem of intake procedure for new patients requesting non-urgent care at a mental health institution. These design practices are typically associated with commercial applications, but they were employed here for a redesign of the intake system for a flexible information flow[5]. Both the original and new intake procedures were modeled as a colored Petri net simulation, which generated results (average, low and high) for both flow time and service time. A similar theme plays out in which combines business process modeling and Petri net theory with the purpose of improving large-scale software system design [6]. The chosen process is the Design & Engineering Methodology for Organizations (DEMO), which "studies communication, information, and action within the context of an organization". The system is then graphically represented using Petri net. Of interest is the example where a medical center's patient admission system is modeled using this approach and analyzed using existing Petri net tools for structural issues such as deadlock and conflict [7][8] [10].

In this paper, we generally focused on the Petri net model in the healthcare record where data and information are easily viable in regarding different unit of any health organization with convenience and security. Here several approaches are made to analyze Petri nets such as the enumeration of all possible states; reachability tree which identifies different nodes and change in the standard of Petri nets with cloud security [11][12].Moreover, the formal model is described below for with more clarity.

2 A formal model of Petri net representing health care record.

Petri nets is a mathematical modeling of parallel and distributed system for solving a graphical documentation for integrated and validated that include choice, duplication, and coincidental execution. Petri nets offer widely mathematical applications of discrete and continuous event execution semiotics, with an efficient mathematical analysis processing theory[9] [Carl Adam Petri].

A formal basic Petri net N holds two kinds of nodes, P and T, accordingly called places and transition, a set $F \subseteq (P \times T) \cup (T \times P)$the nodes directly connected with arcs, the marking of initializing $M_0 : P \to N$ that set of places is mapping into set N is totally non-negative integers.

The concept of Petri net is offer to variety of token nations. Tokens have own identification method, which possibly data have random values. The places contain complex data type security method. Appling to a formal model of Petri Net representing healthcare Record is tuple $\sum, P, T, A, H, Q, L, W, I$ where

$\sum$ is a finite set of non-empty set the type of initialization data value operations and function should be used in arc expression, guard, P Places is a finite set, T transition is a finite set, A arcs is a finite set $: P \cap T = P \cap A = T \cap A = \emptyset$,$H$ is a function node $H: A \to (P \times T) \cup (T \times P)$. Q is mapping $Q: P \to \sum$. The function Q mapping every place p to a kinds Q(p), however that per token on p might have a data value be part of Q(p). L is guard function. T is characterize from into expression specific $\forall t \in T$ type($L(t)$) = Boolean and type($H\ ar(L(t)) \subseteq \sum$. Per each transition $t \in T$.the Boolean expression is a guard of t , there is all variable has kind that be part of $\sum$. W is a function of arc expression. A is characterize into expression such that:$\forall a \in A$: type $(W(a) = Q(p)M\ Q$ and type of $(H\ ar(W(a)) \subseteq \sum$. There p is the place of $H(a)$. Per each arc $a \in A$. The type of $W(a)$ is the multiset $Q(p)M\ Q$, however measure that $W(a)$ necessity appraise to multiset accomplished kind of modification place p. furthermore, all variable in an arc expression $W(a)$ has in $\sum$. I is function of initialization. its characterize by P within expression such that $\forall\ p \in P$: type $(I(p) = Q(p)M\ Q. I$ maps every place $p \in P$ within expression that might be type of $Q(p)M\ Q$. A set place followed by a set of transition such as place (P): $(P1), (P2), (P3), (P4), (P5), (P6), (P$ and transition (T): $(T1), (T2), (T3), (T4), (T5), (T6), (T7), (T8)$. Moreover, the initial marking as M_0 $(0,1,0,0,0,0,0,0)$. The set of input and output secure the patient information record integrated and validated implementation and persistent storage system with CRUD (create, retrieve, update, and delete)in the medical device networking system is done by matrix for as in table I and table II and figure 1. The result is $M_0\{1,0,0,0,0,0,0,0\}$.

Table 1. Place Specification

Name	Specification
P1	Physician
P2	Patient connect with physician
P3	Medical superintendent receives the record packet
P4	Nurse receives the record packet
P5	verifying the destination node packed and is ready to send the record
P6	Place Discard
P7	Pharmacist has received record packet
P8	All data record is updated

Table 2. Transition Specification

Name	Specification
T1	Physician updated the patient record
T2	Patient record is send to the medical superintendent
T3	Medical superintendent check the record
T4	Nurse create the new record
T5	Nurse is allotment the record number of patient
T6	The record verification in case its destination
T7	The pharmacist is transmit record to the medical superintendent
T8	Physician have up to date record of the physician

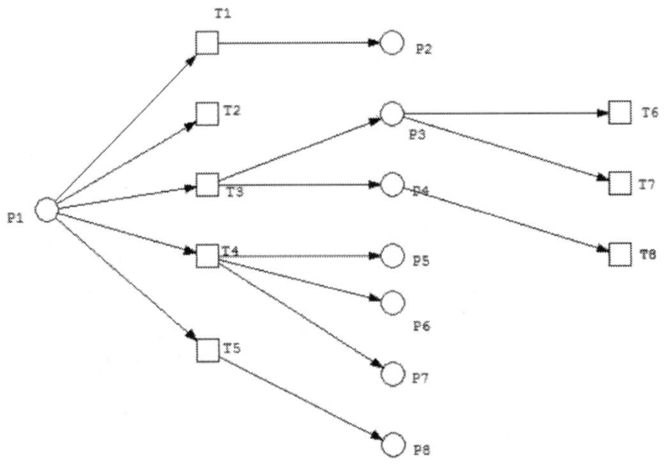

Fig1. Diagram of medical device networking.

$$\textbf{Input Metrics} \begin{bmatrix} 0 & 0 & 0 & 0 & 0 & 0 & 0 & 0 \\ 1 & 0 & 0 & 0 & 0 & 0 & 0 & 0 \\ 0 & 0 & 1 & 0 & 0 & 1 & 1 & 0 \\ 0 & 0 & 1 & 0 & 0 & 0 & 0 & 1 \\ 0 & 0 & 0 & 1 & 0 & 0 & 0 & 0 \\ 0 & 0 & 0 & 1 & 0 & 0 & 0 & 0 \\ 0 & 0 & 0 & 1 & 0 & 0 & 0 & 0 \\ 0 & 0 & 0 & 0 & 1 & 0 & 0 & 0 \end{bmatrix}$$

$$\textbf{Output Metrics} \begin{bmatrix} \mathbf{1} & \mathbf{1} & \mathbf{1} & \mathbf{1} & \mathbf{1} & \mathbf{0} & \mathbf{0} & \mathbf{0} \\ \mathbf{0} & \mathbf{0} & \mathbf{0} & \mathbf{0} & \mathbf{0} & \mathbf{0} & \mathbf{0} & \mathbf{0} \\ \mathbf{0} & \mathbf{0} & \mathbf{0} & \mathbf{0} & \mathbf{0} & \mathbf{1} & \mathbf{1} & \mathbf{0} \\ \mathbf{0} & \mathbf{0} & \mathbf{0} & \mathbf{0} & \mathbf{0} & \mathbf{0} & \mathbf{0} & \mathbf{1} \\ \mathbf{0} & \mathbf{0} & \mathbf{0} & \mathbf{0} & \mathbf{0} & \mathbf{0} & \mathbf{0} & \mathbf{0} \\ \mathbf{0} & \mathbf{0} & \mathbf{0} & \mathbf{0} & \mathbf{0} & \mathbf{0} & \mathbf{0} & \mathbf{0} \\ \mathbf{0} & \mathbf{0} & \mathbf{0} & \mathbf{0} & \mathbf{0} & \mathbf{0} & \mathbf{0} & \mathbf{0} \\ \mathbf{0} & \mathbf{0} & \mathbf{0} & \mathbf{0} & \mathbf{0} & \mathbf{0} & \mathbf{0} & \mathbf{0} \end{bmatrix}$$

Petri net input and output matrix representation of net, here is $P \times T \; and \; T \times P$ (p rows and t columns), p is the number of place and t is the number of transition.

3 Conclusion

In conclusion, we precisely presented a formal security model which can be used to analyze the information flow in health care system. The entities present in this system can be assigned different security levels belonging to a given security encryption technology. Furthermore, every information is assigned a security level which captures the confidentiality level in any healthcare record. It is also potential to specify in a formal way different security strategies for the movement of entities with a system and information flow is smooth. The resulting formal model can then be represented by a suitable formal model, and its dynamic properties analyzed using the existing verification methods and tools developed for Petri nets.

Acknowledgements: This work was supported by National Natural Science Foundation of China Grant No.61603273, by Tianjin Application Foundation and Advanced Technology Research Project under Grant No. 14JCQNJC00300, and by Natural Science Foundation of Tianjin under Grant No. 16JCYBJC18500.

References

[1] X. Liu, Y. Xia, W. Yang, and F. Yang, "Secure and Efficient Querying over Personal Health Records in Cloud Computing," Neurocomputing, 2017.
[2] A. R. Khushk and X. Li, "Petri net modeling of encrypted information flow in federated cloud," J. Phys. Conf. Ser., vol. 887, no. 1, 2017.
[3] X. Allamigeon, V. Bœuf, and S. Gaubert, "Stationary solutions of discrete and continuous Petri nets," Perform. Eval., vol. 113, pp. 1–12, 2017.
[4] S. Whittaker, "Augmenting Petri Nets to Model Health-Care Protocols by," no. September 2011.
[5] G. Smith, "A New Type System for Secure Information Flow."
[6] A. Technische, U. Eindhoven, and D. View, "Petri-net-based workflow management software Petri-net-based Workflow Management Software," no. May 2014.
[7] H. Huang and Q. Zhou, "Petri-net-based modeling and resolving of black hole attack in WMN," Proc. - Int. Comput. Softw. Appl. Conf., pp. 409–414, 2012.
[8] M. Li, S. Yu, Y. Zheng, K. Ren, and W. Lou, "Supplementary Material - Scalable and secure sharing of personal health records in cloud computing using attribute-based encryption," IEEE Trans. Parallel Distrib. Syst., vol. 24, no. 1, pp. 131–143, 2013.
[9] W. Brauer and W. Reisig, "Carl Adam Petri and ' Petri Nets,'" pp. 1–7, 1962.
[10] W. Zeng, M. Koutny, and P. Watson, "Verifying secure information flow in federated clouds," Proc. Int. Conf. Cloud Comput. Technol. Sci. CloudCom, vol. 2015–February, no. February, pp. 78–85, 2015.
[11] W. Zeng, C. Mu, and M. Koutny, "COMPUTING SCIENCE A Flow Sensitive Security Model for Cloud Computing Systems," no. June 2013.
[12] P. Watson, "COMPUTING SCIENCE," no. September 2011.

AUTHOR INDEX

AUTHOR INDEX